SELECTED PLAYS OF

Sean O'Casey

Selected Plays of

SEAN O'CASEY

Selected and with Foreword
by *the Author*

Introduction
by *John Gassner*

GEORGE BRAZILLER / NEW YORK / 1955

—photo by Alfred Eris

Genius without Fetters

ONE CONSEQUENCE OF consorting for some time with O'Casey's work is that one loses control for the workaday world. The experience is delightful, but it is poor preparation for journeyman's work such as the writing of a preface to a collection of plays. O'Casey can do the one thing to critics that shouldn't be done—he can inebriate them. It is doubtful, moreover, that he would regret unchaining anyone from the cast-iron moorings of criticism for the greater glory of a carouse. In a worrying mood, he once wrote that "the Gael will be pickled in penance." But when the question is one of leavening life, O'Casey is one Gael who cannot swim in the brine of repentance.

Fortunately, the critic too needn't be repentant for yielding to the heady companionship of his subject, and the pleasure of introducing O'Casey to his readers—to, I hope, more readers than he already has—is more important than taking a

v

frosty measure of his work. Certainly there can be no other intelligent purpose in publishing a collection of his plays than to facilitate acquaintance with the world's greatest and most distinctive living playwright whose work is rarely seen on the stage while faceless mediocrities glut the marketplace for drama. The occasion for printing this compilation, moreover, is a happy one. O'Casey, who was born in 1884, has attained the biblical age of three score and ten. Considering the difficulties and unlikelihood of survival in his youth, one is moved to salute him for one more accomplishment.

The plays in this volume were selected by O'Casey. A lively debate could be held over the wisdom of some of his omissions and some of his choices, but O'Casey himself has only this to say about the selection:

> *I don't know why I selected them any more than I know why I wrote them. To explain these things would be to explain life and that you, nor I, nor anyone else can do. For better or worse, they are part of the Will to life. The nine plays represent my varying mood in outlook on life and in the varying manners and techniques of the stage.*

In any case, here is God's plenty, including the indispensable selections, *The Shadow of a Gun-*

man, *Juno and the Paycock* and *The Plough and the Stars,* over which there can be no disagreement. In one way or another, and regardless of our own preference, O'Casey's selections make up a true testament.

It is customary, of course, to maintain that a playwright's place is on the stage, as indeed it is. But if he is not to be found on it, there is all the more reason for looking for him in the library. We have every reason to regret that O'Casey's plays have had few professional productions since the nineteen-twenties. But in a theatre poorly suited to the prime requirement of keeping masterpieces on display, productions have not been exactly lavished upon Ibsen, Strindberg, and Chekhov either. They, too, along with the great Greeks, have become largely books for us. For immortality, indeed, the great playwrights need to interest us as readers as well as playgoers. They are dependent upon the theatre of the mind as well as upon the theatre of the boards. For all our regrets, therefore, we should not be wholly dismayed that we must get at O'Casey's plays in books. It may turn out that we shall be pleased, too, for if ever there was a modern playwright whose works read as well as they play or that read well regardless of how they play, it is O'Casey. Readers, however, may need some introduction to a playwright when they are not introduced to him by players and, for that matter, by that spirit of expectancy which bridges the distance between the play and the public whenever we are gathered in the theatre. Let us therefore make some preliminary acquaintance with the dramatist O'Casey. And may those readers (surely not many) who have read some of my earlier comments on him forgive any repetitions they encounter. Repetition is a tribute criticism often pays to genius.

WHEN O'Casey arrived at Dublin's Abbey Theatre in the decade of the twenties a rough-hewn, almost forty-year-old candidate for discovery by William Butler Yeats and Lady Gregory, he brought with him two worlds not usually considered compatible—the worlds of fact and fancy, of depressing necessity and of soaring and melodious imagination. To resolve these two worlds has been the life-work of O'Casey. Their coexistence and conflict will be found in all his work. There is only this difference: The exigent realities of the Dublin of his youth dominate the early work that culminated in the two realistic masterpieces *Juno and the Paycock* and *The Plough and the Stars*. The ascent of the imagination, never a flight from reality but a poetic expression of the author's stormy marriage to life, becomes marked in his later work, to which the divided play *The Silver Tassie,* a half-realistic and half-expressionist protest against war, was a rather thunderous overture in 1927.

There has been debate ever since then as to

which world has proved most congenial to the author's talent. As will be evident from this volume of plays selected by himself, O'Casey favors his non-realistic style, whereas many admirers elect the realistic mode as the one most favorable to effectiveness in his case. There is no doubt in my mind that the most memorable characterizations, such as those of the greatly tried mother-wife Juno and her peacock Captain Boyle and the inimitable Fluther Good at the time of the Easter Rising, belong chiefly to O'Casey's realistic phase. But anyone who is impervious to the weird magic of the later plays, where abstruseness sometimes diminishes character and attenuates dramatic action, not only loses precious qualities of wild fancy, passion, and music rare in the modern theatre, but may not have actually derived all that there was to be derived from the early plays. For, as I have said, O'Casey brought *both* his worlds with him when he became a playwright, and first won a reputation as a realist.

It is of one dramatist that we must speak when we observe the antinomies of naturalism and romanticism, realism and fantastication, particularization and rhetoric in his total work. We should know that we embraced the poet when we embraced the realist in the early plays. And there is good reason to believe that we reject the realist we favored in them when we reject the poet and theatrician who makes himself so conspicuous in the later works. We may criticize in these a tendency toward abstractness and oversimplification and deplore some turgidness in them, but it is actually the writer who is so open to these charges who also fascinates us with his dramatic enterprise, with his idealism, fancy and eloquence. More than a quarter of a century has passed since he deliberately renounced the realistic style and technique which brought him international fame. We can no longer, therefore, presume that we know or can think intelligently about his dramatic art by minimizing the importance of the non-realistic plays in the O'Casey canon. The present collection therefore gives them their due place. And when we read them we discover, I believe, that the same voice is speaking, the same music is being made, and the same winged excess, whether of sympathy or anger, of eloquence or laughter, is present in all the plays, both the realistic and the non-realistic ones. And it is worth noting, too, that it is not merely the most fanciful and hortatory plays but the early universally praised, realistic ones that have lain under some interdict of non-production. It is not just the former that have been regarded as too formidable for the commercial stage. One of the advantages of this collection is that it reveals an underlying unity and acquaints us with the total dramatist.

WHAT SHALL WE SAY about this writer but that he is, in a sense, a stranger in the commercial theatre because he is too big for it. He became almost inevitably a stranger as the English-speaking theatre became constricted in heart and imagination after the nineteen-twenties precisely when he was growing more impassioned and imaginative. He came to demand more and more of the theatre just when it was inclined to give less and less. In all his capacities as visionary, dramatist, poet, and theatrician he became wilder while the theatre became tamer. He cast off all fetters, including those of realistic dramaturgy, and his stride lengthened. The theatre, dangling many chains around its feet, including the heaviest of all—its chain of gold, could not keep pace with him. And that condition, which is the theatre's disgrace and O'Casey's misfortune, is also O'Casey's glory and a reader's warrant of pleasure. For the fact is that O'Casey's plays constitute the most exciting dramatic writing in the English language we have had since Shaw completed *Saint Joan,* if not indeed since the disappearance of the Elizabethan stage.

There are various ways of describing O'Casey's talent. I have found it necessary, for example, to proffer a negative description and discourage a sociological interpretation of his work. This interpretation is possible, of course, for he has often dealt with conditions of poverty and injustice, and with social and political struggles, but it is too constricting. It can dispose us to base favor or disfavor of the playwright on shallow premises.

He is too much of a rhapsodist to be a good sociologist. He brings personal passion rather than cold analysis to his subject matter. Unlike Shaw, he is not even a dramatist of ideas and he has made no claims to being one. We may say that regardless of his affirmative, sometimes even strutting, manner he is an inquirer rather than expounder when theories and premises are involved. He questions conventional beliefs and counters not with reasoned opinions (although he has called himself a "Rationalist"), but with another faith.

O'Casey's opinions in the plays are emotional rejections, enthusiasms, and visions. He is actually wary of "ideas" and likes to show us that they do not abide the test of action. The articulate "Labour" humanitarianism of Jerry in *Juno and the Paycock* and the half-baked Socialist convictions of the Covey in *The Plough and the Stars* are mordantly exposed by O'Casey. And the conflict of "ideas" is amusingly caricatured in *Within the Gates* when a fanatical atheist and a religious fanatic face each other from opposite platforms within Hyde Park. Being O'Casey and not some skin-deep opportunist, he probablly lives by his beliefs more than most people live by theirs. And anything important to an author as sincere as O'Casey must be important in starting or stimulating the pulse of his work. But neither beliefs nor ideas are the work itself. For all his large sympathies with the common man (who, I must say, becomes most uncommon in O'Casey's extravagant and poetically comic and tragic world), he has not written either thesis drama or problem plays. It is quite simply drama—equally incandescent, though not necessarily equally absorbing, when realistic and when not—that he has written. Anyone can tell in very little time what O'Casey is for or against. The important and not always easy thing is to give oneself up to the life and the music on his pages and to the theatre they make together as they meet in the creative process. The life and the music or the music and the life: the former, more in the early plays; the latter, more in the later ones.

Only certain ambivalences apparent in his treatment of the Irish national movement and of life in liberated Ireland require any special explanation, which need not go beyond our saying here that O'Casey has engaged in a lover's quarrel with his land. All the fibres of his being have kept him attached to Ireland, the setting of most of his plays and the source of nearly all his music. But he has been critical of Irish nationalist romanticism as a heady intoxicant for shallow souls and minds, and critical of Irish provincial puritanism, as absurd in his opinion as it is inimical to life. Nationalism became less meaningful to him than the fundamental unity of all desiring and aching mankind. It was not enough to win independence from England. One had to win independence from want and

xiii

pharisaism, too. The rift between O'Casey and Ireland started when the young zealot, who once or twice nearly lost his life for the national cause, began to incorporate the two primary struggles for subsistence and personal freedom in his work.

The struggle for bread and security, not to be evaded by patriotic mouthings or patriotism without content, appears most directly and effectively in *Juno and the Paycock* and *The Plough and the Stars.* It is something about which O'Casey could report at first hand as a charter member of the Dublin poor who lost his father at the age of three, was nobly underfed in childhood on a diet of hard bread and tea, and moved on from pittance to pittance as factory boy in a chandlery, dock worker, and stone breaker on a road-building crew after the age of thirteen. The other struggle—for a full and free life of the body and soul—appears in greater diffusion throughout his work. But it is especially strong in the later plays, appearing as the theme of the delightful *Cock-a-doodle-Dandy,* as well as of the one-acter *Bedtime Story,* as the source of the glorious humor of *Purple Dust,* and as the afflatus of *Within the Gates.* Scorn of hypocrisy and timidity, and sometimes a wild fantastication seemingly presided over by the great god Pan himself, characterize his protest against the suppression of life by rigid moralism and social conformity.

Independent Ireland has been troublesome to

O'Casey, and O'Casey, who fought for national independence in the Irish Citizen's Army, has been troublesome to Ireland ever since a patriotic riot was staged against *The Plough and the Stars* at its second public Abbey Theatre performance in 1926. They have been heroic opponents and it would appear to me that they cannot let each other alone as if they knew "deep down" that they are worthy of each other's mettle. Ireland certainly doesn't ignore O'Casey: He is constantly assailed in the Irish press. For all that, too, the Abbey has managed to produce *The Silver Tassie* at least twice, even though the original rejection of that play by Yeats and other Abbey directors caused the rupture between O'Casey and the Irish National Theatre. And it was his native Ireland that in 1943 first staged one of his most inflammatory dramas *Red Roses for Me* professionally. (In the United States we praise O'Casey, and he has long had the zealous support of such influential critics as Brooks Atkinson, George Jean Nathan, and Richard Watts, Jr., but we do not produce his plays. Though our producers often intend to, they discover that they cannot afford a production. Only off-Broadway groups, such as Margo Jones's arena theatre in Dallas or the Greenwich Village company that staged *The Plough and the Stars* in 1953, have managed a production now and then. In America, it would appear, we have to be poor before we can afford O'Casey.) O'Casey, on the other hand, never lets Ireland alone. His plays and his superbly written series of autobiographical books have been full to the brim with the bittersweet drink of this debauch of love and hate ever since he exiled himself to England a quarter of a century ago.

It is plain, then, that we must take cognizance of this relationship between man and country. Not merely, however, in order to understand the specific criticism of "manners" and politics to be found in a number of his plays, but in order to understand O'Casey's universality. Ireland is the chief symbol of his sense of outrage at the existence of human folly and evil. Ireland is also a symbol of humanity and delight in the world's wonders—the greatest of which, he believes, is mankind itself when it is releasing or endeavoring to release flesh and spirit. We may wonder how he has been able to reconcile his ideal of splendid individuality with a specific endorsement of political communism, if indeed it has been politics rather than some inviolate dream that has won his allegiance. And Irishmen may also wonder how he has been able to remain so close to Ireland, bringing so close a caress to the land with his word-music and portraits (especially of women), and yet spare it so little. But the answer is simple. O'Casey is too big for a small consistency. We might say of him as Whitman said of himself that he contains continents and that if he contradicts himself, well then he contradicts himself. His true consistency lies in the largeness of his genius.

I HAVE ELSEWHERE expressed this view by referring to him as a baroque dramatic poet who belongs to the spacious days of the English theatre in the company of Marlowe, Shakespeare and Ben Jonson more than he does to the contemporary theatre of small-beer sentiment and limited horizons. That is why he is so disturbing to the modern stage and why, at the same time, his work reads so well once we have got over the strangeness of the Irish dialect or the typographical representation of it. The former hod-carrier brought himself up on Shakespeare and the Bible, and he developed his feeling for dialogue and drama in a Dublin environment where the gesture of life was often broad and the speech torrential. The Abbey Theatre of his youth, which was the theatre of Synge's peasant plays, also breathed an ample spirit, whether of lyricism or humor. To its wild rustic notes, he was to add the still wilder notes and heartbeats of the city streets, a broader humor, and a deeper passion in general. The rest of his education, an immersion in the nationalist and working-class movements of southern Ireland, was mainly an education in turbulence.

From his unorthodox initiations into art and from a temperament unbridled in formative years by the genteel tradition come the main features of his work. O'Casey has been unable to accept the theatre as a settled institution requiring circumspect speech and action and neat form. He, on the contrary, has allowed the jagged and glittering chips of his anger and laughter or Rabelaisian levity to fly where they will. He has broken every mold of drama, since none could contain his dramatic impulse for long. We find him first variously using and extending the techniques and styles of realism in *Juno and the Paycock* and *The Plough and the Stars*, moving from family drama and a remarkable mixture of the comic and tragic modes in the former to symphonic episodic drama in the latter. Next we find him splitting dramatic style in two in *The Silver Tassie*, mingling realism and expressionism there; next, writing morality drama of epic proportions in *Within the Gates*, poetic and symbolic farce in *Purple Dust*, satiric fancy in *Cock-a-doodle Dandy* and *Time to Go*, and a variety of other kinds of drama in these and other plays. There is little point in attaching labels to them. It is important only to know that one is in the presence of an extraordinary imagination both poetic and theatrical, both verbal and visual— which is a sure sign of genius in a playwright.

That imagination is variable, too. Sometimes it produces an intensification of plausible characterization and events, as in *Juno and the Paycock* and *The Plough and the Stars*. We then get O'Casey's poetic, high-voltage realism. Sometimes the imagination leads to creative abstraction and we get poetic and high-voltage symbolism. Or O'Casey turns to the invention of wild and beautiful improbabilities, and the results are indefinable, although we call them fantasy. And whether growing naturally out of the playwright's material, superimposed by allegorical intention, or just freely invented, the poetic invention receives support from a fine flamboyance, a personal bravura both comic and heroic. A histrionic sensibility, indeed, is ever present in his work; it is thoroughly delightful when comic, if sometimes out of control when heroic. And whether or not always acceptable, it is plainly natural to O'Casey; its appearance has unmistakable spontaneity. He has been called "a genuine flamboyant" by no less weighty an authority than the London *Times Literary Supplement*.

A histrionic manifestation is his rhetoric. Whether motivated by characterization, as so admirably in the early plays, or whipped up more arbitrarily by the author's own excitations, this rhetoric is *music,* therefore forgivable, and *theatre,* therefore useful. It adds a dramatic dimension lacking in the work of tinny playwrights to which we have been accustomed in the commonplace theatre. There may be some deliberately typed characters in his plays, there may be rather stock characters in the later ones, such as the comic Englishmen of *Purple Dust,* but there can be no commonplace ones when O'Casey's rhetoric rings out. If the talk doesn't always quite *make* the man, it does not fail to *elevate* him. And if sometimes the writing doesn't yield a meaning one can parse out of sentences, the sound and the rhythm create an enchantment where enchantment is needed and the scene must be uplifted. To want to dispense with such rhetoric, I have said elsewhere, is an error—it is tantamount to wanting to ban an orchestra because the kettledrums are loud. Volume is inherent in the orchestra located in O'Casey's larynx. He has used language as though he were writing not for our modern picture-frame stage, but for the Elizabethan platform on which most of our great English drama was created. The music associated with his rhetoric is also dramatically important. His characters are often to be found "lilting" when they are most alive—that is, when they are most strongly concerned with their feelings. And working in the great Elizabethan stage tradition, O'Casey makes arias out of his emotions, whether he execrates evil or celebrates life.

Still, no matter how carefully we particularize this not easily definable playwright's attributes, it is certain that we shall not make him less disconcerting to those who have lukewarm or fastidious temperaments or have artificially cultivated a so-called classical taste. To look too precisely for the nature of his power seems to me like trying to figure out the electro-magnetic field after having been knocked down by lightning. It is only by responding to the whole effect he endeavors to exert that we may get to know him. And if a total response cannot be forced from a public by fiat, it may well be elicited from us by O'Casey's own example. Wherever we find him in his work, we can be sure that *he* has not withheld himself.

August 12, 1954

On Playwriting

LOTS OF PEOPLE YEARN to be writers; why, I don't know, for all other talents are as important, and have artistry in themselves—the tractor driver, the printer, the farm hand, the railroad worker, the miner. Each does something another couldn't do: like these, hard work is the stuff a writer's job is made on. Since God said "By the sweat of his face shall man eat bread," there's been no escape from hard work for anyone who hasn't a big unearned income; and these have always been challenged by God and man.

When I stepped from hard manual work to writing, I just stepped from one kind of hard work to another. I found a kindred thrill in helping to place the last tile on the roof of a house newly built as I find now in putting down the last word of a finished play or biographical volume. There is satisfaction in all things done well. Writing is a gift as is the flair for science, for farming, for building, for teaching, for business, for statesmanship; unique in itself, equal to all other gifts, but no more important than any other eager use of man's energy and imagination.

So I set out to become a playwright, partly because, when I was a lad, paper-covered plays could be bought for a penny each. Most of them were worthless, and are now forgotten; but there were ones by Goldsmith, Sheridan, and Boucicault (later came plays of Shakespeare), and these had a good influence in setting me on the right road. They inured me into the method of building up a story through the medium of conversation alone, and to this day I find it hard to read a novel contentedly, unless it be of the best, its greatness forcing itself well into the fibres of the mind.

Before Curtain-Rise

O'CASEY HAS A GOOD NAME in some places and a very bad one in others. No one can go through life without getting a bad name from someone somewhere. It is the vivifying lot of anyone who tries to do anything new: to paint his hall-door with a new color; to learn to play a fiddle; or to write a new-mannered play. Old friends will shake sage heads, and say, He's going beyond himself; he is to be pitied. And if the playright says a word against, or ventures a laugh at, the commoner and cosiest thoughts of those who live around him, there is an agonised uproar, and vicious cries go up to God.

Those who try to do things mustn't let themselves be bothered overmuch by a bad name or a good one; mustn't let themselves be puffed up by a clap on the back or frightened by a knock on the snout. It isn't possible, of course, not to feel joy at a clap on the back, not to feel some kind of pain from a knock on the snout. As a playwright, I have received knocks when the hair was brown and the face young-looking; and I'm still getting them when I am old and grey and full of tears. Well, not quite full of tears, for within me the laugh comes and goes and always comes again. As well, one can hit back, and land, at times, many a gregorian slashing blow on the conk of him who tries to trip, or on one who aims a blow below the belt.

The knocks mentioned aren't those taps given by the accredited critics of the drama whose integrity as regards the Drama must be equal to that of the playwright, and who are as eager as the playwright himself that the play shoved on the stage should be worthy of the Theater when its best banner, blazoned with the Drama's honors, is flying from its turrets. Indeed, few of them fail to notice, or even to praise, any quick rhythmic patter of steady feet even momentarily appearing through the clumsy action of a stumbling play. These are the opinions that the Drama cannot do without, however we playwrights may wince at some of the comments, for they have been woven into long experience and a wide knowledge of the things belonging to the peace and war of the Theater.

No, not these, but those resentful of any harm to their petted humbug, closeted cliché, or pietistic stutter, frightened of losing their fear, who shout out under the name of God to shut tight the mouth that tries to utter some whisper of the truth. All sorts and conditions of men, all ranks, from a Lord Chamberlain of his late Majesty of England, who didn't like the theme of one play, to the [leftist] Mister Mike Gold up in New York, who didn't like the theme of another, or the playwright either. Well, the only retort to a boo is a bah!

In a number of his plays, Yeats, the poet brings in music from the flute, zither, drum, and gong— elegant sounds, and beautiful too. I, too, have tried to bring in the music of the flute, the fiddle, and the drum; not in the actual instruments, not through them, but by an occasional song, and by the lilt in the dialogue; by weaving into the emotional action of the plays the shrill or plaintive notes of the flute and the reckless rally that the drums of life so often give.

Well, here are the plays, and as the curtain rises, let me say quickly that they have had, at least, the grand quality of causing the commotion of clapping of hands, and the commotion, too, of hatred, fear, and loud cries to God for help to kill them dead from fanatics and fools; first in Dublin, Cork, Limerick, and Galway, then down in London, then up north in Newcastle-on-Tyne; in America, in Houston, down in Texas, up in Boston in Massachusetts (Boston well forgiven because it was the cradle of the great prose-poet, Emerson);

across Europe, in Vienna and Berlin. Strike up
the drums! Come on, Yeats—sing out your song!

> *Those fanatics all that we would undo;*
> *Down the fanatic, down the clown;*
> *Down, down, hammer them down,*
> *Down to the tune of O'Donnell Abu.*

July, 1954

CONTENTS

Contents

A TRAGEDY IN TWO ACTS

The Shadow of a Gunman

CHARACTERS IN THE PLAY

DONAL DAVOREN
SEUMAS SHIELDS, *a pedlar*
TOMMY OWENS   *Residents in*
ADOLPHUS GRIGSON   *the Tenement*
MRS. GRIGSON
MINNIE POWELL
MR. MULLIGAN, *the landlord*
MR. MAGUIRE, *soldier of the I.R.A.*
MRS. HENDERSON   *Residents of an*
MR. GALLOGHER   *adjoining Tenement*
AN AUXILIARY

SCENE

A room in a tenement in Hilljoy Square, Dublin.
Some hours elapse between the two acts. The period of
the Play is May 1920.

ACT I

A Return Room in a tenement house in Hilljoy Square. At the back two large windows looking out into the yard ; they occupy practically the whole of the back wall space. Between the windows is a cupboard, on the top of which is a pile of books. The doors are open, and on these are hanging a number of collars and ties. Running parallel with the windows is a stretcher bed ; another runs at right angles along the wall at right. At the head of this bed is a door leading to the rest of the house. The wall on the left runs diagonally, so that the fireplace — which is in the centre — is plainly visible. On the mantelshelf to the right is a statue of the Virgin, to the left a statue of the Sacred Heart, and in the centre a crucifix. Around the fireplace are a few common cooking utensils. In the centre of the room is a table, on which are a typewriter, a candle and candlestick, a bunch of wild flowers in a vase, writing materials and a number of books. There are two chairs, one near the fireplace and one at the table. The aspect of the place is one of absolute untidiness, engendered on the one hand by the congenital slovenliness of Seumas Shields, and on the other by the temperament of Donal Davoren, making it appear impossible to effect an improvement in such a place.

Davoren is sitting at the table typing. He is about thirty. There is in his face an expression that seems to indicate an eternal war between weakness and strength ; there is in the lines of the brow and chin an indication of a desire for activity, while in his eyes there is visible an unquenchable tendency towards rest. His struggle through life has been a hard one, and his efforts have been handicapped by an inherited and self-developed devotion to " the might of design, the mystery of colour, and the belief in the redemption of all things by beauty everlasting ". His life

*would drive him mad were it not for the fact that he never knew
any other.   He bears upon his body the marks of the struggle for
existence and the efforts towards self-expression.*

*Seumas Shields, who is in the bed next the wall to the right,
is a heavily built man of thirty-five ; he is dark-haired and
sallow-complexioned.   In him is frequently manifested the superstition, the fear and the malignity of primitive man.*

Davoren [lilting an air as he composes] :

> Or when sweet Summer's ardent arms outspread,
> Entwined with flowers,
> Enfold us, like two lovers newly wed,
> Thro' ravish'd hours —
> Then sorrow, woe and pain lose all their powers,
> For each is dead, and life is only ours.

> [*A woman's figure appears at the window and taps loudly
> on one of the panes ; at the same moment there is loud
> knocking at the door.*

Voice of Woman at Window. Are you awake, Mr. Shields
— Mr. Shields, are you awake ? Are you goin' to get
up to-day at all, at all ?

Voice at the Door. Mr. Shields, is there any use of callin'
you at all ? This is a nice nine o'clock : do you know
what time it is, Mr. Shields ?

Seumas [loudly]. Yus !

Voice at the Door. Why don't you get up, then, an' not
have the house turned into a bedlam tryin' to waken
you ?

Seumas [shouting]. All right, all right, all right ! The
way these oul' ones bawl at a body ! Upon my soul !
I'm beginnin' to believe that the Irish People are still

in the stone age. If they could they'd throw a bomb at you.

Davoren. A land mine exploding under the bed is the only thing that would lift you out of it.

Seumas [*stretching himself*]. Oh-h-h. I was fast in the arms of Morpheus — he was one of the infernal deities, son of Somnus, wasn't he?

Davoren. I think so.

Seumas. The poppy was his emblem, wasn't it?

Davoren. Ah, I don't know.

Seumas. It's a bit cold this morning, I think, isn't it?

Davoren. It's quite plain I'm not going to get much quietness in this house.

Seumas [*after a pause*]. I wonder what time is it?

Davoren. The Angelus went some time ago.

Seumas [*sitting up in bed suddenly*]. The Angelus! It couldn't be that late, could it? I asked them to call me at nine so that I could get Mass before I went on my rounds. Why didn't you give us a rap?

Davoren. Give you a rap! Why, man, they've been thundering at the door and hammering at the window for the past two hours, till the house shook to its very foundations, but you took less notice of the infernal din than I would take of the strumming of a grasshopper.

Seumas. There's no fear of you thinking of any one else when you're at your poetry. The land of Saints and Scholars 'ill shortly be a land of bloody poets. [*Anxiously*] I suppose Maguire has come and gone?

Davoren. Maguire ? No, he hasn't been here — why, did you expect him ?

Seumas [*in a burst of indignation*]. He said he'd be here at nine. " Before the last chime has struck," says he, " I'll be coming in on the door," and it must be — what time is it now ?

Davoren. Oh, it must be half-past twelve.

Seumas. Did anybody ever see the like of the Irish People ? Is there any use of tryin' to do anything in this country ? Have everything packed and ready, have everything packed and ready, have . . .

Davoren. And have you everything packed and ready ?

Seumas. What's the use of having anything packed and ready when he didn't come ? [*He rises and dresses himself.*] No wonder this unfortunate country is as it is, for you can't depend upon the word of a single individual in it. I suppose he was too damn lazy to get up ; he wanted the streets to be well aired first. —Oh, Kathleen ni Houlihan, your way's a thorny way.

Davoren. Ah me ! alas, pain, pain ever, for ever !

Seumas. That's from Shelley's *Prometheus Unbound.* I could never agree with Shelley, not that there's anything to be said against him as a poet — as a poet — but . . .

Davoren. He flung a few stones through stained-glass windows.

Seumas. He wasn't the first nor he won't be the last to do that, but the stained-glass windows — more than

ever of them — are here still, and Shelley is doing a
jazz dance down below.

> [*He gives a snarling laugh of pleasure.*

Davoren [*shocked*]. And you actually rejoice and are ex-
ceedingly glad that, as you believe, Shelley, the sensitive, high-minded, noble-hearted Shelley, is suffering
the tortures of the damned.

Seumas. I rejoice in the vindication of the Church and
Truth.

Davoren. Bah. You know as little about truth as anybody else, and you care as little about the Church as
the least of those that profess her faith ; your religion
is simply the state of being afraid that God will torture
your soul in the next world as you are afraid the
Black and Tans will torture your body in this.

Seumas. Go on, me boy ; I'll have a right laugh at you
when both of us are dead.

Davoren. You're welcome to laugh as much as you like
at me when both of us are dead.

Seumas [*as he is about to put on his collar and tie*]. I don't
think I need to wash meself this morning ; do I look
all right ?

Davoren. Oh, you're all right ; it's too late now to start
washing yourself. Didn't you wash yourself yesterday
morning ?

Seumas. I gave meself a great rub yesterday. [*He proceeds
to pack various articles into an attaché case — spoons, forks,
laces, thread, etc.*] I think I'll bring out a few of the
braces too ; damn it, they're well worth sixpence each ;
there's great stuff in them — did you see them ?

Davoren. Yes, you showed them to me before.

Seumas. They're great value ; I only hope I'll be able to get enough o' them. I'm wearing a pair of them meself — they'd do Cuchullian, they're so strong. [*Counting the spoons*] There's a dozen in each of these parcels — three, six, nine — damn it, there's only eleven in this one. I better try another. Three, six, nine — my God, there's only eleven in this one too, and one of them bent ! Now I suppose I'll have to go through the whole bloody lot of them, for I'd never be easy in me mind thinkin' there'd be more than a dozen in some o' them. And still we're looking for freedom — ye gods, it's a glorious country ! [*He lets one fall, which he stoops to pick up.*] Oh, my God, there's the braces after breakin'.

Davoren. That doesn't look as if they were strong enough for Cuchullian.

Seumas. I put a heavy strain on them too sudden. There's that fellow Maguire never turned up, either ; he's almost too lazy to wash himself. [*As he is struggling with the braces the door is hastily shoved in and Maguire rushes in with a handbag.*] This is a nice nine o'clock. What's the use of you coming at this hour o' the day ? Do you think we're going to work be moonlight ? If you weren't goin' to come at nine couldn't you say you weren't. . . .

Maguire. Keep your hair on ; I just blew in to tell you that I couldn't go to-day at all. I have to go to Knocksedan.

Seumas. Knocksedan ! An' what, in the name o' God, is bringin' you to Knocksedan ?

Maguire. Business, business.   I'm going out to catch
butterflies.

Seumas. If you want to make a cod of anybody, make a
cod of somebody else, an' don't be tryin' to make a
cod o' me.   Here I've had everything packed an'
ready for hours ; you were to be here at nine, an' you
wait till just one o'clock to come rushin' in like a mad
bull to say you've got to go to Knocksedan !   Can't
you leave Knocksedan till to-morrow ?

Maguire. Can't be did, can't be did, Seumas ; if I
waited till to-morrow all the butterflies might be dead.
I'll leave this bag here till this evening. [*He puts the bag
in a corner of the room.*]   Good-bye . . . ee.
                    [*He is gone before Seumas is aware of it.*

Seumas [*with a gesture of despair*]. Oh, this is a hopeless
country !   There's a fellow that thinks that the four
cardinal virtues are not to be found outside an Irish
Republic.   I don't want to boast about myself — I
don't want to boast about myself, and I suppose I
could call meself as good a Gael as some of those that
are knocking about now — knocking about now — as
good a Gael as some that are knocking about now, —
but I remember the time when I taught Irish six
nights a week, when in the Irish Republican Brotherhood I paid me rifle levy like a man, an' when the
Church refused to have anything to do with James
Stephens, I tarred a prayer for the repose of his soul
on the steps of the Pro-Cathedral.   Now, after all me
work for Dark Rosaleen, the only answer you can get
from a roarin' Republican to a simple question is
" good-bye . . . ee ".   What, in the name o' God,
can be bringin' him to Knocksedan ?

Davoren. Hadn't you better run out and ask him?

Seumas. That's right, that's right — make a joke about it! That's the Irish People all over — they treat a joke as a serious thing and a serious thing as a joke. Upon me soul, I'm beginning to believe that the Irish People aren't, never were, an' never will be fit for self-government. They've made Balor of the Evil Eye King of Ireland, an' so signs on it there's neither conscience nor honesty from one end of the country to the other. Well, I hope he'll have a happy day in Knocksedan. [*A knock at the door.*] Who's that?

[Another knock.

Seumas [*irritably*]. Who's that; who's there?

Davoren [*more irritably*]. Halt and give the countersign — damn it, man, can't you go and see?
> [*Seumas goes over and opens the door. A man of about sixty is revealed, dressed in a faded blue serge suit; a half tall hat is on his head. It is evident that he has no love for Seumas, who denies him the deference he believes is due from a tenant to a landlord. He carries some papers in his hand.*

The Landlord [*ironically*]. Good-day, Mr. Shields; it's meself that hopes you're feelin' well — you're lookin' well, anyhow — though you can't always go be looks nowadays.

Seumas. It doesn't matter whether I'm lookin' well or feelin' well; I'm all right, thanks be to God.

The Landlord. I'm very glad to hear it.

Seumas. It doesn't matter whether you're glad to hear it or not, Mr. Mulligan.

The Landlord. You're not inclined to be very civil, Mr. Shields.

Seumas. Look here, Mr. Mulligan, if you come here to raise an argument, I've something to do — let me tell you that.

The Landlord. I don't come here to raise no argument ; a person ud have small gains argufyin' with you — let me tell you that.

Seumas. I've no time to be standin' here gostherin' with you — let me shut the door, Mr. Mulligan.

The Landlord. You'll not shut no door till you've heard what I've got to say.

Seumas. Well, say it then, an' go about your business.

The Landlord. You're very high an' mighty, but take care you're not goin' to get a drop. What a baby you are not to know what brings me here ! Maybe you thought I was goin' to ask you to come to tea.

Davoren. Ah me ! alas, pain, pain ever, for ever !

Seumas. Are you goin' to let me shut the door, Mr. Mulligan ?

The Landlord. I'm here for me rent ; you don't like the idea of bein' asked to pay your just an' lawful debts.

Seumas. You'll get your rent when you learn to keep your rent-book in a proper way.

The Landlord. I'm not goin' to take any lessons from you, anyhow.

Seumas. I want to have no more talk with you, Mr. Mulligan.

The Landlord. Talk or no talk, you owe me eleven weeks' rent, an' it's marked down again' you in black an' white.

Seumas. I don't care a damn if it was marked down in green, white, an' yellow.

The Landlord. You're a terribly independent fellow, an' it ud be fitter for you to be less funny an' stop tryin' to be billickin' honest an' respectable people.

Seumas. Just you be careful what you're sayin', Mr. Mulligan.   There's law in the land still.

The Landlord. Be me sowl there is, an' you're goin' to get a little of it now.   [*He offers the papers to Seumas*] Them's for you.

Seumas [*hesitating to take them*]. I want to have nothing to do with you, Mr. Mulligan.

The Landlord [*throwing the papers in the centre of the room*]. What am I better ?   It was the sorry day I ever let you come into this house.   Maybe them notices to quit will stop your writin' letters to the papers about me an' me house.

Davoren. For goodness' sake, bring the man in, and don't be discussing the situation like a pair of primitive troglodytes.

Seumas [*taking no notice*]. Writing letters to the papers is my business, an' I'll write as often as I like, when I like, an' how I like.

The Landlord. You'll not write about this house at all events.   You can blow about the state of the yard, but you took care to say nothin' about payin' rent :

oh no, that's not in your line. But since you're not satisfied with the house, you can pack up an' go to another.

Seumas. I'll go, Mr. Mulligan, when I think fit, an' no sooner.

The Landlord. Not content with keeping the rent, you're startin' to bring in lodgers — [*to Davoren*] not that I'm sayin' anythin' again' you, sir. Bringin' in lodgers without as much as be your leave — what's the world comin' to at all that a man's house isn't his own? But I'll soon put a stop to your gallop, for on the twenty-eight of the next month out you go, an' there'll be few sorry to see your back.

Seumas. I'll go when I like.

The Landlord. I'll let you see whether you own the house or no.

Seumas. I'll go when I like!

The Landlord. We'll see about that.

Seumas. We'll see.

The Landlord. Ay, we'll see.
              [*The Landlord goes out and Seumas shuts the door.*

The Landlord [*outside*]. Mind you, I'm in earnest; you'll not stop in this house a minute longer than the twenty-eight.

Seumas [*with a roar*]. Ah, go to hell!

Davoren [*pacing the room as far as the space will permit*]. What in the name of God persuaded me to come to such a house as this?

Seumas. It's nothing when you're used to it; you're too

thin-skinned altogether. The oul' sod's got the wind up about you, that's all.

Davoren. Got the wind up about me !

Seumas. He thinks you're on the run. He's afraid of a raid, and that his lovely property'll be destroyed.

Davoren. But why, in the name of all that's sensible, should he think that I'm on the run ?

Seumas. Sure they all think you're on the run. Mrs. Henderson thinks it, Tommy Owens thinks it, Mrs. an' Mr. Grigson think it, an' Minnie Powell thinks it too. [*Picking up his attaché case*] I'd better be off if I'm goin' to do anything to-day.

Davoren. What are we going to do with these notices to quit ?

Seumas. Oh, shove them up on the mantelpiece behind one of the statues.

Davoren. Oh, I mean what action shall we take ?

Seumas. I haven't time to stop now. We'll talk about them when I come back. . . . I'll get me own back on that oul' Mulligan yet. I wish to God they would come an' smash his rookery to pieces, for it's all he thinks of, and, mind you, oul' Mulligan would call himself a descendant of the true Gaels of Banba — [*as he goes out*] :

> Oh, proud were the chieftains of famed Inisfail.
> Is truagh gan oidher 'na Vfarradh.
> The stars of our sky an' the salt of our soil —

Oh, Kathleen ni Houlihan, your way's a thorny way !
[*He goes out.*

Davoren [*returning to the table and sitting down at the type-writer*]. Oh, Donal Og O'Davoren, your way's a thorny way. Your last state is worse than your first. Ah me, alas ! Pain, pain ever, for ever. Like thee, Prometheus, no change, no pause, no hope. Ah, life, life, life ! [*There is a gentle knock at the door.*] Another Fury come to plague me now ! [*Another knock, a little louder.*

Davoren. You can knock till you're tired.

[*The door opens and Minnie Powell enters with an easy confidence one would not expect her to possess from her gentle way of knocking. She is a girl of twenty-three, but the fact of being forced to earn her living, and to take care of herself, on account of her parents' early death, has given her a force and an assurance beyond her years. She has lost the sense of fear (she does not know this), and, consequently, she is at ease in all places and before all persons, even those of a superior education, so long as she meets them in the atmosphere that surrounds the members of her own class. Her hair is brown, neither light nor dark, but partaking of both tints according to the light or shade she may happen to be in. Her well-shaped figure — a rare thing in a city girl — is charmingly dressed in a brown tailor-made costume, her stockings and shoes are a darker brown tint than the costume, and all are crowned by a silk tam-o'-shanter of a rich blue tint.*

Minnie. Are you in, Mr. Shields ?

Davoren [*rapidly*]. No, he's not, Minnie ; he's just gone out — if you run out quickly you're sure to catch him.

Minnie. Oh, it's all right, Mr. Davoren, you'll do just

as well ; I just come in for a drop o' milk for a cup
o' tea ; I shouldn't be troublin' you this way, but I'm
sure you don't mind.

Davoren [*dubiously*]. No trouble in the world ; delighted,
I'm sure. [*Giving her the milk*] There, will you have
enough ?

Minnie. Plenty, lashins, thanks. Do you be all alone all
the day, Mr. Davoren ?

Davoren. No, indeed ; I wish to God I was.

Minnie. It's not good for you then. I don't know how
you like to be by yourself — I couldn't stick it long.

Davoren [*wearily*]. No ?

Minnie. No, indeed ; [*with rapture*] there's nothin' I'm
more fond of than a Hooley. I was at one last Sunday
— I danced rings round me ! Tommy Owens was
there — you know Tommy Owens, don't you ?

Davoren. I can't say I do.

Minnie. D'ye not ? The little fellow that lives with his
mother in the two-pair back — [*ecstatically*] he's a
gorgeous melodeon player !

Davoren. A gifted son of Orpheus, eh ?

Minnie [*who never heard of Orpheus*]. You've said it, Mr.
Davoren : the son of poor oul' Battie Owens, a
weeshy, dawny, bit of a man that was never sober an'
was always talkin' politics. Poor man, it killed him in
the long run.

Davoren. A man should always be drunk, Minnie, when
he talks politics — it's the only way in which to make
them important.

Minnie. Tommy takes after the oul' fellow, too ; he'd talk from morning till night when he has a few jars in him. [*Suddenly ; for like all of her class, Minnie is not able to converse very long on the one subject, and her thoughts spring from one thing to another*] Poetry is a grand thing, Mr. Davoren, I'd love to be able to write a poem — a lovely poem on Ireland an' the men o' '98.

Davoren. Oh, we've had enough of poems, Minnie, about '98, and of Ireland, too.

Minnie. Oh, there's a thing for a Republican to say ! But I know what you mean : it's time to give up the writing an' take to the gun. [*Her roving eye catches sight of the flowers in the vase*] What's Mr. Shields doin' with the oul' weeds ?

Davoren. Those aren't Shields', they're mine. Wild flowers is a kindlier name for them, Minnie, than weeds. These are wild violets, this is an *Arum maculatum*, or Wake Robin, and these are Celandines, a very beautiful flower related to the buttercups. [*He quotes*] :

> One day, when Morn's half-open'd eyes
> Were bright with Spring sunshine —
> My hand was clasp'd in yours, dear love,
> And yours was clasp'd in mine —
> We bow'd as worshippers before
> The Golden Celandine.

Minnie. Oh, aren't they lovely, an' isn't the poem lovely, too ! I wonder, now, who she was.

Davoren [*puzzled*]. She, who ?

Minnie. Why, the . . . [*roguishly*] Oh, be the way you don't know.

Davoren. Know ? I'm sure I don't know.

Minnie. It doesn't matter, anyhow — that's your own business ; I suppose I don't know her.

Davoren. Know her — know whom ?

Minnie [*shyly*]. Her whose hand was clasped in yours, an' yours was clasped in hers.

Davoren. Oh, that — that was simply a poem I quoted about the Celandine, that might apply to any girl — to you, for instance.

Minnie [*greatly relieved, coming over and sitting beside Davoren*]. But you have a sweetheart, all the same, Mr. Davoren, haven't you ?

Davoren. I ? No, not one, Minnie.

Minnie. Oh, now, you can tell that to some one else ; aren't you a poet an' aren't all the girls fond o' poets ?

Davoren. That may be, but all the poets aren't fond of girls.

Minnie. They are in the story-books, ay, and fond of more than one, too. [*With a questioning look*] Are you fond of them, Mr. Davoren ?

Davoren. Of course I like girls, Minnie, especially girls who can add to their charms by the way in which they dress, like you, for instance.

Minnie. Oh, now, you're on for coddin' me, Mr. Davoren.

Davoren. No, really, Minnie, I'm not ; you are a very charming little girl indeed.

Minnie. Then if I'm a charmin' little girl, you ought to be able to write a poem about me.

Davoren [*who has become susceptible to the attractiveness of Minnie, catching her hand*]. And so I will, so I will, Minnie ; I have written them about girls not half so pretty as yourself.

Minnie. Ah, I knew you had one, I knew you had one now.

Davoren. Nonsense. Every girl a poet writes about isn't his sweetheart ; Annie Laurie wasn't the sweetheart of Bobbie Burns.

Minnie. You needn't tell me she wasn't ; " An' for bonnie Annie Laurie I'd lay me down an' die ". No man ud lay down an' die for any but a sweetheart, not even for a wife.

Davoren. No man, Minnie, willingly dies for anything.

Minnie. Except for his country, like Robert Emmet.

Davoren. Even he would have lived on if he could ; he died not to deliver Ireland. The British Government killed him to save the British nation.

Minnie. You're only jokin' now ; you'd die for your country.

Davoren. I don't know so much about that.

Minnie. You would, you would, you would — I know what you are.

Davoren. What am I ?

Minnie [*in a whisper*]. A gunman on the run !

Davoren [*too pleased to deny it*]. Maybe I am, and maybe I'm not

Minnie. Oh, I know, I know, I know. Do you never be afraid ?

Davoren. Afraid ! Afraid of what ?

Minnie. Why, the ambushes of course ; *I'm* all of a tremble when I hear a shot go off, an' what must it be in the middle of the firin' ?

Davoren [*delighted at Minnie's obvious admiration ; leaning back in his chair, and lighting a cigarette with placid affectation*]. I'll admit one does be a little nervous at first, but a fellow gets used to it after a bit, till, at last, a gunman throws a bomb as carelessly as a schoolboy throws a snowball.

Minnie [*fervently*]. I wish it was all over, all the same. [*Suddenly, with a tremor in her voice*] You'll take care of yourself, won't you, won't you, Donal — I mean, Mr. Davoren ?

Davoren [*earnestly*]. Call me Donal, Minnie ; we're friends, great friends now — [*putting his arm around her*] go on, Minnie, call me Donal, let me hear you say Donal.

Minnie. The place badly needs a tidyin' up . . . Donal — there now, are you satisfied ? [*Rapidly, half afraid of Davoren's excited emotions*] But it really does, it's in an awful state. To-morrow's a half-day, an' I'll run in an' straighten it up a bit.

Davoren [*frightened at the suggestion*]. No, no, Minnie, you're too pretty for that sort of work ; besides, the people of the house would be sure to start talking about you.

Minnie. An' do you think Minnie Powell cares whether

they'll talk or no? She's had to push her way through life up to this without help from any one, an' she's not goin' to ask their leave, now, to do what she wants to do.

Davoren [*forgetting his timidity in the honest joy of appreciating the independent courage of Minnie*]. My soul within art thou, Minnie! A pioneer in action as I am a pioneer in thought. The two powers that shall " grasp this sorry scheme of things entire, and mould life nearer to the heart's desire ". Lovely little Minnie, and brave as well ; brave little Minnie, and lovely as well !

[*His disengaged hand lifts up her bent head, and he looks earnestly at her ; he is stooping to kiss her, when Tommy Owens appears at the door, which Minnie has left partially open. Tommy is about twenty-five years of age. He is small and thin ; his words are uttered in a nasal drawl ; his voice is husky, due to frequent drinks and perpetual cigarette-smoking. He tries to get rid of the huskiness by an occasional cough. Tommy is a hero-worshipper, and, like many others, he is anxious to be on familiar terms with those who he thinks are braver than he is himself, and whose approbation he tries to win by an assumption equal to their own. He talks in a staccato manner. He has a few drinks taken — it is too early to be drunk — that make him talkative. He is dressed in a suit of dungarees, and gives a gentle cough to draw attention to his presence.*]

Tommy. I seen nothin' — honest — thought you was learnin' to typewrite — Mr. Davoren teachin' you. I seen nothin' else — s'help me God !

Minnie. We'd be hard put to it if we minded what you seen, Tommy Owens.

Tommy. Right, Minnie, Tommy Owens has a heart —
Evenin', Mr. Davoren — don't mind me comin' in —
I'm Tommy Owens — live up in the two-pair back,
workin' in Ross an' Walpole's — Mr. Shields knows
me well ; you needn't be afraid o' me, Mr. Davoren.

Davoren. Why should I be afraid of you, Mr. Owens, or
of anybody else ?

Tommy. Why should you, indeed ?　We're all friends
here — Mr. Shields knows me well — all you've got
to say is, "Do you know Tommy Owens ?" an'
he'll tell you the sort of a man Tommy Owens is.
There's no flies on Tommy — got me ?

Minnie. For goodness' sake, Tommy, leave Mr. Davoren
alone — he's got enough burgeons on him already.

Tommy. Not a word, Minnie, not a word — Mr.
Davoren understands me well, as man to man.　It's
"Up the Republic" all the time — eh, Mr. Davoren ?

Davoren. I know nothing about the Republic ; I have
no connection with the politics of the day, and I don't
want to have any connection.

Tommy. You needn't say no more — a nod's as good as
a wink to a blind horse — you've no meddlin' or
makin' with it, good, bad, or indifferent, pro nor con ;
I know it an' Minnie knows it — give me your hand.
[*He catches Davoren's hand*] Two firm hands clasped
together will all the power outbrave of the heartless
English tyrant, the Saxon coward an' knave. That's
Tommy Owens' hand, Mr. Davoren, the hand of a
man, a man — Mr. Shields knows me well.

　　　　　　　　　　　　　[*He breaks into song.*

High upon the gallows tree stood the noble-hearted three,
By the vengeful tyrant stricken in their bloom ;
But they met him face to face with the spirit of their race,
And they went with souls undaunted to their doom !

Minnie [*in an effort to quell his fervour*]. Tommy Owens, for
goodness' sake . . .

Tommy [*overwhelming her with a shout*] :

God save Ireland ses the hayros, God save Ireland ses we all,
Whether on the scaffold high or the battle-field we die,
Oh, what matter when for Ayryinn dear we fall !

[*Tearfully*] Mr. Davoren, I'd die for Ireland !

Davoren. I know you would, I know you would, Tommy.

Tommy. I never got a chance — they never gave me a
chance — but all the same I'd be there if I was called
on — Mr. Shields knows that — ask Mr. Shields, Mr.
Davoren.

Davoren. There's no necessity, Tommy ; I know you're
the right stuff if you got the chance, but remember that
" he also serves who only stands and waits ".

Tommy [*fiercely*]. I'm bloody well tired o' waitin' — we're
all tired o' waitin'. Why isn't every man in Ireland
out with the I.R.A. ? Up with the barricades, up
with the barricades ; it's now or never, now an' for
ever, as Sarsfield said at the battle o' Vinegar Hill.
Up with the barricades — that's Tommy Owens —
an' a penny buys a whistle. Let them as thinks
different say different — what do you say, Mr.
Davoren ?

Davoren. I say, Tommy, you ought to go up and get your

dinner, for if you wait much longer it won't be worth eating.

Tommy. Oh, damn the dinner ; who'd think o' dinner an' Ireland fightin' to be free ? — not Tommy Owens, anyhow. It's only the Englishman who's always thinkin' of his belly.

Minnie. Tommy Owens !

Tommy. Excuse me, Miss Powell, in the ardure ov me anger I disremembered there was a lady present.

> [*Voices are heard outside, and presently Mrs. Henderson comes into the room, followed by Mr. Gallogher, who, however, lingers at the door, too timid to come any farther. Mrs. Henderson is a massive woman in every way ; massive head, arms, and body ; massive voice, and a massive amount of self-confidence. She is a mountain of good nature, and during the interview she behaves towards Davoren with deferential self-assurance. She dominates the room, and seems to occupy the whole of it. She is dressed poorly but tidily, wearing a white apron and a large shawl. Mr. Gallogher, on the other hand, is a spare little man with a spare little grey beard and a thin, nervous voice. He is dressed as well as a faded suit of blue will allow him to be. He is obviously ill at ease during his interview with Davoren. He carries a hard hat, much the worse for wear, under his left arm, and a letter in his right hand.*

Mrs. Henderson [*entering the room*]. Come along in, Mr. Gallicker, Mr. Davoren won't mind ; it's him as can put you in the way o' havin' your wrongs righted ; come on in, man, an' don't be so shy — Mr. Davoren is wan ov ourselves that stands for govermint ov the people with the people by the people. You'll find

you'll be as welcome as the flowers in May. Good
evenin', Mr. Davoren, an' God an' His holy angels be
between you an' all harm.

Tommy [*effusively*]. Come on, Mr. Gallicker, an' don't be
a stranger — we're all friends here — anything special
to be done or particular advice asked, here's your man
here.

Davoren [*subconsciously pleased, but a little timid of the belief
that he is connected with the gunmen*]. I'm very busy just
now, Mrs. Henderson, and really . . .

Mrs. Henderson [*mistaking the reason of his embarrassment*].
Don't be put out, Mr. Davoren, we won't keep you
more nor a few minutes. It's not in me or in Mr.
Gallicker to spoil sport. Him an' me was young once,
an' knows what it is to be strolling at night in the
pale moonlight, with arms round one another. An'
I wouldn't take much an' say there's game in Mr.
Gallicker still, for I seen, sometimes, a dangerous cock
in his eye. But we won't keep you an' Minnie long
asunder ; he's the letter an' all written. You must
know, Mr. Davoren — excuse me for not introducin'
him sooner — this is Mr. Gallicker, that lives in the
front drawin'-room ov number fifty-five, as decent an'
honest an' quiet a man as you'd meet in a day's walk.
An' so signs on it, it's them as 'ill be imposed upon —
read the letter, Mr. Gallicker.

Tommy. Read away, Mr. Gallicker, it will be attended
to, never fear ; we know our own know, eh, Mr.
Davoren ?

Minnie. Hurry up, Mr. Gallicker, an' don't be keeping
Mr. Davoren.

Mrs. Henderson. Give him time, Minnie Powell. Give him time. You must know in all fairity, Mr. Davoren, that the family livin' in the next room to Mr. Gallicker — the back drawin'-room, to be particular — am I right or am I wrong, Mr. Gallicker?

Mr. Gallogher. You're right, Mrs. Henderson, perfectly right, indeed — that's the very identical room.

Mrs. Henderson. Well, Mr. Davoren, the people in the back drawin'-room, or, to be more particular, the residents — that's the word that's writ in the letter — am I right or am I wrong, Mr. Gallicker?

Mr. Gallogher. You're right, Mrs. Henderson, perfectly accurate — that's the very identical word.

Mrs. Henderson. Well, Mr. Davoren, the residents in the back drawin'-room, as I aforesaid, is nothin' but a gang o' tramps that oughtn't to be allowed to associate with honest, decent, quiet, respectable people. Mr. Gallicker has tried to reason with them, and make them behave themselves — which in my opinion they never will — however, that's only an opinion, an' not legal — ever since they have made Mr. Gallicker's life a HELL! Mr. Gallicker, am I right or am I wrong?

Mr. Gallogher. I'm sorry to say you're right, Mrs. Henderson, perfectly right — not a word of exaggeration.

Mrs. Henderson. Well, now, Mr. Gallicker, seein' as I have given Mr. Davoren a fair account ov how you're situated, an' ov these tramps' cleverality, I'll ask you to read the letter, which I'll say, not because you're there, or that you're a friend o' mine, is as good a letter as was decomposed by a scholar. Now, Mr. Gallicker, an' don't forget the top sayin'.

[*Mr. Gallogher prepares to read ; Minnie leans forward to listen ; Tommy takes out a well-worn note-book and a pencil stump, and assumes a very important attitude.*

Tommy. One second.   Mr. Gallicker, is this the twenty-first or twenty-second ?

Mr. Gallogher. The twenty-first, sir.

Tommy. Thanks ; proceed, Mr. Gallicker.

Mr. Gallogher [*with a few preliminary tremors, reads the letter. Reading*] :

" To All to Whom These Presents Come,
Greeting
" Gentlemen of the Irish Republican Army . . ."

Mrs. Henderson. There's a beginnin' for you, Mr. Davoren.

Minnie. That's some swank.

Tommy. There's a lot in that sayin', mind you ; it's a hard wallop at the British Empire.

Mrs. Henderson [*proudly*]. Go on, Mr. Gallicker.

Mr. Gallogher [*reading*] :

" I wish to call your attention to the persecution me and my family has to put up with in respect of and appertaining to the residents of the back drawing-room of the house known as fifty-five, Saint Teresa Street, situate in the Parish of St. Thomas, in the Borough and City of Dublin. This persecution started eighteen months ago — or to be precise — on the tenth day of the sixth month, in the year nineteen hundred and twenty."

Mrs. Henderson. That's the word I was trying to think ov — precise — it cuts the ground from under their feet — so to speak.

Mr. Gallogher [*reading*] :

   " We, the complainants, resident on the ground floor, deeming it disrespectable . . ."

Mrs. Henderson [*with an emphatic nod*]. Which it was.

Mr. Gallogher [*reading*] :

   " Deeming it disrespectable to have an open hall door, and to have the hall turned into a playground, made a solemn protest, and, in consequence, we the complainants aforesaid has had no peace ever since. Owing to the persecution, as aforesaid specified, we had to take out a summons again them some time ago as there was no Republican Courts then ; but we did not proceed again them as me and my wife — to wit, James and Winifred Gallogher — has a strong objection to foreign Courts as such. We had peace for some time after that, but now things have gone from bad to worse. The name calling and the language is something abominable . . ."

Mrs. Henderson [*holding out her hand as a constable would extend his to stop a car that another may pass*]. Excuse me, Mr. Gallicker, but I think the word " shockin' " should be put in there after abominable ; for the language used be these tramps has two ways o' bein' looked at — for it's abominable to the childer an' shockin' to your wife — am I right or am I wrong, Mr. Davoren ?

Tommy [*judicially*]. Shockin' is a right good word, with a great deal o' meanin', an' . . .

Mrs. Henderson [*with a deprecating gesture that extinguishes Tommy*]. Tommy, let Mr. Davoren speak ; whatever Mr. Davoren ses, Julia Henderson'll abide be.

Davoren [*afraid to say anything else*]. I think the word might certainly be introduced with advantage.

Mrs. Henderson. Go over there, Mr. Gallicker, an' put in the word shockin', as aforesaid.

[*Gallogher goes over to the table, and with a great deal of difficulty enters the word.*

Tommy [*to Mr. Gallogher as he writes*]. Ey, there's two k's in shockin' !

Mr. Gallogher [*reading*] :

" The language is something abominable and shocking. My wife has often to lock the door of the room to keep them from assaulting her. If you would be so kind as to send some of your army or police down to see for themselves we would give them full particulars. I have to be always from home all day, as I work with Mr. Hennessy, the harness maker of the Coombe, who will furnish all particulars as to my unvarnished respectability, also my neighbours. The name of the resident-tenant who is giving all this trouble and who, pursuant to the facts of the case aforesaid, mentioned, will be the defendant, is Dwyer. The husband of the aforesaid Mrs. Dwyer, or the aforesaid defendant, as the case may be, is a seaman, who is coming home shortly, and we beg The Irish Republican Army to note that the said Mrs. Dwyer says he will settle us when he comes home. While leaving it entirely in the hands of the gentlemen of The Republican Army, the defendant, that is to say, James Gallogher of fifty-five St. Teresa Street, ventures to say that he thinks he has made out a Primmy Fashy Case against Mrs. Dwyer and all her heirs, male and female as aforesaid mentioned in the above written schedule.

" *N.B.* — If you send up any of your men, please tell them to bring their guns. I beg to remain the humble servant and devoted admirer of the Gentlemen of the Irish Republican Army.

" Witness my hand this tenth day of the fifth month of the year nineteen hundred and twenty.

" JAMES GALLOGHER."

Mr. Gallogher [*with a modest cough*]. Ahem.

Mrs. Henderson. There's a letter for you, Mr. Davoren !

Tommy. It's the most powerfullest letter I ever heard read.

Minnie. It wasn't you, really, that writ it, Mr. Gallicker ?

Mrs. Henderson. Sinn Fein Amhain : him an' him only, Minnie. I seen him with me own two eyes when me an' Winnie — Mrs. Gallicker, Mr. Davoren, aforesaid as appears in the letter — was havin' a chat be the fire.

Minnie. You'd never think it was in him to do it.

Mrs. Henderson. An' to think that the likes ov such a man is to have the sowl-case worried out ov him by a gang o' tramps ; but it's in good hands now, an' instead ov them settlin' yous, Mr. Gallicker, it's yous 'ill settle them. Give the letter to Mr. Davoren, an' we'll be goin'.

[*Gallogher gives the letter to Davoren.*

Mrs. Henderson [*moving towards the door*]. I hope you an' Mr. Shields is gettin' on all right together, Mr. Davoren.

Davoren. Fairly well, thanks, Mrs. Henderson. We don't see much of each other. He's out during the day, and I'm usually out during the evening.

Mrs. Henderson. I'm afraid he'll never make a fortune out ov what he's sellin'. He'll talk above an hour over a pennorth o' pins. Every time he comes to our place I buy a package o' hairpins from him to give him a little encouragement. I 'clare to God I have as many pins

now as ud make a wire mattress for a double bed. All
the young divils about the place are beginnin' to make
a jeer ov him, too ; I gave one ov them a mallavogin'
the other day for callin' him oul' hairpins !

Mr. Gallogher [*venturing an opinion*]. Mr. Shields is a man
of exceptional mental capacity, and is worthy of a more
dignified position.

Mrs. Henderson. Them words is true, Mr. Gallicker, and
they aren't. For to be wise is to be a fool, an' to be a
fool is to be wise.

Mr. Gallogher [*with deprecating tolerance*]. Oh, Mrs. Henderson, that's a parrotox.

Mrs. Henderson. It may be what a parrot talks, or a black-
bird, or, for the matter of that, a lark — but it's what
Julia Henderson thinks, any . . . whisht, is that a
Stop Press ?
   [*Outside is heard the shriek of a newsboy calling " Stop
   Press ".*

Mrs. Henderson. Run out, Tommy, an' get it till we see
what it is.

Tommy. I haven't got a make.

Mrs. Henderson. I never seen you any other way, an' you'll
be always the same if you keep follyin' your Spear-
mints, an' your Bumble Bees an' your Night Patrols.
[*Shouting to someone outside*] Is that a *Stop Press*, Mrs.
Grigson ?

Voice outside. Yis ; an ambush out near Knocksedan.

Mrs. Henderson. That's the stuff to give them. [*Loudly*]
Was there anybody hurted ?

Voice outside. One poor man killed — some chap named Maguire, the paper says.

Davoren [*agitated*]. What name did she say ?

Minnie. Maguire ; did you know him, Mr. Davoren ?

Davoren. Yes — no, no ; I didn't know him, no, I didn't know him, Minnie.

Minnie. I wonder is it the Maguire that does be with Mr. Shields ?

Davoren. Oh no, not at all, it couldn't be.

Mrs. Henderson. Knocksedan ? That's in the County Sligo, now, or I'm greatly mistaken — am I right, Mr. Gallicker, or am I wrong ?

Mr. Gallogher [*who knows perfectly well that it is in the County Dublin, but dare not correct Mrs. Henderson*]. That's where it is — Knocksedan, that's the very identical county.

Mrs. Henderson. Well, I think we better be makin' a move, Mr. Gallicker ; we've kep' Mr. Davoren long enough, an' you'll find the letter'll be in good hans.
  [*Mr. Gallogher and Mrs. Henderson move towards the door, which when he reaches it Mr. Gallogher grips, hesitates, buttons his coat, and turns to Davoren.*

Mr. Gallogher. Mr. Davoren, sir, on behalf ov meself, James Gallicker, an' Winifred, Mrs. Gallicker, wife ov the said James, I beg to offer, extend an' furnish our humble an' hearty thanks for your benevolent goodness in interferin' in the matter specified, particularated an' expanded upon in the letter, mandamus or schedule, as the case may be. An' let me interpretate to you on behalf ov meself an' Winifred Gallicker, that when-

ever you visit us you will be supernally positive ov a
hundred thousand welcomes — ahem.

Mrs. Henderson [*beaming with pride for the genius of her friend*].
There's a man for you, Mr. Davoren! You forgot
to mention Biddy and Shaun, Mr. Gallicker — [*to
Davoren*] his two children — it's himself has them
trained well. It ud make your heart thrill like an
alarm clock to hear them singin' " Faith ov Our
Fathers " an' " Wrap the Green Flag Roun' Me ".

Mr. Gallogher [*half apologetically and half proudly*]. Faith an'
Fatherland, Mrs. Henderson, Faith and Fatherland.

Mrs. Henderson. Well, good-day, Mr. Davoren, an' God
keep you an' strengthen all the men that are fightin' for
Ireland's freedom.   [*She and Gallogher go out.*

Tommy. I must be off too ; so-long, Mr. Davoren, an'
remember that Tommy Owens only waits the call.
                              [*He goes out too.*

Davoren. Well, Minnie, we're by ourselves once more.

Minnie. Wouldn't that Tommy Owens give you the
sick — only waitin' to hear the call ! Ah, then it'll
take all the brass bands in the country to blow the call
before Tommy Owens ud hear it. [*She looks at her
wristlet watch.*] Sacred Heart, I've only ten minutes
to get back to work ! I'll have to fly ! Quick, Mr.
Davoren, write me name in typewritin' before I go —
just " Minnie ".   [*Davoren types the name.*

Minnie [*shyly but determinedly*]. Now yours underneath —
just " Donal ". [*Davoren does so.*] Minnie, Donal ;
Donal, Minnie ; good-bye now.

Davoren. Here, what about your milk ?

Minnie. I haven't time to take it now.   [*Slyly*] I'll come for
it this evening.   [*They both go towards the door.*

Davoren. Minnie, the kiss I didn't get.

Minnie. What kiss ?

Davoren. When we were interrupted ; you know, you
little rogue, come, just one.

Minnie. Quick, then.
    [*Davoren kisses her and she runs out. Davoren returns
    thoughtfully to the table.*

Davoren. Minnie, Donal ; Donal, Minnie. Very pretty,
but very ignorant. A gunman on the run ! Be careful,
be careful, Donal Davoren. But Minnie is attracted to
the idea, and I am attracted to Minnie. And what
danger can there be in being the shadow of a gunman ?

CURTAIN

ACT II

The same as in Act I. But it is now night. Seumas is in the bed that runs along the wall at back. Davoren is seated near the fire, to which he has drawn the table. He has a fountain-pen in his hand, and is attracted in thought towards the moon, which is shining in through the windows. An open writing-pad is on the table at Davoren's elbow. The bag left by Maguire is still in the same place.

Davoren :

> The cold chaste moon, the Queen of Heaven's bright isles,
> Who makes all beautiful on which she smiles ;
> That wandering shrine of soft yet icy flame,
> Which ever is transformed yet still the same.

Ah, Shelley, Shelley, you yourself were a lovely human orb shining through clouds of whirling human dust. " She makes all beautiful on which she smiles." Ah, Shelley, she couldn't make this thrice accursed room beautiful. Her beams of beauty only make its horrors more full of horrors still. There is an ugliness that can be made beautiful, and there is an ugliness that can only be destroyed, and this is part of that ugliness. Donal, Donal, I fear your last state is worse than your first.

> *[He lilts a verse, which he writes on the pad before him.*

> When night advances through the sky with slow
>   And solemn tread,
> The queenly moon looks down on life below,
>   As if she read
> Man's soul, and in her scornful silence said :
>   All beautiful and happiest things are dead.

35

Seumas [*sleepily*]. Donal, Donal, are you awake ? [*A pause.*]   Donal, Donal, are you asleep ?

Davoren. I'm neither awake nor asleep : I'm thinking.

Seumas. I was just thinkin', too — I was just thinkin', too, that Maguire is sorry now that he didn't come with me instead of going to Knocksedan. He caught something besides butterflies — two of them he got, one through each lung.

Davoren. The Irish people are very fond of turning a serious thing into a joke ; that was a serious affair — for poor Maguire.

Seumas [*defensively*]. Why didn't he do what he arranged to do ? Did he think of me when he was goin' to Knocksedan ? How can he expect me to have any sympathy with him now ?

Davoren. He can hardly expect that now that he's dead.

Seumas. The Republicans 'll do a lot for him, now. How am I goin' to get back the things he has belongin' to me, either ? There's some of them in that bag over there, but that's not quarter of what he had ; an' I don't know where he was stoppin', for he left his old digs a week or so ago — I suppose there's nothing to be said about my loss ; I'm to sing dumb.

Davoren. I hope there's nothing else in the bag, besides thread and hairpins.

Seumas. What else ud be in it ? . . . I can't sleep properly ever since they put on this damned curfew. A minute ago I thought I heard some of the oul' ones standin' at the door ; they won't be satisfied till they bring a raid on the house ; an' they never begin to stand at the door till after curfew. . . . Are you gone to bed, Donal ?

Davoren. No ; I'm trying to finish this poem.

Seumas [*sitting up in bed*]. If I was you I'd give that game up ; it doesn't pay a working-man to write poetry. I don't profess to know much about poetry — I don't profess to know much about poetry — about poetry — I don't know much about the pearly glint of the morning dew, or the damask sweetness of the rare wild rose, or the subtle greenness of the serpent's eye — but I think a poet's claim to greatness depends upon his power to put passion in the common people.

Davoren. Ay, passion to howl for his destruction. The People ! Damn the people ! They live in the abyss, the poet lives on the mountain-top ; to the people there is no mystery of colour : it is simply the scarlet coat of the soldier ; the purple vestments of a priest ; the green banner of a party ; the brown or blue overalls of industry. To them the might of design is a three-roomed house or a capacious bed. To them beauty is for sale in a butcher's shop. To the people the end of life is the life created for them ; to the poet the end of life is the life that he creates for himself ; life has a stifling grip upon the people's throat — it is the poet's musician. The poet ever strives to save the people ; the people ever strive to destroy the poet. The people view life through creeds, through customs, and through necessities ; the poet views creeds, customs, and necessities through life. The people . . .

Seumas [*suddenly, and with a note of anxiety in his voice*]. Whisht ! What's that ? Is that the tappin' again ?

Davoren. Tappin'. What tappin' ?

Seumas [*in an awed whisper*]. This is the second night I heard that tappin' ! I believe it bodes no good to me. There, do you hear it again — a quiet, steady, mysterious tappin' on the wall.

Davoren. I hear no tappin'.

Seumas. It ud be better for me if you did. It's a sure sign of death when nobody hears it but meself.

Davoren. Death ! What the devil are you talking about, man ?

Seumas. I don't like it at all ; there's always something like that heard when one of our family dies.

Davoren. I don't know about that ; but I know there's a hell of a lot of things heard when one of your family lives.

Seumas. God between us an' all harm ! Thank God I'm where I ought to be — in bed. . . . It's always best to be in your proper place when such things happen — Sacred Heart ! There it is again ; do you not hear it now ?

Davoren. Ah, for God's sake go asleep.

Seumas. Do you believe in nothing ?

Davoren. I don't believe in tappin'.

Seumas. Whisht, it's stopped again ; I'll try to go asleep for fear it ud begin again.

Davoren. Ay, do ; and if it starts again I'll be sure to waken you up.   [*A pause.*

Seumas. It's very cold to-night. Do you feel cold ?

Davoren. I thought you were goin' asleep ?

Seumas. The bloody cold won't let me. . . . You'd want a pair of pyjamas on you. [*A pause.*] Did you ever wear pyjamas, Donal ?

Davoren. No, no, no.

Seumas. What kind of stuff is in them ?

Davoren [*angrily*]. Oh, it depends on the climate ; in India, silk ; in Italy, satin ; and the Eskimo wears them made from the skin of the Polar bear.

Seumas [*emphatically*]. If you take my advice you'll get into bed — that poem is beginnin' to get on your nerves.

Davoren [*extinguishing the candle with a vicious blow*]. Right ; I'm going to bed now, so you can shut up.
    [*Visibility is still maintained from the light of the moon.*

Seumas. I was goin' to say something when you put out the light — what's this it was ? — um, um, oh, ay : when I was comin' in this evenin' I saw Minnie Powell goin' out. If I was you I wouldn't have that one comin' in here.

Davoren. She comes in ; I don't bring her in, do I ?

Seumas. The oul' ones'll be talkin', an' once they start you don't know how it'll end. Surely a man that has read Shelley couldn't be interested in an ignorant little bitch that thinks of nothin' but jazz dances, fox-trots, picture theatres an' dress.

Davoren. Right glad I am that she thinks of dress, for she thinks of it in the right way, and makes herself a pleasant picture to the eye. Education has been wasted on many persons, teaching them to talk only, but leaving them with all their primitive instincts. Had poor Minnie received an education she would have been an artist. She is certainly a pretty girl. I'm sure she is a good girl, and I believe she is a brave girl.

Seumas. A Helen of Troy come to live in a tenement ! You think a lot about her simply because she thinks a lot about you, an' she thinks a lot about you because she looks upon you as a hero — a kind o' Paris . . . she'd give the world an' all to be gaddin' about with a gunman. An' what ecstasy it ud give her if after a bit you were shot or hanged ; she'd be able to go about then — like a good many more — singin', " I do not mourn me darlin' lost, for he fell in his Jacket Green ". An' then, for a year an' a day, all round her hat she'd wear the Tri-coloured Ribbon O, till she'd pick up an' marry someone else — possibly a British Tommy with a Mons Star. An' as for bein' brave, it's easy to be that when you've no cause for cowardice ; I wouldn't care to have me life dependin' on brave little Minnie Powell — she wouldn't sacrifice a jazz dance to save it.

Davoren [*sitting on the bed and taking off his coat and vest, preparatory to going to bed*]. There ; that's enough about Minnie Powell. I'm afraid I'll soon have to be on the run out of this house, too ; it is becoming painfully obvious that there is no peace to be found here.

Seumas. Oh, this house is all right ; barrin' the children, it does be quiet enough. Wasn't there children in the last place you were in too ?

Davoren. Ay, ten ; [*viciously*] and they were all over forty. [*A pause as Davoren is removing his collar and tie.*

Seumas. Everything is very quiet now ; I wonder what time is it ?

Davoren. The village cock hath thrice done salutation to the morn.

Seumas. Shakespeare, Richard the III, Act Five, Scene III. It was Ratcliffe said that to Richard just before the battle of Bosworth. . . . How peaceful the heavens look now with the moon in the middle ; you'd never think there were men prowlin' about tryin' to shoot each other. I don't know how a man who has shot any one can sleep in peace at night.

Davoren. There's plenty of men can't sleep in peace at night now unless they know that they have shot somebody.

Seumas. I wish to God it was all over. The country is gone mad. Instead of counting their beads now they're countin' bullets ; their Hail Marys and paternosters are burstin' bombs — burstin' bombs, an' the rattle of machine-guns ; petrol is their holy water ; their Mass is a burnin' buildin' ; their De Profundis is " The Soldiers' Song ", an' their creed is, I believe in the gun almighty, maker of heaven an' earth — an' it's all for " the glory o' God an' the honour o' Ireland ".

Davoren. I remember the time when you yourself believed in nothing but the gun.

Seumas. Ay, when there wasn't a gun in the country ; I've a different opinion now when there's nothin' but guns in the country. . . . An' you daren't open your mouth, for Kathleen ni Houlihan is very different now to the woman who used to play the harp an' sing

" Weep on, weep on, your hour is past ", for she's a ragin' divil now, an' if you only look crooked at her you're sure of a punch in th' eye. But this is the way I look at it — I look at it this way : You're not goin' — you're not goin' to beat the British Empire — the British Empire, by shootin' an occasional Tommy at the corner of an occasional street. Besides, when the Tommies have the wind up — when the Tommies have the wind up they let bang at everything they see — they don't give a God's curse who they plug.

Davoren. Maybe they ought to get down off the lorry and run to the Records Office to find out a man's pedigree before they plug him.

Seumas. It's the civilians that suffer ; when there's an ambush they don't know where to run. Shot in the back to save the British Empire, an' shot in the breast to save the soul of Ireland. I'm a Nationalist meself, right enough — a Nationalist right enough, but all the same — I'm a Nationalist right enough ; I believe in the freedom of Ireland, an' that England has no right to be here, but I draw the line when I hear the gunmen blowin' about dyin' for the people, when it's the people that are dyin for the gunmen ! With all due respect to the gunmen, I don't want them to die for me.

Davoren. Not likely ; you object to any one of them deliberately dying for you for fear that one of these days you might accidentally die for one of them.

Seumas. You're one of the brave fellows that doesn't fear death.

Davoren. Why should I be afraid of it ? It's all the same

to me how it comes, where it comes, or when it comes.
I leave fear of death to the people that are always
praying for eternal life ; " Death is here and death is
there, death is busy everywhere ".

Seumas. Ay, in Ireland. Thanks be to God I'm a daily
communicant. There's a great comfort in religion ;
it makes a man strong in time of trouble an' brave in
time of danger. No man need be afraid with a crowd
of angels round him ; thanks to God for His Holy
religion !

Davoren. You're welcome to your angels ; philosophy is
mine ; philosophy that makes the coward brave ; the
sufferer defiant ; the weak strong ; the . . .
  [*A volley of shots is heard in a lane that runs parallel with
  the wall of the back-yard. Religion and philosophy are
  forgotten in the violent fear of a nervous equality.*

Seumas. Jesus, Mary, an' Joseph, what's that ?

Davoren. My God, that's very close.

Seumas. Is there no Christianity at all left in the country ?

Davoren. Are we ever again going to know what peace
and security are ?

Seumas. If this continues much longer I'll be nothing
but a galvanic battery o' shocks.

Davoren. It's dangerous to be in and it's equally dangerous
to be out.

Seumas. This is a dangerous spot to be in with them
windows ; you couldn't tell the minute a bullet ud
come in through one of them — through one of them,
an' hit the — hit the — an' hit the . . .

Davoren [*irritably*]. Hit the what, man ?

Seumas. The wall.

Davoren. Couldn't you say that at first without making a song about it ?

Seumas [*suddenly*]. I don't believe there's horses in the stable at all.

Davoren. Stable ! What stable are you talking about ?

Seumas. There's a stable at the back of the house with an entrance from the yard ; it's used as a carpenter's shop. Didn't you often hear the peculiar noises at night ? They give out that it's the horses shakin' their chains.

Davoren. And what is it ?

Seumas. Oh, there I'll leave you !

Davoren. Surely you don't mean . . .

Seumas. But I do mean it.

Davoren. You do mean what ?

Seumas. I wouldn't — I wouldn't be surprised — wouldn't be surprised — surprised . . .

Davoren. Yes, yes, surprised — go on.

Seumas. I wouldn't be surprised if they were manu-facturin' bombs there.

Davoren. My God, that's a pleasant contemplation ! The sooner I'm on the run out of this house the better. How is it you never said anything about this before ?

Seumas. Well — well, I didn't want — I didn't want to — to . . .

Davoren. You didn't want to what ?

Seumas. I didn't want to frighten you.

Davoren [*sarcastically*]. You're bloody kind !
[*A knock at the door ; the voice of Mrs. Grigson heard.*

Mrs. Grigson. Are you asleep, Mr. Shields ?

Seumas. What the devil can she want at this hour of the
night ? [*To Mrs. Grigson*] No, Mrs. Grigson, what
is it ?

Mrs. Grigson [*opening the door and standing at the threshold.
She is a woman about forty, but looks much older. She is
one of the cave-dwellers of Dublin, living as she does in a
tenement kitchen, to which only an occasional sickly beam of
sunlight filters through a grating in the yard ; the consequent
general dimness of her abode has given her a habit of peering
through half-closed eyes. She is slovenly dressed in an old
skirt and bodice ; her face is grimy, not because her habits
are dirty — for, although she is untidy, she is a clean woman
— but because of the smoky atmosphere of her room. Her hair
is constantly falling over her face, which she is as frequently
removing by rapid movements of her right hand*]. He hasn't
turned up yet, an' I'm stiff with the cold waitin' for
him.

Seumas. Mr. Grigson, is it ?

Mrs. Grigson. Adolphus, Mr. Shields, after takin' his
tea at six o'clock — no, I'm tellin' a lie — it was
before six, for I remember the Angelus was ringin' out
an' we sittin' at the table — after takin' his tea he
went out for a breath o' fresh air, an' I haven't seen
sign or light of him since. 'Clare to God me heart is

up in me mouth, thinkin' he might be shot be the Black an' Tans.

Seumas. Aw, he'll be all right, Mrs. Grigson. You ought to go to bed an' rest yourself ; it's always the worst that comes into a body's mind ; go to bed, Mrs. Grigson, or you'll catch your death of cold.

Mrs. Grigson. I'm afraid to go to bed, Mr. Shields, for I'm always in dread that some night or another, when he has a sup taken, he'll fall down the kitchen stairs an' break his neck. Not that I'd be any the worse if anything did happen to him, for you know the sort he is, Mr. Shields ; sure he has me heart broke.

Seumas. Don't be downhearted, Mrs. Grigson ; he may take a thought one of these days an' turn over a new leaf.

Mrs. Grigson. Sorra leaf Adolphus 'll ever turn over, he's too far gone in the horns for that now. Sure no one ud mind him takin' a pint or two, if he'd stop at that, but he won't ; nothin' could fill him with beer, an' no matter how much he may have taken, when he's taken more he'll always say, " Here's the first to-day ".

Davoren [to Seumas]. Christ ! Is she going to stop talking there all the night ?

Seumas. 'Sh, she'll hear you ; right enough, the man has the poor woman's heart broke.

Davoren. And because he has her heart broken, she's to have the privilege of breaking everybody else's.

Mrs. Grigson. Mr. Shields.

Seumas. Yes ?

Mrs. Grigson. Do the insurance companies pay if a man is shot after curfew ?

Seumas. Well, now, that's a thing I couldn't say, Mrs. Grigson.

Mrs. Grigson [*plaintively*]. Isn't he a terrible man to be takin' such risks, an' not knowin' what'll happen to him.   He knows them Societies only want an excuse to do people out of their money — is it after one, now, Mr. Shields ?

Seumas. Aw, it must be after one, Mrs. Grigson.

Mrs. Grigson [*emphatically*]. Ah, then, if I was a young girl again I'd think twice before gettin' married.   Whisht ! There's somebody now — it's him, I know be the way he's fumblin'.
  [*She goes out a little way.   Stumbling steps are heard in the hall.*

Mrs. Grigson [*outside*]. Is that you, Dolphie, dear ?
  [*After a few moments Adolphus, with Mrs. Grigson hold-ing his arm, stumbles into the room.*

Mrs. Grigson. Dolphie, dear, mind yourself.

Adolphus [*he is a man of forty-five, but looks, relatively, much younger than Mrs. Grigson.   His occupation is that of a solicitor's clerk.   He has all the appearance of being well fed ; and, in fact, he gets most of the nourishment, Mrs. Grigson getting just enough to give her strength to do the necessary work of the household.   On account of living most of his life out of the kitchen, his complexion is fresh, and his movements, even when sober, are livelier than those of his wife.   He is comfort-ably dressed ; heavy top-coat, soft trilby hat, a fancy coloured scarf about his neck, and he carries an umbrella*]. I'm all right ; do you see anything wrong with me ?

Mrs. Grigson. Of course you're all right, dear ; there's no one mindin' you.

Adolphus Grigson. Mindin' me, is it, mindin' me ? He'd want to be a good thing that ud mind me. There's a man here — a man, mind you, afraid av nothin' — not in this bloody house anyway.

Mrs. Grigson [*imploringly*]. Come on downstairs, Dolphie, dear ; sure there's not one in the house ud say a word to you.

Adolphus Grigson. Say a word to me, is it ? He'd want to be a good thing that ud say anything to Dolphus Grigson. [*Loudly*] Is there anyone wants to say anything to Dolphus Grigson ? If there is, he's here — a man, too — there's no blottin' it out — a man.

Mrs. Grigson. You'll wake everybody in the house ; can't you speak quiet.

Adolphus Grigson [*more loudly still*]. What do I care for anybody in the house ? Are they keepin' me ; are they givin' me anything ? When they're keepin' Grigson it'll be time enough for them to talk. [*With a shout*] I can tell them Adolphus Grigson wasn't born in a bottle !

Mrs. Grigson [*tearfully*]. Why do you talk like that, dear ? We all know you weren't born in a bottle.

Adolphus Grigson. There's some of them in this house think that Grigson was born in a bottle.

Davoren [*to Seumas*]. A most appropriate place for him to be born in.

Mrs. Grigson. Come on down to bed, now, an' you can talk about them in the mornin'.

Grigsor. I'll talk about them, now ; do you think I'm afraid of them ? Dolphus Grigson's afraid av nothin', creepin' or walkin', — if there's any one in the house thinks he's fit to take a fall out av Adolphus Grigson, he's here — a man ; they'll find that Grigson's no soft thing.

Davoren. Ah me, alas ! Pain, pain ever, for ever.

Mrs. Grigson. Dolphie, dear, poor Mr. Davoren wants to go to bed.

Davoren. Oh, she's terribly anxious about poor Mr. Davoren, all of a sudden.

Grigson [*stumbling towards Davoren, and holding out his hand*]. Davoren ! He's a man. Leave it there, mate. You needn't be afraid av Dolphus Grigson ; there never was a drop av informer's blood in the whole family av Grigson. I don't know what you are or what you think, but you're a man, an' not like some of the goughers in this house, that ud hang you. Not referrin' to you, Mr. Shields.

Mrs. Grigson. Oh, you're not deludin' to Mr. Shields.

Seumas. I know that, Mr. Grigson ; go on down, now, with Mrs. Grigson, an' have a sleep.

Grigson. I tie meself to no woman's apron strings, Mr. Shields ; I know how to keep Mrs. Grigson in her place ; I have the authority of the Bible for that. I know the Bible from cover to cover, Mr. Davoren, an' that's more than some in this house could say. And what does the Holy Scripture say about woman ? It says, " The woman shall be subject to her husband ", an' I'll see that Mrs. Grigson keeps the teachin' av the

Holy Book in the letter an' in the spirit. If you're ever in trouble, Mr. Davoren, an' Grigson can help — I'm your man — have you me ?

Davoren. I have you, Mr. Grigson, I have you.

Grigson. Right ; I'm an Orangeman, an' I'm not ashamed av it, an' I'm not afraid av it, but I can feel for a true man, all the same — have *you* got me, Mr. Shields ?

Seumas. Oh, we know you well, Mr. Grigson ; many a true Irishman was a Protestant — Tone, Emmet an' Parnell.

Grigson. Mind you, I'm not sayin' as I agree with them you've mentioned, Mr. Shields, for the Bible forbids it, an' Adolphus Grigson 'll always abide be the Bible. Fear God an' honour the King — that's written in Holy Scripture, an' there's no blottin' it out. [*Pulling a bottle out of his pocket*] But here, Mr. Davoren, have a drink, just to show there's no coolness.

Davoren. No, no, Mr. Grigson, it's too late now to take anything. Go on down with Mrs. Grigson, and we can have a chat in the morning.

Grigson. Sure you won't have a drink ?

Davoren. Quite sure — thanks all the same.

Grigson [*drinking*]. Here's the first to-day ! To all true men, even if they were born in a bottle. Here's to King William, to the battle av the Boyne ; to the Hobah Black Chapter — that's my Lodge, Mr. Davoren ; an' to The Orange Lily O.

[*Singing in a loud shout :*

An' dud ya go to see the show, each rose an' pinkadilly O,
To feast your eyes an' view the prize won be the Orange
Lily O.
The Vic'roy there, so debonair, just like a daffadilly O,
With Lady Clarke, blithe as a lark, approached the Orange
Lily O.
        Heigh Ho the Lily O,
        The Royal, Loyal Lily O,
Beneath the sky what flower can vie with Erin's Orange
Lily O !

Davoren. Holy God, isn't this terrible !

Grigson [*singing*] :

The elated Muse, to hear the news, jumped like a Connaught
filly O,
As gossip Fame did loud proclaim the triumph av the
Lily O.
The Lowland field may roses yield, gay heaths the High-
lands hilly O ;
But high or low no flower can show like Erin's Orange
Lily O.
        Heigh Ho the Lily O,
        The Royal, Loyal Lily O,
Beneath the sky what flower can vie with Erin's Or . . .

[*While Grigson has been singing, the sound of a rapidly
moving motor is heard, faintly at first, but growing
rapidly louder, till it apparently stops suddenly somewhere very near the house, bringing Grigson's song to an
abrupt conclusion. They are all startled, and listen
attentively to the throbbing of the engines, which can be
plainly heard. Grigson is considerably sobered, and
anxiously keeps his eyes on the door. Seumas sits up in
bed and listens anxiously. Davoren, with a shaking
hand, lights the candle, and begins to search hurriedly
among the books and papers on the table.*

Grigson [*with a tremor in his voice*]. There's no need to be afraid, they couldn't be comin' here.

Mrs. Grigson. God forbid ! It ud be terrible if they came at this hour ov the night.

Seumas. You never know now, Mrs. Grigson ; they'd rush in on you when you'd be least expectin' them. What, in the name o' God, is goin' to come out of it all ? Nobody now cares a traneen about the orders of the Ten Commandments ; the only order that anybody minds now is, " Put your hands up ". Oh, it's a hopeless country.

Grigson. Whisht ; do you hear them talking outside at the door ? You're sure of your life nowhere now ; it's just as safe to go everywhere as it is to anywhere. An' they don't give a damn whether you're a loyal man or not. If you're a Republican they make you sing " God save the King ", an' if you're loyal they'll make you sing the " Soldiers' Song ". The singin' ud be all right if they didn't make you dance afterwards.

Mrs. Grigson. They'd hardly come here unless they heard something about Mr. Davoren.

Davoren. About me ! What could they hear about me ?

Grigson. You'll never get some people to keep their mouths shut. I was in the Blue Lion this evening, an' who do you think was there, blowin' out av him, but that little blower, Tommy Owens ; there he was tellin' everybody that *he* knew where there was bombs ; that *he* had a friend that was a General in the I.R.A. ; that *he* could tell them what the Staff was thinkin' av doin' ; that *he* could lay his hand on tons av revolvers ; that they wasn't a mile from where he was livin', but that *he* knew his own know, an' would keep it to himself.

Seumas. Well, God blast the little blower, anyway ; it's the like ov him that deserves to be plugged ! [*To Davoren*] What are you lookin' for among the books, Donal ?

Davoren. A letter that I got to-day from Mr. Gallogher and Mrs. Henderson ; I'm blessed if I know where I put it.

Seumas [*peevishly*]. Can't you look for it in the mornin' ?

Davoren. It's addressed to the Irish Republican Army, and, considering the possibility of a raid, it would be safer to get rid of it.
   [*Shots again heard out in the lane, followed by loud shouts of Halt, halt, halt !*

Grigson. I think we had better be gettin' to bed, Debby ; it's not right to be keepin' Mr. Davoren an' Mr. Shields awake.

Seumas. An' what made them give you such a letter as that ; don't they know the state the country is in ? An' you were worse to take it.   Have you got it ?

Davoren. I can't find it anywhere ; isn't this terrible !

Grigson. Good-night, Mr. Davoren ; good-night, Mr. Shields.

Mrs. Grigson. Good-night, Mr. Shields ; good-night, Mr. Davoren.
   [*They go out.   Seumas and Davoren are too much concerned about the letter to respond to their good-nights.*

Seumas. What were you thinkin' of when you took such a

letter as that? Ye gods, has nobody any brains at all, at all? Oh, this is a hopeless country. Did you try in your pockets?

Davoren [*searching in his pockets*]. Oh, thanks be to God, here it is.

Seumas. Burn it now, an', for God's sake, don't take any letters like that again. . . . There's the motor goin' away; we can sleep in peace now for the rest of the night. Just to make sure of everything now, have a look in that bag o' Maguire's: not that there can be anything in it.

Davoren. If there's nothing in it, what's the good of looking?

Seumas. It won't kill you to look, will it?
[*Davoren goes over to the bag, puts it on the table, opens it, and jumps back, his face pale and his limbs trembling.*

Davoren. My God, it's full of bombs, Mills bombs!

Seumas. Holy Mother of God, you're jokin'!

Davoren. If the Tans come you'll find whether I'm jokin' or no.

Seumas. Isn't this a nice pickle to be in? St. Anthony, look down on us!

Davoren. There's no use of blaming St. Anthony; why did you let Maguire leave the bag here?

Seumas. Why did I let him leave the bag here; why did I let him leave the bag here! How did I know what was in it? Didn't I think there was nothin' in it but spoons an' hairpins? What'll we do now; what'll we do now? Mother o' God, grant there'll be no raid

to-night.   I knew things ud go wrong when I missed
Mass this mornin'.

Davoren. Give over your praying and let us try to think
of what is best to be done.   There's one thing certain :
as soon as morning comes I'm on the run out of this
house.

Seumas. Thinkin' of yourself, like the rest of them.
Leavin' me to bear the brunt of it.

Davoren. And why shouldn't you bear the brunt of it ?
Maguire was no friend of mine ; besides, it's your
fault ; you knew the sort of a man he was, and you
should have been on your guard.

Seumas. Did I know he was a gunman ; did I know he
was a gunman ; did I know he was a gunman ?
Did . . .

Davoren. Do you mean to tell me that . . .

Seumas. Just a moment . . .

Davoren. You didn't know . . .

Seumas. Just a moment . . .

Davoren. That Maguire was connected with . . .

Seumas [*loudly*]. Just a moment ; can't . . .

Davoren. The Republican Movement ?   What's the use
of trying to tell damn lies !
    [*Minnie Powell rushes into the room.   She is only partly
    dressed, and has thrown a shawl over her shoulders.
    She is in a state of intense excitement.*

Minnie. Mr. Davoren, Donal, they're all round the
house ; they must be goin' to raid the place ; I was

lookin' out of the window an' I seen them ; I do be on the watch every night ; have you anything ? If you have . . .

[*There is heard at street door a violent and continuous knocking, followed by the crash of glass and the beating of the door with rifle butts.*

Minnie. There they are, there they are, there they are !

[*Davoren reclines almost fainting on the bed ; Seumas sits up in an attitude of agonized prayerfulness ; Minnie alone retains her presence of mind. When she sees their panic she becomes calm, though her words are rapidly spoken, and her actions are performed with decisive celerity.*

Minnie. What is it ; what have you got ; where are they ?

Davoren. Bombs, bombs, bombs ; my God ! in the bag on the table there ; we're done, we're done !

Seumas. Hail, Mary, full of grace — pray for us miserable sinners — Holy St. Anthony, do you hear them batterin' at the door — now an' at the hour of our death — say an act of contrition, Donal — there's the glass gone !

Minnie. I'll take them to my room ; maybe they won't search it ; if they do aself, they won't harm a girl. Good-bye . . . Donal.

[*She glances lovingly at Donal — who is only semi- conscious — as she rushes out with the bag.*

Seumas. If we come through this I'll never miss a Mass again ! If it's the Tommies it won't be so bad, but if it's the Tans, we're goin' to have a terrible time.

[*The street door is broken open and heavy steps are heard in the hall, punctuated with shouts of* " 'Old the light

*'ere", " Put 'em up", etc. An Auxiliary opens the
door of the room and enters, revolver in one hand and
electric torch in the other.   His uniform is black, and he
wears a black beret.*

The Auxiliary. 'Oo's 'ere ?

Seumas [*as if he didn't know*]. Who — who's that ?

The Auxiliary [*peremptorily*]. 'Oo's 'ere ?

Seumas. Only two men, mister ; me an' me mate in
t'other bed.

The Auxiliary. Why didn't you open the door ?

Seumas. We didn't hear you knockin', sir.

The Auxiliary. You must be a little awd of 'earing, ay ?

Seumas. I had rheumatic fever a few years ago, an' ever
since I do be a — I do be a little deaf sometimes.

The Auxiliary [*to Davoren*]. 'Ow is it you're not in bed ?

Davoren. I was in bed ; when I heard the knockin' I got
up to open the door.

The Auxiliary. You're a koind blowke, you are.   De-
loighted, like, to have a visit from us, ay ?   Ay ?
[*Threatening to strike him*] Why down't you answer ?

Davoren. Yes, sir.

The Auxiliary. What's your name ?

Davoren. Davoren, Dan Davoren, sir.

The Auxiliary. You're not an Irishman, are you ?

Davoren. I-I-I was born in Ireland.

The Auxiliary. Ow, you were, were you ; Irish han'
proud of it, ay ? [*To Seumas*] What's *your* name ?

Seumas. Seuma . . . Oh no ; Jimmie Shields, sir.

The Auxiliary. Ow, you're a selt [*he means a Celt*], one of the seltic race that speaks a lingo of its ahn, and that's going to overthrow the British Empire — I don't think ! 'Ere, where's your gun ?

Seumas. I never had a gun in me hand in me life.

The Auxiliary. Now ; you wouldn't know what a gun is if you sawr one, I suppowse. [*Displaying his revolver in a careless way*] 'Ere, what's that ?

Seumas. Oh, be careful, please, be careful.

The Auxiliary. Why, what 'ave I got to be careful abaht ?

Seumas. The gun ; it-it-it might go off.

The Auxiliary. An' what prawse if it did ; it can easily be relowded. Any ammunition 'ere ? What's in that press ? [*He searches and scatters contents of press.*

Seumas. Only a little bit o' grub ; you'll get nothin' here, sir ; no one in the house has any connection with politics.

The Auxiliary. Now ? I've never met a man yet that didn't say that, but we're a little bit too ikey now to be kidded with that sort of talk.

Seumas. May I go an' get a drink o' water ?

The Auxiliary. You'll want a barrel of watah before you're done with us. [*The Auxiliary goes about the room examining places*] 'Ello, what's 'ere ? A statue o' Christ ! An' a Crucifix ! You'd think you was in a bloomin' monastery.

[*Mrs. Grigson enters, dressed disorderly and her hair awry.*

Mrs. Grigson. They're turning the place upside-down. Upstairs an' downstairs they're makin' a litter of everything ! I declare to God, it's awful what law-abidin' people have to put up with. An' they found a pint bottle of whisky under Dolphie's pillow, an' they're drinkin' every drop of it — an' Dolphie 'll be like a devil in the mornin' when he finds he has no curer.

The Auxiliary [*all attention when he hears the word whisky*]. A bottle of whisky, ay ? 'Ere, where do you live — quick, where do you live ?

Mrs. Grigson. Down in the kitchen — an' when you go down will you ask them not to drink — oh, he's gone without listenin' to me.

> [*While Mrs. Grigson is speaking the Auxiliary rushes out.*]

Seumas [*anxiously to Mrs. Grigson*]. Are they searchin' the whole house, Mrs. Grigson ?

Mrs. Grigson. They didn't leave a thing in the kitchen that they didn't flitter about the floor ; the things in the cupboard, all the little odds an' ends that I keep in the big box, an . . .

Seumas. Oh, they're a terrible gang of blaguards — did they go upstairs ? — they'd hardly search Minnie Powell's room — do you think would they, Mrs. Grigson ?

Mrs. Grigson. Just to show them the sort of a man he was, before they come in, Dolphie put the big Bible on the table, open at the First Gospel of St. Peter, second chapter, an' marked the thirteenth to the seventeenth verse in red ink — you know the passages, Mr. Shields — [*quoting*] :

"Submit yourselves to every ordinance of man for the Lord's sake : whether it be to the king, as supreme ; or unto governors, as unto them that are sent by him for the punishment of evildoers, an' for the praise of them that do well. . . . Love the brotherhood. Fear God. Honour the King."

An' what do you think they did, Mr. Shields ? They caught a hold of the Bible an' flung it on the floor — imagine that, Mr. Shields — flingin' the Bible on the floor ! Then one of them says to another — " Jack," says he, " have you seen the light ; is your soul saved ? " An' then they grabbed hold of poor Dolphie, callin' him Mr. Moody an' Mr. Sankey, an' wanted him to offer up a prayer for the Irish Republic ! An' when they were puttin' me out, there they had the poor man sittin' up in bed, his hands crossed on his breast, his eyes lookin' up at the ceilin', an' he singin' a hymn — " We shall meet in the Sweet Bye an' Bye " — an' all the time, Mr. Shields, there they were drinkin' his whisky ; there's torture for you, an' they all laughin' at poor Dolphie's terrible sufferins.

Davoren. In the name of all that's sensible, what did he want to bring whisky home with him for ? They're bad enough sober, what'll they be like when they're drunk ?

Mrs. Grigson [plaintively]. He always brings a drop home with him — he calls it his medicine.

Seumas [still anxious]. They'll hardly search all the house ; do you think they will, Mrs. Grigson ?

Mrs. Grigson. An' we have a picture over the mantelpiece of King William crossing the Boyne, an' do you know what they wanted to make out, Mr. Shields, that it was Robert Emmet, an' the picture of a sacret society !

Seumas. She's not listenin' to a word I'm sayin'! Oh, the country is hopeless an' the people is hopeless.

Davoren. For God's sake tell her to go to hell out of this — she's worse than the Auxsie.

Seumas [*thoughtfully*]. Let her stay where she is; it's safer to have a woman in the room. If they come across the bombs I hope to God Minnie 'll say nothin'.

Davoren. We're a pair of pitiable cowards to let poor Minnie suffer when we know that we and not she are to blame.

Seumas. What else can we do, man? Do you want us to be done in? If you're anxious to be riddled, I'm not. Besides, they won't harm her, she's only a girl, an' so long as she keeps her mouth shut it'll be all right.

Davoren. I wish I could be sure of that.

Seumas. D'ye think are they goin', Mrs. Grigson? What are they doin' now?

Mrs. Grigson [*who is standing at the door, looking out into the hall*]. There's not a bit of me that's not shakin' like a jelly!

Seumas. Are they gone upstairs, Mrs. Grigson? Do you think, Mrs. Grigson, will they soon be goin'?

Mrs. Grigson. When they were makin' poor Dolphie sit up in the bed, I 'clare to God I thought every minute I'd hear their guns goin' off, an' see poor Dolphie stretched out dead in the bed— whisht, God bless us, I think I hear him moanin'!

Seumas. You might as well be talking to a stone ! They're all hopeless, hopeless, hopeless ! She thinks she hears him moanin' ! It's bloody near time somebody made him moan !

Davoren [*with a sickly attempt at humour*]. He's moaning for the loss of his whisky.

> [*During the foregoing dialogue the various sounds of a raid — orders, the tramping of heavy feet, the pulling about of furniture, etc., are heard. Now a more definite and sustained commotion is apparent. Loud and angry commands of " Go on ", " Get out and get into the lorry ", are heard, mingled with a girl's voice — it is Minnie's — shouting bravely, but a little hysterically, " Up the Republic ".*

Mrs. Grigson [*from the door*]. God save us, they're takin' Minnie, they're takin' Minnie Powell ! [*Running out*] What in the name of God can have happened ?

Seumas. Holy Saint Anthony grant that she'll keep her mouth shut.

Davoren [*sitting down on the bed and covering his face with his hands*]. We'll never again be able to lift up our heads if anything happens to Minnie.

Seumas. For God's sake keep quiet or somebody'll hear you ; nothin'll happen to her, nothin' at all — it'll be all right if she only keeps her mouth shut.

Mrs. Grigson [*running in*]. They're after gettin' a whole lot of stuff in Minnie's room ! Enough to blow up the whole street, a Tan says ! God to-night, who'd have ever thought that of Minnie Powell !

Seumas. Did she say anything, is she sayin' anything, what's she sayin', Mrs. Grigson ?

Mrs. Grigson. She's shoutin' " Up the Republic " at the top of her voice. An' big Mrs. Henderson is fightin' with the soldiers — she's after nearly knockin' one of them down, an' they're puttin' her into the lorry too.

Seumas. God blast her ! Can she not mind her own business ? What does she want here — didn't she know there was a raid on ? Is the whole damn country goin' mad ? They'll open fire in a minute an' innocent people'll be shot !

Davoren. What way are they using Minnie, Mrs. Grigson ; are they rough with her ?

Mrs. Grigson. They couldn't be half rough enough ; the little hussy, to be so deceitful ; she might as well have had the house blew up ! God to-night, who'd think it was in Minnie Powell !

Seumas. Oh, grant she won't say anything !

Mrs. Grigson. There they're goin' away now ; ah, then I hope they'll give that Minnie Powell a coolin'.

Seumas. God grant she won't say anything ! Are they gone, Mrs. Grigson ?

Mrs. Grigson. With her fancy stockins, an' her pompoms, an' her crêpe de chine blouses ! I knew she'd come to no good !

Seumas. God grant she'll keep her mouth shut! Are they gone, Mrs. Grigson ?

Mrs. Grigson. They're gone, Mr. Shields, an' here's poor Dolphie an' not a feather astray on him. Oh, Dolphie, dear, you're all right, thanks to God; I thought you'd never see the mornin'.

Grigson [*entering without coat or vest*]. Of course I'm all right; what ud put a bother on Dolphie Grigson? — not the Tans anyway!

Mrs. Grigson. When I seen you stretched out on the bed, an' you . . . singin' a hymn . . .

Grigson [*fearful of possible humiliation*]. Who was singin' a hymn? D'ye hear me talkin' to you — where did you hear me singin' a hymn?

Mrs. Grigson. I was only jokin', Dolphie, dear; I . . .

Grigson. Your place is below, an' not gosterin' here to men; down with you quick!

[*Mrs. Grigson hurriedly leaves the room.*

Grigson [*nonchalantly taking out his pipe, filling it, lighting it, and beginning to smoke*]. Excitin' few moments, Mr. Davoren; Mrs. G. lost her head completely — panic-stricken. But that's only natural, all women is very nervous. The only thing to do is to show them that they can't put the wind up you; show the least sign of fright an' they'd walk on you, simply walk on you. Two of them come down — " Put them up ", revolvers under your nose — you know, the usual way. " What's all the bother about?" says I, quite calm. " No bother at all," says one of them, " only this gun might go off an' hit somebody — have you me? " says he. " What if it does," says I, " a man can only die once, an' you'll find Grigson won't squeal." " God, you're a cool one," says the other, " there's no blottin' it out."

Seumas. That's the best way to take them ; it only makes things worse to show that you've got the wind up. " Any ammunition here ? " says the fellow that come in here. " I don't think so," says I, " but you better have a look." " No back talk," says he, " or you might get plugged." " I don't know of any clause," says I, " in the British Constitution that makes it a crime for a man to speak in his own room," — with that, he just had a look round, an' off he went.

Grigson. If a man keeps a stiff upper front — Merciful God, there's an ambush !

[*Explosions of two bursting bombs are heard on the street outside the house, followed by fierce and rapid revolver and rifle fire. People are heard rushing into the hall, and there is general clamour and confusion. Seumas and Davoren cower down in the room ; Grigson, after a few moments' hesitation, frankly rushes out of the room to what he conceives to be the safer asylum of the kitchen. A lull follows, punctuated by an odd rifle-shot ; then comes a peculiar and ominous stillness, broken in a few moments by the sounds of voices and movement. Questions are heard being asked : " Who was it was killed ? " " Where was she shot ?" which are answered by: "Minnie Powell " ; " She went to jump off the lorry an' she was shot"; " She's not dead, is she ? " ; " They say she's dead — shot through the buzzom ! "*

Davoren [*in a tone of horror-stricken doubt*]. D'ye hear what they're sayin', Shields, d'ye hear what they're sayin' ? — Minnie Powell is shot.

Seumas. For God's sake speak easy, an' don't bring them in here on top of us again.

Davoren. Is that all you're thinking of ? Do you realize that she has been shot to save us ?

Seumas. Is it my fault ; am I to blame ?

Davoren. It is your fault and mine, both ; oh, we're a pair of dastardly cowards to have let her do what she did.

Seumas. She did it off her own bat — we didn't ask her to do it.
  [*Mrs. Grigson enters.   She is excited and semi-hysterical, and sincerely affected by the tragic occurrence.*

Mrs. Grigson [*falling down in a sitting posture on one of the beds*]. What's goin' to happen next ! Oh, Mr. Davoren, isn't it terrible, isn't it terrible ! Minnie Powell, poor little Minnie Powell's been shot dead ! They were raidin' a house a few doors down, an' had just got up in their lorries to go away, when they was ambushed. You never heard such shootin' ! An' in the thick of it, poor Minnie went to jump off the lorry she was on, an' she was shot through the buzzom. Oh, it was horrible to see the blood pourin' out, an' Minnie moanin'. They found some paper in her breast, with " Minnie " written on it, an' some other name they couldn't make out with the blood ; the officer kep' it. The ambulance is bringin' her to the hospital, but what good's that when she's dead ! Poor little Minnie, poor little Minnie Powell, to think of you full of life a few minutes ago, an' now she's dead !

Davoren. Ah me, alas ! Pain, pain, pain ever, for ever ! It's terrible to think that little Minnie is dead, but it's still more terrible to think that Davoren and Shields are alive ! Oh, Donal Davoren, shame is your portion now till the silver cord is loosened and the golden bowl be broken.   Oh, Davoren, Donal Davoren, poet and poltroon, poltroon and poet !

Seumas [*solemnly*]. I knew something ud come of the tappin' on the wall !

CURTAIN

A TRAGEDY IN THREE ACTS

Juno and the Paycock

CHARACTERS IN THE PLAY

"Captain" Jack Boyle
Juno Boyle, *his wife*
Johnny Boyle ⎫
 ⎬ *their children*
Mary Boyle ⎭
"Joxer" Daly
Mrs. Maisie Madigan
"Needle" Nugent, *a tailor*
Mrs. Tancred
Jerry Devine
Charles Bentham, *a school teacher*
An Irregular Mobilizer
Two Irregulars
A Coal-block Vendor
A Sewing Machine Man
Two Furniture Removal Men
Two Neighbours

Residents in the Tenement

SCENE

Act I.—The living apartment of a two-roomed tenancy of the Boyle family, in a tenement house in Dublin.

Act II.—The same.

Act III.—The same.

A few days elapse between Acts I and II, and two months between Acts II and III.

During Act III the curtain is lowered for a few minutes to denote the lapse of one hour.

Period of the play, 1922.

ACT I

The living-room of a two-room tenancy occupied by the Boyle family in a tenement house in Dublin. Left, a door leading to another part of the house ; left of door a window looking into the street ; at back a dresser ; farther to right at back, a window looking into the back of the house. Between the window and the dresser is a picture of the Virgin ; below the picture, on a bracket, is a crimson bowl in which a floating votive light is burning. Farther to the right is a small bed partly concealed by cretonne hangings strung on a twine. To the right is the fireplace ; near the fireplace is a door leading to the other room. Beside the fireplace is a box containing coal. On the mantelshelf is an alarm clock lying on its face. In a corner near the window looking into the back is a galvanized bath. A table and some chairs. On the table are breakfast things for one. A teapot is on the hob and a frying-pan stands inside the fender. There are a few books on the dresser and one on the table. Leaning against the dresser is a long-handled shovel — the kind invariably used by labourers when turning concrete or mixing mortar. Johnny Boyle is sitting crouched beside the fire. Mary with her jumper off — it is lying on the back of a chair — is arranging her hair before a tiny mirror perched on the table. Beside the mirror is stretched out the morning paper, which she looks at when she isn't gazing into the mirror. She is a well-made and good-looking girl of twenty-two. Two forces are working in her mind — one, through the circumstances of her life, pulling her back ; the other, through the influence of books she has read, pushing her forward. The opposing forces are apparent in her speech and her manners, both of which are degraded by her environment, and improved by her acquaintance — slight though it be — with literature. The time is early forenoon.

Mary [*looking at the paper*]. On a little bye-road, out beyant Finglas, he was found.

> [*Mrs. Boyle enters by door on right ; she has been shopping and carries a small parcel in her hand. She is forty-five years of age, and twenty years ago she must have been a pretty woman ; but her face has now assumed that look which ultimately settles down upon the faces of the women of the working-class ; a look of listless monotony and harassed anxiety, blending with an expression of mechanical resistance. Were circumstances favourable, she would probably be a handsome, active and clever woman.*]

Mrs. Boyle. Isn't he come in yet ?

Mary. No, mother.

Mrs. Boyle. Oh, he'll come in when he likes ; struttin' about the town like a paycock with Joxer, I suppose. I hear all about Mrs. Tancred's son is in this mornin's paper.

Mary. The full details are in it this mornin' ; seven wounds he had — one entherin' the neck, with an exit wound beneath the left shoulder-blade ; another in the left breast penethratin' the heart, an' . . .

Johnny [*springing up from the fire*]. Oh, quit that readin', for God's sake ! Are yous losin' all your feelin's ? It'll soon be that none of you'll read anythin' that's not about butcherin' !

> [*He goes quickly into the room on left.*

Mary. He's gettin' very sensitive, all of a sudden !

Mrs. Boyle. I'll read it myself, Mary, by an' by, when I come home. Everybody's sayin' that he was a Die-hard — thanks be to God that Johnny had nothin' to do with him this long time. . . . [*Opening the parcel and taking out some sausages, which she places on a plate*] Ah, then, if that father o' yours doesn't come in soon for his breakfast, he may go without any ; I'll not wait much longer for him.

Mary. Can't you let him get it himself when he comes in ?

Mrs. Boyle. Yes, an' let him bring in Joxer Daly along with him ? Ay, that's what he'd like, an' that's what he's waitin' for — till he thinks I'm gone to work, an' then sail in with the boul' Joxer, to burn all the coal an' dhrink all the tea in the place, to show them what a good Samaritan he is ! But I'll stop here till he comes in, if I have to wait till to-morrow mornin'.

Voice of Johnny inside. Mother !

Mrs. Boyle. Yis ?

Voice of Johnny. Bring us in a dhrink o' wather.

Mrs. Boyle. Bring in that fella a dhrink o' wather, for God's sake, Mary.

Mary. Isn't he big an' able enough to come out an' get it himself ?

Mrs. Boyle. If you weren't well yourself you'd like some-body to bring you in a dhrink o' wather.

[*She brings in drink and returns.*

Mrs. Boyle. Isn't it terrible to have to be waitin' this way ! You'd think he was bringin' twenty poun's a week into the house the way he's going on. He wore

out the Health Insurance long ago, he's afther wearin'
out the unemployment dole, an', now, he's thryin' to
wear out me ! An' constantly singin', no less, when
he ought always to be on his knees offerin' up a
Novena for a job !

Mary [*tying a ribbon fillet-wise around her head*]. I don't like
this ribbon, ma ; I think I'll wear the green — it looks
betther than the blue.

Mrs. Boyle. Ah, wear whatever ribbon you like, girl, only
don't be botherin' me. I don't know what a girl on
strike wants to be wearin' a ribbon round her head for,
or silk stockins on her legs either ; it's wearin' them
things that make the employers think they're givin'
yous too much money.

Mary. The hour is past now when we'll ask the employers' permission to wear what we like.

Mrs. Boyle. I don't know why you wanted to walk out
for Jennie Claffey ; up to this you never had a good
word for her.

Mary. What's the use of belongin' to a Trades Union if
you won't stand up for your principles ? Why did
they sack her ? It was a clear case of victimization.
We couldn't let her walk the streets, could we ?

Mrs. Boyle. No, of course yous couldn't — yous wanted
to keep her company. Wan victim wasn't enough.
When the employers sacrifice wan victim, the Trades
Unions go wan betther be sacrificin' a hundred.

Mary. It doesn't matther what you say, ma — a principle's
a principle.

Mrs. Boyle. Yis ; an' when I go into oul' Murphy's to-morrow, an' he gets to know that, instead o' payin' all, I'm goin' to borry more, what'll he say when I tell him a principle's a principle? What'll we do if he refuses to give us any more on tick?

Mary. He daren't refuse — if he does, can't you tell him he's paid?

Mrs. Boyle. It's lookin' as if he was paid, whether he refuses or no.

[*Johnny appears at the door on left. He can be plainly seen now; he is a thin, delicate fellow, something younger than Mary. He has evidently gone through a rough time. His face is pale and drawn; there is a tremulous look of indefinite fear in his eyes. The left sleeve of his coat is empty, and he walks with a slight halt.*

Johnny. I was lyin' down; I thought yous were gone. Oul' Simon Mackay is thrampin' about like a horse over me head, an' I can't sleep with him — they're like thunder-claps in me brain! The curse o' — God forgive me for goin' to curse!

Mrs. Boyle. There, now; go back an' lie down again, an' I'll bring you in a nice cup o' tay.

Johnny. Tay, tay, tay! You're always thinkin' o' tay. If a man was dyin', you'd thry to make him swally a cup o' tay!   [*He goes back.*

Mrs. Boyle. I don't know what's goin' to be done with him. The bullet he got in the hip in Easter Week was bad enough, but the bomb that shatthered his arm in the fight in O'Connell Street put the finishin' touch on him. I knew he was makin' a fool of himself. God knows I went down on me bended knees to him not to go agen the Free State.

Mary. He stuck to his principles, an', no matther how you may argue, ma, a principle's a principle.

Voice of Johnny. Is Mary goin' to stay here ?

Mary. No, I'm not goin' to stay here ; you can't expect me to be always at your beck an' call, can you ?

Voice of Johnny. I won't stop here be meself !

Mrs. Boyle. Amn't I nicely handicapped with the whole o' yous ! I don't know what any o' yous ud do without your ma. [*To Johnny*] Your father'll be here in a minute, an' if you want anythin', he'll get it for you.

Johnny. I hate assin' him for anythin'. . . . He hates to be assed to stir. . . . Is the light lightin' before the picture o' the Virgin ?

Mrs. Boyle. Yis, yis ! The wan inside to St. Anthony isn't enough, but he must have another wan to the Virgin here !
  [*Jerry Devine enters hastily. He is about twenty-five, well set, active and earnest. He is a type, becoming very common now in the Labour Movement, of a mind knowing enough to make the mass of his associates, who know less, a power, and too little to broaden that power for the benefit of all. Mary seizes her jumper and runs hastily into room left.*

Jerry [*breathless*]. Where's the Captain, Mrs. Boyle, where's the Captain ?

Mrs. Boyle. You may well ass a body that : he's wherever Joxer Daly is — dhrinkin' in some snug or another.

Jerry. Father Farrell is just afther stoppin' to tell me to run up an' get him to go to the new job that's goin' on in Rathmines ; his cousin is foreman o' the job, an' Father Farrell was speakin' to him about poor Johnny an' his father bein' idle so long, an' the foreman told Father Farrell to send the Captain up an' he'd give him a start — I wondher where I'd find him ?

Mrs. Boyle. You'll find he's ayther in Ryan's or Foley's.

Jerry. I'll run round to Ryan's — I know it's a great house o' Joxer's.   [*He rushes out.*

Mrs. Boyle [*piteously*]. There now, he'll miss that job, or I know for what ! If he gets win' o' the word, he'll not come back till evenin', so that it'll be too late. There'll never be any good got out o' him so long as he goes with that shouldher-shruggin' Joxer. I killin' meself workin', an' he sthruttin' about from mornin' till night like a paycock !

> [*The steps of two persons are heard coming up a flight of stairs. They are the footsteps of Captain Boyle and Joxer. Captain Boyle is singing in a deep, sonorous, self-honouring voice.*

The Captain. Sweet Spirit, hear me prayer ! Hear . . . oh . . . hear . . . me prayer . . . hear, oh, hear . . . Oh, he . . . ar . . . oh, he . . . ar . . . me . . . pray . . . er !

Joxer [*outside*]. Ah, that's a darlin' song, a daaarlin' song !

Mrs. Boyle [*viciously*]. Sweet spirit hear his prayer ! Ah, then, I'll take me solemn affeydavey, it's not for a job he's prayin' !

> [*She sits down on the bed so that the cretonne hangings hide her from the view of those entering.*

> [*The Captain comes slowly in. He is a man of about sixty ; stout, grey-haired and stocky. His neck is short,*

and his head looks like a stone ball that one sometimes
sees on top of a gate-post.   His cheeks, reddish-purple, are
puffed out, as if he were always repressing an almost
irrepressible ejaculation.   On his upper lip is a crisp,
tightly cropped moustache ; he carries himself with the
upper part of his body slightly thrown back, and his
stomach slightly thrust forward.   His walk is a slow,
consequential strut.   His clothes are dingy, and he wears
a faded seaman's-cap with a glazed peak.

Boyle [*to Joxer, who is still outside*]. Come on, come on in,
Joxer ; she's gone out long ago, man.   If there's
nothing else to be got, we'll furrage out a cup o' tay,
anyway.   It's the only bit I get in comfort when she's
away.   'Tisn't Juno should be her pet name at all,
but Deirdre of the Sorras, for she's always grousin'.

[*Joxer steps cautiously into the room. He may be younger*
than the Captain but he looks a lot older. His face is
like a bundle of crinkled paper ; his eyes have a cunning
twinkle ; he is spare and loosely built ; he has a habit
of constantly shrugging his shoulders with a peculiar
twitching movement, meant to be ingratiating. His face
is invariably ornamented with a grin.

Joxer. It's a terrible thing to be tied to a woman that's
always grousin'.   I don't know how you stick it — it
ud put years on me.   It's a good job she has to be so
ofen away, for [*with a shrug*] when the cat's away, the
mice can play !

Boyle [*with a commanding and complacent gesture*]. Pull over
to the fire, Joxer, an' we'll have a cup o' tay in a
minute.

Joxer. Ah, a cup o' tay's a darlin' thing, a daaarlin' thing
— the cup that cheers but doesn't . . .

[*Joxer's rhapsody is cut short by the sight of Juno coming forward and confronting the two cronies. Both are stupefied.*

Mrs. Boyle [*with sweet irony — poking the fire, and turning her head to glare at Joxer*]. Pull over to the fire, Joxer Daly, an' we'll have a cup o' tay in a minute ! Are you sure, now, you wouldn't like an egg ?

Joxer. I can't stop, Mrs. Boyle ; I'm in a desperate hurry, a desperate hurry.

Mrs. Boyle. Pull over to the fire, Joxer Daly ; people is always far more comfortabler here than they are in their own place.

[*Joxer makes hastily for the door. Boyle stirs to follow him ; thinks of something to relieve the situation — stops, and says suddenly :* Joxer !

Joxer [*at door ready to bolt*]. Yis ?

Boyle. You know the foreman o' that job that's goin' on down in Killesther, don't you, Joxer ?

Joxer [*puzzled*]. Foreman — Killesther ?

Boyle [*with a meaning look*]. He's a butty o' yours, isn't he ?

Joxer [*the truth dawning on him*]. The foreman at Killesther — oh yis, yis. He's an oul' butty o' mine — oh, he's a darlin' man, a daarlin' man.

Boyle. Oh, then, it's a sure thing. It's a pity we didn't go down at breakfast first thing this mornin'— we might ha' been working now ; but you didn't know it then.

Joxer [*with a shrug*]. It's betther late than never.

Boyle. It's nearly time we got a start, anyhow ; I'm fed up knockin' round, doin' nothin'. He promised you —gave you the straight tip ?

Joxer. Yis. " Come down on the blow o' dinner," says he, " an' I'll start you, an' any friend you like to brin' with you." " Ah," says I, " you're a darlin' man, a daaarlin' man."

Boyle. Well, it couldn't come at a betther time — we're a long time waitin' for it.

Joxer. Indeed we were ; but it's a long lane that has no turnin'.

Boyle. The blow up for dinner is at one — wait till I see what time it 'tis.
    [*He goes over to the mantelpiece, and gingerly lifts the clock.*

Mrs. Boyle. Min' now, how you go on fiddlin' with that clock — you know the least little thing sets it asthray.

Boyle. The job couldn't come at a betther time ; I'm feelin' in great fettle, Joxer. I'd hardly believe I ever had a pain in me legs, an' last week I was nearly crippled with them.

Joxer. That's betther an' betther ; ah, God never shut wan door but He opened another !

Boyle. It's only eleven o'clock ; we've lashins o' time. I'll slip on me oul' moleskins afther breakfast, an' we can saunther down at our ayse. [*Putting his hand on the shovel*] I think, Joxer, we'd betther bring our shovels ?

Joxer. Yis, Captain, yis ; it's betther to go fully prepared an' ready for all eventualities. You bring your
long-tailed shovel, an' I'll bring me navvy. We
mighten' want them, an', then agen, we might : for
want of a nail the shoe was lost, for want of a shoe the
horse was lost, an' for want of a horse the man was
lost — aw, that's a darlin' proverb, a daarlin' . . .

[*As Joxer is finishing his sentence, Mrs. Boyle approaches
the door and Joxer retreats hurriedly. She shuts the
door with a bang.*

Boyle [*suggestively*]. We won't be long pullin' ourselves
together agen when I'm working for a few weeks.

[*Mrs. Boyle takes no notice.*

Boyle. The foreman on the job is an oul' butty o'
Joxer's ; I have an idea that I know him meself. [*Silence*]
. . . There's a button off the back o' me moleskin
trousers. . . . If you leave out a needle an' thread
I'll sew it on meself. . . . Thanks be to God, the
pains in me legs is gone, anyhow !

Mrs. Boyle [*with a burst*]. Look here, Mr. Jacky Boyle,
them yarns won't go down with Juno. I know you an'
Joxer Daly of an oul' date, an' if you think you're
able to come it over me with them fairy tales, you're
in the wrong shop.

Boyle [*coughing subduedly to relieve the tenseness of the situation*].
U-u-u-ugh !

Mrs. Boyle. Butty o' Joxer's ! Oh, you'll do a lot o'
good as long as you continue to be a butty o' Joxer's !

Boyle. U-u-u-ugh !

Mrs. Boyle. Shovel ! Ah, then, me boyo, you'd do far

more work with a knife an' fork than ever you'll do
with a shovel ! If there was e'er a genuine job goin'
you'd be dh'other way about — not able to lift your
arms with the pains in your legs ! Your poor wife
slavin' to keep the bit in your mouth, an' you gallivantin' about all the day like a paycock !

Boyle. It ud be betther for a man to be dead, betther for
a man to be dead.

Mrs. Boyle [*ignoring the interruption*]. Everybody callin' you
" Captain ", an' you only wanst on the wather, in an
oul' collier from here to Liverpool, when anybody, to
listen or look at you, ud take you for a second Christo
For Columbus !

Boyle. Are you never goin' to give us a rest ?

Mrs. Boyle. Oh, you're never tired o' lookin' for a rest.

Boyle. D'ye want to dhrive me out o' the house ?

Mrs. Boyle. It ud be easier to dhrive you out o' the house
than to dhrive you into a job. Here, sit down an'
take your breakfast — it may be the last you'll get,
for I don't know where the next is goin' to come from.

Boyle. If I get this job we'll be all right.

Mrs. Boyle. Did ye see Jerry Devine ?

Boyle [*testily*]. No, I didn't see him.

Mrs. Boyle. No, but you seen Joxer. Well, he was here
lookin' for you.

Boyle. Well, let him look !

Mrs. Boyle. Oh, indeed, he may well look, for it ud be
hard for him to see you, an' you stuck in Ryan's snug.

Boyle. I wasn't in Ryan's snug — I don't go into Ryan's.

Mrs. Boyle. Oh, is there a mad dog there ? Well, if you weren't in Ryan's you were in Foley's.

Boyle. I'm telling you for the last three weeks I haven't tasted a dhrop of intoxicatin' liquor. I wasn't in ayther wan snug or dh'other — I could swear that on a prayer-book — I'm as innocent as the child unborn !

Mrs. Boyle. Well, if you'd been in for your breakfast you'd ha' seen him.

Boyle [*suspiciously*]. What does he want me for ?

Mrs. Boyle. He'll be back any minute an' then you'll soon know.

Boyle. I'll dhrop out an' see if I can meet him.

Mrs. Boyle. You'll sit down an' take your breakfast, an' let me go to me work, for I'm an hour late already waitin' for you.

Boyle. You needn't ha' waited, for I'll take no breakfast — I've a little spirit left in me still !

Mrs. Boyle. Are you goin' to have your breakfast — yes or no ?

Boyle [*too proud to yield*]. I'll have no breakfast — yous can keep your breakfast. [*Plaintively*] I'll knock out a bit somewhere, never fear.

Mrs. Boyle. Nobody's goin' to coax you — don't think that.

   [*She vigorously replaces the pan and the sausages in the press.*

Boyle. I've a little spirit left in me still.

                              [*Jerry Devine enters hastily.*

Jerry. Oh, here you are at last ! I've been searchin' for you everywhere. The foreman in Foley's told me you hadn't left the snug with Joxer ten minutes before I went in.

Mrs. Boyle. An' he swearin' on the holy prayer-book that he wasn't in no snug !

Boyle [*to Jerry*]. What business is it o' yours whether I was in a snug or no ? What do you want to be gallopin' about afther me for ? Is a man not to be allowed to leave his house for a minute without havin' a pack o' spies, pimps an' informers cantherin' at his heels ?

Jerry. Oh, you're takin' a wrong view of it, Mr. Boyle ; I simply was anxious to do you a good turn. I have a message for you from Father Farrell : he says that if you go to the job that's on in Rathmines, an' ask for Foreman Managan, you'll get a start.

Boyle. That's all right, but I don't want the motions of me body to be watched the way an asthronomer ud watch a star. If you're folleyin' Mary aself, you've no pereeogative to be folleyin' me. [*Suddenly catching his thigh*] U-ugh, I'm afther gettin' a terrible twinge in me right leg !

Mrs. Boyle. Oh, it won't be very long now till it travels into your left wan. It's miraculous that whenever he scents a job in front of him, his legs begin to fail him ! Then, me bucko, if you lose this chance, you may go an' furrage for yourself !

Jerry. This job'll last for some time too, Captain, an' as soon as the foundations are in, it'll be cushy enough.

Boyle. Won't it be a climbin' job ? How d'ye expect me

to be able to go up a ladder with these legs ? An', if I get up aself, how am I goin' to get down agen ?

Mrs. Boyle [*viciously*]. Get wan o' the labourers to carry you down in a hod ! You can't climb a laddher, but you can skip like a goat into a snug !

Jerry. I wouldn't let myself be let down that easy, Mr. Boyle ; a little exercise, now, might do you all the good in the world.

Boyle. It's a docthor you should have been, Devine — maybe you know more about the pains in me legs than meself that has them ?

Jerry [*irritated*]. Oh, I know nothin' about the pains in your legs ; I've brought the message that Father Farrell gave me, an' that's all I can do.

Mrs. Boyle. Here, sit down an' take your breakfast, an' go an' get ready ; an' don't be actin' as if you couldn't pull a wing out of a dead bee.

Boyle. I want no breakfast, I tell you ; it ud choke me afther all that's been said. I've a little spirit left in me still.

Mrs. Boyle. Well, let's see your spirit, then, an' go in at wanst an' put on your moleskin trousers !

Boyle [*moving towards the door on left*]. It ud be betther for a man to be dead ! U-ugh ! There's another twinge in me other leg ! Nobody but meself knows the sufferin' I'm goin' through with the pains in these legs o' mine !

[*He goes into the room on left as Mary comes out with her hat in her hand.*

Mrs. Boyle. I'll have to push off now, for I'm terrible

late already, but I was determined to stay an' hunt
that Joxer this time.   [*She goes off.*

Jerry. Are you going out, Mary?

Mary. It looks like it when I'm putting on my hat,
doesn't it?

Jerry. The bitther word agen, Mary.

Mary. You won't allow me to be friendly with you;
if I thry, you deliberately misundherstand it.

Jerry. I didn't always misundherstand it; you were often
delighted to have the arms of Jerry around you.

Mary. If you go on talkin' like this, Jerry Devine, you'll
make me hate you!

Jerry. Well, let it be either a weddin' or a wake!
Listen, Mary, I'm standin' for the Secretaryship of our
Union. There's only one opposin' me; I'm popular
with all the men, an' a good speaker — all are sayin'
that I'll get elected.

Mary. Well?

Jerry. The job's worth three hundred an' fifty pounds a
year, Mary. You an' I could live nice an' cosily on
that; it would lift you out o' this place an' . . .

Mary. I haven't time to listen to you now — I have to go.
                [*She is going out, when Jerry bars the way.*

Jerry [*appealingly*]. Mary, what's come over you with me
for the last few weeks? You hardly speak to me, an'
then only a word with a face o' bittherness on it. Have
you forgotten, Mary, all the happy evenins that were
as sweet as the scented hawthorn that sheltered the
sides o' the road as we sauntered through the country?

Mary. That's all over now. When you get your new job, Jerry, you won't be long findin' a girl far betther than I am for your sweetheart.

Jerry. Never, never, Mary! No matther what happens, you'll always be the same to me.

Mary. I must be off; please let me go, Jerry.

Jerry. I'll go a bit o' the way with you.

Mary. You needn't, thanks; I want to be by meself.

Jerry [*catching her arm*]. You're goin' to meet another fella; you've clicked with someone else, me lady!

Mary. That's no concern o' yours, Jerry Devine; let me go!

Jerry. I saw yous comin' out o' the Cornflower Dance Class, an' you hangin' on his arm — a thin, lanky strip of a Micky Dazzler, with a walkin'-stick an' gloves!

Voice of Johnny [*loudly*]. What are you doin' there — pullin' about everything!

Voice of Boyle [*loudly and viciously*]. I'm puttin' on me moleskin trousers!

Mary. You're hurtin' me arm! Let me go, or I'll scream, an' then you'll have the oul' fella out on top of us!

Jerry. Don't be so hard on a fella, Mary, don't be so hard.

Boyle [*appearing at the door*]. What's the meanin' of all this hillabaloo?

Mary. Let me go, let me go !

Boyle. D'ye hear me — what's all this hillabaloo about ?

Jerry [*plaintively*]. Will you not give us one kind word, one kind word, Mary ?

Boyle. D'ye hear me talkin' to yous ? What's all this hillabaloo for ?

Jerry. Let me kiss your hand, your little, tiny, white hand !

Boyle. Your little, tiny, white hand — are you takin' leave o' your senses, man ?

[*Mary breaks away and rushes out.*

Boyle. This is nice goins on in front of her father !

Jerry. Ah, dhry up, for God's sake ! [*He follows Mary.*

Boyle. Chiselurs don't care a damn now about their parents, they're bringin' their fathers' grey hairs down with sorra to the grave, an' laughin' at it, laughin' at it. Ah, I suppose it's just the same every-where — the whole worl's in a state o' chassis ! [*He sits by the fire*] Breakfast ! Well, they can keep their breakfast for me. Not if they were down on their bended knees would I take it — I'll show them I've a little spirit left in me still ! [*He goes over to the press, takes out a plate and looks at it*] Sassige ! Well, let her keep her sassige. [*He returns to the fire, takes up the teapot and gives it a gentle shake*] The tea's wet right enough.

[*A pause ; he rises, goes to the press, takes out the sausage, puts it on the pan, and puts both on the fire. He attends the sausage with a fork.*

Boyle [*singing*] :

When the robins nest agen,
And the flowers are in bloom,
When the Springtime's sunny smile seems to banish all
    sorrow an' gloom ;
Then me bonny blue-ey'd lad, if me heart be true till then —
He's promised he'll come back to me,
When the robins nest agen !

  [*He lifts his head at the high note, and then drops his eyes
    to the pan.*

Boyle [*singing*] :

        When the . . .

  [*Steps are heard approaching ; he whips the pan off the fire
    and puts it under the bed, then sits down at the fire. The
    door opens and a bearded man looking in says :*

You don't happen to want a sewin' machine ?

Boyle [*furiously*]. No, I don't want e'er a sewin' machine !
  [*He returns the pan to the fire, and commences to sing again.*

Boyle [*singing*] :

        When the robins nest agen,
        And the flowers they are in bloom,
        He's . . .

            [*A thundering knock is heard at the street door.*

Boyle. There's a terrible tatheraraa — that's a stranger —
  that's nobody belongin' to the house.

                      [*Another loud knock.*

Joxer [*sticking his head in at the door*]. Did ye hear them
  tatherarahs ?

Boyle. Well, Joxer, I'm not deaf.

Johnny [*appearing in his shirt and trousers at the door on left ;*

his face is anxious and his voice is tremulous]. Who's that at the door ; who's that at the door ? Who gave that knock — d'ye yous hear me — are yous deaf or dhrunk or what ?

Boyle [*to Johnny*]. How the hell do I know who 'tis ? Joxer, stick your head out o' the window an' see.

Joxer. An' mebbe get a bullet in the kisser ? Ah, none o' them thricks for Joxer ! It's betther to be a coward than a corpse !

Boyle [*looking cautiously out of the window*]. It's a fella in a thrench coat.

Johnny. Holy Mary, Mother o' God, I . . .

Boyle. He's goin' away — he must ha' got tired knockin'.
                    [*Johnny returns to the room on left.*

Boyle. Sit down an' have a cup o' tay, Joxer.

Joxer. I'm afraid the missus ud pop in on us agen before we'd know where we are. Somethin's tellin' me to go at wanst.

Boyle. Don't be superstitious, man ; we're Dublin men, an'. not boyos that's only afther comin' up from the bog o' Allen — though if she did come in, right enough, we'd be caught like rats in a thrap.

Joxer. An' you know the sort she is — she wouldn't listen to reason — an' wanse bitten twice shy.

Boyle [*going over to the window at back*]. If the worst came to the worst, you could dart out here, Joxer ; it's only a dhrop of a few feet to the roof of the return room, an' the first minute she goes into dh'other room I'll give you the bend, an' you can slip in an' away.

Joxer [*yielding to the temptation*]. Ah, I won't stop very long anyhow. [*Picking up a book from the table*] Whose is the buk ?

Boyle. Aw, one o' Mary's ; she's always readin' lately — nothin' but thrash, too. There's one I was lookin' at dh'other day : three stories, The Doll's House, Ghosts, an' The Wild Duck — buks only fit for chiselurs !

Joxer. Didja ever rade *Elizabeth, or Th' Exile o' Sibayria ?* . . . Ah, it's a darlin' story, a daarlin' story !

Boyle. You eat your sassige, an' never min' *Th' Exile o' Sibayria.*
[*Both sit down ; Boyle fills out tea, pours gravy on Joxer's plate, and keeps the sausage for himself.*

Joxer. What are you wearin' your moleskin trousers for ?

Boyle. I have to go to a job, Joxer. Just afther you'd gone, Devine kem runnin' in to tell us that Father Farrell said if I went down to the job that's goin' on in Rathmines I'd get a start

Joxer. Be the holy, that's good news !

Boyle. How is it good news ? I wondher if you were in my condition, would you call it good news ?

Joxer. I thought . . .

Boyle. You thought ! You think too sudden sometimes, Joxer. D'ye know, I'm hardly able to crawl with the pains in me legs !

Joxer. Yis, yis ; I forgot the pains in your legs. I know you can do nothin' while they're at you.

Boyle. You forgot ; I don't think any of yous realize the

state I'm in with the pains in me legs.   What ud
happen if I had to carry a bag o' cement ?

Joxer. Ah, any man havin' the like of them pains id be
down an' out, down an' out.

Boyle. I wouldn't mind if he had said it to meself ; but,
no, oh no, he rushes in an' shouts it out in front o'
Juno, an' you know what Juno is, Joxer.   We all know
Devine knows a little more than the rest of us, but
he doesn't act as if he did ; he's a good boy, sober,
able to talk an' all that, but still . . .

Joxer. Oh ay ; able to argufy, but still . . .

Boyle. If he's runnin' afther Mary, aself, he's not goin'
to be runnin' afther me.   Captain Boyle's able to take
care of himself.   Afther all, I'm not gettin' brought
up on Virol.   I never heard him usin' a curse ; I don't
believe he was ever dhrunk in his life — sure he's not
like a Christian at all !

Joxer. You're afther takin' the word out o' me mouth —
afther all, a Christian's natural, but he's unnatural.

Boyle. His oul' fella was just the same — a Wicklow man.

Joxer. A Wicklow man !   That explains the whole thing.
I've met many a Wicklow man in me time, but I never
met wan that was any good.

Boyle. " Father Farrell," says he, " sent me down to tell
you."   Father Farrell ! . . . D'ye know, Joxer, I
never like to be beholden to any o' the clergy.

Joxer. It's dangerous, right enough.

Boyle. If they do anything for you, they'd want you to
be livin' in the Chapel. . . . I'm goin' to tell you

somethin', Joxer, that I wouldn't tell to anybody else
— the clergy always had too much power over the people
in this unfortunate country.

Joxer. You could sing that if you had an air to it !

Boyle [*becoming enthusiastic*]. Didn't they prevent the people
in " '47 " from seizin' the corn, an' they starvin' ;
didn't they down Parnell ; didn't they say that hell
wasn't hot enough nor eternity long enough to punish
the Fenians ? We don't forget, we don't forget them
things, Joxer. If they've taken everything else from
us, Joxer, they've left us our memory.

Joxer [*emotionally*]. For mem'ry's the only friend that
grief can call its own, that grief . . . can . . . call
. . . its own !

Boyle. Father Farrell's beginnin' to take a great intherest
in Captain Boyle ; because of what Johnny did for his
country, says he to me wan day. It's a curious way to
reward Johnny be makin' his poor oul' father work.
But that's what the clergy want, Joxer — work, work,
work for me an' you ; havin' us mulin' from mornin'
till night, so that they may be in betther fettle when
they come hoppin' round for their dues ! Job ! Well,
let him give his job to wan of his hymn-singin',
prayer-spoutin', craw-thumpin' Confraternity men !
   [*The voice of a coal-block vendor is heard chanting in the
   street.*

Voice of Coal Vendor. Blocks . . . coal-blocks ! Blocks
. . . coal-blocks !

Joxer. God be with the young days when you were
steppin' the deck of a manly ship, with the win'
blowin' a hurricane through the masts, an' the only

sound you'd hear was, " Port your helm ! " an' the
only answer, " Port it is, sir ! "

Boyle. Them was days, Joxer, them was days. Nothin'
was too hot or too heavy for me then. Sailin' from the
Gulf o' Mexico to the Antanartic Ocean. I seen
things, I seen things, Joxer, that no mortal man should
speak about that knows his Catechism. Ofen, an'
ofen, when I was fixed to the wheel with a marlin-
spike, an' the wins blowin' fierce an' the waves lashin'
an' lashin', till you'd think every minute was goin' to
be your last, an' it blowed, an' blowed — blew is
the right word, Joxer, but blowed is what the sailors
use. . . .

Joxer. Aw, it's a darlin' word, a daarlin' word.

Boyle. An', as it blowed an' blowed, I ofen looked up
at the sky an' assed meself the question — what is the
stars, what is the stars ?

Voice of Coal Vendor. Any blocks, coal-blocks ; blocks,
coal-blocks !

Joxer. Ah, that's the question, that's the question —
what is the stars ?

Boyle. An' then, I'd have another look, an' I'd ass meself
— what is the moon ?

Joxer. Ah, that's the question — what is the moon, what
is the moon ?

[*Rapid steps are heard coming towards the door. Boyle
makes desperate efforts to hide everything ; Joxer rushes to
the window in a frantic effort to get out ; Boyle begins
to innocently lilt " Oh, me darlin' Jennie, I will be
thrue to thee ", when the door is opened, and the black
face of the Coal Vendor appears.*

The Coal Vendor. D'yes want any blocks?

Boyle [*with a roar*]. No, we don't want any blocks!

Joxer [*coming back with a sigh of relief*]. That's afther puttin'
the heart across me — I could ha' sworn it was Juno.
I'd bestter be goin', Captain; you couldn't tell the
minute Juno'd hop in on us.

Boyle. Let her hop in; we may as well have it out first
as at last. I've made up me mind — I'm not goin' to
do only what she damn well likes.

Joxer. Them sentiments does you credit, Captain; I
don't like to say anything as between man an' wife,
but I say as a butty, as a butty, Captain, that you've
stuck it too long, an' that it's about time you showed
a little spunk.

> How can a man die bestter than facin' fearful odds,
> For th' ashes of his fathers an' the temples of his gods?

Boyle. She has her rights — there's no one denyin' it,
but haven't I me rights too?

Joxer. Of course you have — the sacred rights o' man!

Boyle. Today, Joxer, there's goin' to be issued a proclamation be me, establishin' an independent Republic,
an' Juno'll have to take an oath of allegiance.

Joxer. Be firm, be firm, Captain; the first few minutes'll
be the worst: — if you gently touch a nettle it'll sting
you for your pains; grasp it like a lad of mettle, an' as
soft as silk remains!

Voice of Juno outside. Can't stop, Mrs. Madigan — I
haven't a minute!

Joxer [*flying out of the window*]. Holy God, here she is!

Boyle [*packing the things away with a rush in the press*]. I knew that fella ud stop till she was in on top of us !
[*He sits down by the fire.*
[*Juno enters hastily ; she is flurried and excited.*

Juno. Oh, you're in — you must have been only afther comin' in ?

Boyle. No, I never went out.

Juno. It's curious, then, you never heard the knockin'.
[*She puts her coat and hat on bed.*

Boyle. Knockin' ? Of course I heard the knockin'.

Juno. An' why didn't you open the door, then ? I suppose you were so busy with Joxer that you hadn't time.

Boyle. I haven't seen Joxer since I seen him before. Joxer ! What ud bring Joxer here ?

Juno. D'ye mean to tell me that the pair of yous wasn't collogin' together here when me back was turned ?

Boyle. What ud we be collogin' together about ? I have somethin' else to think of besides collogin' with Joxer. I can swear on all the holy prayer-books . . .

Mrs. Boyle. That you weren't in no snug ! Go on in at wanst now, an' take off that moleskin trousers o' yours, an' put on a collar an' tie to smarten yourself up a bit. There's a visitor comin' with Mary in a minute, an' he has great news for you.

Boyle. A job, I suppose ; let us get wan first before we start lookin' for another.

Mrs. Boyle. That's the thing that's able to put the win' up you. Well, it's no job, but news that'll give you the chance o' your life.

Boyle. What's all the mysthery about ?

Mrs. Boyle. G'win an' take off the moleskin trousers when you're told !   [*Boyle goes into room on left.*
[*Mrs. Boyle tidies up the room, puts the shovel under the bed, and goes to the press.*

Mrs. Boyle. Oh, God bless us, looka the way everything's thrun about ! Oh, Joxer was here, Joxer was here !
[*Mary enters with Charlie Bentham ; he is a young man of twenty-five, tall, good-looking, with a very high opinion of himself generally. He is dressed in a brown coat, brown knee-breeches, grey stockings, a brown sweater, with a deep blue tie ; he carries gloves and a walking-stick.*

Mrs. Boyle [*fussing round*]. Come in, Mr. Bentham ; sit down, Mr. Bentham, in this chair ; it's more comfortabler than that, Mr. Bentham. Himself'll be here in a minute ; he's just takin' off his trousers.

Mary. Mother !

Bentham. Please don't put yourself to any trouble, Mrs. Boyle — I'm quite all right here, thank you.

Mrs. Boyle. An' to think of you knowin' Mary, an' she knowin' the news you had for us, an' wouldn't let on ; but it's all the more welcomer now, for we were on our last lap !

Voice of Johnny inside. What are you kickin' up all the racket for ?

Boyle [*roughly*]. I'm takin' off me moleskin trousers !

Johnny. Can't you do it, then, without lettin' th' whole

house know you're takin off your trousers ?   What
d'ye want puttin' them on an' takin' them off again ?

Boyle. Will you let me alone, will you let me alone ?
Am I never goin' to be done thryin' to please th' whole
o' yous ?

Mrs Boyle [*to Bentham*]. You must excuse th' state o' th'
place, Mr. Bentham ; th' minute I turn me back that
man o' mine always makes a litther o' th' place, a litther
o' th' place.

Bentham. Don't worry, Mrs. Boyle ; it's all right, I
assure . . .

Boyle [*inside*]. Where's me braces ; where in th' name o'
God did I leave me braces ? . . . Ay, did you see where
I put me braces ?

Johnny [*inside, calling out*]. Ma, will you come in here an'
take da away ou' o' this or he'll dhrive me mad.

Mrs. Boyle [*going towards the door*]. Dear, dear, dear, that
man'll be lookin' for somethin' on th' day o' Judgement. [*Looking into room and calling to Boyle*] Look at
your braces, man, hangin' round your neck !

Boyle [*inside*]. Aw, Holy God !

Mrs. Boyle [*calling*]. Johnny, Johnny, come out here for a
minute.

Johnny. Ah, leave Johnny alone, an' don't be annoyin'
him !

Mrs. Boyle. Come on, Johnny, till I inthroduce you to Mr.
Bentham. [*To Bentham*] My son, Mr. Bentham ; he's
afther goin' through the mill. He was only a chiselur
of a Boy Scout in Easter Week, when he got hit in the

hip ; and his arm was blew off in the fight in O'Connell Street. [*Johnny comes in.*] Here he is, Mr. Bentham ; Mr. Bentham, Johnny. None can deny he done his bit for Irelan', if that's goin' to do him any good.

Johnny [*boastfully*]. I'd do it agen, ma, I'd do it agen ; for a principle's a principle.

Mrs. Boyle. Ah, you lost your best principle, me boy, when you lost your arm ; them's the only sort o' principles that's any good to a workin' man.

Johnny. Ireland only half free'll never be at peace while she has a son left to pull a trigger.

Mrs. Boyle. To be sure, to be sure — no bread's a lot betther than half a loaf. [*Calling loudly in to Boyle*] Will you hurry up there ?
     [*Boyle enters in his best trousers, which aren't too good, and looks very uncomfortable in his collar and tie.*

Mrs. Boyle. This is me husband ; Mr. Boyle, Mr. Bentham.

Bentham. Ah, very glad to know you, Mr. Boyle. How are you ?

Boyle. Ah, I'm not too well at all ; I suffer terrible with pains in me legs. Juno can tell you there what . . .

Mrs. Boyle. You won't have many pains in your legs when you hear what Mr. Bentham has to tell you.

Bentham. Juno ! What an interesting name ! It reminds one of Homer's glorious story of ancient gods and heroes.

Boyle. Yis, doesn't it ? You see, Juno was born an' christened in June ; I met her in June ; we were married in June, an' Johnny was born in June, so wan day I says to her, " You should ha' been called Juno," an' the name stuck to her ever since.

Mrs. Boyle. Here, we can talk o' them things agen ; let Mr. Bentham say what he has to say now.

Bentham. Well, Mr. Boyle, I suppose you'll remember a Mr. Ellison of Santry — he's a relative of yours, I think.

Boyle [*viciously*]. Is it that prognosticator an' procrastinator ! Of course I remember him.

Bentham. Well, he's dead, Mr. Boyle . . .

Boyle. Sorra many'll go into mournin' for him.

Mrs. Boyle. Wait till you hear what Mr. Bentham has to say, an' then, maybe, you'll change your opinion.

Bentham. A week before he died he sent for me to write his will for him. He told me that there were two only that he wished to leave his property to : his second cousin, Michael Finnegan of Santry, and John Boyle, his first cousin, of Dublin.

Boyle [*excitedly*]. Me, is it me, me ?

Bentham. You, Mr. Boyle ; I'll read a copy of the will that I have here with me, which has been duly filed in the Court of Probate.

　　　[*He takes a paper from his pocket and reads :*

6th February 1922

This is the last Will and Testament of William Ellison, of Santry, in the County of Dublin. I hereby order and wish my property to be sold and divided as follows :—

£20 to the St. Vincent de Paul Society.

£60 for Masses for the repose of my soul (5s. for each Mass).

The rest of my property to be divided between my first and second cousins.

I hereby appoint Timothy Buckly, of Santry, and Hugh Brierly, of Coolock, to be my Executors.

> (*Signed*)   WILLIAM ELLISON.
> HUGH BRIERLY.
> TIMOTHY BUCKLY.
> CHARLES BENTHAM, N.T.

Boyle [*eagerly*]. An' how much'll be comin' out of it, Mr. Bentham ?

Bentham. The Executors told me that half of the property would be anything between £1500 and £2000.

Mary. A fortune, father, a fortune !

Johnny. We'll be able to get out o' this place now, an' go somewhere we're not known.

Mrs. Boyle. You won't have to trouble about a job for awhile, Jack.

Boyle [*fervently*]. I'll never doubt the goodness o' God agen.

Bentham. I congratulate you, Mr. Boyle.

> [*They shake hands.*

Boyle. An' now, Mr. Bentham, you'll have to have a wet.

Bentham. A wet ?

Boyle. A wet — a jar — a boul !

Mrs. Boyle. Jack, you're speakin' to Mr. Bentham, an' not to Joxer.

Boyle [*solemnly*]. Juno . . . Mary . . . Johnny . . . we'll have to go into mournin' at wanst. . . . I never expected that poor Bill ud die so sudden. . . . Well, we all have to die some day . . . you, Juno, to-day . . . an' me, maybe, to-morrow. . . . It's sad, but it can't be helped. . . . Requiescat in pace . . . or, usin' our oul' tongue like St. Patrick or St. Bridget, Guh sayeree jeea ayera !

Mary. Oh, father, that's not Rest in Peace ; that's God save Ireland.

Boyle. U-u-ugh, it's all the same — isn't it a prayer ? . . . Juno, I'm done with Joxer ; he's nothin' but a prognosticator an' a . . .

Joxer [*climbing angrily through the window and bounding into the room*]. You're done with Joxer, are you ? Maybe you thought I'd stop on the roof all the night for you ! Joxer out on the roof with the win' blowin' through him was nothin' to you an' your friend with the collar an' tie !

Mrs. Boyle. What in the name o' God brought you out on the roof ; what were you doin' there ?

Joxer [*ironically*]. I was dhreamin' I was standin' on the bridge of a ship, an' she sailin' the Antartic Ocean, an' it blowed, an' blowed, an' I lookin' up at the sky an' sayin', what is the stars, what is the stars ?

Mrs. Boyle [*opening the door and standing at it*]. Here, get ou' o' this, Joxer Daly ; I was always thinkin' you had a slate off.

Joxer [*moving to the door*]. I have to laugh every time I look at the deep-sea sailor ; an' a row on a river ud make him sea-sick !

Boyle. Get ou' o' this before I take the law into me own hands !

Joxer [*going out*]. Say aw rewaeawr, but not good-bye. Lookin' for work, an' prayin' to God he won't get it !   [*He goes.*

Mrs. Boyle. I'm tired tellin' you what Joxer was ; maybe now you see yourself the kind he is.

Boyle. He'll never blow the froth off a pint o' mine agen, that's a sure thing. Johnny . . . Mary . . . you're to keep yourselves to yourselves for the future. Juno, I'm done with Joxer. . . . I'm a new man from this out. . . .

[*Clasping Juno's hand, and singing emotionally :*

O, me darlin' Juno, I will be thrue to thee ;
Me own, me darlin' Juno, you're all the world to me.

CURTAIN

ACT II

*The same, but the furniture is more plentiful, and of a vulgar
nature. A glaringly upholstered armchair and lounge ; cheap
pictures and photos everywhere. Every available spot is ornamented with huge vases filled with artificial flowers. Crossed
festoons of coloured paper chains stretch from end to end of ceiling.
On the table is an old attaché case. It is about six in the evening, and two days after the First Act. Boyle, in his shirt-sleeves,
is voluptuously stretched on the sofa ; he is smoking a clay pipe.
He is half asleep. A lamp is lighting on the table. After a few
moments' pause the voice of Joxer is heard singing softly outside
at the door — "Me pipe I'll smoke, as I dhrive me moke — are you
there, Mor . . . ee . . . ar . . . i . . . teee ! "*

Boyle [*leaping up, takes a pen in his hand and busies himself with papers*]. Come along, Joxer, me son, come
along.

Joxer [*putting his head in*]. Are you be yourself ?

Boyle. Come on, come on ; that doesn't matther ; I'm
masther now, an' I'm goin' to remain masther.
                                                    [*Joxer comes in.*

Joxer. How d'ye feel now, as a man o' money ?

Boyle [*solemnly*]. It's a responsibility, Joxer, a great responsibility.

Joxer. I suppose 'tis now, though you wouldn't think it.

Boyle. Joxer, han' me over that attackey case on the table
there. [*Joxer hands the case.*] Ever since the Will was

104

passed I've run hundhreds o' dockyments through me hans — I tell you, you have to keep your wits about you.   [*He busies himself with papers.*

Joxer. Well, I won't disturb you ; I'll dhrop in when . . .

Boyle [*hastily*]. It's all right, Joxer, this is the last one to be signed to-day. [*He signs a paper, puts it into the case, which he shuts with a snap, and sits back pompously in the chair.*] Now, Joxer, you want to see me ; I'm at your service — what can I do for you, me man ?

Joxer. I've just dhropped in with the £3 : 5s. that Mrs. Madigan riz on the blankets an' table for you, an' she says you're to be in no hurry payin' it back.

Boyle. She won't be long without it ; I expect the first cheque for a couple o' hundhred any day. There's the five bob for yourself — go on, take it, man ; it'll not be the last you'll get from the Captain. Now an' agen we have our differ, but we're there together all the time.

Joxer. Me for you, an' you for me, like the two Musketeers.

Boyle. Father Farrell stopped me to-day an' tole me how glad he was I fell in for the money.

Joxer. He'll be stoppin' you ofen enough now ; I suppose it was " Mr." Boyle with him ?

Boyle. He shuk me be the han' . . .

Joxer [*ironically*]. I met with Napper Tandy, an' he shuk me be the han' !

Boyle. You're seldom asthray, Joxer, but you're wrong shipped this time. What you're sayin' of Father

Farrell is very near to blasfeemey. I don't like any one to talk disrespectful of Father Farrell.

Joxer. You're takin' me up wrong, Captain ; I wouldn't let a word be said agen Father Farrell — the heart o' the rowl, that's what he is ; I always said he was a darlin' man, a daarlin' man.

Boyle. Comin' up the stairs who did I meet but that bummer, Nugent. " I seen you talkin' to Father Farrell," says he, with a grin on him. " He'll be folleyin' you," says he, " like a Guardian Angel from this out " — all the time the oul' grin on him, Joxer.

Joxer. I never seen him yet but he had that oul' grin on him !

Boyle. " Mr. Nugent," says I, " Father Farrell is a man o' the people, an', as far as I know the History o' me country, the priests was always in the van of the fight for Irelan's freedom."

Joxer [*fervently*] :

> Who was it led the van, Soggart Aroon ?
> Since the fight first began, Soggart Aroon ?

Boyle. " Who are you tellin' ? " says he. " Didn't they let down the Fenians, an' didn't they do in Parnell ? An' now . . ." " You ought to be ashamed o' yourself," says I, interruptin' him, " not to know the History o' your country." An' I left him gawkin' where he was.

Joxer. Where ignorance 's bliss 'tis folly to be wise ; I wondher did he ever read the Story o' Irelan'.

Boyle. Be J. L. Sullivan ? Don't you know he didn't.

Joxer. Ah, it's a darlin' buk, a daarlin' buk !

Boyle. You'd betther be goin', now, Joxer; his Majesty, Bentham, 'll be here any minute, now.

Joxer. Be the way things is lookin', it'll be a match between him an' Mary. She's thrun over Jerry altogether. Well, I hope it will, for he's a darlin' man.

Boyle. I'm glad you think so — I don't. [*Irritably*] What's darlin' about him?

Joxer [*nonplussed*]. I only seen him twiced; if you want to know me, come an' live with me.

Boyle. He's too dignified for me — to hear him talk you'd think he knew as much as a Boney's Oraculum. He's given up his job as teacher, an' is goin' to become a solicitor in Dublin — he's been studyin' law. I suppose he thinks I'll set him up, but he's wrong shipped. An' th' other fella — Jerry's as bad. The two o' them ud give you a pain in your face, listenin' to them; Jerry believin' in nothin', an' Bentham believin' in everythin'. One that says all is God an' no man; an' th' other that says all is man an' no God!

Joxer. Well, I'll be off now.

Boyle. Don't forget to dhrop down afther awhile; we'll have a quiet jar, an' a song or two.

Joxer. Never fear.

Boyle. An' tell Mrs. Madigan that I hope we'll have the pleasure of her organization at our little enthertainment.

Joxer. Righto; we'll come down together. [*He goes out.* [*Johnny comes from room on left, and sits down moodily at the fire. Boyle looks at him for a few moments, and shakes his head. He fills his pipe.*

Voice of Juno at the door. Open the door, Jack ; this thing has me nearly kilt with the weight.

   [*Boyle opens the door. Juno enters carrying the box of a gramophone, followed by Mary carrying the horn and some parcels. Juno leaves the box on the table and flops into a chair.*

Juno. Carryin' that from Henry Street was no joke.

Boyle. U-u-ugh, that's a grand-lookin' insthrument — how much was it ?

Juno. Pound down, an' five to be paid at two shillins a week.

Boyle. That's reasonable enough.

Juno. I'm afraid we're runnin' into too much debt ; first the furniture, an' now this.

Boyle. The whole lot won't be much out of £2000.

Mary. I don't know what you wanted a gramophone for — I know Charlie hates them ; he says they're destructive of real music.

Boyle. Desthructive of music — that fella ud give you a pain in your face. All a gramophone wants is to be properly played ; its thrue wondher is only felt when everythin's quiet — what a gramophone wants is dead silence !

Mary. But, father, Jerry says the same ; afther all, you can only appreciate music when your ear is properly trained.

Boyle. That's another fella ud give you a pain in your face. Properly thrained ! I suppose you couldn't appreciate football unless your fut was properly thrained.

Mrs. Boyle [*to Mary*]. Go on in ower that an' dress, or Charlie'll be in on you, an' tea nor nothing'll be ready.   [*Mary goes into room left.*

Mrs. Boyle [*arranging table for tea*]. You didn't look at our new gramophone, Johnny?

Johnny. 'Tisn't gramophones I'm thinking of.

Mrs. Boyle. An' what is it you're thinkin' of, allanna?

Johnny. Nothin', nothin', nothin'.

Mrs. Boyle. Sure, you must be thinkin' of somethin'; it's yourself that has yourself the way y'are; sleepin' wan night in me sisther's, an' the nex' in your father's brother's — you'll get no rest goin' on that way.

Johnny. I can rest nowhere, nowhere, nowhere.

Mrs. Boyle. Sure, you're not thryin' to rest anywhere.

Johnny. Let me alone, let me alone, let me alone, for God's sake.   [*A knock at street door.*

Mrs. Boyle [*in a flutter*]. Here he is; here's Mr. Bentham!

Boyle. Well, there's room for him; it's a pity there's not a brass band to play him in.

Mrs. Boyle. We'll han' the tea round, an' not be clusthered round the table, as if we never seen nothin'. [*Steps are heard approaching, and Juno, opening the door, allows Bentham to enter.*

Juno. Give your hat an' stick to Jack, there . . . sit down, Mr. Bentham . . . no, not there . . . in th' easy chair be the fire . . . there, that's betther. Mary'll be out to you in a minute.

Boyle [*solemnly*]. I seen be the paper this mornin' that Consols was down half per cent. That's serious, min' you, an' shows the whole counthry's in a state o' chassis.

Mrs. Boyle. What's Consols, Jack ?

Boyle. Consols ? Oh, Consols is — oh, there's no use tellin' women what Consols is — th' wouldn't undherstand.

Bentham. It's just as you were saying, Mr. Boyle . . .

        [*Mary enters, charmingly dressed.*

Bentham. Oh, good evening, Mary ; how pretty you're looking !

Mary [*archly*]. Am I ?

Boyle. We were just talkin' when you kem in, Mary ; I was tellin' Mr. Bentham that the whole counthry's in a state o' chassis.

Mary [*to Bentham*]. Would you prefer the green or the blue ribbon round me hair, Charlie ?

Mrs. Boyle. Mary, your father's speakin'.

Boyle [*rapidly*]. I was jus' tellin' Mr. Bentham that the whole counthry's in a state o' chassis.

Mary. I'm sure you're frettin', da, whether it is or no.

Mrs. Boyle. With all our churches an' religions, the worl's not a bit the betther.

Boyle [*with a commanding gesture*]. Tay !

        [*Mary and Mrs. Boyle dispense the tea.*

Mrs. Boyle. An' Irelan's takin' a leaf out o' the worl's buk ; when we got the makin' of our own laws I thought we'd never stop to look behind us, but instead of that we never stopped to look before us ! If the people ud folley up their religion betther there'd be a betther chance for us — what do you think, Mr. Bentham ?

Bentham. I'm afraid I can't venture to express an opinion on that point, Mrs. Boyle ; dogma has no attraction for me.

Mrs. Boyle. I forgot you didn't hold with us : what's this you said you were ?

Bentham. A Theosophist, Mrs. Boyle.

Mrs. Boyle. An' what in the name o' God's a Theosophist ?

Boyle. A Theosophist, Juno, 's a — tell her, Mr. Bentham, tell her.

Bentham. It's hard to explain in a few words : Theosophy's founded on The Vedas, the religious books of the East. Its central theme is the existence of an allpervading Spirit — the Life-Breath. Nothing really exists but this one Universal Life-Breath. And whatever even seems to exist separately from this Life-Breath, doesn't really exist at all. It is all vital force in man, in all animals, and in all vegetation. This Life-Breath is called the Prawna.

Mrs. Boyle. The Prawna ! What a comical name !

Boyle. Prawna ; yis, the Prawna. [*Blowing gently through his lips*] That's the Prawna !

Mrs. Boyle. Whist, whist, Jack.

Bentham. The happiness of man depends upon his sympathy with this Spirit. Men who have reached a high state of excellence are called Yogi. Some men become Yogi in a short time, it may take others millions of years.

Boyle. Yogi! I seen hundhreds of them in the streets o' San Francisco.

Bentham. It is said by these Yogi that if we practise certain mental exercises that we would have powers denied to others — for instance, the faculty of seeing things that happen miles and miles away.

Mrs. Boyle. I wouldn't care to meddle with that sort o' belief; it's a very curious religion, altogether.

Boyle. What's curious about it? Isn't all religions curious? — if they weren't, you wouldn't get any one to believe them. But religions is passin' away — they've had their day like everything else. Take the real Dublin people, f'rinstance: they know more about Charlie Chaplin an' Tommy Mix than they do about SS. Peter an' Paul!

Mrs. Boyle. You don't believe in ghosts, Mr. Bentham?

Mary. Don't you know he doesn't, mother?

Bentham. I don't know that, Mary. Scientists are beginning to think that what we call ghosts are sometimes seen by persons of a certain nature. They say that sensational actions, such as the killing of a person, demand great energy, and that that energy lingers in the place where the action occurred. People may live in the place and see nothing, when someone may come along whose personality has some peculiar connection with the energy of the place, and, in a flash, the person sees the whole affair.

Johnny [*rising swiftly, pale and affected*]. What sort o' talk is this to be goin' on with ? Is there nothin' betther to be talkin' about but the killin' o' people ? My God, isn't it bad enough for these things to happen without talkin' about them !

[*He hurriedly goes into the room on left.*

Bentham. Oh, I'm very sorry, Mrs. Boyle ; I never thought . . .

Mrs. Boyle [*apologetically*]. Never mind, Mr. Bentham, he's very touchy.

[*A frightened scream is heard from Johnny inside.*

Mrs. Boyle. Mother of God, what's that ?

[*He rushes out again, his face pale, his lips twitching, his limbs trembling.*

Johnny. Shut the door, shut the door, quick, for God's sake ! Great God, have mercy on me ! Blessed Mother o' God, shelter me, shelther your son !

Mrs. Boyle [*catching him in her arms*]. What's wrong with you ? What ails you ? Sit down, sit down, here, on the bed . . . there now . . . there now.

Mary. Johnny, Johnny, what ails you ?

Johnny. I seen him, I seen him . . . kneelin' in front o' the statue . . . merciful Jesus, have pity on me !

Mrs. Boyle [*to Boyle*]. Get him a glass o' whisky . . . quick, man, an' don't stand gawkin'.

[*Boyle gets the whisky.*

Johnny. Sit here, sit here, mother . . . between me an'
the door.

Mrs. Boyle. I'll sit beside you as long as you like, only
tell me what was it came across you at all ?

Johnny [*after taking some drink*]. I seen him. . . . I seen
Robbie Tancred kneelin' down before the statue . . .
an' the red light shinin' on him . . . an' when I
went in . . . he turned an' looked at me . . . an' I
seen the wouns bleedin' in his breast. . . . Oh, why
did he look at me like that ? . . . it wasn't my fault
that he was done in. . . . Mother o' God, keep him
away from me !

Mrs. Boyle. There, there, child, you've imagined it all.
There was nothin' there at all — it was the red light
you seen, an' the talk we had put all the rest into
your head. Here, dhrink more o' this — it'll do you
good. . . . An', now, stretch yourself down on the
bed for a little. [*To Boyle*] Go in, Jack, an' show him
it was only in his own head it was.

Boyle [*making no move*]. E-e-e-e-eh ; it's all nonsense ; it
was only a shadda he saw.

Mary. Mother o' God, he made me heart lep !

Bentham. It was simply due to an over-wrought imagination — we all get that way at times.

Mrs. Boyle. There, dear, lie down in the bed, an' I'll
put the quilt across you . . . e-e-e-eh, that's it . . .
you'll be as right as the mail in a few minutes.

Johnny. Mother, go into the room an' see if the light's
lightin' before the statue.

Mrs. Boyle [*to Boyle*]. Jack, run in an' see if the light's
lightin' before the statue.

Boyle [*to Mary*]. Mary, slip in an' see if the light's lightin' before the statue.   [*Mary hesitates to go in.*

Bentham. It's all right ; Mary, I'll go.

> [*He goes into the room ; remains for a few moments, and returns.*

Bentham. Everything's just as it was — the light burning bravely before the statue.

Boyle. Of course ; I knew it was all nonsense.

> [*A knock at the door.*

Boyle [*going to open the door*]. E-e-e-e-eh.

> [*He opens it, and Joxer, followed by Mrs. Madigan, enters. Mrs. Madigan is a strong, dapper little woman of about forty-five ; her face is almost always a widespread smile of complacency. She is a woman who, in manner at least, can mourn with them that mourn, and rejoice with them that do rejoice. When she is feeling comfortable, she is inclined to be reminiscent ; when others say anything, or following a statement made by herself, she has a habit of putting her head a little to one side, and nodding it rapidly several times in succession, like a bird pecking at a hard berry. Indeed, she has a good deal of the bird in her, but the bird instinct is by no means a melodious one. She is ignorant, vulgar and forward, but her heart is generous withal. For instance, she would help a neighbour's sick child ; she would probably kill the child, but her intention would be to cure it ; she would be more at home helping a drayman to lift a fallen horse. She is dressed in a rather soiled grey dress and a vivid purple blouse ; in her hair is a huge comb, ornamented with huge coloured beads. She enters with a gliding step, beaming smile and nodding head. Boyle receives them effusively.*

Boyle. Come on in, Mrs. Madigan ; come on in ; I was

afraid you weren't comin'. . . . [*Slyly*] There's some people able to dhress, ay, Joxer?

Joxer. Fair as the blossoms that bloom in the May, an' sweet as the scent of the new-mown hay. . . . Ah, well she may wear them.

Mrs. Madigan [*looking at Mary*]. I know some as are as sweet as the blossoms that bloom in the May — oh, no names, no pack dhrill!

Boyle. An' now I'll inthroduce the pair o' yous to Mary's intended : Mr. Bentham, this is Mrs. Madigan, an oul' back-parlour neighbour, that, if she could help it at all, ud never see a body shuk!

Bentham [*rising, and tentatively shaking the hand of Mrs. Madigan*]. I'm sure, it's a great pleasure to know you, Mrs. Madigan.

Mrs. Madigan. An' I'm goin' to tell you, Mr. Bentham, you're goin' to get as nice a bit o' skirt in Mary, there, as ever you seen in your puff. Not like some of the dhressed-up dolls that's knockin' about lookin' for men when it's a skelpin' they want. I remember, as well as I remember yestherday, the day she was born — of a Tuesday, the 25th o' June, in the year 1901, at thirty-three minutes past wan in the day be Foley's clock, the pub at the corner o' the street. A cowld day it was too, for the season o' the year, an' I remember sayin' to Joxer, there, who I met comin' up th' stairs, that the new arrival in Boyle's ud grow up a hardy chiselur if it lived, an' that she'd be somethin' one o' these days that nobody suspected, an' so signs on it, here she is to-day, goin' to be married to a young man lookin' as if he'd be fit to commensurate in any position in life it ud please God to call him!

Boyle [*effusively*]. Sit down, Mrs. Madigan, sit down, me oul' sport. [*To Bentham*] This is Joxer Daly, Past Chief Ranger of the Dear Little Shamrock Branch of the Irish National Foresters, an oul' front-top neighbour, that never despaired, even in the darkest days of Ireland's sorra.

Joxer. Nil desperandum, Captain, nil desperandum.

Boyle. Sit down, Joxer, sit down. The two of us was ofen in a tight corner.

Mrs. Boyle. Ay, in Foley's snug !

Joxer. An' we kem out of it flyin', we kem out of it flyin', Captain.

Boyle. An' now for a dhrink — I know yous won't refuse an oul' friend.

Mrs. Madigan [*to Juno*]. Is Johnny not well, Mrs. . . .

Mrs. Boyle [*warningly*]. S-s-s-sh.

Mrs. Madigan. Oh, the poor darlin'.

Boyle. Well, Mrs. Madigan, is it tea or what ?

Mrs. Madigan. Well, speakin' for meself, I jus' had me tea a minute ago, an' I'm afraid to dhrink any more — I'm never the same when I dhrink too much tay. Thanks, all the same, Mr. Boyle.

Boyle. Well, what about a bottle o' stout or a dhrop o' whisky ?

Mrs. Madigan. A bottle o' stout ud be a little too heavy for me stummock afther me tay. . . . A-a-ah, I'll thry the ball o' malt. [*Boyle prepares the whisky.*

Mrs. Madigan. There's nothin' like a ball o' malt occasional like — too much of it isn't good. [*To Boyle, who is adding water*] Ah, God, Johnny, don't put too much wather on it ! [*She drinks.*] I suppose yous'll be lavin' this place.

Boyle. I'm looking for a place near the sea ; I'd like the place that you might say was me cradle, to be me grave as well. The sea is always callin' me.

Joxer. She is callin', callin', callin', in the win' an' on the sea.

Boyle. Another dhrop o' whisky, Mrs. Madigan ?

Mrs. Madigan. Well, now, it ut be hard to refuse seein' the suspicious times that's in it.

Boyle [*with a commanding gesture*]. Song ! . . . Juno . . . Mary . . . " Home to Our Mountains " !

Mrs. Madigan [*enthusiastically*]. Hear, hear !

Joxer. Oh, tha's a darlin' song, a daarlin' song !

Mary [*bashfully*]. Ah no, da ; I'm not in a singin' humour.

Mrs. Madigan. Gawn with you, child, an' you only goin' to be marrid ; I remember as well as I remember yestherday, — it was on a lovely August evenin', exactly, according' to date, fifteen years ago, come the Tuesday folleyin' the nex' that's comin' on, when me own man — *the Lord be good to him* — an' me was sitting' shy together in a doty little nook on a counthry road, adjacent to The Stiles. " That'll scratch your lovely, little white neck," says he, ketchin' hould of a danglin' bramble branch, holdin' clusters of the loveliest flowers you ever seen, an' breakin' it off, so that his arm fell,

accidental like, roun' me waist, an' as I felt it tightenin',
an' tightenin', an' tightenin', I thought me buzzom
was every minute goin' to burst out into a roystherin'
song about

> The little green leaves that were shakin' on the threes,
> The gallivantin' butterflies, an' buzzin' o' the bees ! "

Boyle. Ordher for the song !

Juno. Come on, Mary — we'll do our best.
  [*Juno and Mary stand up, and choosing a suitable position,
  sing simply " Home to Our Mountains ".*
  [*They bow to company, and return to their places.*

Boyle [*emotionally, at the end of song*]. Lull . . . me . . .
  to . . . rest !

Joxer [*clapping his hands*]. Bravo, bravo ! Darlin' girulls,
  darlin' girulls !

Mrs. Madigan. Juno, I never seen you in betther form.

Bentham. Very nicely rendered indeed.

Mrs. Madigan. A noble call, a noble call !

Mrs. Boyle. What about yourself, Mrs. Madigan ?
  [*After some coaxing, Mrs. Madigan rises, and in a
  quavering voice sings the following verse :*

> If I were a blackbird I'd whistle and sing ;
> I'd follow the ship that my thrue love was in ;
> An' on the top riggin', I'd there build me nest,
> An' at night I would sleep on me Willie's white breast !

  [*Becoming husky, amid applause, she sits down.*

Mrs. Madigan. Ah, me voice is too husky now, Juno ;
  though I remember the time when Maisie Madigan

could sing like a nightingale at matin' time. I remember as well as I remember yestherday, at a party given to celebrate the comin' of the first chiselur to Annie an' Benny Jimeson — who was the barber, yous may remember, in Henrietta Street, that, afther Easter Week, hung out a green, white an' orange pole, an', then, when the Tans started their Jazz dancin', whipped it in agen, an' stuck out a red, white an' blue wan instead, givin' as an excuse that a barber's pole was strictly non-political — singin' " An' You'll Remember Me ", with the top notes quiverin' in a dead hush of pethrified attention, folleyed be a clappin' o' hans that shuk the tumblers on the table, an' capped by Jimeson, the barber, sayin' that it was the best rendherin' of " You'll Remember Me " he ever heard in his natural !

Boyle [*peremptorily*]. Ordher for Joxer's song !

Joxer. Ah no, I couldn't ; don't ass me, Captain.

Boyle. Joxer's song, Joxer's song— give us wan of your shut-eyed wans.

[*Joxer settles himself in his chair ; takes a drink ; clears his throat ; solemnly closes his eyes, and begins to sing in a very querulous voice :*

She is far from the lan' where her young hero sleeps,
An' lovers around her are sighing   [*He hesitates.*
An' lovers around her are sighin' . . . sighin' . . . sighin' . . .
                                                      [*A pause.*

Boyle [*imitating Joxer*] :

And lovers around her are sighing !

What's the use of you thryin' to sing the song if you don't know it ?

Mary. Thry another one, Mr. Daly — maybe you'd be more fortunate.

Mrs. Madigan. Gawn, Joxer; thry another wan.

Joxer [*starting again*] :

I have heard the mavis singin' his love song to the morn;
I have seen the dew-dhrop clingin' to the rose jus' newly
born; but . . . but . . . [*frantically*] To the rose jus'
newly born . . . newly born . . . born.

Johnny. Mother, put on the gramophone, for God's sake, an' stop Joxer's bawlin'.

Boyle [*commandingly*]. Gramophone ! . . . I hate to see fellas thryin' to do what they're not able to do.
[*Boyle arranges the gramophone, and is about to start it, when voices are heard of persons descending the stairs.*

Mrs. Boyle [*warningly*]. Whisht, Jack, don't put it on, don't put it on yet; this must be poor Mrs. Tancred comin' down to go to the hospital — I forgot all about them bringin' the body to the church to-night. Open the door, Mary, an' give them a bit o' light.
[*Mary opens the door, and Mrs. Tancred — a very old woman, obviously shaken by the death of her son — appears, accompanied by several neighbours. The first few phrases are spoken before they appear.*

First Neighbour. It's a sad journey we're goin' on, but God's good, an' the Republicans won't be always down.

Mrs. Tancred. Ah, what good is that to me now? Whether they're up or down — it won't bring me darlin' boy from the grave.

Mrs. Boyle. Come in an' have a hot cup o' tay, Mrs. Tancred, before you go.

Mrs. Tancred. Ah, I can take nothin' now, Mrs. Boyle — I won't be long afther him.

First Neighbour. Still an' all, he died a noble death, an' we'll bury him like a king.

Mrs. Tancred. An' I'll go on livin' like a pauper. Ah, what's the pains I suffered bringin' him into the world to carry him to his cradle, to the pains I'm sufferin' now, carryin' him out o' the world to bring him to his grave !

Mary. It would be better for you not to go at all, Mrs. Tancred, but to stay at home beside the fire with some o' the neighbours.

Mrs. Tancred. I seen the first of him, an' I'll see the last of him.

Mrs. Boyle. You'd want a shawl, Mrs. Tancred ; it's a cowld night, an' the win's blowin' sharp.

Mrs. Madigan [*rushing out*]. I've a shawl above.

Mrs. Tancred. Me home is gone now ; he was me only child, an' to think that he was lyin' for a whole night stretched out on the side of a lonely counthry lane, with his head, his darlin' head, that I often kissed an' fondled, half hidden in the wather of a runnin' brook. An' I'm told he was the leadher of the ambush where me nex' door neighbour, Mrs. Mannin', lost her Free State soldier son. An' now here's the two of us oul' women, standin' one on each side of a scales o' sorra, balanced be the bodies of our two dead darlin' sons. [*Mrs. Madigan returns, and wraps a shawl around her.*] God bless you, Mrs. Madigan. . . . [*She moves slowly towards the door*] Mother o' God, Mother o' God, have

pity on the pair of us ! . . . O Blessed Virgin, where
were you when me darlin' son was riddled with bullets,
when me darlin' son was riddled with bullets ! . . .
Sacred Heart of the Crucified Jesus, take away our
hearts o' stone . . . an' give us hearts o' flesh ! . . .
Take away this murdherin' hate . . . an' give us
Thine own eternal love !   [*They pass out of the room.*

Mrs. Boyle [*explanatorily to Bentham*]. That was Mrs.
Tancred of the two-pair back ; her son was found,
e'er yestherday, lyin' out beyant Finglas riddled with
bullets. A Die-hard he was, be all accounts. He was
a nice quiet boy, but lattherly he went to hell, with
his Republic first, an' Republic last an' Republic over
all. He ofen took tea with us here, in the oul' days,
an' Johnny, there, an' him used to be always together.

Johnny. Am I always to be havin' to tell you that he was
no friend o' mine ? I never cared for him, an' he could
never stick me. It's not because he was Commandant
of the Battalion that I was Quarther-Masther of, that
we were friends.

Mrs. Boyle. He's gone now — the Lord be good to him !
God help his poor oul' creature of a mother, for no
matther whose friend or enemy he was, he was her
poor son.

Bentham. The whole thing is terrible, Mrs. Boyle ; but
the only way to deal with a mad dog is to destroy him.

Mrs. Boyle. An' to think of me forgettin' about him
bein' brought to the church to-night, an' we singin' an'
all, but it was well we hadn't the gramophone goin',
anyhow.

Boyle. Even if we had aself. We've nothin' to do with

these things, one way or t'other. That's the Government's business, an' let them do what we're payin' them for doin'.

Mrs. Boyle. I'd like to know how a body's not to mind these things ; look at the way they're afther leavin' the people in this very house. Hasn't the whole house, nearly, been massacreed ? There's young Dougherty's husband with his leg off ; Mrs. Travers that had her son blew up be a mine in Inchegeela, in Co. Cork ; Mrs. Mannin' that lost wan of her sons in ambush a few weeks ago, an' now, poor Mrs. Tancred's only child gone west with his body made a collandher of. Sure, if it's not our business, I don't know whose business it is.

Boyle. Here, there, that's enough about them things ; they don't affect us, an' we needn't give a damn. If they want a wake, well, let them have a wake. When I was a sailor, I was always resigned to meet with a wathery grave ; an' if they want to be soldiers, well, there's no use o' them squealin' when they meet a soldier's fate.

Joxer. Let me like a soldier fall — me breast expandin' to th' ball !

Mrs. Boyle. In wan way, she deserves all she got ; for lately, she let th' Die-hards make an open house of th' place ; an' for th' last couple of months, either when th' sun was risin' or when th' sun was settin', you had C.I.D. men burstin' into your room, assin' you where were you born, where were you christened, where were you married, an' where would you be buried !

Johnny. For God's sake, let us have no more o' this talk.

Mrs. Madigan. What about Mr. Boyle's song before we start th' gramophone ?

Mary [*getting her hat, and putting it on*]. Mother, Charlie and I are goin' out for a little sthroll.

Mrs. Boyle. All right, darlin'.

Bentham [*going out with Mary*]. We won't be long away, Mrs. Boyle.

Mrs. Madigan. Gwan, Captain, gwan.

Boyle. E-e-e-e-eh, I'd want to have a few more jars in me, before I'd be in fettle for singin'.

Joxer. Give us that poem you writ t'other day. [*To the rest*] Aw, it's a darlin' poem, a daarlin' poem.

Mrs. Boyle. God bless us, is he startin' to write poetry !

Boyle [*rising to his feet*]. E-e-e-e-eh.
    [*He recites in an emotional, consequential manner the following verses :*

Shawn an' I were friends, sir, to me he was all in all.
His work was very heavy and his wages were very small.
None betther on th' beach as Docker, I'll go bail,
'Tis now I'm feelin' lonely, for to-day he lies in jail.
He was not what some call pious — seldom at church or
    prayer ;
For the greatest scoundrels I know, sir, goes every Sunday
    there.
Fond of his pint — well, rather, but hated the Boss by
    creed
But never refused a copper to comfort a pal in need.

E-e-e-e-eh.   [*He sits down.*

Mrs. Madigan. Grand, grand ; you should folly that up, you should folly that up.

Joxer. It's a daarlin' poem !

Boyle [*delightedly*]. E-e-e-e-eh.

Johnny. Are yous goin' to put on th' gramophone to night, or are yous not ?

Mrs. Boyle. Gwan, Jack, put on a record.

Mrs. Madigan. Gwan, Captain, gwan.

Boyle. Well, yous'll want to keep a dead silence.
  [*He sets a record, starts the machine, and it begins to play "If you're Irish, come into the Parlour". As the tune is in full blare, the door is suddenly opened by a brisk, little bald-headed man, dressed circumspectly in a black suit ; he glares fiercely at all in the room ; he is "Needle Nugent", a tailor. He carries his hat in his hand.*

Nugent [*loudly, above the noise of the gramophone*]. Are yous goin' to have that thing bawlin' an' the funeral of Mrs. Tancred's son passin' the house ? Have none of yous any respect for the Irish people's National regard for the dead ? [*Boyle stops the gramophone.*

Mrs. Boyle. Maybe, Needle Nugent, it's nearly time we had a little less respect for the dead, an' a little more regard for the livin'.

Mrs. Madigan. We don't want you, Mr. Nugent, to teach us what we learned at our mother's knee. You don't look yourself as if you were dyin' of grief ; if y'ass Maisie Madigan anything, I'd call you a real thrue Die-hard an' live-soft Republican, attendin' Republican funerals in the day, an' stoppin' up half the night makin' suits for the Civic Guards !
  [*Persons are heard running down to the street, some saying, "Here it is, here it is." Nugent withdraws, and the*

rest, except Johnny, go to the window looking into the street, and look out. Sounds of a crowd coming nearer are heard ; portion are singing :

> To Jesus' Heart all burning
> With fervent love for men,
> My heart with fondest yearning
> Shall raise its joyful strain.
> While ages course along,
> Blest be with loudest song
> The Sacred Heart of Jesus
> By every heart and tongue.

Mrs. Boyle. Here's the hearse, here's the hearse !

Boyle. There's t'oul' mother walkin' behin' the coffin.

Mrs. Madigan. You can hardly see the coffin with the wreaths.

Joxer. Oh, it's a darlin' funeral, a daarlin' funeral !

Mrs. Madigan. W'd have a betther view from the street.

Boyle. Yes — this place ud give you a crick in your neck.

> [*They leave the room, and go down. Johnny sits moodily by the fire.*
> [*A young man enters ; he looks at Johnny for a moment.*

The Young Man. Quarther-Masther Boyle.

Johnny [*with a start*]. The Mobilizer !

The Young Man. You're not at the funeral ?

Johnny. I'm not well.

The Young Man. I'm glad I've found you ; you were stoppin' at your aunt's ; I called there but you'd gone. I've to give you an ordher to attend a Battalion Staff meetin' the night afther to-morrow.

Johnny. Where ?

The Young Man. I don't know ; you're to meet me at the Pillar at eight o'clock ; then we're to go to a place I'll be told of to-night ; there we'll meet a mothor that'll bring us to the meeting. They think you might be able to know somethin' about them that gave the bend where Commandant Tancred was shelterin'.

Johnny. I'm not goin', then. I know nothing about Tancred.

The Young Man [*at the door*]. You'd betther come for your own sake — remember your oath.

Johnny [*passionately*]. I won't go ! Haven't I done enough for Ireland ! I've lost me arm, an' me hip's desthroyed so that I'll never be able to walk right agen ! Good God, haven't I done enough for Ireland ?

The Young Man. Boyle, no man can do enough for Ireland !

[*He goes.*

[*Faintly in the distance the crowd is heard saying :*

Hail, Mary, full of grace, the Lord is with Thee ;
Blessed art Thou amongst women, and blessed, etc.

CURTAIN

ACT III

The same as Act II. It is about half-past six on a November evening ; a bright fire burns in the grate ; Mary, dressed to go out, is sitting on a chair by the fire, leaning forward, her hands under her chin, her elbows on her knees. A look of dejection, mingled with uncertain anxiety, is on her face. A lamp, turned low, is lighting on the table. The votive light under the picture of the Virgin gleams more redly than ever. Mrs. Boyle is putting on her hat and coat. It is two months later.

Mrs. Boyle. An' has Bentham never even written to you since — not one line for the past month ?

Mary [*tonelessly*]. Not even a line, mother.

Mrs. Boyle. That's very curious. . . . What came between the two of yous at all ? To leave you so sudden, an' yous so great together. . . . To go away t' England, an' not to even leave you his address. . . . The way he was always bringin' you to dances, I thought he was mad afther you. Are you sure you said nothin' to him ?

Mary. No, mother — at least nothing that could possibly explain his givin' me up.

Mrs. Boyle. You know you're a bit hasty at times, Mary, an' say things you shouldn't say.

Mary. I never said to him what I shouldn't say, I'm sure of that.

Mrs. Boyle. How are you sure of it ?

Mary. Because I love him with all my heart and soul, mother. Why, I don't know ; I often thought to myself that he wasn't the man poor Jerry was, but I couldn't help loving him, all the same.

Mrs. Boyle. But you shouldn't be frettin' the way you are ; when a woman loses a man, she never knows what she's afther losin', to be sure, but, then, she never knows what she's afther gainin', either. You're not the one girl of a month ago — you look like one pinin' away. It's long ago I had a right to bring you to the doctor, instead of waitin' till to-night.

Mary. There's no necessity, really, mother, to go to the doctor ; nothing serious is wrong with me — I'm run down and disappointed, that's all.

Mrs. Boyle. I'll not wait another minute ; I don't like the look of you at all. . . . I'm afraid we made a mistake in throwin' over poor Jerry. . . . He'd have been betther for you than that Bentham.

Mary. Mother, the best man for a woman is the one for whom she has the most love, and Charlie had it all.

Mrs. Boyle. Well, there's one thing to be said for him — he couldn't have been thinkin' of the money, or he wouldn't ha' left you . . . it must ha' been somethin' else.

Mary [*wearily*]. I don't know . . . I don't know, mother . . . only I think . . .

Mrs. Boyle. What d'ye think ?

Mary. I imagine . . . he thought . . . we weren't . . . good enough for him.

Mrs. Boyle. An' what was he himself, only a school teacher ? Though I don't blame him for fightin' shy of people like that Joxer fella an' that oul' Madigan wan — nice sort o' people for your father to inthroduce to a man like Mr. Bentham. You might have told me all about this before now, Mary ; I don't know why you like to hide everything from your mother ; you knew Bentham, an' I'd ha' known nothin' about it if it hadn't bin for the Will ; an' it was only to-day, afther long coaxin', that you let out that he's left you.

Mary. It would have been useless to tell you — you wouldn't understand.

Mrs. Boyle [*hurt*]. Maybe not. . . . Maybe I wouldn't understand. . . . Well, we'll be off now.
          [*She goes over to door left, and speaks to Boyle inside.*

Mrs. Boyle. We're goin' now to the doctor's. Are you goin' to get up this evenin' ?

Boyle [*from inside*]. The pains in me legs is terrible ! It's me should be poppin' off to the doctor instead o' Mary, the way I feel.

Mrs. Boyle. Sorra mend you ! A nice way you were in last night — carried in in a frog's march, dead to the world. If that's the way you'll go on when you get the money it'll be the grave for you, an asylum for me and the Poorhouse for Johnny.

Boyle. I thought you were goin' ?

Mrs. Boyle. That's what has you as you are — you can't bear to be spoken to. Knowin' the way we are, up to our ears in debt, it's a wondher you wouldn't ha' got up to go to th' solicitor's an' see if we could ha' gotten a little o' the money even.

Boyle [*shouting*]. I can't be goin' up there night, noon an' mornin', can I? He can't give the money till he gets it, can he? I can't get blood out of a turnip, can I?

Mrs. Boyle. It's nearly two months since we heard of the Will, an' the money seems as far off as ever. . . . I suppose you know we owe twenty pouns to oul' Murphy?

Boyle. I've a faint recollection of you tellin' me that before.

Mrs. Boyle. Well, you'll go over to the shop yourself for the things in future — I'll face him no more.

Boyle. I thought you said you were goin'?

Mrs. Boyle. I'm goin' now; come on, Mary.

Boyle. Ey, Juno, ey!

Mrs. Boyle. Well, what d'ye want now?

Boyle. Is there e'er a bottle o' stout left?

Mrs. Boyle. There's two o' them here still.

Boyle. Show us in one o' them an' leave t'other there till I get up. An' throw us in the paper that's on the table, an' the bottle o' Sloan's Liniment that's in th' drawer.

Mrs. Boyle [*getting the liniment and the stout*]. What paper is it you want — the *Messenger*?

Boyle. Messenger! The *News o' the World*!
[*Mrs. Boyle brings in the things asked for, and comes out again.*

Mrs. Boyle [*at door*]. Mind the candle, now, an' don't burn the house over our heads. I left t'other bottle o' stout on the table.

[*She puts bottle of stout on table. She goes out with Mary. A cork is heard popping inside.*

[*A pause ; then outside the door is heard the voice of Joxer lilting softly : " Me pipe I'll smoke, as I dhrive me moke . . . are you . . . there . . . Mor . . . ee . . . ar . . . i . . . teee ! " A gentle knock is heard, and after a pause the door opens, and Joxer, followed by Nugent, enters.*

Joxer. Be God, they must be all out ; I was thinkin' there was somethin' up when he didn't answer the signal. We seen Juno an' Mary goin', but I didn't see him, an' it's very seldom he escapes me.

Nugent. He's not goin' to escape me — he's not goin' to be let go to the fair altogether.

Joxer. Sure, the house couldn't hould them lately ; an' he goin' about like a mastherpiece of the Free State counthry ; forgettin' their friends ; forgettin' God — wouldn't even lift his hat passin' a chapel ! Sure they were bound to get a dhrop ! An' you really think there's no money comin' to him afther all ?

Nugent. Not as much as a red rex, man ; I've been a bit anxious this long time over me money, an' I went up to the solicitor's to find out all I could — ah, man, they were goin' to throw me down the stairs. They toul' me that the oul' cock himself had the stairs worn away comin' up afther it, an' they black in the face tellin' him he'd get nothin'. Some way or another that the Will is writ he won't be entitled to get as much as a make !

Joxer. Ah, I thought there was somethin' curious about the whole thing ; I've bin havin' sthrange dhreams for the last couple o' weeks. An' I notice that that Bentham fella doesn't be comin' here now — there must be somethin' on the mat there too. Anyhow, who, in the name o' God, ud leave anythin' to that oul' bummer ? Sure it ud be unnatural. An' the way Juno an' him's been throwin' their weight about for the last few months ! Ah, him that goes a borrowin' goes a sorrowin' !

Nugent. Well, he's not goin' to throw his weight about in the suit I made for him much longer. I'm tellin' you seven pouns aren't to be found growin' on the bushes these days.

Joxer. An' there isn't hardly a neighbour in the whole street that hasn't lent him money on the strength of what he was goin' to get, but they're after backing the wrong horse. Wasn't it a mercy o' God that I'd nothin' to give him ! The softy I am, you know, I'd ha' lent him me last juice ! I must have had somebody's good prayers. Ah, afther all, an honest man's the noblest work o' God !   [*Boyle coughs inside.*

Joxer. Whisht, damn it, he must be inside in bed.

Nugent. Inside o' bed or outside of it, he's goin' to pay me for that suit, or give it back — he'll not climb up my back as easily as he thinks.

Joxer. Gwan in at wanst, man, an' get it off him, an' don't be a fool.

Nugent [*going to door left, opening it and looking in*]. Ah, don't disturb yourself, Mr. Boyle ; I hope you're not sick ?

Boyle. Th' oul' legs, Mr. Nugent, the oul' legs.

Nugent. I just called over to see if you could let me have anything off the suit ?

Boyle. E-e-e-eh, how much is this it is ?

Nugent. It's the same as it was at the start — seven pouns.

Boyle. I'm glad you kem, M. Nugent ; I want a good heavy top-coat — Irish frieze, if you have it. How much would a top-coat like that be, now ?

Nugent. About six pouns.

Boyle. Six pouns — six an' seven, six an' seven is thirteen — that'll be thirteen pouns I'll owe you.
     [*Joxer slips the bottle of stout that is on the table into his pocket. Nugent rushes into the room, and returns with suit on his arm ; he pauses at the door.*

Nugent. You'll owe me no thirteen pouns. Maybe you think you're betther able to owe it than pay it !

Boyle [*frantically*]. Here, come back to hell ower that — where're you goin' with them clothes o' mine ?

Nugent. Where am I goin' with them clothes o' yours ? Well, I like your damn cheek !

Boyle. Here, what am I goin' to dhress meself in when I'm goin' out ?

Nugent. What do I care what you dhress yourself in ! You can put yourself in a bolsther cover, if you like.
          [*He goes towards the other door, followed by Joxer.*

Joxer. What'll he dhress himself in !   Gentleman Jack an' his frieze coat !   [*They go out.*

Boyle [*inside*]. Ey, Nugent ; ey, Mr. Nugent, Mr. Nugent !

[*After a pause Boyle enters hastily, buttoning the braces of his moleskin trousers ; his coat and vest are on his arm ; he throws these on a chair and hurries to the door on right.*

Boyle. Ey, Mr. Nugent, Mr. Nugent !

Joxer [*meeting him at the door*]. What's up, what's wrong, Captain ?

Boyle. Nugent's been here an' took away me suit — the only things I had to go out in !

Joxer. Tuk your suit — for God's sake ! An' what were you doin' while he was takin' them ?

Boyle. I was in bed when he stole in like a thief in the night, an' before I knew even what he was thinkin' of, he whipped them from the chair an' was off like a redshank !

Joxer. An' what, in the name o' God, did he do that for ?

Boyle. What did he do it for ? How the hell do I know what he done it for ? — jealousy an' spite, I suppose.

Joxer. Did he not say what he done it for ?

Boyle. Amn't I afther tellin' you that he had them whipped up an' was gone before I could open me mouth ?

Joxer. That was a very sudden thing to do ; there mus' be somethin' behin' it. Did he hear anythin', I wondher ?

Boyle. Did he hear anythin' ? — you talk very queer, Joxer — what could he hear ?

Joxer. About you not gettin' the money, in some way or t'other ?

Boyle. An' what ud prevent me from gettin' th' money ?

Joxer. That's jus' what I was thinkin' — what ud prevent you from gettin' the money — nothin', as far as I can see.

Boyle [*looking round for bottle of stout, with an exclamation*]. Aw, holy God !

Joxer. What's up, Jack ?

Boyle. He must have afther lifted the bottle o' stout that Juno left on the table !

Joxer [*horrified*]. Ah no, ah no ; he wouldn't be afther doin' that now.

Boyle. An' who done it then ? Juno left a bottle o' stout here, an' it's gone — it didn't walk, did it ?

Joxer. Oh, that's shockin' ; ah, man's inhumanity to man makes countless thousands mourn !

Mrs. Madigan [*appearing at the door*]. I hope I'm not disturbin' you in any discussion on your forthcomin' legacy — if I may use the word — an' that you'll let me have a barny for a minute or two with you, Mr. Boyle.

Boyle [*uneasily*]. To be sure, Mrs. Madigan — an oul' friend's always welcome.

Joxer. Come in the evenin', come in th' mornin' ; come when you're assed, or come without warnin', Mrs. Madigan.

Boyle. Sit down, Mrs. Madigan.

Mrs. Madigan [*ominously*]. Th' few words I have to say can be said standin'. Puttin' aside all formularies, I suppose you remember me lendin' you some time ago three pouns that I raised on blankets an' furniture in me uncle's?

Boyle. I remember it well. I have it recorded in me book — three pouns five shillins from Maisie Madigan, raised on articles pawned; an', item: fourpence, given to make up the price of a pint, on th' principle that no bird ever flew on wan wing; all to be repaid at par, when the ship comes home.

Mrs. Madigan. Well, ever since I shoved in the blankets I've been perishing with th' cowld, an' I've decided, if I'll be too hot in th' nex' world aself, I'm not goin' to be too cowld in this wan; an' consequently, I want me three pouns, if you please.

Boyle. This is a very sudden demand, Mrs. Madigan, an' can't be met; but I'm willin' to give you a receipt in full, in full.

Mrs. Madigan. Come on, out with th' money, an' don't be jack-actin'.

Boyle. You can't get blood out of a turnip, can you?

Mrs. Madigan [*rushing over and shaking him*]. Gimme me money, y'oul' reprobate, or I'll shake the worth of it out of you!

Boyle. Ey, houl' on, there; houl' on, there! You'll wait for your money now, me lassie!

Mrs. Madigan [*looking around the room and seeing the gramophone*]. I'll wait for it, will I? Well, I'll not wait long;

if I can't get th' cash, I'll get th' worth of it.

[*She catches up the gramophone.*

Boyle. Ey, ey, there, wher'r you goin' with that?

Mrs. Madigan. I'm goin' to th' pawn to get me three quid five shillins; I'll brin' you th' ticket, an' then you can do what you like, me bucko.

Boyle. You can't touch that, you can't touch that! It's not my property, an' it's not ped for yet!

Mrs. Madigan. So much th' betther. It'll be an ayse to me conscience, for I'm takin' what doesn't belong to you. You're not goin' to be swankin' it like a paycock with Maisie Madigan's money — I'll pull some o' th' gorgeous feathers out o' your tail!

[*She goes off with the gramophone.*

Boyle. What's th' world comin' to at all? I ass you, Joxer Daly, is there any morality left anywhere?

Joxer. I wouldn't ha' believed it, only I seen it with me own two eyes. I didn't think Maisie Madigan was that sort of woman; she has either a sup taken, or she's heard somethin'.

Boyle. Heard somethin' — about what, if it's not any harm to ass you?

Joxer. She must ha' heard some rumour or other that you weren't goin' to get th' money'

Boyle. Who says I'm not goin' to get th' money?

Joxer. Sure, I don't know — I was only sayin'.

Boyle. Only sayin' what?

Joxer. Nothin'.

Boyle. You were goin' to say somethin' — don't be a twisther.

Joxer [*angrily*]. Who's a twisther ?

Boyle. Why don't you speak your mind, then ?

Joxer. You never twisted yourself — no, you wouldn't know how !

Boyle. Did you ever know me to twist ; did you ever know me to twist ?

Joxer [*fiercely*]. Did you ever do anythin' else ! Sure, you can't believe a word that comes out o' your mouth.

Boyle. Here, get out, ower o' this ; I always knew you were a prognosticator an' a procrastinator !

Joxer [*going out as Johnny comes in*]. The anchor's weighed, farewell, ree . . . mem . . . ber . . . me. Jacky Boyle, Esquire, infernal rogue an' damned liar.

Johnny. Joxer an' you at it agen ? — when are you goin' to have a little respect for yourself, an' not be always makin' a show of us all ?

Boyle. Are you goin' to lecture me now ?

Johnny. Is mother back from the doctor yet, with Mary ?
  [*Mrs. Boyle enters ; it is apparent from the serious look on her face that something has happened. She takes off her hat and coat without a word and puts them by. She then sits down near the fire, and there is a few moments' pause.*

Boyle. Well, what did the doctor say about Mary ?

Mrs. Boyle [*in an earnest manner and with suppressed agitation*].

Sit down here, Jack ; I've something to say to you
. . . about Mary.

Boyle [*awed by her manner*]. About . . . Mary ?

Mrs. Boyle. Close that door there and sit down here.

Boyle [*closing the door*]. More throuble in our native land,
is it ? [*He sits down.*]   Well, what is it ?

Mrs. Boyle. It's about Mary.

Boyle. Well, what about Mary — there's nothin' wrong
with her, is there ?

Mrs. Boyle. I'm sorry to say there's a gradle wrong with
her.

Boyle. A gradle wrong with her !   [*Peevishly*] First
Johnny an' now Mary ; is the whole house goin' to
become an hospital !   It's not consumption, is it ?

Mrs. Boyle. No . . . it's not consumption . . . it's
worse.

Johnny. Worse !   Well, we'll have to get her into some
place ower this, there's no one here to mind her.

Mrs. Boyle. We'll all have to mind her now.   You might
as well know now, Johnny, as another time.   [*To
Boyle*] D'ye know what the doctor said to me about her,
Jack ?

Boyle. How ud I know — I wasn't there, was I ?

Mrs. Boyle. He told me to get her married at wanst.

Boyle. Married at wanst !   An' why did he say the like
o' that ?

Mrs. Boyle. Because Mary's goin' to have a baby in a short
time.

Boyle. Goin' to have a baby ! — my God, what'll Bentham say when he hears that ?

Mrs. Boyle. Are you blind, man, that you can't see that it was Bentham that has done this wrong to her ?

Boyle [*passionately*]. Then he'll marry her, he'll have to marry her !

Mrs. Boyle. You know he's gone to England, an' God knows where he is now.

Boyle. I'll folly him, I'll folly him, an' bring him back, an' make him do her justice. The scoundrel, I might ha' known what he was, with his yogees an' his prawna !

Mrs. Boyle. We'll have to keep it quiet till we see what we can do.

Boyle. Oh, isn't this a nice thing to come on top o' me, an' the state I'm in ! A pretty show I'll be to Joxer an' to that oul' wan, Madigan ! Amn't I afther goin' through enough without havin' to go through this !

Mrs. Boyle. What you an' I'll have to go through'll be nothin' to what poor Mary'll have to go through ; for you an' me is middlin' old, an' most of our years is spent ; but Mary'll have maybe forty years to face an' handle, an' every wan of them'll be tainted with a bitther memory.

Boyle. Where is she ? Where is she till I tell her off ? I'm tellin' you when I'm done with her she'll be a sorry girl !

Mrs. Boyle. I left her in me sister's till I came to speak to you. You'll say nothin' to her, Jack ; ever since she left school she's earned her livin', an' your fatherly care never throubled the poor girl.

Boyle. Gwan, take her part agen her father ! But I'll let you see whether I'll say nothin' to her or no ! Her an' her readin' ! That's more o' th' blasted nonsense that has the house fallin' down on top of us ! What did th' likes of her, born in a tenement house, want with readin' ? Her readin's afther bringin' her to a nice pass — oh, it's madnin', madnin', madnin' !

Mrs. Boyle. When she comes back say nothin' to her, Jack, or she'll leave this place.

Boyle. Leave this place ! Ay, she'll leave this place, an' quick too !

Mrs. Boyle. If Mary goes, I'll go with her.

Boyle. Well, go with her ! Well, go, th' pair o' yous ! I lived before I seen yous, an' I can live when yous are gone. Isn't this a nice thing to come rollin' in on top o' me afther all your prayin' to St. Anthony an' The Little Flower ! An' she's a Child o' Mary, too — I wonder what'll the nuns think of her now ? An' it'll be bellows'd all over th' disthrict before you could say Jack Robinson ; an' whenever I'm seen they'll whisper, " That's th' father of Mary Boyle that had th' kid be th' swank she used to go with ; d'ye know, d'ye know ? " To be sure they'll know — more about it than I will meself !

Johnny. She should be dhriven out o' th' house she's brought disgrace on !

Mrs. Boyle. Hush, you, Johnny. We needn't let it be bellows'd all over the place ; all we've got to do is to leave this place quietly an' go somewhere where we're not known, an' nobody'll be th' wiser.

Boyle. You're talkin' like a two-year-oul', woman. Where'll we get a place ou' o' this ? — places aren't that easily got.

Mrs. Boyle. But, Jack, when we get the money . . .

Boyle. Money — what money ?

Mrs. Boyle. Why, oul' Ellison's money, of course.

Boyle. There's no money comin' from oul' Ellison, or any one else. Since you've heard of wan throuble, you might as well hear of another. There's no money comin' to us at all — the Will's a wash-out !

Mrs. Boyle. What are you sayin', man — no money ?

Johnny. How could it be a wash-out ?

Boyle. The boyo that's afther doin' it to Mary done it to me as well. The thick made out the Will wrong ; he said in th' Will, only first cousin an' second cousin, instead of mentionin' our names, an' now any one that thinks he's a first cousin or second cousin t'oul' Ellison can claim the money as well as me, an' they're springin' up in hundreds, an' comin' from America an' Australia, thinkin' to get their whack out of it, while all the time the lawyers is gobblin' it up, till there's not as much as ud buy a stockin' for your lovely daughter's baby !

Mrs. Boyle. I don't believe it, I don't believe it, I don't believe it !

Johnny. Why did you say nothin' about this before ?

Mrs. Boyle. You're not serious, Jack ; you're not serious !

Boyle. I'm tellin' you the scholar, Bentham, made a banjax o' th' Will ; instead o' sayin', " th' rest o' me property to be divided between me first cousin, Jack Boyle, an' me second cousin, Mick Finnegan, o' Santhry ", he writ down only, " me first an' second cousins ", an' the world an' his wife are afther th' property now.

Mrs. Boyle. Now I know why Bentham left poor Mary in th' lurch ; I can see it all now — oh, is there not even a middlin' honest man left in th' world ?

Johnny [*to Boyle*]. An' you let us run into debt, an' you borreyed money from everybody to fill yourself with beer ! An' now you tell us the whole thing's a washout ! Oh, if it's thrue, I'm done with you, for you're worse than me sisther Mary !

Boyle. You hole your tongue, d'ye hear ? I'll not take any lip from you. Go an' get Bentham if you want satisfaction for all that's afther happenin' us.

Johnny. I won't hole me tongue, I won't hole me tongue ! I'll tell you what I think of you, father an' all as you are . . . you . . .

Mrs. Boyle. Johnny, Johnny, Johnny, for God's sake, be quiet !

Johnny. I'll not be quiet, I'll not be quiet ; he's a nice father, isn't he ? Is it any wondher Mary went asthray, when . . .

Mrs. Boyle. Johnny, Johnny, for my sake be quiet — for your mother's sake !

Boyle. I'm goin' out now to have a few dhrinks with th' last few makes I have, an' tell that lassie o' yours not to be here when I come back ; for if I lay me eyes on her, I'll lay me hans on her, an' if I lay me hans on her, I won't be accountable for me actions !

Johnny. Take care somebody doesn't lay his hands on you — y'oul' . . .

Mrs. Boyle. Johnny, Johnny !

Boyle [*at door, about to go out*]. Oh, a nice son, an' a nicer daughter, I have. [*Calling loudly upstairs*] Joxer, Joxer, are you there ?

Joxer [*from a distance*]. I'm here, More . . . ee . . . aar . . . i . . . tee !

Boyle. I'm goin' down to Foley's — are you comin' ?

Joxer. Come with you ? With that sweet call me heart is stirred ; I'm only waiting for the word, an' I'll be with you, like a bird !

         [*Boyle and Joxer pass the door going out.*

Johnny [*throwing himself on the bed*]. I've a nice sisther, an' a nice father, there's no bettin' on it. I wish to God a bullet or a bomb had whipped me ou' o' this long ago ! Not one o' yous, not one o' yous, have any thought for me !

Mrs. Boyle [*with passionate remonstrance*]. If you don't whisht, Johnny, you'll drive me mad. Who has kep' th' home together for the past few years — only me ? An' who'll have to bear th' biggest part o' this throuble but me ? — but whinin' an' whingin' isn't goin' to do any good.

Johnny. You're to blame yourself for a gradle of it — givin' him his own way in everything, an' never assin' to check him, no matther what he done. Why didn't you look afther th' money ? why . . .

     [*There is a knock at the door ; Mrs. Boyle opens it ; Johnny*
      rises on his elbow to look and listen ; two men enter.

First Man. We've been sent up be th' Manager of the Hibernian Furnishing Co., Mrs. Boyle, to take back the furniture that was got a while ago.

Mrs. Boyle. Yous'll touch nothin' here — how do I know who yous are ?

First Man [*showing a paper*]. There's the ordher, ma'am. [*Reading*] A chest o' drawers, a table, wan easy an' two ordinary chairs ; wan mirror ; wan chestherfield divan, an' a wardrobe an' two vases. [*To his comrade*] Come on, Bill, it's afther knockin'-off time already.

Johnny. For God's sake, mother, run down to Foley's an' bring father back, or we'll be left without a stick.
                    [*The men carry out the table.*

Mrs. Boyle. What good would it be ? — you heard what he said before he went out.

Johnny. Can't you thry ? He ought to be here, an' the like of this goin' on.
          [*Mrs. Boyle puts a shawl around her, as Mary enters.*

Mary. What's up, mother ? I met men carryin' away the table, an' everybody's talking about us not gettin' the money after all.

Mrs. Boyle. Everythin's gone wrong, Mary, everythin'. We're not gettin' a penny out o' the Will, not a penny — I'll tell you all when I come back ; I'm goin' for your father.   [*She runs out.*

Johnny [*to Mary, who has sat down by the fire*]. It's a wondher you're not ashamed to show your face here, afther what has happened.
          [*Jerry enters slowly ; there is a look of earnest hope on his
          face. He looks at Mary for a few moments.*

Jerry [*softly*]. Mary !   [*Mary does not answer.*

Jerry. Mary, I want to speak to you for a few moments, may I ?

> [*Mary remains silent ; Johnny goes slowly into room on left.*

Jerry. Your mother has told me everything, Mary, and I have come to you. . . . I have come to tell you, Mary, that my love for you is greater and deeper than ever. . . .

Mary [*with a sob*]. Oh, Jerry, Jerry, say no more ; all that is over now ; anything like that is impossible now !

Jerry. Impossible ? Why do you talk like that, Mary ?

Mary. After all that has happened.

Jerry. What does it matter what has happened ? We are young enough to be able to forget all those things. [*He catches her hand*] Mary, Mary, I am pleading for your love. With Labour, Mary, humanity is above everything ; we are the Leaders in the fight for a new life. I want to forget Bentham, I want to forget that you left me — even for a while.

Mary. Oh, Jerry, Jerry, you haven't the bitter word of scorn for me after all.

Jerry [*passionately*]. Scorn ! I love you, love you, Mary !

Mary [*rising, and looking him in the eyes*]. Even though . . .

Jerry. Even though you threw me over for another man ; even though you gave me many a bitter word !

Mary. Yes, yes, I know ; but you love me, even though . . . even though . . . I'm . . . goin' . . . goin'

. . . [*He looks at her questioningly, and fear gathers in his eyes.*] Ah, I was thinkin' so. . . . You don't know everything !

Jerry [*poignantly*]. Surely to God, Mary, you don't mean that . . . that . . . that . . .

Mary. Now you know all, Jerry ; now you know all !

Jerry. My God, Mary, have you fallen as low as that ?

Mary. Yes, Jerry, as you say, I have fallen as low as that.

Jerry. I didn't mean it that way, Mary . . . it came on me so sudden, that I didn't mind what I was sayin'. . . . I never expected this — your mother never told me. . . . I'm sorry . . . God knows, I'm sorry for you, Mary.

Mary. Let us say no more, Jerry ; I don't blame you for thinkin' it's terrible. . . . I suppose it is. . . . Everybody'll think the same . . . it's only as I expected — your humanity is just as narrow as the humanity of the others.

Jerry. I'm sorry, all the same. . . . I shouldn't have troubled you. . . . I wouldn't if I'd known. . . . If I can do anything for you . . . Mary . . . I will.
[*He turns to go, and halts at the door.*

Mary. Do you remember, Jerry, the verses you read when you gave the lecture in the Socialist Rooms some time ago, on Humanity's Strife with Nature ?

Jerry. The verses — no ; I don't remember them.

Mary. I do. They're runnin' in me head now —

An' we felt the power that fashion'd
All the lovely things we saw,
That created all the murmur
Of an everlasting law,
Was a hand of force an' beauty,
With an eagle's tearin' claw.

Then we saw our globe of beauty
Was an ugly thing as well,
A hymn divine whose chorus
Was an agonizin' yell ;
Like the story of a demon,
That an angel had to tell ;

Like a glowin' picture by a
Hand unsteady, brought to ruin :
Like her craters, if their deadness
Could give life unto the moon ;
Like the agonizing horror
Of a violin out of tune.

[*There is a pause, and Devine goes slowly out.*

Johnny [*returning*]. Is he gone ?

Mary. Yes.   [*The two men re-enter.*

First Man. We can't wait any longer for t'oul' fella —
sorry, Miss, but we have to live as well as th' nex'
man.   [*They carry out some things.*

Johnny. Oh, isn't this terrible ! . . . I suppose you
told him everything . . . couldn't you have waited
for a few days ? . . . he'd have stopped th' takin' of
the things, if you'd kep' your mouth shut. Are you
burnin' to tell every one of the shame you've brought
on us ?

Mary [*snatching up her hat and coat*]. Oh, this is unbearable !
                    [*She rushes out.*

First Man [re-entering]. We'll take the chest o' drawers next — it's the heaviest.
> [*The votive light flickers for a moment, and goes out.*

Johnny [in a cry of fear]. Mother o' God, the light's afther goin' out !

First Man. You put the win' up me the way you bawled that time. The oil's all gone, that's all.

Johnny [with an agonizing cry]. Mother o' God, there's a shot I'm afther gettin' !

First Man. What's wrong with you, man ? Is it a fit you're takin' ?

Johnny. I'm afther feelin' a pain in me breast, like the tearin' by of a bullet !

First Man. He's goin' mad — it's a wondher they'd leave a chap like that here by himself.
> [*Two Irregulars enter swiftly ; they carry revolvers ; one goes over to Johnny ; the other covers the two furniture men.*

First Irregular [to the men, quietly and incisively]. Who are you ? — what are yous doin' here ? — quick !

First Man. Removin' furniture that's not paid for.

Irregular. Get over to the other end of the room an' turn your faces to the wall — quick !
> [*The two men turn their faces to the wall, with their hands up.*

Second Irregular [to Johnny]. Come on, Sean Boyle, you're wanted ; some of us have a word to say to you.

Johnny. I'm sick, I can't — what do you want with me ?

Second Irregular. Come on, come on ; we've a distance to go, an' haven't much time — come on.

Johnny. I'm an oul' comrade — yous wouldn't shoot an oul' comrade.

Second Irregular. Poor Tancred was an oul' comrade o' yours, but you didn't think o' that when you gave him away to the gang that sent him to his grave. But we've no time to waste ; come on — here, Dermot, ketch his arm. [*To Johnny*] Have you your beads ?

Johnny. Me beads ! Why do you ass me that, why do you ass me that ?

Second Irregular. Go on, go on, march !

Johnny. Are yous goin' to do in a comrade ? — look 'at me arm, I lost it for Ireland.

Second Irregular. Commandant Tancred lost his life for Ireland.

Johnny. Sacred Heart of Jesus, have mercy on me ! Mother o' God, pray for me — be with me now in the agonies o' death ! . . . Hail, Mary, full o' grace . . . the Lord is . . . with Thee.

   [*They drag out Johnny Boyle, and the curtain falls. When it rises again the most of the furniture is gone. Mary and Mrs. Boyle, one on each side, are sitting in a darkened room, by the fire ; it is an hour later.*

Mrs. Boyle. I'll not wait much longer . . . what did they bring him away in the mothor for ? Nugent says he thinks they had guns . . . is me throubles never goin' to be over ? . . . If anything ud happen to poor Johnny, I think I'd lose me mind. . . . I'll go to the

Police Station, surely they ought to be able to do somethin'.   [*Below is heard the sound of voices.*

Mrs. Boyle. Whisht, is that something?   Maybe, it's your father, though when I left him in Foley's he was hardly able to lift his head.   Whisht!
  [*A knock at the door, and the voice of Mrs. Madigan, speaking very softly*]: Mrs. Boyle, Mrs. Boyle.
                              [*Mrs. Boyle opens the door.*

Mrs. Madigan. Oh, Mrs. Boyle, God an' His Blessed Mother be with you this night!

Mrs. Boyle [*calmly*]. What is it, Mrs. Madigan?   It's Johnny — something about Johnny.

Mrs. Madigan. God send it's not, God send it's not Johnny!

Mrs. Boyle. Don't keep me waitin', Mrs. Madigan; I've gone through so much lately that I feel able for anything.

Mrs. Madigan. Two polismen below wantin' you.

Mrs. Boyle. Wantin' me; an' why do they want me?

Mrs. Madigan. Some poor fella's been found, an' they think it's, it's . . .

Mrs. Boyle. Johnny, Johnny!

Mary [*with her arms round her mother*]. Oh, mother, mother, me poor, darlin' mother.

Mrs. Boyle. Hush, hush, darlin'; you'll shortly have your own throuble to bear.   [*To Mrs. Madigan*] An' why do the polis think it's Johnny, Mrs. Madigan?

Mrs. Madigan. Because one o' the doctors knew him when he was attendin' with his poor arm.

Mrs. Boyle. Oh, it's thrue, then ; it's Johnny, it's me son, me own son !

Mary. Oh, it's thrue, it's thrue what Jerry Devine says — there isn't a God, there isn't a God ; if there was He wouldn't let these things happen !

Mrs. Boyle. Mary, Mary, you musn't say them things. We'll want all the help we can get from God an' His Blessed Mother now ! These things have nothin' to do with the Will o' God. Ah, what can God do agen the stupidity o' men !

Mrs. Madigan. The polis want you to go with them to the hospital to see the poor body — they're waitin' below.

Mrs. Boyle. We'll go. Come, Mary, an' we'll never come back here agen. Let your father furrage for himself now ; I've done all I could an' it was all no use — he'll be hopeless till the end of his days. I've got a little room in me sisther's where we'll stop till your throuble is over, an' then we'll work together for the sake of the baby.

Mary. My poor little child that'll have no father !

Mrs. Boyle. It'll have what's far betther — it'll have two mothers.

A Rough Voice shouting from below. Are yous goin' to keep us waitin' for yous all night ?

Mrs. Madigan [*going to the door, and shouting down*]. Take your hour, there, take your hour ! If yous are in such a hurry, skip off, then, for nobody wants you here —

if they did yous wouldn't be found. For you're the
same as yous were undher the British Government —
never where yous are wanted ! As far as I can see, the
Polis as Polis, in this city, is Null an' Void !

Mrs. Boyle. We'll go, Mary, we'll go ; you to see your
poor dead brother, an' me to see me poor dead son !

Mary. I dhread it, mother, I dhread it !

Mrs. Boyle. I forgot, Mary, I forgot ; your poor oul'
selfish mother was only thinkin' of herself. No, no,
you mustn't come — it wouldn't be good for you. You
go on to me sisther's an' I'll face th' ordeal meself.
Maybe I didn't feel sorry enough for Mrs. Tancred
when her poor son was found as Johnny's been found
now — because he was a Die-hard ! Ah, why didn't I
remember that then he wasn't a Diehard or a Stater,
but only a poor dead son ! It's well I remember all
that she said — an' it's my turn to say it now : What
was the pain I suffered, Johnny, bringin' you into the
world to carry you to your cradle, to the pains I'll
suffer carryin' you out o' the world to bring you to
your grave ! Mother o' God, Mother o' God, have
pity on us all ! Blessed Virgin, where were you when
me darlin' son was riddled with bullets, when me
darlin' son was riddled with bullets ? Sacred Heart
o' Jesus, take away our hearts o' stone, and give us
hearts o' flesh ! Take away this murdherin' hate, an'
give us Thine own eternal love !

[*They all go slowly out.*
[*There is a pause ; then a sound of shuffling steps on the
stairs outside. The door opens and Boyle and Joxer, both
of them very drunk, enter.*

Boyle. I'm able to go no farther. . . . Two polis, ey

. . . what were they doin' here, I wondher? . . . Up to no good, anyhow . . . an' Juno an' that lovely daughter o' mine with them. [*Taking a sixpence from his pocket and looking at it*] Wan single, solitary tanner left out of all I borreyed. . . . [*He lets it fall.*] The last o' the Mohicans. . . . The blinds is down, Joxer, the blinds is down!

Joxer [*walking unsteadily across the room, and anchoring at the bed*]. Put all . . . your throubles . . . in your oul' kit-bag . . . an' smile . . . smile . . . smile!

Boyle. The counthry'll have to steady itself . . . it's goin' . . . to hell. . . . Where'r all . . . the chairs . . . gone to . . . steady itself, Joxer. . . . Chairs'll . . . have to . . . steady themselves. . . . No matther . . . what any one may . . . say. . . . Irelan' sober . . . is Irelan' . . . free.

Joxer [*stretching himself on the bed*]. Chains . . . an' . . . slaveree . . . that's a darlin' motto . . . a daaarlin' . . . motto!

Boyle. If th' worst comes . . . to th' worse . . . I can join a . . . flyin' . . . column. . . . I done . . . me bit . . . in Easther Week . . . had no business . . . to . . . be . . . there . . . but Captain Boyle's Captain Boyle!

Joxer. Breathes there a man with soul . . . so . . . de . . . ad . . . this . . . me . . . o . . . wn, me nat . . . ive l . . . an'!

Boyle [*subsiding into a sitting posture on the floor*]. Commandant Kelly died . . . in them . . . arms . . . Joxer. . . . Tell me Volunteer Butties . . . says he . . . that . . . I died for . . . Irelan'!

Joxer. D'jever rade Willie . . . Reilly . . . an' his own . . . Colleen . . . Bawn? It's a darlin' story, a daarlin' story !

Boyle. I'm telling you . . . Joxer . . . th' whole worl's . . . in a terr . . . ible state o' . . . chassis !

CURTAIN

A Tragedy in Four Acts

The Plough and the Stars

To the gay
laugh of my mother at the
gate of the grave

CHARACTERS IN THE PLAY

JACK CLITHEROE (*a bricklayer*), *Commandant in the Irish Citizen Army*

NORA CLITHEROE, *his wife*

PETER FLYNN (*a labourer*), *Nora's uncle*

THE YOUNG COVEY (*a fitter*), *Clitheroe's cousin*

BESSIE BURGESS (*a street fruit-vendor*)

MRS. GOGAN (*a charwoman*)

MOLLSER, *her consumptive child*

FLUTHER GOOD (*a carpenter*)

Residents in the Tenement

LIEUT. LANGON (*a Civil Servant*), *of the Irish Volunteers*

CAPT. BRENNAN (*a chicken butcher*), *of the Irish Citizen Army*

CORPORAL STODDART, *of the Wiltshires*

SERGEANT TINLEY, *of the Wiltshires*

ROSIE REDMOND, *a daughter of " the Digs "*

A BAR-TENDER

A WOMAN

THE FIGURE IN THE WINDOW

———

ACT I.—The living-room of the Clitheroe flat in a Dublin tenement.

ACT II.—A public-house, outside of which a meeting is being held.

ACT III.—The street outside the Clitheroe tenement.

ACT IV.—The room of Bessie Burgess.

———

TIME.—Acts I and II, November 1915 ; Acts III and IV, Easter Week, 1916. A few days elapse between Acts III and IV.

ACT I

The home of the Clitheroes. It consists of the front and back drawing-rooms in a fine old Georgian house, struggling for its life against the assaults of time, and the more savage assaults of the tenants. The room shown is the back drawing-room, wide, spacious, and lofty. At back is the entrance to the front drawing-room. The space, originally occupied by folding doors, is now draped with casement cloth of a dark purple, decorated with a design in reddish-purple and cream. One of the curtains is pulled aside, giving a glimpse of front drawing-room, at the end of which can be seen the wide, lofty windows looking out into the street. The room directly in front of the audience is furnished in a way that suggests an attempt towards a finer expression of domestic life. The large fireplace on right is of wood, painted to look like marble (the original has been taken away by the landlord). On the mantelshelf are two candle-sticks of dark carved wood. Between them is a small clock. Over the clock is hanging a calendar which displays a picture of " The Sleeping Venus ". In the centre of the breast of the chimney hangs a picture of Robert Emmet. On the right of the entrance to the front drawing-room is a copy of " The Gleaners ", on the opposite side a copy of " The Angelus ". Underneath " The Gleaners " is a chest of drawers on which stands a green bowl filled with scarlet dahlias and white chrysanthemums. Near to the fireplace is a settee which at night forms a double bed for Clitheroe and Nora. Underneath " The Angelus " are a number of shelves containing saucepans and a frying-pan. Under these is a table on which are various articles of delf ware. Near the end of the room, opposite to the fireplace is a gate-legged table, covered with a cloth. On top of the table a huge cavalry sword is lying. To the right is a door which leads to a lobby

from which the staircase leads to the hall. The floor is covered
with a dark green linoleum. The room is dim except where it is
illuminated from the glow of the fire. Through the window of
the room at back can be seen the flaring of the flame of a gasolene
lamp giving light to workmen repairing the street. Occasionally
can be heard the clang of crowbars striking the setts. Fluther
Good is repairing the lock of door, Right. A claw-hammer is
on a chair beside him, and he has a screw-driver in his hand. He
is a man of forty years of age, rarely surrendering to thoughts
of anxiety, fond of his " oil " but determined to conquer the
habit before he dies. He is square-jawed and harshly featured ;
under the left eye is a scar, and his nose is bent from a smashing
blow received in a fistic battle long ago. He is bald, save for a
few peeping tufts of reddish hair around his ears ; and his upper
lip is hidden by a scrubby red moustache, embroidered here and
there with a grey hair. He is dressed in a seedy black suit, cotton
shirt with a soft collar, and wears a very respectable little black
bow. On his head is a faded jerry hat, which, when he is excited,
he has a habit of knocking farther back on his head, in a series
of taps. In an argument he usually fills with sound and fury
generally signifying a row. He is in his shirt-sleeves at present,
and wears a soiled white apron, from a pocket in which sticks a
carpenter's two-foot rule. He has just finished the job of putting
on a new lock, and, filled with satisfaction, he is opening and
shutting the door, enjoying the completion of a work well done.
Sitting at the fire, airing a white shirt, is Peter Flynn. He is a
little, thin bit of a man, with a face shaped like a lozenge ; on
his cheeks and under his chin is a straggling wiry beard of a dirty-
white and lemon hue. His face invariably wears a look of
animated anguish, mixed with irritated defiance, as if everybody
was at war with him, and he at war with everybody. He is
cocking his head in a way that suggests resentment at the presence
of Fluther, who pays no attention to him, apparently, but is
really furtively watching him. Peter is clad in a singlet, white

whipcord knee-breeches, and is in his stocking-feet.

A voice is heard speaking outside of door, Left [it is that of Mrs. Gogan].

Mrs. Gogan [*outside*]. Who are you lookin' for, sir ? Who ? Mrs. Clitheroe ? . . . Oh, excuse me. Oh ay, up this way. She's out, I think : I seen her goin'. Oh, you've somethin' for her ; oh, excuse me. You're from Arnott's. . . . I see. . . . You've a parcel for her. . . . Righto. . . . I'll take it. . . . I'll give it to her the minute she comes in. . . . It'll be quite safe. . . . Oh, sign that. . . . Excuse me. . . . Where ? . . . Here ? . . . No, there ; righto. Am I to put Maggie or Mrs. ? What is it ? You dunno ? Oh, excuse me.

> [*Mrs. Gogan opens the door and comes in. She is a doleful-looking little woman of forty, insinuating manner and sallow complexion. She is fidgety and nervous, terribly talkative, has a habit of taking up things that may be near her and fiddling with them while she is speaking. Her heart is aflame with curiosity, and a fly could not come into nor go out of the house without her knowing. She has a draper's parcel in her hand, the knot of the twine tying it is untied. Peter, more resentful of this intrusion than of Fluther's presence, gets up from the chair, and without looking around, his head carried at an angry cock, marches into the room at back.*

Mrs. Gogan [*removing the paper and opening the cardboard box it contains*]. I wondher what's that now ? A hat ! [*She takes out a hat, black, with decorations in red and gold.*] God, she's goin' to th' divil lately for style ! That hat, now, cost more than a penny. Such notions of upper-osity she's gettin'. [*Putting the hat on her head*] Oh, swank, what ! [*She replaces it in parcel.*

Fluther. She's a pretty little Judy, all the same.

Mrs. Gogan. Ah, she is, an' she isn't. There's prettiness an' prettiness in it. I'm always sayin' that her skirts are a little too short for a married woman. An' to see her, sometimes of an evenin', in her glad-neck gown would make a body's blood run cold. I do be ashamed of me life before her husband. An' th' way she thries to be polite, with her " Good mornin', Mrs. Gogan," when she's goin' down, an' her " Good evenin', Mrs. Gogan," when she's comin' up. But there's politeness an' politeness in it.

Fluther. They seem to get on well together, all th' same.

Mrs. Gogan. Ah, they do, an' they don't. The pair o' them used to be like two turtle doves always billin' an' cooin'. You couldn't come into th' room but you'd feel, instinctive like, that they'd just been afther kissin' an' cuddlin' each other. . . . It often made me shiver, for, afther all, there's kissin' an' cuddlin' in it. But I'm thinkin' he's beginnin' to take things more quietly ; the mysthery of havin' a woman's a mysthery no longer. . . . She dhresses herself to keep him with her, but it's no use — afther a month or two, th' wondher of a woman wears off.

Fluther. I dunno, I dunno. Not wishin' to say anything derogatory, I think it's all a question of location : when a man finds th' wondher of one woman beginnin' to die, it's usually beginnin' to live in another.

Mrs. Gogan. She's always grumblin' about havin' to live in a tenement house. " I wouldn't like to spend me last hour in one, let alone live me life in a tenement," says she. " Vaults," says she, " that are hidin' th'

dead, instead of homes that are sheltherin' th' livin'."
" Many a good one," says I, " was reared in a tenement
house." Oh, you know, she's a well-up little lassie,
too ; able to make a shillin' go where another would
have to spend a pound. She's wipin' th' eyes of th'
Covey an' poor oul' Pether — everybody knows that
— screwin' every penny she can out o' them, in ordher
to turn th' place into a babby-house. An' she has
th' life frightened out o' them ; washin' their face,
combin' their hair, wipin' their feet, brushin' their
clothes, thrimmin' their nails, cleanin' their teeth —
God Almighty, you'd think th' poor men were undher-
goin' penal servitude.

Fluther [*with an exclamation of disgust*]. A-a-ah, that's
goin' beyond th' beyonds in a tenement house. That's
a little bit too derogatory.

[*Peter enters from room, Back, head elevated and resentful
fire in his eyes ; he is still in his singlet and trousers,
but is now wearing a pair of unlaced boots — possibly
to be decent in the presence of Mrs. Gogan. He places
the white shirt, which he has carried in on his arm, on
the back of a chair near the fire, and, going over to the
chest of drawers, he opens drawer after drawer, looking
for something ; as he fails to find it he closes each drawer
with a snap ; he pulls out pieces of linen neatly folded,
and bundles them back again any way.*

Peter [*in accents of anguish*]. Well, God Almighty, give me
patience !

[*He returns to room, Back, giving the shirt a vicious turn
as he passes.*

Mrs. Gogan. I wondher what he is foostherin' for now ?

Fluther. He's adornin' himself for th' meeting to-night.

[*Pulling a handbill from his pocket and reading*] " Great Demonstration an' torchlight procession around places in th' city sacred to th' memory of Irish Patriots, to be concluded be a meetin', at which will be taken an oath of fealty to th' Irish Republic. Formation in Parnell Square at eight o'clock." Well, they can hold it for Fluther. I'm up th' pole ; no more dhrink for Fluther. It's three days now since I touched a dhrop, an' I feel a new man already.

Mrs. Gogan. Isn't oul' Peter a funny-lookin' little man ? . . . Like somethin' you'd pick off a Christmas Tree. . . . When he's dhressed up in his canonicals, you'd wondher where he'd been got. God forgive me, when I see him in them, I always think he must ha' had a Mormon for a father ! He an' th' Covey can't abide each other ; th' pair o' them is always at it, thryin' to best each other. There'll be blood dhrawn one o' these days.

Fluther. How is it that Clitheroe himself, now, doesn't have anythin' to do with th' Citizen Army ? A couple o' months ago, an' you'd hardly ever see him without his gun, an' th' Red Hand o' Liberty Hall in his hat.

Mrs. Gogan. Just because he wasn't made a Captain of. He wasn't goin' to be in anything where he couldn't be conspishuous. He was so cocksure o' being made one that he bought a Sam Browne belt, an' was always puttin' it on an' standin' at th' door showing it off, till th' man came an' put out th' street lamps on him. God, I think he used to bring it to bed with him ! But I'm tellin' you herself was delighted that that cock didn't crow, for she's like a clockin' hen if he leaves her sight for a minute.

[*While she is talking, she takes up book after book from the table, looks into each of them in a near-sighted way, and then leaves them back. She now lifts up the sword, and proceeds to examine it.*

Mrs. Gogan. Be th' look of it, this must ha' been a general's sword. . . . All th' gold lace an' th' fine figaries on it. . . . Sure it's twiced too big for him.

Fluther. A-ah; it's a baby's rattle he ought to have, an' he as he is with thoughts tossin' in his head of what may happen to him on th' day o' judgement.
[*Peter has entered, and seeing Mrs. Gogan with the sword, goes over to her, pulls it resentfully out of her hands, and marches into the room, Back, without speaking.*

Mrs. Gogan [*as Peter whips the sword*]. Oh, excuse me ! . . . [*To Fluther*] Isn't he th' surly oul' rascal !

Fluther. Take no notice of him. . . . You'd think he was dumb, but when you get his goat, or he has a few jars up, he's vice versa.   [*He coughs.*

Mrs. Gogan [*she has now sidled over as far as the shirt hanging on the chair*]. Oh, you've got a cold on you, Fluther.

Fluther [*carelessly*]. Ah, it's only a little one.

Mrs. Gogan. You'd want to be careful, all th' same. I knew a woman, a big lump of a woman, red-faced an' round-bodied, a little awkward on her feet ; you'd think, to look at her, she could put out her two arms an' lift a two-storied house on th' top of her head ; got a ticklin' in her throat, an' a little cough, an' the' next mornin' she had a little catchin' in her chest, an' they had just time to wet her lips with a little rum, an' off she went.
[*She begins to look at and handle the shirt.*

Fluther [*a little nervously*]. It's only a little cold I have ; there's nothing derogatory wrong with me.

Mrs. Gogan. I dunno ; there's many a man this minute lowerin' a pint, thinkin' of a woman, or pickin' out a winner, or doin' work as you're doin', while th' hearse dhrawn be th' horses with the black plumes is dhrivin' up to his own hall door, an' a voice that he doesn't hear is muttherin' in his ear, " Earth to earth, an' ashes t' ashes, an' dust to dust."

Fluther [*faintly*]. A man in th' pink o' health should have a holy horror of allowin' thoughts o' death to be festherin' in his mind, for — [*with a frightened cough*] be God, I think I'm afther gettin' a little catch in me chest that time — it's a creepy thing to be thinkin' about.

Mrs. Gogan. It is, an' it isn't ; it's both bad an' good. . . . It always gives meself a kind o' thresspassin' joy to feel meself movin' along in a mournin' coach, an' me thinkin' that, maybe, th' next funeral 'll be me own, an' glad, in a quiet way, that this is somebody else's.

Fluther. An' a curious kind of a gaspin' for breath — I hope there's nothin' derogatory wrong with me.

Mrs. Gogan [*examining the shirt*]. Frills on it, like a woman's petticoat.

Fluther. Suddenly gettin' hot, an' then, just as suddenly, gettin' cold.

Mrs. Gogan [*holding out the shirt towards Fluther*]. How would you like to be wearin' this Lord Mayor's night-dhress, Fluther ?

Fluther [*vehemently*]. Blast you an' your nightshirt ! Is a man fermentin' with fear to stick th' showin' off to him of a thing that looks like a shinin' shroud ?

Mrs. Gogan. Oh, excuse me !
[*Peter has again entered, and he pulls the shirt from the hands of Mrs. Gogan, replacing it on the chair. He returns to room.*

Peter [*as he goes out*]. Well, God Almighty, give me patience !

Mrs. Gogan [*to Peter*]. Oh, excuse me !
[*There is heard a cheer from the men working outside on the street, followed by the clang of tools being thrown down, then silence. The glare of the gasolene light diminishes and finally goes out.*

Mrs. Gogan [*running into the back room to look out of the window*]. What's the men repairin' th' streets cheerin' for ?

Fluther [*sitting down weakly on a chair*]. You can't sneeze but that oul' one wants to know th' why an' th' wherefore. . . . I feel as dizzy as bedamned ! I hope I didn't give up th' beer too suddenly.
[*The Covey comes in by door, Right. He is about twenty-five, tall, thin, with lines on his face that form a perpetual protest against life as he conceives it to be. Heavy seams fall from each side of nose, down around his lips, as if they were suspenders keeping his mouth from falling. He speaks in a slow, wailing drawl; more rapidly when he is excited. He is dressed in dungarees, and is wearing a vividly red tie. He flings his cap with a gesture of disgust on the table, and begins to take off his overalls.*

Mrs. Gogan [*to the Covey, as she runs back into the room*]. What's after happenin', Covey ?

The Covey [*with contempt*]. Th' job's stopped. They've been mobilized to march in th' demonstration to-night undher th' Plough an' th' Stars. Didn't you hear them cheerin', th' mugs ! They have to renew their political baptismal vows to be faithful in seculo seculorum.

Fluther [*forgetting his fear in his indignation*]. There's no reason to bring religion into it. I think we ought to have as great a regard for religion as we can, so as to keep it out of as many things as possible.

The Covey [*pausing in the taking off of his dungarees*]. Oh, you're one o' the boys that climb into religion as high as a short Mass on Sunday mornin's ? I suppose you'll be singin' songs o' Sion an' songs o' Tara at th' meetin', too.

Fluther. We're all Irishmen, anyhow ; aren't we ?

The Covey [*with hand outstretched, and in a professional tone*]. Look here, comrade, there's no such thing as an Irishman, or an Englishman, or a German or a Turk ; we're all only human bein's. Scientifically speakin', it's all a question of the accidental gatherin' together of mollycewels an' atoms.

[*Peter comes in with a collar in his hand. He goes over to mirror, Left, and proceeds to try to put it on.*

Fluther. Mollycewels an' atoms ! D'ye think I'm goin' to listen to you thryin' to juggle Fluther's mind with complicated cunundhrums of mollycewels an' atoms ?

The Covey [*rather loudly*]. There's nothin' complicated in it. There's no fear o' th' Church tellin' you that

mollycewels is a stickin' together of millions of atoms
o' sodium, carbon, potassium o' iodide, etcetera, that,
accordin' to th' way they're mixed, make a flower, a
fish, a star that you see shinin' in th' sky, or a man
with a big brain like me, or a man with a little brain
like you !

Fluther [*more loudly still*]. There's no necessity to be
raisin' your voice ; shoutin's no manifestin' forth of a
growin' mind.

Peter [*struggling with his collar*]. God, give me patience
with this thing. . . . She makes these collars as stiff
with starch as a shinin' band o' solid steel ! She does
it purposely to thry an' twart me. If I can't get it on
th' singlet, how, in th' Name o' God, am I goin' to
get it on th' shirt ?

The Covey [*loudly*]. There's no use o' arguin' with you ;
it's education you want, comrade.

Fluther. The Covey an' God made th' world, I suppose,
wha' ?

The Covey. When I hear some men talkin' I'm inclined
to disbelieve that th' world's eight-hundhred million
years old, for it's not long since th' fathers o' some o'
them crawled out o' th' sheltherin' slime o' the sea.

Mrs. Gogan [*from room at back*]. There, they're afther
formin' fours, an' now they're goin' to march away.

Fluther [*scornfully*]. Mollycewels ! [*He begins to untie his
apron*] What about Adam an' Eve ?

The Covey. Well, what about them ?

Fluther [*fiercely*]. What about them, you ?

The Covey. Adam an' Eve ! Is that as far as you've got ?
Are you still thinkin' there was nobody in th' world
before Adam an' Eve ? [*Loudly*] Did you ever hear,
man, of th' skeleton of th' man o' Java ?

Peter [*casting the collar from him*]. Blast it, blast it, blast
it !

Fluther [*viciously folding his apron*]. Ah, you're not goin' to
be let tap your rubbidge o' thoughts into th' mind o'
Fluther.

The Covey. You're afraid to listen to th' thruth !

Fluther. Who's afraid ?

The Covey. You are !

Fluther. G'way, you wurum !

The Covey. Who's a worum ?

Fluther. You are, or you wouldn't talk th' way you're
talkin'.

The Covey. Th' oul', ignorant savage leppin' up in you,
when science shows you that th' head of your god is an
empty one. Well, I hope you're enjoyin' th' blessin' o'
havin' to live be th' sweat of your brow.

Fluther. You'll be kickin' an' yellin' for th' priest yet,
me boyo. I'm not goin' to stand silent an' simple
listenin' to a thick like you makin' a maddenin'
mockery o' God Almighty. It 'ud be a nice derogatory
thing on me conscience, an' me dyin', to look back in
rememberin' shame of talkin' to a word-weavin' little
ignorant yahoo of a red flag Socialist !

Mrs. Gogan [*she has returned to the front room, and has*

wandered around looking at things in general, and is now in front of the fireplace looking at the picture hanging over it]. For God's sake, Fluther, dhrop it ; there's always th' makin's of a row in th' mention of religion . . . [*Looking at picture*] God bless us, it's a naked woman !

Fluther [*coming over to look at it*]. What's undher it ? [*Reading*] " Georgina : The Sleepin' Vennis ". Oh, that's a terrible picture ; oh, that's a shockin' picture ! Oh, th' one that got that taken, she must have been a prime lassie !

Peter [*who also has come over to look, laughing, with his body bent at the waist, and his head slightly tilted back*]. Hee, hee, hee, hee, hee !

Fluther [*indignantly, to Peter*]. What are you hee, hee-in' for ? That' a nice thing to be hee, hee-in' at. Where's your morality, man ?

Mrs. Gogan. God forgive us, it's not right to be lookin' at it.

Fluther. It's nearly a derogatory thing to be in th' room where it is.

Mrs. Gogan [*giggling hysterically*]. I couldn't stop any longer in th' same room with three men, afther lookin' at it !   [*She goes out.*

[*The Covey, who has divested himself of his dungarees, throws them with a contemptuous motion on top of Peter's white shirt.*

Peter [*plaintively*]. Where are you throwin' them ? Are you thryin' to twart an' torment me again ?

The Covey. Who's thryin' to twart you ?

Peter [*flinging the dungarees violently on the floor*]. You're not goin' to make me lose me temper, me young Covey.

The Covey [*flinging the white shirt on the floor*]. If you're Nora's pet, aself, you're not goin' to get your way in everything.

Peter [*plaintively, with his eyes looking up at the ceiling*]. I'll say nothin'. . . . I'll leave you to th' day when th' all-pitiful, all-merciful, all-lovin' God 'll be handin' you to th' angels to be rievin' an' roastin' you, tearin' an' tormentin' you, burnin' an' blastin' you!

The Covey. Aren't you th' little malignant oul' bastard, you lemon-whiskered oul' swine!

[*Peter runs to the sword, draws it, and makes for the Covey, who dodges him around the table ; Peter has no intention of striking, but the Covey wants to take no chances.*

The Covey [*dodging*]. Fluther, hold him, there. It's a nice thing to have a lunatic like this lashin' around with a lethal weapon!

[*The Covey darts out of the room, Right, slamming the door in the face of Peter.*

Peter [*battering and pulling at the door*]. Lemme out, lemme out ; isn't it a poor thing for a man who wouldn't say a word against his greatest enemy to have to listen to that Covey's twartin' animosities, shovin' poor, patient people into a lashin' out of curses that darken his soul with th' shadow of th' wrath of th' last day!

Fluther. Why d'ye take notice of him? If he seen you didn't, he'd say nothin' derogatory.

Peter. I'll make him stop his laughin' an' leerin', jibin' an' jeerin' an' scarifyin' people with his corner-boy insinuations ! . . . He's always thryin' to rouse me : if it's not a song, it's a whistle ; if it isn't a whistle, it's a cough. But you can taunt an' taunt — I'm laughin' at you ; he, hee, hee, hee, hee, heee !

The Covey [*singing through the keyhole*] :

    Dear harp o' me counthry, in darkness I found thee,
    The dark chain of silence had hung o'er thee long —

Peter [*frantically*]. Jasus, d'ye hear that ? D'ye hear him soundin' forth his divil-souled song o' provocation ?

The Covey [*singing as before*] :

    When proudly, me own island harp, I unbound thee,
    An' gave all thy chords to light, freedom an' song !

Peter [*battering at door*]. When I get out I'll do for you, I'll do for you, I'll do for you !

The Covey [*through the keyhole*]. Cuckoo-oo !
    [*Nora enters by door, Right. She is a young woman of twenty-two, alert, swift, full of nervous energy, and a little anxious to get on in the world. The firm lines of her face are considerably opposed by a soft, amorous mouth and gentle eyes. When her firmness fails her, she persuades with her feminine charm. She is dressed in a tailor-made costume, and wears around her neck a silver fox fur.*

Nora [*running in and pushing Peter away from the door*]. Oh, can I not turn me back but th' two o' yous are at it like a pair o' fightin' cocks ! Uncle Peter . . . Uncle Peter . . . UNCLE PETER !

Peter [*vociferously*]. Oh, Uncle Peter, Uncle Peter be damned ! D'ye think I'm goin' to give a free pass to th' young Covey to turn me whole life into a Holy Manual o' penances an' martyrdoms ?

The Covey [*angrily rushing into the room*]. If you won't exercise some sort o' conthrol over that Uncle Peter o' yours, there'll be a funeral, an' it won't be me that'll be in th' hearse !

Nora [*between Peter and the Covey, to the Covey*]. Are yous always goin' to be tearin' down th' little bit of respectability that a body's thryin' to build up ? Am I always goin' to be havin' to nurse yous into th' hardy habit o' thryin' to keep up a little bit of appearance ?

The Covey. Why weren't you here to see th' way he run at me with th' sword ?

Peter. What did you call me a lemon-whiskered oul' swine for ?

Nora. If th' two o' yous don't thry to make a generous altheration in your goin's on, an' keep on thryin' t' inaugurate th' customs o' th' rest o' th' house into this place, yous can flit into other lodgin's where your bowsey battlin' 'ill meet, maybe, with an encore.

Peter [*to Nora*]. Would you like to be called a lemon-whiskered oul' swine ?

Nora. If you attempt to wag that sword of yours at anybody again, it'll have to be taken off you an' put in a safe place away from babies that don't know th' danger o' them things.

Peter [*at entrance to room, Back*]. Well, I'm not goin' to let anybody call me a lemon-whiskered oul' swine.

[*He goes in.*

Fluther [*trying the door*]. Openin' an' shuttin' now with a well-mannered motion, like a door of a select bar in a high-class pub.

Nora [*to the Covey, as she lays table for tea*]. An', once for all, Willie, you'll have to thry to deliver yourself from th' desire of provokin' oul' Pether into a wild forgetfulness of what's proper an' allowable in a respectable home.

The Covey. Well, let him mind his own business, then. Yestherday, I caught him hee-hee-in' out of him an' he readin' bits out of Jenersky's *Thesis on th' Origin, Development, an' Consolidation of th' Evolutionary Idea of th' Proletariat.*

Nora. Now, let it end at that, for God's sake ; Jack 'll be in any minute, an' I'm not goin' to have th' quiet of his evenin' tossed about in an everlastin' uproar between you an' Uncle Pether. [*To Fluther*] Well, did you manage to settle th' lock, yet, Mr. Good ?

Fluther [*opening and shutting door*]. It's betther than a new one, now, Mrs. Clitheroe ; it's almost ready to open and shut of its own accord.

Nora [*giving him a coin*]. You're a whole man. How many pints will that get you ?

Fluther [*seriously*]. Ne'er a one at all, Mrs. Clitheroe, for Fluther's on th' wather waggon now. You could stan' where you're stannin' chantin', " Have a glass o' malt, Fluther ; Fluther, have a glass o' malt," till th' bells would be ringin' th' ould year out an' th' New Year in, an' you'd have as much chance o' movin' Fluther as a tune on a tin whistle would move a deaf man an' he dead.

[*As Nora is opening and shutting door, Mrs. Bessie Burgess
appears at it. She is a woman of forty, vigorously built.
Her face is a dogged one, hardened by toil, and a little
coarsened by drink. She looks scornfully and viciously at
Nora for a few moments before she speaks.*

Bessie. Puttin' a new lock on her door . . . afraid her
poor neighbours ud break through an' steal. . . . [*In
a loud tone*] Maybe, now, they're a damn sight more
honest than your ladyship . . . checkin' th' children
playin' on th' stairs . . . gettin' on th' nerves of your
ladyship. . . . Complainin' about Bessie Burgess
singin' her hymns at night, when she has a few up.
. . . [*She comes in half-way on the threshold, and screams*]
Bessie Burgess 'll sing whenever she damn well likes !
[*Nora tries to shut door, but Bessie violently shoves it in,
and, gripping Nora by the shoulders, shakes her.*

Bessie. You little over-dressed throllope, you, for one
pin I'd paste th' white face o' you !

Nora [*frightened*]. Fluther, Fluther !

Fluther [*running over and breaking the hold of Bessie from Nora*].
Now, now, Bessie, Bessie, leave poor Mrs. Clitheroe
alone ; she'd do no one any harm, an' minds no one's
business but her own.

Bessie. Why is she always thryin' to speak proud things,
an' lookin' like a mighty one in th' congregation o' th'
people !
[*Nora sinks frightened on to the couch as Jack Clitheroe
enters. He is a tall, well-made fellow of twenty-five.
His face has none of the strength of Nora's. It is a face
in which is the desire for authority, without the power
to attain it.*

Clitheroe [*excitedly*]. What's up ? what's afther happenin' ?

Fluther. Nothin', Jack.   Nothin'.   It's all over now.
Come on, Bessie, come on.

Clitheroe [*to Nora*]. What's wrong, Nora ?   Did she say
anything to you ?

Nora. She was bargin' out of her, an' I only told her to
g'up ower o' that to her own place ; an' before I knew
where I was, she flew at me like a tiger, an' thried to
guzzle me !

Clitheroe [*going to door and speaking to Bessie*]. Get up to your
own place, Mrs. Burgess, and don't you be interferin'
with my wife, or it'll be th' worse for you. . . . Go
on, go on !

Bessie [*as Clitheroe is pushing her out*]. Mind who you're
pushin', now. . . . I attend me place o' worship,
anyhow . . . not like some o' them that go to neither
church, chapel nor meetin'-house. . . . If me son was
home from th' threnches he'd see me righted.

        [*Bessie and Fluther depart, and Clitheroe closes the door.*

Clitheroe [*going over to Nora, and putting his arm round her*].
There, don't mind that old bitch, Nora, darling ; I'll
soon put a stop to her interferin'.

Nora. Some day or another, when I'm here be meself,
she'll come in an' do somethin' desperate.

Clitheroe [*kissing her*]. Oh, sorra fear of her doin' anythin'
desperate.   I'll talk to her to-morrow when she's sober.
A taste o' me mind that'll shock her into the sensibility of behavin' herself !

        [*Nora gets up and settles the table. She sees the dungarees
        on the floor and stands looking at them, then she turns to*

the Covey, who is reading Jenersky's " Thesis " at the fire.

Nora. Willie, is that th' place for your dungarees ?

The Covey [getting up and lifting them from the floor]. Ah, they won't do th' floor any harm, will they ?
> [*He carries them into room, Back.*

Nora [calling]. Uncle Peter, now, Uncle Peter ; tea's ready.
> [*Peter and the Covey come in from room, Back ; they all sit down to tea. Peter is in full dress of the Foresters : green coat, gold braided ; white breeches, top boots, frilled shirt. He carries the slouch hat, with the white ostrich plume, and the sword in his hands. They eat for a few moments in silence, the Covey furtively looking at Peter with scorn in his eyes. Peter knows it and is fidgety.*

The Covey [provokingly]. Another cut o' bread, Uncle Peter ?   [*Peter maintains a dignified silence.*

Clitheroe. It's sure to be a great meetin' to-night. We ought to go, Nora.

Nora [decisively]. I won't go, Jack ; you can go if you wish.   [*A pause.*

The Covey. D'ye want th' sugar, Uncle Peter ?

Peter [explosively]. Now, are you goin' to start your thryin' an' your twartin' again ?

Nora. Now, Uncle Peter, you musn't be so touchy ; Willie has only assed you if you wanted th' sugar.

Peter. He doesn't care a damn whether I want th' sugar or no. He's only thryin' to twart me !

Nora [*angrily, to the Covey*]. Can't you let him alone, Willie ? If he wants the sugar, let him stretch his hand out an' get it himself !

The Covey [*to Peter*]. Now, if you want the sugar, you can stretch out your hand and get it yourself !

Clitheroe. To-night is th' first chance that Brennan has got of showing himself off since they made a Captain of him — why, God only knows. It'll be a treat to see him swankin' it at th' head of the Citizen Army carryin' th' flag of the Plough an' th' Stars. . . . [*Looking roguishly at Nora*] He was sweet on you, once, Nora ?

Nora. He may have been. . . . I never liked him. I always thought he was a bit of a thick.

The Covey. They're bringin' nice disgrace on that banner now.

Clitheroe [*remonstratively*]. How are they bringin' disgrace on it ?

The Covey [*snappily*]. Because it's a Labour flag, an' was never meant for politics. . . . What does th' design of th' field plough, bearin' on it th' stars of th' heavenly plough, mean, if it's not Communism ? It's a flag that should only be used when we're buildin' th' barricades to fight for a Workers' Republic !

Peter [*with a puff of derision*]. P-phuh.

The Covey [*angrily*]. What are you phuhin' out o' you for ? Your mind is th' mind of a mummy. [*Rising*] I betther go an' get a good place to have a look at Ireland's warriors passin' by.

      [*He goes into room, Left, and returns with his cap.*

Nora [*to the Covey*]. Oh, Willie, brush your clothes before you go.

The Covey. Oh, they'll do well enough.

Nora. Go an' brush them ; th' brush is in th' drawer there.
[*The Covey goes to the drawer, muttering, gets the brush, and starts to brush his clothes.*

The Covey [*singing at Peter, as he does so*] :

> Oh, where's th' slave so lowly,
> Condemn'd to chains unholy,
> Who, could he burst his bonds at first,
> Would pine beneath them slowly ?
>
> We tread th' land that . . . bore us,
> Th' green flag glitters . . . o'er us,
> Th' friends we've tried are by our side,
> An' th' foe we hate . . . before us !

Peter [*leaping to his feet in a whirl of rage*]. Now, I'm tellin' you, me young Covey, once for all, that I'll not stick any longer these tittherin' taunts of yours, rovin' around to sing your slights an' slandhers, reddenin' th' mind of a man to th' thinkin' an' sayin' of things that sicken his soul with sin ! [*Hysterically ; lifting up a cup to fling at the Covey*] Be God, I'll——

Clitheroe [*catching his arm*]. Now then, none o' that, none o' that !

Nora. Uncle Pether, Uncle Pether, UNCLE PETHER !

The Covey [*at the door, about to go out*]. Isn't that th' malignant oul' varmint ! Lookin' like th' illegitimate son of an illegitimate child of a corporal in th' Mexican army ! [*He goes out.*

Peter [*plaintively*]. He's afther leavin' me now in such a state of agitation that I won't be able to do meself justice when I'm marchin' to th' meetin'.

Nora [*jumping up*]. Oh, for God's sake, here, buckle your sword on, and go to your meetin', so that we'll have at least one hour of peace !

[*She proceeds to belt on the sword.*

Clitheroe [*irritably*]. For God's sake hurry him up ou' o' this, Nora.

Peter. Are yous all goin' to thry to start to twart me now ?

Nora [*putting on his plumed hat*]. S-s-sh. Now, your hat's on, your house is thatched ; off you pop !

[*She gently pushes him from her.*

Peter [*going, and turning as he reaches the door*]. Now, if that young Covey——

Nora. Go on, go on.   [*He goes.*
    [*Clitheroe sits down in the lounge, lights a cigarette, and looks thoughtfully into the fire. Nora takes the things from the table, placing them on the chest of drawers. There is a pause, then she swiftly comes over to him and sits beside him.*

Nora [*softly*]. A penny for them, Jack !

Clitheroe. Me ? Oh, I was thinkin' of nothing.

Nora. You were thinkin' of th' . . . meetin' . . . Jack. When we were courtin' an' I wanted you to go, you'd say, " Oh, to hell with meetin's," an' that you felt lonely in cheerin' crowds when I was absent. An' we weren't a month married when you began that you couldn't keep away from them.

Clitheroe. Oh, that's enough about th' meetin'. It looks as if you wanted me to go, th' way you're talkin'. You were always at me to give up th' Citizen Army, an' I gave it up ; surely that ought to satisfy you.

Nora. Ay, you gave it up — because you got th' sulks when they didn't make a Captain of you. It wasn't for my sake, Jack.

Clitheroe. For your sake or no, you're benefitin' by it, aren't you ? I didn't forget this was your birthday, did I ? [*He puts his arms around her*] And you liked your new hat ; didn't you, didn't you ?

　　　　　　　　　　[*He kisses her rapidly several times.*

Nora [*panting*]. Jack, Jack ; please, Jack ! I thought you were tired of that sort of thing long ago.

Clitheroe. Well, you're finding out now that I amn't tired of it yet, anyhow. Mrs. Clitheroe doesn't want to be kissed, sure she doesn't ? [*He kisses her again*] Little, little red-lipped Nora !

Nora [*coquettishly removing his arm from around her*]. Oh, yes, your little, little red-lipped Nora's a sweet little girl when th' fit seizes you ; but your little, little red-lipped Nora has to clean your boots every mornin', all the same.

Clitheroe [*with a movement of irritation*]. Oh, well, if we're goin' to be snotty !　　　　　　　　　　　　　　[*A pause.*

Nora. It's lookin' like as if it was you that was goin' to be . . . snotty ! Bridlin' up with bittherness, th' minute a body attempts t'open her mouth.

Clitheroe. Is it any wondher, turnin' a tendher sayin' into a meanin' o' malice an' spite !

Nora. It's hard for a body to be always keepin' her mind bent on makin' thoughts that'll be no longer than th' length of your own satisfaction.   [*A pause.*

Nora [*standing up*]. If we're goin' to dhribble th' time away sittin' here like a pair o' cranky mummies, I'd be as well sewin' or doin' something about th' place.
  [*She looks appealingly at him for a few moments ; he doesn't speak. She swiftly sits down beside him, and puts her arm around his neck.*

Nora [*imploringly*]. Ah, Jack, don't be so cross !

Clitheroe [*doggedly*]. Cross ? I'm not cross ; I'm not a bit cross. It was yourself started it.

Nora [*coaxingly*]. I didn't mean to say anything out o' the way. You take a body up too quickly, Jack. [*In an ordinary tone as if nothing of an angry nature had been said*] You didn't offer me me evenin' allowance yet.
  [*Clitheroe silently takes out a cigarette for her and himself and lights both.*

Nora [*trying to make conversation*]. How quiet th' house is now ; they must be all out.

Clitheroe [*rather shortly*]. I suppose so.

Nora [*rising from the seat*]. I'm longin' to show you me new hat, to see what you think of it. Would you like to see it ?

Clitheroe. Ah, I don't mind.
  [*Nora suppresses a sharp reply, hesitates for a moment, then gets the hat, puts it on, and stands before Clitheroe.*

Nora. Well, how does Mr. Clitheroe like me new hat ?

Clitheroe. It suits you, Nora, it does right enough.

[*He stands up, puts his hand beneath her chin, and tilts her head up. She looks at him roguishly. He bends down and kisses her.*

Nora. Here, sit down, an' don't let me hear another cross word out of you for th' rest o' the night.

[*They sit down.*

Clitheroe [*with his arms around her*]. Little, little, red-lipped Nora !

Nora [*with a coaxing movement of her body towards him*]. Jack !

Clitheroe [*tightening his arms around her*]. Well ?

Nora. You haven't sung me a song since our honeymoon. Sing me one now, do . . . please, Jack !

Clitheroe. What song ? " Since Maggie Went Away " ?

Nora. Ah, no, Jack, not that ; it's too sad. " When You said You Loved Me."

[*Clearing his throat, Clitheroe thinks for a moment, and then begins to sing. Nora, putting an arm around him, nestles her head on his breast and listens delightedly.*

Clitheroe [*singing verses following to the air of " When You and I were Young, Maggie "*] :

> Th' violets were scenting th' woods, Nora,
>   Displaying their charm to th' bee,
> When I first said I lov'd only you, Nora,
>   An' you said you lov'd only me !
>
> Th' chestnut blooms gleam'd through th' glade,
>   Nora,
>   A robin sang loud from a tree,
> When I first said I lov'd only you, Nora,
>   An' you said you lov'd only me !

Th' golden-rob'd daffodils shone, Nora,
  An' danc'd in th' breeze on th' lea,
When I first said I lov'd only you, Nora,
  An' you said you lov'd only me !

Th' trees, birds, an' bees sang a song, Nora,
  Of happier transports to be,
When I first said I lov'd only you, Nora,
  An' you said you lov'd only me !

> *[Nora kisses him.*
> *[A knock is heard at the door, Right ; a pause as they listen. Nora clings closely to Clitheroe. Another knock, more imperative than the first.*

Clitheroe. I wonder who can that be, now ?

Nora [a little nervous]. Take no notice of it, Jack ; they'll go away in a minute. *[Another knock, followed by a voice.*

Voice. Commandant Clitheroe, Commandant Clitheroe, are you there ? A message from General Jim Connolly.

Clitheroe. Damn it, it's Captain Brennan.

Nora [anxiously]. Don't mind him, don't mind, Jack. Don't break our happiness. . . . Pretend we're not in. Let us forget everything to-night but our two selves !

Clitheroe [reassuringly]. Don't be alarmed, darling ; I'll just see what he wants, an' send him about his business.

Nora [tremulously]. No, no. Please, Jack ; don't open it. Please, for your own little Nora's sake !

Clitheroe [rising to open the door]. Now don't be silly, Nora.
> *[Clitheroe opens door, and admits a young man in the full uniform of the Irish Citizen Army — green suit ; slouch green hat caught up at one side by a small Red Hand*

badge ; Sam Browne belt, with a revolver in the holster.
He carries a letter in his hand. When he comes in he
smartly salutes Clitheroe. The young man is Captain
Brennan.

Capt. Brennan [*giving the letter to Clitheroe*]. A dispatch
from General Connolly.

Clitheroe [*reading. While he is doing so, Brennan's eyes are*
fixed on Nora, who droops as she sits on the lounge]. " Commandant Clitheroe is to take command of the eighth
battalion of the I.C.A. which will assemble to proceed
to the meeting at nine o'clock. He is to see that all
units are provided with full equipment ; two days'
rations and fifty rounds of ammunition. At two
o'clock A.M. the army will leave Liberty Hall for a
reconnaissance attack on Dublin Castle. — Com.-Gen.
Connolly."

Clitheroe. I don't understand this. Why does General
Connolly call me Commandant ?

Capt. Brennan. Th' Staff appointed you Commandant,
and th' General agreed with their selection.

Clitheroe. When did this happen ?

Capt. Brennan. A fortnight ago.

Clitheroe. How is it word was never sent to me ?

Capt. Brennan. Word was sent to you. . . . I meself
brought it.

Clitheroe. Who did you give it to, then ?

Capt. Brennan [*after a pause*]. I think I gave it to Mrs.
Clitheroe, there.

Clitheroe. Nora, d'ye hear that ?   [*Nora makes no answer.*

Clitheroe [*there is a note of hardness in his voice*]. Nora . . .
Captain Brennan says he brought a letter to me from
General Connolly, and that he gave it to you. . . .
Where is it ? What did you do with it ?

Nora [*running over to him, and pleadingly putting her arms
around him*]. Jack, please, Jack, don't go out to-night an'
I'll tell you ; I'll explain everything. . . . Send him
away, an' stay with your own little red-lipp'd Nora.

Clitheroe [*removing her arms from around him*]. None o' this
nonsense, now ; I want to know what you did with
th' letter ?   [*Nora goes slowly to the lounge and sits down.*

Clitheroe [*angrily*]. Why didn't you give me th' letter ?
What did you do with it ? . . . [*He shakes her by the
shoulder*] What did you do with th' letter ?

Nora [*flaming up*]. I burned it, I burned it ! That's what
I did with it ! Is General Connolly an' th' Citizen
Army goin' to be your only care ? Is your home goin'
to be only a place to rest in ? Am I goin' to be only
somethin' to provide merry-makin' at night for you ?
Your vanity'll be th' ruin of you an' me yet. . . .
That's what's movin' you : because they've made an
officer of you, you'll make a glorious cause of what
you're doin', while your little red-lipp'd Nora can go
on sittin' here, makin' a companion of th' loneliness of
th' night !

Clitheroe [*fiercely*]. You burned it, did you ? [*He grips her
arm*] Well, me good lady——

Nora. Let go — you're hurtin' me !

Clitheroe. You deserve to be hurt. . . . Any letter that comes to me for th' future, take care that I get it. . . . D'ye hear — take care that I get it !

[*He goes to the chest of drawers and takes out a Sam Browne belt, which he puts on, and then puts a revolver in the holster. He puts on his hat, and looks towards Nora. While this dialogue is proceeding, and while Clitheroe prepares himself, Brennan softly whistles " The Soldiers' Song ".*

Clitheroe [*at door, about to go out*]. You needn't wait up for me ; if I'm in at all, it won't be before six in th' morning.

Nora [*bitterly*]. I don't care if you never come back !

Clitheroe [*to Capt. Brennan*]. Come along, Ned.

[*They go out ; there is a pause. Nora pulls the new hat from her head and with a bitter movement flings it to the other end of the room. There is a gentle knock at door, Right, which opens, and Mollser comes into the room. She is about fifteen, but looks to be only about ten, for the ravages of consumption have shrivelled her up. She is pitifully worn, walks feebly, and frequently coughs. She goes over to Nora.*

Mollser [*to Nora*]. Mother's gone to th' meetin', an' I was feelin' terrible lonely, so I come down to see if you'd let me sit with you, thinkin' you mightn't be goin' yourself. . . . I do be terrible afraid I'll die sometime when I'm be meself. . . . I often envy you, Mrs. Clitheroe, seein' th' health you have, an' th' lovely place you have here, an' wondherin' if I'll ever be sthrong enough to be keepin' a home together for a man. Oh, this must be some more o' the Dublin Fusiliers flyin' off to the front.

[*Just before Mollser ceases to speak, there is heard in the distance the music of a brass band playing a regiment to the boat on the way to the front. The tune that is being played is " It's a Long Way to Tipperary " ; as the band comes to the chorus, the regiment is swinging into the street by Nora's house, and the voices of the soldiers can be heard lustily singing the chorus of the song.*

It's a long way to Tipperary, it's a long way to go ;
It's a long way to Tipperary, to th' sweetest girl I know !
Goodbye Piccadilly, farewell Leicester Square.
It's a long, long way to Tipperary, but my heart's right there !

[*Nora and Mollser remain silently listening. As the chorus ends and the music is faint in the distance again, Bessie Burgess appears at door, Right, which Mollser has left open.*

Bessie [*speaking in towards the room*]. There's th' men marchin' out into th' dhread dimness o' danger, while th' lice is crawlin' about feedin' on th' fatness o' the land ! But yous'll not escape from th' arrow that flieth be night, or th' sickness that wasteth be day. . . . An' ladyship an' all, as some o' them may be, they'll be scattered abroad, like th' dust in th' darkness !

[*Bessie goes away ; Nora steals over and quietly shuts the door. She comes back to the lounge and wearily throws herself on it beside Mollser.*

Mollser [*after a pause and a cough*]. Is there anybody goin', Mrs. Clitheroe, with a titther o' sense ?

CURTAIN

A commodious public-house at the corner of the street in which the meeting is being addressed from Platform No. 1. It is the south corner of the public-house that is visible to the audience. The counter, beginning at Back about one-fourth of the width of the space shown, comes across two-thirds of the length of the stage, and, taking a circular sweep, passes out of sight to Left. On the counter are beer-pulls, glasses, and a carafe. The other three-fourths of the Back is occupied by a tall, wide, two-paned window. Beside this window at the Right is a small, box-like, panelled snug. Next to the snug is a double swing door, the entrance to that particular end of the house. Farther on is a shelf on which customers may rest their drinks. Underneath the windows is a cushioned seat. Behind the counter at Back can be seen the shelves running the whole length of the counter. On these shelves can be seen the end (or the beginning) of rows of bottles. The Barman is seen wiping the part of the counter which is in view. Rosie is standing at the counter toying with what remains of a half of whisky in a wine-glass. She is a sturdy, well-shaped girl of twenty; pretty, and pert in manner. She is wearing a cream blouse, with an obviously suggestive glad neck; a grey tweed dress, brown stockings and shoes. The blouse and most of the dress are hidden by a black shawl. She has no hat, and in her hair is jauntily set a cheap, glittering, jewelled ornament. It is an hour later.

Barman [*wiping counter*]. Nothin' much doin' in your line to-night, Rosie ?

Rosie. Curse o' God on th' haporth, hardly, Tom.   There

isn't much notice taken of a pretty petticoat of a night like this. . . . They're all in a holy mood. Th' solemn-lookin' dials on th' whole o' them an' they marchin' to th' meetin.' You'd think they were th' glorious company of th' saints, an' th' noble army of martyrs thrampin' through th' sthreets of paradise. They're all thinkin' of higher things than a girl's garthers. . . . It's a tremendous meetin' ; four platforms they have — there's one o' them just outside opposite th' window.

Barman. Oh, ay ; sure when th' speaker comes [*motioning with his hand*] to th' near end, here, you can see him plain, an' hear nearly everythin' he's spoutin' out of him.

Rosie. It's no joke thrying' to make up fifty-five shillin's a week for your keep an' laundhry, an' then taxin' you a quid for your own room if you bring home a friend for th' night. . . . If I could only put by a couple of quid for a swankier outfit, everythin' in th' garden ud look lovely——

Barman. Whisht, till we hear what he's sayin'.
    [*Through the window is silhouetted the figure of a tall man who is speaking to the crowd. The Barman and Rosie look out of the window and listen.*

The Voice of the Man. It is a glorious thing to see arms in the hands of Irishmen. We must accustom ourselves to the thought of arms, we must accustom ourselves to the sight of arms, we must accustom ourselves to the use of arms. . . . Bloodshed is a cleansing and sanctifying thing, and the nation that regards it as the final horror has lost its manhood. . . . There are many

things more horrible than bloodshed, and slavery is one
of them !

[*The figure moves away towards the Right, and is lost to
sight and hearing.*

Rosie. It's th' sacred thruth, mind you, what that man's
afther sayin'.

Barman. If I was only a little younger, I'd be plungin'
mad into th' middle of it !

Rosie [*who is still looking out of the window*]. Oh, here's the
two gems runnin' over again for their oil !

[*Peter and Fluther enter tumultuously. They are hot, and
full and hasty with the things they have seen and heard.
Emotion is bubbling up in them, so that when they drink,
and when they speak, they drink and speak with the
fullness of emotional passion. Peter leads the way to the
counter.*

Peter [*splutteringly to Barman*]. Two halves . . . [*To
Fluther*] A meetin' like this always makes me feel as
if I could dhrink Loch Erinn dhry !

Fluther. You couldn't feel any way else at a time like
this when th' spirit of a man is pulsin' to be out
fightin' for th' thruth with his feet thremblin' on th'
way, maybe to th' gallows, an' his ears tinglin' with
th' faint, far-away sound of burstin' rifle-shots that'll
maybe whip th' last little shock o' life out of him
that's left lingerin' in his body !

Peter. I felt a burnin' lump in me throat when I heard
th' band playin' " The Soldiers' Song", rememberin'
last hearin' it marchin' in military formation, with th'
people starin' on both sides at us, carryin' with us

th' pride an' resolution o' Dublin to th' grave of Wolfe Tone.

Fluther. Get th' Dublin men goin' an' they'll go on full force for anything that's thryin' to bar them away from what they're wantin', where th' slim thinkin' counthry boyo ud limp away from th' first faintest touch of compromization !

Peter [*hurriedly to the Barman*]. Two more, Tom ! . . . [*To Fluther*] Th' memory of all th' things that was done, an' all th' things that was suffered be th' people, was boomin' in me brain. . . . Every nerve in me body was quiverin' to do somethin' desperate !

Fluther. Jammed as I was in th' crowd, I listened to th' speeches pattherin' on th' people's head, like rain fallin' on th' corn ; every derogatory thought went out o' me mind, an' I said to meself, " You can die now, Fluther, for you've seen th' shadow-dhreams of th' past leppin' to life in th' bodies of livin' men that show, if we were without a titther o' courage for centuries, we're vice versa now ! " Looka here. [*He stretches out his arm under Peter's face and rolls up his sleeve.*] The blood was BOILIN' in me veins !
  [*The silhouette of the tall figure again moves into the frame of the window speaking to the people.*

Peter [*unaware, in his enthusiasm, of the speaker's appearance, to Fluther*]. I was burnin' to dhraw me sword, an' wave an' wave it over me——

Fluther [*overwhelming Peter*]. Will you stop your blatherin' for a minute, man, an' let us hear what he's sayin' !

Voice of the Man. Comrade soldiers of the Irish Volunteers and of the Citizen Army, we rejoice in this terrible

war. The old heart of the earth needed to be warmed
with the red wine of the battlefields. . . . Such
august homage was never offered to God as this : the
homage of millions of lives given gladly for love of
country.   And we must be ready to pour out the same
red wine in the same glorious sacrifice, for without
shedding of blood there is no redemption !

> [*The figure moves out of sight and hearing.*

Fluther [*gulping down the drink that remains in his glass, and
rushing out*]. Come on, man ; this is too good to be
missed !

> [*Peter finishes his drink less rapidly, and as he is going out
> wiping his mouth with the back of his hand he runs into
> the Covey coming in.   He immediately erects his body
> like a young cock, and with his chin thrust forward, and
> a look of venomous dignity on his face, he marches out.*

The Covey [*at counter*]. Give us a glass o' malt, for God's
sake, till I stimulate meself from th' shock o' seein' th'
sight that's afther goin' out !

Rosie [*all business, coming over to the counter, and standing near
the Covey*]. Another one for me, Tommy ; [*to the
Barman*] th' young gentleman's ordherin' it in th'
corner of his eye.

> [*The Barman brings the drink for the Covey, and leaves it
> on the counter.   Rosie whips it up.*

Barman. Ay, houl' on there, houl' on there, Rosie !

Rosie [*to the Barman*]. What are you houldin' on out o'
you for ?   Didn't you hear th' young gentleman say
that he couldn't refuse anything to a nice little bird ?
[*To the Covey*] Isn't that right, Jiggs ? [*The Covey says
nothing.*] Didn't I know, Tommy, it would be all

right ? It takes Rosie to size a young man up, an' tell th' thoughts that are thremblin' in his mind. Isn't that right, Jiggs ?

[*The Covey stirs uneasily, moves a little farther away, and pulls his cap over his eyes.*

Rosie [*moving after him*]. Great meetin' that's gettin' held outside. Well, it's up to us all, anyway, to fight for our freedom.

The Covey [*to Barman*]. Two more, please. [*To Rosie*] Freedom ! What's th' use o' freedom, if it's not economic freedom ?

Rosie [*emphasizing with extended arm and moving finger*]. I used them very words just before you come in. " A lot o' thricksters," says I, " that wouldn't know what freedom was if they got it from their mother." . . . [*To Barman*] Didn't I, Tommy ?

Barman. I disremember.

Rosie. No, you don't disremember. Remember you said, yourself, it was all " only a flash in th' pan." Well, " flash in th' pan, or no flash in th' pan," says I, " they're not goin' to get Rosie Redmond," says I, " to fight for freedom that wouldn't be worth winnin' in a raffle ! "

The Covey. There's only one freedom for th' workin' man : conthrol o' th' means o' production, rates of exchange, an' th' means of disthribution. [*Tapping Rosie on the shoulder*] Look here, comrade, I'll leave here to-morrow night for you a copy of Jenersky's *Thesis on the Origin, Development, an' Consolidation of the Evolutionary Idea of the Proletariat.*

Rosie [*throwing off her shawl on to the counter, and showing an exemplified glad neck, which reveals a good deal of a white bosom*]. If y'ass Rosie, it's heartbreakin' to see a young fella thinkin' of anything, or admirin' anything, but silk thransparent stockin's showin' off the shape of a little lassie's legs !

> [*The Covey, frightened, moves a little away.*

Rosie [*following on*]. Out in th' park in th' shade of a warm summery evenin', with your little darlin' bridie to be, kissin' an' cuddlin' [*she tries to put her arm around his neck*], kissin' an' cuddlin', ay ?

The Covey [*frightened*]. Ay, what are you doin' ? None o' that, now ; none o' that. I've something else to do besides shinannickin' afther Judies !

> [*He turns away, but Rosie follows, keeping face to face with him.*

Rosie. Oh, little duckey, oh, shy little duckey ! Never held a mot's hand, an' wouldn't know how to tittle a little Judy ! [*She clips him under the chin.*] Tittle him undher th' chin, tittle him undher th' chin !

The Covey [*breaking away and running out*]. Ay, go on, now ; I don't want to have any meddlin' with a lassie like you !

Rosie [*enraged*]. Jasus, it's in a monasthery some of us ought to be, spendin' our holidays kneelin' on our adorers, tellin' our beads, an' knockin' hell out of our buzzums !

The Covey [*outside*]. Cuckoo-oo !

> [*Peter and Fluther come in again, followed by Mrs. Gogan, carrying a baby in her arms. They go over to the counter.*

Peter [*with plaintive anger*]. It's terrible that young Covey can't let me pass without proddin' at me ! Did you hear him murmurin' " cuckoo " when we were passin' ?

Fluther [*irritably*]. I wouldn't be everlastin' cockin' me ear to hear every little whisper that was floatin' around about me ! It's my rule never to lose me temper till it would be dethrimental to keep it. There's nothin' derogatory in th' use o' th' word " cuckoo ", is there ?

Peter [*tearfully*]. It's not th' word ; it's th' way he says it : he never says it straight out, but murmurs it with curious quiverin' ripples, like variations on a flute !

Fluther. Ah, what odds if he gave it with variations on a thrombone ! [*To Mrs. Gogan*] What's yours goin' to be, ma'am ?

Mrs. Gogan. Ah, a half o' malt, Fluther.

Fluther [*to Barman*]. Three halves, Tommy.
                    [*The Barman brings the drinks.*

Mrs. Gogan [*drinking*]. The Foresthers' is a gorgeous dhress ! I don't think I've seen nicer, mind you, in a pantomime. . . . Th' loveliest part of th' dhress, I think, is th' osthrichess plume. . . . When yous are goin' along, an' I see them wavin' an' noddin' an' waggin', I seem to be lookin' at each of yous hangin' at th' end of a rope, your eyes bulgin' an' your legs twistin' an' jerkin', gaspin' an' gaspin' for breath while yous are thryin' to die for Ireland !

Fluther. If any o' them is hangin' at the end of a rope, it won't be for Ireland !

Peter. Are you goin' to start th' young Covey's game o' proddin' an' twartin' a man ? There's not many that's talkin' can say that for twenty-five years he never missed a pilgrimage to Bodenstown !

Fluther. You're always blowin' about goin' to Bodenstown. D'ye think no one but yourself ever went to Bodenstown ?

Peter [*plaintively*]. I'm not blowin' about it ; but there's not a year that I go there but I pluck a leaf off Tone's grave, an' this very day me prayer-book is nearly full of them.

Fluther [*scornfully*]. Then Fluther has a vice versa opinion of them that put ivy leaves into their prayer-books, scabbin' it on th' clergy, an' thryin' to out-do th' haloes o' th' saints be lookin' as if he was wearin' around his head a glittherin' aroree boree allis ! [*Fiercely*] Sure, I don't care a damn if you slep' in Bodenstown ! You can take your breakfast, dinner, an' tea on th' grave in Bodenstown, if you like, for Fluther !

Mrs. Gogan. Oh, don't start a fight, boys, for God's sake ; I was only sayin' what a nice costume it is — nicer than th' kilts, for, God forgive me, I always think th' kilts is hardly decent.

Fluther. Ah, sure, when you'd look at him, you'd wondher whether th' man was makin' fun o' th' costume, or th' costume was makin' fun o' th' man !

Barman. Now, then, thry to speak asy, will yous ? We don't want no shoutin' here.

[*The Covey followed by Bessie Burgess comes in. They go over to the opposite end of the counter, and direct their gaze on the other group.*]

The Covey [*to Barman*]. Two glasses o' malt.

Peter. There he is, now ; I knew he wouldn't be long till he folleyed me in.

Bessie [*speaking to the Covey, but really at the other party*]. I can't for th' life o' me undherstand how they can call themselves Catholics, when they won't lift a finger to help poor little Catholic Belgium.

Mrs. Gogan [*raising her voice*]. What about poor little Catholic Ireland ?

Bessie [*over to Mrs. Gogan*]. You mind your own business, ma'am, an' stupefy your foolishness be gettin' dhrunk.

Peter [*anxiously*]. Take no notice of her ; pay no attention to her. She's just tormentin' herself towards havin' a row with somebody.

Bessie. There's a storm of anger tossin' in me heart, thinkin' of all th' poor Tommies, an' with them me own son, dhrenched in water an' soaked in blood, gropin' their way to a shattherin' death, in a shower o' shells ! Young men with th' sunny lust o' life beamin' in them, layin' down their white bodies, shredded into torn an' bloody pieces, on th' althar that God Himself has built for th' sacrifice of heroes !

Mrs. Gogan. Isn't it a nice thing to have to be listenin' to a lassie an' hangin' our heads in a dead silence, knowin' that some persons think more of a ball of malt than they do of th' blessed saints.

Fluther. Whisht ; she's always dangerous an' derogatory when she's well oiled. Th' safest way to hindher her from havin' any enjoyment out of her spite, is to dip our thoughts into the fact of her bein' a female person that has moved out of th' sight of ordinary sensible people.

Bessie. To look at some o' th' women that's knockin' about, now, is a thing to make a body sigh. . . . A woman on her own, dhrinkin' with a bevy o' men, is hardly an example to her sex. . . . A woman dhrinkin' with a woman is one thing, an' a woman dhrinkin' with herself is still a woman — flappers may be put in another category altogether — but a middle-aged married woman makin' herself th' centre of a circle of men is as a woman that is loud an' stubborn, whose feet abideth not in her own house.

The Covey [*to Bessie*]. When I think of all th' problems in front o' th' workers, it makes me sick to be lookin' at oul' codgers goin' about dhressed up like green-accoutred figures gone asthray out of a toyshop !

Peter. Gracious God, give me patience to be listenin' to that blasted young Covey proddin' at me from over at th' other end of th' shop !

Mrs. Gogan [*dipping her finger in the whisky, and moistening with it the lips of her baby*]. Cissie Gogan's a woman livin' for nigh on twenty-five years in her own room, an' beyond biddin' th' time o' day to her neighbours, never yet as much as nodded her head in th' direction of other people's business, while she knows some as are never content unless they're standin' senthry over other people's doin's !
  [*Bessie is about to reply, when the tall, dark figure is again silhouetted against the window, and the voice of the speaker is heard speaking passionately.*

Voice of Speaker. The last sixteen months have been the most glorious in the history of Europe. Heroism has come back to the earth. War is a terrible thing, but war is not an evil thing. People in Ireland dread war

because they do not know it.   Ireland has not known
the exhilaration of war for over a hundred years.   When
war comes to Ireland she must welcome it as she would
welcome the Angel of God !

[*The figure passes out of sight and hearing.*

The Covey [*towards all present*]. Dope, dope. There's only
one war worth havin' : th' war for th' economic
emancipation of th' proletariat.

Bessie. They may crow away out o' them ; but it ud be
fitther for some o' them to mend their ways, an' cease
from havin' scouts out watchin' for th' comin' of th'
Saint Vincent de Paul man, for fear they'd be nailed
lowerin' a pint of beer, mockin' th' man with an angel
face, shinin' with th' glamour of deceit an' lies !

Mrs. Gogan. An' a certain lassie standin' stiff behind her
own door with her ears cocked listenin' to what's being
said, stuffed till she's sthrained with envy of a neighbour thryin' for a few little things that may be got be
hard sthrivin' to keep up to th' letther an' th' law,
an' th' practices of th' Church !

Peter [*to Mrs. Gogan*]. If I was you, Mrs. Gogan, I'd parry
her jabbin' remarks be a powerful silence that'll keep
her tantalizin' words from penethratin' into your
feelin's.   It's always betther to leave these people to
th' vengeance o' God !

Bessie. Bessie Burgess doesn't put up to know much,
never havin' a swaggerin' mind, thanks be to God, but
goin' on packin' up knowledge accordin' to her conscience : precept upon precept, line upon line ; here
a little, an there a little.   But ⌊*with a passionate swing of
her shawl*⌋, thanks be to Christ, she knows when she

was got, where she was got, an' how she was got ;
while there's some she knows, decoratin' their finger
with a well-polished weddin' ring, would be hard put
to it if they were assed to show their weddin' lines !

Mrs. Gogan [*plunging out into the centre of the floor in a wild
tempest of hysterical rage*]. Y' oul' rip of a blasted liar, me
weddin' ring's been well earned be twenty years be th'
side o' me husband, now takin' his rest in heaven,
married to me be Father Dempsey, in th' Chapel o'
Saint Jude's, in th' Christmas Week of eighteen
hundhred an' ninety-five ; an' any kid, livin' or dead,
that Jinnie Gogan's had since, was got between th'
bordhers of th' Ten Commandments ! . . . An' that's
more than some o' you can say that are kep' from th'
dhread o' desthruction be a few drowsy virtues, that
th' first whisper of temptation lulls into a sleep, that'll
know one sin from another only on th' day of their
last anointin', an' that use th' innocent light o' th'
shinin' stars to dip into th' sins of a night's diversion !

Bessie [*jumping out to face Mrs. Gogan, and bringing the palms
of her hands together in sharp claps to emphasize her remarks*].
Liar to you, too, ma'am, y' oul' hardened thresspasser on
other people's good nature, wizenin' up your soul in
th' arts o' dodgeries, till every dhrop of respectability
in a female is dhried up in her, lookin' at your ready-
made manœuverin' with th' menkind !

Barman. Here, there ; here, there ; speak asy there. No
rowin' here, no rowin' here, now.

Fluther [*trying to calm Mrs. Gogan*]. Now Jinnie, Jinnie,
it's a derogatory thing to be smirchin' a night like this
with a row ; it's rompin' with th' feelin's of hope we
ought to be, instead o' bein' vice versa !

Peter [*trying to quiet Bessie*]. I'm terrible dawny, Mrs. Burgess, an' a fight leaves me weak for a long time aftherwards. . . . Please, Mrs. Burgess, before there's damage done, thry to have a little respect for yourself.

Bessie [*with a push of her hand that sends Peter tottering to the end of the shop*]. G'way, you little sermonizing, little yella-faced, little consequential, little pudgy, little bum, you !

Mrs. Gogan [*screaming*]. Fluther, leggo ! I'm not goin' to keep an unresistin' silence, an' her scattherin' her festherin' words in me face, stirrin' up every dhrop of decency in a respectable female, with her restless rally o' lies that would make a saint say his prayer backwards !

Bessie [*shouting*]. Ah, everybody knows well that th' best charity that can be shown to you is to hide th' thruth as much as our thrue worship of God Almighty will allow us !

Mrs. Gogan [*frantically*]. Here, houl' th' kid, one o' yous ; houl' th' kid for a minute ! There's nothin' for it but to show this lassie a lesson or two. . . . [*To Peter*] Here, houl' th' kid, you. [*Before Peter is aware of it, she places the infant in his arms.*]

Mrs. Gogan [*to Bessie, standing before her in a fighting attitude*]. Come on, now, me loyal lassie, dyin' with grief for little Catholic Belgium ! When Jinnie Gogan's done with you, you'll have a little leisure lyin' down to think an' pray for your king an' counthry !

Barman [*coming from behind the counter, getting between the women, and proceeding to push them towards the door*]. Here, now, since yous can't have a little friendly argument quietly, you'll get out o' this place in quick time.   Go

on, an' settle your differences somewhere else — I don't
want to have another endorsement on me licence.

Peter [*anxiously, over to Mrs. Gogan*]. Here, take your kid
back, ower this. How nicely I was picked, now, for it
to be plumped into me arms !

The Covey. She knew who she was givin' it to, maybe.

Peter [*hotly to the Covey*]. Now, I'm givin' you fair warnin',
me young Covey, to quit firin' your jibes an' jeers at
me. . . . For one o' these days, I'll run out in front
o' God Almighty an' take your sacred life !

Barman [*pushing Bessie out after Mrs. Gogan*]. Go on, now ;
out you go.

Bessie [*as she goes out*]. If you think, me lassie, that Bessie
Burgess has an untidy conscience, she'll soon show you
to th' differ !

Peter [*leaving the baby down on the floor*]. Ay, be Jasus, wait
there, till I give her back her youngster ! [*He runs to
the door.*] Ay, there, ay ! [*He comes back.*] There, she's
afther goin' without her kid. What are we goin' to do
with it, now ?

The Covey. What are we goin' to do with it ? Bring it
outside an' show everybody what you're afther findin' !

Peter [*in a panic to Fluther*]. Pick it up, you, Fluther, an'
run afther her with it, will you ?

Fluther. What d'ye take Fluther for ? You must think
Fluther's a right gom. D'ye think Fluther's like yourself, destitute of a titther of undherstandin' ?

Barman [*imperatively to Peter*]. Take it up, man, an' run

out afther her with it, before she's gone too far.
You're not goin' to leave th' bloody thing here, are you ?

Peter [*plaintively, as he lifts up the baby*]. Well, God
Almighty, give me patience with all th' scorners,
tormentors, an' twatters that are always an' ever
thryin' to goad me into prayin' for their blindin' an'
blastin' an' burnin' in th' world to come !

[He goes out.

Fluther. God, it's a relief to get rid o' that crowd.
Women is terrible when they start to fight.   There's no
holdin' them back.   [*To the Covey*] Are you goin' to
have anything ?

The Covey. Ah, I don't mind if I have another half.

Fluther [*to Barman*]. Two more, Tommy, me son.

[The Barman gets the drinks.

Fluther. You know, there's no conthrollin' a woman
when she loses her head.

   [*Rosie enters and goes over to the counter on the side nearest
   to Fluther.*

Rosie [*to Barman*]. Divil a use o' havin' a thrim little leg
on a night like this ; things was never worse. . . .
Give us a half till to-morrow, Tom, duckey.

Barman [*coldly*]. No more to-night, Rosie ; you owe me
for three already.

Rosie [*combatively*]. You'll be paid, won't you ?

Barman. I hope so.

Rosie. You hope so !   Is that th' way with you, now ?

Fluther [*to Barman*]. Give her one ; it'll be all right.

Rosie [*clapping Fluther on the back*]. Oul' sport !

Fluther. Th' meetin' should be soon over, now.

The Covey. Th' sooner th' betther.   It's all a lot o' blasted nonsense, comrade.

Fluther. Oh, I wouldn't say it was all nonsense.   Afther all, Fluther can remember th' time, an' him only a dawny chiselur, bein' taught at his mother's knee to be faithful to th' Shan Van Vok !

The Covey. That's all dope, comrade ; th' sort o' thing that workers are fed on be th' Boorzwawzee.

Fluther [*a little sharply*]. What's all dope ?   Though I'm sayin' it that shouldn't : [*catching his cheek with his hand, and pulling down the flesh from the eye*] d'ye see that mark there, undher me eye ? . . . A sabre slice from a dragoon in O'Connell Street !   [*Thrusting his head forward towards Rosie*] Feel that dint in th' middle o' me nut !

Rosie [*rubbing Fluther's head, and winking at the Covey*]. My God, there's a holla !

Fluther [*putting on his hat with quiet pride*]. A skelp from a bobby's baton at a Labour meetin' in th' Phœnix Park !

The Covey. He must ha' hitten you in mistake.   I don't know what you ever done for th' Labour movement.

Fluther [*loudly*]. D'ye not ?   Maybe, then, I done as much, an' know as much about th' Labour movement as th' chancers that are blowin' about it !

Barman. Speak easy, Fluther, thry to speak easy.

The Covey. There's no necessity to get excited about it, comrade.

Fluther [*more loudly*]. Excited ?   Who's gettin' excited ?

There's no one gettin' excited ! It would take something more than a thing like you to flutther a feather
o' Fluther. Blatherin', an', when all is said, you know
as much as th' rest in th' wind up !

The Covey. Well, let us put it to th' test, then, an' see
what you know about th' Labour movement : what's
the mechanism of exchange ?

Fluther [*roaring, because he feels he is beaten*]. How th' hell
do I know what it is ? There's nothin' about that in
th' rules of our Thrades Union !

Barman. For God's sake, thry to speak easy, Fluther.

The Covey. What does Karl Marx say about th' Relation
of Value to th' Cost o' Production ?

Fluther [*angrily*]. What th' hell do I care what he says ?
I'm Irishman enough not to lose me head be follyin'
foreigners !

Barman. Speak easy, Fluther.

The Covey. It's only waste o' time talkin' to you, comrade.

Fluther. Don't be comradin' me, mate. I'd be on me
last legs if I wanted you for a comrade.

Rosie [*to the Covey*]. It seems a highly rediculous thing to
hear a thing that's only an inch or two away from a
kid, swingin' heavy words about he doesn't know th'
meanin' of, an' uppishly thryin' to down a man like
Misther Fluther here, that's well flavoured in th'
knowledge of th' world he's livin' in.

The Covey [*savagely to Rosie*]. Nobody's askin' you to be
buttin' in with your prate. . . . I have you well
taped, me lassie. . . . Just you keep your opinions
for your own place. . . . It'll be a long time before

th' Covey takes any insthructions or reprimandin' from a prostitute !

Rosie [*wild with humiliation*]. You louse, you louse, you ! . . . You're no man. . . . You're no man . . . I'm a woman, anyhow, an' if I'm a prostitute aself, I have me feelin's. . . . Thryin' to put his arm around me a minute ago, an' givin' me th' glad eye, th' little wrigglin' lump o' desolation turns on me now, because he saw there was nothin' doin'. . . . You louse, you ! If I was a man, or you were a woman, I'd bate th' puss o' you !

Barman. Ay, Rosie, ay ! You'll have to shut your mouth altogether, if you can't learn to speak easy !

Fluther [*to Rosie*]. Houl' on there, Rosie ; houl' on there. There's no necessity to flutther yourself when you're with Fluther. . . . Any lady that's in th' company of Fluther is goin' to get a fair hunt. . . . This is outside your province. . . . I'm not goin' to let you demean yourself be talkin' to a tittherin' chancer. . . . Leave this to Fluther — this is a man's job. [*To the Covey*] Now, if you've anything to say, say it to Fluther, an', let me tell you, you're not goin' to be pass-remarkable to any lady in my company.

The Covey. Sure I don't care if you were runnin' all night afther your Mary o' th' Curlin' Hair, but, when you start tellin' luscious lies about what you done for th' Labour movement, it's nearly time to show y'up !

Fluther [*fiercely*]. Is it you show Fluther up? G'way, man, I'd beat two o' you before me breakfast !

The Covey [*contemptuously*]. Tell us where you bury your dead, will you ?

Fluther [*with his face stuck into the face of the Covey*]. Sing a little less on th' high note, or, when I'm done with you, you'll put a Christianable consthruction on things, I'm tellin' you !

The Covey. You're a big fella, you are.

Fluther [*tapping the Covey threateningly on the shoulder*]. Now, you're temptin' Providence when you're temptin' Fluther !

The Covey [*losing his temper, and bawling*]. Easy with them hands, there, easy with them hands ! You're startin' to take a little risk when you commence to paw the Covey !
> [*Fluther suddenly springs into the middle of the shop, flings his hat into the corner, whips off his coat, and begins to paw the air.*

Fluther [*roaring at the top of his voice*]. Come on, come on, you lowser ; put your mits up now, if there's a man's blood in you ! Be God, in a few minutes you'll see some snots flyin' around, I'm tellin' you. . . . When Fluther's done with you, you'll have a vice versa opinion of him ! Come on, now, come on !

Barman [*running from behind the counter and catching hold of the Covey*]. Here, out you go, me little bowsey. Because you got a couple o' halves you think you can act as you like. [*He pushes the Covey to the door*] Fluther's a friend o' mine, an' I'll not have him insulted.

The Covey [*struggling with the Barman*]. Ay, leggo, leggo there ; fair hunt, give a man a fair hunt ! One minute with him is all I ask ; one minute alone with him, while you're runnin' for th' priest an' th' doctor.

Fluther [*to the Barman*]. Let him go, let him go, Tom : let him open th' door to sudden death if he wants to !

Barman [*to the Covey*]. Go on, out you go an' do th' bowsey somewhere else. [*He pushes the Covey out and comes back.*

Rosie [*getting Fluther's hat as he is putting on his coat*]. Be God, you put th' fear o' God in his heart that time ! I thought you'd have to be dug out of him. . . . Th' way you lepped out without any of your fancy side-steppin' ! " Men like Fluther," say I to meself, " is gettin' scarce nowadays."

Fluther [*with proud complacency*]. I wasn't goin' to let meself be malignified by a chancer. . . . He got a little bit too derogatory for Fluther. . . . Be God, to think of a cur like that comin' to talk to a man like me !

Rosie [*fixing on his hat*]. Did j'ever !

Fluther. He's lucky he got off safe. I hit a man last week, Rosie, an' he's fallin' yet !

Rosie. Sure, you'd ha' broken him in two if you'd ha' hitten him one clatther !

Fluther [*amorously, putting his arm around Rosie*]. Come on into th' snug, me little darlin', an' we'll have a few dhrinks before I see you home.

Rosie. Oh, Fluther, I'm afraid you're a terrible man for th' women.
  [*They go into the snug as Clitheroe, Captain Brennan, and Lieut. Langon of the Irish Volunteers enter hurriedly. Captain Brennan carries the banner of The Plough and*

the Stars, and Lieut. Langon a green, white, and orange
Tri-colour.   They are in a state of emotional excitement.
Their faces are flushed and their eyes sparkle ;   they
speak rapidly, as if unaware of the meaning of what they
said.   They have been mesmerized by the fervency of the
speeches.

Clitheroe [*almost pantingly*].   Three glasses o' port !
[The Barman brings the drinks.

Capt. Brennan.   We won't have long to wait now.

Lieut. Langon.   Th' time is rotten ripe for revolution.

Clitheroe.   You have a mother, Langon.

Lieut. Langon.   Ireland is greater than a mother.

Capt. Brennan.   You have a wife, Clitheroe.

Clitheroe.   Ireland is greater than a wife.

Lieut. Langon.   Th' time for Ireland's battle is now — th'
place for Ireland's battle is here.
[*The tall, dark figure again is silhouetted against the*
window.   The three men pause and listen.

Voice of the Man.   Our foes are strong, but strong as they
are, they cannot undo the miracles of God, who ripens
in the heart of young men the seeds sown by the young
men of a former generation.   They think they have
pacified Ireland ;   think they have foreseen everything ;
think they have provided against everything ;   but the
fools, the fools, the fools ! — they have left us our
Fenian dead, and, while Ireland holds these graves,
Ireland, unfree, shall never be at peace !

Capt. Brennan [*catching up The Plough and the Stars*].   Im-
prisonment for th' Independence of Ireland !

Lieut. Langon [*catching up the Tri-colour*]. Wounds for th' Independence of Ireland !

Clitheroe. Death for th' Independence of Ireland !

The Three [*together*]. So help us God !

> [*They drink. A bugle blows the Assembly. They hurry out. A pause. Fluther and Rosie come out of the snug ; Rosie is linking Fluther, who is a little drunk. Both are in a merry mood.*

Rosie. Come on home, ower o' that, man. Are you afraid or what ? Are you goin' to come home, or are you not ?

Fluther. Of course I'm goin' home. What ud ail me that I wouldn't go ?

Rosie [*lovingly*]. Come on, then, oul' sport.

Officer's Voice [*giving command outside*]. Irish Volunteers, by th' right, quick march !

Rosie [*putting her arm round Fluther and singing*] :

> I once had a lover, a tailor, but he could do nothin' for me,
> An' then I fell in with a sailor as strong an' as wild as th' sea.
> We cuddled an' kissed with devotion, till th' night from th' mornin' had fled ;
> An' there, to our joy, a bright bouncin' boy
> Was dancin' a jig in th' bed !
>
> Dancin' a jig in th' bed, an' bawlin' for butther an' bread.
> An' there, to our joy, a bright bouncin' boy
> Was dancin' a jig in th' bed !
>
> > [*They go out with their arms round each other.*

Clitheroe's Voice [*in command outside*]. Dublin Battalion of the Irish Citizen Army, by th' right, quick march !

CURTAIN

ACT III

The corner house in a street of tenements : it is the home of the Clitheroes. The house is a long, gaunt, five-story tenement ; its brick front is chipped and scarred with age and neglect. The wide and heavy hall door, flanked by two pillars, has a look of having been charred by a fire in the distant past. The door lurches a little to one side, disjointed by the continual and reckless banging when it is being closed by most of the residents. The diamond-paned fanlight is destitute of a single pane, the frame- work alone remaining. The windows, except the two looking into the front parlour [Clitheroe's room], are grimy, and are draped with fluttering and soiled fragments of lace curtains. The front parlour windows are hung with rich, comparatively, casement cloth. Five stone steps lead from the door to the path on the street. Branching on each side are railings to prevent people from falling into the area. At the left corner of the house runs a narrow lane, bisecting the street, and connecting it with another of the same kind. At the corner of the lane is a street lamp.

As the house is revealed, Mrs. Gogan is seen helping Mollser to a chair, which stands on the path beside the railings, at the left side of the steps. She then wraps a shawl around Mollser's shoulders. It is some months later.

Mrs. Gogan [*arranging shawl around Mollser*]. Th' sun'll do you all th' good in th' world. A few more weeks o' this weather, an' there's no knowin' how well you'll be. . . . Are you comfy, now ?

Mollser [*weakly and wearily*]. Yis, ma ; I'm all right.

Mrs. Gogan. How are you feelin' ?

Mollser. Betther, ma, betther. If th' horrible sinkin' feelin' ud go, I'd be all right.

Mrs. Gogan. Ah, I wouldn't put much pass on that. Your stomach maybe's out of ordher. . . . Is th' poor breathin' any betther, d'ye think ?

Mollser. Yis, yis, ma ; a lot betther.

Mrs. Gogan. Well, that's somethin' anyhow. . . . With th' help o' God, you'll be on th' mend from this out. . . . D'your legs feel any sthronger undher you, d'ye think ?

Mollser [*irritably*]. I can't tell, ma. I think so. . . . A little.

Mrs. Gogan. Well, a little aself is somethin'. . . . I thought I heard you coughin' a little more than usual last night. . . . D'ye think you were ?

Mollser. I wasn't, ma, I wasn't.

Mrs. Gogan. I thought I heard you, for I was kep' awake all night with th' shootin'. An' thinkin' o' that mad-man, Fluther, runnin' about through th' night lookin' for Nora Clitheroe to bring her back when he heard she'd gone to folly her husband, an' in dhread any minute he might come staggerin' in covered with bandages, splashed all over with th' red of his own blood, an' givin' us barely time to bring th' priest to hear th' last whisper of his final confession, as his soul was passin' through th' dark doorway o' death into th' way o' th' wondherin' dead. . . . You don't feel cold, do you ?

Mollser. No, ma ; I'm all right.

Mrs. Gogan. Keep your chest well covered, for that's th'

delicate spot in you . . . if there's any danger, I'll
whip you in again. . . . [*Looking up the street*] Oh,
here's th' Covey an' oul' Pether hurryin' along. God
Almighty, sthrange things is happenin' when them two
is pullin' together.

> [*The Covey and Peter come in, breathless and excited.*

Mrs. Gogan [*to the two men*]. Were yous far up th' town ?
Did yous see any sign o' Fluther or Nora ? How is
things lookin' ? I hear they're blazin' away out o' th'
G.P.O. That th' Tommies is sthretched in heaps
around Nelson's Pillar an' th' Parnell Statue, an' that
th' pavin' sets in O'Connell Street is nearly covered be
pools o' blood.

Peter. We seen no sign o' Nora or Fluther anywhere.

Mrs. Gogan. We should ha' held her back be main force
from goin' to look for her husband. . . . God knows
what's happened to her — I'm always seein' her
sthretched on her back in some hospital, moanin' with
th' pain of a bullet in her vitals, an' nuns thryin' to
get her to take a last look at th' crucifix !

The Covey. We can do nothin'. You can't stick your
nose into O'Connell Street, an' Tyler's is on fire.

Peter. An' we seen th' Lancers——

The Covey [*interrupting*]. Throttin' along, heads in th' air ;
spurs an' sabres jinglin', an' lances quiverin', an'
lookin' as if they were assin' themselves, " Where's
these blighters, till we get a prod at them ? " when
there was a volley from th' Post Office that stretched
half o' them, an' sent th' rest gallopin' away wondherin'
how far they'd have to go before they'd feel safe.

Peter [*rubbing his hands*]. "Damn it," says I to meself, "this looks like business!"

The Covey. An' then out comes General Pearse an' his staff, an', standin' in th' middle o' th' street, he reads th' Proclamation.

Mrs. Gogan. What proclamation?

Peter. Declarin' an Irish Republic.

Mrs. Gogan. Go to God!

Peter. The gunboat *Helga's* shellin' Liberty Hall, an' I hear the people livin' on th' quays had to crawl on their bellies to Mass with th' bullets that were flyin' around from Boland's Mills.

Mrs. Gogan. God bless us, what's goin' to be th' end of it all!

Bessie [*looking out of the top window*]. Maybe yous are satisfied now; maybe yous are satisfied now. Go on an' get guns if yous are men — Johnny get your gun, get your gun, get your gun! Yous are all nicely shanghaied now; th' boyo hasn't a sword on his thigh now! Oh, yous are all nicely shanghaied now!

Mrs. Cogan [*warningly to Peter and the Covey*]. S-s-sh, don't answer her. She's th' right oul' Orange bitch! She's been chantin' "Rule, Britannia" all th' mornin'.

Peter. I hope Fluther hasn't met with any accident, he's such a wild card.

Mrs. Gogan. God grant it; but last night I dreamt I seen gettin' carried into th' house a sthretcher with a figure lyin' on it, stiff an' still, dhressed in th' habit of Saint Francis. An, then, I heard th' murmurs of a crowd no one could see sayin' th' litany for th' dead; an' then it got so dark that nothin' was seen but th' white face of th' corpse, gleamin' like a white wather-lily floatin' on th' top of a dark lake.   Then a tiny whisper thrickled into me ear, sayin', "Isn't the face very like th' face o' Fluther?" an' then, with a thremblin' flutther, th' dead lips opened, an', although I couldn't hear, I knew they were sayin', "Poor oul' Fluther, afther havin' handed in his gun at last, his shakin' soul moored in th' place where th' wicked are at rest an' th' weary cease from throublin'."

Peter [*who has put on a pair of spectacles, and has been looking down the street*]. Here they are, be God, here they are; just afther turnin' th' corner — Nora an' Fluther!

The Covey. She must be wounded or something — he seems to be carryin' her.

    [*Fluther and Nora enter.   Fluther has his arm around her and is half leading, half carrying her in.   Her eyes are dim and hollow, her face pale and strained-looking; her hair is tossed, and her clothes are dusty.*

Mrs. Gogan [*running over to them*]. God bless us, is it wounded y'are, Mrs. Clitheroe, or what?

Fluther. Ah, she's all right, Mrs. Gogan; only worn out from thravellin' an' want o' sleep.   A night's rest, now, an' she'll be as fit as a fiddle.   Bring her in, an' make her lie down.

Mrs. Gogan [*to Nora*]. Did you hear e'er a whisper o' Mr. Clitheroe?

Nora [*wearily*]. I could find him nowhere, Mrs. Gogan. None o' them would tell me where he was.   They told me I shamed my husband an' th' women of Ireland be carryin' on as I was. . . . They said th' women must learn to be brave an' cease to be cowardly. . . . Me who risked more for love than they would risk for hate. . . . [*Raising her voice in hysterical protest*] My Jack will be killed, my Jack will be killed ! . . . He is to be butchered as a sacrifice to th' dead !

Bessie [*from upper window*]. Yous are all nicely shanghaied now ! Sorra mend th' lasses that have been kissin' an' cuddlin' their boys into th' sheddin' of blood ! . . . Fillin' their minds with fairy tales that had no beginnin', but, please God, 'll have a bloody quick endin' ! . . . Turnin' bitther into sweet, an' sweet into bitther. . . . Stabbin' in th' back th' men that are dyin' in th' threnches for them ! It's a bad thing for any one that thries to jilt th' Ten Commandments, for judgements are prepared for scorners an' sthripes for th' back o' fools ! [*Going away from window as she sings :*]

> Rule, Britannia, Britannia rules th' waves,
> Britons never, never, never shall be slaves !

Fluther [*with a roar up at the window*]. Y'ignorant oul' throllope, you !

Mrs. Gogan [*to Nora*]. He'll come home safe enough to you, you'll find, Mrs. Clitheroe ; afther all, there's a power o' women that's handed over sons an' husbands to take a runnin' risk in th' fight they're wagin'.

Nora. I can't help thinkin' every shot fired 'll be fired at Jack, an' every shot fired at Jack 'll be fired at me. What do I care for th' others ? I can think only of me own self. . . . An' there's no woman gives a son or a husband to be killed — if they say it, they're lyin', lyin', against God, Nature, an' against themselves ! . . . One blasted hussy at a barricade told me to go home an' not be thryin' to dishearten th' men. . . .

That I wasn't worthy to bear a son to a man that was out fightin' for freedom. . . . I clawed at her, an' smashed her in th' face till we were separated. . . . I was pushed down th' street, an' I cursed them — cursed the rebel ruffians an' Volunteers that had dhragged me ravin' mad into th' sthreets to seek me husband !

Peter. You'll have to have patience, Nora. We all have to put up with twarthers an' tormentors in this world.

The Covey. If they were fightin' for anything worth while, I wouldn't mind.

Fluther [*to Nora*]. Nothin' derogatory 'll happen to Mr. Clitheroe. You'll find, now, in th' finish up it'll be vice versa.

Nora. Oh, I know that wherever he is, he's thinkin' of wantin' to be with me. I know he's longin' to be passin' his hand through me hair, to be caressin' me neck, to fondle me hand an' to feel me kisses clingin' to his mouth. . . . An' he stands wherever he is because he's brave ? [*Vehemently*] No, but because he's a coward, a coward, a coward !

Mrs. Gogan. Oh, they're not cowards anyway.

Nora [*with denunciatory anger*]. I tell you they're afraid to say they're afraid ! . . . Oh, I saw it, I saw it, Mrs. Gogan. . . . At th' barricade in North King Street I saw fear glowin' in all their eyes. . . . An' in th' middle o' th' sthreet was somethin' huddled up in a horrible tangled heap. . . . His face was jammed again th' stones, an' his arm was twisted round his back. . . . An' every twist of his body was a cry against th' terrible thing that had happened to him. . . . An' I saw they were afraid to look at it. . . .

An' some o' them laughed at me, but th' laugh was a
frightened one. . . . An' some o' them shouted at
me, but th' shout had in it th' shiver o' fear. . . . I
tell you they were afraid, afraid, afraid !

Mrs. Gogan [*leading her towards the house*]. Come on in,
dear. If you'd been a little longer together, th' wrench
asundher wouldn't have been so sharp.

Nora. Th' agony I'm in since he left me has thrust away
every rough thing he done, an' every unkind word he
spoke ; only th' blossoms that grew out of our lives
are before me now ; shakin' their colours before me
face, an' breathin' their sweet scent on every thought
springin' up in me mind, till, sometimes, Mrs. Gogan,
sometimes I think I'm goin' mad !

Mrs. Gogan. You'll be a lot betther when you have a
little lie down.

Nora [*turning towards Fluther as she is going in*]. I don't
know what I'd have done, only for Fluther. I'd have
been lyin' in th' streets, only for him. . . . [*As she
goes in*] They have dhriven away th' little happiness
life had to spare for me. He has gone from me for
ever, for ever. . . . Oh, Jack, Jack, Jack !

> [*She is led in by Mrs. Gogan as Bessie comes out with a
> shawl around her shoulders. She passes by them with
> her head in the air. When they have gone in, she gives
> a mug of milk to Mollser silently.*

Fluther. Which of yous has th' tossers ?

The Covey. I have.

Bessie [*as she is passing them to go down the street*]. You an'
your Leadhers an' their sham-battle soldiers has landed
a body in a nice way, havin' to go an' ferret out a bit

o' bread God knows where. . . . Why aren't yous in th' G.P.O. if yous are men ? It's paler an' paler yous are gettin'. . . . A lot o' vipers, that's what th' Irish people is !   [*She goes out.*

Fluther. Never mind her. . . . [*To the Covey*] Make a start an' keep us from th' sin o' idleness. [*To Mollser*] Well, how are you to-day, Mollser, oul' son ? What are you dhrinkin', milk ?

Mollser. Grand, Fluther, grand, thanks. Yis, milk.

Fluther. You couldn't get a betther thing down you. . . . This turn-up has done one good thing, anyhow ; you can't get dhrink anywhere, an' if it lasts a week, I'll be so used to it that I won't think of a pint.

The Covey [*who has taken from his pocket two worn coins and a thin strip of wood about four inches long*]. What's th' bettin' ?

Peter. Heads, a juice.

Fluther. Harps, a tanner.
[*The Covey places the coins on the strip of wood, and flips them up into the air. As they jingle on the ground the distant boom of a big gun is heard. They stand for a moment listening.*

Fluther. What th' hell's that ?

The Covey. It's like th' boom of a big gun !

Fluther. Surely to God they're not goin' to use artillery on us ?

The Covey [*scornfully*]. Not goin' ! [*Vehemently*] Wouldn't they use anything on us, man ?

Fluther. Aw, holy Christ, that's not playin' th' game !

Peter [*plaintively*]. What would happen if a shell landed here now ?

The Covey [*ironically*]. You'd be off to heaven in a fiery chariot.

Peter. In spite of all th' warnin's that's ringin' around us, are you goin' to start your pickin' at me again ?

Fluther. Go on, toss them again, toss them again. . . . Harps, a tanner.

Peter. Heads, a juice.   [*The Covey tosses the coins.*

Fluther [*as the coins fall*]. Let them roll, let them roll. Heads, be God !
> [*Bessie runs in excitedly. She has a new hat on her head, a fox fur round her neck over her shawl, three umbrellas under her right arm, and a box of biscuits under her left. She speaks rapidly and breathlessly.*

Bessie. They're breakin' into th' shops, they're breakin' into th' shops ! Smashin' th' windows, battherin' in th' doors, an' whippin' away everything ! An' th' Volunteers is firin' on them. I seen two men an' a lassie pushin' a piano down th' sthreet, an' th' sweat rollin' off them thryin' to get it up on th' pavement ; an' an oul' wan that must ha' been seventy lookin' as if she'd dhrop every minute with th' dint o' heart beatin', thryin' to pull a big double bed out of a broken shop-window ! I was goin' to wait till I dhressed meself from th' skin out.

Mollser [*to Bessie, as she is going in*]. Help me in, Bessie ; I'm feelin' curious.
> [*Bessie leaves the looted things in the house, and, rapidly returning, helps Mollser in.*

The Covey. Th' selfishness of that one — she waited till she got all she could carry before she'd come to tell anyone !

Fluther [*running over to the door of the house and shouting in to Bessie*]. Ay, Bessie, did you hear of e'er a pub gettin' a shake up ?

Bessie [*inside*]. I didn't hear o' none.

Fluther [*in a burst of enthusiasm*]. Well, you're goin' to hear of one soon !

The Covey. Come on, man, an' don't be wastin' time.

Peter [*to them as they are about to run off*]. Ay, ay, are you goin' to leave me here ?

Fluther. Are you goin' to leave yourself here ?

Peter [*anxiously*]. Didn't yous hear her sayin' they were firin' on them ?

The Covey and Fluther [*together*]. Well ?

Peter. Supposin' I happened to be potted ?

Fluther. We'd give you a Christian burial, anyhow.

The Covey [*ironically*]. Dhressed up in your regimentals.

Peter [*to the Covey, passionately*]. May th' all-lovin' God give you a hot knock one o' these days, me young Covey, tuthorin' Fluther up now to be tiltin' at me, an' crossin' me with his mockeries an' jibin' !
[*A fashionably dressed, middle-aged, stout woman comes hurriedly in, and makes for the group. She is almost fainting with fear.*

The Woman. For Gawd's sake, will one of you kind men show any safe way for me to get to Wrathmines ? . . .

I was foolish enough to visit a friend, thinking the howl thing was a joke, and now I cawn't get a car or a tram to take me home — isn't it awful ?

Fluther. I'm afraid, ma'am, one way is as safe as another.

Woman. And what am I gowing to do ? Oh, isn't this awful ? . . . I'm so different from others. . . . The mowment I hear a shot, my legs give way under me — I cawn't stir, I'm paralysed — isn't it awful ?

Fluther [*moving away*]. It's a derogatory way to be, right enough, ma'am.

Woman [*catching Fluther's coat*]. Creeping along the street there, with my head down and my eyes half shut, a bullet whizzed past within an inch of my nowse. . . . I had to lean against the wall for a long time, gasping for breath — I nearly passed away — it was awful ! . . . I wonder, would you kind men come some of the way and see me safe ?

Fluther. I have to go away, ma'am, to thry an' save a few things from th' burnin' buildin's.

The Covey. Come on, then, or there won't be anything left to save.   [*The Covey and Fluther hurry away.*

Woman [*to Peter*]. Wasn't it an awful thing for me to leave my friend's house ? Wasn't it an idiotic thing to do ? . . . I haven't the slightest idea where I am. . . . You have a kind face, sir. Could you possibly come and pilot me in the direction of Wrathmines ?

Peter [*indignantly*]. D'ye think I'm goin' to risk me life throttin' in front of you ? An' maybe get a bullet that would gimme a game leg or something that would

leave me a jibe an' a jeer to Fluther an' th' young
Covey for th' rest o' me days !

[*With an indignant toss of his head he walks into the house.*

The Woman [*going out*]. I know I'll fall down in a dead
faint if I hear another shot go off anyway near me —
isn't it awful !

[*Mrs. Gogan comes out of the house pushing a pram before
her. As she enters the street, Bessie rushes out, follows
Mrs. Gogan, and catches hold of the pram, stopping Mrs.
Gogan's progress.*

Bessie. Here, where are you goin' with that ? How
quick you were, me lady, to clap your eyes on th'
pram. . . . Maybe you don't know that Mrs. Sullivan, before she went to spend Easther with her people
in Dunboyne, gave me sthrict injunctions to give an
accasional look to see if it was still standin' where it
was left in th' corner of th' lobby.

Mrs. Gogan. That remark of yours, Mrs. Bessie Burgess,
requires a little considheration, seein' that th' pram
was left on our lobby, an' not on yours ; a foot or two
a little to th' left of th' jamb of me own room door ;
nor is it needful to mention th' name of th' person
that gave a squint to see if it was there th' first thing
in th' mornin', an' th' last thing in th' stillness o' th'
night ; never failin' to realize that her eyes couldn't be
goin' wrong, be sthretchin' out her arm an' runnin'
her hand over th' pram, to make sure that th' sight was
no deception ! Moreover, somethin's tellin' me that
th' runnin' hurry of an inthrest you're takin' in it now
is a sudden ambition to use th' pram for a purpose
that a loyal woman of law an' ordher would stagger
away from !

[*She gives the pram a sudden push that pulls Bessie forward.*

Bessie [*still holding the pram*]. There's not as much as one body in th' house that doesn't know that it wasn't Bessie Burgess that was always shakin' her voice complainin' about people leavin' bassinettes in th' way of them that, week in an' week out, had to pay their rent, an' always had to find a regular accommodation for her own furniture in her own room. . . . An' as for law an' ordher, puttin' aside th' harp an' shamrock, Bessie Burgess 'll have as much respect as she wants for th' lion an' unicorn !

Peter [*appearing at the door*]. I think I'll go with th' pair of yous an' see th' fun. A fella might as well chance it, anyhow.

Mrs. Gogan [*taking no notice of Peter, and pushing the pram on another step*]. Take your rovin' lumps o' hands from pattin' th' bassinette, if you please, ma'am ; an', steppin' from th' threshold of good manners, let me tell you, Mrs. Burgess, that's it's a fat wondher to Jennie Gogan that a lady-like singer o' hymns like yourself would lower her thoughts from sky-thinkin' to sthretch out her arm in a sly-seekin' way to pinch anything dhriven asthray in th' confusion of th' battle our boys is makin' for th' freedom of their counthry !

Peter [*laughing and rubbing his hands together*]. Hee, hee, hee, hee, hee ! I'll go with th' pair o' yous an' give yous a hand.

Mrs. Gogan [*with a rapid turn of her head as she shoves the pram forward*]. Get up in th' prambulator an' we'll wheel you down.

Bessie [*to Mrs. Gogan*]. Poverty an' hardship has sent Bessie Burgess to abide with sthrange company, but she

always knew them she had to live with from backside
to breakfast time ; an' she can tell them, always
havin' had a Christian kinch on her conscience, that a
passion for thievin' an' pinchin' would find her soul a
foreign place to live in, an' that her present intention is
quite th' lofty-hearted one of pickin' up anything
shaken up an' scatthered about in th' loose confusion
of a general plundher !

[By this time they have disappeared from view. Peter is
following, when the boom of a big gun in the distance
brings him to a quick halt.

Peter. God Almighty, that's th' big gun again ! God
forbid any harm would happen to them, but sorra
mind I'd mind if they met with a dhrop in their mad
endeyvours to plundher an' desthroy.

[He looks down the street for a moment, then runs to the
hall door of the house, which is open, and shuts it with a
vicious pull ; he then goes to the chair in which Mollser
had sat, sits down, takes out his pipe, lights it and
begins to smoke with his head carried at a haughty angle.
The Covey comes staggering in with a ten-stone sack of
flour on his back. On the top of the sack is a ham. He
goes over to the door, pushes it with his head, and finds
he can't open it ; he turns slightly in the direction of
Peter.

The Covey [to Peter]. Who shut th' door ? . . . [He kicks
at it] Here, come on an' open it, will you ? This isn't
a mot's hand-bag I've got on me back.

Peter. Now, me young Covey, d'ye think I'm goin' to be
your lackey ?

The Covey [angrily]. Will you open th' door, y'oul'——

Peter [shouting]. Don't be assin' me to open any door,

don't be assin' me to open any door for you. . . .
Makin' a shame an' a sin o' th' cause that good men
are fightin' for. . . . Oh, God forgive th' people that,
instead o' burnishin' th' work th' boys is doin' to-day
with quiet honesty an' patience, is revilin' their
sacrifices with a riot of lootin' an' roguery !

The Covey. Isn't your own eyes leppin' out o' your head
with envy that you haven't th' guts to ketch a few o'
th' things that God is givin' to His chosen people ?
. . . Y'oul' hypocrite, if everyone was blind you'd
steal a cross off an ass's back !

Peter [*very calmly*]. You're not going to make me lose me
temper ; you can go on with your proddin' as long as
you like ; goad an' goad an' goad away ; hee, hee, heee !
I'll not lose me temper.

        [*Somebody opens door and the Covey goes in.*

The Covey [*inside, mockingly*]. Cuckoo-oo !

Peter [*running to the door and shouting in a blaze of passion
as he follows the Covey in*]. You lean, long, lanky lath
of a lowsey bastard. . . . [*Following him in*] Lowsey
bastard, lowsey bastard !

    [*Bessie and Mrs. Gogan enter, the pride of a great joy
illuminating their faces. Bessie is pushing the pram,
which is filled with clothes and boots ; on the top of the
boots and clothes is a fancy table, which Mrs. Gogan is
holding on with her left hand, while with her right hand
she holds a chair on the top of her head. They are heard
talking to each other before they enter.*

Mrs. Gogan [*outside*]. I don't remember ever havin' seen
such lovely pairs as them, [*they appear*] with th' pointed
toes an' th' cuban heels.

Bessie. They'll go grand with th' dhresses we're afther liftin', when we've stitched a sthray bit o' silk to lift th' bodices up a little bit higher, so as to shake th' shame out o' them, an' make them fit for women that hasn't lost themselves in th' nakedness o' th' times.

[*They fussily carry in the chair, the table, and some of the other goods. They return to bring in the rest.*

Peter [*at door, sourly to Mrs. Gogan*]. Ay, you. Mollser looks as if she was goin' to faint, an' your youngster is roarin' in convulsions in her lap.

Mrs. Gogan [*snappily*]. She's never any other way but faintin' !

[*She goes to go in with some things in her arms, when a shot from a rifle rings out. She and Bessie make a bolt for the door, which Peter, in a panic, tries to shut before they have got inside.*

Mrs. Gogan. Ay, ay, ay, you cowardly oul' fool, what are you thryin' to shut th' door on us for ?

[*They retreat tumultuously inside. A pause ; then Captain Brennan comes in supporting Lieutenant Langon, whose arm is around Brennan's neck. Langon's face, which is ghastly white, is momentarily convulsed with spasms of agony. He is in a state of collapse, and Brennan is almost carrying him. After a few moments Clitheroe, pale, and in a state of calm nervousness, follows, looking back in the direction from which he came, a rifle, held at the ready, in his hands.*

Capt. Brennan [*savagely to Clitheroe*]. Why did you fire over their heads ? Why didn't you fire to kill ?

Clitheroe. No, no, Bill ; bad as they are they're Irish men an' women.

Capt. Brennan [*savagely*]. Irish be damned ! Attackin' an'
mobbin' th' men that are riskin' their lives for them.
If these slum lice gather at our heels again, plug one o'
them, or I'll soon shock them with a shot or two
meself !

Lieut. Langon [*moaningly*]. My God, is there ne'er an
ambulance knockin' around anywhere ? . . . Th'
stomach is ripped out o' me ; I feel it — o-o-oh,
Christ !

Capt. Brennan. Keep th' heart up, Jim ; we'll soon get
help, now.
[*Nora rushes wildly out of the house and flings her arms
round the neck of Clitheroe with a fierce and joyous
insistence. Her hair is down, her face is haggard, but
her eyes are agleam with the light of happy relief.*

Nora. Jack, Jack, Jack ; God be thanked . . . be
thanked. . . . He has been kind and merciful to
His poor handmaiden. . . . My Jack, my own Jack,
that I thought was lost is found, that I thought was
dead is alive again ! . . . Oh, God be praised for
ever, evermore ! . . . My poor Jack. . . . Kiss me,
kiss me, Jack, kiss your own Nora !

Clitheroe [*kissing her, and speaking brokenly*]. My Nora ; my
little, beautiful Nora, I wish to God I'd never left
you.

Nora. It doesn't matter — not now, not now, Jack. It
will make us dearer than ever to each other. . . . Kiss
me, kiss me again.

Clitheroe. Now, for God's sake, Nora, don't make a
scene.

Nora. I won't, I won't ; I promise, I promise, Jack ;

honest to God. I'll be silent an' brave to bear th' joy
of feelin' you safe in my arms again. . . . It's hard
to force away th' tears of happiness at th' end of an
awful agony.

Bessie [from the upper window]. Th' Minsthrel Boys aren't
feelin' very comfortable now. Th' big guns has knocked
all th' harps out of their hands.   General Clitheroe 'd
rather be unlacin' his wife's bodice than standin'
at a barricade . . . An' th' professor of chicken-
butcherin' there, finds he's up against somethin' a
little tougher even than his own chickens, an' that's
sayin' a lot !

Capt. Brennan [up to Bessie]. Shut up, y'oul' hag !

Bessie [down to Brennan]. Choke th' chicken, choke th'
chicken, choke th' chicken !

Lieut. Langon. For God's sake, Bill, bring me some place
where me wound 'll be looked afther. . . . Am I to
die before anything is done to save me ?

Capt. Brennan [to Clitheroe]. Come on, Jack. We've got to
get help for Jim, here — have you no thought for his
pain an' danger ?

Bessie. Choke th' chicken, choke th' chicken, choke th'
chicken !

Clitheroe [to Nora]. Loosen me, darling, let me go.

Nora [clinging to him]. No, no, no, I'll not let you go !
Come on, come up to our home, Jack, my sweetheart,
my lover, my husband, an' we'll forget th' last few
terrible days ! . . . I look tired now, but a few hours
of happy rest in your arms will bring back th' bloom

of freshness again, an' you will be glad, you will be
glad, glad . . . glad !

Lieut. Langon. Oh, if I'd kep' down only a little longer,
I mightn't ha' been hit ! Everyone else escapin', an'
me gettin' me belly ripped asundher ! . . . I couldn't
scream, couldn't even scream. . . . D'ye think I'm
really badly wounded, Bill ? Me clothes seem to be
all soakin' wet. . . . It's blood . . . My God, it must
be me own blood !

Capt. Brennan [*to Clitheroe*]. Go on, Jack, bid her good-
bye with another kiss, an' be done with it ! D'ye want
Langon to die in me arms while you're dallyin' with
your Nora ?

Clitheroe [*to Nora*]. I must go, I must go, Nora. I'm sorry
we met at all. . . . It couldn't be helped — all other
ways were blocked be th' British. . . . Let me go,
can't you, Nora ? D'ye want me to be unthrue to me
comrades ?

Nora. No, I won't let you go. . . . I want you to be
thrue to me, Jack. . . . I'm your dearest comrade ;
I'm your thruest comrade. . . . They only want th'
comfort of havin' you in th' same danger as themselves. . . . Oh, Jack, I can't let you go !

Clitheroe. You must, Nora, you must.

Nora. All last night at th' barricades I sought you, Jack.
. . . I didn't think of th' danger — I could only think
of you. . . . I asked for you everywhere. . . . Some
o' them laughed. . . . I was pushed away, but I
shoved back. . . . Some o' them even sthruck me.
. . . an' I screamed an' screamed your name !

Clitheroe [*in fear her action would give him future shame*].

What possessed you to make a show of yourself, like that? . . . What way d'ye think I'll feel when I'm told my wife was bawlin' for me at th' barricades? What are you more than any other woman?

Nora. No more, maybe; but you are more to me than any other man, Jack. . . . I didn't mean any harm, honestly, Jack. . . . I couldn't help it. . . . I shouldn't have told you. . . . My love for you made me mad with terror.

Clitheroe [angrily]. They'll say now that I sent you out th' way I'd have an excuse to bring you home. . . . Are you goin' to turn all th' risks I'm takin' into a laugh?

Lieut. Langon. Let me lie down, let me lie down, Bill; th' pain would be easier, maybe, lyin' down. . . . Oh, God, have mercy on me!

Capt. Brennan [to Langon]. A few steps more, Jim, a few steps more; thry to stick it for a few steps more.

Lieut. Langon. Oh, I can't, I can't, I can't!

Capt. Brennan [to Clitheroe]. Are you comin', man, or are you goin' to make an arrangement for another honeymoon? . . . If you want to act th' renegade, say so, an' we'll be off!

Bessie [from above]. Runnin' from th' Tommies — choke th' chicken. Runnin' from th' Tommies — choke th' chicken!

Clitheroe [savagely to Brennan]. Damn you, man, who wants to act th' renegade? [*To Nora*] Here, let go your hold; let go, I say!

Nora [clinging to Clitheroe, and indicating Brennan]. Look, Jack, look at th' anger in his face; look at th' fear glintin' in his eyes. . . . He himself's afraid, afraid, afraid ! . . . He wants you to go th' way he'll have th' chance of death sthrikin' you an' missin' him ! . . . Turn round an' look at him, Jack, look at him, look at him ! . . . His very soul is cold . . . shiverin' with th' thought of what may happen to him. . . . It is his fear that is thryin' to frighten you from recognizin' th' same fear that is in your own heart !

Clitheroe [struggling to release himself from Nora]. Damn you, woman, will you let me go !

Capt. Brennan [fiercely, to Clitheroe]. Why are you beggin' her to let you go ? Are you afraid of her, or what ? Break her hold on you, man, or go up, an' sit on her lap !   [Clitheroe trying roughly to break her hold.

Nora [imploringly]. Oh, Jack. . . . Jack. . . . Jack !

Lieut. Langon [agonisingly]. Brennan, a priest ; I'm dyin', I think, I'm dyin' !

Clitheroe [to Nora]. If you won't do it quietly, I'll have to make you ! [To Brennan] Here, hold this gun, you, for a minute.   [He hands the gun to Brennan.

Nora [pitifully]. Please, Jack. . . . You're hurting me, Jack. . . . Honestly. . . . Oh, you're hurting . . . me ! . . . I won't, I won't, I won't ! . . . Oh, Jack, I gave you everything you asked of me. . . . Don't fling me from you, now !
    [He roughly loosens her grip, and pushes her away from him.
    Nora sinks to the ground and lies there.

Nora [weakly]. Ah, Jack. . . . Jack. . . . Jack !

Clitheroe [taking the gun back from Brennan]. Come on, come on.

[*They go out. Bessie looks at Nora lying on the street, for a few moments, then, leaving the window, she comes out, runs over to Nora, lifts her up in her arms, and carries her swiftly into the house. A short pause, then down the street is heard a wild, drunken yell ; it comes nearer, and Fluther enters, frenzied, wild-eyed, mad, roaring drunk. In his arms is an earthen half-gallon jar of whisky ; streaming from one of the pockets of his coat is the arm of a new tunic shirt ; on his head is a woman's vivid blue hat with gold lacing, all of which he has looted.*

Fluther [*singing in a frenzy*] :

Fluther's a jolly good fella ! . . . Fluther's a jolly good fella !
Up th' rebels ! . . . That nobody can deny !

[*He beats on the door.*
Get us a mug or a jug, or somethin', some o' yous, one o' yous, will yous, before I lay one o' yous out ! . . . [*Looking down the street*] Bang an' fire away for all Fluther cares. . . . [*Banging at door*] Come down an' open th' door, some of yous, one o' yous, will yous, before I lay some o' yous out ! . . . Th' whole city can topple home to hell, for Fluther !

[*Inside the house is heard a scream from Nora, followed by a moan.*

Fluther [*singing furiously*] :

That nobody can deny, that nobody can deny,
For Fluther's a jolly good fella, Fluther's a jolly good fella,
Fluther's a jolly good fella . . . Up th' rebels !   That nobody can deny !

[*His frantic movements cause him to spill some of the whisky out of the jar.*
Blast you, Fluther, don't be spillin' th' precious liquor ! [*He kicks at the door.*] Ay, give us a mug or a

jug, or somethin', one o' yous, some o' yous, will yous, before I lay one o' yous out !

[*The door suddenly opens, and Bessie, coming out, grips him by the collar.*

Bessie [*indignantly*]. You bowsey, come in ower o' that. . . . I'll thrim your thricks o' dhrunken dancin' for you, an' none of us knowin' how soon we'll bump into a world we were never in before !

Fluther [*as she is pulling him in*]. Ay, th' jar, th' jar, th' jar !

[*A short pause, then again is heard a scream of pain from Nora. The door opens and Mrs. Gogan and Bessie are seen standing at it.*

Bessie. Fluther would go, only he's too dhrunk. . . . Oh, God, isn't it a pity he's so dhrunk ! We'll have to thry to get a docthor somewhere.

Mrs. Gogan. I'd be afraid to go. . . . Besides, Mollser's terrible bad. I don't think you'll get a docthor to come. It's hardly any use goin'.

Bessie [*determinedly*]. I'll risk it. . . . Give her a little of Fluther's whisky. . . . It's th' fright that's brought it on her so soon. . . . Go on back to her, you.

[*Mrs. Gogan goes in, and Bessie softly closes the door. She is moving forward, when the sound of some rifle shots, and the tok, tok, tok of a distant machine-gun bring her to a sudden halt. She hesitates for a moment, then she tightens her shawl round her, as if it were a shield, then she firmly and swiftly goes out.*

Bessie [*as she goes out*]. Oh, God, be Thou my help in time o' throuble. An' shelter me safely in th' shadow of Thy wings !

CURTAIN

ACT IV

*The living-room of Bessie Burgess. It is one of two small attic
rooms [the other, used as a bedroom, is to the Left], the ceiling
slopes up towards the back, giving to the apartment a look of
compressed confinement. In the centre of the ceiling is a small
skylight. There is an unmistakable air of poverty bordering on
destitution. The paper on the walls is torn and soiled, particu-
larly near the fire where the cooking is done, and near the washstand where the washing is done. The fireplace is to the Left.
A small armchair near fire. One small window at Back. A
pane of this window is starred by the entrance of a bullet.
Under the window to the Right is an oak coffin standing on
two kitchen chairs. Near the coffin is a home-manufactured
stool, on which are two lighted candles. Beside the window
is a worn-out dresser on which is a small quantity of delf.
Tattered remains of cheap lace curtains drape the window.
Standing near the window on Left is a brass standard-lamp with
a fancy shade ; hanging on the wall near the same window is a
vividly crimson silk dress, both of which have been looted. A
door on Left leading to the bedroom. Another opposite giving a
way to the rest of the house. To the Left of this door a common
washstand. A tin kettle, very black, and an old saucepan inside
the fender. There is no light in the room but that given from the
two candles and the fire. The dusk has well fallen, and the
glare of the burning buildings in the town can be seen through
the window, in the distant sky. The Covey and Fluther have
been playing cards, sitting on the floor by the light of the candles
on the stool near the coffin. When the curtain rises the Covey
is shuffling the cards, Peter is sitting in a stiff, dignified way*

beside him, and Flalther is kneeling beside the window, cautiously looking out. It is a few days later.

Fluther [*furtively peeping out of the window*]. Give them a good shuffling. . . . Th' sky's gettin' reddher an' reddher. . . . You'd think it was afire. . . . Half o' th' city must be burnin'.

The Covey. If I was you, Fluther, I'd keep away from that window. . . . It's dangerous, an', besides, if they see you, you'll only bring a nose on th' house.

Peter. Yes ; an' he knows we had to leave our own place th' way they were riddlin' it with machine-gun fire. . . . He'll keep on pimpin' an' pimpin' there, till we have to fly out o' this place too.

Fluther [*ironically*]. If they make any attack here, we'll send you out in your green an' glory uniform, shakin' your sword over your head, an' they'll fly before you as th' Danes flew before Brian Boru !

The Covey [*placing the cards on the floor, after shuffling them*]. Come on, an' cut.
        [*Fluther comes over, sits on floor, and cuts the cards.*

The Covey [*having dealt the cards*]. Spuds up again.
        [*Nora moans feebly in room on Left.*

Fluther. There, she's at it again. She's been quiet for a long time, all th' same.

The Covey. She was quiet before, sure, an' she broke out again worse than ever. . . . What was led that time ?

Peter. Thray o' Hearts, Thray o' Hearts, Thray o' Hearts.

Fluther. It's damned hard lines to think of her dead-born kiddie lyin' there in th' arms o' poor little Mollser. Mollser snuffed it sudden too, afther all.

The Covey. Sure she never got any care. How could she get it, an' th' mother out day an' night lookin' for work, an' her consumptive husband leavin' her with a baby to be born before he died !

Voices in a lilting chant to the Left in a distant street. Red Cr . . . oss, Red Cr . . . oss ! . . . Ambu . . . lance, Ambu . . . lance !

The Covey [to Fluther]. Your deal, Fluther.

Fluther [shuffling and dealing the cards]. It'll take a lot out o' Nora — if she'll ever be th' same.

The Covey. Th' docthor thinks she'll never be th' same ; thinks she'll be a little touched here. [*He touches his forehead.*] She's ramblin' a lot ; thinkin' she's out in th' counthry with Jack ; or gettin' his dinner ready for him before he comes home ; or yellin' for her kiddie. All that, though, might be th' chloroform she got. . . . I don't know what we'd have done only for oul' Bessie : up with her for th' past three nights, hand runnin'.

Fluther. I always knew there was never anything really derogatory wrong with poor oul' Bessie. [*To Peter, who is taking a trick*] Ay, houl' on, there, don't be so damn quick — that's my thrick.

Peter. What's your thrick ? It's my thrick, man.

Fluther [loudly]. How is it your thrick ?

Peter [answering as loudly]. Didn't I lead th' deuce !

Fluther. You must be gettin' blind, man ; don't you see th' ace ?

Bessie [*appearing at door of room, Left ; in a tense whisper*].
D'ye want to waken her again on me, when she's just
gone asleep ?   If she wakes will yous come an' mind
her ?   If I hear a whisper out o' one o' yous again, I'll
. . . gut yous !

The Covey [*in a whisper*]. S-s-s-h.   She can hear anything
above a whisper.

Peter [*looking up at the ceiling*]. Th' gentle an' merciful
God 'll give th' pair o' yous a scawldin' an' a scarifyin'
one o' these days !
   [*Fluther takes a bottle of whisky from his pocket, and takes a
   drink.*

The Covey [*to Fluther*]. Why don't you spread that out,
man, an' thry to keep a sup for to-morrow ?

Fluther. Spread it out ?   Keep a sup for to-morrow ?
How th' hell does a fella know there'll be any to-
morrow ?   If I'm goin' to be whipped away, let me be
whipped away when it's empty, an' not when it's half
full !   [*To Bessie, who has seated herself in an armchair at
the fire*] How is she, now, Bessie ?

Bessie. I left her sleeping quietly.   When I'm listenin' to
her babblin', I think she'll never be much betther than
she is.   Her eyes have a hauntin' way of lookin' in
instead of lookin' out, as if her mind had been lost
alive in madly minglin' memories of th' past. . . .
[*Sleepily*] Crushin' her thoughts . . . together . . . in
a fierce . . . an' fanciful . . . [*she nods her head and
starts wakefully*] idea that dead things are livin', an'
livin' things are dead. . . . [*With a start*] Was that
a scream I heard her give ?   [*Reassured*] Blessed God, I
think I hear her screamin' every minute !   An' it's
only there with me that I'm able to keep awake.

The Covey. She'll sleep, maybe, for a long time, now. Ten there.

Fluther. Ten here. If she gets a long sleep, she might be all right. Peter's th' lone five.

The Covey. Whisht! I think I hear somebody movin' below. Whoever it is, he's comin' up.

> *A pause. Then the door opens and Captain Brennan comes into the room. He has changed his uniform for a suit of civvies. His eyes droop with the heaviness of exhaustion; his face is pallid and drawn. His clothes are dusty and stained here and there with mud. He leans heavily on the back of a chair as he stands.*

Capt. Brennan. Mrs. Clitheroe; where's Mrs. Clitheroe? I was told I'd find her here.

Bessie. What d'ye want with Mrs. Clitheroe?

Capt. Brennan. I've a message, a last message for her from her husband.

Bessie. Killed! He's not killed, is he!

Capt. Brennan [*sinking stiffly and painfully on to a chair*]. In th' Imperial Hotel; we fought till th' place was in flames. He was shot through th' arm, an' then through th' lung. . . . I could do nothin' for him — only watch his breath comin' an' goin' in quick, jerky gasps, an' a tiny sthream o' blood thricklin' out of his mouth, down over his lower lip. . . . I said a prayer for th' dyin', an' twined his Rosary beads around his fingers. . . . Then I had to leave him to save meself. . . . [*He shows some holes in his coat*] Look at th' way a machine-gun tore at me coat, as I belted out o' th' buildin' an' darted across th' sthreet for shelter. . . .

An' then, I seen The Plough an' th' Stars fallin' like
a shot as th' roof crashed in, an' where I'd left poor
Jack was nothin' but a leppin' spout o' flame !

Bessie [*with partly repressed vehemence*]. Ay, you left him !
You twined his Rosary beads round his fingers, an'
then you run like a hare to get out o' danger !

Capt. Brennan. I took me chance as well as him. . . .
He took it like a man. His last whisper was to
" Tell Nora to be brave ; that I'm ready to meet my
God, an' that I'm proud to die for Ireland."   An'
when our General heard it he said that " Commandant
Clitheroe's end was a gleam of glory."   Mrs. Clitheroe's
grief will be a joy when she realizes that she has had a
hero for a husband.

Bessie. If you only seen her, you'd know to th' differ.
     [*Nora appears at door, Left. She is clad only in her
     nightdress ; her hair, uncared for some days, is hanging
     in disorder over her shoulders. Her pale face looks paler
     still because of a vivid red spot on the tip of each cheek.
     Her eyes are glimmering with the light of incipient
     insanity ; her hands are nervously fiddling with her
     nightgown. She halts at the door for a moment, looks
     vacantly around the room, and then comes slowly in. The
     rest do not notice her till she speaks.*

Nora [*in a quiet and monotonous tone*]. No . . . Not there,
Jack. . . . I can feel comfortable only in our own
familiar place beneath th' bramble tree. . . . We
must be walking for a long time ; I feel very, very
tired. . . . Have we to go farther, or have we passed
it by ? [*Passing her hand across her eyes*] Curious mist on
my eyes. . . . Why don't you hold my hand, Jack.
. . . [*Excitedly*] No, no, Jack, it's not. Can't you see

it's a goldfinch.   Look at th' black-satiny wings with
th' gold bars, an' th' splash of crimson on its head.
. . . [*Wearily*] Something ails me, something ails
me. . . . Don't kiss me like that ; you take my breath
away, Jack. . . . Why do you frown at me ? . . .
You're going away, and [*frightened*] I can't follow you.
Something's keeping me from moving. . . . [*Crying
out*] Jack, Jack, Jack !

Bessie [*who has gone over and caught Nora's arm*]. Now, Mrs.
Clitheroe, you're a terrible woman to get up out of
bed. . . . You'll get cold if you stay here in them
clothes.

Nora. Cold ?   I'm feelin' very cold ; it's chilly out
here in th' counthry. . . . [*Looking around frightened*]
What place is this ?   Where am I ?

Bessie [*coaxingly*]. You're all right, Nora ; you're with
friends, an' in a safe place.   Don't you know your
uncle an' your cousin, an' poor oul' Fluther ?

Peter [*about to go over to Nora*]. Nora, darlin', now——

Fluther [*pulling him back*]. Now, leave her to Bessie, man.
A crowd 'll only make her worse.

Nora [*thoughtfully*]. There is something I want to remember, an' I can't.   [*With agony*] I can't, I can't, I
can't !   My head, my head !   [*Suddenly breaking from
Bessie, and running over to the men, and gripping Fluther by
the shoulders*] Where is it ?   Where's my baby ?   Tell
me where you've put it, where've you hidden it ?   My
baby, my baby ; I want my baby !   My head, my
poor head. . . . Oh, I can't tell what is wrong with
me.   [*Screaming*] Give him to me, give me my husband !

Bessie. Blessin' o' God on us, isn't this pitiful !

Nora [*struggling with Bessie*]. I won't go away for you ; I won't. Not till you give me back my husband. [*Screaming*] Murderers, that's what yous are ; murderers, murderers !

Bessie. S-s-sh. We'll bring Mr. Clitheroe back to you, if you'll only lie down an' stop quiet. . . . [*Trying to lead her in*] Come on, now, Nora, an' I'll sing something to you.

Nora. I feel as if my life was thryin' to force its way out of my body. . . . I can hardly breathe . . . I'm frightened, I'm frightened, I'm frightened ! For God's sake, don't leave me, Bessie. Hold my hand, put your arms around me !

Fluther [*to Brennan*]. Now you can see th' way she is, man.

Peter. An' what way would she be if she heard Jack had gone west ?

The Covey [*to Peter*]. Shut up, you, man !

Bessie [*to Nora*]. We'll have to be brave, an' let patience clip away th' heaviness of th' slow-movin' hours, rememberin' that sorrow may endure for th' night, but joy cometh in th' mornin'. . . . Come on in, an' I'll sing to you, an' you'll rest quietly.

Nora [*stopping suddenly on her way to the room*]. Jack an' me are goin' out somewhere this evenin'. Where I can't tell. Isn't it curious I can't remember. . . . Maura, Maura, Jack, if th' baby's a girl ; any name you like, if th' baby's a boy ! . . . He's there. [*Screaming*] He's there, an' they won't give him back to me !

Bessie. S-ss-s-h, darlin', s-ssh. I won't sing to you, if you're not quiet.

Nora [*nervously holding Bessie*]. Hold my hand, hold my hand, an' sing to me, sing to me !

Bessie. Come in an' lie down, an' I'll sing to you.

Nora [*vehemently*]. Sing to me, sing to me ; sing, sing !

Bessie [*singing as she leads Nora into room*] :

> Lead, kindly light, amid th' encircling gloom,
> > Lead Thou me on.
> Th' night is dark an' I am far from home,
> > Lead Thou me on.
> Keep Thou my feet, I do not ask to see
> Th' distant scene — one step enough for me.
>
> So long that Thou hast blessed me, sure Thou still
> > Wilt lead me on ;

> > > > > > [*They go in.*

Bessie [*singing in room*] :

> O'er moor an' fen, o'er crag an' torrent, till
> > Th' night is gone.
> An' in th' morn those angel faces smile
> That I have lov'd long since, an' lost awhile !

The Covey [*to Brennan*]. Now that you've seen how bad she is, an' that we daren't tell her what has happened till she's betther, you'd best be slippin' back to where you come from.

Capt. Brennan. There's no chance o' slippin' back now, for th' military are everywhere : a fly couldn't get through. I'd never have got here, only I managed to change me uniform for what I'm wearin'. . . . I'll have to take me chance, an' thry to lie low here for a while.

The Covey [*frightened*]. There's no place here to lie low. Th' Tommies 'll be hoppin' in here, any minute !

Peter [*aghast*]. An' then we'd all be shanghaied !

The Covey. Be God, there's enough afther happenin' to us!

Fluther [*warningly, as he listens*]. Whisht, whisht, th' whole o' yous. I think I heard th' clang of a rifle butt on th' floor of th' hall below. [*All alertness.*] Here, come on with th' cards again. I'll deal.

[*He shuffles and deals the cards to all.*

Fluther. Clubs up. [*To Brennan*] Thry to keep your hands from shakin', man. You lead, Peter. [*As Peter throws out a card*] Four o' Hearts led.

[*The door opens and Corporal Stoddart of the Wiltshires enters in full war kit; steel helmet, rifle and bayonet, and trench tool. He looks round the room. A pause and a palpable silence.*

Fluther [*breaking the silence*]. Two tens an' a five.

Corporal Stoddart. 'Ello. [*Indicating the coffin*] This the stiff?

The Covey. Yis.

Corporal Stoddart. Who's gowing with it? Ownly one allowed to gow with it, you know.

The Covey. I dunno.

Corporal Stoddart. You dunnow?

The Covey. I dunno.

Bessie [*coming into the room*]. She's afther slippin' off to sleep again, thanks be to God. I'm hardly able to keep me own eyes open. [*To the soldier*] Oh, are yous goin' to take away poor little Mollser?

Corporal Stoddart. Ay; 'oo's agowing with 'er?

Bessie. Oh, th' poor mother, o' course. God help her, it's a terrible blow to her !

Fluther. A terrible blow ? Sure, she's in her element now, woman, mixin' earth to earth, an' ashes t'ashes an' dust to dust, an' revellin' in plumes an' hearses, last days an' judgements !

Bessie [*falling into chair by the fire*]. God bless us ! I'm jaded !

Corporal Stoddart. Was she plugged ?

The Covey. Ah, no ; died o' consumption.

Corporal Stoddart. Ow, is that all ? Thought she moight 'ave been plugged.

The Covey. Is that all ? Isn't it enough ? D'ye know, comrade, that more die o' consumption than are killed in th' wars ? An' it's all because of th' system we're livin' undher ?

Corporal Stoddart. Ow, I know. I'm a Sowcialist moiself, but I 'as to do my dooty.

The Covey [*ironically*]. Dooty ! Th' only dooty of a Socialist is th' emancipation of th' workers.

Corporal Stoddart. Ow, a man's a man, an 'e 'as to foight for 'is country, 'asn't 'e ?

Fluther [*aggressively*]. You're not fightin' for your counthry here, are you ?

Peter [*anxiously, to Fluther*]. Ay, ay, Fluther, none o' that, none o' that !

The Covey. Fight for your counthry ! Did y'ever read, comrade, Jenersky's *Thesis on the Origin, Development, an' Consolidation of th' Evolutionary Idea of the Proletariat* ?

Corporal Stoddart. Ow, cheese it, Paddy, cheese it !

Bessie [*sleepily*]. How is things in th' town, Tommy ?

Corporal Stoddart. Ow, I fink it's nearly hover. We've got 'em surrounded, and we're clowsing in on the bloighters. Ow, it was only a little bit of a dawg-foight.
  [*The sharp ping of the sniper's rifle is heard, followed by a squeal of pain.*

Voices to the Left in a chant. Red Cr . . . oss, Red Cr . . . oss ! Ambu . . . lance, Ambu . . . lance !

Corporal Stoddart [*excitedly*]. Christ, that's another of our men 'it by that blawsted sniper ! 'E's knocking abaht 'ere, somewheres. Gawd, when we gets th' bloighter, we'll give 'im the cold steel, we will. We'll jab the belly aht of 'im, we will !
  [*Mrs. Gogan comes in tearfully, and a little proud of the importance of being directly connected with death.*

Mrs. Gogan [*to Fluther*]. I'll never forget what you done for me, Fluther, goin' around at th' risk of your life settlin' everything with th' undhertaker an' th' cemetery people. When all me own were afraid to put their noses out, you plunged like a good one through hummin' bullets, an' they knockin' fire out o' th' road, tinklin' through th' frightened windows, an' splashin' themselves to pieces on th' walls ! An' you'll find, that Mollser, in th' happy place she's gone to, won't forget to whisper, now an' again, th' name o' Fluther.

Corporal Stoddart. Git it aht, mother, git it aht.

Bessie [*from the chair*]. It's excusin' me you'll be, Mrs.

Gogan, for not stannin' up, seein' I'm shaky on me feet for want of a little sleep, an' not desirin' to show any disrespect to poor little Mollser.

Fluther. Sure, we all know, Bessie, that it's vice versa with you.

Mrs. Gogan [*to Bessie*]. Indeed, it's meself that has well chronicled, Mrs. Burgess, all your gentle hurryin's to me little Mollser, when she was alive, bringin' her somethin' to dhrink, or somethin' t'eat, an' never passin' her without liftin' up her heart with a delicate word o' kindness.

Corporal Stoddart [*impatiently, but kindly*]. Git it aht, git it aht, mother.
[*The Covey, Fluther, Brennan, and Peter carry out the coffin, followed by Mrs. Gogan.*

Corporal Stoddart [*to Bessie, who is almost asleep*]. 'Ow many men is in this 'ere 'ouse ? [*No answer. Loudly*] 'Ow many men is in this 'ere 'ouse ?

Bessie [*waking with a start*]. God, I was nearly asleep ! . . . How many men ? Didn't you see them ?

Corporal Stoddart. Are they all that are in the 'ouse ?

Bessie. Oh, there's none higher up, but there may be more lower down. Why ?

Corporal Stoddart. All men in the district 'as to be rounded up. Somebody's giving 'elp to the snipers, and we 'as to take precautions. If I 'ad my woy, I'd make 'em all join hup, and do their bit ! But I suppowse they and you are all Shinners.

Bessie [*who has been sinking into sleep, waking up to a sleepy vehemence*]. Bessie Burgess is no Shinner, an' never had no thruck with anything spotted be th' fingers o' th' Fenians ; but always made it her business to harness herself for Church whenever she knew that God Save the King was goin' to be sung at t'end of th' service ; whose only son went to th' front in th' first contingent of the Dublin Fusiliers, an' that's on his way home carryin' a shatthered arm that he got fightin' for his King an' counthry !

> [*Her head sinks slowly forward again. Peter comes into the room ; his body is stiffened and his face is wearing a comically indignant look. He walks to and fro at the back of the room, evidently repressing a violent desire to speak angrily. He is followed in by Fluther, the Covey, and Brennan, who slinks into an obscure corner of the room, nervous of notice.*

Fluther [*after an embarrassing pause*]. Th' air in th' sthreet outside's shakin' with the firin' o' rifles an' machine-guns. It must be a hot shop in th' middle o' th' scrap.

Corporal Stoddart. We're pumping lead in on 'em from every side, now ; they'll soon be shoving up th' white flag.

Peter [*with a shout*]. I'm tellin' you either o' yous two lowsers 'ud make a betther hearse-man than Peter ; proddin' an' pokin' at me an' I helpin' to carry out a corpse !

Fluther. It wasn't a very derogatory thing for th' Covey to say that you'd make a fancy hearse-man, was it ?

Peter [*furiously*]. A pair o' redjesthered bowseys pondherin' from mornin' till night on how they'll get a chance to break a gap through th' quiet nature of a man that's always endeavourin' to chase out of him any sthray thought of venom against his fella-man !

The Covey. Oh, shut it, shut it, shut it !

Peter. As long as I'm a livin' man, responsible for me thoughts, words, an' deeds to th' Man above, I'll feel meself instituted to fight again' th' sliddherin' ways of a pair o' picaroons, whisperin', concurrin', concoctin', an' conspirin' together to rendher me unconscious of th' life I'm thryin' to live !

Corporal Stoddart [*dumbfounded*]. What's wrong, Daddy ; wot 'ave they done to you ?

Peter [*savagely to the Corporal*]. You mind your own business! What's it got to do with you, what's wrong with me ?

Bessie [*in a sleepy murmur*]. Will yous thry to conthrol yourselves into quietness ? Yous'll waken her . . . up . . . on . . . me . . . again.   [*She sleeps.*

Fluther. Come on, boys, to th' cards again, an' never mind him.

Corporal Stoddart. No use of you gowing to start cawds ; you'll be gowing out of 'ere, soon as Sergeant comes.

Fluther. Goin' out o' here ? An' why're we goin' out o' here ?

Corporal Stoddart. All men in district to be rounded up, and 'eld in till the scrap is hover.

Fluther. An' where're we goin' to be held in ?

Corporal Stoddart. They're puttin 'em in a church.

The Covey. A church?

Fluther. What sort of a church? Is it a Protestan' Church?

Corporal Stoddart. I dunnow ; I suppowse so.

Fluther [*dismayed*]. Be God, it'll be a nice thing to be stuck all night in a Protestan' Church !

Corporal Stoddart. Bring the cawds ; you moight get a chance of a goime.

Fluther. Ah, no, that wouldn't do. . . . I wondher? [*After a moment's thought*] Ah, I don't think we'd be doin' anything derogatory be playin' cards in a Protestan' Church.

Corporal Stoddart. If I was you I'd bring a little snack with me ; you moight be glad of it before the mawning. [*Sings*] :

> I do loike a snoice mince poy,
> I do loike a snoice mince poy !

[*The snap of the sniper's rifle rings out again, followed simultaneously by a scream of pain. Corporal Stoddart goes pale, and brings his rifle to the ready, listening.*

Voices chanting to the Right. Red Cro . . . ss, Red Cro . . . ss ! Ambu . . . lance, Ambu . . . lance !
[*Sergeant Tinley comes rapidly in, pale, agitated, and fiercely angry.*

Corporal Stoddart [*to Sergeant*]. One of hour men 'it, Sergeant ?

Sergeant Tinley. Private Taylor ; got 'it roight through the chest, 'e did ; an 'ole in front of 'im as 'ow you could put your fist through, and 'arf 'is back blown

awoy ! Dum-dum bullets they're using. Gang of
Hassassins potting at us from behind roofs. That's
not playing the goime : why down't they come into
the owpen and foight fair !

Fluther [*unable to stand the slight*]. Fight fair ! A few
hundhred scrawls o' chaps with a couple o' guns an'
Rosary beads, again' a hundhred thousand thrained
men with horse, fut, an' artillery . . . an' he wants us
to fight fair ! [*To Sergeant*] D'ye want us to come out
in our skins an' throw stones ?

Sergeant Tinley [*to Corporal*]. Are these four all that are
'ere ?

Corporal Stoddart. Four ; that's all, Sergeant.

Sergeant Tinley [*vindictively*]. Come on, then ; get the
blighters aht. [*To the men*] 'Ere, 'op it aht ! Aht
into the streets with you, and if a snoiper sends another
of our men west, you gow with 'im ! [*He catches
Fluther by the shoulder*] Gow on, git aht !

Fluther. Eh, who are you chuckin', eh ?

Sergeant Tinley [*roughly*]. Gow on, git aht, you blighter.

Fluther. Who are you callin' a blighter to, eh ? I'm a
Dublin man, born an' bred in th' city, see ?

Sergeant Tinley. I down't care if you were Broin Buroo ;
git aht, git aht.

Fluther [*halting as he is going out*]. Jasus, you an' your guns !
Leave them down, an' I'd beat th' two o' yous without
sweatin' !
  [*Peter, Brennan, the Covey, and Fluther, followed by the
  soldiers, go out. Bessie is sleeping heavily on the chair by*

*the fire. After a pause, Nora appears at door, Left, in
her nightdress. Remaining at door for a few moments
she looks vaguely around the room. She then comes in
quietly, goes over to the fire, pokes it, and puts the kettle
on. She thinks for a few moments, pressing her hand to
her forehead. She looks questioningly at the fire, and then
at the press at back. She goes to the press, opens it, takes
out a soiled cloth and spreads it on the table. She then
places things for tea on the table.*

Nora. I imagine th' room looks very odd somehow. . . . I
was nearly forgetting Jack's tea. . . . Ah, I think I'll
have everything done before he gets in. . . . [*She lilts
gently, as she arranges the table.*]

> Th' violets were scenting th' woods, Nora,
>   Displaying their charms to th' bee,
> When I first said I lov'd only you, Nora,
>   An' you said you lov'd only me.

> Th' chestnut blooms gleam'd through th' glade,
>   Nora,
>   A robin sang loud from a tree,
> When I first said I lov'd only you, Nora,
>   An' you said you lov'd only me.

> [*She pauses suddenly, and glances round the room.*

Nora [*doubtfully*]. I can't help feelin' this room very
strange. . . . What is it ? . . . What is it ? . . . I
must think. . . . I must thry to remember. . . .

Voices chanting in a distant street. Ambu . . . lance,
Ambu . . . lance ! Red Cro . . . ss, Red Cro . . . ss !

Nora [*startled and listening for a moment, then resuming the
arrangement of the table*] :

Trees, birds, an' bees sang a song, Nora,
Of happier transports to be,
When I first said I lov'd only you, Nora,
An' you said you lov'd only me.

[*A burst of rifle fire is heard in a street near by, followed
by the rapid rok, tok, tok of a machine-gun.*

Nora [*staring in front of her and screaming*]. Jack, Jack,
Jack ! My baby, my baby, my baby !

Bessie [*waking with a start*]. You divil, are you afther
gettin' out o' bed again !
[*She rises and runs towards Nora, who rushes to the
window, which she frantically opens.*

Nora [*at window, screaming*]. Jack, Jack, for God's sake,
come to me !

Soldiers [*outside, shouting*]. Git away, git away from that
window, there !

Bessie [*seizing hold of Nora*]. Come away, come away,
woman, from that window !

Nora [*struggling with Bessie*]. Where is it ; where have you
hidden it ? Oh, Jack, Jack, where are you ?

Bessie [*imploringly*]. Mrs. Clitheroe, for God's sake, come
away !

Nora [*fiercely*]. I won't ; he's below. Let . . . me . . .
go ! You're thryin' to keep me from me husband.
I'll follow him. Jack, Jack, come to your Nora !

Bessie. Hus-s-sh, Nora, Nora ! He'll be here in a
minute. I'll bring him to you, if you'll only be quiet
— honest to God, I will.
[*With a great effort Bessie pushes Nora away from the*

window, the force used causing her to stagger against it herself. Two rifle shots ring out in quick succession. Bessie jerks her body convulsively ; stands stiffly for a moment, a look of agonized astonishment on her face, then she staggers forward, leaning heavily on the table with her hands.

Bessie [*with an arrested scream of fear and pain*]. Merciful God, I'm shot, I'm shot, I'm shot ! . . . Th' life's pourin' out o' me ! [*To Nora*] I've got this through . . . through you . . . through you, you bitch, you ! . . . O God, have mercy on me ! . . . [*To Nora*] You wouldn't stop quiet, no, you wouldn't, you wouldn't, blast you ! Look at what I'm afther gettin', look at what I'm afther gettin' . . . I'm bleedin' to death, an' no one's here to stop th' flowin' blood ! [*Calling*] Mrs. Gogan, Mrs. Gogan ! Fluther, Fluther, for God's sake, somebody, a doctor, a doctor !
    [*She staggers frightened towards the door, to seek for aid, but, weakening half-way across the room, she sinks to her knees, and bending forward, supports herself with her hands resting on the floor. Nora is standing rigidly with her back to the wall opposite, her trembling hands held out a little from the sides of her body, her lips quivering, her breast heaving, staring wildly at the figure of Bessie.*

Nora [*in a breathless whisper*]. Jack, I'm frightened. . . . I'm frightened, Jack. . . . Oh, Jack, where are you ?

Bessie [*moaningly*]. This is what's afther comin' on me for nursin' you day an' night. . . . I was a fool, a fool, a fool ! Get me a dhrink o' wather, you jade, will you ? There's a fire burnin' in me blood ! [*Pleadingly*] Nora, Nora, dear, for God's sake, run out an' get Mrs. Gogan, or Fluther, or somebody to bring a doctor, quick, quick, quick ! [*As Nora does not stir*] Blast you, stir yourself, before I'm gone !

Nora. Oh, Jack, Jack, where are you ?

Bessie [*in a whispered moan*]. Jesus Christ, me sight's goin' ! It's all dark, dark ! Nora, hold me hand !
   [*Bessie's body lists over and she sinks into a prostrate position on the floor.*

Bessie. I'm dyin', I'm dyin' . . . I feel it. . . . Oh God, oh God ! [*She feebly sings*]

> I do believe, I will believe
>   That Jesus died for me ;
> That on th' cross He shed His blood,
>   From sin to set me free. . . .
>
> I do believe . . . I will believe
>   . . . Jesus died . . . me ;
> . . . th' cross He shed . . . blood,
>   From sin . . . free.

   [*She ceases singing, and lies stretched out, still and very rigid. A pause. Then Mrs. Gogan runs hastily in.*

Mrs. Gogan [*quivering with fright*]. Blessed be God, what's afther happenin' ? [*To Nora*] What's wrong, child, what's wrong ? [*She sees Bessie, runs to her and bends over the body*] Bessie, Bessie ! [*She shakes the body*] Mrs. Burgess, Mrs. Burgess ! [*She feels Bessie's forehead*] My God, she's as cold as death. They're afther murdherin' th' poor inoffensive woman !
   [*Sergeant Tinley and Corporal Stoddart enter agitatedly, their rifles at the ready.*

Sergeant Tinley [*excitedly*]. This is the 'ouse. That's the window !

Nora [*pressing back against the wall*]. Hide it, hide it; cover it up, cover it up!

Sergeant Tinley [*going over to the body*]. 'Ere, what's this? Who's this? [*Looking at Bessie*] Oh Gawd, we've plugged one of the women of the 'ouse.

Corporal Stoddart. Whoy the 'ell did she gow to the window? Is she dead?

Sergeant Tinley. Oh, dead as bedamned. Well, we couldn't afford to toike any chawnces.

Nora [*screaming*]. Hide it, hide it; don't let me see it! Take me away, take me away, Mrs. Gogan!
    [*Mrs. Gogan runs into room, Left, and runs out again with a sheet which she spreads over the body of Bessie.*

Mrs. Gogan [*as she spreads the sheet*]. Oh, God help her, th' poor woman, she's stiffenin' out as hard as she can! Her face has written on it th' shock o' sudden agony, an' her hands is whitenin' into th' smooth shininess of wax.

Nora [*whimperingly*]. Take me away, take me away; don't leave me here to be lookin' an' lookin' at it!

Mrs. Gogan [*going over to Nora and putting her arm around her*]. Come on with me, dear, an' you can doss in poor Mollser's bed, till we gather some neighbours to come an' give th' last friendly touches to Bessie in th' lonely layin' of her out.
    [*Mrs. Gogan and Nora go slowly out.*

Corporal Stoddart [*who has been looking around, to Sergeant Tinley*]. Tea here, Sergeant. Wot abaht a cup of scald?

Sergeant Tinley. Pour it aht, Stoddart, pour it aht. I could scoff hanything just now.

> [*Corporal Stoddart pours out two cups of tea, and the two soldiers begin to drink. In the distance is heard a bitter burst of rifle and machine-gun fire, interspersed with the boom, boom of artillery. The glare in the sky seen through the window flares into a fuller and a deeper red.*

Sergeant Tinley. There gows the general attack on the Powst Office.

Voices in a distant street. Ambu . . . lance, Ambu . . . lance ! Red Cro . . . ss, Red Cro . . . ss !

> [*The voices of soldiers at a barricade outside the house are heard singing :*

> They were summoned from the 'illside,
> They were called in from the glen,
> And the country found 'em ready
> At the stirring call for men.
> Let not tears add to their 'ardship,
> As the soldiers pass along,
> And although our 'eart is breaking,
> Make it sing this cheery song.

Sergeant Tinley and Corporal Stoddart [*joining in the chorus, as they sip the tea*] :

> Keep the 'owme fires burning,
> While your 'earts are yearning ;
> Though your lads are far away
> They dream of 'owme ;
> There's a silver loining
> Through the dark cloud shoining,
> Turn the dark cloud inside out,
> Till the boys come 'owme !

CURTAIN

A Tragi-comedy in Four Acts

The Silver Tassie

To Eileen
with the yellow daffodils
in the green vase

CHARACTERS IN THE PLAY
(As they appear)

SYLVESTER HEEGAN
MRS. HEEGAN, *his wife*
SIMON NORTON
SUSIE MONICAN
MRS. FORAN
TEDDY FORAN, *her husband*
HARRY HEEGAN, D.C.M., *Heegan's son*
JESSIE TAITE
BARNEY BAGNAL
THE CROUCHER
1ST SOLDIER
2ND SOLDIER
3RD SOLDIER
4TH SOLDIER
THE CORPORAL
THE VISITOR
THE STAFF-WALLAH
1ST STRETCHER-BEARER
2ND STRETCHER-BEARER
1ST CASUALTY
2ND CASUALTY
SURGEON FORBY MAXWELL
THE SISTER OF THE WARD

————

ACT I.—Room in Heegan's home.
ACT II.—Somewhere in France (*later on*).
ACT III.—Ward in a Hospital (*a little later on*).
ACT IV.—Room in Premises of Avondale Football Club
(*later on still*).

ACT I

*The eating, sitting, and part sleeping room of the Heegan family.
A large window at back looks on to a quay, from which can be
seen the centre mast of a steamer, at the top of which gleams a white
light. Another window at right looks down on a side street.
Under the window at back, plumb in the centre, is a stand, the
legs gilded silver and the top gilded gold ; on the stand is a
purple velvet shield on which are pinned a number of silver
medals surrounding a few gold ones. On each side of the shield
is a small vase holding a bunch of artificial flowers. The shield is
draped with red and yellow ribbons. To the left of the stand
is a bed covered with a bedspread of black striped with vivid
green. To the right of the stand is a dresser and chest of drawers
combined. The fireplace is to the left. Beside the fireplace is a
door leading to a bedroom, another door which gives access to the
rest of the house and the street, on the right. At the corner left is
a red coloured stand resembling an easel, having on it a silver-
gilt framed picture photograph of Harry Heegan in football
dress, crimson jersey with yellow collar and cuffs and a broad
yellow belt, black stockings, and yellow football boots. A table
on which are a half-pint bottle of whisky, a large parcel of bread
and meat sandwiches, and some copies of English illustrated
magazines.*

*Sylvester Heegan and Simon Norton are sitting by the fire.
Sylvester Heegan is a stockily built man of sixty-five ; he has
been a docker all his life since first the muscles of his arms could
safely grip a truck, and even at sixty-five the steel in them is only
beginning to stiffen.*

*Simon Norton is a tall man, originally a docker too, but by a
little additional steadiness, a minor effort towards self-education,*

a natural, but very slight superior nimbleness of mind, has risen in the Company's estimation and has been given the position of checker, a job entailing as many hours of work as a docker, almost as much danger, twice as much responsibility, and a corresponding reduction in his earning powers. He is not so warmly, but a little more circumspectly dressed than Sylvester, and in his manner of conduct and speech there is a hesitant suggestion of greater refinement than in those of Sylvester, and a still more vague indication that he is aware of it. This timid semi-conscious sense of superiority, which Simon sometimes forgets, is shown frequently by a complacent stroking of a dark beard which years are beginning to humiliate. The night is cold, and Simon and Sylvester occasionally stretch longingly towards the fire. They are fully dressed and each has his topcoat and hat beside him, as if ready to go out at a moment's notice. Susie Monican is standing at the table polishing a Lee-Enfield rifle with a chamois cloth ; the butt of the rifle is resting on the table. She is a girl of twenty-two, well-shaped limbs, challenging breasts, all of which are defiantly hidden by a rather long dark blue skirt and bodice buttoning up to the throat, relieved by a crimson scarf around her neck, knotted in front and falling down her bosom like a man's tie. She is undeniably pretty, but her charms are almost completely hidden by her sombre, ill-fitting dress, and the rigid manner in which she has made her hair up declares her unflinching and uncompromising modesty. Just now she is standing motionless, listening intently, looking towards the door on right.

Mrs. Heegan is standing at the window at right, listening too, one hand pulling back the curtain, but her attention, taken from the window, is attracted to the door. She is older than Sylvester, stiffened with age and rheumatism ; the end of her life is unknowingly lumbering towards a rest : the impetus necessity has given to continual toil and striving is beginning to slow down, and everything she has to do is done with a quiet

*mechanical persistence.   Her inner ear cannot hear even a faint
echo of a younger day.   Neither Sylvester nor Simon has noticed
the attentive attitude of Mrs. Heegan or Susie, for Sylvester,
with one arm outstretched crooked at the elbow, is talking with
subdued intensity to Simon.*

Sylvester. I seen him do it, mind you.   I seen him do it.

Simon. I quite believe you, Sylvester.

Sylvester. Break a chain across his bisseps !   [*With pantomime action*] Fixes it over his arm . . . bends it up
. . . a little strain . . . snaps in two . . . right
across his bisseps !

Susie. Shush you, there !
     [*Mrs. Heegan goes out with troubled steps by door.   The
     rest remain still for a few moments.*

Sylvester. A false alarm.

Simon. No cause for undue anxiety ;   there's plenty of
time yet.

Susie [*chanting as she resumes the polishing of rifle*] :
     Man walketh in a vain shadow, and disquieteth him-
          self in vain :
     He heapeth up riches, and cannot tell who shall
          gather them.
     [*She sends the chant in the direction of Sylvester and Simon,
     Susie coming close to the two men and sticking an angry
     face in between them.*

Susie. When the two of yous stand quiverin' together on
the dhread day of the Last Judgement, how will the two
of yous feel if yous have nothin' to say but " he broke
a chain across his bisseps " ?   Then the two of you'll

know that the wicked go down into hell, an' all the people who forget God !

[*She listens a moment, and leaving down the rifle, goes out by door left.*

Sylvester. It's persecutin', that tambourine theology of Susie's. I always get a curious, sickenin' feelin', Simon, when I hear the Name of the Supreme Bein' tossed into the quietness of a sensible conversation.

Simon. The day he won the Cross Country Championship of County Dublin, Syl, was a day to be chronicled.

Sylvester. In a minor way, yes, Simon. But the day that caps the chronicle was the one when he punched the fear of God into the heart of Police Constable 63 C under the stars of a frosty night on the way home from Terenure.

Simon. Without any exaggeration, without any exaggeration, mind you, Sylvester, that could be called a memorable experience.

Sylvester. I can see him yet [*he gets up, slides from side to side, dodging and parrying imaginary blows*] glidin' round the dazzled Bobby, cross-ey'd tryin' to watch him.

Simon [*tapping his pipe resolutely on the hob*]. Unperturbed, mind you, all the time.

Sylvester. An' the hedges by the road-side standin' stiff in the silent cold of the air, the frost beads on the branches glistenin' like toss'd-down diamonds from the breasts of the stars, the quietness of the night stimulated to a fuller stillness by the mockin' breathin' of Harry, an' the heavy, ragin' pantin' of the Bobby, an' the quickenin' beats of our own hearts afraid, of hopin' too little or hopin' too much.

[*During the last speech by Sylvester, Susie has come in with a bayonet, and has commenced to polish it.*

Susie. We don't go down on our knees often enough ; that's why we're not able to stand up to the Evil One : we don't go down on our knees enough. . . . I can hear some persons fallin' with a splash of sparks into the lake of everlastin' fire. . . . An account of every idle word shall be given at the last day.

[*She goes out again with rifle.*

Susie [*bending towards Simon and Sylvester as she goes*]. God is listenin' to yous ; God is listenin' to yous !

Sylvester. Dtch, dtch, dtch. People ought to be forcibly restrained from constantly cannonadin' you with the name of the Deity.

Simon. Dubiety never brush'd a thought into my mind, Syl, while I was waitin' for the moment when Harry would stretch the Bobby hors dee combaa on the ground.

Sylvester [*resuming his pantomime actions*]. There he was staggerin', beatin' out blindly, every spark of energy panted out of him, while Harry feinted, dodg'd, side-stepp'd, then suddenly sail'd in an' put him asleep with . . .

Simon. A right-handed hook to the jaw !⎫
Sylvester. A left-handed hook to the jaw !⎭ [*together*].

Sylvester [*after a pause*]. A left-handed hook to the jaw, Simon.

Simon. No, no, Syl, a right-handed hook to the jaw.

[*Mrs. Foran runs quickly in by the door with a frying-pan in her hand, on which is a steak. She comes to the fire,*

pushing, so as to disturb the two men. She is one of the
many gay, careworn women of the working-class.

Mrs. Foran [*rapidly*]. A pot of clothes is boilin' on the fire
above, an' I knew yous wouldn't mind me slappin' a
bit of a steak on here for a second to show him, when
he comes in before he goes away, that we're mindful of
his needs, an' I'm hopeful of a dream to-night that
the sea's between us, not lookin' very haggard in the
mornin' to find the dream a true one. [*With satisfied
anticipation*]
    For I'll be single again, yes, I'll be single again ;
    An' I eats what I likes, . . . an' I drinks what I
    likes,
    An' I likes what I likes, when I'm——
[*Stopping suddenly*] What's the silence for ?

Sylvester [*slowly and decidedly*]. I was at the fight, Simon,
an' I seen him givin' a left-handed hook to the jaw.

Mrs. Foran. What fight ?

Simon [*slowly and decidedly*]. I was there too, an' I saw him
down the Bobby with a right-handed hook to the jaw.

Mrs. Foran. What Bobby ?   [*A pause.*

Sylvester. It was a close up, an' I don't know who'd know
better if it wasn't the boy's own father.

Mrs. Foran. What boy . . . what father ?

Sylvester. Oh, shut up, woman, an' don't be smotherin'
us with a shower of questions.

Susie [*who has entered on the last speech, and has started to
polish a soldier's steel helmet*]. Oh, the miserableness of
them that don't know the things that belong unto
their peace.   They try one thing after another, they try

everything, but they never think of trying God. [*Coming nearer to them.*] Oh, the happiness of knowing that God's hand has pick'd you out for heaven. [*To Mrs. Foran*] What's the honey-pot kiss of a lover to the kiss of righteousness and peace ?

[*Mrs. Foran, embarrassed, goes over to window.*

Susie [*turning to Simon*]. Simon, will you not close the dandy door of the public-house and let the angels open the pearly gates of heaven for you ?

Sylvester. We feel very comfortable where we are, Susie.

Susie. Don't mock, Sylvester, don't mock. You'd run before a great wind, tremble in an earthquake, and flee from a fire ; so don't treat lightly the still, small voice calling you to repentance and faith.

Sylvester [*with appeal and irritation*]. Oh, do give over worryin' a man, Susie.

Susie. God shows His love by worrying, and worrying, and worrying the sinner. The day will come when you will call on the mountains to cover you, and then you'll weep and gnash your teeth that you did not hearken to Susie's warning. [*Putting her hands appealingly on his shoulders*] Sylvester, if you pray long enough, and hard enough, and deep enough, you'll get the power to fight and conquer Beelzebub.

Mrs. Foran. I'll be in a doxological mood to-night, not because the kingdom of heaven 'll be near me, but because my husband 'll be far away, and to-morrow [*singing*] :

I'll be single again, yes, single again ;
An' I goes where I likes, an' I does what I likes,
An' I likes what I likes now I'm single again !

Simon. Go on getting Harry's things ready, Susie, and defer the dosing of your friends with canticles till the time is ripe with rest for them to listen quietly.

[*Simon and Sylvester are very self-conscious during Susie's talk to them. Simon empties his pipe by tapping the head on the hob of the grate. He then blows through it. As he is blowing through it, Sylvester is emptying his by tapping it on the hob ; as he is blowing it Simon taps his again ; as Simon taps Sylvester taps with him, and then they look into the heads of the pipes and blow together.*

Susie. It must be mercy or it must be judgement : if not mercy to-day it may be judgement to-morrow. He is never tired of waiting and waiting and waiting ; and watching and watching and watching ; and knocking and knocking and knocking for the sinner — you, Sylvester, and you, Simon — to turn from his wickedness and live. Oh, if the two of you only knew what it was to live ! Not to live leg-staggering an' belly-creeping among the pain-spotted and sin-splashed desires of the flesh ; but to live, oh, to live swift-flying from a holy peace to a holy strength, and from holy strength to a holy joy, like the flashing flights of a swallow in the deep beauty of a summer sky.

[*Simon and Sylvester shift about, self-conscious and uneasy.*

Susie [*placing her hand first on Simon's shoulder and then on Sylvester's*]. The two of you God's elegant swallows ; a saved pair ; a loving pair strong-wing'd, freed from the gin of the snarer, tip of wing to tip of wing, flying fast or darting swift together to the kingdom of heaven.

Simon [*expressing a protecting thought to Sylvester*]. One of the two of us should go out and hunt back the old woman from the perishing cold of watching for the return of Harry.

Sylvester. She'll be as cold as a naked corpse, an' unstinted watchin' won't bring Harry back a minute sooner. I'll go an' drive her back. [*He rises to go*] I'll be back in a minute, Susie.

Simon [*hurriedly*]. Don't bother, Syl, I'll go ; she won't be farther than the corner of the street ; you go on toasting yourself where you are. [*He rises*] I'll be back in a minute, Susie.

Mrs. Foran [*running to the door*]. Rest easy the two of you, an' I'll go, so as to give Susie full time to take the sin out of your bones an' put you both in first-class form for the kingdom of heaven.   [*She goes out.*

Susie. Sinners that jeer often add to the glory of God : going out, she gives you, Sylvester, and you, Simon, another few moments, precious moments — oh, how precious, for once gone, they are gone for ever — to listen to the warning from heaven.

Simon [*suddenly*]. Whisht, here's somebody coming, I think ?

Sylvester. I'll back this is Harry comin' at last.
     [*A pause as the three listen.*

Sylvester. No, it's nobody.

Simon. Whoever it was 's gone by.

Susie. Oh, Syl, oh, Simon, don't try to veil the face of God with an evasion. You can't, you can't cod God. This may be your last chance before the pains of hell encompass the two of you. Hope is passing by ;

salvation is passing by, and glory arm-in-arm with her. In the quietness left to you go down on your knees and pray that they come into your hearts and abide with you for ever. . . . [*With fervour, placing her left hand on Simon's shoulder and her right hand on Sylvester's, and shaking them*] Get down on your knees, get down on your knees, get down on your knees and pray for conviction of sin, lest your portion in David become as the portion of the Canaanites, the Amorites, the Perizzites and the Jebusites !

Sylvester. Eh, eh, Susie ; cautious now — you seem to be forgettin' yourself.

Simon. Desist, Susie, desist. Violence won't gather people to God. It only ingenders hostility to what you're trying to do.

Sylvester. You can't batter religion into a man like that.

Simon. Religion is love, but that sort of thing is simply a nullification of religion.

Susie. Bitterness and wrath in exhortation is the only hope of rousing the pair of yous into a sense of coming and everlasting penalties.

Sylvester. Well, give it a miss, give it a miss to me now. Don't try to claw me into the kingdom of heaven. An' you only succeed in distempering piety when you try to mangle it into a man's emotions.

Simon. Heaven is all the better, Susie, for being a long way off.

Sylvester. If I want to pray I do it voluntarily, but I'm not going to be goaded an' goaded into it.

Susie. I go away in a few days to help to nurse the

wounded, an' God's merciful warnings may depart along with me, then sin'll usher the two of you into Gehenna for all eternity. Oh, if the two of you could only grasp the meaning of the word eternity! [*Bending down and looking up into their faces*] Time that had no beginning and never can have an end — an' there you'll be — two cockatrices creeping together, a desolation, an astonishment, a curse and a hissing from everlasting to everlasting.   [*She goes into room.*

Sylvester. Cheerful, what! Cockatrices — be-God, that's a good one, Simon!

Simon. Always a trying thing to have to listen to one that's trying to push the kingdom of God into a reservation of a few yards.

Sylvester. A cockatrice! Now where did she manage to pick up that term of approbation, I wonder?

Simon. From the Bible. An animal somewhere mentioned in the Bible, I think, that a serpent hatched out of a cock's egg.

Sylvester. A cock's egg! It couldn't have been the egg of an ordinary cock. Not the male of what we call a hen?

Simon. I think so.

Sylvester. Well, be-God, that's a good one! You know Susie'll have to be told to disintensify her soul-huntin', for religion even isn't an excuse for saying that a man'll become a cockatrice.

Simon. In a church, somehow or other, it seems natural enough, and even in the street it's all right, for one thing is as good as another in the wide-open ear of the air, but in the delicate quietness of your own home it, it——

Sylvester. Jars on you !

Simon. Exactly !

Sylvester. If she'd only confine her glory-to-God business to the festivals, Christmas, now, or even Easter, Simon, it would be recommendable ; for a few days before Christmas, like the quiet raisin' of a curtain, an' a few days after, like the gentle lowerin' of one, there's nothing more . . . more——

Simon. Appropriate. . . .

Sylvester. Exhilaratin' than the singin' of the Adestay Fidellis.

Simon. She's damned pretty, an' if she dressed herself justly, she'd lift some man's heart up, an' toss down many another.   It's a mystery now, what affliction causes the disablement, for most women of that kind are plain, an' when a woman's born plain she's born good.   I wonder what caused the peculiar bend in Susie's nature ?   Narrow your imagination to the limit and you couldn't call it an avocation.

Sylvester [*giving the head of his pipe a sharp, quick blow on the palm of his hand to clear it*]. Adoration.

Simon. What ?

Sylvester. Adoration, Simon, accordin' to the flesh. . . . She fancied Harry and Harry fancied Jessie, so she hides her rage an' loss in the love of a scorchin' Gospel.

Simon. Strange, strange.

Sylvester. Oh, very curious, Simon.

Simon. It's a problem, I suppose.

Sylvester. An inconsolable problem, Simon.
[*Mrs. Foran enters by door, helping in Mrs. Heegan, who is
pale and shivering with cold.*

Mrs. Heegan [*shivering and shuddering*]. U-u-uh, I feel the
stream of blood that's still trickling through me old
veins icifyin' fast ; u-uh.

Mrs. Foran. Madwoman, dear, to be waitin' out there on
the quay an' a wind risin' as cold as a stepmother's
breath, piercin' through your old bones, mockin' any
effort a body would make to keep warm, an' [*suddenly
rushing over to the fireplace in an agony of dismay, scattering
Simon and Sylvester, and whipping the frying-pan off the
fire*] — The steak, the steak ; I forgot the blasted
steak an' onions fryin' on the fire ! God Almighty,
there's not as much as a bead of juice left in either of
them. The scent of the burnin' would penetrate to
the street, an' not one of you'd stir a hand to lift them
out of danger. Oh, look at the condition they're in.
Even the gospel-gunner couldn't do a little target
practice by helpin' the necessity of a neighbour. [*As
she goes out*] I can hear the love for your neighbours
almost fizzlin' in your hearts.

Mrs. Heegan [*pushing in to the fire, to Simon and Sylvester*].
Push to the right and push to the left till I get to the
fosterin' fire. Time eatin' his heart out, an' no sign of
him yet. The two of them, the two of my legs is
numb . . . an' the wind's risin' that'll make the sea
heave an' sink under the boat to-night, under shaded
lights an' the submarines about. [*Susie comes in, goes
over to window, and looks out.*] Hours ago the football
match must have been over, an' no word of him yet,

an' all drinkin' if they won, an' all drinkin' if they
lost ; with Jessie hitchin' on after him, an' no one
thinkin' of me an' the maintenance money.

Sylvester. He'll come back in time ; he'll have to come
back ; he must come back.

Simon. He got the goals, Mrs. Heegan, that won the
last two finals, and it's only fair he'd want to win this,
which'll mean that the Cup won before two——

Sylvester [*butting in*]. Times hand runnin'.

Simon. Two times consecutively before, makin' the Cup
the property of the Club.

Sylvester. Exactly !

Mrs. Heegan. The chill's residin' in my bones, an' feelin's
left me just the strength to shiver. He's overstayed
his leave a lot, an' if he misses now the tide that's
waitin', he skulks behind desertion from the colours.

Susie. On Active Service that means death at dawn.

Mrs. Heegan. An' my governmental money grant would
stop at once.

Susie. That would gratify Miss Jessie Taite, because you
put her weddin' off with Harry till after the duration
of the war, an' cut her out of the allowance.

Sylvester [*with a sickened look at Simon*]. Dtch, dtch, dtch,
the way the women wag the worst things out of
happenings ! [*To the women*] My God Almighty, he'll
be back in time an' fill yous all with disappointment.

Mrs. Heegan. She's coinin' money workin' at munitions,
an' doesn't need to eye the little that we get from

Harry ; for one evening hurryin' with him to the pictures she left her bag behind, an' goin' through it what would you think I found ?

Susie. A saucy book, now, or a naughty picture ?

Mrs. Heegan. Lion and Unicorn standin' on their Jew ay mon draw. With all the rings an' dates, an' rules an' regulations.

Simon. What was it, Mrs. Heegan ?

Mrs. Heegan. Spaced an' lined ; signed an' signatured ; nestlin' in a blue envelope to keep it warm.

Sylvester [*testily*]. Oh, sing it out, woman, an' don't be takin' the value out of what you're goin' to tell us.

Mrs. Heegan. A Post Office Savings Bank Book.

Sylvester. Oh, hairy enough, eh ?

Simon. How much, Mrs. Heegan ?

Mrs. Heegan. Pounds an' shillings with the pence missin' ; backed by secrecy, an' security guaranteed by Act of Parliament.

Sylvester [*impatiently*]. Dtch, dtch. Yes, yes, woman, but how much was it ?

Mrs. Heegan. Two hundred an' nineteen pounds, sixteen shillings, an' no pence.

Sylvester. Be-God, a nice little nest-egg, right enough !

Susie. I hope in my heart that she came by it honestly, and that she remembers that it's as true now as when it was first spoken that it's harder for a camel to go through the eye of a needle than for a rich person to enter the kingdom of heaven.

Simon. And she hidin' it all under a veil of silence, when there wasn't the slightest fear of any of us bein' jealous of her.

> [*A tumult is heard on the floor over their heads, followed by a crash of breaking delf. They are startled, and listen attentively.*

Mrs. Heegan [*breaking the silence*]. Oh, there he's at it again. An' she sayin' that he was a pattern husband since he came home on leave, merry-making with her an' singin' dolorously the first thing every mornin'. I was thinkin' there'd be a rough house sometime over her lookin' so well after his long absence . . . you'd imagine now, the trenches would have given him some idea of the sacredness of life !

> [*Another crash of breaking delfware.*

Mrs. Heegan. An' the last week of his leave she was too fond of breakin' into song in front of him.

Sylvester. Well, she's gettin' it now for goin' round heavin' her happiness in the poor man's face.

> [*A crash, followed by screams from Mrs. Foran.*

Susie. I hope he won't be running down here as he often does.

Simon [*a little agitated*]. I couldn't stay here an' listen to that ; I'll go up and stop him : he might be killing the poor woman.

Mrs. Heegan. Don't do anything of the kind, Simon ; he might down you with a hatchet or something.

Simon. Phuh, I'll keep him off with the left and hook him with the right. [*Putting on his hat and coat as he goes to the door.*] Looking prim and careless 'll astonish him.   Monstrous to stay here, while he may be killing the woman.

Mrs. Heegan [*to Simon as he goes out*]. For God's sake mind yourself, Simon.

Sylvester [*standing beside closed door on right with his ear close to one of the panels, listening intently*]. Simon's a tidy little man with his fists, an' would make Teddy Foran feel giddy if he got home with his left hook. [*Crash.*] I wonder is that Simon knockin' down Foran, or Foran knockin' down Simon?

Mrs. Heegan. If he came down an' we had the light low, an' kept quiet, he might think we were all out.

Sylvester. Shush.   I can hear nothin' now.   Simon must have awed him.   Quiet little man, but when Simon gets goin'.   Shush?   No, nothin' . . . Something unusual has happened.   O, oh, be-God!
   [*The door against which Sylvester is leaning bursts suddenly in.   Sylvester is flung headlong to the floor, and Mrs. Foran, her hair falling wildly over her shoulders, a cut over her eye, frantic with fear, rushes in and scrambles in a frenzy of haste under the bed.   Mrs. Heegan, quickened by fear, runs like a good one, followed by Susie, into the room, the door of which they bang after them.   Sylvester hurriedly fights his way under the bed with Mrs. Foran.*

Mrs. Foran [*speaking excitedly and jerkily as she climbs under the bed*]. Flung his dinner into the fire — and started to smash the little things in the room.   Tryin' to save the dresser, I got a box in the eye.   I locked the door on him as I rushed out, an' before I was half-way down, he had one of the panels flyin' out with — a hatchet!

Sylvester [*under the bed — out of breath*]. Whythehell

didn'tyou sing out beforeyousent thedoor flyin' inontop o' me !

Mrs. Foran. How could I an' I flyin' before danger to me — life ?

Sylvester. Yes, an'you'vegot meinto a nice extremity now !

Mrs. Foran. An' I yelled to Simon Norton when he had me — down, but the boyo only ran the faster out of the — house !

Sylvester. Oh, an' the regal-like way he went out to fight ! Oh, I'm findin' out that everyone who wears a cocked hat isn't a Napoleon !

[Teddy Foran, Mrs. Foran's husband, *enters by door, with a large, fancy, vividly yellow-coloured bowl, ornamented with crimson roses, in one hand and a hatchet in the other. He is big and powerful, rough and hardy. A man who would be dominant in a public-house, and whose opinions would be listened to with great respect. He is dressed in the khaki uniform of a soldier home on leave.*

Teddy. Under the bed, eh ? Right place for a guilty conscience. I should have thrown you out of the window with the dinner you put before me. Out with you from under there, an' come up with your husband.

Susie [*opening suddenly door right, putting in her head, pulling it back and shutting door again*]. God is looking at you, God is looking at you !

Mrs. Foran. I'll not budge an inch from where I am.

Teddy [*looking under the bed and seeing Sylvester*]. What are you doin' there encouragin' her against her husband ?

Sylvester. You've no right to be rippin' open the poor woman's life of peace with violence.

Teddy [*with indignation*]. She's my wife, isn't she ?

Mrs. Foran. Nice thing if I lose the sight of my eye with the cut you gave me !

Teddy. She's my wife, isn't she ? An' you've no legal right to be harbourin' her here, keepin' her from her household duties. Stunned I was when I seen her lookin' so well after me long absence. Blowin' her sighin' in me face all day, an' she sufferin' the tortures of hell for fear I'd miss the boat !

Sylvester. Go on up to your own home ; you've no right to be violatin' this place.

Teddy. You'd like to make her your cheery amee, would you ? It's napoo, there, napoo, you little pip-squeak. I seen you an' her goin' down the street arm-in-arm.

Sylvester. Did you expect to see me goin' down the street leg-in-leg with her ?

Teddy. Thinkin' of her Ring-papers instead of her husband. [*To Mrs. Foran*] I'll teach you to be rippling with joy an' your husband goin' away ! [*He shows the bowl.*] Your weddin' bowl, look at it ; pretty, isn't it ? Take your last eyeful of it now, for it's goin' west quick !

Susie [*popping her head in again*]. God is watching you, God is watching you !

Mrs. Foran [*appealingly*]. Teddy, Teddy, don't smash the poor weddin' bowl.

Teddy [*smashing the bowl with a blow of the hatchet*]. It would be a pity, wouldn't it ? Damn it, an' damn you. I'm off now to smash anything I missed, so that you'll have

a gay time fittin' up the little home again by the time
your loving husband comes back.   You can come an'
have a look, an' bring your mon amee if you like.

[*He goes out, and there is a pause as Mrs. Foran and
Sylvester peep anxiously towards the door.*

Sylvester. Cautious, now cautious ; he might be lurking
outside that door there, ready to spring on you the
minute you show'd your nose !

Mrs. Foran. Me lovely little weddin' bowl, me lovely
little weddin' bowl !

[*Teddy is heard breaking things in the room above.*

Sylvester [*creeping out from under the bed*]. Oh, he is gone
up.   He was a little cow'd, I think, when he saw me.

Mrs. Foran. Me little weddin' bowl, wrapp'd in tissue
paper, an' only taken out for a few hours every
Christmas — me poor little weddin' bowl.

Susie [*popping her head in*]. God is watching — oh, he's
gone !

Sylvester [*jubilant*]. Vanished !   He was a little cow'd, I
think, when he saw me.

[*Mrs. Heegan and Susie come into the room.*

Mrs. Foran. He's makin' a hash of every little thing we
have in the house, Mrs. Heegan.

Mrs. Heegan. Go inside to the room, Mrs. Foran, an' if
he comes down again, we'll say you ran out to the
street.

Mrs. Foran [*going into room*]. My poor little weddin' bowl
that I might have had for generations !

Susie [*who has been looking out of the window, excitedly*].

They're comin', they're comin' : a crowd with a concertina ; some of them carrying Harry on their
shoulders, an' others are carrying that Jessie Taite too,
holding a silver cup in her hands. Oh, look at the
shameful way she's showing her legs to all who like
to have a look at them !

Mrs. Heegan. Never mind Jessie's legs — what we have to
do is to hurry him out in time to catch the boat.

   [*The sound of a concertina playing in the street outside has
   been heard, and the noise of a marching crowd. The
   crowd stop at the house. Shouts are heard — " Up the
   Avondales ! " ; " Up Harry Heegan and the Avondales ! " Then steps are heard coming up the stairs,
   and first Simon Norton enters, holding the door cere-
   moniously wide open to allow Harry to enter, with his
   arm around Jessie, who is carrying a silver cup joyously,
   rather than reverentially, elevated, as a priest would
   elevate a chalice. Harry is wearing khaki trousers, a
   military cap stained with trench mud, a vivid orange-
   coloured jersey with black collar and cuffs. He is twenty-
   three years of age, tall, with the sinewy muscles of a
   manual worker made flexible by athletic sport. He is a
   typical young worker, enthusiastic, very often boisterous,
   sensible by instinct rather than by reason. He has gone
   to the trenches as unthinkingly as he would go to the
   polling booth. He isn't naturally stupid ; it is the
   stupidity of persons in high places that has stupefied him.
   He has given all to his masters, strong heart, sound lungs,
   healthy stomach, lusty limbs, and the little mind that
   education has permitted to develop sufficiently to make all
   the rest a little more useful. He is excited now with the
   sweet and innocent insanity of a fine achievement, and the
   rapid lowering of a few drinks.*

[*Jessie is twenty-two or so, responsive to all the animal impulses of life.   Ever dancing around, in and between the world, the flesh, and the devil.   She would be happy climbing with a boy among the heather on Howth Hill, and could play ball with young men on the swards of the Phoenix Park.   She gives her favour to the prominent and popular.   Harry is her favourite : his strength and speed have won the Final for his club, he wears the ribbon of the D.C.M.   It is a time of spiritual and animal exaltation for her.*

[*Barney Bagnal, a soldier mate of Harry's, stands a little shyly near the door, with a pleasant, good-humoured grin on his rather broad face.   He is the same age as Harry, just as strong, but not so quick, less finely formed, and not so sensitive ; able to take most things quietly, but savage and wild when he becomes enraged.   He is fully dressed, with topcoat buttoned on him, and he carries Harry's on his arm.*

Harry [*joyous and excited*]. Won, won, won, be-God ; by the odd goal in five.   Lift it up, lift it up, Jessie, sign of youth, sign of strength, sign of victory !

Mrs. Heegan [*to Sylvester*]. I knew, now, Harry would come back in time to catch the boat.

Harry [*to Jessie*]. Leave it here, leave it down here, Jessie, under the picture, the picture of the boy that won the final.

Mrs. Heegan. A parcel of sandwiches, a bottle of whisky, an' some magazines to take away with you an' Barney, Harry.

Harry. Napoo sandwiches, an' napoo magazines : look at the cup, eh ?   The cup that Harry won, won by the

odd goal in five ! [*To Barney*] The song that the little
Jock used to sing, Barney, what was it ? The little
Jock we left shrivellin' on the wire after the last push.

Barney. " Will ye no come back again ? "

Harry. No, no, the one we all used to sing with him,
" The Silver Tassie ". [*Pointing to cup*] There it is,
the Silver Tassie, won by the odd goal in five, kicked
by Harry Heegan.

Mrs. Heegan. Watch your time, Harry, watch your time.

Jessie. He's watching it, he's watching it — for God's
sake don't get fussy, Mrs. Heegan.

Harry. They couldn't take their beatin' like men. . . .
Play the game, play the game, why the hell couldn't
they play the game ? [*To Barney*] See the President
of the Club, Dr. Forby Maxwell, shaking hands with
me, when he was giving me the cup, " Well done,
Heegan ! " The way they yell'd and jump'd when
they put in the equalizing goal in the first half !

Barney. Ay, a fluke, that's what it was ; a lowsey fluke.

Mrs. Heegan [*holding Harry's coat up for him to put it on*].
Here, your coat, Harry, slip it on while you're talkin'.

Harry [*putting it on*]. All right, keep smiling, don't fuss.
[*To the rest*] Grousing the whole time they were chas-
ing the ball ; an' when they lost it, " Referee, referee,
offside, referee . . . foul there ; ey, open your eyes,
referee ! "

Jessie. And we scream'd and shouted them down with
" Play the game, Primrose Rovers, play the game ! "

Barney. You ran them off their feet till they nearly stood
still.

Mrs. Foran [*has been peeping twice in timidly from the room and now comes in to the rest*]. Somebody run up an' bring Teddy down for fear he'd be left behind.

Sylvester [*to Harry*]. Your haversack an' trench tools, Harry ; haversack first, isn't it ?

Harry [*fixing his haversack*]. Haversack, haversack, don't rush me. [*To the rest*] But when I got the ball, Barney, once I got the ball, the rain began to fall on the others. An' the last goal, the goal that put us one ahead, the winning goal, that was a-a-eh-a stunner !

Barney. A beauty, me boy, a hot beauty.

Harry. Slipping by the back rushing at me like a mad bull, steadying a moment for a drive, seeing in a flash the goalie's hands sent with a shock to his chest by the force of the shot, his half-stunned motion to clear, a charge, and then carrying him, the ball and all with a rush into the centre of the net !

Barney [*enthusiastically*]. Be-God, I did get a thrill when I seen you puttin' him sittin' on his arse in the middle of the net !

Mrs. Foran [*from the door*]. One of yous do go up an' see if Teddy's ready to go.

Mrs. Heegan [*to Harry*]. Your father 'll carry your kit-bag, an' Jessie 'll carry your rifle as far as the boat.

Harry [*irritably*]. Oh, damn it, woman, give your wailin' over for a minute !

Mrs. Heegan. You've got only a few bare minutes to spare, Harry.

Harry. We'll make the most of them, then. [*To Barney*]

Out with one of them wine-virgins we got in " The Mill in the Field ", Barney, and we'll rape her in a last hot moment before we set out to kiss the guns !

[*Simon has gone into room and returned with a gun and a kit-bag. He crosses to where Barney is standing.*

Barney [*taking a bottle of wine from his pocket*]. Empty her of her virtues, eh ?

Harry. Spill it out, Barney, spill it out. . . . [*Seizing Silver Cup, and holding it towards Barney*] Here, into the cup, be-God. A drink out of the cup, out of the Silver Tassie !

Barney [*who has removed the cap and taken out the cork*]. Here she is now. . . . Ready for anything, stripp'd to the skin !

Jessie. No double-meaning talk, Barney.

Susie [*haughtily, to Jessie*]. The men that are defending us have leave to bow themselves down in the House of Rimmon, for the men that go with the guns are going with God.

[*Barney pours wine into the cup for Harry and into a glass for himself.*

Harry [*to Jessie*]. Jessie, a sup for you. [*She drinks from the cup.*] An' a drink for me. [*He drinks.*] Now a kiss while our lips are wet. [*He kisses her.*] Christ, Barney, how would you like to be retreating from the fairest face and [*lifting Jessie's skirt a little*] — and the trimmest, slimmest little leg in the parish ? Napoo, Barney, to everyone but me !

Mrs. Foran. One of you go up, an' try to get my Teddy down.

Barney [lifting Susie's skirt a little]. Napoo, Harry, to everyone but——

Susie [angrily, pushing Barney away from her]. You khaki-
cover'd ape, you, what are you trying to do? Man-
handle the lassies of France, if you like, but put on
your gloves when you touch a woman that seeketh not
the things of the flesh.

Harry [putting an arm round Susie to mollify her]. Now,
Susie, Susie, lengthen your temper for a passing
moment, so that we may bring away with us the breath
of a kiss to the shell-bullied air of the trenches. . . .
Besides, there's nothing to be ashamed of — it's not a
bad little leggie at all.

*Susie [slipping her arm round Harry's neck, and looking
defiantly at Barney].* I don't mind what Harry does; I
know he means no harm, not like other people. Harry's
different.

Jessie. You'll not forget to send me the German helmet
home from France, Harry?

Susie [trying to rest her head on Harry's breast]. I know
Harry, he's different. It's his way. I wouldn't let
anyone else touch me, but in some way or another I can
tell Harry's different.

*Jessie [putting her arm round Harry under Susie's in an effort
to dislodge it].* Susie, Harry wants to be free to keep his
arm round me during his last few moments here, so
don't be pulling him about!

Susie [shrinking back a little]. I was only saying that Harry
was different.

Mrs. Foran. For God's sake, will someone go up for Teddy, or he won't go back at all !

Teddy [*appearing at door*]. Damn anxious for Teddy to go back ! Well, Teddy's goin' back, an' he's left everything tidy upstairs so that you'll not have much trouble sortin' things out. [*To Harry*] The Club an' a crowd's waitin' outside to bring us to the boat before they go to the spread in honour of the final. [*Bitterly*] A party for them while we muck off to the trenches !

Harry [*after a slight pause, to Barney*]. Are you game, Barney ?

Barney. What for ?

Harry. To go to the spread and hang the latch for another night ?

Barney [*taking his rifle from Simon and slinging it over his shoulder*]. No, no, napoo desertin' on Active Service. Deprivation of pay an' the rest of your time in the front trenches. No, no. We must go back !

Mrs. Heegan. No, no, Harry. You must go back.

Simon,
Sylvester, }[*together*]. You must go back.
and Susie

Voices of crowd outside. They must go back !
                 [*The ship's siren is heard blowing.*

Simon. The warning signal.

Sylvester. By the time they get there, they'll be unslinging the gangways !

Susie [*handing Harry his steel helmet*]. Here's your helmet, Harry.   [*He puts it on.*

Mrs. Heegan. You'll all nearly have to run for it now !

Sylvester. I've got your kit-bag, Harry.

Susie. I've got your rifle.

Simon. I'll march in front with the cup, after Conroy with the concertina.

Teddy. Come on : ong avong to the trenches !

Harry [*recklessly*]. Jesus, a last drink, then ! [*He raises the Silver Cup, singing*] :
> Gae bring to me a pint of wine,
> And fill it in a silver tassie ;

Barney [*joining in vigorously*] :
> . . . . a silver tassie.

Harry :
> That I may drink before I go,
> A service to my bonnie lassie.

Barney :
> . . . . bonnie lassie.

Harry :
> The boat rocks at the pier o' Leith,
> Full loud the wind blows from the ferry ;
> The ship rides at the Berwick Law,
> An' I must leave my bonnie Mary !

Barney :
> . . . . . . leave my bonnie Mary !

Harry :
> The trumpets sound, the banners fly,
> The glittering spears are ranked ready ;

Barney :
> . . . glittering spears are ranked ready ;

Harry :

> The shouts of war are heard afar,
> The battle closes thick and bloody.

Barney :

> . . . . . . closes thick and bloody.

Harry :

> It's not the roar of sea or shore,
> That makes me longer wish to tarry,
> Nor shouts of war that's heard afar —
> It's leaving thee, my bonnie lassie !

Barney :

> . . leaving thee, my bonnie lassie !

Teddy. Come on, come on.

> *[Simon, Sylvester, and Susie go out.*

Voices outside :

> Come on from your home to the boat ;
> Carry on from the boat to the camp.
> *[Teddy and Barney go out. Harry and Jessie follow ; as
> Harry reaches the door, he takes his arm from round Jessie
> and comes back to Mrs. Heegan.*

Voices outside. From the camp up the line to the trenches.

Harry [shyly and hurriedly kissing Mrs. Heegan]. Well, good-bye, old woman.

Mrs. Heegan. Good-bye, my son.

> *[Harry goes out. The chorus of " The Silver Tassie ",
> accompanied by a concertina, can be heard growing fainter
> till it ceases. Mrs. Foran goes out timidly. Mrs. Heegan
> pokes the fire, arranges the things in the room, and then
> goes to the window and looks out. After a pause, the loud*

and long blast of the ship's siren is heard. The light on the masthead, seen through the window, moves slowly away, and Mrs. Heegan with a sigh, " Ah dear ", goes over to the fire and sits down. A slight pause, then Mrs. Foran returns to the room.

Mrs. Foran. Every little bit of china I had in the house is lyin' above in a mad an' muddled heap like the flotsum an' jetsum of the seashore !

Mrs. Heegan [*with a deep sigh of satisfaction*]. Thanks be to Christ that we're after managin' to get the three of them away safely.

ACT II

In the war zone : a scene of jagged and lacerated ruin of what was once a monastery. At back a lost wall and window are indicated by an arched piece of broken coping pointing from the left to the right, and a similar piece of masonry pointing from the right to the left. Between these two lacerated fingers of stone can be seen the country stretching to the horizon where the front trenches are. Here and there heaps of rubbish mark where houses once stood. From some of these, lean, dead hands are protruding. Further on, spiky stumps of trees which were once a small wood. The ground is dotted with rayed and shattered shell-holes. Across the horizon in the red glare can be seen the criss-cross pattern of the barbed wire bordering the trenches. In the sky sometimes a green star, sometimes a white star, burns. Within the broken archway to the left is an arched entrance to another part of the monastery, used now as a Red Cross Station. In the wall, right, near the front is a stained-glass window, background green, figure of the Virgin, white-faced, wearing a black robe, lights inside making the figure vividly apparent. Further up from this window is a life-size crucifix. A shell has released an arm from the cross, which has caused the upper part of the figure to lean forward with the released arm outstretched towards the figure of the Virgin. Underneath the crucifix on a pedestal, in red letters, are the words : PRINCEPS PACIS. *Almost opposite the crucifix is a gunwheel to which Barney is tied. At the back, in the centre, where the span of the arch should be, is the shape of a big howitzer gun, squat, heavy underpart, with a long, sinister barrel now pointing towards the front at an angle of forty-five degrees. At the base of the gun a piece of wood is placed on which is chalked,* HYDE PARK CORNER. *On another piece of wood*

near the entrance of the Red Cross Station is chalked, NO
HAWKERS OR STREET CRIES PERMITTED HERE. *In the
near centre is a brazier in which a fire is burning. Crouching
above, on a ramp, is a soldier whose clothes are covered with mud
and splashed with blood. Every feature of the scene seems a little
distorted from its original appearance. Rain is falling steadily ;
its fall worried now and again by fitful gusts of a cold wind. A
small organ is heard playing slow and stately notes as the curtain
rises.*

*After a pause, the Croucher, without moving, intones
dreamily :*

Croucher. And the hand of the Lord was upon me, and
     carried me out in the spirit of the Lord, and set
     me down in the midst of a valley.
     And I looked and saw a great multitude that stood
     upon their feet, an exceeding great army.
     And he said unto me, Son of man, can this exceeding
     great army become a valley of dry bones ?
     [*The music ceases, and a voice, in the part of the monastery
     left standing, intones :* Kyr . . . ie . . . e . . . eleison.
     Kyr . . . ie . . . e . . . eleison, *followed by the answer :*
     Christe . . . eleison.

Croucher [*resuming*]. And I answered, O Lord God, thou
     knowest. And he said, prophesy and say unto
     the wind, come from the four winds a breath and
     breathe upon these living that they may die.
     [*As he pauses the voice in the monastery is heard again :*
     Gloria in excelsis Deo et in terra pax hominibus
     bonae voluntatis.

Croucher [*resuming*]. And I prophesied, and the breath
     came out of them, and the sinews came away from
     them, and behold a shaking, and their bones fell

asunder, bone from his bone, and they died, and the exceeding great army became a valley of dry bones.

[*The voice from the monastery is heard, clearly for the first half of the sentence, then dying away towards the end :* Accendat in nobis Dominus ignem sui amoris, et flammam aeternae caritatis.

[*A group of soldiers come in from fatigue, bunched together as if for comfort and warmth. They are wet and cold, and they are sullen-faced. They form a circle around the brazier and stretch their hands towards the blaze.*

1st Soldier. Cold and wet and tir'd.

2nd Soldier. Wet and tir'd and cold.

3rd Soldier. Tir'd and cold and wet.

4th Soldier [*very like Teddy*]. Twelve blasted hours of ammunition transport fatigue !

1st Soldier. Twelve weary hours.

2nd Soldier. And wasting hours.

3rd Soldier. And hot and heavy hours.

1st Soldier. Toiling and thinking to build the wall of force that blocks the way from here to home.

2nd Soldier. Lifting shells.

3rd Soldier. Carrying shells.

4th Soldier. Piling shells.

1st Soldier. In the falling, pissing rine and whistling wind.

2nd Soldier. The whistling wind and falling, drenching rain.

3rd Soldier. The God-dam rain and blasted whistling wind.

1st Soldier. And the shirkers sife at home coil'd up at ease.

2nd Soldier. Shells for us and pianos for them.

3rd Soldier. Fur coats for them and winding-sheets for us.

4th Soldier. Warm.

2nd Soldier. And dry.

1st Soldier. An' 'appy. [*A slight pause.*

Barney. An' they call it re-cu-per-at-ing !

1st Soldier [*reclining near the fire*]. Gawd, I'm sleepy.

2nd Soldier [*reclining*]. Tir'd and lousy.

3rd Soldier [*reclining*]. Damp and shaking.

4th Soldier [*murmuringly, the rest joining him*]. Tir'd and lousy, an' wet an' sleepy, but mother call me early in the morning.

1st Soldier [*dreamily*]. Wen I thinks of 'ome, I thinks of a field of dysies.

The Rest [*dreamily*]. Wen 'e thinks of 'ome, 'e thinks of a field of dysies.

1st Soldier [*chanting dreamily*] :
  I sees the missus paryding along Walham Green,
  Through the jewels an' silks on the costers' carts,
  Emmie a-pulling her skirt an' muttering,
  " A balloon, a balloon, I wants a balloon ",
  The missus a-tugging 'er on, an' sying,
  " A balloon, for shime, an' your father fighting :
  You'll wait till 'e's 'ome, an' the bands a-plying ! "
  [*He pauses.*

[*Suddenly*] But wy'r we 'ere, wy'r we 'ere — that's wot we wants to know !

2nd Soldier. God only knows — or else, perhaps, a red-cap.

1st Soldier [*chanting*] :
> Tabs'll murmur, 'em an' 'aw, an' sy : " You're 'ere because you're
> Point nine double o, the sixth platoon an' forty-eight battalion,
> The Yellow Plumes that pull'd a bow at Crecy,
> And gave to fame a leg up on the path to glory ;
> Now with the howitzers of the Twenty-first Division,
> Tiking life easy with the Army of the Marne,
> An' all the time the battered Conchie squeals,
> ' It's one or two men looking after business '."

3rd Soldier. An' saves his blasted skin !

1st Soldier [*chanting*]. The padre gives a fag an' softly whispers :
> " Your king, your country an' your muvver 'as you 'ere."
> An' last time 'ome on leave, I awsks the missus :
> " The good God up in heaven, Bill, 'e knows,
> An' I gets the seperytion moneys reg'lar."
>   [*He sits up suddenly.*
> But wy'r we 'ere, wy'r we 'ere, — that's wot I wants to know !

The Rest [*chanting sleepily*]. Why 's 'e 'ere, why 's 'e 'ere — that's wot 'e wants to know !

Barney [*singing to the air of second bar in chorus of* "*Auld Lang Syne*"]. We're here because we're here, because we're here, because we're here !

[*Each slides into an attitude of sleep — even Barney's head droops a little. The Corporal, followed by the Visitor, appears at back. The Visitor is a portly man with a rubicund face ; he is smiling to demonstrate his ease of mind, but the lines are a little distorted with an ever-present sense of anxiety. He is dressed in a semi-civilian, semi-military manner — dark worsted suit, shrapnel helmet, a haversack slung round his shoulder, a brown belt round his middle, black top boots and spurs, and he carries a cane. His head is bent between his shoulders, and his shoulders are crouched a little.*]

Visitor. Yes, to-morrow, I go a little further. Penetrate a little deeper into danger. Foolish, yes, but then it's an experience ; by God, it's an experience. The military authorities are damned strict — won't let a . . . man . . . plunge !

Corporal. In a manner of speakin', sir, only let you see the arses of the guns.

Visitor [*not liking the remark*]. Yes, no ; no, oh yes. Damned strict, won't let a . . . man . . . plunge ! [*Suddenly, with alarm*] What's that, what was that ?

Corporal. Wha' was what ?

Visitor. A buzz, I thought I heard a buzz.

Corporal. A buzz ?

Visitor. Of an aeroplane.

Corporal. Didn't hear. Might have been a bee.

Visitor. No, no ; don't think it was a bee. [*Arranging helmet with his hands*] Damn shrapnel helmet ; skin tight ; like a vice ; hurts the head. Rather be without it ; but, regulations, you know. Military authorities damn particular — won't let a . . . man . . . plunge !

Visitor [*seeing Barney*]. Aha, what have we got here, what have we got here ?

Corporal [*to Barney*]. 'Tshun ! [*To the Visitor*] Regimental misdemeanour, sir.

Visitor [*to Barney*]. Nothing much, boy, nothing much ?

Barney [*chanting softly*] :
    A Brass-hat pullin' the bedroom curtains
    Between himself, the world an' the Estaminay's
      daughter,
    In a pyjama'd hurry ran down an' phon'd
    A Tommy was chokin' an Estaminay cock,
    An' I was pinch'd as I was puttin' the bird
    Into a pot with a pint of peas.

Corporal [*chanting hoarsely*] :
    And the hens all droop, for the loss has made
    The place a place of desolation !

Visitor [*reprovingly, to the Corporal*]. Seriously, Corporal, seriously, please. Sacred, sacred : property of the citizen of a friendly State, sacred. On Active Service, serious to steal a fowl, a cock. [*To Barney*] The uniform, the cause, boy, the corps. Infra dignitatem, boy, infra dignitatem.

Barney. Wee, wee.

Visitor [*pointing to reclining soldiers*]. Taking it easy, eh ?

Corporal. Done in ; transport fatigue ; twelve hours.

Visitor. Um, not too much rest, corporal. Dangerous.

Keep 'em moving much as possible. Too much rest —
bad. Sap, sap, sap.

Corporal [*pointing to the left*]. Bit of monastery left intact.
Hold services there ; troops off to front line. Little
organ plays.

Visitor. Splendid. Bucks 'em up. Gives 'em peace.
  [*A Staff Officer enters suddenly, passing by the Visitor with
  a springing hop, so that he stands in the centre with the
  Visitor on his right and the Corporal on his left. He is
  prim, pert, and polished, superfine khaki uniform, gold
  braid, crimson tabs, and gleaming top-boots. He speaks
  his sentences with a gasping importance.*

Corporal [*stiffening*]. 'Shun ! Staff !

Soldiers [*springing to their feet — the Croucher remains as he is,
  with a sleepy alertness*]. Staff ! 'Shun !

Corporal [*bellowing at the Croucher*]. Eh, you there : 'shun !
Staff !

Croucher [*calmly*]. Not able. Sick. Privilege. Excused
duty.

Staff-Wallah [*reading document*] :
        Battery Brigade Orders, F.A., 31 D 2.

Units presently recuperating, parade eight o'clock P.M.
Attend Lecture organized by Society for amusement
    and mental development, soldiers at front.
Subject : Habits of those living between Frigid Zone
    and Arctic Circle.
Lecturer : Mr. Melville Sprucer.
Supplementary Order : Units to wear gas-masks.
As you were.
  [*The Staff-Wallah departs as he came with a springing hop.*

The Visitor and the Corporal relax, and stroll down towards the R.C. Station. The soldiers relax too, seeking various positions of ease around the fire.

Visitor [*indicating R.C. Station*]. Ah, in here. We'll just pop in here for a minute. And then pop out again.
[*He and the Corporal go into the R.C. Station. A pause.*

1st Soldier [*chanting and indicating that he means the Visitor by looking in the direction of the R.C. Station*] :
The perky bastard's cautious nibbling
In a safe, safe shelter at danger queers me.
Furiously feeling he's up to the neck in
The whirl and the sweep of the front-line fighting.

2nd Soldier [*chanting*] :
In his full-blown, chin-strapp'd, shrapnel helmet,
He'll pat a mug on the back and murmur,
" Here's a stand-fast Tauntonshire before me ",
And the mug, on his feet, 'll whisper " yessir ".

3rd Soldier [*chanting*] :
Like a bride, full-flush'd, 'e'll sit down and listen
To every word of the goddam sermon,
From the cushy-soul'd, word-spreading, yellow-
streaked dud.

Barney [*chanting*]. Who wouldn't make a patch on a
Tommy's backside.   [*A pause.*

1st Soldier. 'Ow long have we been resting 'ere ?

2nd Soldier. A month.

3rd Soldier. Twenty-nine days, twenty-three hours and [*looking at watch*] twenty-three minutes.

4th Soldier. Thirty-seven minutes more'll make it thirty days.

Croucher :

Thirty days hath September, April, June, and November —

November — that's the month when I was born — November.

Not the beginning, not the end, but the middle of November.

Near the valley of the Thames, in the middle of November.

Shall I die at the start, near the end, in the middle of November ?

1st Soldier [*nodding towards the Croucher*]. One more scrap, an' 'e'll be Ay one in the kingdom of the bawmy.

2nd Soldier. Perhaps they have forgotten.

3rd Soldier. Forgotten.

4th Soldier. Forgotten us.

1st Soldier. If the blighters at the front would tame their grousing.

The Rest. Tame their grousing.

2nd Soldier. And the wounded cease to stare their silent scorning.

The Rest. Passing by us, carried cushy on the stretchers.

3rd Soldier. We have beaten out the time upon the duck-board.

4th Soldier. Stiff standing watch'd the sunrise from the firestep.

2nd Soldier. Stiff standing from the firestep watch'd the sunset.

3rd Soldier. Have bless'd the dark wiring of the top with curses.

2nd Soldier. And never a ray of leave.

3rd Soldier. To have a quiet drunk.

1st Soldier. Or a mad mowment to rustle a judy.
> [*3rd Soldier takes out a package of cigarettes; taking one himself he hands the package round. Each takes one, and the man nearest to Barney, kneeling up, puts one in his mouth and lights it for him. They all smoke silently for a few moments, sitting up round the fire.*

2nd Soldier [*chanting very earnestly and quietly*] :
> Would God I smok'd an' walk'd an' watch'd th'
> Dance of a golden Brimstone butterfly,
> To the saucy pipe of a greenfinch resting
> In a drowsy, brambled lane in Cumberland.

1st Soldier :
> Would God I smok'd and lifted cargoes
> From the laden shoulders of London's river-way ;
> Then holiday'd, roaring out courage and movement
> To the muscled machines of Tottenham Hotspur.

3rd Soldier :
> To hang here even a little longer,
> Lounging through fear-swell'd, anxious moments ;
> The hinderparts of the god of battles
> Shading our war-tir'd eyes from his flaming face.

Barney :
> If you creep to rest in a clos'd-up coffin,
> A tail of comrades seeing you safe home ;

Or be a kernel lost in a shell exploding —
It's all, sure, only in a lifetime.

All Together :
Each sparrow, hopping, irresponsible,
Is indentur'd in God's mighty memory ;
And we, more than they all, shall not be lost
In the forgetfulness of the Lord of Hosts.

[*The Visitor and the Corporal come from the Red Cross Station.*

Visitor [*taking out a cigarette-case*]. Nurses too gloomy. Surgeons too serious. Doesn't do.

Corporal. All lying-down cases, sir. Pretty bad.

Visitor [*who is now standing near the crucifix*]. All the more reason make things merry and bright. Lift them out of themselves. [*To the soldiers*] See you all to-morrow at lecture ?

1st Soldier [*rising and standing a little sheepishly before the Visitor*]. Yessir, yessir.

The Rest. Yessir, yessir.

The Visitor. Good. Make it interesting. [*Searching in pocket*] Damn it, have I none ? Ah, saved.

[*He takes a match from his pocket and is about to strike it carelessly on the arm of the crucifix, when the 1st Soldier, with a rapid frightened movement, knocks it out of his hand.*

1st Soldier [*roughly*]. Blarst you, man, keep your peace-white paws from that !

2nd Soldier. The image of the Son of God.

3rd Soldier. Jesus of Nazareth, the King of the Jews.

1st Soldier [*reclining by the fire again*]. There's a Gawd knocking abaht somewhere.

4th Soldier. Wants Him to be sending us over a chit in the shape of a bursting shell.

The Visitor. Sorry put it across you. [*To Corporal*] Too much time to think. Nervy. Time to brood, brood ; bad. Sap. Sap. Sap. [*Walking towards where he came in*] Must return quarters ; rough and ready. Must stick it. There's a war on. Cheerio. Straight down road instead of round hill : shorter ?

Corporal. Less than half as long.

The Visitor. Safe ?

Corporal. Yes. Only drop shells off and on, cross-roads. Ration party wip'd out week ago.

The Visitor. Go round hill. No hurry. General Officer's orders, no unnecessary risks. Must obey. Military Authorities damned particular — won't let a . . . man . . . plunge !

[*He and the Corporal go off. The soldiers in various attitudes are asleep around the fire. After a few moments' pause, two Stretcher-Bearers come in slowly from left, carrying a casualty. They pass through the sleeping soldiers, going towards the Red Cross Station. As they go they chant a verse, and as the verse is ending, they are followed by another pair carrying a second casualty.*]

1st Bearers [*chanting*] :
  Oh, bear it gently, carry it softly —
  A bullet or a shell said stop, stop, stop.
  It's had its day, and it's left the play,
  Since it gamboll'd over the top, top, top.
  It's had its day and it's left the play,
  Since it gamboll'd over the top.

2nd Bearers [*chanting*] :
> Oh, carry it softly, bear it gently —
> The beggar has seen it through, through, through.
> If it 'adn't been 'im, if it 'adn't been 'im,
> It might 'ave been me or you, you, you.
> If it 'adn't been 'im, if it 'adn't been 'im,
> It might 'ave been me or you.

Voice [*inside R.C. Station*]. Easy, easy there ; don't crowd.

1st Stretcher-Bearer [*to man behind*]. Woa, woa there, Bill, 'ouse full.

Stretcher-Bearer [*behind, to those following*]. Woa, woa ; traffic blocked.

> [*They leave the stretchers on the ground.*

The Wounded on the Stretchers [*chanting*] :
> Carry on, carry on to the place of pain,
> Where the surgeon spreads his aid, aid, aid.
> And we show man's wonderful work, well done,
> To the image God hath made, made, made,
> And we show man's wonderful work, well done,
> To the image God hath made !

> When the future hours have all been spent,
> And the hand of death is near, near, near,
> Then a few, few moments and we shall find
> There'll be nothing left to fear, fear, fear,
> Then a few, few moments and we shall find
> There'll be nothing left to fear.

> The power, the joy, the pull of life,
> The laugh, the blow, and the dear kiss,
> The pride and hope, the gain and loss,
> Have been temper'd down to this, this, this,
> The pride and hope, the gain and loss,
> Have been temper'd down to this.

1st Stretcher-Bearer [*to Barney*]. Oh, Barney, have they liced you up because you've kiss'd the Colonel's judy ?

Barney. They lit on me stealin' Estaminay poulthry.

1st Stretcher-Bearer. A hen ?

2nd Stretcher-Bearer. A duck, again, Barney ?

3rd Stretcher-Bearer. A swan this time.

Barney [*chanting softly*] :
    A Brass-hat pullin' the bedroom curtains
    Between himself, the world an' the Estaminay's
        daughter,
    In a pyjama'd hurry ran down and phon'd
    A Tommy was chokin' an Estaminay cock ;
    An' I was pinch'd as I was puttin' the bird
    Into a pot with a pint of peas.

1st Stretcher-Bearer. The red-tabb'd squit !

2nd Stretcher-Bearer. The lousy map-scanner !

3rd Stretcher-Bearer. We must keep up, we must keep up the morale of the awmy.

2nd Stretcher-Bearer [*loudly*]. Does e' eat well ?

The Rest [*in chorus*]. Yes, 'e eats well !

2nd Stretcher-Bearer. Does 'e sleep well ?

The Rest [*in chorus*]. Yes, 'e sleeps well !

2nd Stretcher-Bearer. Does 'e whore well ?

The Rest [*in chorus*]. Yes, 'e whores well !

2nd Stretcher-Bearer. Does 'e fight well ?

The Rest [*in chorus*]. Napoo ; 'e 'as to do the thinking for the Tommies !

Voice [*from the R.C. Station*]. Stretcher Party — carry on !
    [*The Bearers stoop with precision, attach their supports to
       the stretchers, lift them up and march slowly into the
       R.C. Station, chanting.*

Stretcher-Bearers [*chanting*] :
    Carry on — we've one bugled reason why —
    We've 'eard and answer'd the call, call, call.
    There's no more to be said, for when we are dead,
    We may understand it all, all, all.
    There's no more to be said, for when we are dead,
    We may understand it all.
    [*They go out, leaving the scene occupied by the Croucher
       and the soldiers sleeping around the fire. The Corporal
       re-enters. He is carrying two parcels. He pauses, look-
       ing at the sleeping soldiers for a few moments, then
       shouts.*

Corporal [*shouting*]. Hallo, there, you sleepy blighters !
    Number 2, a parcel ; and for you, Number 3. Get a
    move on — parcels !
            [*The Soldiers wake up and spring to their feet.*

Corporal. For you, Number 2. [*He throws a parcel to 2nd
    Soldier.*] Number 3.
               [*He throws the other parcel to 3rd Soldier.*

3rd Soldier [*taking paper from around his parcel*]. Looks like
    a bundle of cigarettes.

1st Soldier. Or a pack of cawds.

4th Soldier. Or a prayer-book.

3rd Soldier [*astounded*]. Holy Christ, it is !

The Rest. What ?

3rd Soldier. A prayer-book !

4th Soldier. In a green plush cover with a golden cross.

Croucher. Open it at the Psalms and sing that we may be saved from the life and death of the beasts that perish.

Barney. Per omnia saecula saeculorum.

2nd Soldier [*who has opened his parcel*]. A ball, be God !

4th Soldier. A red and yellow coloured rubber ball.

1st Soldier. And a note.

2nd Soldier [*reading*]. To play your way to the enemies' trenches when you all go over the top.   Mollie.

1st Soldier. See if it 'ops.
  [*The 2nd Soldier hops the ball, and then kicks it from him.
  The Corporal intercepts it, and begins to dribble it
  across the stage.   The 3rd Soldier tries to take it from
  him.   The Corporal shouts " Offside, there ! "   They
  play for a few minutes with the ball, when suddenly the
  Staff-Wallah springs in and stands rigidly in centre.*

Corporal [*stiff to attention as he sees the Staff-Wallah*]. 'Shun.
  Staff !
  [*All the soldiers stiffen.   The Croucher remains motion-
  less.*

Corporal [*shouting to the Croucher*]. You : 'shun.   Staff !

Croucher. Not able.   Sick.   Excused duty.

Staff-Wallah [*reading document*] :
  Brigade Orders, C/X 143.   B/Y 341.   Regarding gas-
  masks.   Gas-masks to be worn round neck so as to
  lie in front $2\frac{1}{2}$ degrees from socket of left shoulder-

blade, and 2¾ degrees from socket of right shoulder-
blade, leaving bottom margin to reach ¼ of an inch
from second button of lower end of tunic.   Order to
take effect from 6 A.M. following morning of date
received.   Dismiss !

> [*He hops out again, followed by Corporal.*

1st Soldier [*derisively*].   Comprenneemoy.

3rd Soldier.   Tray bong.

2nd Soldier [*who is standing in archway, back, looking scornfully
after the Staff-Wallah, chanting*] :
    Jazzing back to his hotel he now goes gaily,
    Shelter'd and safe where the clock ticks tamely.
    His backside warming a cushion, down-fill'd,
    Green clad, well splash'd with gold birds red-beak'd.

1st Soldier :
    His last dim view of the front-line sinking
    Into the white-flesh'd breasts of a judy ;
    Cuddling with proud, bright, amorous glances
    The thing salved safe from the mud of the trenches.

2nd Soldier :
    His tunic reared in the lap of comfort
    Peeps at the blood-stain'd jackets passing,
    Through colour-gay bars of ribbon jaunty,
    Fresh from a posh shop snug in Bond Street.

Croucher :
    Shame and scorn play with and beat them,
    Till we anchor in their company ;
    Then the decorations of security
    Become the symbols of self-sacrifice.

> [*A pause.*

2nd Soldier :

> A warning this that we'll soon be exiles
> From the freedom chance of life can give,
> To the front where you wait to be hurried breath-
>   less,
> Murmuring how, how do you do, to God.

3rd Soldier :

> Where hot with the sweat of mad endeavour,
> Crouching to scrape a toy-deep shelter,
> Quick-tim'd by hell's fast, frenzied drumfire
> Exploding in flaming death around us.

2nd Soldier :

> God, unchanging, heart-sicken'd, shuddering,
> Gathereth the darkness of the night sky
> To mask His paling countenance from
> The blood dance of His self-slaying children.

3rd Soldier :

> Stumbling, swiftly cursing, plodding,
> Lumbering, loitering, stumbling, grousing,
> Through mud and rain, and filth and danger,
> Flesh and blood seek slow the front line.

2nd Soldier :

> Squeals of hidden laughter run through
> The screaming medley of the wounded
> Christ, who bore the cross, still weary,
> Now trails a rope tied to a field gun.

> [*As the last notes of the chanting are heard the Corporal comes
> rapidly in ; he is excited but steady ; pale-faced and
> grim.*

Corporal. They attack. Along a wide front the enemy
attacks. If they break through it may reach us even
here.

Soldiers [*in chorus as they all put on gas-masks*]. They attack.
The enemy attacks.

Corporal. Let us honour that in which we do put our
trust.

Soldiers [*in chorus*] :
     That it may not fail us in our time of need.
     [*The Corporal goes over to the gun and faces towards it,
     standing on the bottom step. The soldiers group around,
     each falling upon one knee, their forms crouched in a
     huddled act of obeisance. They are all facing the gun with
     their backs to the audience. The Croucher rises and joins
     them.*

Corporal [*singing*] :
     Hail, cool-hardened tower of steel emboss'd
     With the fever'd, figment thoughts of man ;
     Gnardian of our love and hate and fear,
     Speak for us to the inner ear of God !

Soldiers :
     We believe in God and we believe in thee.

Corporal :
     Dreams of line, of colour, and of form ;
     Dreams of music dead for ever now ;
     Dreams in bronze and dreams in stone have gone
     To make thee delicate and strong to kill.

Soldiers :
     We believe in God and we believe in thee.

Corporal :
     Jail'd in thy steel are hours of merriment
     Cadg'd from the pageant-dream of children's play ;
     Too soon of the motley stripp'd that they may sweat
     With them that toil for the glory of thy kingdom.

Soldiers :

    We believe in God and we believe in thee.

Corporal :

    Remember our women, sad-hearted, proud-fac'd,
    Who've given the substance of their womb for
      shadows ;
    Their shrivel'd, empty breasts war tinselléd
    For patient gifts of graves to thee.

Soldiers :

    We believe in God and we believe in thee.

Corporal :

    Dapple those who are shelter'd with disease,
    And women labouring with child,
    And children that play about the streets,
    With blood of youth expiring in its prime.

Soldiers :

    We believe in God and we believe in thee.

Corporal :

    Tear a gap through the soul of our mass'd enemies ;
    Grant them all the peace of death ;
    Blow them swiftly into Abram's bosom,
    And mingle them with the joys of paradise !

Soldiers :

    For we believe in God and we believe in thee.

    [*The sky has become vexed with a crimson glare, mixed with
      yellow streaks, and striped with pillars of rising brown
      and black smoke. The Staff-Wallah rushes in, turbulent
      and wild, with his uniform disordered.*

Staff-Wallah :

    The enemy has broken through, broken through,
      broken through !
    Every man born of woman to the guns, to the guns.

Soldiers :

　　To the guns, to the guns, to the guns !

Staff-Wallah :

　　Those at prayer, all in bed, and the swillers drinking
　　　deeply in the pubs.

Soldiers :

　　To the guns, to the guns.

Staff-Wallah :

　　All the batmen, every cook, every bitch's son that
　　　hides
　　A whiff of courage in his veins,
　　Shelter'd vigour in his body,
　　That can run, or can walk, even crawl —
　　Dig him out, dig him out, shove him on —

Soldiers :

　　To the guns !

　　[*The Soldiers hurry to their places led by the Staff-Wallah
　　　to the gun. The gun swings around and points to the
　　　horizon ; a shell is swung into the breech and a flash
　　　indicates the firing of the gun, searchlights move over the
　　　red glare of the sky ; the scene darkens, stabbed with
　　　distant flashes and by the more vivid flash of the gun
　　　which the Soldiers load and fire with rhythmical move-
　　　ments while the scene is closing. Only flashes are seen ;
　　　no noise is heard.*

ACT III

The upper end of an hospital ward. At right angles from back wall are two beds, one covered with a red quilt and the other with a white one. From the centre of the head of each bed is an upright having at the top a piece like a swan's neck, curving out over the bed, from which hangs a chain with a wooden cross-piece to enable weak patients to pull themselves into a sitting posture. To the left of these beds is a large glass double-door which opens on to the ground : one of the doors is open and a lovely September sun, which is setting, gives a glow to the garden.

Through the door two poplar trees can be seen silhouetted against the sky. To the right of this door is another bed covered with a black quilt. Little white discs are fixed to the head of each bed : on the first is the number 26, on the second 27, and on the third 28. Medical charts hang over each on the wall. To the right is the fireplace, facing down the ward. Farther on, to the right of the fire, is a door of a bathroom. In the corner, between the glass door and the fire, is a pedestal on which stands a statue of the Blessed Virgin ; under the statue is written, " Mater Misericordiae, ora pro nobis ". An easy-chair, on which are rugs, is near the fire. In the centre is a white, glass-topped table on which are medicines, drugs, and surgical instruments. On one corner is a vase of flowers. A locker is beside the head, and a small chair by the foot of each bed. Two electric lights, green-shaded, hang from the ceiling, and a bracket light with a red shade projects from the wall over the fireplace. It is dusk, and the two lights suspended from the ceiling are lighted. The walls are a brilliant white.

Sylvester is in the bed numbered " 26 " ; he is leaning upon his elbow looking towards the glass door.

317

*Simon, sitting down on the chair beside bed numbered " 27 ",
is looking into the grounds.*

Sylvester [*after a pause*]. Be God, isn't it a good one !

Simon. Almost, almost, mind you, Sylvester, incomprehensible.

Sylvester. To come here and find Susie Monican fashion'd
like a Queen of Sheba. God moves in a mysterious
way, Simon.

Simon. There's Surgeon Maxwell prancing after her now.

Sylvester [*stretching to see*]. Heads together, eh ? Be God,
he's kissing her behind the trees ! Oh, Susannah,
Susannah, how are the mighty fallen, and the weapons
of war perished !
> [*Harry Heegan enters crouched in a self-propelled invalid
> chair ; he wheels himself up to the fire. Sylvester slides
> down into the bed, and Simon becomes interested in a book
> that he takes off the top of his locker. Harry remains
> for a few moments beside the fire, and then wheels himself
> round and goes out as he came in ; Sylvester raises himself
> in the bed, and Simon leaves down the book to watch
> Harry.*

Sylvester. Down and up, up and down.

Simon. Up and down, down and up.

Sylvester. Never quiet for a minute.

Simon. Never able to hang on to an easy second.

Sylvester. Trying to hold on to the little finger of life.

Simon. Half-way up to heaven.

Sylvester. And him always thinking of Jessie.

Simon. And Jessie never thinking of him.

> [*Susie Monican, in the uniform of a V.A.D. nurse, enters the ward by the glass door. She is changed, for it is clear that she has made every detail of the costume as attractive as possible. She has the same assertive manner, but dignity and a sense of importance have been added. Her legs, encased in silk stockings, are seen (and shown) to advantage by her short and smartly cut skirt. Altogether she is now a very handsome woman. Coming in she glances at the bed numbered 28, then pauses beside Sylvester and Simon.*

Susie. How is Twenty-eight ?

Simon and Sylvester [*together*]. Travelling again.

Susie. Did he speak at all to you ?

Sylvester. Dumb, Susie, dumb.

Simon. Brooding, Susie ; brooding, brooding.

Sylvester. Cogitatin', Susie ; cogitatin', cogitatin'.

Susie [*sharply, to Sylvester*]. It's rediculous, Twenty-six, for you to be in bed. The Sister's altogether too indulgent to you. Why didn't you pair of lazy devils entice him down to sit and cogitate under the warm wing of the sun in the garden ?

Sylvester. Considerin' the low state of his general health.

Simon. Aided by a touch of frost in the air.

Sylvester. Thinkin' it over we thought it might lead——

Simon. To him getting an attack of double pneumonia.

Sylvester and Simon [*together*]. An' then he'd go off like —
[*they blow through their lips*] poof — the snuff of a
candle !

Susie. For the future, during the period you are patients
here, I am to be addressed as " Nurse Monican ", and
not as " Susie ". Remember that, the pair of you,
please.
    [*Harry wheels himself in again, crossing by her, and, going
    over to the fire, looks out into grounds.*

Susie [*irritatedly, to Sylvester*]. Number Twenty-six, look
at the state of your quilt   You must make an effort to
keep it tidy.   Dtch, dtch, dtch, what would the Matron
say if she saw it !

Simon [*with a nervous giggle*]. He's an uneasy divil, Nurse
Monican.

Susie [*hotly, to Simon*]. Yours is as bad as his, Twenty-
seven.   You mustn't lounge on your bed ; it must be
kept perfectly tidy [*she smoothes the quilts*]. Please don't
make it necessary to mention this again.   [*To Harry*]
Would you like to go down for a little while into
the garden, Twenty-eight ?
                    [*Harry crouches silent and moody.*

Susie [*continuing*]. After the sober rain of yesterday it is
good to feel the new grace of the yellowing trees, and
to get the fresh smell of the grass.
    [*Harry wheels himself round and goes out by the left.*

Susie [*to Sylvester as she goes out*]. Remember, Twenty-six,
if you're going to remain in a comatose condition,
you'll have to keep your bed presentable.   [*A pause.*

Sylvester [*mimicking Susie*]. Twenty-six, if you're going to remeen in a comatowse condition, you'll have to keep your bed in a tidy an' awdahly mannah.

Simon. Dtch, dtch, dtch, Twenty-seven, it's disgriceful. And as long as you're heah, in the capacity of a patient, please remember I'm not to be addressed as " Susie ", but as " Nurse Monican ".

Sylvester. Twenty-seven, did you tike the pills the doctah awdahed ?

Voice of Susie, left. Twenty-six !

Sylvester. Yes, Nurse ?

Voice of Susie. Sister says you're to have a bawth at once ; and you, Twenty-seven, see about getting it ready for him.   *[A fairly long pause.*

Sylvester [angrily]. A bawth : well, be God, that's a good one ! I'm not in a fit condition for a bath !
         [Another pause.

Sylvester [earnestly, to Simon]. You haven't had a dip now for nearly a week, while I had one only the day before yesterday in the late evening : it must have been you she meant, Simon.

Simon. Oh, there was no dubiety about her bellowing out Twenty-six, Syl.

Sylvester [excitedly]. How the hell d'ye know, man, she didn't mix the numbers up ?

Simon. Mix the numbers up ! How could the woman mix the numbers up ?

Sylvester. How could the woman mix the numbers up ! What could be easier than to say Twenty-six instead of

Twenty-seven ?   How could the woman mix the
numbers up !   Of course the woman could mix the
numbers up !

Simon. What d'ye expect me to do — hurl myself into a
bath that was meant for you ?

Sulvester. I don't want you to hurl yourself into anything ;
but you don't expect me to plunge into a bath that
maybe wasn't meant for me ?

Simon. Nurse Monican said Twenty-six, and when you
can alter that, ring me up and let me know.
[*A pause ; then Simon gets up and goes toward bathroom
door.*

Sylvester [*snappily*]. Where are you leppin' to now ?

Simon. I want to get the bath ready.

Sylvester. You want to get the bawth ready !   Turn the
hot cock on, and turn the cold cock on for Number
Twenty-six, mixin' them the way a chemist would
mix his medicines — sit still, man, till we hear the
final verdict.
[*Simon sits down again.   Susie comes in left, and, passing
to the door leading to grounds, pauses beside Simon and
Sylvester.*

Susie [*sharply*]. What are the two of you doing ?   Didn't
I tell you, Twenty-six, that you were to take a bawth ;
and you, Twenty-seven, that you were to get it ready
for him ?

Sylvester [*sitting brightly up in bed*]. Oh, just goin' to spring
up, Nurse Monican, when you popped in.

Susie. Well, up with you, then, and take it. [*To Simon*] You go and get it ready for him.

> [*Simon goes into the bathroom.*

Sylvester [*venturing a last hope as Susie goes towards the entrance to grounds*]. I had a dip, Nurse, only the day before yesterday in the late evening.

Susie [*as she goes out*]. Have another one now, please.

> [*The water can be heard flowing in the bathroom, and a light cloud of steam comes out by the door which Simon has left open.*

Sylvester [*mimicking Susie*]. Have another one, now, please ! One to be taken before and after meals. The delicate audacity of the lip of that one since she draped her shoulders with a crimson cape !

> [*Simon appears and stands leaning against the side of the bathroom door.*

Simon [*gloating*]. She's steaming away now, Sylvester, full cock.

Sylvester [*scornfully, to Simon*]. Music to you, the gurgling of the thing, music to you. Gaugin' the temperature for me. Dtch, dtch, dtch [*sitting up*], an hospital's the last place that God made. Be damn it, I wouldn't let a stuffed bird stay in one !

Simon. Come on, man, before the hot strength bubbles out of it.

Sylvester [*getting out of bed*]. Have you the towels hot an' everything ready for me to spring into ?

Simon [*with a bow*]. Everything's ready for your enjoyment, Sir.

Sylvester [*as he goes towards the bathroom*]. Can't they be content with an honest to God cleanliness, an' not be tryin' to gild a man with soap and water.

Simon [*with a grin, as Sylvester passes*]. Can I do anything more for you, Sir ?

Sylvester [*almost inarticulate with indignation, as he goes in*]. Now I'm tellin' you, Simon Norton, our cordiality's gettin' a little strained !

> [*Harry wheels himself in, goes again to the fireplace, and looks into grounds. Simon watches him for a moment, takes a package of cigarettes from his pocket and lights one.*

Simon [*awkwardly, to Harry*]. Have a fag, Harry, oul' son ?

Harry. Don't want one ; tons of my own in the locker.

Simon. Like me to get you one ?

Harry. I can get them myself if I want one. D'ye think my arms are lifeless as well as my legs ?

Simon. Far from that. Everybody's remarking what a great improvement has taken place in you during the last few days.

Harry. Everybody but myself.

Simon. What with the rubbing every morning and the rubbing every night, and now the operation to-morrow as a grand finally, you'll maybe be in the centre of the football field before many months are out.

Harry [*irritably*]. Oh, shut up, man ! It's a miracle I want — not an operation. The last operation was to give life to my limbs, but no life came, and again I felt the horrible sickness of life only from the waist up. [*Raising his voice*] Don't stand there gaping at me, man.

Did you never before clap your eyes on a body dead
from the belly down ? Blast you, man, why don't you
shout at me, " While there's life there's hope " !
> [Simon edges away to his corner. Susie comes in by the
> glass door and goes over to the table.

Harry [to Susie]. A package of fags. Out of the locker.
Will you, Susie ?
> [Susie goes to Harry's locker, gets the cigarettes and gives
> them to him. As he lights the cigarette, his right arm
> gives a sudden jerk.

Susie. Steady. What's this ?

Harry [with a nervous laugh]. Barred from my legs it's
flowing back into my arms. I can feel it slyly creeping
into my fingers.

Voice of Patient, out left [plaintively]. Nurse !

Susie [turning her head in direction of the voice]. Shush, you
Twenty-three ; go asleep, go asleep.

Harry. A soft, velvety sense of distance between my
fingers and the things I touch.

Susie. Stop thinking of it. Brooding checks the chance of
your recovery. A good deal may be imagination.

Harry [peevishly]. Oh, I know the different touches of
iron [he touches the bed-rail] ; of wood [he touches the
chair] ; of flesh [he touches his cheek] ; and to my fingers
they're giving the same answers — a feeling of numb
distance between me and the touches of them all.

Voice of Patient, out left. Nurse !

Susie. Dtch, dtch. Go asleep, Twenty-three.

Voice, out left. The stab in the head is worse than ever, Nurse.

Susie. You've got your dose of morphia, and you'll get no more.   You'll just have to stick it.

> [*Resident Surgeon Forby Maxwell enters from the grounds. He is about thirty years of age, and good-looking.   His white overalls are unbuttoned, showing war ribbons on his waistcoat, flanked by the ribbon of the D.S.O.   He has a careless, jaunty air, and evidently takes a decided interest in Susie.   He comes in singing softly.*]

Surgeon Maxwell :
> Stretched on the couch, Jessie fondled her dress,
> That hid all her beauties just over the knee ;
> And I wondered and said, as I sigh'd, " What a shame,
> That there's no room at all on the couch there for me."

Susie [*to Surgeon Maxwell*]. Twenty-three's at it again.

Surgeon Maxwell. Uh, hopeless case.   Half his head in Flanders.   May go on like that for another month.

Susie. He keeps the patients awake at night.

Simon. With his " God have mercys on me ", running after every third or fourth tick of the clock.

Harry. 'Tisn't fair to me, 'tisn't fair to me ; I must get my bellyful of sleep if I'm ever going to get well.

Surgeon Maxwell. Oh, the poor devil won't trouble any of you much longer.   [*Singing*] :
> Said Jess, with a light in the side of her eyes,
> " A shrewd, mathematical fellow like you,
> With an effort of thought should be able to make
> The couch wide enough for the measure of two."

Susie. Dtch, dtch, Surgeon Maxwell.

Surgeon Maxwell [*singing*] :
I fixed on a plan, and I carried it through,
And the eyes of Jess gleam'd as she whisper'd to
me :
" The couch, made for one, that was made to hold
two,
Has, maybe, been made big enough to hold three ! "
[*Surgeon Maxwell catches Susie's hand in his. Sylvester
bursts in from the bathroom, and rushes to his bed,
colliding with the Surgeon as he passes him.*

Surgeon Maxwell. Hallo, hallo there, what's this ?

Sylvester [*flinging himself into bed, covering himself rapidly
with the clothes, blowing himself warm*]. Pooh, pooh, I
feel as if I was sittin' on the doorstep of pneumonia !
Pooh, oh !

Surgeon Maxwell [*to Sylvester*]. We'll have a look at you
in a moment, Twenty-six, and see what's wrong with
you.
[*Sylvester subsides down into the bed, and Simon edges
towards the entrance to grounds, and stands looking into
the grounds, or watching Surgeon Maxwell examining
Sylvester.*

Surgeon Maxwell [*to Harry, who is looking intently out into
the grounds*]. Well, how are we to-day, Heegan ?

Harry. I imagine I don't feel quite so dead in myself as
I've felt these last few days back.

Surgeon Maxwell. Oh, well, that's something.

Harry. Sometimes I think I feel a faint, fluttering kind
of a buzz in the tops of my thighs.

Surgeon Maxwell [*touching Harry's thigh*]. Where, here?

Harry. No; higher up, doctor; just where the line is that leaves the one part living and the other part dead.

Surgeon Maxwell. A buzz?

Harry. A timid, faint, fluttering kind of a buzz.

Surgeon Maxwell. That's good. There might be a lot in that faint, fluttering kind of a buzz.

Harry [*after a pause*]. I'm looking forward to the operation to-morrow.

Surgeon Maxwell. That's the way to take it. While there's life there's hope [*with a grin and a wink at Susie*]. And now we'll have a look at Twenty-six.
> [*Harry, when he hears " while there's life there's hope ",
> wheels himself madly out left; half-way out he turns his
> head and stretches to look out into the grounds, then he
> goes on.*

Susie. Will the operation to-morrow be successful?

Surgeon Maxwell. Oh, of course; very successful.

Susie. Do him any good, d'ye think?

Surgeon Maxwell. Oh, blast the good it'll do him.
> [*Susie goes over to Sylvester in the bed.*

Susie [*to Sylvester*]. Sit up, Twenty-six, Surgeon Maxwell wants to examine you.

Sylvester [*sitting up with a brave effort but a woeful smile*]. Righto. In the pink!
> [*Surgeon Maxwell comes over, twirling his stethoscope.
> Simon peeps round the corner of the glass door.*

Susie [*to Surgeon Maxwell*]. What was the cause of the row between the Matron and Nurse Jennings ? [*To Sylvester*] Open your shirt, Twenty-six.

Surgeon Maxwell [*who has fixed the stethoscope in his ears, removing it to speak to Susie*]. Caught doing the tango in the Resident's arms in the Resident's room. Naughty girl, naughty girl. [*To Sylvester*] Say " ninety-nine ".

Sylvester. Ninety-nine.

Susie. Oh, I knew something like that would happen. Daughter of a Dean, too.

Surgeon Maxwell [*to Sylvester*]. Say " ninety-nine ".

Sylvester. Ninety-nine.   U-u-uh, it's gettin' very cold here, sitting up !

Surgeon Maxwell [*to Sylvester*]. Again.   Don't be frightened ; breathe quietly.

Sylvester. Ninety-nine.   Cool as a cucumber, Doctor. Ninety-nine.

Surgeon Maxwell [*to Susie*]. Damn pretty little piece.   Not so pretty as you, though.

Sylvester [*to Surgeon Maxwell*]. Yesterday Doctor Joyce, givin' me a run over, said to a couple of medical men that were with him lookin' for tips, that the thing was apparently yieldin' to treatment, and that an operation wouldn't be necessary.

Surgeon Maxwell. Go on ; ninety-nine, ninety-nine.

Sylvester. Ninety-nine, ninety-nine.

Surgeon Maxwell [*to Susie*]. Kicks higher than her head, and you should see her doing the splits.

Sylvester [*to Surgeon Maxwell*]. Any way of gettin' rid of it'll do for me, for I'm not one of them that'll spend a night before an operation in a crowd of prayers.

Susie. Not very useful things to be doing and poor patients awaiting attention.

Surgeon Maxwell [*putting stethoscope into pocket*]. He'll do all right ; quite fit.   Great old skin.   [*To Sylvester*] You can cover yourself up, now.   [*To Susie*] And don't tell me, Nurse Susie, that you've never felt a thrill or left a bedside for a kiss in a corner.   [*He tickles her under the arm*.]   Kiss in a corner, Nurse !

Susie [*pleased, but coy*]. Please don't, Doctor Maxwell, please.

Surgeon Maxwell [*tickling her again as they go out*]. Kiss in a corner ; ta-ra-ra-ra, kiss in a corner !   [*A pause.*

Sylvester [*to Simon*]. Simon, were you listenin' to that conversation ?

Simon. Indeed I was.

Sylvester. We have our hands full, Simon, to keep alive. Think of sinkin' your body to the level of a hand that, ta-ra-ra-ra, would plunge a knife into your middle, haphazard, hurryin' up to run away after a thrill from a kiss in a corner.   Did you see me dizzied an' wastin' me time pumpin' ninety-nines out of me, unrecognized, quiverin' with cold an' equivocation !

Simon. Everybody says he's a very clever fellow with the knife.

Sylvester. He'd gouge out your eye, saw off your arm, lift a load of vitals out of your middle, rub his hands, keep down a terrible desire to cheer lookin' at the ruin, an' say, " Twenty-six, when you're a little better, you'll feel a new man ! "

[Mrs. Heegan, Mrs. Foran, and Teddy enter from the grounds. Mrs. Foran is leading Teddy, who has a heavy bandage over his eyes, and is dressed in the blue clothes of military hospitals.

Mrs. Foran [to Teddy]. Just a little step here, Ted ; upsh ! That's it ; now we're on the earth again, beside Simon and Sylvester. You'd better sit here.

[She puts him sitting on a chair.

Sylvester [to Mrs. Heegan, as she kisses him]. Well, how's the old woman, eh ?

Mrs. Heegan. A little anxious about poor Harry.

Simon. He'll be all right. To-morrow'll tell a tale.

Susie [coming in, annoyed]. Who let you up here at this hour ? Twenty-eight's to have an operation to-morrow, and shouldn't be disturbed.

Mrs. Heegan. Sister Peter Alcantara said we might come up, Nurse.

Mrs. Foran [loftily]. Sister Peter Alcantara's authority ought to be good enough, I think.

Mrs. Heegan. Sister Peter Alcantara said a visit might buck him up a bit.

Mrs. Foran. Sister Peter Alcantara knows the responsibility she'd incur by keeping a wife from her husband and a mother from her son.

Susie. Sister Peter Alcantara hasn't got to nurse him.

And remember, nothing is to be said that would make his habit of introspection worse than it is.

Mrs. Foran [*with dignity*]. Thanks for the warnin', Nurse, but them kind of mistakes is unusual with us.

> [*Susie goes out left, as Harry wheels himself rapidly in. Seeing the group, he stops suddenly, and a look of disappointment comes on to his face.*

Mrs. Heegan [*kissing Harry*]. How are you, son?

Mrs. Foran. I brought Teddy, your brother in arms, up to see you, Harry.

Harry [*impatiently*]. Where's Jessie? I thought you were to bring her with you?

Mrs. Heegan. She's comin' after us in a moment.

Harry. Why isn't she here now?

Mrs. Foran. She stopped to have a word in the grounds with someone she knew.

Harry. It was Barney Bagnal, was it? Was it Barney Bagnal?

Teddy. Maybe she wanted to talk to him about gettin' the V.C.

Harry. What V.C.? Who's gettin' the V.C.?

Teddy. Barney. Did he not tell you? [*Mrs. Foran prods his knee.*] What's up?

Harry [*intensely, to Teddy*]. What's he gettin' it for? What's he gettin' the V.C. for?

Teddy. For carryin' you wounded out of the line of fire. [*Mrs. Foran prods his knee.*] What's up?

Harry [*in anguish*]. Christ Almighty, for carryin' me wounded out of the line of fire!

Mrs. Heegan [*rapidly*]. Harry, I wouldn't be thinkin' of anything till we see what the operation'll do to-morrow.

Simon [*rapidly*]. God, if it gave him back the use even of one of his legs.

Mrs. Foran [*rapidly*]. Look at all the places he could toddle to, an' all the things he could do then with the prop of a crutch.

Mrs. Heegan. Even at the worst, he'll never be dependin' on anyone, for he's bound to get the maximum allowance.

Simon. Two quid a week, isn't it?

Sylvester. Yes, a hundred per cent total incapacitation.

Harry. She won't come up if one of you don't go down and bring her up.

Mrs. Heegan. She's bound to come up, for she's got your ukelele.

Harry. Call her up, Simon, call her up — I must see Jessie.

[*Simon goes over to the door leading to the grounds, and looks out.*

Mrs. Foran [*bending over till her face is close to Harry's*]. The drawn look on his face isn't half as bad as when I seen him last.

Mrs. Heegan [*bending and looking into Harry's face*]. Look, the hollows under his eyes is fillin' up, too.

Teddy. I'm afraid he'll have to put Jessie out of his head, for when a man's hit in the spine . . . [*Mrs. Foran prods his knee.*] What's up, woman?

Harry [*impatiently, to Simon*]. Is she coming? Can you see her anywhere?

Simon. I see someone like her in the distance, under the trees.

Harry. Call her; can't you give her a shout, man?

Simon [*calling*]. Jessie. Is that you, Jessie? Jessie-e!

Mrs. Heegan [*to Harry*]. What time are you goin' under the operation?

Harry [*to Simon*]. Call her again, call her again, can't you!

Simon [*calling*]. Jessie, Jessie-e!

Teddy. Not much of a chance for an injury to the spine, for . . .

Mrs. Foran [*putting her face close to Teddy's*]. Oh, shut up, you!

Harry. Why did you leave her in the grounds? Why didn't you wait till she came up with you?

Mrs. Foran [*going over to Simon and calling*]. Jessie, Jessie-e!

Jessie's Voice, in distance. Yehess!

Mrs. Foran [*calling*]. Come up here at once; we're all waitin' for you!

Jessie's Voice. I'm not going up!

Mrs. Foran [*calling*]. Bring up that ukelele here at once, miss!

Jessie's Voice. Barney 'll bring it up!

[*Harry, who has been listening intently, wheels himself rapidly to where Simon and Mrs. Foran are, pushing through them hurriedly.*

Harry [*calling loudly*]. Jessie ! Jessie ! Jessie-e !

Mrs. Foran. Look at that, now ; she's runnin' away, the young rip !

Harry [*appealingly*]. Jessie, Jessie-e !
   [*Susie enters quickly from left. She goes over to Harry and pulls him back from the door.*

Susie [*indignantly*]. Disgraceful ! Rousing the whole ward with this commotion ! Dear, dear, dear, look at the state of Twenty-eight. Come along, come along, please ; you must all go at once.

Harry. Jessie's coming up for a minute, Nurse.

Susie. No more to come up. We've had enough for one night, and you for a serious operation to-morrow. Come on, all out, please.
   [*Susie conducts Mrs. Heegan, Mrs. Foran, and Teddy out left.*

Mrs. Foran [*going out*]. We're goin', we're goin', thank you. A nice way to treat the flotsum and jetsum of the battlefields !

Susie [*to Harry*]. To bed now, Twenty-eight, please. [*To Simon*] Help me get him to bed, Twenty-seven.
   Susie pushes Harry to his bed, right ; Simon brings portion of a bed-screen which he places around Harry, hiding him from view.

Susie [*turning to speak to Sylvester, who is sitting up in bed, as she arranges screen*]. You're going to have your little operation in the morning, so you'd better go to sleep too.
   [*Sylvester goes pale and a look of dismay and fear crawls over his face.*

Susie. Don't funk it now. They're not going to turn you inside out. It'll be over in ten minutes.

Sylvester [*with a groan*]. When they once get you down your only hope is in the infinite mercy of God!

Simon. If I was you, Sylvester, I wouldn't take this operation too seriously. You know th' oul' song — Let Me like a Soldier Fall! If I was you, I'd put it completely out of me mind.

Sylvester [*subsiding on to the pillow — with an agonised look on his face*]. Let me like a soldier fall! Did anyone ever hear th' equal o' that! Put it out of me mind completely! [*He sits up, and glares at Simon.*] Eh, you, look! If you can't think sensibly, then thry to think without talkin'! [*He sinks back on the pillow again.*] Let me like a soldier fall. Oh, it's not a fair trial for a sensible man to be stuck down in a world like this!

[*Sylvester slides down till he lies prone and motionless on the bed. Harry is in bed now. Simon removes the screen, and Susie arranges Harry's quilt for the night.*

Susie [*to Simon*]. Now run and help get the things together for supper. [*Simon goes out left.*] [*Encouragingly to Harry*] After the operation, a stay in the air of the Convalescent may work wonders.

Harry. If I could mingle my breath with the breeze that blows from every sea, and over every land, they wouldn't widen me into anything more than the shrivell'd thing I am.

Susie [*switching off the two hanging lights, so that the red light over the fireplace alone remains*]. Don't be foolish, Twenty-eight. Wheeling yourself about among the beeches and the pines, when the daffodils are hanging out their blossoms, you'll deepen your chance in the courage and renewal of the country.

[*The bell of a Convent in grounds begins to ring for Compline.*

Harry [*with intense bitterness*]. I'll say to the pine, " Give me the grace and beauty of the beech " ; I'll say to the beech, " Give me the strength and stature of the pine ". In a net I'll catch butterflies in bunches ; twist and mangle them between my fingers and fix them wriggling on to mercy's banner. I'll make my chair a Juggernaut, and wheel it over the neck and spine of every daffodil that looks at me, and strew them dead to manifest the mercy of God and the justice of man !

Susie [*shocked*]. Shush, Harry, Harry !

Harry. To hell with you, your country, trees, and things, you jibbering jay !

Susie [*as she is going out*]. Twenty-eight !

Harry [*vehemently*]. To hell with you, your country, trees, and things, you jibbering jay !

[*Susie looks at him, pauses for a few moments, as if to speak, and then goes out.*

[*A pause ; then Barney comes in by door from grounds. An overcoat covers his military hospital uniform of blue. His left arm is in a sling. Under his right arm he carries a ukelele, and in his hand he has a bunch of flowers. Embarrassed, he goes slowly to Harry's bed, drops the flowers at the foot, then he drops the ukelele there.*

Barney [*awkwardly*]. Your ukelele. An' a bunch of flowers from Jessie.   [*Harry remains motionless on the bed.*

Barney. A bunch of flowers from Jessie, and . . . your . . . ukelele.

> [*The Sister of the Ward enters, left, going to the chapel for Compline. She wears a cream habit with a white coif ; a large set of Rosary beads hangs from her girdle. She pauses on her way, and a brass Crucifix flashes on her bosom.*

Sister [*to Harry*]. Keeping brave and hopeful, Twenty-eight ?

Harry [*softly*]. Yes, Sister.

Sister. Splendid. And we've got a ukelele too. Can you play it, my child ?

Harry. Yes, Sister.

Sister. Splendid. You must play me something when you're well over the operation. [*To Barney*] Standing guard over your comrade, Twenty-two, eh ?

Barney [*softly and shyly*]. Yes, Sister.

Sister. Grand. Forasmuch as ye do it unto the least of these my brethren, ye do it unto me. Well, God be with you both, my children. [*To Harry*] And Twenty-eight, pray to God, for wonderful He is in His doing toward the children of men.

> [*Calm and dignified she goes out into the grounds.*

Barney [*pausing as he goes out left*]. They're on the bed ; the ukelele, and the bunch of flowers from . . . Jessie.

> [*The Sisters are heard singing in the Convent the hymn of Salve Regina.*

Sisters :
> Salve Regina, mater misericordiae ;
> Vitae dulcedo et spes nostra, salve !

Ad te clamamus, exules filii Hevae ;
Ad te suspiramus, gementes et flentes in hac lacry-
   marum valle.
Eia ergo Advocata nostra,
Illos tuos misericordes oculos ad nos converte,
Et Jesum, benedictum fructum ventris tui—

Harry. God of the miracles, give a poor devil a chance,
give a poor devil a chance !

Sisters :
Nobis post hoc exsilium ostende,
O clemens, o pia, o dulcis Virgo Maria !

ACT IV

A room of the dance hall of the Avondale Football Club. At back, left, cutting corners of the back and side walls, is the arched entrance, divided by a slim pillar, to the dance hall. This entrance is hung with crimson and black striped curtains; whenever these are parted the dancers can be seen swinging or gliding past the entrance if a dance be taking place at the time. Over the entrance is a scroll on which is printed : " Up the Avondales ! " The wall back has a wide, tall window which opens to the garden, in which the shrubs and some sycamore trees can be seen. It is hung with apple-green casement curtains, which are pulled to the side to allow the window to be open as it is at present. Between the entrance to hall and the window is a Roll of Honour containing the names of five members of the Club killed in the war. Underneath the Roll of Honour a wreath of laurel tied with red and black ribbon. To the front left is the fireplace. Between the fireplace and the hall entrance is a door on which is an oval white enamel disc with " Caretaker " painted on it. To the right a long table, covered with a green cloth, on which are numerous bottles of wine and a dozen glasses. On the table, too, is a telephone. A brown carpet covers the floor. Two easy and one ordinary chairs are in the room. Hanging from the ceiling are three lanterns; the centre one is four times the length of its width, the ones at the side are less than half as long as the centre lantern and hang horizontally; the lanterns are black, with a broad red stripe running down the centre of the largest and across those hanging at each side, so that, when they are lighted, they suggest an illuminated black cross with an inner one of gleaming red. The hall is vividly decorated with many coloured lanterns, looped with coloured streamers.

When the scene is revealed the curtains are drawn, and the band can be heard playing a fox-trot. Outside in the garden, near the window, Simon and Sylvester can be seen smoking, and Teddy is walking slowly up and down the path. The band is heard playing for a few moments, then the curtains are pulled aside, and Jessie, with Barney holding her hand, comes in and walks rapidly to the table where the wine is standing. They are quickly followed by Harry, who wheels himself a little forward, then stops, watching them. The curtains part again, and Mrs. Heegan is seen watching Harry. Simon and Sylvester, outside, watch those in the room through the window. Barney wears a neat navy-blue suit, with a rather high, stiff collar and black tie. Pinned on the breast of his waistcoat are his war medals, flanked by the Victoria Cross. Harry is also wearing his medals. Jessie has on a very pretty, rather tight-fitting dance frock, with the sleeves falling widely to the elbow, and cut fairly low on her breast. All the dancers, and Harry too, wear coloured, fantastically shaped paper hats.

Jessie [*hot, excited, and uneasy, as with a rapid glance back she sees the curtains parted by Harry*]. Here he comes prowling after us again ! His watching of us is pulling all the enjoyment out of the night. It makes me shiver to feel him wheeling after us.

Barney. We'll watch for a chance to shake him off, an' if he starts again we'll make him take his tangled body somewhere else. [*As Harry moves forward from the curtained entrance*] Shush, he's comin' near us. [*In a louder tone to Jessie*] Red wine, Jessie, for you, or white wine ?

Harry. Red wine first, Jessie, to the passion and the power and the pain of life, an' then a drink of white wine to the melody that is in them all !

Jessie. I'm so hot.

Harry. I'm so cold ; white wine for the woman warm to make her cold ; red wine for the man that's cold to make him warm !

Jessie. White wine for me.

Harry. For me the red wine till I drink to men puffed up with pride of strength, for even creeping things can praise the Lord !

Barney [*gently to Harry, as he gives a glass of wine to Jessie*]. No more for you now, Harry.

Harry [*mockingly*]. Oh, please, your lusty lordship, just another, an' if I seek a second, smack me well. [*Wheeling his chair viciously against Barney*] Get out, you trimm'd-up clod. There's medals on my breast as well as yours ! [*He fills a glass.*]

Jessie. Let us go back to the dancing, Barney. [*Barney hesitates.*] Please, Barney, let us go back to the dancing !

Harry. To the dancing, for the day cometh when no man can play. And legs were made to dance, to run, to jump, to carry you from one place to another ; but mine can neither walk, nor run, nor jump, nor feel the merry motion of a dance. But stretch me on the floor fair on my belly, and I will turn over on my back, then wriggle back again on to my belly ; and that's more than a dead, dead man can do !

Barney. Jessie wants to dance, an' so we'll go, and leave you here a little.

Harry. Cram pain with pain, and pleasure cram with pleasure. I'm going too. You'd cage me in from seeing you dance, and dance, and dance, with Jessie close to you, and you so close to Jessie. Though you wouldn't think it, yes, I have — I've hammer'd out many a merry measure upon a polish'd floor with a sweet, sweet heifer. [*As Barney and Jessie are moving away he catches hold of Jessie's dress*] Her name? Oh, any name will do — we'll call her Jessie !

Jessie. Oh, let me go. [*To Barney*] Barney, make him let me go, please.

    [*Barney, without a word, removes Harry's hand from Jessie's dress. Jessie and Barney then go out to the dance hall through the curtained entrance. After a while Mrs. Heegan slips away from the entrance into the hall. After a moment's pause Harry follows them into the hall. Simon and Sylvester come in from the garden, leaving Teddy still outside smoking and walking to and fro in the cautious manner of the blind. Simon and Sylvester sit down near the fire and puff in silence for a few moments.*

Sylvester [*earnestly*]. I knew it. I knew it, Simon — strainin' an' strainin' his nerves ; driftin' an' driftin' towards an hallucination !

Simon. Jessie might try to let him down a little more gently, but it would have been better, I think, if Harry hadn't come here to-night.

Sylvester. I concur in that, Simon. What's a decoration to an hospital is an anxiety here.

Simon. To carry life and colour to where there's nothing but the sick and helpless is right ; but to carry the sick and helpless to where there's nothing but life and colour is wrong.   [*The telephone bell rings.*

Sylvester. There's the telephone bell ringing.

Simon. Oh, someone 'll come in and answer it in a second.

Sylvester. To join a little strength to a lot of weakness is what I call sensible ; but to join a little weakness to a lot of strength is what I call a . . .

Simon. A cod.

Sylvester. Exactly.   [*The telephone continues to ring.*

Sylvester. There's that telephone ringin' still.

Simon. Oh, someone 'll come in and answer it in a second.
[*Teddy has groped his way to French window.*

Teddy. The telephone's tinklin', boys.

Sylvester. Thanks, Teddy.   We hear it, thanks.   [*To Simon*] When he got the invitation from the Committay to come, wearin' his decorations, me an' the old woman tried to persuade him that, seein' his condition, it was better to stop at home, an' let me represent him, but [*with a gesture*] no use !
[*Teddy resumes his walk to and fro.*

Simon. It was natural he'd want to come, since he was the means of winning the Cup twice before for them, leading up to their keeping the trophy for ever by the win of a year ago.

Sylvester. To bring a boy so helpless as him, whose memory of agility an' strength time hasn't flattened down, to a place wavin' with joy an' dancin', is simply, simply——

Simon. Devastating, I'd say.

Sylvester. Of course it is ! Is that god-damn telephone goin' to keep ringin' all night ?

> [*Mrs. Foran enters from hall quickly.*

Mrs. Foran. Miss Monican says that one of you is to answer the telephone, an' call her if it's anything important.

Sylvester [*nervously*]. I never handled a telephone in my life.

Simon. I chanced it once and got so hot and quivery that I couldn't hear a word, and didn't know what I was saying myself.

Mrs. Foran. Have a shot at it and see.

> [*The three of them drift over to the telephone.*

Sylvester. Chance it again, Simon, an' try to keep steady.

> [*As Simon stretches his hand to the receiver.*

Sylvester. Don't rush, don't rush, man, an' make a mess of it. Take it in your stride.

Simon [*pointing to receiver*]. When you lift this down, you're connected, I think.

Sylvester. No use of thinkin' on this job. Don't you turn the handle first ?

Simon [*irritably*]. No, you don't turn no handle, man !

Mrs. Foran. Let Simon do it now ; Simon knows.

> [*Simon tremblingly lifts down the receiver, almost letting it fall.*

Sylvester. Woa, woa, Simon ; careful, careful !

Simon [*speaking in receiver*]. Eh, hallo ! Eh, listen there. Eh, hallo ! listen.

Sylvester. You listen, man, an' give the fellow at the other end a chance to speak.

Simon. If you want me to manipulate the thing, let me manipulate it in tranquillity.

Mrs. Foran [*to Sylvester*]. Oh, don't be puttin' him out, Sylvester.

Simon [*waving them back*]. Don't be crushing in on me ; give me room to manipulate the thing.

> [*Dead silence for some moments.*

Mrs. Foran. Are you hearin' anything from the other end ?

Simon. A kind of a buzzing and a roaring noise.

> [*Sylvester suddenly gives the cord a jerk and pulls the receiver out of Simon's hand.*

[*Angrily*] What the hell are you trying to do, man ? You're after pulling it right out of my mit.

Sylvester [*heatedly*]. There was a knot or a twist an' a tangle in it that was keepin' the sound from travellin'.

Simon. If you want me to work the thing properly, you'll have to keep yourself from interfering. [*Resuming surlily*] Eh, hallo, listen, yes ? Ha ! ha ! ha ! ha ! Yes, yes, yes. No, no, no. Cheerio ! Yes. Eh, hallo, listen, eh. Hallo.

Sylvester. What is it ? What're they sayin' ?

Simon [*hopelessly, taking the receiver from his ear*]. I don't seem to be able to hear a damn sound.

Sylvester. An' Holy God, what are you yessin' and noin' and cherioin' out of you for then ?

Simon. You couldn't stand here like a fool and say nothing, could you ?

Sylvester. Show it to me, Simon, show it to me — you're not holdin' it at the proper angle.

Mrs. Foran. Give it to Syl, Simon ; it's a delicate contrivance that needs a knack in handlin'.

Sylvester [*as he is taking the receiver from Simon and carefully placing it to his ear*]. You have always to preserve an eqwee-balance between the speakin' mouth and the hearin' ear. [*Speaking into receiver*] Hallo ! Anybody there at the other end of this ? Eh, wha's that ? Yes, yes, I've got you [*taking the receiver from his ear and speaking to Simon and Mrs. Foran*] : Something like wine, or dine, or shine, or something — an' a thing that's hummin'.

Simon. I can see no magnificent meaning jumping out of that !

Mrs. Foran. They couldn't be talkin' about bees, could they ?

Sylvester [*scornfully*]. Bees ! No, they couldn't be talkin' about bees ! That kind of talk, Mrs. Foran, only tends to confuse matters. Bees ! Dtch, dtch, dtch — the stupidity of some persons is . . . terrifyin' !

Simon. Ask them quietly what they want.

Sylvester [*indignantly*]. What the hell's the use of askin' them that, when I can hear something only like a thing that's hummin' ?

Mrs. Foran. It wouldn't be, now, comin', or even bummin' ?

Sylvester. It might even possibly be drummin'. Personally, Mrs. Foran, I think, since you can't help, you might try to keep from hinderin'.

Simon. Put it back, Syl, where it was, an' if it rings again, we'll only have to slip quietly out of this.

Mrs. Foran. Yes, put it back, an' say it never rang.

Sylvester Where was it? Where do I put it back?

Simon. On that thing stickin' out there. Nice and gently now.

> [*Sylvester cautiously puts receiver back. They look at the telephone for a few moments, then go back to the fire, one by one. Sylvester stands with his back to it; Simon sits in a chair, over the back of which Mrs. Foran leans.*

Mrs. Foran. Curious those at the other end of the telephone couldn't make themselves understood.

Simon. Likely they're not accustomed to it, and it's a bit difficult if you're not fully conscious of its manipulation.

Sylvester. Well, let them study an' study it then, or abide by the consequences, for we can't be wastin' time teachin' them.

> [*The curtains at entrance of dance hall are pulled aside, and Teddy, who has disappeared from the garden a little time before, comes in. As he leaves the curtains apart, the dancers can be seen gliding past the entrance in the movements of a tango. Teddy comes down, looks steadily but vacantly towards the group around the fire, then goes over carefully to the table, where he moves his hand about till it touches a bottle, which he takes up in one hand, feeling it questioningly with the other.*

Simon. How goes it, Teddy ?

Teddy [*with a vacant look towards them*]. Sylvester — Simon
— well. What seest thou, Teddy ? Thou seest not
as man seeth. In the garden the trees stand up ; the
green things showeth themselves and fling out flowers
of divers hues. In the sky the sun by day and the moon
and the stars by night — nothing. In the hall the
sound of dancing, the eyes of women, grey and blue
and brown and black, do sparkle and dim and sparkle
again. Their white breasts rise and fall, and rise again.
Slender legs, from red and black, and white and green,
come out, go in again — nothing. Strain as you may,
it stretches from the throne of God to the end of the
hearth of hell.

Simon. What ?

Teddy. The darkness.

Simon [*knowing not what to say*]. Yes, oh yes.

Teddy [*holding up a bottle of wine*]. What colour, Syl ?
It's all the same, but I like the red the best.

Mrs. Foran [*going over to Teddy*]. Just one glass, dear, and
you'll sit down quietly an' take it in sips.
   [*Mrs. Foran fills a glass of wine for Teddy, leads him to a
   chair, puts him sitting down, and gives the glass of wine
   carefully to him. The band in the hall has been playing,
   and through the parted curtains the dancers are seen
   gliding past. Jessie moves by now in the arms of Barney,
   and in a few moments is followed along the side of the
   hall by Harry wheeling himself in his chair and watching
   them. Mrs. Foran and the two men look on and become
   more attentive when among the dancers Susie, in the arms
   of Surgeon Maxwell, Jessie partnered with Barney, and
   Harry move past.*

Sylvester [*as Susie goes by*]. Susie Monican's lookin' game enough to-night for anything.

Simon. Hardly remindful of her one-time fear of God.

Sylvester [*as Jessie goes by followed by Harry*]. There he goes, still followin' them.

Simon. And Jessie's looking as if she was tired of her maidenhood, too.

Mrs. Foran. The thin threads holdin' her dress up sidlin' down over her shoulders, an' her catchin' them up again at the tail end of the second before it was too late.

Simon [*grinning*]. And Barney's hand inching up, inching up to pull them a little lower when they're sliding down.

Mrs. Foran. Astonishin' the way girls are advertisin' their immodesty. Whenever one of them sits down, in my heart I pity the poor men havin' to view the disedifyin' sight of the full length of one leg couched over another.

Teddy [*forgetful*]. A damn nice sight, all the same, I think.

Mrs. Foran [*indignantly*]. One would imagine such a thought would jar a man's mind that had kissed good-bye to the sight of his eyes.

Teddy. Oh, don't be tickin' off every word I say !

Mrs. Foran [*after an astonished pause, whipping the glass out of Teddy's hand*]. Damn the drop more, now, you'll get for the rest of the evenin'.
   [*The band suddenly stops playing, and the couples seen just then through the doorway stop dancing and look attentively*

up the hall. After a slight pause, Harry in his chair,
pushed by Susie, comes in through the entrance ; his face
is pale and drawn, his breath comes in quick faint gasps,
and his head is leaning sideways on the back of the chair.
Mrs. Heegan is on one side of Harry, and Surgeon
Maxwell, who is in dinner-jacket style of evening dress,
wearing his medals, including the D.S.O., walks on the
other. Harry is wheeled over near the open window.
Barney and Jessie, standing in the entrance, look on and
listen.

Maxwell. Here near the window. [*To Mrs. Heegan*]
He'll be all right, Mrs. Heegan, in a second ; a little
faint — too much excitement. When he recovers a
little, I'd get him home.

Harry [*faintly but doggedly*]. Napoo home, napoo. Not
yet. I'm all right. I'll spend a little time longer in
the belly of an hour bulgin' out with merriment.
Carry on.

Maxwell. Better for you to go home, Heegan.

Harry. When they drink to the Club from the Cup —
the Silver Tassie — that I won three times, three
times for them — that first was filled to wet the lips
of Jessie and of me — I'll go, but not yet. I'm all
right ; my name is yet only a shadow on the Roll of
Honour.

Mrs. Heegan. Come home, Harry ; you're gettin' your
allowance only on the understandin' that you take care
of yourself.

Harry. Get the Cup. I'll mind it here till you're ready
to send it round to drink to the Avondales — on the
table here beside me. Bring the Cup ; I'll mind it
here on the table beside me.

Maxwell. Get the Cup for him, someone.

[*Simon goes to the hall and returns with the Cup, which he gives to Harry.*

Harry [*holding the Cup out*]. A first drink again for me, for me alone this time, for the shell that hit me bursts for ever between Jessie and me. [*To Simon*] Go on, man, fill out the wine !

Maxwell [*to Simon*]. A little — just a glass. Won't do him any harm. [*To Harry*] Then you'll have to remain perfectly quiet, Heegan.

Harry. The wine — fill out the wine !

Simon [*to Harry*]. Red wine or white ?

Harry. Red wine, red like the faint remembrance of the fires in France ; red wine like the poppies that spill their petals on the breasts of the dead men. No, white wine, white like the stillness of the millions that have removed their clamours from the crowd of life. No, red wine ; red like the blood that was shed for you and for many for the commission of sin ! [*He drinks the wine.*] Steady, Harry, and lift up thine eyes unto the hills. [*Roughly to those around him*] What are you all gaping at ?

Maxwell. Now, now, Heegan — you must try to keep quiet.

Susie. And when you've rested and feel better, you will sing for us a Negro Spiritual, and point the melody with the ukelele.

Mrs. Heegan. Just as he used to do.

Sylvester. Behind the trenches.

Simon. In the Rest Camps.

Mrs. Foran. Out in France.

Harry. Push your sympathy away from me, for I'll have none of it. [*He wheels his chair quickly towards the dance hall.*] Go on with the dancing and keep the ball a-rolling. [*Calling loudly at the entrance*] Trumpets and drum begin! [*The band begins to play.*] Dance and dance and dance. [*He listens for a moment.*] Sink into merriment again, and sling your cares to God! [*He whirls round in the chair to the beat of the tune. Dancers are seen gliding past entrance.*] Dear God, I can't. [*He sinks sideways on his chair.*] I must, must rest. [*He quietly recites :*]

> For a spell here I will stay,
> Then pack up my body and go —
> For mine is a life on the ebb,
> Yours a full life on the flow !

[*Harry goes over to far side of window and looks out into garden. Mrs. Heegan is on his right and Teddy on his left ; Simon and Sylvester a little behind, looking on. Mrs. Foran to the right of Mrs. Heegan. Surgeon Maxwell and Susie, who are a little to the front, watch for a moment, then the Surgeon puts his arm round Susie and the pair glide off into the dance hall.*

[*When Surgeon Maxwell and Susie glide in to the motions of the dance through the entrance into the dance hall, the curtains are pulled together. A few moments' pause. Teddy silently puts his hand on Harry's shoulder, and they both stare into the garden.*

Simon. The air'll do him good.

Sylvester. An' give him breath to sing his song an' play the ukelele.

Mrs. Heegan. Just as he used to do.

Sylvester. Behind the trenches.

Simon. In the Rest Camps.

Mrs. Foran. Out in France.

Harry. I can see, but I cannot dance.

Teddy. I can dance, but I cannot see.

Harry. Would that I had the strength to do the things I see.

Teddy. Would that I could see the things I've strength to do.

Harry. The Lord hath given and the Lord hath taken away.

Teddy. Blessed be the name of the Lord.

Mrs. Foran. I do love the ukelele, especially when it goes tinkle, tinkle, tinkle in the night-time.

Sylvester. Bringin' before you glistenin' bodies of blacks, coilin' themselves an' shufflin' an' prancin' in a great jungle dance ; shakin' assegais an' spears to the rattle, rattle, rattle an' thud, thud, thud of the tom-toms.

Mrs. Foran. There's only one possible musical trimmin' to the air of a Negro Spiritual, an' that's the tinkle, tinkle, tinkle of a ukelele.

Harry, The rising sap in trees I'll never feel.

Teddy. The hues of branch or leaf I'll never see.

Harry. There's something wrong with life when men can walk.

Teddy. There's something wrong with life when men can see.

Harry. I never felt the hand that made me helpless.

Teddy. I never saw the hand that made me blind.

Harry. Life came and took away the half of life.

Teddy. Life took from me the half he left with you.

Harry. The Lord hath given and the Lord hath taken away.

Teddy. Blessed be the name of the Lord.
[*Susie comes quickly in by entrance, goes over to the table and, looking at several bottles of wine, selects one. She is going hurriedly back, when, seeing Harry, she goes over to him.*

Susie [*kindly*]. How are you now, Harry?

Harry. All right, thank you.

Susie. That's good.
[*Susie is about to hurry away, when Mrs. Foran stops her with a remark.*

Mrs. Foran [*with a meaning gesture*]. He's takin' it cushy till you're ready to hear him singin' his Negro Spiritual, Miss.

Susie. Oh, God, I'd nearly forgotten that. They'll be giving out the balloons at the next dance, and when that fox-trot's over he'll have to come in and sing us the Spiritual.

Mrs. Heegan. Just as he used to do.

Simon. Behind the trenches.

Sylvester. In the Rest Camps.

Mrs. Foran. Out in France.

Susie. As soon as the Balloon Dance is over, Harry, out through the garden and in by the front entrance with you, so that you'll be ready to start as they all sit down. And after the song, we'll drink to the Club from the Silver Tassie.

> [*She hurries back to the hall with the bottle of wine.*

Mrs. Foran. I'm longin' to hear Harry on the ukelele.

Harry. I hope I'll be able to do justice to it.

Mrs. Heegan. Of course you will, Harry.

Harry [*nervously*]. Before a crowd. Forget a word and it's all up with you.

Simon. Try it over now, softly; the sound couldn't carry as far as the hall.

Sylvester. It'll give you confidence in yourself.

Harry [*to Simon*]. Show us the ukelele, Simon.

> [*Simon gets the ukelele and gives it to Harry.*

Teddy. If I knew the ukelele it might wean me a little way from the darkness.

> [*Harry pulls a few notes, tuning the ukelele, then he softly sings.*

Harry :

Swing low, sweet chariot, comin' for to carry me home,

Swing low, sweet chariot, comin' for to carry me home.

I looked over Jordan, what did I see, comin' for to carry me home ?

A band of angels comin' after me — comin' for to carry me home.

> [*A voice in the hall is heard shouting through a megaphone.*

Voice. Balloons will be given out now !   Given out now
— the balloons !

Mrs. Foran [*excitedly*]. They're goin' to send up the
balloons !   They're going to let the balloons fly now !

Harry [*singing*] :
    Swing low, sweet chariot, comin' for to carry me
      home.
    Swing low, sweet chariot, comin' for to carry me
      home.

Mrs. Foran [*as Harry is singing*]. Miss Monican wants us
all to see the flyin' balloons.
    [*She catches Teddy's arm and runs with him into the hall.*

Simon. We must all see the flyin' balloons.

Mrs. Heegan [*running into hall*]. Red balloons and black
balloons.

Simon [*following Mrs. Heegan*]. Green balloons and blue
balloons.

Sylvester [*following Simon*]. Yellow balloons and puce
balloons.
    [*All troop into the hall, leaving the curtains apart, and
    Harry alone with his ukelele.   Through the entrance
    various coloured balloons that have been tossed into the
    air can be seen, mid sounds of merriment and excitement.*

Harry [*softly and slowly*]. Comin' for to carry me home.
    [*He throws the ukelele into an armchair, sits still for a
    moment, then goes to the table, takes up the Silver Cup,
    and wheels himself into the garden.*
    [*After a pause Barney looks in, then enters pulling Jessie by
    the hand, letting the curtains fall together again.   Then
    he goes quickly to window, shuts and bolts it, drawing-to*

one half of the curtains, goes back to Jessie, catches her hand again, and tries to draw her towards room on the left. During the actions that follow the dance goes merrily on in the hall.

Jessie [*holding up a broken shoulder-strap and pulling back towards the hall*]. Barney, no. God, I'd be afraid he might come in on us alone.
[*Hands part the curtains and throw in coloured streamers that encircle Jessie and Barney.*

Barney. Damn them ! . . . He's gone, I tell you, to sing the song an' play the ukelele.

Jessie [*excited and afraid*]. See, they're watching us. No, Barney. You mustn't. I'll not go ! [*Barney seizes Jessie in his arms and forces her towards the door on the left.*] You wouldn't be good. I'll not go into that room.

Barney. I will be good, I tell you ! I just want to be alone with you for a minute.
[*Barney loosens Jessie's other shoulder-strap, so that her dress leaves her shoulders and bosom bare.*

Jessie [*near the door left, as Barney opens it*]. You've loosened my dress — I knew you weren't going to be good. [*As she kisses him passionately*] Barney, Barney — you shouldn't be making me do what I don't want to do !

Barney [*holding her and trying to pull her into room*]. Come on, Jessie, you needn't be afraid of Barney — we'll just rest a few minutes from the dancing.
[*At that part of the window uncurtained Harry is seen peering in. He then wheels his chair back and comes on to the centre of the window-frame with a rush, bursting*

*the catch and speeding into the room, coming to a halt,
angry and savage, before Barney and Jessie.*

Harry. So you'd make merry over my helplessness in
front of my face, in front of my face, you pair of
cheats ! You couldn't wait till I'd gone, so that my
eyes wouldn't see the joy I wanted hurrying away from
me over to another ? Hurt her breast pulling your
hand quick out of her bodice, did you ? [*To Jessie*]
Saved you in the nick of time, my lady, did I ? [*To
Barney*] Going to enjoy yourself on the same little
couch where she, before you formed an image in her
eye, acted the part of an amateur wife, and I acted the
part of an amateur husband — the black couch with
the green and crimson butterflies, in the yellow bushes,
where she and me often tired of the things you're
dangling after now !

Jessie. He's a liar, he's a liar, Barney ! He often tried it
on with coaxing first and temper afterwards, but it
always ended in a halt that left him where he started.

Harry. If I had my hands on your white neck I'd leave
marks there that crowds of kisses from your Barney
wouldn't moisten away.

Barney. You half-baked Lazarus, I've put up with you
all the evening, so don't force me now to rough-handle
the bit of life the Jerries left you as a souvenir !

Harry. When I wanted to slip away from life, you
brought me back with your whispered " Think of the
tears of Jess, think of the tears of Jess ", but Jess has
wiped away her tears in the ribbon of your Cross,
and this poor crippled jest gives a flame of joy to the
change ; but when you get her, may you find in her
the pressed-down emptiness of a whore !

Barney [*running over and seizing Harry*]. I'll tilt the leaking life out of you, you jealous, peering pimp !

Jessie [*trying to hold Barney back*]. Barney, Barney, don't ! don't !

Harry [*appealingly*]. **Barney, Barney !** My heart — you're stopping it !

Jessie [*running to entrance and shouting in*]. Help ! help ! They're killing each other !
[*In the hall the dance stops. Surgeon Maxwell runs in, followed by Susie, Simon, Sylvester, Mrs. Foran, Mrs. Heegan, and lastly Teddy finding his way over to the window. Dancers gather around entrance and look on.*
[*Surgeon Maxwell, running over, separates Barney from Harry.*

Maxwell. What's this ? Come, come — we can't have this sort of thing going on.

Mrs. Heegan. He was throttlin' him, throttlin' a poor helpless creature, an' if anything happens, he and that painted slug Jessie Taite 'll be held accountable !

Maxwell. This can't be allowed to go on. You'll have to bring him home. Any more excitement would be dangerous.

Mrs. Heegan. This is what he gets from Jessie Taite for sittin' on the stairs through the yawnin' hours of the night, racin' her off to the play an' the pictures, an' plungin' every penny he could keep from me into presents for the consolidation of the courtship !

Maxwell. Bring the boy home, woman, bring the boy home.

Sylvester [*fiercely to Jessie*]. And money of mine in one of the gewgaws scintillatin' in her hair !

Jessie. What gewgaw ? What gewgaw ?
[*Coloured streamers are thrown in by those standing at entrance, which fall on and encircle some of the group around Harry.*

Sylvester. The tiarara I gave you two Christmases ago with the yellow berries and the three flutterin' crimson swallows !

Harry [*faintly and bitterly, with a hard little laugh*]. Napoo Barney Bagnal and napoo Jessie Taite. A merry heart throbs coldly in my bosom ; a merry heart in a cold bosom — or is it a cold heart in a merry bosom ? [*He gathers a number of the coloured streamers and winds them round himself and chair.*] Teddy ! [*Harry catches Teddy by the sleeve and winds some more streamers round him.*] Sing a song, man, and show the stuff you're made of !

Maxwell [*catching hold of Mrs. Heegan's arm*]. Bring him home, woman. [*Maxwell catches Sylvester's arm.*] Get him home, man.

Harry. Dear God, this crippled form is still your child. [*To Mrs. Heegan*] Dear mother, this helpless thing is still your son. Harry Heegan, me, who, on the football field, could crash a twelve-stone flyer off his feet. For this dear Club three times I won the Cup, and grieve in reason I was just too weak this year to play again. And now, before I go, I give you all the Cup, the Silver Tassie, to have and to hold for ever, evermore. [*From *his chair he takes the Cup with the two sides hammered close together, and holds it out to them.*] Mangled and bruised as I am bruised and mangled. Hammered free from all its comely shape. Look, there is Jessie writ, and here is Harry, the one name safely separated from the other. [*He flings it on the floor.*] Treat it kindly. With care it may be opened out, for Barney there to drink to Jess, and Jessie there to drink to Barney.

Teddy. Come, Harry, home to where the air is soft. No longer can you stand upon a hill-top ; these empty eyes of mine can never see from one. Our best is all behind us — what's in front we'll face like men, dear comrade of the blood-fight and the battle-front !

Harry. What's in front we'll face like men ! [*Harry goes out by the window, Sylvester pushing the chair, Teddy's hand on Harry's shoulder, Mrs. Heegan slowly following. Those left in the room watch them going out through the garden, turning to the right till they are all out of sight. As he goes out of window*] The Lord hath given and man hath taken away !

Teddy [*heard from the garden*]. Blessed be the name of the Lord !
  [*The band in the hall begins to play again. Those in hall begin to dance.*

Maxwell. Come on, all, we've wasted too much time already.

Susie [*to Jessie, who is sitting quietly in a chair*]. Come on, Jessie — get your partner ; [*roguishly*] you can have a quiet time with Barney later on. '

Jessie. Poor Harry !

Susie. Oh nonsense ! If you'd passed as many through your hands as I, you'd hardly notice one. [*To Jessie*] Jessie, Teddy Foran and Harry Heegan have gone to live their own way in another world. Neither I nor you can lift them out of it. No longer can they do the things we do. We can't give sight to the blind or make the lame walk. We would if we could. It is the misfortune of war. As long as wars are waged, we shall be vexed by woe ; strong legs shall be made useless and bright eyes made dark. But we, who have come through the fire unharmed, must go on living. [*Pulling Jessie from the chair*] Come along, and take your part in life ! [*To Barney*] Come along, Barney, and take your partner into the dance !

> [*Barney comes over, puts his arm round Jessie, and they dance into the hall. Susie and Surgeon Maxwell dance together. As they dance the Waltz " Over the Waves ", som eremain behind drinking. Two of these sing the song to the same tune as the dance.*]

Maxwell :

> Swing into the dance,
> Take joy when it comes, ere it go ;
> For the full flavour of life
> Is either a kiss or a blow.
> He to whom joy is a foe,
> Let him wrap himself up in his woe ;
> For he is a life on the ebb,
> We a full life on the flow !

> [*All in the hall dance away with streamers and balloons flying. Simon and Mrs. Foran sit down and watch the*

*fun through the entrance.   Mrs. Foran lights a cigarette
and smokes.   A pause as they look on.*

Mrs. Foran. It's a terrible pity Harry was too weak to
stay an' sing his song, for there's nothing I love more
than the ukelele's tinkle, tinkle in the night-time.

CURTAIN

SONGS AND CHANTS IN
THE SILVER TASSIE

1st CHANT.

Intonation

I sees the mis - sus paryd-ing a - long Wal-ham Green, Through the jewels

Mediation

an' silks on the cos - ters' carts, Em - mie a - pull - ing her skirt

Ending

an' mut - ter - ing, "A bal - loon, a bal-loon, I wants a bal - loon",

The mis-sus . . . an' your fa-ther fight-ing : You'll wait . . that's wot we wants to know !

Tabs 'll . . . for - ty-eight bat-ta-lion, The Yel-low . . . leg up on the path to glo-ry;

Now with . . . Ar-my of the Marne, An' all the time . . . two men looking after business.

The padre . . . muv-ver 'as you 'ere." An' last time . . . sep-er-y-tion mon-eys reg'-lar.

But wy - 'r we 'ere, wy - 'r we 'ere—that's wot I wants to know !

365

2nd CHANT.

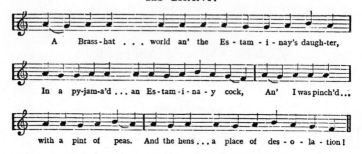

A   Brass-hat ... world an' the Es - tam - i - nay's daugh-ter,

In   a   py-jam-a'd ... an Es - tam - i - na - y cock,   An'   I was pinch'd ...

with   a   pint of   peas.   And the hens ... a   place of   des - o - la - tion!

3rd CHANT.

The   perk - y ... queers me. Furi - ous - ly   feel - ing ... front-line fight - ing.

In   his   full-blown, ... mur-mur, "Here's a stand-fast ... whis - per "yes - sir".

Like   a   bride, ... ser - mon, From the cush - y   ... Tom-my's back-side.

4th CHANT.

Jazz - ing back to   his   ho - tel   he now goes gai - ly, Shel - ter'd

and   safe where   the   clock   ticks   tame - ly.   His   back - side warm - ing

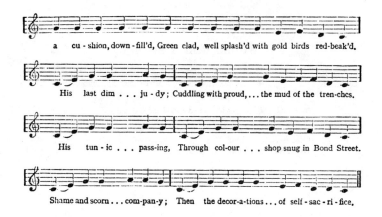

a   cu - shion, down - fill'd, Green clad, well splash'd with gold birds red-beak'd.

His   last dim . . . ju - dy ; Cuddling with proud, . . . the mud of the tren-ches.

His   tun - ic . . . pass-ing, Through col-our . . . shop snug in Bond Street.

Shame and scorn . . . com-pan-y ;   Then   the decor-a-tions . . . of self - sac - ri - fice.

5th CHANT.

A   warn-ing . . . give,   To the front . . . do, to   God.

God, un-chang-ing, . . . night sky   To mask . . . His self-slay-ing chil-dren.

Stumbling, swiftly . . . grous-ing,   Through mud . . . seek slow the front line.

Squeals of hid - den . . . wounded—Christ who bore . . . tied to a field gun.

WOULD GOD I SMOK'D.

Would God I smok'd and walk'd and watch'd - - The dance of a
Would God I smok'd and lift - ed car - goes From the lad - en
To hang here ev - en a lit - tle lon - ger, Loung - ing
If you creep to rest in a clos'd-up cof - fin, A tail of
Each spar - row, hop - ping, ir - re - sponsible, Is in - den - tur'd

gol - den Brim - stone but - ter - fly, - - To the
shoul - ders of Lon - don's riv - er - way; - - Then
through fear - swell'd, anx - ious moments; The
com - rades see - ing you safe home; - Or be a
in God's migh - ty mem - o - ry; . - And we,

sau - cy pipe of a green - finch rest - ing In a
holi - day'd, roar - ing out courage and move-ment To the
hin - der - parts of the god of bat - tles Shading our
ker - nel lost in a shell ex - plod - ing— It's all,
more than they all, shall not be lost In the for-

drowsy, brambled lane in Cumber - land. In Cumber - land.
mus - cled ma-chines of Tottenham Hotspur. Of Tottenham Hotspur.
war - tir'd eyes from his flam - ing face. From his flaming face.
sure, on - ly in a life - time. A life - time.
get - ful - ness of the Lord of Hosts. Of the Lord of Hosts.

STRETCHER-BEARERS' SONG.

Oh, bear it gent-ly, car-ry it soft-ly—A bull-et or a shell said stop, stop, stop. It's had its day, and it's left the play, Since it gam-boll'd ov-er the top, top, top. It's had its day and it's left the play, Since it gam-boll'd o · · ver the top.

SONG TO THE GUN.

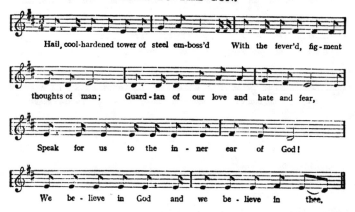

Hail, cool-hardened tower of steel em-boss'd With the fever'd, fig-ment thoughts of man; Guard-ian of our love and hate and fear, Speak for us to the in-ner ear of God! We be-lieve in God and we be-lieve in thee.

THE ENEMY HAS BROKEN THROUGH

The en-em-y has brok-en through, brok-en through, brok-en through! Ev-ery man born of wo-man to the guns, to the guns. To the guns, to the guns, to the guns! Those at prayer, all in bed and the swillers drinking deeply in the pubs. To the guns, to the guns. All the bat-men, ev-ery cook, ev-ery bitch's son that hides A whiff of cour-age in his veins, Shelter'd vig-our in his bod-y, That can run, or can walk, ev-en crawl— · · · Dig him out, dig him out, shove him on— · · · To the guns!

SURGEON'S SONG.

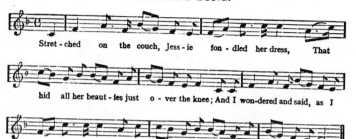

Stret - ched on the couch, Jess - ie fon - dled her dress, That

hid all her beaut - ies just o - ver the knee; And I won-dered and said, as I

sigh'd, "What a shame, That there's no room at all on the couch there for me."

A MORALITY IN FOUR SCENES

Within the Gates

CHARACTERS IN THE PLAY

THE DREAMER
OLDER CHAIR ATTENDANT
YOUNGER CHAIR ATTENDANT
THE BISHOP
THE BISHOP'S SISTER
THE ATHEIST
THE POLICEWOMAN
1ST NURSEMAID
2ND NURSEMAID
A GUARDSMAN
A GARDENER
1ST EVANGELIST
2ND EVANGELIST
THE YOUNG WOMAN
A YOUNG SALVATION ARMY OFFICER
THE OLD WOMAN
A MAN WEARING A BOWLER HAT
THE MAN WITH THE STICK (*afterwards, an umbrella*)
MAN WEARING A TRILBY HAT
MAN WEARING A STRAW ONE (*afterwards, a cap*)
A CROWD OF THE DOWN-AND-OUT

A Chorus of Young Men and Maidens

SCENE I

Within a Park.
On a Spring Morning.

SCENE II

Within a Park.
On a Summer Noon.

SCENE III

Within a Park.
On an Autumn Evening.

SCENE IV

Within a Park.
On a Winter's Night.

Spring. Morning.

Within a Park on a Spring morning.

A clear, light-blue sky, against which is shown, in places, the interlaced dark-brown branches of trees, dotted with green, yellow, and red buds.

The green sward in front slopes up towards the back, but in no way high enough to prevent a view of the spaciousness of the Park behind. In the centre of the slope are a few wide steps leading to the top, where, a little to one side, stands a War Memorial in the form of a steel-helmeted soldier, the head bent on the breast, skeleton-like hands leaning on the butt-end of a rifle. Bushes allow the figure to be seen only from the waist up. The body and arms of the figure are shaped in a sharply defined way ; the hat a wide circle ; and the features are cut in long, sharp, and angular lines. The figure stands out grey against the blue sky and the green shrubs, and seems to be shrinking back from the growing interests brought into being by new life and her thrusting activities.

The rise of the slope is sprinkled with large, formalized figures of daffodils.

At the foot of the slope are paths branching to the right and to the left, that on the left flowing into a wider one encircling the Park lake, from which can be occasionally heard the cries of the water-fowl swimming on the water or preening themselves on the banks.

Birds are heard singing in a subdued but busy way, as they search for food or build their nests.

Formally shaped chairs are here and there, and one or two stiff and dignified-looking benches are near the foot of the slope.

*They are painted so as to mingle with the colours of the scene,
and are hardly noticeable. The scheme of colour is a delicate
green and light blue, patterned by the yellow daffodils and the
bare, bud-dotted branches of the trees.*

*As the gates are opening, the Dreamer enters, and passes
through them into the Park. He is gazing with an intensely
dreaming expression at a paper which he holds in his left hand.
His right hand, holding a short pencil, moves in a gentle, dreamy
way, beating time, as he murmurs the opening bars of " Our
Mother the Earth is a Maiden Again ". He crosses out as the
Chorus enters, singing, followed by various people, who move
about at the back, up, down, and about the paths, without
jostle or confusion.*

*A Chorus of Young Boys and Girls, representing trees and
flowers, enter, singing.*

*First, a girl whose skirt represents a white crocus, veined
with blue ; next, a boy in black on whose breast is a stylized
pattern of a beech-tree leaf ; then a girl whose skirt represents
a blue cornflower ; next, a boy on whose breast is a formally
shaped oak leaf ; then a girl whose skirt represents a daffodil ;
next, a boy on whose breast is the pattern of a maple leaf.*

*The Chorus remain in front, while the crowd move about as
they listen, or when they join in the singing.*

Chorus [*singing*] :

    Our mother the Earth is a maiden again, young, fair,
       and a maiden again.

    Our mother the Earth is a maiden again, she's young,
       fair, and a maiden again.

    Her thoughts are a dance as she seeks out her Bride-
       groom, the Sun, through the lovely confusion of
       singing of birds, and of blossom and bud.

    She feels the touch of his hand on her hair, on her
       cheeks ; in the budding of trees,

She feels the kiss of his love on her mouth, on her
breast, as she dances along,

Crowd [joining in] :
Through the lovely confusion of singing of birds, and
of blossom and bud.
Her thoughts are a dance as she seeks out her Bride-
groom, the Sun, through the lovely confusion of
singing of birds, and of blossom and bud.

Chorus :
She hears the fiercely sung song of the birds, busy
building new homes in the hedge ;
She hears a challenge to life and to death as she
dances along,

Crowd [joining in] :
Through the lovely confusion of singing of birds, and
of blossom and bud.
Her thoughts are a dance as she seeks out her Bride-
groom, the Sun, through the lovely confusion of
singing of birds, and of blossom and bud.

Chorus and Crowd :
Our mother the Earth is a maiden again, young,
fair, and a maiden again.

[While the last line is being sung, the Crowd and the
Chorus go out by different ways, leaving only the two
Chair Attendants dusting the chairs and arranging them.
One is young and thin and the other is old and stocky,
and both are in the last lap of physical decay. One has a
stiff right leg, and the other has a stiff left one. They
are dressed in long, khaki-coloured cotton coats, and wear
peaked caps.

Older One. 'Ow's the poor old leg, todye, 'Erbert ?

Young One. Oh Gord ! 'Ow's yours ?

Older One. Aw — sime wye, with honours ! I seen thet poet chap atryin' to cadge a chire again ; sits dahn on one till 'e sees me comin' in the distance.

Young One [*not listening — pensively*]. Wot'll we do when we file to be able to walk ! 'En this singin' gets me dahn. 'Eartless for a crahwd to sing when a man's in misery.

Older One [*testily*]. Don't let us think of them things ! It's our destiny. But I 'ates that poet chap ; I 'ates 'im ! 'Ate 'is liveliness. Fair cheek 'e 'as. A bum — that's wot 'e 'is. Wouldn't do a dye's work for Gord Almighty. I'd say it to 'is fice, I would.

Young One. Look aht ! 'Ere 'e is.
> [*The Dreamer comes down the grass slope, crosses over, and sits down on a bench. He watches the Two Attendants. He is a young man, lithely built, though a little thin and pale now from a hard time ; but he carries himself buoyantly. His features are rugged ; his eyes bright, sometimes flashing in an imaginative mood, but usually quiet and dreamy-looking. His head is covered with a soft black, broad-brimmed hat, and he is wearing a tightly-belted trench mackintosh. Outside the trench coat, around his neck, is a light, vivid orange scarf.*

Dreamer [*suddenly*]. Here, you two derelict worshippers of fine raiment — when are you going to die ?

Older One [*angrily*]. Mind your own business, see ! We 'as more right to life than you 'as. We work — you don't - eh, Godfrey ?

Young One. My oath, we 'as !

Dreamer. No one has a right to life who doesn't fight to make it greater. I've watched you fawning on the bishop and on every good coat that sits down on a chair.

Young One. You mind your own business !

[*The Young Woman comes down the slope and crosses the sward to go out to the left. She has a preoccupied and rather anxious look on her face, and appears to be searching for someone.*

[*She is very pretty, and her figure would make most young men immediately forget the seventh commandment. Her face is a little pale, but this paleness is hidden by a cautious and clever make-up. She has an intelligent look, which is becoming a little worn by contact with the selfishness and meanness of the few clients that have patronised her ; for these, though unable to resist the desire to have her, hate her subconsciously before they go with her, and consciously detest her when their desires have been satisfied. She has read a little, but not enough ; she has thought a little, but not enough ; she is deficient in self-assurance, and is too generous and sensitive to be a clever whore, and her heart is not in the business.*

[*Convent tales of punishments reserved for the particular sins tangled round sex expression have left in her mind lusty images of hellfire. She is dressed in a black tailored suit, topped by a scarlet hat. On the hat is an ornament, in black, of a crescent ; and the hip of her dress is decorated with a scarlet one. The Dreamer sees her, rises, and is about to follow her. She stops and faces him.*

Young Woman. I am troubled ; I am anxious ; please don't follow me.

Dreamer. I shall follow after loveliness all the days of my life.

Young Woman. Not just now, please ; I do not want you. [*She turns to go ; he follows slowly. She turns, to say hysterically*] Go away, please !

[*She goes out. He returns, crestfallen, to his seat on the bench. The Attendants snigger.*

Older One. The likes of 'er ain't for the likes of 'im.

Young One [*to the Dreamer*]. A fine choke-off, wha' ?

[*Dreamer rises, catches each by the coat-collar, and shakes them.*

Dreamer [*roughly*]. Ye lost ones ! Will ye starve and droop and die without a dream ? Even the lame and the halt can hunt out a shrine ! Will ye mock at the better ones who refuse to die like sheep ?

Attendants [*together*]. Eh, there, leggo ! Someone call a perliceman !

[*The Atheist comes in from a path above, sees the angry scene, and hurries down to stop it.*

Atheist [*catching the Dreamer by the arm*]. Now then, friend, now then ; let withered life die in its own sour way, without pushing it to a sudden and unprovided end !

Dreamer [*pushing the Attendants from him — one to the right, the other to the left*]. Away, and cower in your corner, till life hoodooes you out of the misery you both love ! Away, the pair of you, who make a nightmare of the dream of God !

[*The Attendants slink off, one to the right, the other to the left. The Dreamer and the Atheist sit on the bench together.*

Atheist [*warningly*]. Take care, friend : you'd pay as high a penalty for hurting hopelessness as you would for a life of promise or one of proved production.

Dreamer. I know ; I lost my temper. Never mind that now. I've seen her ; she passed by here just before you came.

Atheist [*rising*]. Passed by 'ere ? I'm off in the opposite direction.

Dreamer [*stopping him*]. No fear of meeting her ; she won't come back. I tried to keep her, but she wouldn't stay a second.

Atheist. Oh, lay off the young lass, Dreamer. Let 'er go 'er own wye — up the hill of life or dahn it.

Dreamer. She's too lonely to be left alone, Ned ; and too pretty ; intelligent, too, as you say.

Atheist [*impatiently*]. I know all that ! She 'as a fine mind, if she'd only use it the right way. But it's forever darting forward, back ; to the left to-day, to the right to-morrow — no 'uman being could stand it. I'm glad I'm only her step-da.

Dreamer. Who is, and where is, her real daddy ?

Atheist. Stoodent of theology, the story goes : fell in love with a pretty housemaid, and she responded. When the mother knew what was abaht to happen, she knocked at the college gate, but was driven off. When a few years old, the kid was shoved into a church institoo-tion, where the nuns, being what she was — a child of sin —, paid her special attention ; an' the terrors an' dangers of hell became the child's chief enjoyment !

Dreamer. Good God ! [*Earnestly*] Ned, we must never ease off the fight for a life that is free from fear !

Atheist. Never, Dreamer, never. Then the mother married an Irish dragoon, a brave, decent man,

Dreamer, home from the front on leave ; had a star-
lit time with the warrior for a week ; then the dragoon
disappeared in one of those vanishing advances from
the front line an' the widow settles dahn on 'er pension.

Dreamer. Then she fastened on to you, eh ?

Atheist. To tell the truth, it was I fastened on to 'er.
Even when I met 'er, she was still the kind of woman
would make a man long for something to 'appen — you
know, Dreamer ?

Dreamer. Ay, I know — too damned well !

Atheist. Then I delivered the child from the church in-
stitootion, sayin' I was the father. I did my best for
'er, takin' awye a supernatural 'eaven from over 'er 'ead,
an' an unnatural 'ell from under 'er feet ; but she never
quite escaped. D'ye know, one time, the lass near
knew the whole of Pine's *Age of Reason* off by 'eart !

Dreamer. And did you bring her into touch with song ?

Atheist. Song ? Oh, I had no time for song !

Dreamer. You led her from one darkness into another,
man. [*He rises and walks about — angrily*] Will none of
you ever guess that man can study man, or worship
God, in dance and song and story ! [*Appealingly*] Ah,
Ned, if you could but see her with the eyes of youth,
you would not let her live so lonely.

Atheist. I helped her all I could. Out of the earnings of
a first-class carpenter, I gave 'er a good education, an'
taught 'er a lot myself ; but it was all no good — she
refused to think as I did. The 'ome's broken up, now,
and I'm not eager to try to get it together agine.

Dreamer. How broken up ?

Atheist. You see, when the maid came close to woman-
hood, the mother turned religious, an' begun to 'ate
the kid, sayin' that while the kid was there, 'er sin was
ever in front of 'er fice.   Then she took to drink an'
violence.

Dreamer. A sweet home for a girl coming also to woman-
hood !

Atheist. After a long time of patient endoorance, one
day the girl ups an', withaht a word, goes ; an' a
month after, I goes too ; so 'ere she is, her whole
life a desire for a bright time of it ; an' 'ere I am, a
speaker rending the strands of superstition's web thet
keeps poor men from movin'.

Dreamer. Give the lovely lass one more chance, speaker ;
live the last years of your life with loveliness.

Atheist. Not damn likely ; the longer I'm by myself,
the more I likes it.
  [*While they have been speaking the last few words, the Man
    with the Stick has appeared on the slope above.*

Man with Stick [*calling down to Atheist*]. 'Ave you got to-
night's speech ready, Ned ?

Atheist [*taking note-book from a pocket*]. Not yet, Bill.

Man with Stick. Get a move on : we 'as to bounce the
idea of a Gord from men's minds, so make it strong.
  [*The Two Chair Attendants limp in, carrying a chair
    between them.   They set it down, stand panting for a
    while, then the Older One begins to give it a dust, the
    Man with the Stick watching them contemptuously, and
    dubiously shaking his grey head.*

Man with Stick [*going close to Older Attendant*]. 'Ere, 'ave you an inquirin' mind, friend ?

Older One. Eh ? Wot ?

Man with Stick. I asks if you 'as an inquirin' mind. [*He taps the chair with the stick.*] Wot is this ? A chair. Does thet tell you all abaht it ? No. Wot's it myde of ? Wood. Nah, if it was myde of cork it would be lighter ; but if it was myde of lead it would be 'eavier — see ?

Older One. Ay ?

Man with Stick. Ay ? Not ay, but wye ?

Older One. Wye ? Wot wye ?

Man with Stick [*impatiently*]. Wot wye ! Listen, man. [*Hitting the chair with stick.*] Wood ; 'ard. Nah wye's the chair 'ard ? Is it doo to density, or is it not ?

Older One. I don't ask no questions of chairs.

Young One. We 'as to attend to our werk, see ?

Man with Stick [*woe in his voice*]. No brrine !
   [*The two Nursemaids, the Under One pushing the fine pram, appear behind Man with the Stick.*

Younger Nursemaid [*imperiously*]. Gangway there !
   [*The pram strikes his heels, and he jumps aside, his mouth opening for an angry exclamation ; but when he sees the splendid pram, he closes it without saying a word. The Upper Nursemaid picks out a chair farthest from the others. The Chair Attendants run over bearing a chair between them for the Under Maid, and the Older One dusts both the chairs vigorously.*

Older One [*after dusting*]. Now, miss. Nice day, miss.

Upper Nursemaid [*shortly*]. Very nice.

Older One. To cart such a byeby abaht's a responsible thing, I'd say, miss.

Upper Nursemaid [*stiffly*]. I suppose so. I don't feel it. [*She sees his dirty hand is resting on the pram.*] Take that dirty paw off the pram at once ! This is a countess's baby !

Older One [*pulling his hand away as if the pram was red-hot*]. Oh, excuse me, miss. I forgot for the minute !

Upper Nursemaid [*loftily*]. Go away ; we're season tickets ; go away !

> [*The Attendant slinks off from the pram as the Bishop, followed by his Sister, appears coming down the slope from behind the Memorial. The Policewoman strolls in from the path on the left.*

Atheist [*mockingly — over to the Nursemaids*]. Must be careful of a countess's byeby !

Upper Nursemaid [*with great dignity*]. A countess's byeby's a considerytion, I'd like you all to know.

> [*The Bishop and his Sister come down among the crowd. The Bishop is a heavily built man of sixty or so. His head, his feet, and hands are large ; his voice, once deep and sonorous, has become a little husky. The pretentious briskness of his movements is an attempt to hide from others the fact that he is beginning to fail. He is anxious to show to all he meets that he is an up-to-the-present-minute clergyman, and that those who wear the stole are, on the whole, a lusty, natural, broad-minded, cheery crowd. He is in a black cassock, wears a purple stock round his neck, and his head is covered with a purple biretta or a scarlet one. A black ribbon is round his neck, and from the ends of this, which meet on his chest,*

hangs a large red cross, on which is a white figure of the Saviour.

[*His Sister is a few years younger, grey-haired, stiff, and formal. She has more common sense than her brother, but, while there is a suggestion of good-nature about the Bishop, there is no suggestion whatever of softness about the form or manner of his Sister. Her dress is of grey stuff, stiff like steel.*

Bishop [*breezily*]. Hello, boys ; good morning, Constable. [*To Nursemaids*] Hello, girls !

Attendants [*together*]. 'Ello, your reverence.

Policewoman [*with a dignified salute*]. Morning, sir.

Bishop [*buoyantly*]. Glorious nip of crispness in the air of a Spring morning, isn't there ?

Policewoman. Exhilarating, I'd say.

Older One. Gits a man goin'.

Younger One [*lilting*]. Yes, let me like a soldier fall, dideray diderum dideree.

Bishop. Flowers appear on the earth ; the time of singing of birds is come, and the voice of the turtle is heard in the land — God speaking of Spring, friends !

Policewoman. Quate, sir.

Young One. 'Its it off nacely, sir.

Dreamer [*to the Bishop*]. Not God, but a poet speaking of Spring, sir. Render to God the things that are God's and to the poet the things that are his.

Bishop [*to the Dreamer — smilingly*]. God is in all, and God is all things, sir.

Atheist [*combatively*]. Would the reverend en' learned

gentleman tell us poor people 'oo is Gord, wot 'e is, en' where 'e is located ?

Policewoman [*to the Atheist, stiffly*]. You keep your almighty arguments for your meetings.

Older One [*viciously*]. 'Ear, 'ear !

Bishop [*to Policewoman — graciously*]. Never mind, Constable ; there are always those who never will give thanks to God for life.

Dreamer. Always, when there are those who have no life for which to thank Him.

> [*Two prowling Evangelists come shuffling in.* *Each has a frame strapped to his body from which rise two upright pieces between which is a poster, looking like a square banner over their heads.* *On the first one, in red, is the phrase Once to Die, and on the second, in black, Then the Judgement.*
>
> *The First Evangelist has a lemon-shaped head, staring, stupid-looking eyes, shrunken cheeks, surly lines round a wide mouth, and ears that stick out from the side of his head.*
>
> *The Second has a big head, coarse face, heavy, hanging lips, and a small snubby nose.* *As he chants, he continually blinks his eyes.* *Both are shabbily dressed, and look, for all the world, like sullen, long-forgotten clowns.* *They shuffle in among the disputants, each pointing to the warning posters over their heads.*

1st Evangelist. Once to Die.

2nd Evangelist. After that The Judgement.

1st Evangelist [*chanting*] :
> Is it well with thy soul ?
> Is it well, is it well with thy soul ?

2nd Evangelist [*chanting*] :
   It is well with my soul.
   It is well, it is well with my soul.

   [*They chant themselves out, looking back to gather the others into the warning they give.*

Atheist [*mockingly — to the Bishop*]. Two more Richmonds in the field !

Young One [*encouraging the Bishop*]. Never you mind 'im or them, sir ; — go on torking abaht the Spring en' the birds !   [*The birds sing merrily.*

Bishop [*joyously*]. Listen ! The busy birds warbling a sylvan sonata. Facing out life with a song ! No shaking of the head here in denial of God's goodness and glory. Sursum corda — lift up your hearts !

Dreamer. We lift them up unto the birds.

Older One [*gushingly*]. The birds bring a man 'ope. Even with the doo 'eavy on the grass, a feller begins to feel spry en' elevated when they stert their chirruping.

Policewoman. Not a daht abaht it.

Bishop's Sister. Gilbert, come and look at the swans.

Bishop [*with conviction — to the Policewoman*]. Do you know, Constable, that, to an observing mind, it seems to be conclusive that the most beautiful part of God's creation — apart from man, of course —

Policewoman. Quate — setting man en' woman aside for a moment.

Bishop. Quite. The most beautiful part of God's manifold creation is, undoubtedly, the birds !

[*The Bishop lifts his head and looks up at the sky ; then the Policewoman does the same, and, lastly, the two Chair Attendants lift their heads and crane their necks in an upward look.*

Bishop. Brave little birds.

Policewoman. Beautiful little birds.

Attendants [*together*]. Beautiful, innocent little birds.

Man with Stick [*suddenly leaning forward — imperatively*]. 'Ere, 'ow do birds resist the lawrs of gravitation ? Come, quick — the lot of you — think !
               [*They all lower their heads again, together.*

Young One [*enthusiastically*]. Never you mind 'im, sir. Wot you says reminds man that Gord watches even over the fall of the sparrer !

Atheist [*mockingly*]. Ay, an' the fall of the 'awk on the sparrer to tear it to pieces !

Older One [*hotly*]. You shut your rotten mouth, will you ! Warnt to 'ear yourself torkin', torkin', do you ? Try to look at things in perspective, carn't you ? Wot's you or me in the general scheme of things, eh ? Speck o' dust, blide o' grass, a nought, a nothing. Wish Jimmy Douglas of the *Daily Express* was 'ere to 'ear you. 'E's the man would stun you both with truth ! [*To his fellow Attendant*] Wot d'ye sye, Godfrey ?

Young One. 'E's a man as knows 'oo's 'oo en' wot's wot.

Older One. You bet 'e does. 'Ow on a 'olidye, sitting by the sea, under the stars, wot 'e sawr en' wot 'e 'eard. 'Ow 'e marvelled at the star dust 'e could see en' the star dust 'e couldn't see ; en' 'ow 'e was filled with terror en' fear as 'e 'eard the clock of eternity ticking !

Dreamer. It won't be long, old man, till you hear the clock of eternity ticking !

Older One [*stormily*]. Wot if it won't ? It ain't the end, is it ?

Dreamer [*rising from the bench — fervently*]. Kill off the withered mind, the violently-stupid, O Lord, who having nothing to give, have nothing to get !

Bishop's Sister [*pulling Bishop's cassock*]. Gilbert, do come to watch the swans !

Older One [*catching hold of Dreamer's sleeve — violently*]. Thinkin' thet life doesn't keep agoing on when it ends ! I yells it aht, I yells it aht — death's only the gytewye to a fuller en' a nobler life !

Dreamer [*angrily shaking off the Attendant's hold*]. Take that dead hand off me ! There are some here equal in value to a countess's baby. [*He shoves the Attendant roughly from him so that he lurches back against the pram.*] Be off, and die, and keep a holy distance from the quick and the lively !

Young One [*bawling to the Older One*]. 'Erbert, eh, mind the countess's byeby !

Atheist [*mockingly — to the Nursemaid*]. Lady, lady, this is no place for a countess's byeby !

Policewoman [*going to the Nursemaid*]. 'E's right ; better conduct it to a calmer locality.

[*The two Nursemaids rise hurriedly, cross over the sward, preceded by the Policewoman, and disappear with the pram behind the trees to the left.*

Bishop's Sister [*plucking at his cassock*]. You see, Gilbert ! A bishop should be in the midst of the incense, in the sanctuary, safe away from the sour touch of common humanity.

Bishop [*jovially*]. Nonsense, dear ! I lose no dignity in getting close to the common people. Get them to talk with us ; laugh and joke with us ; and then we can expect them to pray with us.

Atheist [*over to the Bishop*]. Prayer ? For what ? To whom ?
　Old memories, faiths infirm and dead,
　Ye fools ; for which among you deems
　His prayer can alter green to red,
　Or stones to bread ?

Bishop's Sister [*pulling the Bishop away*]. You but mould mockery from the profane thoughts of others. Come and watch the swans. Remember what happened to you in your student days !
　[*The Bishop, at the last phrase, stiffens, his face clenches, and he goes off with his Sister without another word.*

Atheist [*as the Bishop is pulled out*]. He 'as a better charnce with the swans than 'e 'as with us !

Man with Stick [*calling from top of slope*]. 'Ere, are you comin' to look up wot it says in *The Origin of the Idea of a God* ?

Atheist [*rising to go*]. Must be off, Dreamer. Will you come a bit of the way ?

Dreamer. No ; I've got a song shaping in my mind, and I must think it out : Song of the Down-and-Out.

Atheist [*indtfferently*]. Oh, hymn for the unemployed ?

Dreamer. No, no ; not the unemployed. They remain

men in their misfortune. I keen those who whine
through to-day and dread to-morrow; who would for
ever furl the flag of life; who fear any idea common
thought hasn't had time to bless; those who have a
sigh for a song and a sad sigh for a drumbeat.

Atheist. A fair crowd, Dreamer. Well, so-long for the
present.

Dreamer. See you at the old place, and we'll have coffee
and a sandwich?

Atheist. I'll be there.

> [*He goes off with the Man with the Stick. The Dreamer
> takes out a note-book, and writes in it. The Gardener
> appears behind, trimming the shrubs with a pair of
> shears. The Dreamer then strolls up to watch him, the
> two Chair Attendants put some chairs in order.*

Older One [*attempting brightness*]. I listened to the wireless
last night, Godfrey.

Young One. 'Eard anything worth while?

Older One. Part of Pageant of England. Wunnerful!
Mide me feel prahd to be en Englishman!

Young One. Wot was it abaht?

Older One. The guys as was once kings en stytesmen wot
mide us all wot we is. Mide me thrill, it did, to 'ear
the sahnd of Drike's drum!

Young One. 'Oo's drum?

Older One. Drike's. The bloke wot beat the Spanish
Armyda, en' drove them back to Spine. A ghost-
drum is alwyes 'eard beatin' whenever England's in
dineger.

Young One [*scornfully*]. Superstition !

> [*In the distance are heard faint sounds of the sombre music of the Down-and-Out chant, saddened with the slow beat of a muffled drum. The Attendants stand stiff, a look of fright on their faces.*

Attendants [*together*]. The drum-beat of the Down-and-Out !

Older One [*to his companion*]. Wot'r you stiffenin' for ?

Young One [*tensely*]. I warn't stiffenin'. [*A pause.*] Wot'r you styrin' at ?

Older One [*tensely*]. I warn't styrin'. Didja hear anything ?

Younger One [*tensely*]. No, nothing ; did you ?

Older One. Nothing.

> [*They go slowly by each other, one to the left, the other to the right, and go out — a deeper limp coming into each lame leg, keeping time to the distant chant and drum-beat.*
> [*The Dreamer is watching the Gardener working, handling the blossoms.*

Dreamer. Happy man to be handling the purple, blue, and yellow of the blossoms.

Gardener. Let them live and let them die, for I'm not thinking of blossoms at all.

Dreamer. What are you thinking of then ?

Gardener. Of a dance I take a sweet little lass to, when the sun goes in and the stars come out.

Dreamer. I envy you the handling of a flower by day and of a girl by night.

Gardener. When the dance ends, I go to her little flat, her

very own flat, where [*he lilts*] She'll be the honey-
suckle, I'll be the bee !

Dreamer. I hope a bee that never leaves a sting behind.

Gardener. You should see her — a beauty ! Thinks I'll
marry her ; I'm too young to marry yet. Mad to have
a kid — matrimony's signature tune ; but not for me,
though. An odd lass. A little too serious. Says
she wants a chance sometimes to sit and wonder.

Dreamer [*musingly*]. I hear a song in what you've said.

Gardener [*surprised*]. A song ? In what ?

Dreamer. In the flowers, heaven, and the girl.

Gardener. You do, do you ? Funny !
  [*The Gardener goes on arranging the flowers, while the
    Dreamer slowly goes off till he is hidden behind the
    shrubs. After a pause, the Gardener begins to sing.*

A fig for th' blossoms th' biggest vase can hold,
The flow'rs that face the world shy, the ones that face
  it bold.
Men may praise them and worship them as something
  fine and rare,
Lounging through their gorgeous perfumes so deftly
  hidden there.
But I'll never wonder though some in glee disclose
The white of whitest lily, the red of reddest rose ;
For I'll fold in my arms a girl as bright as she is gay,
And tonight the primrose path of love will be a
  wonder way !
  [*Couples, linking arms, enter from different points, mix and
    cross by each other, parade about, keeping time with the tune
    as they join in the singing. The Gardener moves out of
    sight. The Young Woman is seen moving hurriedly*

among the couples, taking no heed of the singing, weaving a way through the couples without spoiling the ordered movements, but she doesn't keep in time with the lilt. She looks anxious, and appears to be searching for someone. She disappears while the song is being sung.

The Crowd of Couples [singing] :
When Adam first corner'd Eve, he stood bewildered there,
For he saw beauty shining through a mist of golden hair ;
But Eve quickly coaxed him on, and show'd him woman's way,
And so the lover and his lass are king and queen to-day !

So here's to the lasses who bow in beauty's fane,
Who kiss in costly parlour or kiss in country lane ;
Let man bend his back to work or bend down his knee to pray,
Still the primrose path of love will ever be a wonder way !

[*When the couples go, the only ones left are the Guardsman and the Nursemaid, and the Man with the Stick. The Nursemaid and the Guardsman, who has his arm round her, go to a bench. He sits down, and as the Nursemaid proceeds to do the same, he catches her, and sweeps her on to his knee. The Man with the Stick, who has been at the butt of the slope shaking his head contemptuously at the singing, now comes down to where the couple is seated, and swings his stick in disdain.*

Man with Stick [*scornfully — swinging the stick*]. Nonsense ! A lot of it is all nonsense, nonsense !

Guardsman. Lot of wot ?

Man with Stick. Babble abaht life ! Life, man, life ! Before we can get sense into it, we've gotta know its meaning : wot it is, where it came from, where it goes.

Guardsman. Where wot goes ?

Man with Stick. Life, man, life !

Nursemaid [*indignantly*]. You push off. We want to be left alone. We've important things to talk abaht, so push off, please !

Man with Stick [*taken aback*]. Oh ? If you ain't eager to learn the truth, I'll push off — [*he sees the Two Evangelists approaching, displaying their placards*] now ! [*Muttering as he goes*] Bumptious, brazen ignorance !
  [*The Two Evangelists prowl forward, looking left and right for sinners. They spy the Guardsman and the Nursemaid, and shuffle over slowly to them.*

1st Evangelist [*to the Couple*]. Remember, brother and sister, it's a terrible thing when it comes.

Guardsman. Wot is ? When wot comes ?

1st Evangelist. Death, brother, Death !

2nd Evangelist. An' after death The Judgement !

1st Evangelist. Oh, be converted before it is too late.

2nd Evangelist. Before it is too, too late, too late.

1st Evangelist. It may be upon you to-day, in an hour, in a moment.

Guardsman. Wot mye ?

1st Evangelist. Death, brother, death !

Nursemaid [*indignantly*]. We want to be left alone.

We've important business to talk about an' do, so push off, please.

1st Evangelist. Left alone ! Devil's desire that, sister. You won't be left alone in hell.

Guardsman [*rising angrily, and pushing them away*]. Here, git ! We wants privacy, so git !

Nursemaid [*rising from bench as he is about to sit down again, having got rid of the Evangelists*]. Let's sit dahn on th' grass, 'Arry — it's more comfortable.

Guardsman. So it is.
> [*They recline on the slope. He puts his arms round her, kisses her, and is about to kiss again, when the Police-woman appears opposite, and stares reprovingly at them. She goes over to them.*

Policewoman. You can't do the like of that 'ere. Control yourselves. It doesn't allow such conduct in a public place.

Guardsman [*embarrassed, but trying to be defiant*]. Wot dorsen't ?

Policewoman [*sharply*]. Th' lawr, young man, the lawr !
> [*The Couple rise, and go off embarrassed, followed by the Policewoman. As they go off, the Young Woman and the Atheist appear at the top of the slope, and come down it.*

Guardsman [*to the Nursemaid, as they go off*]. As I was asayin', th' orderly officer says to me, Private Odgerson, says 'e, seein' as you're a man of intelligence, says 'e, en' th' best shot in the battalion, 'e says, we warnt your edvice, 'e says, in a kinda fix we're in —
>   [*They disappear.*

Young Woman [*indicating a bench to the Atheist*]. I'll sit down on a seat, Dad, for a minute. My legs are giving way under me. Let me sit down a second.

Atheist [*irritably — as they sit down*]. You shouldn't have rushed after me the way you did. En' 'urry up — I've gotta read up some things in *The Origin of the Idea of a God*.

Young Woman [*between breaths*]. I was afraid, if I didn't run, I'd lose sight of you, and I wanted to see you.

Atheist [*as he helps the Young Woman to sit down*]. Damn stupid to rush yourself into a heart attack.

Young Woman [*frightened*]. There's a shadow passing over my eyes again ! [*Grasping the Atheist's arm*] Dad, I'm afraid I'm far from well.

Atheist [*soothingly*]. Just a little flutter from over-exertion, that's all. All our hearts jump at times.

Young Woman [*vehemently*]. I tell you it's deeper than that, an' I'll croak suddenly, sooner or later. The other night I had a man with me, an' when I was half stripped it came on me as he was coming over to paw me. In a mist I saw the fright in his eyes, saw him huddling his clothes on an' hurrying away. Then I fell down. In a faint I fell down, till the morning came an' brought up the woman below to find me still in a faint where I fell down.

Atheist. Excitement, over-excitement.

Young Woman [*hysterically*]. If I have to die, I'll die game : I'll die dancing !

Atheist. Hush ! Not so loud — we're in a park.

Young Woman [*persuasively catching hold of his arm*]. I want you to help me, Dad; I'll go mad if I have to live alone any longer.

Atheist [*firmly*]. No, no; no more of that. Live your own life. I'm not your father, so cut out the daddy business.

Young Woman [*moving closer to him*]. You crept into a father's place when you took me away from the nuns who were moulding my life round the sin of my mother. You made me call you Dad when you saved me from their crosses, their crowns, and their canes, and lifted my hands up in salute to the sun and the moon and the stars. [*She puts an arm around him.*] You'll give me one more chance, won't you? You will, you will!

Atheist [*restlessly*]. I did that twice before, and, as soon as you felt well, you hurried off, leaving me with rooms I didn't want and furniture I couldn't sell.

Young Woman [*leaning wearily against his shoulder*]. I can't live alone any longer, Dad. When I lie down in bed and stretch out in search of sleep, the darkness reddens into a glow from the fire that can never be quenched.

Atheist [*impatiently*]. Oh, the old, false, foolish fear again!

Young Woman. Green-eyed, barrel-bellied men glare and grin at me; huge-headed, yellow-eyed women beckon to me out of the glow from the fire that can never be quenched. Black-feathered owls, with eyes like great white moons, peck at me as they fly through the glow from the fire that can never be quenched. Save me, Dad, oh, save me!

Atheist [*scornful and angry*]. The hell en' red-fire for ever talk of the nuns ! They frame the world en' fill life with it, till we eat, sleep, work, en' play for ever in the smoke of hell !

Young Woman [*humbly*]. It will be only for awhile, Dad, for I'm going to marry the Gardener. He's not much, but, at least, he is safety, and, maybe, peace too.

Atheist [*impatiently*]. For Gord's sike, put 'im aht of your little 'ead, girl ! 'E 'as as much intention of marryin' you as I have.

Young Woman. We're to go to a dance to-night, and afterwards we'll settle everything.

Atheist [*positively*]. I'm tellin' you all 'e wants is a good en' warm time free o' cost.

[*A handsome young Salvation Army Officer enters from the right above, crosses slope, and comes down towards a seat some distance away from the Young Woman and the Atheist. He is trying to read a book as he walks along. He is wearing a yellow mackintosh, which is open, showing the red jersey of a Staff Officer. The Officer glances at the Young Woman as he passes, and she returns the look. He sits down on a seat and steals a furtive look at the Young Woman. He meets her eyes and lowers his glance to the ground. He again glances at her, at her face, and then at her legs.*

Young Woman [*turning her thoughts away from the Officer, and pressing close to the Atheist, as she puts an arm coaxingly round his neck*]. You'll do what I ask you, this once, Dad, only this once, won't you ?

Atheist [*firmly removing her arm from around his neck*]. No, never again. Swing along on your own sweet way, and leave your dad out of it.

Young Woman [*tensely*]. You won't ? You won't, Dad ?

Atheist [*in a tone of finality*]. No, I won't !
　　[*There is a pause, during which the Young Woman, with
　　tightened lips and a sullen look in her eyes, stares in front
　　of her.*

Young Woman [*suddenly thrusting her face close to the Atheist's*].
I believe in God, see ! And that in the beginning He
created heaven and earth.

Atheist [*moving his face away from the Young Woman's*]. I see,
I see.

Young Woman [*following the face of the Atheist with her own,
while the Salvation Army Officer listens intently to what she
is saying*]. And in the resurrection of the dead, when
they that have done good shall go into life everlasting,
and they that have done evil into everlasting fire !
　　[*The Atheist rises from the bench without a word, and goes
　　up the centre path to the slope, and passes out.*

Young Woman [*rising, follows him part of the way, and speaks
loudly after him*]. And I believe that God's near them
who need His help, and helps them who ask His help
— see !

S.A. Officer [*softly and prayerfully*]. God be praised !
　　[*The Young Woman returns to the bench, sinks down on it,
　　and begins to cry softly and resentfully. The Salvation
　　Army Officer after a moment's hesitation comes over,
　　looking with a shy interest at the pretty legs displayed by
　　a disarranged skirt, and then slowly sits down beside her.*

S.A. Officer [*earnestly*]. No need to cry, sister, for no one
trusts to God in vain.

Young Woman [*resentfully*]. Oh, go away ; I'm miserable, for he that's gone is the only real friend I have in the world.

S.A. Officer. God is your only friend.

Young Woman. I've not called upon Him for years, and He will not hasten to hear me now.

S.A. Officer [*putting his hand gently on her knee*]. God would empty heaven of His angels rather than let the humblest penitent perish.

Young Woman [*in low tones*]. If I ask for help, will He hear?

S.A. Officer. He will hear.

Young Woman. And hearing, will He listen?

S.A. Officer. Hearing, He will listen.

Young Woman [*grasping his arm appealingly*]. And listening, will He grant what the sinner asks, to save the sinner from a life of sin?

S.A. Officer [*fervently, as he caresses her knee*]. God is able to save to the uttermost all them that come to Him.

Young Woman [*earnestly, after a few moments' thought*]. I'll pray and pray and pray till all that's done's annulled, and all that is to do is blessed by God's agreement.

S.A. Officer [*fervently and softly*]. God be praised, sister!

Young Woman [*becoming conscious that he is caressing her knee*]. Oh, God, don't do that, please! You'll make a ladder, and silk stockings aren't easy to get.
 [*She pushes his hand away, pulls down her skirt, and looks at him questioningly. He stands up, embarrassed, and fidgets with his cap.*

S.A. Officer [*nervously*]. I must go on, now, to our meeting.

Will you come? [*She is silent.*] No? Some other time, then. I should like to keep in touch with you. Very much indeed. Sister, you are not very far from God. Good-bye.

Young Woman [*in a tired voice, void of interest*]. Good-bye.

[*He turns up the centre path, looks back for a moment at the Young Woman, then crosses the slope, and goes out. She leans her arm on the arm of the bench, and shades her eyes wearily with her hand. After a few moments have passed, the Gardener enters carrying a tall, slender May-pole, painted black. On the top of the pole is a hoop from which hang long green, blue, and rich yellow ribbons. He fixes it in the centre of the sward. The Young Woman, with a long sigh, raises her head, sees the Gardener. She runs over to him, and flings her arms around his neck.*

Gardener [*astonished*]. What has brought you here? Aren't you working?

Young Woman. No, I've given it up.

Gardener. Why?

Young Woman. You know well enough, you know well enough. How often have I told you that the swine of a manager brings good-looking girls, one at a time, to a silent storeroom to sort chemises, and then sends his slimy paw flickering around under their skirts. When he made a clutch at me, I came away.

Gardener [*peevishly*]. Oh, you should have fenced him off as every girl does with a man like that. What are you going to do if you can't get another job?

Young Woman [*coaxingly*]. That's why I wanted to speak

to you.   You'll have to live with me ; I'm frightened, I'm frightened to live alone any longer.

Gardener [*suspiciously*].   Live with you — how live with you ?

Young Woman [*with calm confidence*].   Marry me, Ned.   You want me or you do not want me.   I'm not going to be just a dance number for you any longer.   Do you want me or do you not ?

Gardener [*nervously*].   Look here, Jannice, I'm busy getting ready for some damned fools to practise folk-dancing. They're trying to make England merry again.   So I've no time to talk to you now, dear.

Young Woman [*impetuously*].   Do you want me or do you not want me ?

Gardener [*coaxingly*].   Of course, I want you, but we can talk about this to-night.

Young Woman.   No, now ; what we say now will last our lives out.   There will only be our two selves — for awhile ; we needn't have a kid till we can afford one. [*Appealingly*] You will, you will, Ned ; this means everything to me, everything.
     [*At the beginning of the Young Woman's appeal, the Man
        with the Stick appears on the slope above, and halts to
        listen.*

Gardener.   A kid !   Oh, be sensible, woman, for God's sake !   We can't talk of these things here.

Young Woman [*vehemently*].   Oh, be a man, Ned, be a man, and, if you want a thing, take a risk to get it !   I want something for what I mean to give.   Answer me — is it yes or no !

Gardener [*roughly removing her arms*]. Buzz off, I tell you. I'll see you to-night.

Young Woman. Answer the question : yes or no, yes or no, yes or no !

Gardener [*with a shout*]. No !
   [*The Young Woman looks at him silently for a few moments, then turns away, and goes out, her face tense, but her lips quivering.   The Gardener returns his attention to the Maypole.*

Man with Stick [*from top of slope*]. You've lost something, friend, you've lost a lot.   If I was young as you, I'd ha' carried 'er 'ome !

Gardener [*resentfully*]. Mind your own affairs.   I've got my werk to do.

Man with Stick [*extending the stick towards the Maypole*]. 'Ere, d'ye know what that there pole is a symbol of — what it represents ?

Gardener [*surlily*]. No, en' don't want to know.

Man with Stick. You oughter then ;   knowledge is power, my friend.   It represents life, new life about to be born ;   fertility ;   th' urge wot was in the young lass you hunted away.

Gardener [*mockingly*]. You don't say !

Man with Stick. Ay ;   en' Pharaoh 'ad one, en' on May Day used to pull it up with golden cords, en' orl the people darnced rahnd it.

Gardener. 'Ow d'ye know ?   You weren't there.

Man with Stick. Scholars were, man.   Ask any scholar, en' 'e'll tell you the sime.

Gardener [*stepping back to view the Maypole*]. I'm not concerned with what Pharaoh did or didn't do.

[*A group of lively Boys and Girls run in, and catch in their hands the ribbons hanging from the Maypole. They are dressed in fancy folk-dress. They dance round the pole, keeping time to the first part of the folk-tune "Haste to the Wedding". Then they suddenly stop as the Young Woman enters from the direction by which she left, closely followed by the Policewoman. The Young Woman is sobbing softly. The Gardener and the Man with the Stick stare at them. They cross over.*]

Policewoman [*complacently*]. I caught you in the act that time, my lyedy.

Young Woman [*sobbing*]. It was he spoke to me, miss ; on my word of honour, it was he spoke to me first.

Policewoman. On your word of honour ! Tell that to the magistrite when you're in front of 'im. If I'm eny kind of a guesser, you'll not solicit eny more young en' innocent men for a month to come.

[*The two of them pass out. The Gardener and the Man with the Stick stare after them. The Folk-Dancers begin again, and dance through the second part of the tune, "Haste to the Wedding".*]

THE GATES CLOSE

SCENE II

Summer noon. The same as the preceding one on a noonday in summer. The colours now are mainly golden glows, tinged with a gentle red. The green on the sward still lingers, but it, too, is tinted with a golden yellow. Instead of daffodils, big-faced hollyhocks, yellow, white, and red, peep out at life from the shrubbery. The Memorial, touched by the sun, now resembles a giant clad in gleaming steel.

The Dreamer enters as the gates open, and passes through them into the Park. He has a thoughtful look on his face, and is gazing at a piece of manuscript in his hand. His right hand moves gently as he beats time with the song that is being sung. People are moving about, all gay with a sensuous enjoyment of the loveliness of the day. They are singing at the top of their bent. The Dreamer passes through them, and goes out.

People [*singing*] :
> Ye who are haggard and giddy with care, busy
> counting your profit and losses,
> Showing the might of your name unto God in the
> gay-coloured page of a cheque book ;
> Storing the best of your life in a drawer of your desk
> at the office :

> Bellow good-bye to the buggerin' lot 'n come out
> To bow down the head 'n bend down the knee to the
> bee, the bird, 'n the blossom,
> Bann'ring the breast of the earth with a wonderful
> beauty !

407

Ye who are twisting a prayer from your thoughts in
the dimness and gloom of the churches,

Lighting your candle-petitions away to chalk-
coloured virgins and martyrs,

Racking your life for the hope of a cosy corner in
heaven :

All Crowd Together :
Bellow, etc.

Some of the Crowd :

Ye who in senates, and Parliaments, talk, talk on
through the day 'n the night-time,

Talk, and still talk, and still talk, and talk on through
the hundreds of centuries passing,

Till the wide ear of the wide world is deafen'd with
wisdom !

Bellow, etc.

[*When the song has ended, the Atheist, the Man wearing the
Trilby Hat, and the Man with the Stick are seen arguing together. On a bench towards the back sit the
two Nursemaids, between them the pram enfolding the
countess's baby. The Bishop is on a seat nearer the front.
He has been reading a book, but this is now lying open
on his knee, and he is bending forward to hear the better
what is being said by the disputants. The two Chair
Attendants are lying, half asleep, at the foot of the slope.*

Man wearing Trilby. An 'eathen song ! Say wot you
like, you'll find every man at 'eart is religious.

Atheist. Look, brother, no question can be solved by a
generalization. All men are not religious no more'n
all men are liars. The more a man uses 'is mind, the
less 'e uses Gord.

Man wearing Trilby. If we was to set aside Deity, we'd let loose all manner of evil among ourselves — everyone knows that. There'd be no authority nowhere.

Bishop [*speaking over to them*]. Our friend is right : there must be the few who rule and the many whose duty it is to obey, or there would be an end to order.

Atheist [*to the Bishop*]. It 'as been the few rebels life gave us, the ones who forgot to obey, that have rushed the world ahead ! You think of Copernicus, Galileo, en' Darwin — rebels against the thought en' dooty of the time. [*He points an accusing finger at the Bishop.*] There isn't a single rebel in your calendar of saints !

Bishop. Nonsense, friend.

Man with Stick [*with a long-drawn, impatient sigh*]. Aw, wot's the use of arguin' with 'im !

Atheist [*to Bishop*]. 'Ere, d'ye believe that the ten commandments constitoot a competent rule of life en' conduct ?

Bishop [*smiling indulgently*]. I'd venture to say they do, sir.

Man wearing Trilby. I'd sye so, too.

Nursemaid [*joining in*]. Of course they does.

Atheist [*mockingly*]. Christian countries don't seem to think so, then, for even England, dooring the last thirty years, 'as myde over two thousand lawrs, covering sixteen thousand pages of cep imperial octavo, a tidy addition to the lawr of loving your neighbour as yourself, sir.

Man with Stick [*gleefully*]. En' they ain't finished miking them yet !

Man wearing Trilby. Where's your authority for thet ?

Man with Stick. [*angrily*]. Where's your authority for wot you sye?

Man wearing Trilby [*firmly*]. The Bible, sir; the 'Oly Book, every word inspired, every verse infallible.

Attendants [*together*]. 'Ear, 'ear!

Nursemaid [*with calm conviction*]. Even from time immemorial, the Bible 'as myde truth pline to all people.

Man with Stick [*taking a few steps to go in disgust, and returning to thrust his face close to that of the Man wearing the Trilby*]. Aw, come on, Jenner; I'm off — no brrains! [*He taps his stick heatedly on the ground, and makes to go; he hesitates for a moment, then returns and comes close to Man wearing Trilby.*] 'Ere, d'ye believe the Bible where it syes the whyle swallowed Jonah?

Man wearing Trilby. 'Course I does.

Man with Stick. You does!

Nursemaid. En' wye wouldn't 'e?

Man wearing Trilby [*tapping Man with Stick on the chest*]. If the Bible said Jonah swallowed the whyle, I'd believe it; but I'm not asked to believe anything so absurd.

Man with Stick [*catching the Atheist's arm, and drawing him away*]. Aw, come on, man! We're just wastin' our knowledge 'ere.   [*They go off.*

Attendants [*as they are going — together*]. Booh!

Bishop [*raising a hand to silence the boobing*]. Friends, let our misguided brothers go in peace. [*To Man wearing Trilby*] I shouldn't harp too much on the whale story, friend; it's but an allegory, you know.

Man wearing Trilby [*indignantly*]. Is that all you know about it ! The Bible says the whyle swallowed Jonah, son of Amittae. It's a plyne fact, en' you should be ashymed to derny it. [*He crosses to go out ; halts ; and turns to glare at the Bishop.*] Tyke warnin', you, at wot 'appened to Jonah, son of Amittae, for you're worse'n 'e was !   [*He goes out.*

Nursemaid [*consolingly — to Bishop*]. Never mind 'im, sir ; 'e don't know wot 'e's asaying of.

Older One. Ignorance torkin'.

Young One. Just ignorance.

Bishop [*cheerfully*]. Never mind ! [*He goes over to the Nursemaids.*] Aha, here we have the fair countess's baby. No guile here. The world hasn't been long enough yet with the young lamb. [*To Upper Nurse-maid*] And where's your boy-friend — that gallant guardsman I've seen you with so often ?

Nursemaid [*after a moment's hesitation*]. We ain't on speaking terms, sir ; he misbehaved himself by takin' walks with another girl.

   [*The head and half the body of the Guardsman has appeared above the bushes at top of the slope. He stares down at the Nursemaid, dodging down whenever he thinks anyone might see him.*

Bishop. Oh ? Maybe he is sorry.

Under Nursemaid [*to Bishop*]. 'E is, sir. It's agettin' 'im dahn. [*To Upper Nursemaid*] I'd try to forgive 'im, Greeta, even if 'e was to blime. You never knows wot a quarrel 'll lead to — mye mean a parting for ever !

Bishop. In this life, we have to forgive many things.

Under Nursemaid. Besides, 'e asserted thet it was 'is sister.

Upper Nursemaid [*indignantly*]. 'Is sister ! I seen them in the bushes when 'e was atuckin' 'er into 'im. No ; I'm determined to be adamant. I don't allow for deception. When 'e knew how to respect me, 'e 'ad me ; when 'e doesn't, 'e 'asn't ; en' I'm determined to be adamant !

Under Nursemaid [*catching a glimpse of the soldier's head as it pops up and down — excitedly*]. 'E's behind the 'edge awatching us, Greeta ! Oh, 'is fice 'as altered, worn en' unhappy like — Greeta, 'ave a 'eart : 'e is suffering !

Bishop. Do be kind to him, dear.

Under Nursemaid. I feel for 'im when I see the sorrowful look in 'is eyes. You are 'ard, Greeta.

Upper Nursemaid [*rising and tidying the pram, preparatory to moving away*]. A little suffering'll do 'im good. No, Reeta ; unless 'e writes en' apologizes humbly ; unless 'e writes en' explines ; unless 'e writes en' asks me to forgive 'im, 'e'll never 'ave a chance of being with yours truly agine !

    [*She goes off, pushing the pram, stiff and dignified, never glancing at where the head of the Guardsman is gaping over the bushes. She is followed by the other Nursemaid, shaking her head, and sending a sympathetic glance to the soldier. When they have gone, the Guardsman comes down the slope to follow ; but the Bishop halts him by catching his arm in a friendly way.*]

Bishop [*sympathetically*]. Friend, a little kindly advice to you : write a humble letter of apology to your sweetheart. Then there'll be harmony, and everything in the garden'll look lovely. [*Smilingly*] Your conduct calls for an apology, you know.

Guardsman [*coldly*]. Ow, does it ? [*Angrily*] En' wot the 'ell is it to you wether it does or not ? Powkin' your big nose into other people's business. You keep off my affyres, see !

[*He goes angrily off after the Nurses, leaving the good Bishop embarrassed.*

Older One [*with almost tearful sympathy*]. Wot a shime, sir ! You see wot 'appens when religion's lost. Upsets the mind. There ought to be some lawr to mike people respect religion.

Young One. We goes to church reglar, don't we, 'Erbert ? We was brought up thet wye, wasn't we, 'Erbert ? Respectful like.

Bishop [*feelingly*]. I know ; I guessed it from the first.

Older One [*slyly*]. Where's the lyedy as is always with you, sir ?

Bishop [*slyly, too*]. I gave her — what do you call it ? — I gave her the slip, to-day. My sister, you know ; she's too cautious ; afraid I'll come to harm by being familiar with the common people.

Older One. Harm ! Ahar har ! [*He chuckles at the idea.*] Harm !

Young One. Nice thing to see a clergyman merry an' bright, an' ready to tork to 'umble men, like us — isn't it, 'Erbert ?

Older One. I concur with thet.

Bishop [*gaily*]. Oh, the Church isn't altogether so solemn an institution as many people seem to think — she can laugh, sing, and skip — at a suitable time, at a suitable time.

Older One. I always said the clergy was 'uman — didn't I, Godfrey ?

Young One. Often en' often.

Older One [*confidently*]. We've a friend 'ere — d'ye know thet, Godfrey ?

Young One. The gentleman's got a kind 'eart, I'd sye.

Older One. You've only got to look at 'is fine fice to see thet. [*Affectionately linking his arm in that of the Bishop, an act which makes the Bishop stiffen a little in doubt.*] At the moment, sir, the pire of us is in a bad wye, a bad wye ; we 'ave lost our jobs, en' don't know wot to do. A pahnd or two, now, would 'elp a lot — wouldn't it, Godfrey ?

Young One. I'd sye so.

Bishop [*growing stiffer, and withdrawing his arm from the contact of the Older Attendant's*]. No, no, please. My sister deals with all matters of help to the needy. Apply to her. If she approves, she'll assist you. One must be careful in the dispensation of charity.

Older One [*peevishly*]. Aw, your sister wouldn't be no good to us ! She wouldn't listen right. She'd warnt to know the why en' wherefore of everything.

Bishop [*firmly*]. And rightly so, friend. The giving away of money is a great responsibility. She'd be very angry if I did what you ask.

Older One, She'd never know, sir.   Me nor Godfrey
would never sye a word — would we, Godfrey ?

Young One. We'd keep it dark, orlright.

Bishop [*decisively*]. No no ; a rule is a rule, so let us
change the subject.   [*A silent pause.*

Older One [*bitterly*]. Chynge the subject !   En' why did
you coax innercent people into queuein' up behind
the idea of the clergy bein' 'uman ? [*Hotly*] Whaja
warnt to force your company on them as didn't warnt
it !

Young One. I knew it all along.   The clergy alwyes fail
when they're asked a pline question.

Older One [*indignantly*]. 'Op en' skip en' jump !   Here's
one as 'opes they'll 'op outa this place ! [*The Bishop
sits down on a bench, takes out his book, and begins to read
again.*]   Ow, we're goin' to read, are we ?   Well, if I
was asittin' on a bench, en' got a 'int to go, I'd push
off — wouldn't you, Godfrey ?

Young One. Quick !

Bishop [*with quiet determination*]. I choose this place in
which to rest, and I shall go when I think it dignified
to do so.   [*He resumes his reading.*

Older One [*recklessly and loudly — to the Young One*]. Know
wot I'd like to do, Godfrey, honest ?   Gambol a gime
with en 'eifer in front of a clergyman, strite, I
would !   Show 'im a little of the gaiety of life, strite,
I would !

Young One. Don't know as it would shock them, 'Erbert
— I bet they 'as their 'ectic moments on the sly !

Older One. You bet they 'as ! Wot do they do in their palaces when the lamps is lighted en' the blinds is drawn ? We eats, they eats ; we drinks, they drinks ; we sleeps, they sleeps ; but wot do they do in their palaces when the lamps is lighted en' the blinds is drawn ?

[*The Young Woman enters, and, after a glance at the Bishop, sits down on a bench directly opposite him. She takes out mirror and puff from her handbag, and gives her face a few deft touches.*

Young One [*giving a few stiff steps of a dance — echoing the Older Attendant*]. Ay, wot do they do in their palaces when the lamps is lighted en' the blinds is drawn !

Older One [*poking him in the side to draw his attention to the Young Woman*]. Look, Godfrey, oh, look ! Wot a peach ! 'Ow would you like to tuck 'er up at night, Godfrey ?

[*Lines of ugly joy swarm over their faces at the delightful thought, while they stare brazenly at the Young Woman. Suddenly, in the near distance, is heard the roll of a muffled drum, and the mournful chant of the Down-and-Out. The scene seems to grow dark and the air chilly. The two Attendants stiffen, and lines of fright chase away the lines of joy from their faces. The Young Woman, frightened too, turns pale, half rises from her seat, and stares into the distance.*

Down-and-Out [*chanting in the near distance*] :
Life has pass'd us by to the loud roll of her drum,
With her waving flags of green and yellow held high,
All starr'd with the golden, flaming names of her
  most mighty children.   [*The chant fades away.*

[*The two Attendants slink out, bent-backed and silent, one to the right, the other to the left, as the chant fades away. The Young Woman, shivering, sinks slowly down on to the seat again. There is a pause. She is very attractive, sitting there in her tailor-made coat and her bright hat. Her slim legs looking slimmer in their elegant silk stockings are for all to see from the knees down. The Bishop suddenly sighs, closes the book he has been reading, puts it in his pocket, and, turning a little round, sees the Young Woman. He looks at her pretty face, thoughtfully bent towards the ground, at her neatly dressed body, and, finally, his eyes linger a little over the slim legs visible from the knees down. An old interest seems to stir in him as he looks at her. Ashamed, he turns his head away for a few moments. He looks at her again, first at her face, then at her body, and then, more consciously, at her legs. He turns his gaze away again and moves uneasily in his seat, lets his head sink forward till his chin rests on his breast. He lifts his head and looks at her ; she turns at the same time, and they stare at each other for a moment ; then the Bishop's head sinks down on his breast again.*

[*Suddenly the Young Woman rises swiftly, as if she had come to a sudden resolution, hurries to where the Bishop is, sits down on the bench beside him, and, catching his arm, speaks to him imploringly.*

Young Woman [*appealingly*]. I want you to help me. You are near to God, but I am out of reach.

Bishop [*frightened*]. Oh, my child, I'm afraid I can help only those whom I know.

Young Woman. Listen to me, listen to me, first. My heart is bad, and doctors say that death may seize me at any moment, and take me out of life. There's a young man who loves me, and is going to marry me, but I want you to come with me to see him, and make him marry me at once.

Bishop [*bewildered*]. But I know nothing about you or about him.

Young Woman. You will, please, you must; you are a man after God's own heart — you'll help a young girl whose one chance is help at once.

Bishop [*frightened to be seen talking to the girl — looking round him nervously*]. Why do you run to the priest for help only when you begin to feel the terrible consequences of your shame?

Young Woman [*irritated at the Bishop's thought*]. Oh, I'm not going to have a kid, man, if that's what you mean. Nothing like that for me yet, thank you! It's because I'd love to have one that I came to you; — to save me from falling into the condition that could never give me one.

Bishop. But you can't discuss such things with a man and a perfect stranger, girl.

Young Woman. You're neither a man nor a stranger: you are a priest of the most high God.

Bishop [*frightened and petulant*]. Oh, be sensible, girl! Go and talk these things with your father and mother.

Young Woman [*bitterly*]. I never knew my father, and my mother drinks, and hates me.

Bishop [*reprovingly*]. You mustn't talk like that about

your mother.   Whatever she may be, she should be sacred to you.

Young Woman [*impatiently*]. Sacred to me !   A mother can be sacred only when she makes herself sacred to her children ; — can't you understand that, man ?

Bishop [*coldly*]. I have no help to offer you, and I must ask you to go away, please.

Young Woman [*impulsively sitting down beside him*]. Do listen to me, please do, Lord Bishop.   I've seen you laughing and talking with common people, and it gave me heart to speak to you.

Bishop [*in his best manner ; putting his hand on her knee and patting it*]. Go and live with your mother, and show her you realize what a mother really is.   Work steadily, cultivate thrifty habits, and in a few years' time you'll be able to face marriage far more brightly and firmly than you could possibly face it now.

Young Woman [*trembling and agitated, pushing his hand from her knee*]. Oh, piping out of you the same old rot that I've heard a thousand times — mother, work, and thrift !   [*Indignantly*] If you knew what a rip she was, I wonder if you'd like to live with her ?   I wonder, if you were a girl, and good-looking, would you bray about the happiness of work ?   [*Raising her voice a little*] Do you know why I had to fly out of the two last jobs I was in, had to — d'ye hear — had to fly out of them ?

Bishop [*taking a book from his pocket and beginning to read — coldly*]. I do not want to know the reason.

Young Woman [*vehemently*]. Because I wouldn't let the manager see how I looked with nothing on.   Oh, you hide behind your book when facts frighten you. There's many an old graven image has made a girl dance out of her job and chance the streets, sooner than strip herself for his benefit, with nine hours a day and three pounds a week added on to the pleasure.

Bishop [*from behind his book*]. You mustn't annoy me in this way. Please leave me in peace.

Young Woman [*vehemently*]. It's the truth. Can't you put your book down for a second and listen? [*She pushes the book aside.*] Come with me to the shop, and I'll bring you face to face with the man!

Bishop [*beginning to read again*]. Be good enough to go away, please.

Young Woman [*imploringly*]. Please listen to me! Are you afraid to find a lie in what you think to be the truth, or the truth in what you think to be a lie? Come and tell the manager you're my friend, and make him give me back the job I have had to leave. Oh, do, do, please!
    [*The Bishop still remains behind the shelter of his book.*

Young Woman [*after a pause*]. Won't you help me?

Bishop [*in cold and final tones*]. No.

Young Woman [*with quiet bitterness*]. I suppose you'd have helped me had I let you go on handling my knee.

Bishop [*in cold and tense voice*]. If you don't go away at once, I'll have you handed over to the police for annoying me!
    [*The Young Woman sits silent and shocked for a few moments, looking fixedly at the Bishop.*

Young Woman [*mockingly*]. Oh, hand me over to a policeman, would you ? I see. Easy way of getting over a
difficulty by handing it over to a policeman. [*She stands
up.*] Get back, get back, please ; gangway, gangway,
there — policemen making a gangway for Jesus Christ !
[*The Bishop stiffens himself behind his book. With intense
scorn and bitterness*] You and your goodness are of no use
to God ! If Christ came again, He'd have to call, not
the sinners, but the righteous to repentance. Go out
into the sun, and pick the yellow primroses ! Take
your elegant and perfumed soul out of the stress, the
stain, the horrid cries, the noisy laugh of life ; and go
out into the sun to pick the yellow primroses ! When
you go to where your God is throned, tell the gaping
saints you never soiled a hand in Jesu's service. Tell
them a pretty little lass, well on her way to hell, once
tempted you to help her ; but you saved yourself by
the calm and cunning of a holy mind, an' went out
into the sun to pick the yellow primroses, leaving her,
sin-soddened, in the strain, the stain, the horrid cries,
an' the noisy laugh of life. Tell them you were ever
calm before the agony in other faces, an', an' the tip of
your finger never touched a brow beaded with a bloody
sweat !

[*The horrified Bishop suddenly closes his book, and rises from
his seat to go away, but the Young Woman with a
vigorous push from her hand, sends him sitting down in
the seat again.*

Young Woman [*passionately, thrusting her face close to the
Bishop's*]. A tired Christ would be afraid to lean on your
arm. Your Christ wears a bowler hat, carries a cane,
twiddles his lavender gloves, an' sends out gilt-edged
cards of thanks to callers. Out with you, you old

shivering sham, an' go away into the sun to pick the yellow primroses !

[*As the Young Woman is speaking her last few sentences the Old Woman enters. She is pale and haggard, and vicious lines harden the look of her mouth. Her hair is white, but her black eyes are still undimmed by age. Her thin body is still upright, showing that in her youth she was slim and vigorous, and her face still shelters traces of what were once very good looks. Her boots, though polished, are old and broken, and everything about her, though old and patched and shabby, is clean and neat. Constant, quiet drinking has made her a little incoherent in her thoughts. In one hand she carries a small wreath of red poppies and laurel leaves, which has a bunch of violets where the wreath is tied together by a bow of black ribbon. She has heard the voice of the Young Woman, and comes down to where the girl is speaking, gripping her roughly by the arm as the Young Woman is about to go away from the Bishop.*]

Old Woman [*to the Young Woman*]. Putting yourself again on the market for men, are you ? Piling up money, and not a penny nor the thought of a penny for your lonely and suffering mother. [*As the Young Woman tries to free herself*] No use your trying to get away. [*She drops the wreath on the ground, and holds the girl tighter.*] I have you and I hold you till I get a little to help me on in life for a day or two !

Young Woman [*doggedly*]. I haven't any money ; and, even if I had, I wouldn't part with a penny to you, for all you want it for is drink !

Old Woman [*furiously*]. Drink ! Hear that now ! Is it any wonder God has given her a heart that may go phut any minute ! [*Over to the Bishop*] Hear what she says, you ? That I want the money for drink !

Young Woman [*with a frightened laugh*]. Let me go, will you ? If my heart does go phut, I'll go game, see ! Pass out dancing — see ?
    [*The Old Woman claws at the girl's hat, pulls it off, and flings it on the ground.*

Old Woman [*wildly*]. Want the money for drink, do I ? I'll tear every stitch on you into ribbons !

Young Woman [*appealing*]. Please, please, Mother, don't ruin the few little decent things I have to wear !
    [*The Bishop gets up from his seat, goes over to the struggling Women, and tries to separate them.*

Bishop [*trying to restore peace*]. For shame, for shame ! Mother and daughter, — for shame, for shame !
    [*As soon as she hears the Bishop's voice the Old Woman releases her hold on the girl, and stares at the Bishop. The Young Woman, excited and exhausted, sinks into a seat a little distance away. The Bishop returns the Old Woman's look for a moment, and then rather hastily returns to his seat and resumes the reading of his book. The Old Woman's eyes follow the Bishop and, after a moment's hesitation, she comes up close to him.*

Old Woman [*looking fixedly at the Bishop — murmuringly*]. Your voice has a strange echo in it. Behind that wizened face is hidden a look of the first young man who conquered me on a Sunday night, after the ora pro nobis people had pulled down their blinds and were slinking into sleep. There under a yellow moon, among the shadows by a grove of birch trees, on a bed of flattened bluebells, one of the prettiest fillies that ever wore a skirt was jockeyed into sin, and out of the rapture and the risk came this girl who dares to fancy men more than she does her own mother. [*Suddenly*] Is your name Gilbert ?

Bishop [*over the top of his book — looking very uneasy*]. Go away, you wretched and forgotten creature. My name is not Gilbert !

Old Woman [*still staring at him — murmuring*]. I'm not much to look at now ; but the man who first got the better of me's a big jack-a-dandy in the church, for I saw him once in a holy procession, helping to sing a canticle, a purple cape hanging from his shoulders. [*Suddenly pushing the Bishop's book aside*] Eh, you, is your name Gilbert ?

Bishop [*roughly*]. Get away, get away, woman. My name is not Gilbert. Get away, get away, I tell you !

[*The Old Woman goes over to the Young Woman, limping, sitting on a seat. The Bishop leans forward with his elbows on his knees and his head in his hands.*

Old Woman [*to the Young Woman — whiningly*]. Why don't you try to be decent to your poor mother ? She won't trouble you for long. I feel a few more months will see the end of me.

Young Woman [*savagely*]. I'd dance and sing if I thought you'd die in an hour !

Old Woman [*wildly*]. You'd dance and sing if I died in an hour ? Hear that, now ? Dance and sing ? How can God listen to such a saying and not strike you dead ? [*Over to the Bishop*] Didja hear what she said ? — dance and sing if I died in an hour ? Come over and bruise her hopes with a grim curse from God.

Bishop [*his hands covering his face*]. Oh, hush, hush, woman ; hush and go home.

Old Woman [*wrathful at the Bishop's indifference*]. Hush, hush, and go home you ! Hear what she said to me, said to her mother ? Dance if I died in an hour, and you take her part. You ought to be driven helter-skelter out of everything holy. Hush you, and go home, with your ora pro pugeree mugeree rigmarolum ! [*Turning violently on the Young Woman*] In league with you, is he ? [*She seizes hold of the Young Woman and shakes her violently.*] Dance if I was dead to-day, or died to-morrow, would you ?

Young Woman [*terrified*]. Mother, mind ; don't — I didn't mean anything !

Old Woman [*shaking her more violently still*]. I think of nothing but drink, do I not ?

Young Woman [*hysterically*]. My heart, my heart — you'll be the death of me !

　　[*The Dreamer appears on the slope above and looks on at those below.*

Old Woman [*fiercely flinging her back so that the girl falls on her knees*]. I'll teach you a little of the duty a daughter owes to her mother !

　　[*She raises a hand to strike the girl, but the Dreamer, who has come close, seizes her, and prevents her arm from falling. The Bishop rises, makes a step forward to interfere, but stops in hesitation.*

Dreamer [*gently shaking the Old Woman*]. Now then, now then — what's this ?

　　[*The Young Woman pulls herself on to a seat. She is panting for breath. She reclines down on the bench, closing her eyes, while trying to regain her breath.*

Young Woman [*her eyes closed — between breaths*]. Get her away ; send her away, for God's sake !

Dreamer [*firmly conducting the Old Woman out*]. Go away ; go home, old woman, better go home. Let the old pray by the fire, and leave a way for the young to live.

Old Woman [*murmuringly, as she goes out*]. No pity in the young ; only waiting for time to hustle us off. [*She brushes with her hand the laurel wreath she has picked up from the ground.*] The bad present, and the good absent ; the shame living, and the pride buried ; gone from my grasp and my sight in the flame and smoke of the war. Oh, Jesus, is there no rest to be found anywhere !

    [*The Old Woman goes out, and the Dreamer, returning to the Young Woman, sees the Bishop beckoning to him. He goes to him.*

Bishop [*anxiously*]. Do you think she'll be all right ?

Dreamer. Yes ; she'll be herself again in a few minutes.

Bishop [*handing the Dreamer three pound notes*]. Steal over and slip these in her handbag. Don't mention me. I've no real interest in her, you understand ? Still I pity her in a way. I must go now. It's all the money I have with me. I'll return this way again, later on. [*He turns to go, wheels, and grasps the Dreamer's arm tight.*] Please don't be anyway cruel to her. She is — God's child.

Dreamer. I'll watch her till she has recovered.

Bishop. Thanks.

[*The Bishop goes up the slope. The Dreamer steals over to where the Young Woman is reclining on the bench. He takes up her handbag; sees the Bishop's back is turned; slips one of the notes into his pocket, and the other two into the handbag. When the Bishop reaches the top of the slope, he turns back to look at the Young Woman. The Dreamer waves a hand reassuringly, and the Bishop goes out. The Dreamer goes to the Young Woman, and sits down beside her.*

Dreamer [*to the Young Woman*]. Feeling a little better now?

Young Woman [*still panting a little*]. Bit better now. It's my heart — goes curious now when anything happens. Please sit down beside me for a minute or two.

Dreamer. For a year and a day, if you like.
   [*He sits beside her and takes her hand in his and strokes it.*

Young Woman [*bitterly*]. I'll go off in one of these attacks yet. Nice thing to have for a mother, isn't she? I love the dear silver that shines in her hair! Feeling better, now, anyhow. [*Slyly*] Well, how do you like the hand?

Dreamer. Lovely — like a blue-veined, pink-tipp'd lily.

Young Woman [*taking her hand away*]. Well, let it go for a minute, till I straighten myself up a little.
   [*She arranges her hat, smoothes the folds of her skirt, gives a few touches to her blouse, and sits down again.*

Young Woman. I'm a little more presentable now.

Dreamer [*moving a hand semi-circularly over her breasts*]. There's a wrinkle or two in your blouse still.

Young Woman [*taking his hand away*]. Now, now ! Dad's spoken about you. Not the real Dad, — never saw my real father ; don't even know who or what he was. Hard lines, isn't it ?

Dreamer. It doesn't matter very much now, dear.

Young Woman. My second Dad — the Atheist, you know — calls you a poet. How do you live ?

Dreamer. Oh, I sell an odd article, or, maybe, a song or a story, and so manage to live an austere life. But oughtn't you to go home and have a rest ? I'll see you safe there.

Young Woman [*slyly*]. Tuck me up, and sing me to sleep with one of your songs ?

Dreamer [*earnestly*]. I'd love to ! [*He rises and catches her by an arm.*] Come ! Don't let this rosy chance be pulled to bits by prudence. Come, sweet lass, and let's transmute vague years of life into a glowing hour of love !

Young Woman [*pulling her arm free, and speaking somewhat sharply*]. Not so quick, please ! Men are always ready to rush a pretty woman into love, looking for joy, and behold, trouble. Supposing I go and give, what do I get ?

Dreamer. I'll pay your merry kindness with a song.

Young Woman [*a little scornfully*]. A song ! A puff of scented air ! You're out on the hunt for bargains, young man. Go with a priest for a prayer and with a poet for a song ! It's a poor offer, young sir.

Dreamer [*sitting beside her. Earnestly — close to the Young Woman's face*]. Young lady, many great queens and many grand ladies have joyfully snared themselves in the golden meshes of a poet's song !

Young Woman [*laughingly*]. Well, I'm neither a great queen nor a grand lady ; I'm not even a clergyman's daughter.

Dreamer. To me you're a great lady and a grand queen, and it was for you I wrote the song.

Young Woman [*a little recklessly*]. Well, let's see if your little song can snare the hapless heart of a pretty little maiden.

Dreamer. Wait till we get to your flat, so that I can kiss you between the verses.

Young Woman. Oh, you're travelling quick along your own little road, young singer. Sing it now or sing it never.

Dreamer [*resignedly*]. Oh, all right, then. We'll call it by your name — what is it ?

Young Woman. Just Jannice.

Dreamer. What a pretty name ! Well, we'll call the song just *Jannice*. [*He gives a shy little cough and sings. He is standing now, with one foot on the seat of the bench*] :
> Her legs are as pliant and slim
> As fresh, golden branches of willow ;
> I see lustre of love on each limb,
> Looking down from the heights of a pillow !
> Looking **down** from the **heights** of a pillow !

Tossed by a soft breeze in the spring,
The blooms of an apple tree billow ;
And her breasts are as lovely to me,
Looking down from the heights of a pillow,
Looking down from the heights of a pillow !

Gay, white apple-blossoms her breast,
Her legs golden branches of willow ;
I'd enjoy for a year and a day
Looking down from the heights of a pillow,
Looking down from the heights of a pillow !

Dreamer [*after a pause — expectantly*]. Well ?

Young Woman [*not satisfied, but pleased withal on account of the praise that is in it*]. A pretty song, young singer, but its grace and meaning are hardly a fit for me. I cannot live, or even hope, on the sweet sound of a song. Have you nothing else to offer ?

Dreamer [*reluctantly*]. I could give you a pound.

Young Woman. A pound ! A small gift of gold for a grand lady or a great queen ! Have you nothing more ?

Dreamer [*rather wearily*]. A few shillings for a meal to-day and a meal to-morrow.

Young Woman [*laying a hand almost affectionately on his arm. He covers her hand with his*]. Keep the little you have for yourself, young singer, for your life seems uncertain as my own.
  [*The Bishop has strolled in, and now sits on the bench opposite, apparently reading his book, but really watching the Young Woman. She gives him a hasty, scornful glance.*

Dreamer [*tightening his grip on her hand*]. Well, at least, let me walk across the park with you.

Young Woman [*releasing her hand, and rising*] No, no ; I don't want you. Why do you keep insisting that I need you with me ?

Dreamer. I am thinking, not of your need, but of my own, Jannice.
[*The young Salvation Army Officer enters, and comes down the slope slowly. He keeps looking at the Young Woman.*

Young Woman [*to Dreamer*]. That is selfish. Your way, young singer, though bright with song, is dim with danger. At the end of the way, I might find myself even lower than I am. There is no peace with you. [*She indicates the Salvation Army Officer.*] Here is a real friend who offers peace as a child might offer a friend a new-blown daisy.

Dreamer. His voice is not the voice of peace, but of fear.
[*The Young Woman goes to meet the young Salvation Army Officer.*

Young Woman [*gaily*] :
Good morrow, good morrow, young sir ;
Let's sanction this bold, sunny weather,
By lying aside in the shade,
And cooling warm feelings together !

S.A. Officer [*seriously*]. God's blessing on you, sister, though your thoughtless manner is fashioned to the woe of the world.

Young Woman [*putting her arms round the neck of the Salvation Army Officer — recklessly*]. Oh, come out of the gloom for a moment, dear ! Come into the sun, and kiss me with the kisses of thy mouth !

S.A. Officer [*gently removing the arms of the Young Woman*]. Our ways are not your ways, sister ; we have been led to turn our eyes aside from the gaudy beckoning of the world's vanities.

Young Woman [*a little abashed*]. Sometimes it is very hard to choose. If I lodge where you do, can your people be my people, and your God my God ?

S.A. Officer [*eagerly*]. Ah, if you only will it, sister, it is so ! Out of self, into Christ, into glory ! It is as simple as that, sister.

Bishop [*over to the Salvation Army Officer — sharply*]. The saints didn't find it quite so simple, my young friend.

S.A. Officer [*to Young Woman*]. Never heed him, sister. He would hide God's countenance with a cloud of ritual. Come with me : the yoke is easy ; the burden light.

Young Woman. To peace ?

S.A. Officer. To peace that is perfect, and peace everlasting.

Young Woman. I will go a little way to hear more of the peace that seems so far away. [*She takes the arm of the Salvation Army Officer, and bows mockingly to the Bishop*] Good-bye, old man, who, saving yourself, had no time to save others.

> [*The Bishop does not reply, but sits sadly on the bench looking down towards the ground. The Dreamer sits sadly on the bench opposite, watching the Young Woman go with the Salvation Army Officer. The air of " Jannice " is heard softly, either on flute or fiddle. The Salvation Army Officer and the Young Woman go slowly up the*

slope. When they reach the top, and are about to go off, the Young Woman turns and looks down towards the Dreamer.

Young Woman [*down to the Dreamer*]. I have not quite forgotten your sweet song, young singer !

[*The two go out.*

THE GATES CLOSE

The same part of the Park on an Autumn evening. The sky now is a deep rich crimson, faintly touched at the horizon with golden yellow; while the upper part has a plainly-visible and sweeping border of purple and mauve. The leaves of the trees are red and yellow, the trunks a rich bronze. Now and again, one of them flutters to the ground. At the back, against the slope, are a number of tall, gaunt sunflowers, something like those shown to us by Van Gogh. The figure of the Soldier now shows a deep black against the crimson hue of the sky. Chairs having coloured cloth seats and backs are here and there.

The Two Attendants, looking more haggard and decayed than ever, are lying, apparently asleep, on the slope.

Before the gates open, a band, somewhere in the Park, is heard playing " Land of Hope and Glory ". The music is quite clear and definite, but when the Park is in view the music becomes fainter, as if it was being played at some distance away. The music ceases when the Young Woman and the Dreamer appear.

Older One [*suddenly rousing up and leaning on his elbow to listen*]. " Land of 'Ope en' Glory " ! There's not much of the glory left, en' none of the 'ope. [*He nudges his sleeping companion.*] Eh, Godfrey, 'ear wot they're playin' ? [*Younger Attendant grunts sleepily.*] " Land of 'Ope en' Glory " ! Wot d'ye think of that ?

Young One [*in a sleepy mutter*]. Aw, wot they plays don't concern us.

Older One [*somewhat sharply*]. 'Course it concerns us! Why aren't we part of the 'ope en' the glory? There's that Dreamer, the Atheist, the Man with the Stick, and that gay-dressed young 'eifer goin' abaht good en' proper, denyin' of Gord en' all as is His; en' 'ere we are, two God-fearin', upright men, en' wot's the misery for? [*The Young Attendant takes no notice, so he pokes him.*] Two God-fearin' men, Godfrey, I syes.

Young One [*drowsily*]. Yeh; two God-fearin' young men, ri' enough. I wanna go asleep.

Older One [*bending over and giving him a shake — impatiently*]. Not tykin' no interest in public affaires helps us dahn. Is there a Gord or ain't there? [*His head falls on his breast for a few moments, and he falls back a little in sleepiness, but jerks himself upright again.*] Wot I said before, I syes again: There'll be nothing left if we lift th' pahnd off th' gold stannard. [*He shakes the Younger Attendant again.*] I 'olds we're ruined if we go off th' gold stannard! [*He sinks slowly down on the slope, weary, and full of sleep.*]   [*A pause.*

Young One [*suddenly sitting up*]. En' I syes no! Give the British pahnd a charnce in the world's market. While we keep on sterling, we lose our gold in masses. I 'olds we're ruined, if we don't go off the stannard.
                                        [*He sinks down.*

Older One [*sleepily*]. I 'olds we're ruined if we does!
   [*They both apparently sink into sleep as the Young Woman and the Dreamer appear above, and come down the slope, passing the sleeping figures by. She is pale, but her eyes are asparkle, though she has the Dreamer by the arm, and leans a little on him.*

Young Woman [*as she is coming down*]. I shouldn't have taken the wine, Dreamer. It has made me unsteady, inclining me to see the world fairer than I should.

Dreamer. It was good wine, then. You see clearly, for wine is the mirror of the heart.

Young Woman. I feel uneasy, feeling so much joy.

Dreamer [*setting her on a seat*]. Wait for me here, Jannice. I must cash the cheque I got this morning. I won't be from you over half an hour.

Young Woman. I wish you wouldn't go, dear Dreamer. Alone, I feel afraid of myself. [*A little roguishly*] Supposing when you are gone, Salvation's Officer comes and I go with him?

Dreamer. I'm not afraid of him : there's no peace or joy for you where he is. To him, peace may bring joy ; to such as you, only joy can give you peace.

Young Woman. Still, stay here, Dreamer. I've two pounds I found suddenly in my bag this morning.

Dreamer. Keep them. I'll go. The music of the band will keep you company till I come again. A kiss !

[*He kisses her, and goes, waving back from the top of the slope, while she reclines a little sleepily on the seat, as the Man wearing the Trilby comes hurriedly in, followed as quickly by the Man with the Stick ; he is followed a little more slowly by the Atheist, a Man wearing a Bowler Hat, and a Man wearing a Straw Hat — commonly called " a boater ". They come together, and form an arguing group. Each, excepting the Atheist, carries a big newspaper under an arm.*]

Man with Stick [*calling to Man wearing Trilby*]. Eh, stand your ground ! If we wants knorledge, we must ask questions.

Man wearing Trilby [*halting, and letting the rest come up to him*]. Let there be an end of mockery, then.

Man wearing Bowler. Yes ; let's conduct the debate with decorum.

Man with Stick. I wasn't mockin' enyone — I was only mockin' Genesis.

Man wearing Trilby. Well, Genesis is part of me, en' I'm part of Genesis.

Man with Stick [*looking at the sky, and giving a long, impatient sigh*]. Uuh !

Atheist [*gently to Man wearing Trilby*]. You see, friend, your arguments for existence of a Gord can't be the cause of belief, for the reason that the belief was there before them ; and this belief was born into the mind of primitive man by ignorance and fear.

Man wearing Straw Hat. So you say !

Atheist [*turning to him*]. And so say the most eminent anthropologists we have. [*To Man wearing Trilby*] You, my friend, are arguing for the arguments usually set forth to prove the belief, and not for the belief itself which existed before the arguments — see ?

Man with Stick. 'E don't warnt to see !

Man wearing Trilby. All I syes is use your eyes, use your ears, use your brine, en' wot's the explyenation of all the wunnerful things we sees en' 'ears arahnd us — on the earth en' above us in the sky — en' I syes Gord myde them orl !

Man with Stick [*impatiently*]. Ah, wot we warnt to know, man, is who myde Gord !

Man wearing Straw Hat [*pushing in truculently*]. 'E always existed ! In the beginning all things was myde by 'im, en' withaht 'im was not enything myde wot was myde !

Man with Stick [*with another look at the sky*]. Aw, aw — we're back to Genesis again !

Atheist [*quietly and firmly*]. There never was a beginning, friend. Nothing 'as been myde, en' everything's been evolved out of matter, energy, en' force ; forms chynging, but substance remineing the syme.

Man with Stick [*tapping the ground affirmatively*]. 'Course they 'as.

Man wearing Trilby [*hesitant*]. Yes ; in a way, yes ; but even Einstein syes —

Man with Stick [*interrupting fiercely*]. Aw, we're not responsible for wot Einstein syes !

Atheist [*deprecatingly — to Man with Stick*]. Patience, brother.

Man wearing Trilby. Wot first created this matter en' this energy en' this force you speak abaht ? If it was always, 'ow was it always, en' where was it always ? We gets nowhere when we syes thet wot's to come comes aht of wot is, en' wot is, is aht of wot was : it only mystifies a man ; so I syes in the beginning, before enything wot is was, was Gord, en' it was 'e manipulated energy en' force to mike us wot we are.

Young Woman [*who has been listening abstractedly for some time — running a little unsteadily over to them, and pushing her way into the group*]. And aren't you fellows a fine example of what we are ! [*To Atheist*] No beginning ? As it was in the beginning, is now, and ever shall be ; world without end. Amen. See ?

Man with Stick [*indignantly*]. You mustn't interrupt, young woman ! Your mind isn't able to comprehend wot we're torking abaht.

Young Woman. And yours is ? Why, the wisdom each of you has, taken together, would fit on a spoon. [*She pushes them about a little wildly.*] Oh, go away, you little chirrupers, and leave the Park to peace. Let a quiet place enjoy the quietness it gives.

Atheist [*moving off*]. The discussion's ended, gentlemen, for the present. Go and read your papers.

[*He goes off.*

[*The four men, Man with Stick, Man wearing Trilby, Man wearing Bowler, and Man wearing Straw Hat, sit down on the seats having coloured cloth seats and backs. The seats are so placed that if a line was drawn to each of them, the lines would make an X. They take the papers from under their arms, spread them out, and begin to read. Each of the newspapers on the page facing outwards has one large word only. One has Murder, another Rape, another Suicide, on the fourth Divorce. The Young Woman returns, still a little unsteady, to the bench. As the men read, the Band is heard softly playing " London Bridge is Falling Down ". As the tune is played for the second time, the Man wearing the Straw Hat sings the words half to himself.*

Man wearing Straw Hat [*singing*] :
    London Bridge is falling down, falling down, falling down,
    London Bridge is falling down, my fair lady.

Man wearing Bowler [*with complacent dignity — singing*] :
    Build it up with gold and silver, gold and silver, gold and silver,
    Build it up with gold and silver, my fair lady.

Young Woman [*singing with distinct note of denial*] :
    Gold and silver will not do, will not do, will not do,
    Gold and silver will not do, my fair lady.

Man wearing Straw Hat [*singing a little sadly*] :
    Gold and silver's grown a god, grown a god, grown
        a god,
    Gold and silver's grown a god, my fair lady.

Young Woman [*standing up, stamping her foot, and singing
    fiercely*] :
    Let it fall to pieces then, pieces then, pieces then,
    Let it fall to pieces then, my fair lady !

Older One [*rising from the slope to lean on his elbow — in a
    protesting, whining snarl*]. Wot's yous warnt to make
    such a row when two poor men is tryin' to sleep awye
    the worries of the world !
                    [*The Older Attendant sinks down to sleep again.*

Young Woman [*mockingly — after watching the Readers for a
    few moments*]. Let every sound be hushed, for the
    oblate fathers are busy reading the gospel for the day.
    Furnishing their minds with holy thoughts, and
    storing wisdom there.   Let us pray !   Oh, Lucifer,
    Lucifer, who has caused all newspapers to be written
    for our learning — stars of the morning and stars of
    the evening — grant we may so read them that we
    may always find a punch in them, hot stuff in them,
    and sound tips in them ; so that, outwardly in our
    bodies and inwardly in our souls, we may get closer
    and closer to thee !   [*Indignantly*] Why the hell don't
    you all say Amen !

Man wearing Trilby [*to Young Woman*]. Hush, woman : we
    want quietness when our minds are busy.

Young Woman [*rising and moving about among the Readers recklessly*]. I've had a few drinks, but what about it ! A short life and a merry one ! My heart's due to stop beating any minute now, but what about it ! [*She contemplates the Readers.*] Devoted, body and soul, to the love of learning. Listen : Jannice is going to die dancing. [*Vehemently*] Are all you damn perishers deaf and dumb ?

Man wearing Bowler [*with irritation*]. Oh, go away ; we want to read in peace.

Young Woman [*singing softly, but a little drunkenly*] :
 Stirr'd by a soft breeze in the Spring,
 The blooms of an apple tree billow ;
 And her breast is as fragrant to me,
 Looking down from the height of a pillow,
 Looking down from the height of a pillow !
 [*She coughs, becomes a little breathless, and presses a hand to her side.*
I'm a sick woman. [*She bends her head down on her breast.*] Death has touched me, and is telling me to be ready ; take your things off, and come with me. [*Defiantly*] I'll not give in, I'll not hold back. And when I go, should God's angels beckon me up or push me down, I'll go game. [*Horrified*] Jesu, Son of Mary, what'm I saying ? I'll fold all the things done in this life round me like a mantle, and wait for judgement.
 [*She sinks down on a seat, and stares thoughtfully in front of her.*

Man with Stick [*reading from behind the paper marked Murder*]. The condemned man, who is to be hanged for cutting a woman into bits, ate a hearty breakfast, spent an edifying time with the chaplain, smoked a cigarette while being pinioned, and walked with a goose-step to the gallows.

Rest of the Readers [*in chorus*]. Walked with a goose-step to the gallows.

Man with Straw Hat [*reading from behind the paper marked Suicide*]. The dead man left a letter saying, I have ruined thousands and have made many mad ; I have shaken hands with Dukes and Duchesses ; before I put the pistol-point to my ear and scatter my brains, I kiss the pictures of my little darlings ; knowing that, while all men condemn, all men will understand.

Rest of the Readers [*in chorus*]. All men will understand.

Young Woman [*getting up from the bench with a half-hysterical laugh*]. Never say die till you're dead ! [*She looks at the Readers.*]   Rape, murder, and suicide !   A bit of a change from the life of the saints. [*Loudly to the Readers*] What will you fellows do when you die, and have to leave it all behind you ?

The Readers [*in chorus*]. Go away, young woman — we want quietness.

Man wearing Bowler [*reading from behind the paper marked Divorce*]. The housemaid said she climbed the ivy, got to the verandah, looked in through the window, saw the co-respondent in bed, the respondent in her camisole trotting towards the bed ; then came darkness, and she would leave the judge and jury to guess the rest.

Rest of the Readers [*in chorus*]. Leave the learned judge and jury to guess the rest.

   [*While the last phrase is being chorused by the Readers, the*

Bishop appears on the slope above, looking down anxiously at the Young Woman.

Bishop [*from the slope above*]. Jannice !

Young Woman [*up to the Bishop*]. Are you following me still ? [*Angrily*] Go away, go away and leave me in peace ! Let me run my race in my own way. Don't be mousing after me.

Bishop [*pleadingly*]. I want to help you, Jannice ; let me help you !

Young Woman [*loudly*]. Go away, I tell you ; I want no God's grenadier running after me. [*In a half-scream*] Go away ! [*The Bishop goes back to the Memorial, and the Young Woman again contemplates the Readers.*] What are you all seeking ? You look like a silent gang of monkeys searching for fleas !

The Readers [*in chorus*]. Go away ; we want to read our papers in peace !

Young Woman [*softly and thoughtfully*]. Most important thing, too, is peace ; most important. Peace most pure and peace most perfect, due to the children of the Prince of Peace. [*Recklessly*] But what have I to do with peace ! When I come to the temple of peace, the veil of the temple turns to steel ! Is there no one far enough from the way of the world to take an interval of rest, and have a look at me ? [*The tune of " The Danube Waltz " has been heard for a few moments before, played softly by the Band. She begins to dance to the tune, in and out among the Readers.*] Now, you deaf and dumb perishers, have a look at a lovely pair of legs, if you're not blind as well ! [*She lifts her skirts as she dances, and makes her movements keep time with the tune.*

The Readers look over the tops of their papers and watch her.]
All interested now ? Well, what do you think of
them — saucy, eh ? [*Slapping her left leg*] This one's
lovely. [*Slapping the right one*] This divine ! [*She stops
breathless, and scans them scornfully. The music slowly
fades away. Breathless and scornful*] You bunch of high-
minded toads, don't look at me long, for there's only
venom for a woman in the things ye think of her. The
dear joy of a sin ye turn to a sting and a bruising. [*She
half sinks on a seat.*] Oh, my heart, my heart's restless
again ! [*She speaks in a lower tone to the Readers.*] In your
looking after a woman there is no kindliness ; before
ye no image of loveliness, neither can ye hear the sound
of a song as ye follow her, for your desire's but a
venomous heat and a shame and a bruising !

[*She sinks down, pale, breathless, and frightened, on the
seat. The Readers return to their reading ; and take no
more notice of her.*

Man wearing Bowler [*reading from behind his paper*]. The
great cricketer, unbuckling his pads, said, You may
take it from me that out there somewhere is a supreme,
infinitely wise mind, which we call God, behind everything.· God won't let the English people dahn. He'll
keep our wicket up, and the bat of faith will drive
the bad ball of unbelief far away over the boundary of
England !

Man with Stick [*with scornful disgust*]. Wot the 'ell does a
cricketer know abaht them abstruse things !

Young Woman [*who has been moving uneasily on the bench*]. I
can't breathe, I can't breathe ! [*She pulls the neck of her
bodice open.*] It's on me again, but I'll go game, I'll go
game. Eyes front up or down ! [*The Bishop begins to*

*come down slowly towards the Young Woman. In a panic of
fear]* Dance, sing, and strip for the fun of the thing —
that's all they want from a woman ! A sigh, a sob of
pain, a thought higher than their own from a woman,
and they're all hurrying home. *[Turning towards the
Readers]* God damn you, will none of you stir to help
when you see a Christian in danger ! *[She calls out in a
semi-scream]* Dreamer, Dreamer — where's the Dreamer !
 *[She sinks down half fainting on the bench. The Bishop
  comes quickly to her, now, and chafes her hands. The
  Readers have risen from their seats, have folded up their
  newspapers, and now come to where the Young Woman
  and the Bishop are, forming a semicircle around them.*

Bishop *[gently and fervently]*. Jannice, my little Jannice,
I've come to help you ; everything will be all right
soon. *[Addressing the Readers]* Don't gather round,
friends. Leave the girl to me. I'll watch over her.
[As they don't stir — sharply] Leave us alone, I say, and
don't stand there, staring like apes ! *[All but the Man
with the Stick go silently and slowly out. To Man with the
Stick]* Didn't you hear me tell you to go away, man ?

Man with Stick *[indignantly]*. 'Oo are you to sye come en'
'e cometh, en' go en' 'e goeth ? Wot she warnts is a
doctor, en' not a pryer !

Bishop *[in a burst of fury — using some of the strength of his
younger days, and pushing him out roughly]*. Oh, go to
hell !
 *[He returns to the Young Woman as she recovers slightly,
  looking up at him without any confidence in her look.*

Bishop *[returning a little to formal speech, but softly, and with
feeling]*. You are ill, my child ; and you are lonely.
You have forgotten God for a few moments, but He

sends you His help in time of trouble ; and, through
me, unworthy messenger, a share of His sympathy and
love.

[*He sits down beside her. She recovers a little, sits up,
and stretches out a hand to him, which he takes in his
own, and strokes gently.*

Young Woman [*with a sigh of relief*]. I'm glad you came. I
was very lonely. My heart's beating a bit steadier
now, thank God.

Bishop [*gently patting her hand*]. That's good, now ; that's
good.

Young Woman [*regaining confidence*]. A lot steadier now. I
think it's more fear than anything else. I've had a
hard time of it ; and I get into a panic whenever my
heart gives a double-time beat. I feel nearly normal
again.

Bishop [*encouragingly*]. That's good. Keep calm for a little
while and you'll soon be all right.

Young Woman. I'm waiting for the Dreamer. He'll be
here shortly, and then I'll be safe again.

Bishop [*still stroking her hand — a little coldly*]. My child,
I shouldn't think too much of the Dreamer, or make
a friend of him. The things he writes give scandal,
and tend to undermine morality and overthrow
tradition. He is a bad influence, my child.

Young Woman [*taking her hand out of the Bishop's — firmly*].
I won't hear a word said against the Dreamer. He
was the only one from whom I got courage and help.
The Atheist, when he acted as my dad, was kind, too,
in his own self-interested way. [*She looks innocently*

into the Bishop's face.] I never saw my real father. Mother often said he had a high place in your church ; but he never had the courage to come and claim his child.

Bishop [*coldly*]. From what I saw of her, your mother isn't to be trusted.

Young Woman [*emphatically*]. Well, the Dreamer is. He is as poor as I am, but he gaily shares with me his money and his joy. So, you see, he is more important to me than the God you praise.

Bishop [*shocked*]. You mustn't say such things, my child ! I am here to help you, showing how kind and gentle God can be to — er — a straying lamb seeking in devious ways to find a way back to the waiting flock.

Young Woman [*fretfully*]. Oh, the flock doesn't care a damn whether I'm in or out, man. The flock ! So long as they get their four meals a day, with a gay hour after, and a cosy fire in the winter, they'll never stretch a neck to see where a ram or a ewe has wandered.

Bishop [*soothingly*]. Well, never mind, now, and don't let your thoughts irritate you into any excitement, child. What you need most, now, is rest, and a chance to live a sober and a quiet life.

Young Woman [*more irritably than ever*]. And follow the commandments of God — always trying to crimp people into piety. You cross, crown, and anchor boys expect the very linnets to sing hymns in their spare time. The Salvation Army Officer, too, has the same gloomy glimpse of life. Miserere, miserere, all the **way** to heaven !

Bishop. Hush. Forget everything but your own help-lessness ; and don't get excited.

Young Woman [*vehemently*]. I have to get a little farther away from the devil before I try to get a little nearer to God. I've a long way to travel yet before the white and holy candles are lit, and the golden incense scattered.

Bishop. My child, the sinner is always nearer to God than the sinner dares to think.

Young Woman [*a little hysterically*]. Amen, and let us get to business. Make me safe and make me happy, and I'll give sweet thanks to God. Why've you been following me about for days ? I sought you once, and you sent me empty away. Why do you want to help me now ? [*Indicating sleeping Attendants*] Why don't you try to help those poor sleeping devils there ?

Bishop [*a little impatiently*]. Oh, it would be waste of time to think of them.

Young Woman. They're still God's children, aren't they ?

Bishop [*more impatiently*]. We'll see about them another time. You seem to be an interesting case — young and intelligent. You don't seem to be an ordinary — eh — what shall I say ?

Young Woman [*bitterly*]. Oh, a whore ! You may as well say it as think it. [*The Bishop is shocked at the girl's bluntness. He stiffens, and stays silent. Looking intently at the Bishop's face*] What was it made you light on me, I wonder ? There are hundreds of girls, some of them better, some of them worse, than me, and it's curious that I should be the lucky dip. [*The Bishop remains silent.*] Well, go on ; open up the overture, and play us something nice.

Bishop [*trying to control his impatience*]. My child, your present way of life is an evil one. I wish to give you a chance to turn aside from it ; so please try to be decently attentive, and listen seriously to what I am about to say.

Young Woman [*with a half-suppressed giggle*]. Wine's beginning to take effect again. I had a wild time all this week with the Dreamer. He got an advance on a book that's to be published soon, and he's gone for another advance now. [*She prods the Bishop's breast.*] If he comes back before our treaty's signed, I'm off, and you won't see me again till what he gets is gone : so go ahead, and strike a light, and let us see the way we're walking.

Bishop [*with gloomy indignation*]. I can't listen any longer to these frivolous remarks. You have no pity for yourself. You have gone too far away for any helping hand to reach. I will leave you alone. [*He rises from the bench to go.*] I have done my best. I will leave you alone.

Young Woman [*catching his cassock — pleadingly*]. No, no ; don't go away. I will listen ; I will listen quietly ; I promise. Be kind, and help me. I do want to try to do what is lawful and right. In God's name, be kind, dear Bishop.

Bishop [*rather sternly*]. Listen, child, then, and be serious. When trying to help you, I must be careful of what others may think.

Young Woman. Why have you to be careful ? Can't you yourself pray, or push yourself out of the fear of what may be said about you ? What does it matter how many say a man's a sinner if God thinks him a saint ?

Bishop [*very annoyed*]. I can't waste time going into those questions now. You said you were going to be serious. Well, then, one more flippant word and I leave you, never to turn a thought to you again.

Young Woman [*earnestly*]. I will be serious ; I promise. I fix my face, and am serious. I'll do anything you ask me to do.
    [*She pulls gently at his cassock, and he slowly resumes his seat on the bench beside her.*

Bishop [*with some embarrassment*]. I'm about to say something now which, I fear, will sound very unpleasant to you, perhaps even harsh and ungenerous ; something that will bite deeply into all that you may think to be a pleasure. [*He puts a hand gently and appealingly on her shoulder.*] God alone knows, my dear daughter, how deep is my desire to save you !

Young Woman [*with calm and innocent confidence*]. Oh, with your power and position, you should be able to push me into a job that wouldn't make the change such a sad one.

Bishop [*taking his hand from her shoulder, and speaking harshly*]. I wouldn't think of getting you a place till, after a year or two of trial, I felt certain you had learned how to behave yourself.   [*A pause and a tense silence.*

Young Woman [*with a stifled sob of humiliation*]. I see. [*A pause.*] How am I to live through the two years ?

Bishop [*forcing himself to speak harshly*]. I've arranged that a pious Sisterhood should receive you into their Hostel, where the Reverend Mother will care for you, watch over you, and help you to live with becoming circumspection. In return, when you begin to feel at home, you can make yourself useful to the good Sisters.

Young Woman [*with tightened lips*]. I see.

> [*The Policewoman enters, crosses in front of the Young Woman and the Bishop, and looks fixedly and wonderingly at the pair of them. The Young Woman looks down at her feet and the Bishop stares in front of him.*

Policewoman [*speaking towards the Bishop*]. Nice die, m'lud.

Bishop. I beg your pardon?

Policewoman. Said it was a nice die, m'lud.

Bishop [*stammeringly*]. Oh yes, quite; lovely day, beautiful day; yes, indeed, a very beautiful day. [*The Policewoman, watching them as long as possible, goes slowly out. Appealingly*] Why do you keep silent? Take your chance, take your last chance; for God's sake take your last chance. [*The Young Woman sits silent.*] Do you hear me? The offer I have made is a good offer. In it is peace, and a fair hope of better things to come. Go on, girl, speak; make up your mind, make up your mind.

Young Woman [*rising with hysterical laughter that rouses the sleeping Attendants, who lean on their elbows, watching*]. Wine's beginning to take effect again. Your old mind must be worn out thinking of such a wonderful plan. He lifted me up and set me down in the midst of a holy sisterhood. Refugium peccatorum, but not for me, thank you kindly. [*She bows mockingly to the Bishop.*] Chained fast to prayer and firm to fasting! [*She puts her face near the Bishop's.*] Not for me, thank you kindly!

Bishop [*with intense feeling*]. What will you do when your good looks go, and you lose the means to earn your bread?

Young Woman [*with a snarling look on her face as she thrusts it close to the Bishop's*]. Die, I dare say, while you heap up

hopes in the books of a bank, and carry your faith about
in a coffin !

> [*She hurriedly opens her handbag, takes out two notes, and
> holds them close to the Bishop's nose. The Two Attendants
> are now alert, and are watching intently.*

Young Woman [*viciously*]. See, old purple buttons — the
last two between all I need and me ! [*She rolls each into
the shape of a crumpled ball, and calls to the Attendants.*]
Eh, you there — up, and see what God has sent you !
[*She flings a crumpled note to each of them. They open them,
smoothe them out, and put them joyously into their pockets.
To the Bishop — recklessly*] I fling my wealth away !
[*She points a finger at the Bishop's nose.*] Faith in God, old
purple buttons, faith in God ! Be merry, man, for a
minute, for you'll be a long time dead ! [*The Bishop,
full of sorrow and disappointment, mixed with shame, bends
forward on the seat, and rests his head in his hands. The Young
Woman dances round with mock stateliness as she sings words
to the tune of " Little Brown Jug ". The Two Chair
Attendants, as far as their game legs will allow, imitate her
in a reckless manner, beating out time, one with his good right
leg, and the other with his good left one. Singing and dancing
round with mock stateliness*] :

> Sing and dance, dance and sing,
> Brief life should be a joyous thing ;
> The minds that are to troubles wed
> Are fit to host but with the dead !
> Ha ha ha, you and me, till we both have ceased to be,
> Sling out woe, hug joy instead,
> For we will be a long time dead !

Chair Attendants [*joining vigorously in*] :

> Sling aht woe, 'ug joy instead,
> For we will be a long time dead !

Young Woman [*singing*] :

Life is born and has its day,
Sings a song, then slinks away ;
Speaks a word — the word is said,
Then hurries off to join the dead !
Ha ha ha, you and me, till we both have ceased to be,
Sling out woe, hug joy instead,
For we will be a long time dead !

Attendants [*joining in*] :

Sling aht woe, 'ug joy instead,
For we will be a long time dead !

[*During the singing of the second verse of the song the
Atheist has made his appearance on the top of the slope,
and stands there watching what is going on below. As
the Young Woman is ending the latter verse of the song,
the drum-beat and chant of the Down-and-Out is heard
in the near distance, coming nearer and nearer. The
Chair Attendants hear it, stiffen with fear, and end the
chorus weakly. Then the Young Woman recognizes it,
and stands stiff, frightened, while she listens intently.
Together.*]   The drum-beat and chant of the Down-
and-Out !

*The scene grows dark and chilly, and even the Bishop
shivers, though the Atheist seems not to notice the change.
The sky seems to turn a cold grey, and against it the
Down-and-Out pass by. They are all grey, vague
figures of young and old men and women, hopelessness
graven on every grey face. They go by in a rather slow
shuffling march, chanting their miserere to the monotonous
tap, tap of the drum-beat. They go behind the Atheist,
but he stands there, indifferent to march or chant. The
Attendants sink down to their knees, one on the right of
the grass sward, the other to the left of it.*

Down-and-Outs [*chanting*] :

    We challenge life no more, no more, with our dead
        faith, and our dead hope ;

    We carry furl'd the fainting flag of a dead hope and
        a dead faith.

    Day sings no song, neither is there room for rest
        beside night in her sleeping ;

    We've but a sigh for a song, and a deep sigh for a
        drum-beat.

    Oh where shall we go when the day calls ?

    Oh where shall we sleep when the night falls ?

    We've but a sigh for a song, and a deep sigh for a
        drum-beat !

    [*The Down-and-Out pass out, their song fading out in the
    repetition of the line, " We've but a sigh for a song, and
    a deep sigh for a drum-beat "*.

Bishop [*pointing towards where the Down-and-Out have gone*].
There go God's own aristocracy, the poor in spirit !
Their slogan, Welcome be the Will of God ; their life
of meek obedience and resignation in that state of
poverty unto which it has pleased God to call them, a
testimony that God's in His heaven, all's well with
the world. [*To the Attendants*] Join them, my sons.
[*To Young Woman*] Join them, my daughter, in the spirit
of penitence and prayer !

Atheist [*from the slope above*]. Jannice, stand firm, and
remember that you are the bride of the Dreamer. Tell
him that the world shall be, not what his God wills,
but what fighting man can make it. Tell him you have
given life a dance and the Dreamer has given life a
song !

Bishop [*coming close to the Young Woman, who is leaning for help on the back of a bench*]. They came close, my child, they came close. They will get you some day, if you do not let me save you now.

Young Woman [*with a quivering lip*]. No !

Attendants [*together*]. Save us, sir ; save us !
                    [*The Bishop takes no notice of them.*

Bishop [*bending over the Young Woman*]. The day is fair, my daughter, the day is fair ; but what of the night, when youth has faded, and the shadows fall, and the heart is lonely ?

Young Woman [*tonelessly, but defiantly*]. When youth has gone, when night has fallen, and when the heart is lonely, I will stand and stare steady at a God who has filled the wealthy with good things and has sent the poor empty away.

Bishop [*sorrowfully*]. Don't say such things, child. Come with me, I beg of you to come with me.

Young Woman [*with tight lips*]. No.
       [*The Bishop looks sadly at her for a moment, then turns and
       goes slowly up the slope.*
       [*The Young Salvation Army Officer followed by other
       members of the Army, all in uniform, peaked caps and
       red jerseys, come in, and group themselves in a half-
       circle, near the centre, to the left of the grass sward.
       One of them has a trombone, another a cornet, and a
       third, a big drum. Beside them is raised the red and blue
       and yellow banner of the sect. A small, box-like stand
       is placed on the grass, so that a speaker may be raised a
       little above the crowd. Around them gather various
       people, among them the Man wearing a Bowler Hat, the
       Man wearing a Straw Hat, the Man wearing a Trilby,*

the Nursemaid with her Guardsman, the Attendants,
and the Man with the Stick, who stands off, nearer to the
Atheist, as if for protection. The Young Salvation Army
Officer stands out to watch the Bishop going slowly up
the slope. When he reaches the top, he turns, and speaks
pleadingly down to the Young Woman.

Bishop [*making a quiet sign of the cross*]. My poor child, I ask
you, in the Name of God — come !

Young Woman [*firmly, though her lips quiver a little*]. No !
  [*The Bishop looks sadly at her for a moment, and then turns,*
  goes by the Atheist, and passes out. The Young Woman
  reclines weakly back on the bench, silent and desolate-
  looking. The scene brightens and the birds sing once
  more. The Young Salvation Army Officer goes over close
  to the Young Woman.

S.A. Officer [*to Young Woman*]. The ritualist has left you
in your need, but the evangelist is here to comfort and
help you — if you will. Dear sister, set your foot, by
faith, on the path that leads to the land that is fairer
than day ; where the Father waits to prepare you a
dwelling-place — a house not made with hands, eternal
in the heavens.
  [*She is silent, and stirs not. He quietly signals to the*
  musicians, and they softly play the tune, " There were
  Ninety and Nine ", the rest of the Army and some of the
  crowd singing the words.

Crowd :
  There were ninety and nine that safely lay
  In the shelter of the fold,
  But one was out on the hills away,
  Far off from the gates of gold,

Away on the mountains wild and bare,
Away from the tender Shepherd's care ;
Away from the tender Shepherd's care.

S.A. Officer [*to Young Woman*]. You, sister. But the Lord
was anxious, and would not be satisfied with His ninety
and nine who were safe. So He set out to find His lost
sheep — you, dear sister, you !
    [*He again quietly signals the musicians, who play the air
    again, while the rest sing the words.*

Crowd :
But none of the ransomed ever knew
How deep were the waters crossed,
Nor how dark was the night that the Lord pass'd
    through,
Ere He found His sheep that was lost.
Out in the desert He heard its cry —
Sick and helpless and ready to die ;
Sick and helpless and ready to die.

    [*The Young Woman is visibly affected. She rises from
    the bench, and half turns towards where the Salvation
    Army members are grouped. The Young Salvation Army
    Officer, seeing this, lays a hand gently on her shoulder.*

S.A. Officer [*with uplifted eyes — prayerfully*]. There is a
young sinner with us now who needs the pardon Christ
can give. Let her come to the foot of the cross. She
must struggle down to the cross before she can climb
up to the crown. Brothers and sisters, let us pray that
she may turn from her sin, and be saved ! [*As he is
speaking the Dreamer appears on the top of the slope above, gets
in front of the Atheist, and stands to look at what is happening.*]
Save this wandering lamb, O God, and bring her
safely home !

Salvationists [*in chorus*]. Save her, great and most merciful Redeemer !

S.A. Officer. That the trumpets of the angels may have a new note in their sounding !

Salvationists [*in chorus*]. Save her, great and most merciful Redeemer !

S.A. Officer. That the crown of thorns on the head of the crucified one may shine as the sun in the season of summer !

Salvationists [*in chorus*]. Save her, great and most merciful Redeemer !

S.A. Officer. That the nails in His hands and His feet may gleam like the moon at the full in the season of harvest !

Young Woman [*in a frightened voice*]. Ah, save me from the fire that is never quenched, and give me peace !

Dreamer [*from the slope above*]. Jannice, Jannice, the Dreamer calls !
> [*The air of "Jannice" is faintly heard, as if from a distance. The Young Woman stands listening, and the look of fright fades from her face.*

S.A. Officer [*up to the Dreamer*]. Go your wild way, young man ; for our sister has shut herself away from the pride and vanity of your thoughtless life.

Dreamer [*to S.A. Officer*]. The rose that once has opened can never close again. [*To the Young Woman*] Jannice, here is peace ; peace unharmed by the fire of life. I have that will give another month of gay and crowded life ; of wine and laughter ; joy in our going out and our

coming in ; and the dear pain from the golden flame
of love. Jannice, the Dreamer calls !

[*The tune of " Jannice " is heard much more clearly now.
The Young Woman has retreated away from the Salva-
tionist group ; now the Young Salvation Army Officer
holds out his arms to her, but she backs away from him
and half turns towards the Dreamer.*

S.A. Officer [*sadly*]. Let us all pray silently and together
against the power trying to draw our young sister from
the offer of redemption.

[*The Attendants fall on their knees, and with outspread
fingers cover their faces. The Men Salvationists remove
their caps and bend their heads in an attitude of prayer.
The Women Salvationists do the same, but do not remove
their bonnets. The Young Salvation Army Officer takes
off his cap, and covers his face with one hand. The tune
of " Jannice " is heard clearly.*

Dreamer [*taking a step down the slope*]. Jannice, the Dreamer
calls you to the deep kiss and clutch of love ; to sing
our song with the song that is sung by a thousand stars
of the evening !

[*The Young Woman moves slowly away from the praying
group, gradually quickens her movement, till finally she
runs to be clasped in the arms of the Dreamer ; while the
Atheist looks down on the Salvationists with a slight
twist of mockery disarranging his lips.*

[*The Young Salvation Army Officer glances up, and sees
that the Young Woman is about to go with the Dreamer.
He bends his head on his breast — a picture of disappointment, and, maybe, of vanity cheated of its due. The
Musicians, replacing their caps on their heads, play the
tune of " Ninety and Nine " very softly, and the rest
sing the words as softly, too, for the tune of " Jannice " has*

*faded away as the Young Woman goes into the arms of the
Dreamer, as the Dreamer and the Young Woman pass out
on their way together.*

Oh, sad is the fate of the lamb who strays
Far off from her Shepherd's care,
Leaving fair fields where the sunlight plays
For the gloom of the mountains bare ;
Oh, sad is the Shepherd seeking his sheep,
To find that his lov'd one is nowhere there ;
To find that his lov'd one is nowhere there !

THE GATES CLOSE

Scene IV

A Winter's night in the Park. The colour of the sky is a deep black, brightening from the centre to the horizon to a rich violet, deepening to a full purple hue. To the right, where the purple sky begins to sink into the darkness, is a group of stars ; one red, the other golden, and a third, silver. The trees are quite bare of leaves, and their branches form a pattern against the purple parts of the sky.

Light from an electric lamp behind the War Memorial shines on the head and shoulders of the figure, making them glow like burnished aluminium ; and the bent head appears to be .looking down at the life going on below it.

A Group of Men are standing to the right, looking as if they were directly under the stars. They are the Man wearing a Trilby, the Man wearing a Bowler Hat, the Man who wore a Straw One, but now is wearing a Tweed Cap, the Man with the Stick, and some others. They are all wearing topcoats or mackintoshes, and their collars are pulled up as high as they can go around their throats. The Man with the Stick now carries an Umbrella. As the scene is opening, the latter part of the bugle-call, The Last Post, *is heard sounding in the far distance.*

Man wearing Cap [*to the Others*]. Wot's that, now ?

Man wearing Bowler. Sounds like *The Last Post.*

Man wearing Trilby. It is *The Last Post.*

Man wearing Cap. Wunner where's it from ?

Man wearing Trilby. From the barracks up Kensington way. You can 'ear any sound pline on a still, clear night like this one.

Man wearing Bowler. Creepy sound, 'asn't it? Alwyes mikes me think of grives when I 'ears it.

Man with Umbrella. En' wot if it does? A grive's as common as a crydle, man, en' we've no caurse to be afride of either.

Man wearing Cap. It's easy to talk, but a grive's a grive ; en' with winter 'ere, en' the Park nearly desolyte, the sahnd of *The Last Post* 'as en eerie effect on me.

Man wearing Trilby [suddenly]. 'Ere 'e is agine ! Like 'Amlet's ghost. Wot interest 'as 'e in the girl, I wunner ?

Man with Umbrella. Up to no good, I bet. No bishop ever is. Keep back in the gloom so as 'e won't see.

> [*They retire a little.*
> [*The Bishop comes down the slope, looking from right to left, then stopping to look behind him. His face is grey, and a deep look of worry lines it. He is followed by his Sister, who looks stern and appears to be annoyed.*

Bishop's Sister [with suppressed anger]. Gilbert, for goodness' sake, have sense. Why do you trouble yourself like this for a trollop ?

Bishop [angrily]. Don't call her by that name ; I won't have it, I won't have it !

Bishop's Sister. You're a fool, Gilbert ! She never was your child ; and even if she ever had a claim, she ceased to be your child when we put her into the Institution.

Bishop. Even if she ceased to be my child, she, nevertheless, remains a child of God ; she still has her claim to the kingdom of heaven. I must not forget that now ; I must never forget that again !

Bishop's Sister. If you go on like this much longer, Gilbert, you'll find yourself becoming ridiculous to respectable and important opinion.

Bishop [*vehemently*]. That has been my besetting sin all along — fear of the respectable opinion of others. I renounce it now! She herself has said, What does it matter how many think a man to be a sinner if God believes him to be a saint. That's what she said — to my very face.

Bishop's Sister. Just like the impudent and semi-blas-phemous thing such as she would say!

Bishop [*impatiently*]. Don't waste time talking, woman. [*Catching her arm*] Look at that figure out there in the shadows. [*He points with his finger.*] Can you see? Is it she?

Bishop's Sister [*freeing her arm*]. I refuse to look! What has happened to you, Gilbert, after all these years of forgetfulness? Why do you suddenly so concern your-self with such a trivial thing.

Bishop. A human soul is not a trivial thing.

Bishop's Sister. Some souls are, and well you know it, and she is one of them. I tell you this fancy solicitude of yours is just a sentimental fear of something done years ago in a foolish moment. I tell you, such a soul is a trivial thing to be a torment to you.

Bishop [*sadly*]. Not hers, but our souls, I'm afraid, are the trivial things in the sight of God, and in the minds of brave men. [*Fiercely*] But mine's going to be trivial no longer! I go to seek her, and don't follow me.

Bishop's Sister [*doggedly*]. I will follow you! You're not sensible enough to be left alone.

Bishop [*angrily*]. Go home, woman. Being too sensible
   has been my curse all along. By trying to save my
   honoured soul, I am losing it. Go home, woman, and
   let me find a way to my girl and my God !

   [*He hurries away among the trees to the left, and, after a
   moment's hesitation, his Sister follows him. The Man
   with the Umbrella comes out from the group, and peers
   after them. The others, too, come out of the gloom and
   join the Man with the Umbrella in staring towards the
   direction in which the Bishop and his Sister have gone.
   As they stare, the Guardsman and the Nursemaid, arm-in-
   arm, enter from the opposite direction, and, seeing the
   men staring, are interested, so they join the group of
   peerers.*

Man with Umbrella [*pointing with his umbrella*]. There they
   go, one after the other — foller my leader like.   Thet
   sister of 'is'll 'ave to keep a close eye on 'er brother.
   At 'is age too, runnin' after a girl as might 'ave been
   'is daughter !

Guardsman [*wonderingly*]. 'Oo ?

Man wearing Trilby. Now, now ; the gentleman 'as no
   evil aims in 'is afollowing 'er.   I 'eard 'im sye 'e
   warnted to save 'is soul en' 'ers.

Guardsman [*wonderingly*]. 'Oo's soul, wot soul ?

Man with Umbrella [*contemptuously*]. Soul !   There ain't
   no soul.   Wot you 'ave in your mind is mind ; the
   mind wot conquers time, spice, en' material conditions.

Man wearing Trilby. En' when did mind begin, en' 'oo
   myde it ?

Man with Umbrella. Nothing begins, man ; things like

mind simply appear, sudden like; when, 'ow, or where, we don't know.

Guardsman [*impatiently*]. But what was it arunning after the girl?

Man with Umbrella. That clergyman fella 'oo's been runnin' rahnd tryin' to mike free with ordinary people.

Guardsman [*indignantly*]. 'Im, is it? Th' bloke wot tried to interfere once with me en' my girl. Why didn't some of you tell 'im orf?

Nursemaid [*chucking his arm*]. Aw, come on, Harry.

Guardsman [*impatiently to Nursemaid*]. Wyte a minute, carn't you! [*To the group*] Wot prevented you from atellin' 'im orf? I'd ha' done it. Our company sergeant-major's a fire terror, 'e is. Gives you a feelin' 'e 'ites everyone, 'e does, en' wishes you was dead. But whenever 'e gets me on the rawr, I tells 'im orf, I do, s'elp me!

Man with Umbrella [*with amused scorn*]. You does, does you?

Guardsman [*getting warm to his subject*]. T'other dye, Guardsman Odgerson, 'e syes, wot's th' meanin' of your bed not bein' properly folded? Git your poor mind movin', 'e roars, fer Gord's syke, en' sye wye your bed's not properly folded, 'e syes.

Nursemaid. 'E's en ign'rant barstid, 'e is; we all knows 'im.

Guardsman [*mimicking how he did it*]. I gits 'old of a byenet en' chises 'im rahnd the barrack square till I was caught up by the picket!

Man wearing Trilby. A serious thing to do in the Awmy.

Guardsman. When I was on the carpet before the Myjor,

'e did look fierce. Serious breach of discipline, 'e syes. But, 'e syes, considering the provocytion, 'e syes, admonished, 'e syes, I think will meet the cyse. Agoin' aht, 'e syes to me, private, served 'im right, Guardsman Odgerson ; pity you didn't give 'im a jeb, 'e syes — I know th' bugger !

Nursemaid. A real torf, the myjor, 'e is ; a proper torf. Come on, Harry.

Guardsman. Wyte a minute, carn't you.

Man wearing Trilby. Well, I won't wyte no longer for the Atheist to come en' amuse us with his relativity ideas. I knew 'e wouldn't fyce us aht, for everyone knows spice is one thing en' time is another.

Man with Umbrella. It's not 'im's afryde to come ; it's you're afryde to stye. Spice-time gives a noo meanin' to th' universe. Spice is relative to time, en' time is relative to spice — there's nothin' easier to understand.

Man wearing Trilby [*dubiously*]. Yes, quite ; I gets thet, but—

Man with Umbrella [*interrupting impatiently*]. Wyte, 'old on a second. Don't question me, yet. Listen carefully ; let your mind foller wot I sye, en' you'll get th' idear.

Guardsman. Listen cautiously to wot th' gentleman's asyein' — 'e knows wot 'e's torking abaht.

Nursemaid [*tugging at the Guardsman's sleeve*]. Aw, c'm on, Harry ; you knows I 'as to be back by ten.
              [*The Guardsman takes no notice.*

Man with Umbrella [*pompously*]. Now try to remember that all th' old idears of the cosmos — Greek for all things th' 'uman mind knows of — are buried with Copernicus, Kepler, Newton, en' all that crew.

Guardsman [*emphatically*]. 'Course they is, en' deep too.

Man with Umbrella. Now we all know that the clock created time, en' the measuring-rod created spice, so that there is really neither spice nor time ; but there is such a thing as spice-time. See ? Get that ?

Man wearing Trilby [*with confidence*]. Quite ; that much is perfectly clear.

Man with Umbrella. Right. Now, suppose that one night, when we all slept, th' universe we knows sank down to the size of a football, en' all the clocks began to move a thousand times quicker, — no, slower — it wouldn't mike the slightest difference to us, for we wouldn't realize that any difference 'ad tyken plice, though each of us would live a thousand times longer, en' man couldn't be seen, even under a microscope.

Guardsman [*jocularly*]. Could a woman be seen under a microscope ?

Man wearing Cap [*to Guardsman*]. Levity's outa plice, friend, when men are trying to think out th' truth of things.

Guardsman. But 'ow could th' world sink dahn to th' size of a football ? Doesn't seem a sife thing to me.

Man with Umbrella [*with cold dignity*]. I said *if* it did, friend.

Guardsman [*trying to find a way out*]. Yes ; but if a man couldn't be seen under a microscope, wot abaht 'is kids ?

Man with Umbrella. I simply styted a hypothenuse, friend.

Man wearing Cap [*to Guardsman*]. It's only en hypothenuse, you understand? [*To Man with Umbrella*] But it's en impossible one, I think. D'ye mean that under your hypothenuse, en hour of the clock would stretch aht into ten years of time?

Man with Umbrella. Exactly that in spice-time; en 'undred years if you like.

Man wearing Cap. Wot? Then in your spice-time, a man doin' eight hours would be workin' for eight 'undred years!

Guardsman [*to Man with Umbrella*]. You're barmy, man! Wot abaht th' bloke doin' penal servitude fer life? When is 'e agoin' to get aht? You're barmy, man!

Nursemaid [*to Guardsman — chucking his arm*]. Are you comin', Harry? If you don't 'urry, I'll 'ave to go, en' you'll 'ave to go withaht even a firewell squeeze.

Man with Umbrella [*annoyed — to Guardsman*]. Look, friend, if I was you, I'd go with the girl; for it's pline your mind 'asn't been educyted yet to grasp the complicyted functions of wot we know as spice-time problems.

Guardsman [*with heat*]. 'Oo 'asn't a mind? 'Oo're you to sye I 'asn't a mind? I 'asn't a mind as would warnt to tern th' world into a football. It's a punch on the jawr you warnts for thinkin' people warnts the world to be a football. Wye's there different thoughts in every mind, en' different rules in every country? Becorse people like you 'as th' world turned upside dahn! Wot do I mean when I syes th' world is upside dahn? Why, I means th' whole world is upside dahn, en' ennyone as 'as a mind'll unnerstend me!

Man with Umbrella [*to Guardsman*]. Wite a minute, wite a minute — you've got it all wrong.

Nursemaid [*anxiously — pulling Guardsman's arm*]. Come awye, do ! They'll get you with their tork right on the carpet, in front of the colonel ; so mind yourself, for I warn you, en' everyone knows as 'ow it ain't never allowed by the War Office to tork politics — soldiers is above them things.

Guardsman [*freeing himself — stormily*]. I won't let no blighter sye as 'ow I ain't got no eddicytion to tork of things ! [*To Group*] Where would you muckers be if it warnt for us swaddies, eh ? Poor swaddies rovin' the world, pickin' up fevers, to keep you sife at 'ome, en' 'appy. 'Oo is it does it, I asks ? [*He strikes his chest.*] We blighters, us blokes !

Man with Trilby. Tike it easy, soldier ; tike it easy.

Guardsman [*more stormily still*]. 'Oo was it, en' 'oo is it is holdin' dahn Africar en' Indiar, en' teachin' 'em 'ow to behive theirselves proper, eh ? [*He strikes his breast.*] We blighters, us poor blokes !

Nursemaid [*butting in hotly*]. Yes, en' we done a thing or two for the Chinks of China, too !

Guardsman. Too true, we did !

Nursemaid [*dragging the Guardsman away*]. Come on, come aht — we're wastin' our time torkin' to these silly old cacklers !

Guardsman [*as he is being pulled out*]. If it warn't my dooty to see my gal 'ome sife, I'd mike you muckers do a right-about-wheel en' quick march off the field ; I would, en' proper, too, blimey ; if I was to spend a month in clink for it, s'help me, I would !

[*He and the Nursemaid pass out of view.*

Man with Umbrella. There's en example, a fine example of militarism for us !

Man wearing Bowler [*deprecatingly*]. He wasn't altogether to blime. It was en unfortunate hypothenuse to set before ignorent minds ; en', to me, wholly ahtside respect to things unknowable, which should be left with 'Im 'oo mide things comprehensible en' incomprehensible. Introducin' the universe as a football was a regrettable en' might become a dinegerous conception, even as a mere hypothenuse, as you might sye.

[*While the Man wearing the Bowler Hat has been speaking, the Old Woman comes in slowly and wearily, and now and again gives an unsteady step, as if she had a little drink taken. She plods along till she is beside the Group of Men. She stops and looks rather vacantly at them. She carries a laurel wreath tied with red ribbon.*

Old Woman [*tonelessly*]. Anyone here see a young girl pass ? My daughter ; a poor one ; yes, indeed, regardless of her poor mother. A scarlet crescent on the hip of a black dress ; a black one on the side of a scarlet hat. My dearest daughter. A good mother I've been ; some say too good ; but she doesn't care, never thinks of me. [*To the Group*] Did she pass you by ?

Man wearing Bowler. I shouldn't worry, ma'am ; she'll soon be in good hands — the Bishop is seeking for her.

Old Woman [*cocking an ear*]. The Bishop ? That villain ! He took her part against me — against her own mother. What does he want with her ?

Man wearing Bowler. Don't know, ma'am ; he seemed to be anxious to find her.

Old Woman [*musingly*]. My first husband is now a man

like him.   Somewhere he stands before an altar jewelled with candlelight, wearing a crimson cassock and a golden cope.   And a mean heart is hiding under them.   He left me alone.   Somewhere he's powerful and pompous ;   in some place or other he's brightly hidden away where I can't reach.   [*She sighs.*]   Everything golden is going into the bellies of the worms.

Man wearing Cap. Maybe the Bishop could help you, ma'am.

Old Woman. Him? He'd help no one. God can, though. I never have to raise my voice, for God can hear a whisper better than a thunderclap. Yet a little while, and He'll level down to nothing the stir that still remains around us ; for everything golden is going into the bellies of the worms.

Man wearing Trilby. If I was you, ma'am, I'd go home and have a rest.

Old Woman. There can be no rest nor work nor play where there is no life, and the golden infancy of England's life is tarnishing now in the bellies of the worms. But God can save us, maybe, even at this late hour.

Man with Umbrella [*mockingly*]. Gord's a poor prop for enny one to lean on, ma'am.

Old Woman [*awake and lively at once*]. Who said that about God ? [*To Man with Umbrella — fiercely*] You did, you, you worm ! Is it any wonder we're all as we are, and I'm as I am ? Provoking God to hide His goodness and His mercy. Go away you — [*She raises an arm as if to strike him. He stretches out the hand holding the umbrella to guard himself, and she, with an unexpected jerk, snatches it from him and flings it from her.*] Ah, you'd strike an old woman, would you ; and with a weapon, too ? [*With bitterness*] And to think that all our hero soldiers died that such as you might live ! [*She catches sight of the wreath she is carrying.*] May this little token ease the anger of the dead. [*She wanders over till she is facing the base of the War Memorial. She remains silent before it for a few moments, with head bent ; then speaks tonelessly and sadly.*] A few more moments of time, and Spring'll be dancing among us again ; dancing in gold and purple pavilions of laburnum an' lilac ; the birds'll be busy at building small worlds of their own in the safe an' snug breast of the hedges ; the girls will go rambling round, each big with the thought of the life in the loins of the young men ; but those who are gone shall sink into stillness, deep under the stillness that shelters the dead !

Man wearing Trilby [*removing his hat*]. May they all rest in peace !

Man wearing Bowler [*removing his hat*]. Amen !
    [*The Old Woman lifts the wreath she is carrying, high above her head, much in the same way a priest elevates the Host. Man with Umbrella has picked it up.*

Old Woman [*lifting her head till she faces the Memorial Figure*]. O soldier in bronze, cold guard of remembrance for those who rode out on swift horses to battle, and fell, I lay at thy feet this circle of green and ribbon of red as a signal of shame unto those who've forgotten the dead. [*She bends down and lays the wreath at the foot of the Memorial. Then she sings softly and quietly, without moving, the following verse. Singing :*
    When souls are lin'd out on th' cold Judgement Day,
    To stand shaking and sad in sin's wild disarray ;

When pardon is lost, and all hopes lie in ruin,
May God give a thought to an Irish Dragoon !

Voices [*singing*] :
    May God give a thought to an Irish Dragoon !

Old Woman [*singing*] :
    Who fought on hills high and who fought in lands
        low,
    Till a blustering bullet came swift from a foe,
    And left me alone, though I'll follow full soon
    The path blaz'd to death by an Irish Dragoon !

Voices [*singing*] :
    The path blaz'd to death by her Irish Dragoon !

    [*She turns down and slowly comes towards the Group of
        Men, singing as she goes.*

Old Woman [*singing*] :
    Though God makes the brightest of mornings look
        sad,
    Though He's taken from me all the joys I once had ;
    Though He deny all, let Him grant me one boon,
    To sleep when I die with my Irish Dragoon !

Voices [*singing*] :
    To sleep when she dies with her Irish Dragoon !

    [*As she crosses while singing the last line, the Bishop,
        followed by his Sister, comes in from the opposite side, his
        face full of anxiety and dejection.   He and the Old
        Woman meet when they reach the Group of Men.*

Old Woman [*lifting her head, and seeing the Bishop*]. Ah,
his reverence, the Bishop !   Looking for my daughter,
too.   And what may you want with her, your reverence ?

Bishop's Sister [*getting in front of the Bishop — to Old Woman*]. Get away, woman! He isn't looking for your daughter. She would be the last person he would wish to meet!

Old Woman. Aha, are you another of the night-strollers seeking lightsome contacts in the gloomier parts of the Park?

Bishop's Sister [*furiously*]. How dare you say such a thing! How dare you even hint at such a desire in me, you tumble-down, wicked woman! I do not tread the ways of sin like you or your daughter!

Old Woman. Indeed you don't; but you could, you know, without a risk. No harm could ever come to you.

Bishop's Sister. I am what you never were, never can be — a good woman!

Old Woman. Your misfortune, madam; but there's some compensation in being a stony monument to good conduct and virtue.

Bishop [*coming forward in front of his Sister*]. Go away, you wretched woman, and cease from annoying a Bishop's sister!

Old Woman [*a little confusedly*]. Oh, yes, a bishop; I forgot. Tell me, do you, at festivals, wear a crimson cassock and a golden cope?

Bishop. What I wear concerns you not; so go away.

Old Woman. You've been looking for a girl, haven't you? The one with a red crescent on the hip of a black dress, and a black one to the side of a scarlet hat? She's my daughter.

Bishop [*somewhat sharply*]. I wasn't seeking any girl, woman. No girl at all. I once tried to help your daughter, but it was useless. So I washed my hands of her completely and for ever.

Man wearing Trilby [*coming forward*]. You've forgotten, I think, sir. Remember you asked me if I saw her, some little time ago ?

Bishop [*hesitantly*]. No, no ; I did not.

Bishop's Sister [*quickly*]. If he asked for anyone, it must have been I he was looking for.

Man wearing Trilby [*embarrassed and confused*]. Yes, of course, ma'am ; my mistake. [*He retires again.*

Old Woman [*meditatively — to the Bishop*]. There's a hidden hum in your old voice that carries a wisp of remembrance to me. [*Suddenly*] Is your name Gilbert ?

Bishop [*hastily*]. No, no ; it is not. Nothing like it either.

Bishop's Sister [*quickly*]. His name is not Gilbert ! [*To the world at large*] What are the police doing that undesirable persons are allowed to annoy and molest people in this way !

Bishop [*to Old Woman*]. Go away from us, woman. If our politics were what they should be, you wouldn't be permitted to wander about interfering with people enjoying the innocent pleasures of the Park !

Old Woman [*scornfully*]. Pleasures and politics ! Your politics are husks that only swine will eat ; your power shelters behind a battlement of hunger ; your religion's as holy as a coloured garter round a whore's leg : truth's bent in two, and hope is broken. [*Mourn-fully*] O Jesus ! is there no wisdom to be found anywhere ! All gone with the golden life of England into the bellies of the worms !

[*While she has been saying the last few sentences, she has been going out slowly, with tired steps, and now passes from view.*

Bishop [*turning towards the Group of Men, and trying to appear in no way affected by his scene with the Old Woman*]. Shocking example, friends, of what a woman can become ! Under the influence of drink, I'm afraid. But go on with your discussion, gentlemen — it is a fine thing to see working men trying to elevate and develop their minds.

Man wearing Cap. We've finished it, sir. We have had enough of argument for one dye. We were about to go home when the Old Woman made her appearance.

Bishop's Sister [*to the Men*]. We were going homewards, too, gentlemen, when, as you saw, the half-insane creature interfered with us. Good night to you all. Come along, Gilbert.

Bishop [*suddenly catching his Sister by the arm, and pointing away from himself — agitatedly*]. Look ! That girl going down the path there ! Is that she ? She'll be passing through the light from a lamp in a second, and my old eyes are too dim to be sure. [*A short pause.*] Now ! Quick, quick, look, can't you !

Bishop's Sister [*angrily*]. I won't, I won't look. Think of what you're trying to do, Gilbert : help and kindness are but tortures to girls of her kind and class. Please be sensible and come home !

[*He shakes off a hand she has placed on his arm, and hurries out in the direction of where he thinks he had seen the girl. His Sister remains motionless where she is for a few moments, and then, distractedly, follows him out.*

Man wearing Trilby. See, we were right after all : his name is Gilbert, en' 'e is looking for the girl. There's something curious in it all.

Man with Umbrella. May be something curious in it, but nothing strynge — you don't know bishops as well as I do.

Man wearing Bowler. Odd how, after denying it, she called him Gilbert ; en' 'e, forgetting wot 'e said a second before, called aht to 'er to tell 'im if the passing figure was the girl 'e sought.

Man wearing Cap. Aware of nothing save wot was in their minds — like a man not feeling or hearing ennything when he's unconscious.

Man with Umbrella. Nonsense, man ; 'course you can feel en' 'ear when you're unconscious. You're unconscious when you're asleep, but you still 'ave the faculty of 'earin' en' feeling.

Man wearing Cap. No, sir, no ; all the so-called senses are dormant in a styte of unconsciousness.

Man with Umbrella. Wot abaht en alawm clock agoing off first thing in the mawning ?

Man wearing Cap. You 'ear it only when you become conscious of its striking.

Man in Bowler. 'Ow does it wyeken you up, then ?

Man wearing Cap. It doesn't wyeken you up, it can't

wyeken you up till you become conscious of its sahnd. You understand thet, surely ?

Man wearing Bowler. I understand, but I don't agree. Wot I sye is, while I'm asleep, which is a styte of unconsciousness, I 'ear.

Man with Umbrella. 'Course 'e 'ears !

Man wearing Cap. The styte of unconsciousness implies a condition unaccompanied by conscious experience. We experience something when we 'ear ; 'ow then can we, when we're unconscious, pass into the experience of 'earing ?

Man with Umbrella. You're confusing the issue : let's decide first wot is 'earing : now wot do we mean when we say we 'ear ?

Man wearing Cap. The sense of 'earing exists simply as the sense of feeling exists, manifested, for instance, in pleasure or pine, though we know thet pine is nonexistent, strictly speaking.

Man wearing Bowler [*scornfully*]. Pine non-existent ? Oh, don't be silly, man !

Man with Umbrella [*with disgust*]. Aw, 'e's a giving us Christian Science now !

Man wearing Bowler. Mean to sye you carn't feel the jeb of a pin or the sting of a wasp ?

Man wearing Cap. You can, if you want to feel them.

Man with Umbrella. Can if you — but no one warnts to feel them. Aw ! We're back again at where we sterted.

Man wearing Bowler [*to the Man with Umbrella*]. Wite a

minute, wite a minute ; impatience 'll never get at the truth of things. [*To the Man wearing Cap*] Suppose you cut your finger, wouldn't you feel pine ?

Man wearing Cap. I'm not going to suppose ennything of the kind. As mind willed pine into existence, so mind c'n will pine awye again.

Man with Umbrella [*with impatience*]. Aw !

Man wearing Bowler [*to the Man with Umbrella*]. Wite a minute, wite a minute. [*To the Man wearing Cap*] You said thet if you cut your finger you wouldn't feel pine ?

Man wearing Cap. I never said ennything of the kind.

Man with Umbrella. Never said ennything of the kind ? But we 'eard you syeing it just now, man !

Man wearing Cap. I argued in a general wye, en' I refuse to be refuted by a trivial particular, the genesis of which I deny : immaterially speaking, you carn't cut your finger.

Man with Umbrella [*with consternation*]. Immaterially speaking — carn't cut your finger — oh, mister, mister !

Man wearing Bowler [*suddenly interrupting*]. Hush, hush ; look — she's coming ; the girl the Bishop warnted ; coming with the Dreamer !
      [*They all cease talking, and look towards the point indicated by the Man wearing the Bowler Hat.*
      [*After a moment or two the Young Woman enters with the Dreamer. She is leaning heavily on his arm. Her breathing is quick ; her face is very pale, and in her eyes is a fixed look of fear. The lie of her clothing shows*

that she has dressed hastily. She is dressed as before, in
black, slashed with crimson.

[*The Dreamer wears a vivid orange scarf thrown carelessly*
round his neck and shoulders. He leads the Young
Woman to a bench opposite to where the Group of Men is
standing, and gently helps her to sit down on it. There
is a hushed pause for a few moments.

Young Woman [*tremulously*]. I'm bad, Dreamer; please go
and find the Bishop for me. [*She mechanically arranges*
her dress.] My clothes seem to be on me every way and
any way. [*With a wan smile*] You hurried me into them,
Dreamer, as quick as you hurried me out of them!
Things are twisting before my eyes. [*Frightened*]
Get the Bishop, go for the Bishop!

Dreamer. Aren't you safer in the arms of the Dreamer
than you are at the Bishop's feet?

Young Woman [*tonelessly*]. While I had life — yes; but I
feel close to death now, and I have a lot to answer for,
Dreamer.

Dreamer [*vehemently*]. Not you, fair lass; not you! A
few smiles bestowed on the unworthy is all that you
have to answer for. It is those who disordered your
life with their damned whims; those who have left
a lovely thing lonely and insecure; who have neglected
to nurture the rare: it is we, dear lass, who will have
to answer for all these things!

Young Woman. You were always kind, Dreamer, and, at
least, you led me to where I heard a song. Be kind to
me still, and bring the Bishop here.

[*The Dreamer goes over to the Group of Men who are*
watching him and the Young Woman.

Dreamer [*to the Men*]. Have any of you seen the Bishop lately ?

Man wearing Trilby. 'E was 'ere a short time ago.   [*He points at the Young Woman.*]   En' 'e was looking for 'er.

Dreamer. If any of you see him, send him here — the spot where the Memorial is, near the Bird Sanctuary — please.

Man wearing Bowler. As we go 'ome, if we see 'im, we'll send 'im along.
>   [*They go out by different ways, and the Dreamer goes back to the Young Woman.*

Dreamer. On their way home, if they see him, the men will send the Bishop here.

Young Woman [*agitated*]. You go, too, Dreamer — none of them might meet the Bishop.   Oh, please do !

Dreamer. I don't like to leave you alone, Jannice.

Young Woman [*with a faint smile*]. You will soon have to leave me alone, whether you like it or no.   I will be quite safe here.   No one will bother me now.

Dreamer. Don't stir then till I come back.
>   [*He takes her hand in his, gently kisses it, and goes up the slope, and out.*
>   [*The Young Woman sits on the bench, staring straight before her, looking lonely and unhappy.   She remains alone in the scene for a few moments ; then the Bishop's Sister comes on to the top of the slope, looking from side to side, as if in search of someone.   As she appears above, the Old Woman comes in from the shadows on the left below.   She is greatly bent, and walks with slow and dragging feet.   She shivers as she looks about and catches sight of*

the lonely figure sitting on the bench. She shuffles over to it.

Old Woman [*peering at the figure*]. Have you seen a Bishop strolling about anywhere here recently? He's a friend of mine. I am in sore straits, having no home now, and he may be willing to help me. [*She pauses for an answer, but gets none.*] A man, a comfortable man wearing a cassock adorned with purple buttons, with a scarlet cap on his head. Why don't you answer? [*She peers more closely at the figure, and recognizes the Young Woman.*] Oh, it's you, is it? So here you are, looking very pale, and as if you were settling down for death. Remember now the way you treated your poor mother! No fancy dreams in front of you now — only the last things staring you in the face!

> [*The Bishop's Sister has heard the Old Woman talking, has watched her while she spoke, and now comes down the slope towards them.*

Young Woman [*doggedly — with a vicious look at the Old Woman*]. Anyhow, if I go, I'll go game, and die dancing!

Old Woman [*with some exultation in her voice*]. Looks as if it would be me who would be dancing over your grave, my merry lady!

> [*The Young Woman rises from the bench, and walks unsteadily away from the Old Woman, meeting the Bishop's Sister, who has come down the slope. The Young Woman retreats a few steps from her, so that she is between them both, where she stands shivering.*

Bishop's Sister [*to the Young Woman*]. So I've found you just before the Bishop could come to you. Waiting for his help and pity, are you? Be off out of the Park, and hide yourself, you shameless thing, or I'll send the police to take you out !

Old Woman [*getting in front of the Young Woman, and bowing low in mockery before the Bishop's Sister*]. Salaam, mem pukka memsahib, salaam, and pardon her and pardon me and pardon us all for getting in the way of thy greatness ; and grant us grace to have faith in thy dignity and importance, per benedicite pax hugger muggery ora pro puggery rigmarolum !

Bishop's Sister [*venomously*]. The pair of you ought to be stretched out naked on the ground so that decent women could trample the life out of you !

Old Woman [*confidently*]. Gallant men would lift us up on to our feet again.

Bishop's Sister [*violently*]. Sympathy for such as you would be a sin. The soft and gentle hand of pity must be changed to the punishing hand of bronze !

Old Woman [*remonstrating*]. Oh, sister, sister !

Bishop's Sister [*furiously*]. How dare you call me sister !

Old Woman [*reflectively*]. How savage women can be when God has been unkind and made us plain, so that no man can find a vision in our face.

    [*In the distance is heard the beat of the drum and the faint murmur of the Down-and-Out chant. The Three Women become rigid, and listen intently.*

    [*Down the slope come the tottering Attendants, followed by the Two Evangelists, bent, and with unsteady legs. All their faces are full of fear. They come into the centre, an Evangelist and an Attendant going behind the Bishop's Sister, and an Evangelist and an Attendant behind the Young Woman.*

Evangelists and Attendants [*in chorus, as they come down the slope*]. With drum-beat and chant the Down-and-Out are close upon us !

Bishop's Sister [*with merry rancour*]. Soon they will encompass you round about ; and there will be no way of escape, even for the lady of the good looks !
> [*The Bishop appears on the slope above. He stands so that the light from a lamp falls on him, a sad and dignified figure in his cassock with its purple buttons, and the scarlet biretta on his head. He stretches out an arm over those below, extending two fingers of a hand in blessing, and says in sad and low tones, almost intoning the words :*

Bishop. Benedicti vos a Domino, qui fecit coelum et terram.
> [*He comes slowly down the slope, backed by the chant, louder now, of the Down-and-Outs, and the Young Woman rushes over to him, and falls on her knees.*

Young Woman [*imploringly*]. Bless me, even me, oh ! my father !
> [*With a shiver and a quivering lip, the Bishop stretches an arm over her, extends his fingers to bless her, but his arm falls slowly to his side again, and he remains silent.*
> [*The Dreamer now appears on the slope, and stands in the light where the Bishop had stood before, looking at those below him. The Bishop walks away from the kneeling Young Woman, and stands in the centre, with a group on his right and another on his left.*

1st Evangelist. We have danced no dance, neither have we sought the beauty of any woman ; we have sung no songs, nor have we ever made merry in our hearts.

2nd Evangelist. We have honoured pain ; bound up joy

with sighing ; and multiplied sorrows that men might know Thy mercy and Thy kindness.

Bishop. Grant them pardon, O Lord, and bring them peace !

Dreamer. Let them sink into the grave, O Lord, and never let their like appear on the face of the earth again.

1st Evangelist. Stricken, we struck not back ; we blessed them that cursed us ; and prayed for them that took no note of our misery and want.

Bishop. Grant them pardon, O Lord, and bring them peace !

Dreamer. Let brambles, O Lord, grow thick where they are buried deep ; let the fox and the vixen guard their cubs in the midst of the brambles ; and let children sing and laugh and play where these have moaned in their misery !

[*The Down-and-Outs are here now, spreading over the slope above, and making to come down ; but the Dreamer with outstretched arms bars the way. On their way, and just before coming in on to the slope, they are heard singing.*]

Down-and-Outs [*chanting*] :

Life has pass'd us by to the loud roll of her drum,
With her waving flags of yellow and green held high,
All starr'd with the golden, flaming names of her most mighty children.

Oh, where shall we go when the day calls ?
Oh, where shall we sleep when the night falls ?
We've but a sigh for a song, and a deep sigh for a drum-beat !

[*Their chant changes into a menacing hum, like that of a swarm of wasps, to the tune of the chant, as the rest speak to each other.   The Young Woman goes unsteadily over to the Bishop.*

Young Woman [*imploring*]. Let me not mingle my last moments with this marching misery !

Bishop [*to Young Woman — slow, but with decision*]. You must go where they go, and their sighing shall be your song !

Down-and-Outs [*chanting*] :
    She must be merry no more ; she must walk in the
        midst of the mournful ;
    Who've but a sigh for a song, and a deep sigh for a
        drum-beat !
    [*The Young Woman has stiffened with resentment as she has listened, and now stands facing the Dreamer, looking at him for encouragement.*

Dreamer [*to Young Woman*]. Turn your back swift on the poor, purple-button'd dead-man, whose name is absent from the book of life.   Offer not as incense to God the dust of your sighing, but dance to His glory, and come before His presence with a song !

Young Woman [*with reckless defiance*]. I'll go the last few steps of the way rejoicing ; I'll go, go game, and I'll die dancing !

Dreamer [*exultantly*]. Sing them silent, dance them still, and laugh them into an open shame !
    [*Faintly, as if the tune was heard only in the minds of the Dreamer and the Young Woman, the notes of a dance tune are heard, coming from the subdued playing of a flute and other instruments.   The Young Woman and the*

Dreamer dance to the melody, she a little unsteadily.
They dance for about a minute, then the movements of the
Young Woman become a little uncertain ; she staggers,
recovers herself, dances again, but with faltering steps.
The music of the dance becomes fainter.

Young Woman [*frightened*]. Dreamer, Dreamer, I'm fainting — I think I'm going to die.

Dreamer [*fiercely*]. Sing them silent ; dance them still ;
laugh them into an open shame !

Down-and-Outs [*chanting and coming down a little by the*
centre].
    She must be merry no more ; she must be set in the
        midst of the mournful,
    Who've but a sigh for a song, and a deep sigh for a
        drum-beat.

Dreamer [*fiercely, with his face close to the Young Woman's*].
Sing them silent ; dance them still ; laugh them into
an open shame !

Bishop [*prayerfully as they dance*]. O Lord, who taketh
pleasure in Thy people, let this dance be unto Thee as
a merry prayer offered by an innocent and excited
child !
    [*The tune of the dance is now mournful, and the Dreamer*
    is almost carrying the Young Woman in his arms. They
    dance in this way for a few moments, then the head of the
    Young Woman falls limp, and the Dreamer lifts her in
    his arms, carries her to a soft spot on the green sward,
    and lays her down there.

Young Woman [*almost in a whisper*]. I die, Dreamer, I die,
and there is fear in my heart.

Dreamer [*tenderly*]. Fear nothing : courage in the hearts

of men and women is what God needs most ; and
He will find room for one scarlet blossom among a
thousand white lilies !

[*The Bishop goes unsteadily to where the Young Woman is
lying. He kneels beside her, and takes one of her hands
in his.*

Young Woman [*to the Bishop*]. Guide the hand you hold
into making the sign of the cross, that I may whisper
my trust in the golden mercy of God !

[*The Bishop guides her hand as she makes the sign of the
cross. She lies still and silent. The Down-and-Out
come down the rest of the way, changing the waspish hum
of their voices to the dolorous chant of their miserere.
They spread out, enveloping the Evangelists, the Attendants, and the Old Woman.*

Down-and-Outs [*chanting*] :
We challenge life no more, no more, with our dead
faith and our dead hope ;
We carry furl'd the fainting flags of a dead hope
and a dead faith.
Day sings no song, neither is there room for rest
beside night in her sleeping :
We've but a sigh for a song, and a deep sigh for a
drum-beat !

[*They force the Dreamer back a few paces at first ; but
exerting his strength, he forces a way through them,
scattering them to right and left, as he chants his vigorous
song of defiance and resolution.*

Dreamer :
Way for the strong and the swift and the fearless :
Life that is stirr'd with the fear of its life, let it die ;
Let it sink down, let it die, and pass from our vision
for ever.

Sorrow and pain we shall have, and struggle unend-
   ing :
We shall weave courage with pain, and fight through
   the struggle unending.
Way for the strong and the swift and the fearless :
Life that is stirr'd with the fear of its life, let it die ;
Let it sink down, let it die, and pass from our vision
   for ever !

[*The Dreamer goes up the slope. When he reaches the top,*
he turns, looks down at the still form of the Young
Woman. The Bishop's Sister stands apart, and watches
the Bishop kneeling beside the form of the Young Woman.
She goes over, after a moment's pause, and gently
touches the Bishop's shoulder.

Bishop [*looking up at his Sister*]. Go home, go home, for
Christ's sake, woman, and ask God's mercy on us all !
   [*She looks at the kneeling figure for a moment, then, turning,*
   she goes out without a word.

Bishop [*in low and grief-stricken tones*]. She died making the
sign of the cross !

Dreamer [*looking down to where the Young Woman is lying*].
You fought the good fight, Jannice ; and you kept the
faith : Hail and farewell, sweetheart ; for ever and
for ever, hail and farewell !
   [*The Dreamer turns, and begins to go out slowly. The sky's*
   purple and black changes to a bright grey, pierced with
   golden segments, as if the sun was rising, and a new day
   about to begin. The music, sounding low, of the song
   he sang to her, is heard ; in the middle of the melody the
   gates begin to close slowly, coming together on the last
   few notes of the tune.

THE GATES CLOSE

Music to "WITHIN THE GATES"

Composed and adapted by **HERBERT HUGHES**

SPRING CHORUS

Founded on "Haste to the Wedding"

SCENE I

Allegro giocoso — *Chorus of Girls and Boys*

Our Mother the Earth is a maiden a-gain Young fair and a

maid-en a-gain Our Mother the Earth is a maid-en a-gain She's young fair and a

maid-en a-gain Her thoughts are a dance as she seeks out her

bride-groom the sun through the love-ly con-fus-ion of singing of birds and of

blossom and bud. She feels the touch of his hand on her hair, on her

cheeks, in the bud-ding of trees — She feels the kiss of his love on her

mouth, on her breast as she dan-ces a-long — Through the lovely con-fus-ion of

sing-ing of birds, and of blossom and bud Her thoughts are a dance as she

seeks out her bride-groom the sun through the love-ly con-fus-ion of

singing of birds and of blossom and bud. She hears the fiercely-sung

song of the birds bu-sy building new homes in the hedge She hears a chal-lenge to

490

life and to death as she dan - - ces a - long __ Through the

lovely con-fus-ion of singing of birds and of blossom and bud Her thoughts are a

dance as she seeks out her bride-groom the sun Through the lovely con-fus-ion of

singing of birds and of blossom and bud Our Mother the Earth is a

maid-en a - gain __ Young, fair and a maid-en a-gain. Our Mother the Earth is a

maiden a-gain She's young and is fair and a maiden __ a - gain. __

GARDENER'S SONG

Air: "Moll Roone"

Andante

A fig for the blos-soms th' big-gest vase can hold, Th'

flow'rs that face the world shy the ones that face it bold; Men may

praise them and wor-ship them as some-thing fine and rare, Loung-ing

through their gor-geous per-fume so __ deft - ly hid - den there. But

I'll __ nev - er won - der though some in glee dis-close The

white of whit-est li - ly the red of red-dest rose, For I'll

fold in my arms a girl as bright as she is gay, And to-

- night the prim-rose path of love will be a won-der way!

491

SUMMER CHORUS

Alla marcia

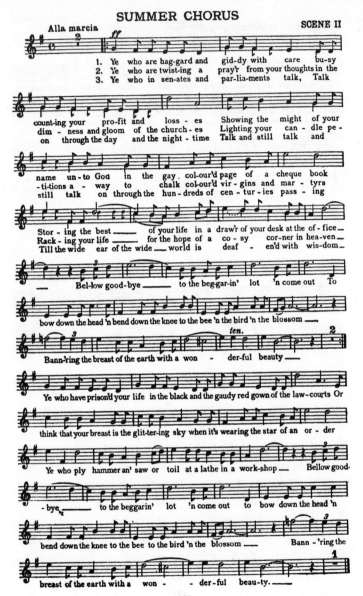

1. Ye who are hag-gard and gid-dy with care bu-sy
2. Ye who are twist-ing a pray'r from your thoughts in the
3. Ye who in sen-ates and par-lia-ments talk, Talk

count-ing your pro-fit and loss - es Showing the might of your
dim - ness and gloom of the church - es Lighting your can - dle pe-
on through the day and the night - time Talk and still talk and

name un-to God in the gay col-our'd page of a cheque book
-ti-tions a - way to chalk col-our'd vir-gins and mar-tyrs
still talk on through the hun - dreds of cen - tur-ies pass - ing

Stor - ing the best ____ of your life in a draw'r of your desk at the of - fice ___
Rack - ing your life ____ for the hope of a co - sy cor-ner in hea-ven ___
Till the wide ear of the wide ___ world is deaf - en'd with wis-dom ___

Bel-low good-bye ____ to the beg-gar-in' lot 'n come out To

bow down the head 'n bend down the knee to the bee 'n the bird 'n the blossom ___

ten.

Bann-'ring the breast of the earth with a won - der-ful beauty ___

Ye who have prison'd your life in the black and the gaudy red gown of the law-courts Or

think that your breast is the glit-ter-ing sky when it's wearing the star of an or - der

Ye who ply hammer an' saw or toil at a lathe in a work-shop ___ Bellow good-

- bye ____ to the beggarin' lot 'n come out to bow down the head 'n

bend down the knee to the bee to the bird 'n the blossom ___ Bann -'ring the

breast of the earth with a won - der-ful beau-ty. ___

492

SONG OF THE DOWN AND OUT

Air: **"The Foggy Dew"**
Quasi Marcia Funebre di Chopin

SCENE II

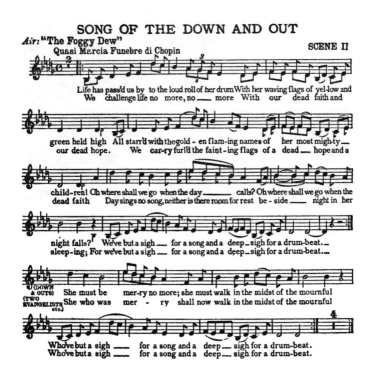

Life has pass'd us by to the loud roll of her drum With her waving flags of yel-low and
We challenge life no more, no —— more With our dead faith and

green held high All starr'd with the gold-en flam-ing names of her most migh-ty ——
our dead hope. We car-ry furl'd the faint-ing flags of a dead —— hope and a

child-ren! Oh where shall we go when the day —— calls? Oh where shall we go when the
dead faith Day sings no song, neither is there room for rest be-side —— night in her

night falls? We've but a sigh —— for a song and a deep —— sigh for a drum-beat. ——
sleep-ing; For we've but a sigh —— for a song and a deep —— sigh for a drum-beat. ——

(DOWN & OUTS) She must be mer-ry no more; she must walk in the midst of the mournful
(TWO EVANGELISTS etc.) She who was mer-ry shall now walk in the midst of the mournful

Who've but a sigh —— for a song and a deep —— sigh for a drum-beat.
Who've but a sigh —— for a song and a deep —— sigh for a drum-beat.

JANNICE

Founded on an Irish tune
Allegretto commodo *The Dreamer sings*

SCENE II

Her legs are as pli-ant and slim As fresh, golden branches of

wil - low; I see lus-tre of love on each limb Look-ing

down from the heights of a pil - low Look-ing down from the heights of a pil - low

Tossed by___ a soft breeze in the spring The blooms of an ap-ple tree

bil - low; And her breasts are as love-ly to me Look-ing

down from the heights of a pil - low Look-ing down from the heights of a pil -

- low Gay white ap-ple blossoms her breast, Her legs golden branches of

wil - low; I'd en - joy for a year and a day Look-ing down from the heights of a pil -

- low; Look - ing down from the heights of a pil - low.

SING AND DANCE

Air: "**Little Brown Jug**" *by R. A. Eastburn*   SCENE III

Allegro moderato

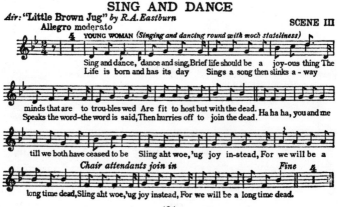

YOUNG WOMAN (*Singing and dancing round with much stateliness*)

Sing and dance, dance and sing, Brief life should be a joy-ous thing The
Life is born and has its day Sings a song then slinks a - way

minds that are to trou-bles wed Are fit to host but with the dead. Ha ha ha, you and me
Speaks the word—the word is said, Then hurries off to join the dead.

till we both have ceased to be Sling aht woe, 'ug joy in-stead, For we will be a

Chair attendants join in   *Fine*

long time dead, Sling aht woe, 'ug joy instead, For we will be a long time dead.

494

THE NINETY AND NINE

ELIZABETH C. CLEPHANE   IRA D. SANKEY

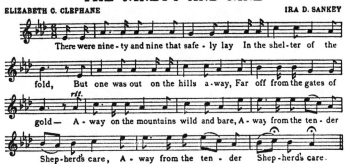

There were nine-ty and nine that safe-ly lay In the shel-ter of the fold, But one was out on the hills a-way, Far off from the gates of gold— A-way on the mountains wild and bare, A-way from the ten-der Shep-herd's care, A-way from the ten-der Shep-herd's care.

THE IRISH DRAGOON

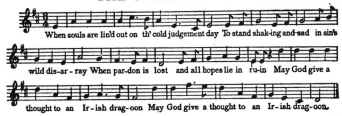

When souls are lin'd out on th' cold judgement day To stand shak-ing and sad in sin's wild dis-ar-ray When par-don is lost and all hopes lie in ru-in May God give a thought to an Ir-ish drag-oon May God give a thought to an Ir-ish drag-oon.

WAY FOR THE STRONG!

SCENE IV

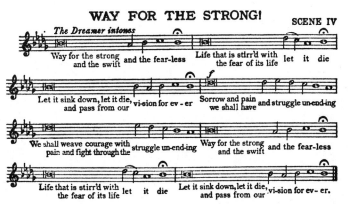

The Dreamer intones

Way for the strong and the swift and the fear-less Life that is stirr'd with the fear of its life let it die Let it sink down, let it die, and pass from our vi-sion for ev-er Sorrow and pain we shall have and struggle un-end-ing We shall weave courage with pain and fight through the struggle un-end-ing Way for the strong and the swift and the fear-less Life that is stirr'd with the fear of its life let it die Let it sink down, let it die, and pass from our vi-sion for ev-er.

495

Purple Dust

To Shivaun

CHARACTERS IN THE PLAY

CYRIL POGES

BASIL STOKE

SOUHAUN, *Cyril's mistress*

AVRIL, *Basil's mistress*

BARNEY, *their manservant*

CLOYNE, *their maidservant*

O'KILLIGAIN, *a foreman stonemason*

1ST WORKMAN

2ND WORKMAN

3RD WORKMAN

REVEREND GEORGE CANON CHREEHEWEL,
    P.P. of Clune na Geera

POSTMASTER

YELLOW-BEARDED MAN

THE FIGURE

THE BULL

SCENES

ACT   I.—A room in an old Tudor mansion
            in Clune na Geera.

ACT II.—The same.

ACT III.—The same.

TIME.—The present.

ACT I

SCENE : *A wide, deep, gloomy room that was once part of the assembly or living room of a Tudor-Elizabethan mansion. The floor is paved with broad black and dull red flagstones. The walls are timbered with oak beams, and beams of the same wood criss-cross each other, forming the roof, so that the room looks somewhat like a gigantic cage. The beams are painted, alternately, black and white so as to show they are there and to draw attention to their beauty ; but the paint makes them too conspicuous and, therefore, ugly.*

On the right is a huge open fireplace, overhung by a huge hood. In the centre of the fireplace is a big iron arm with a swinging cross-piece thrust out like a crane ; from this cross-piece hangs a thick chain to which a big shining copper kettle is attached. At the back are two rather narrow arched doorways, one towards the right, the other towards the left. Between these are two long, deep, mullioned windows. At the right, nearly opposite the fireplace, is a wider arched doorway leading to the entrance hall. Near the fireplace are two straight-backed seats, like infantile church pews, each big enough only to hold one person. A small Elizabethan or Jacobean table is somewhere near the centre of the room. On this table is a vase in which are a collection of violets and primroses, mostly primroses.

It is about seven o'clock of an autumn morning, fine, crisp, and fair.

Three workmen are seen in the room, two with shovels and one with a pickaxe. One with a shovel and the one with the pickaxe are standing near the archway leading to the entrance hall ; the other, with a shovel, is beside the wide fireplace, looking curiously at it. The 1st Workman is a tall, lean man

with a foxy face; the 2nd Workman is tall too, and strongly
built; he has a dreamy look, and has a dark trim beard faintly
touched with grey; the 3rd Workman is stouter than the others,
and not so tall. They are all roughly dressed in soiled clothes,
and wear high rubber boots.

1st Workman [*near the fireplace*]. Well, of all th' wondhers,
to come to live in a house that's half down and it's
wanin' over. Thrickin' th' rotten beams into a look
o' sturdiness with a coat o' white and black paint, an'
they for long a dismal dwellin', even for the gnawin'
beetle an' th' borin' worm.

3rd Workman [*with the pickaxe*]. They like that sort of
thing.

1st Workman. An' th' maid was tellin' me they're goin'
to invest in hins an' cows, an' make th' place self-
supportin'.

3rd Workman. An' th' two o' them business men, rollin'
in money.

1st Workman. Women you're not married to cost a lot
to keep; an' th' two with them'll dip deep into the
oul' men's revenue. Goin' over to London done them
a world o' good.

3rd Workman. Irish, too, an' not a bit ashamed o'
themselves.

1st Workman. Ashamed is it? Isn't th' oulder one
proclaimin' she's straight derived from th' Duke of
Ormond?

3rd Workman. An' we knowin' th' two o' them well as
kids with patched petticoats an' broken shoes, runnin'
round th' lanes o' Killnageera.

1st Workman. God be good to her, anyway, for bringin' a bit o' th' doddherers' money to where it's needed.

3rd Workman. Th' two poor English omadhauns won't have much when th' lasses decide it's time for partin'.

2nd Workman [*who has been silently leaning on his shovel, looking dreamily ahead of him*]. That day'll hasten, for God is good. Our poets of old have said it often : time'll see th' Irish again with wine an' ale on th' table before them ; an' th' English, barefoot, beggin' a crust in a lonely sthreet, an' th' weather frosty.

1st Workman. Afther a reckless life, they need th' peace o' th' country.

3rd Workman [*assuming a listening attitude*]. They're stirrin'.
    [*Mr. Cyril Poges, Souhaun, and Barney come in by one
    entrance at the back; Avril, Basil Stoke, and Cloyne
    from the other; they dance in what they think to be a
    country style, and meet in the centre, throwing their legs
    about while they sing. Avril has a garland of moonfaced
    daisies round her neck and carries a dainty little
    shepherd's crook in her hand; Cyril Poges, a little
    wooden rake with a gaily-coloured handle; Souhaun
    has a little hoe, garlanded with ribbons; Cloyne, a
    dainty little hayfork; Barney, a little reaping-hook;
    and Basil Stoke, a slim-handled little spade. Each wears
    a white smock having on it the stylised picture of an
    animal; on Poges's, a pig; on Basil's, a hen; on
    Souhaun's, a cow; on Avril's, a duck; on Cloyne's, a
    sheep; on Barney's, a cock.
    [*Poges is a man of sixty-five years of age. He was, when
    young, a rather good-looking man, but age has altered
    him a lot. He is now inclined to be too stout, with a*

*broad chest and too prominent belly; his face is a little
too broad, too ruddy, and there are perceptible bags of
flesh under his eyes. He has a large head; getting bald
in front; though behind and over his ears the hair is long,
fairly thick, and tinged with grey. He has a fussy
manner, all business over little things; wants his own
way at all times; and persuades himself that whatever
he thinks of doing must be for the best, and expects
everyone else to agree with him. He is apt to lose his
temper easily, and to shout in the belief that that is the
only way to make other people fall in with his opinions.
He has now persuaded himself that in the country peace
and goodwill are to be found; and expects that everyone
else should find them there too. Under the smock he is
dressed in morning clothes, and he wears a tall hat.*

[*Basil Stoke is a long, thin man of thirty, with a rather
gloomy face which he thinks betokens dignity, made
gloomier still by believing that he is something of a
philosopher. His cheeks are thin and their upper bones
are as sharp as a hatchet. He is clean-shaven, and the
thin hair on his half-bald head is trimly brushed back
from his forehead. His eyes are covered with a pair of
large horn-rimmed glasses. Under the smock he is dressed
in jacket, plus-fours, and he wears a cap.*

[*Souhaun is a woman of thirty-three years of age. She
must have been a very handsome girl and she is still
very good-looking, in a more matronly way. She has
the fine figure of her young friend Avril, but her arms
and her legs have grown a little plumper. She is still
attractive enough to find attention from a good many men,
when her young friend is out of the way. She wears,
under the smock, what a lady would usually wear in the
morning.*

[*Cloyne is a stoutly-built, fine-looking girl of twenty-six or*

so, and wears the servant's dress under her smock, and
has a smart servant's cap on her head.

[*Barney is a middle-aged man with a discontented face and
a muttering manner. Under his smock he wears the usual
dress of a butler.*

[*Avril is dressed, under her smock, in gay pyjamas.*

Poges [*singing*] :

> Rural scenes are now our joy :
> Farmer's boy,
> Milkmaid coy,
> Each like a newly-painted toy,

All :

> In the bosky countrie !

Avril [*singing*] :

> By poor little man the town was made,
> To degrade
> Man and maid ;
> God's green thought in a little green shade
> Made the bosky countrie !

All [*chorus*] :

> Hey, hey, the country's here,
> The country's there,
> It's everywhere !
> We'll have it, now, last thing at night,
> And the very first thing in the morning !

Basil [*singing*] :

> Our music, now, is the cow's sweet moo,
> The pigeon's coo,
> The lark's song too,
> And the cock's shrill cock-a-doodle-doo,

All :

> In the bosky countrie !
> *[chorus]*
> Hey, hey, the country's here,
> The country's there,
> It's everywhere !
> We'll have it, now, last thing at night,
> And the very first thing in the morning !

[*As they are singing the last lines of the chorus for the
second time, those who have come in by the left entrance
go out by the right one ; and those who have come in by
the right entrance go out by the left one.   The workmen
stand silent for a few moments, watching the places where
the singers disappeared.*

1st Workman. Well, God help the poor omadhauns ! It's
a bad sign to see people actin' like that, an' they sober.

3rd Workman. A sthrange crowd, they are, to come
gallivantin' outa the city to a lonely an' inconsiderate
place like this.

1st Workman. At home, now, they'd be sinkin' into their
first sleep ; but because they're in the counthry they
think the thing to do is to get up at the crack o' dawn.

3rd Workman. An' they killin' themselves thryin' to look
as if the counthry loved them all their life.

1st Workman. With the young heifer gaddin' round with
next to nothin' on, goadin' the decency an' circumspection of the place.

3rd Workman. An' her eyes wiltin' when she sees what
she calls her husband, an' widenin' wondherfully
whenever they happen to light on O'Killigain.

1st Workman. A handsome, hefty young sthripling, with a big seam in his arm that he got from a bullet fired in Spain.

3rd Workman. For ever fillin' the place with reckless talk against the composure of the Church in the midst of the way things are now.

2nd Workman. Ay, an' right he is, if ears didn't shut when his mind was speakin'.

1st Workman [*to 2nd Workman*]. If I was you I'd be dumb as well, for Canon Chreehewel's mad to dhrive him outa th' place, with all who hear him.

2nd Workman [*fervently*]. There's ne'er another man to be found as thrue or as clever as him till you touch a city's centre ; an' if he goes, I'll go too.

1st Workman [*a little derisively*]. Me brave fella.

3rd Workman. It's what but they're thryin' to be something else beside themselves.

1st Workman. They'd plunge through any hardship to make themselves believe they are what they never can become.

2nd Workman [*dolorously*]. An' to think of two such soilifyin' females bein' born in Ireland, an' denizenin' themselves here among decent people !

3rd Workman. Whissht ; here's the boss, O'Killigain.

[*O'Killigain comes in from the side entrance, with a short straight-edge in his hand. He is a tall, fair young man twenty-five or twenty-six years old. He has a rough, clearly-cut face ; dogged-looking when he is roused, and handsome when he is in a good humour, which is often enough. He is clean-shaven, showing rather thick but*

finely-formed lips. His hair, though cut short, is thick
and striking. When he speaks of something interesting
him, his hands make graceful gestures. He has had a
pretty rough life, which has given him a great confidence
in himself; and wide reading has strengthened that
confidence considerably. He is dressed in blue dungarees
and wears a deep yellow muffler, marked with blue
decoration, round his neck. He is humming a tune as he
comes in, and goes over towards the men.

O'Killigain [*lilting, as he comes in*] :
 They may rail at this life, from the hour I began it,
 I found it a life full of kindness and bliss ;
 And until they can show me some happier planet,
 More social and bright, I'll content me with this.

 [*To the men*] 'Morra, boys.

All the Men. 'Morra, Jack.

O'Killigain [*with a gesture pointing to where he thinks the*
people of the house may be]. Up yet ?

1st Workman. Up is it ? Ay, an' dancin' all about the
 place.

O'Killigain. Bright colours, in cloth and paint, th' ladies
 want, they say ; jazz pattherns, if possible, say the two
 dear young ladies : well, they'll want pretty bright
 colours to cheer up this morgue.

3rd Workman. It's a strange thing, now, that a man with
 money would like to live in a place lonesome an' cold
 enough to send a shiver through a year-old dead man !

O'Killigain. Because they think it has what they call a
 history. Everything old is sacred in every country.
 Give a house a history, weave a legend round it, let

some titled tomfool live or die in it — and some fool mind will see loveliness in rottenness and ruin.

1st Workman. A nephew of the Duke of Ormond, they say, dhrank himself to death in it, and the super-numary wife of the older codger says she's a direct descendant of the nephew ; and she says they've come from the darkness an' danger of England to settle down in what is really their proper home.

O'Killigain. And they're goin' to have the spoons and forks an' kn⌄ves done with what they say is the Ormond crest ; Ormond's motto will shine out from their notepaper ; and this tumble-down oul' shack is to be christened Ormond Manor.

2nd Workman [savagely]. The English gett, hurryin' off with the ensign privilege of an Irish gentleman !

3rd Workman. Isn't it sthrange how many'll fall for a mere name ? Remember oul' Miss MacWilliam who used to faint with ecstasy the times she told the story of sittin' for a second in the King o' Denmark's chair ; an' oul' Tom Mulligan who swaggered round for years afther the son o' the Earl of Skibbereen had accidentally spit in his eye !

O'Killigain. Well, men, we'd better make a start.

1st Workman [warningly]. Shush ! Here's the flower o' Finea !

[*Avril comes in from the left entrance. She is a pretty girl of twenty-one or so, inclined, at times, to be a little romantic, and is very much aware of her good looks. She is far from being unintelligent, but does little and cares less about developing her natural talents. Her eyes are large and expressive, but sometimes sink into a hardened lustre. She is inclined to think that every good-looking young fellow, rich or poor, should fall for her pretty face and figure, and is a little worried if one of them doesn't. She adopts a free-and-easy and very unnatural attitude when she is talking to workmen. She is dressed now in gay scarlet trousers, widening at the ends, and very tight around her hips and bottom; low-cut black silk bodice, slashed with crimson, half hidden by a red-and-white striped scarf thrown carelessly round her shoulders — and black shoes. She trips over in a slow dancing way to where the workmen are standing, and as she comes in she lilts the first verse of The Maid of Bunclody.*

Avril [*close to the workmen*]. Top o' the mornin', boys !

O'Killigain [*humouring her*]. Same to you, miss, an' many of them, each of them fairer an' finer than the finest of all that ever brought the soft light o' the dawn at the peep o' day into your openin' eyes.

Avril. It's meself that hopes you like the lovely house you're renovatin' ?

O'Killigain. An' tell me who wouldn't like the lovely house we're renovatin' ? It's a dark man he'd be, without a stim o' light, an' destitute o' feelin'.

1st Workman [*enthusiastically*]. Sure, miss, it's dumb with many wondhers we've all been for years that no one o' the well-to-do laid hands suddenly on the house to give it the glory again that musta been here throughout the jewel'd days of the times gone by !

Avril. When it's thoroughly restored it'll be a pleasure an' a pride to the whole district.

O'Killigain [*with just a touch of sarcasm in his voice*]. Sure, when we're done with it wouldn't it be fit for the

shelther an' ayse an' comfort of Nuad of the Silver
Hand, were he with us now, or of the great Fergus
himself of the bright bronze chariots?

Avril. Or even the nephew of Ormond's great Duke, the
warlike ancestor of my very own friend an' distant
cousin?

O'Killigain. An' all the people here who are anything'll
be mad with envy that they hadn't seized holt of it
to make it what it'll soon be shown to be! [*Avril lilts
a reel and dances lightly about the room. The 1st and 3rd
Workmen join in the lilting of the air. As she is passing
O'Killigain he catches her excitedly and whirls her recklessly
round the room till she is breathless, while the two men
quicken the time of the lilting. To Avril while she stands
breathlessly before him*] Bow to your partner. [*Avril bows
to him and he bows to her. Indicating the two men who
lilted the tune of the reel*] Bow, bow to the bards.

> [*She bows to the two men, and when she has bent to the
> bow, O'Killigain gives her a sharp skelp on the behind.
> She straightens herself with a little squeal of pain and
> a sharp cry of indignation, and faces him angrily.*

Avril [*indignantly*]. You low fellow, what did you dare
do that for! How dare you lay your dirty hands on
a real lady! That's the danger of being friendly with
a guttersnipe! Wait till you hear what Mr. Basil
Stoke'll say when he hears what you've done. Get
out of the room, get out of the house — go away, and
never let your ugly face be seen here again!

O'Killigain [*with some mockery in his voice*]. Sure, I meant
no harm, miss; it was simply done in the excitement
of the game. [*To 1st Workman*] Wasn't it, now, Bill?

3rd Workman. Ay was it, miss. Sure, th' poor man lost his caution in the gaiety and the gayer tune.

O'Killigain. I did it all in play ; I thought you'd like it.

Avril [*sarcastically*]. Oh, did you ? Well, I didn't like it, and I don't allow anyone to take advantage of any effort I make to treat workmen as human beings.

2nd Workman [*maliciously*]. If I was asked anything, I'd say I saw a spark of pleasure in the flame of pain that came into her eyes when she was hot !

Avril [*furiously — to the men*]. Be off, you, and let me speak alone to this young man ! I don't require any explanation from such as you ; so be off, and I'll deal with this fellow ! [*The three workmen slide away out of the scene. With a gentler tone in her voice*] Never, never do a thing like that again, young man.

O'Killigain [*with mocking earnestness*]. Never again, young lady. You looked so handsome, gay, and young that my thoughts became as jaunty an' hilarious as your little dancin' feet.

Avril. Never again, mind you — especially when others are here to stand and gape. [*She goes over and feels the muscle of his arm.*] There's too much power in that arm to give a safe and gentle blow to a poor young girl.

O'Killigain. Ashamed I am of the force that sent a hand to hit a girl of grace, fit to find herself walkin' beside all the beauty that ever shone before the eyes o' man since Helen herself unbound her thresses to dance her wild an' willin' way through the sthreets o' Throy !

Avril. It's I that know the truth is only in the shine o' the words you shower on me, as ready to you as the wild flowers a love-shaken, innocent girl would pick in a hurry outa the hedges, an' she on her way to Mass.

O'Killigain. Is it afther tellin' me that you are, an' your own words dancin' out as fair an' fine as the best o' mine ?

Avril. An' why wouldn't they, now, an' me that sang me song, first runnin' me years in, an' runnin' them out, in th' fields an' roads that skirted the threes an' hills o' Killnageera ? But is there an Irishman goin' who hasn't a dint o' wondher in his talkin' ?

O'Killigain. I never met many who had it ; but I got the touch of makin' a song from me mother, who — [*proudly*] — once won a grand gold medal at a Feis for a song of her own, put together between the times of bringin' up six children an' puttin' an odd flower on the grave of the one that died.

Avril. You must sing me a few of your songs sometime.

O'Killigain. Now, if you'd like to listen, an' you think that the time is handy.

Avril. Not now ; we might be disturbed ; but some evening, somewhere away from here.

O'Killigain. I will, an' welcome ; some of them, too, that have been set in a little book, lookin' gay an' grand, for all the world to see. Come ; listen — [*in a mocking whisper*] — and brave the wrath of the gouty, doughty Basil Stoke.

Avril [*with a toss of her head*]. That thing ! [*With bitter contempt*] A toddler thricking with a woman's legs ; a thief without the power to thieve the thing he covets ; a louse burrowing in a young lioness's belly ; a

perjurer in passion ; a gutted soldier bee whose job
is done, and still hangs on to life !

O'Killigain [*embracing her tightly*]. Tonight, or tomorrow
night, then, beside the blasted thorn three.

Avril [*with fright in her voice*]. The blasted thorn tree !
Oh, not there, not there — for evil things sit high, sit
low in its twisty branches ; and lovers, long ago, who
leaned against it lost their love or died. No, no, not
there : a saint himself would shudder if he had to
pass it on a dusky night, with only a sly chit of a
moon in the sky to show the way.

O'Killigain. Oh, foolish girl, there never can be evil
things where love is living. Between the evil things
an' us we'll make the sign of the rosy cross, an' it's
blossomin' again the dead an' dhry thing will be, an'
fruit will follow. We are no' saints, and so can abide
by things that wither, without shudder or sigh, let
the night be dark or dusky. It is for us to make dying
things live once more, and things that wither, leaf and
bloom again. Fix your arm in mine, young and fair
one, and face for life.

Avril [*after a little hesitation*]. Undher the thorn three
then, with you.
　　[*As the sound of voices is heard he holds her tight for a
　　few moments, kisses her several times, then lets her go.
　　He goes over and examines a wall where a telephone is
　　evidently being put in.*
　　[*Avril, all demure, stands at the other end of the room
　　watching him.*
　　[*Souhaun, followed by Poges and Basil, comes into the room.
　　She is carrying a large two-handled earthenware jug in
　　her right hand, and two coloured cushions under her left*

*arm. Cyril Poges is carrying a large coloured picture of
himself in a gold frame ; and Basil Stoke too is bearing
a picture of himself in a silver frame ; he has a hammer
sticking out of his side pocket. Cloyne follows them in
with a six-step A ladder. Poges and Stokes are wearing
gum-boots reaching to their thighs, and bright scarves
round their necks.*

[*Poges and Basil rest the pictures against a wall.*

Souhaun [*to Avril*]. Oh, here you are, with Mr. O'Killigain.
We were wondering where you were. We've a lot to
do, dear, before we can get the house comfortable, so
don't keep Mr. O'Killigain from his work. [*She
leaves the jug down in a corner.*] Filled with gay flowers,
Cyril, this jug'll be just the thing on your quattrocento
desk-bureau.

Poges. Lovely, darling. [*To O'Killigain*] We've been for
a run over the fields, O'Killigain ; lovely ; feel as
fresh as a daisy after it. [*Indicating the boots*] Great
comfort, these boots, in the long damp grass. Saw a
swarm of rabbits — quaint creatures.

Basil. With these and rubber hats and rubber coats,
we'll be able to weather anything. I've got the
hammer. Have you got the nails ?

Poges. I forgot them. I'll get them now.

Basil. And I'll get the string.

[*One goes out left, and the other right.*

Souhaun [*to Cloyne*]. Hold this curtain stuff end, Cloyne,
till we see its width.

[*Cloyne holds one end of the stuff while Souhaun holds the
other. O'Killigain, pretending to be interested, bends
over Cloyne and, stretching out a hand to handle the stuff,*

*half puts his arm around Cloyne's neck, who is very well
pleased.*

O'Killigain. Finely woven as a plover's wing, it is. No
way odd it ud look as a cloak for the lovely Emer ;
an', if it hung from th' sturdy shouldhers of Queen
Maev herself, she'd find a second glory !

Souhaun [*displeased at his covert attention to Cloyne*]. Over
here, Cloyne, please ; hold this end.
        [*Souhaun and Cloyne change places, and O'Killigain bends
        over Souhaun.*

Avril [*to O'Killigain*]. I must have a chat with that man
working for you who knows everything worth knowing
about Ireland's past and present, Mr. O'Killigain.

O'Killigain [*very seriously*]. And please, miss, don't try to
make fun of him. Touch him not with a jibe, for he's
a wandherin' king holdin' th' ages be th' hand.

Souhaun. How could a common worker be a king,
O'Killigain ?

O'Killigain. Easier than for a king to be a common
worker. Th' king o' a world that doesn't exist was a
carpenter.

Avril. Where is the real world to be found, then ?

O'Killigain. Where I have found it often, an' seek to
find it still.

Avril. And where's that place to be found ?

O'Killigain. With the bittherness an' joy blendin' in a
pretty woman's hand ; with the pity in her breast ;
in th' battlin' beauty of her claspin' arms ; an' rest
beside her when th' heart is tired.

Cloyne. Sure, it's only makin' fun of us all he is.

O'Killigain. Softer an' safer than St. Patrick's breastplate is a woman's breast to save a man from the slings of life. [*Singing softly, moving a little away. Slyly towards the women :*]

Come in, or go out, or just stay at the door,
With a girl on each arm an' one standin' before ;
Sure, the more that I have, the more I adore,
For there's life with the lasses,
Says Rory O'More !

Oh, courtin's an illigant, gorgeous affray,
When it's done in the night, or just done in the day ;
When joy has been spent, sure, there's joy still in store ;
For there's life with the lasses,
Says Rory O'More !

When all has been done, though nothin's been said,
Deep in the green grass, or at home in the bed ;
To ev'ry brave effort we'll yield an encore ;
For there's life with the lasses,
Says Rory O'More !

> [*As he ends his song, Poges and Basil return, the one with the nails, the other with the string-wire.*

Poges [*to O'Killigain — briskly*]. The garage is well in hand, isn't it, O'Killigain ?

O'Killigain [*who has tapped the wall, and is shaking his head*]. Yes, well in hands.

Poges [*enthusiastically*]. Good man ; when it's done I'll get a first-class artist over from London to paint and make it exactly like a little Tudor dwelling, so that it won't in any way distort the beauty of the fine old house. What do you say, O'Killigain ? [*O'Killigain is silent.*] Eh ?

O'Killigain. I didn't speak.

Basil [*who has moved over, and is looking ecstatically up at an end wall*]. Early Tudor, I think ; yes, Early Tudor, I'll swear. A great period, a great period. Full of flow, energy, colour, power, imagination, and hilarity.

O'Killigain [*tapping the wall beside him — ironically*]. And this is Middle Tudor — not a doubt about it.

Poges [*looking ecstatically at the other end wall*]. Late Tudor this one, I'm sure. Ah, England had no equal then. Look at the Lionheart, eh ? Smashed the infidel, smashed him out of Jerusalem into the desert places. What was his name, follower of the Prophet ? You remember, Hegira, the white stone, or was it a black stone ? — oh, what was the bounder's name ?

Souhaun [*helpfully*]. Tuttuttankamen, dear ?

Poges [*scornfully*]. Tuttuttankamen ! My God, woman, he was only the other day !

Avril [*more helpfully*]. The Mahdi, dear ?

Poges [*more scornfully*]. The Mahdi ! [*Plaintively*] Is there no one here knows a line of the history of his country !

Basil [*with complacent confidence*]. Genghis Khan.

Poges [*emphatically*]. Genghis Khan ! That was the name of the bounder driven from Jerusalem by the Lion-hearted Richard. A warrior, a hero. And maybe he was actually in this very house. It's all very moving. [*To O'Killigain*] I imagine I hear the clank, clank, clank of armour when I walk the rooms, and see the banners and banneroles, with their quaint designs, fluttering from the walls ! Don't you feel the lovely sensation of — er — er — er — old, unhappy, far-off things, and battles long ago ? [*O'Killigain is silent.*] [*Insistently*] Don't you feel something of all that, O'Killigain, eh ?

O'Killigain [*quietly*]. I let the dead bury their dead.

Souhaun. Oh, don't worry Mr. O'Killigain, Cyril ; he's a workaday worker, and neither understands nor takes an interest in these things.

Poges. Nonsense ; O'Killigain's an intelligent man, and is only too glad to learn a little about the finer things of life ; and to think of great things past and gone is good — isn't that so ?

O'Killigain. Occasionally, perhaps ; but not to live among them. Life as it is, and will be, moves me more.

Poges. Come, come ; we mustn't be always brooding upon the present and the future. Life is too much with us, O'Killigain ; late and soon, getting and spending, we lay waste our powers. But you've never read good old Wordsworth, I suppose ?

O'Killigain. As a matter of fact, I have.

Poges. You have ? Well, that promotes a fellowship between us, eh ? Great man, great man ; but a greater poet, eh ?

O'Killigain [*with some vehemence*]. A tired-out oul' blatherer ; a tumble-down thinker ; a man who made a hiding-place of his own life ; a shadow parading about as the sun ; a poet, sensitive to everything but man ; a bladder blown that sometimes gave a note of music ; a fool who thought the womb of the world was

Wordsworth ; a poet who jailed the striving of man in a moral lullaby ; a snail to whom God gave the gleam of the glowworm ; a poet singing the song of safety first !

Poges [*irritated*]. Oh ! Is that the result of the new schooling ? I'm afraid very few will agree with you, my friend. Well, well, we've more to do than discuss the merit of a poet ; so hasten on the work of building the garage, like a good man.

O'Killigain [*bowing ironically*]. I go, sir.   [*He goes out.*

Poges [*to the others*]. Isn't that a shocking example of bad taste and ignorance ? [*To Souhaun*] There's one of your fine countrymen for you, dear.

Souhaun. Well, Cyril dear, you know you were just trying to show off to him. A few little quotations, drummed into you at school, is all you know of Wordsworth. You're never tired of saying that poetry isn't your cup of tea.

Poges [*angry*]. Modern poetry, modern poetry isn't my cup of tea ; and I don't care who knows it. But I don't deny the past. Tradition — that is our strength in time of trouble ; tradition, follow the traditions, the only things that count in a cultured man's life. Keep as close as we can to the beauties of the past — the, the glory that was Rome and the grandeur that was Greece — Shakespeare knew what he was talking about when he said that.

Basil. Well, by living in this old historic house we're keeping close to the old traditions.

Souhaun [*dubiously*]. It's beginning to feel a little cold and damp to me.

Poges [*astonished and indignant*]. Cold ? What are you talking about ? Damp ? Nonsense. Were it warmer, it would begin to feel uncomfortable. What do you say, Cloyne ?

Cloyne [*who has been dusting the walls with a long-handled duster*]. I feel quite cosy, sir ; though there is a bit of a breeze blowing down the chimney.

Poges [*shivering a little*]. Eh ? Cosy, eh ? Of course you do ; we all do. Think, too, of the loveliness all round us : river, lake, valley, and hill. [*Lilting*] Angels, often pausing here, doubt if Eden were more fair. Here we have the peace of Eden.

Souhaun. And you must admit, dear, that we Irish are a simple, hearty, honest, and obliging people.

Basil [*enthusiastically*]. They're dears. All I've met of them are dears ; so quaint and charming — they are sweet. They need control, though ; they need control.

Poges. I agree. All the Irish are the same. Bit backward perhaps, like all primitive peoples, especially now, for they're missing the example and influence of the gentry ; but delightful people all the same. They need control, though ; oh yes, they need it badly.

Basil. We must get to really know the country ; it's one thing to be sensitive about the country scene, and quite another to understand it.

Poges [*heartily*]. Quite right, Basil. We must get to know the country so that everything in it is natural to us. [*Lilting*] To plough and to sow, to reap and to mow, and to be a farmer's boy-oy-oy. The different trees, for example, to call them by their names the instant we see them.

Avril. In winter or summer.

Poges. Quite. In the summer by their fruits.

Avril. Trees don't have fruits, Cyril.

Poges. Of course not. I mean barks and branches. It will be a joy to say to some ignorant visitor from the city : That tree ? Oh, that's just an oak ; and that one there by the river is a — a——

Avril. Gooseberry tree, Cyril.

Poges. A lilac, or something. [*To Avril*] Don't be funny. This is a serious matter.

Cloyne. We mustn't forget the hens, either, sir.

Poges. Hens ? Yes, of course — the hens. A fine idea. Yes, we'll have to have hens ; a first-class strain, though : nothing else would be of any use.

Cloyne. A first-class strain, of course.

Poges. And a cow as well.

Avril. A cow might be dangerous.

Poges. Dangerous ? Nonsense ; if he was, then we'd simply have to keep him in a cage. [*He sets up the step-ladder, mounts it, and holds up his picture against the wall.*] How does that look ?

Souhaun [*taking no notice*]. First of all, we must get to know the nature and names of all the wild flowers of the district.

Poges [*letting the picture rest on the ground, and turning to the rest*]. Especially the wild flowers that Shakespeare loved — the — the — er — er — [*his eye catches sight of primroses in a little vase on the table*] — the primrose, for instance ; you know — the primrose by the river's brim, a yellow primrose was to him, but it was nothing more ; though we all actually know all there is to be known about the little primrose.

Basil [*letting his picture rest on the ground, leaning over the top so that he at one end of the room and Poges at the other look like preachers in pulpits, panelled with their own portraits*]. That's just ignorant complacency, Cyril. Of course, if we regard, assume, or look at the plant purely as a single entity, then a primrose is a primrose, and there's nothing more to be said about it.

Poges. Well, you can't assume or regard the primrose as an elm tree, can you, old boy ?

Basil [*quickly*]. Don't interrupt me for a minute, please. If we take the primrose, however, into our synthetical consideration, as a whole, or, *a priori*, as a part, with the rest of the whole of natural objects or phenomena, then there is, or may be, or can be a possibility of thinking of the flower as of above the status, or substance, or quality of a fragment ; and, consequently, correlating it with the whole, so that, to a rational thinker, or logical mind, the simple primrose is, or may become, what we may venture to call a universal. See ?

Poges [*bewildered*]. Eh ? Oh yes, yes ; no, no ; yes, yes : eh, what ?

Souhaun [*to Cloyne*]. Cloyne, you'd better go and look after the fires in our room.

[*Cloyne rises and goes out.*

Avril [*with mockery in her voice*]. Hush, listen all — great men are speaking !

Poges [to Basil]. Eh, what the devil are you trying to say, man ?

Avril [with triumphant mockery]. Ah, Cyril, you're caught !

Poges [indignantly]. Caught ?   Who's caught ?   Me ? Nonsense, girl. He has simply compounded a fact with a fallacy. Can I see ? Have I eyes ? Yes. Very well, then.   I see a flower with a root, leaves, and a blossom ; I ask myself, What is it ? I answer, A flower ; I ask, What is it called ?   I answer, A primrose.

Basil [languidly]. So you say, sir.

Poges [vehemently]. So everyone says, sir !

Basil [leaning forward towards Poges]. And what is a flower, sir ?

Poges [furiously]. A flower ?   Good God, sir, a plant ; a contrivance springing out of the earth ; a vegetating combination of root, leaves, and blossom.

Souhaun. Calmly, Cyril, calmly.

Basil [leaning back and closing his eyes wearily]. I knew you'd just say that, sir.   Words ; you're merely using words. Try to think, sir, of a primrose, not as a primrose, but as a simple object, and as a substance outside of yourself.

Poges [half frantic]. Damn it, man, don't I know that a primrose isn't a substance inside of myself !   Tell us how a man is to think of a primrose except as a primrose.   He can't think of it as the dear little, sweet little shamrock of Ireland, can he ?   It is indeed a pitiful humiliation to have to listen to a half-educated fool !

Basil [*angry at last — setting the picture aside and taking a threatening step towards Poges, Avril stepping in front to restrain him*]. A fool ! Do you say I am a fool, sir ? Is a man versed in all the philosophies of the world to be called a fool !

Avril. Basil, dear !

Souhaun [*getting in front of Poges*]. Cyril, darling, do remember that we are having just a little friendly discussion about a common country flower !

Avril [*ironically*]. Basil is only trying to share his great knowledge with us.

Poges. He calls that knowledge, does he ?

Souhaun. We must remember that Basil passed through Oxford, dear.

Poges. I don't care if he crept under it or flew over it ; he's not going to punish me with what he picked up there.

Basil [*a little tearfully*]. Considering that I have read every word written by Hume, Spinoza, Aristotle, Locke, Bacon, Plato, Socrates, and Kant, among others, I think my views ought to receive some respect from an ignorant man.

Poges [*boastfully*]. I was reared any old how ; and here I am today, a money'd man, able to say to almost any man, come, and he cometh, and to almost any other man, go, and he goeth — and quick too ; able to shake hands with lords and earls, and call them by their Christian names. This — [*he touches his forehead*] — and these — [*he holds out his hands*] — did it all, without an inherited penny to help ! [*He looks bale-*

fully at Basil.]   And that's more than some of them
can say.   And I never passed through Oxford !

Souhaun [soothingly — to Basil]. Come, now, go away for
a few minutes, till he's calm again.

Basil [tearfully and wrathfully]. Souhaun and you can see,
Avril, that the virtue of respect and ready veneration
that every right-minded Englishman has for the classic
colleges has gone completely out of him.

Souhaun [soothingly]. There now, there now ; it'll all
come back soon.

Basil [almost weeping]. Whenever he got the chance he
hurried me down to Oxford to meet this professor
and that doctor, itching all over to obtain a degree
honoris causa, in any faculty of Divinity, Science,
Literature, Medicine, or Law !

Poges [scornfully]. And most of them anxious for tips from
the Stock Exchange.   Go away, man, and weep in
silence.   [*He lifts his picture up against the wall.*]   We
have something else to do.   Here, how does that look
there ?

Souhaun [gently pushing Basil out of the room]. There, go,
dear, till you recover yourself.

Basil [going out — loudly]. Quisabit grunniodem expectio
porcum — what can one expect from a pig but a grunt ?

Poges [with the picture against the wall]. There, how does
that look here ?   [*Pityingly*] Poor fool ; juvenile mind,
Souhaun, juvenile mind.   But snappy enough, when
he likes, and I, by cunning investment, having doubled
his income for him.   Ingratitude.   [*Impatiently*] Well,
how does this look here ?

Souhaun. I think the opposite wall would be more suitable, dear.

Avril. Where it is, is best, mother.

Poges. Make up your minds, make up your minds !

Souhaun. Where it is, dear.

Poges. How is it for height ?

Souhaun. A little higher.

Avril. A little lower.

Poges. One of you, one of you !

Souhaun. A little to the right, now.

Avril. A little to the left, now.

Poges [*lowering the picture to the ground*]. Which is it ? How is it ? What is it !
> [*Cloyne comes in with a newspaper in her hand.*

Cloyne [*to Poges*]. Your newspaper, sir — the *Financial Universe.*
> [*She leaves it on the table, and goes out again. Poges breaks open his paper, and is about to look at it when Barney appears at the left entrance. A sound of cackling is heard outside, and the loud lowing of a cow, and the crowing of cocks.*

Poges [*with the paper half spread before him*]. What the hell's that ?

Barney. There's a man outside wants to know if you want any entherprisin' hins ?

Poges. Any what ?

Barney. Any hins, entherprisin' hins ?

Poges [*impatiently*]. What the devil would I want with hins
enterprising or unenterprising ?

Barney. He says it's all over the counthry that you're
searchin' high an' low for entherprisin' hins.

Cloyne [*appearing at the right entrance*]. There's two men
here wantin' to know if you'd buy some prime an'
startlin' cocks, goin' cheap ?

1st Workman [*appearing beside Barney, and shoving him aside
to get in front*]. Excuse me, sir, but there's a friend o'
mine just arrived with a cow that ud do any man good
to see ; a baste with a skin on her as shiny an' soft
as the down on a first-class angel's wing ; an' uddhers
that'll make any man hard put to it to fetch enough
pails to get the milk she gives !

Poges. Hins, cocks, and cows ! [*To 1st Workman*] What
the hell do you take me for — a farmer's boy, or what ?

Souhaun. It's all out of what you said about having hens
and a cow in the place. [*To Cloyne*] And you, you little
fool, must have gossiped it all over the district !

Cloyne. The only one I mentioned it to was Mr. O'Killigain.

1st Workman [*coming over to Poges*]. Listen, sir, whisper,
now : Sthrike for th' honour of St. Patrick, while the
iron's hot, for the cow. An' whisper, don't, for the
love o' God, have anything to do with the hins an'
cocks they're thryin' to palm off on you — there isn't
one o' them that isn't th' essence of a false pretendher !

Souhaun [*angrily — to Cloyne*]. I won't have you gossiping
to O'Killigain, spending time with him you ought to
give getting the house in shape ! The idea of dis-

cussing our private affairs with O'Killigain ! If you
think that O'Killigain has taken a fancy to you, you
never made a bigger mistake, my girl.

Cloyne [*indignantly*]. Indeed, ma'am ? Well, if Mr.
O'Killigain bids me the time o' day, I'll do the same,
without any permission from you, ma'am !

Barney [*impatiently*]. An' what am I goin' to say to the
man who's brought th' entherprisin' hins ?

Poges [*shouting*]. Pack him off about his business !

[*Barney goes out.*

[*To Cloyne*] And you do the same to the man who brought
the startling cocks !

Souhaun [*to Cloyne*]. And no more trespassing on the good
nature of O'Killigain, either !

Cloyne [*turning and facing Souhaun swiftly as she is going out*].
There's a withering old woman, not a hundred miles
from where I am, who ought to take her own advice,
an' keep from thryin' her well-faded thricks of charm
on poor Mr. O'Killigain herself !   [*She goes out.*

Poges [*loudly and complainingly*]. Oh, stop these unseemly
disputes in a house that ought to know only peace and
dignity ! Can't you try to act as the *les grand dames*
and the *les grander monsieurs* must have acted when they
moved about here in this beautiful Tudor house.
While we're in it, let us forget the vile world and all
its ways. [*Angrily — to* 1st *Workman, who has been
tugging at his sleeve for the last few moments*] What the hell
do you want, man ?

1st *Workman* [*earnestly, almost into Poges' ear*]. Listen,
whisper, sir ; take the bull be th' horns, an' get the
cow, before she's gone. An' as for entherprisin' hins,

or cocks that'll do you credit, leave it to me, sir, an'
you'll go about with a hilarious look in your eyes !

Poges [*catching* 1st *Workman by the shoulders, in a rage, and
pushing him out of the room, and down the passage*]. Get out,
get out, you fool, with your hins and cocks and cows !

Souhaun [*quickly* — *to Avril, when Poges has disappeared round
the entrance*]. Go on up, and flatter and comfort your
old fool by ridiculing my old fool ; and, when he's
half himself again, wanting still more comfort and
flattery, wheedle a cheque out of the old prattler.

Avril [*jumping up*]. Splendid idea !   [*She runs off out.*

Souhaun [*calling after her*]. A good one, mind you !
    [*Poges comes back fuming, and brushing his coat where it
    touched the* 1st *Workman.*

Poges. Are we to have no peace down here where peace
was born ? [*He takes up the paper again and begins to
read it.*] Uum. Ha, tin shares up again. Good. [*He
buries his face in the paper.*] If it weren't for the damned
taxes.
    [1st *and* 3rd *Workmen peer around corner of the left
    entrance ; then they come over quickly and smoothly to
    where Poges is buried in his paper, the* 1st *Workman
    standing on his left hand and the* 3rd *Workman on his
    right.*

1st *Workman* [*persuasively* — *towards Poges' paper*]. Listen,
here, sir : if it's genuine poultry you want, that lay
with pride an' animation, an' not poor, insignificant
fowls that set about th' business o' layin' like a
member o' Doyle Eireann makin' his maiden speech,
I have a sthrain o' pullets that'll give you eggs as if
you were gettin' them be steam !

Poges [*angrily — glancing over the top of his paper*]. Go away, go away, man, and don't be driving me mad !

3rd Workman [*towards Poges' paper*]. Oh, the lies that some can tell to gain their own ends ! Sure, sir, everyone knows that his poor hins are harmless ; only venturin' to lay when heavy thundher frightens them into a hasty sign o' life ! But it's meself can give you what you want, with a few lively cocks thrown in, to help them on with the work of furnishing nourishment to the whole world.

Poges. Go away ; when I want poultry, I'll get into touch with the experts in the Department of Agriculture.

1st Workman [*horrified — partly to Poges and partly to Souhaun*]. Oh, listen to that, now ! Didja hear that, ma'am ? The Department of Agriculture, is it ? Wisha, God help your innocence, sir. Sure, it's only a tiny time ago that the same Department sent down a special sthrong covey o' cocks to improve the sthrain, an' only afther a short probation, didn't they give the hins hysterics ?

Poges. Hysterics ? Good God !

3rd Workman. Ay, an' hadn't the frightened farmers to bring guns to bear on the cocks when they found their hins scatthered over hill an' dale, lyin' on their backs with their legs in the air, givin' their last gasp, an' glad to get outa the world they knew so well ! The few mighty ones who survived were that stunned that there wasn't an egg in th' place for years !

Poges [*good-humouredly catching the men by the arm and leading them to the left entrance*]. Now, now, men, I'm busy ;

I've some very important business to think about and can't be bothered with hins !

1st Workman [*as they go out*]. Another time, sir ; but don't think of the Department in this important matther : they'll send you hins'll paralyse the cocks, or cocks that'll paralyse the hins ! [*They go out.*

Poges [*returning, and reading the paper*]. Childlike people, the Irish, aren't they ? Hysterical hins ! Dr. What's-his-name, the fellow who said all man is moved by streams of thought that never enter his head — well, he'd find something to study down here. Well, it's delightful to be in a lovely house, in a lovely country, with nothing to think of but hysterical hins ! [*He suddenly concentrates on something in the paper.*] I must have some of those shares. [*He runs to the telephone and joggles and shakes it.*] What can be the matter with this Exchange ? — I can't hear a sound ! [*To Souhaun*] Call one of the workmen, will you ? I must get through to London at once.

 [*Souhaun runs out to call a workman. In a moment or two the 2nd Workman comes into the room.*

2nd Workman. Is it me you want, sir ?

Poges. Not you especially ; I just want to know if you know, or anyone in the county knows, why I can't connect with the Exchange ?

2nd Workman. Oh, is that all, sir ?

Poges [*snappily*]. Is that all ! Isn't it enough, fool !

2nd Workman [*sharply*]. Who th' hell are you callin' a fool to ?

Poges [*placatingly but with some impatience*]. My good man, please let me know if you can say why the Exchange doesn't answer my call.

2nd Workman. Ask anyone from one end o' the counthry to the other, or even O'Killigain himself, if Philib O'Dempsey's a fool, an' see what they'll say. A sound mind, armed with a firm education for seven long years in a steady school, an' now well fit to stand his ground in any argument, barrin' th' highest philosophies of the greatest minds mendin' th' world !

Poges. My good man, I only asked you a simple question.

2nd Workman [*ignoring the remark*]. Comin' over here, thinkin' that all the glory an' grandeur of the world, an' all the might of man, was stuffed into a bulgin' purse, an' stickin' their tongue out at a race that's oldher than themselves by a little like a thousand years, greater in their beginnin' than they are in their prime ; with us speakin' with ayse the mighty languages o' the world when they could barely gurgle a few sounds, sayin' the rest in the movement of their fingers.

Poges [*shouting in rage*]. Go to the devil, man, and learn manners !

2nd Workman [*going on vehemently, but moving slowly to one of the entrances*]. Hammerin' out handsome golden orna-ments for flowin' cloak an' tidy tunic we were, while you were busy gatherin' dhried grass, an' dyin' it blue, to hide the consternation of your middle parts ; decoratin' eminent books with glowin' colour an' audacious beauty were we, as O'Killigain himself will tell you, when you were still a hundhred score o' years away from even hearin' of the alphabet. [*Beside the entrance.*] Fool ? It's yourself's the fool, I'm sayin',

settlin' down in a place that's only fit for the housin'
o' dead men ! Settlin' here, are you ? Wait till God
sends the heavy rain, and the floods come !

[*He goes out.*

Poges [*to Souhaun*]. There's Erin, the tear and the smile
in her eye for you ! The unmannerly ruffian !
Venomous, too — wanting me to wait till the floods
come ! Cheeking me up to my very face !

Souhaun. Well, it's not a royal face, is it ? You'll have
to learn to be respectful to the people if you want
them to be respectful to you.

Poges [*sarcastically*]. I'll be most deferential in the future.
[*Stormily — to 1st Workman appearing at the entrance*] Well,
what do you want ?

1st Workman. Excuse, but I sailed in, hearin' you were in
a difficulty, an' I wanted to see if I could help.

Poges. Well, I want to know where's the man who is
responsible for putting in this 'phone ?

1st Workman. Why, is there anything wrong with it, sir ?

Poges [*stormily*]. Everything's wrong with it, man ! I
can't get on to the Exchange.

1st Workman. Sure, that's aysily explained : it's not
connected yet.

Poges. It was to be connected first thing this morning.
When will it be connected ?

1st Workman [*cautiously*]. Oh, now, that depends, sir.

Poges. Depends ? Depends on what ?

1st Workman. On how long it'll take to get the sthrame o'

sound from here flowin' safely to whatever other end
there may be fixed for it to be heard in.

Poges [*impatiently*]. Get O'Killigain, get him to come here
at once.

1st Workman. Sure, that's the Postmaster's job — Mr.
O'Killigain has nothing to do with it.

Poges [*shouting*]. Then get me the man that has something
to do with it !

Souhaun [*who has been looking at the coloured curtain stuff and
spreading it out*]. Now, Cyril, see what you think : Is
the red with the green stripe or the green with the red
stripe the most suitable to go with the walls ?
    [*The sound of horses trotting is heard outside, becoming
    plainer, till the sound ceases somewhere close to the house.*

Poges [*to Souhaun — with irritation*]. For goodness' sake,
one thing at a time. [*To 1st Workman*] Go and get the
man that's doing this job.

1st Workman. I'm afraid you'll have to thravel a long way
if you want to get him, sir ; you see, he had to go to
pay his last respects to a dead cousin ; but never fear,
he won't be gone beyond a couple of hours, unless
something out o' the ordinary keeps him away the
whole o' the evenin' an' th' strongest part o' th' night.
    [*Poges sinks down on one of the seats, silent and confounded.*

Cloyne [*appearing at back entrance*]. Th' horses are here
now, sir.

Poges [*sitting up*]. Horses ?   What horses ?

Cloyne. The horses Mr. Basil an' Miss Avril ordhered to
come here.

Souhaun. Basil and Avril are going out for a little canter, Cyril.

Poges [*peevishly*]. But this is not the time to be thinking of amusement ; we have to get the house into some shape. Ask O'Killigain to come here.

Souhaun [*to Cloyne*]. Yes, get O'Killigain, Cloyne ; he has a good eye, and will be able to judge which of these curtain stuffs should go on the windows.
  [*Cloyne goes. O'Killigain appears at the left entrance with an anxious look on his face.*

O'Killigain. Who's going to ride these horses that are outside ?

Souhaun [*haughtily*]. Miss Avril and her friend Mr. Basil Stoke are going to ride them.

O'Killigain. I suppose you know these horses are mettle-some creatures, and need riders at home in the saddle ?

Souhaun [*more haughtily still*]. Miss Avril and her friend learned the art in a London riding-school, and exercised frequently in Richmond Park ; so your kind solicitude is unnecessary, sir.

O'Killigain [*viciously*]. Richmond Park isn't Clune na Geera, ma'am. The horses there are animals ; the horses here are horses. [*Avril comes tripping in, dressed in jersey and jodhpurs, and is followed by Basil, dressed in a dark-green kind of hunting coat, buckskin breeches, and big gleaming top-boots with spurs ; he carries a whip in his hand, and a high, handsome, shining tall hat on his head. With a frightened look at Basil*] Good God !
                    [*He turns on his heel and walks out again.*

Basil [*with complacent conceit — to Souhaun*]. The old ways coming back again to the old house, Souhaun.

Souhaun [*rapturously*]. Isn't it grand, dear ? Don't forget to go through the village.

Avril [*joyously*]. Basil has been so kind, Souhaun, dear ; he has given me a grand cheque.

Souhaun [*giving Basil a kiss and winking at Avril*]. Basil, you're a darling !

Poges [*grumpily*]. Be careful how you handle those horses.

Basil [*haughtily — to Poges*]. Did you say anything, sir ?

Poges [*with some heat*]. I said be careful how you handle those horses !

Basil [*with a mocking bow*]. Thank you, sir ; we'll do our best. [*To Avril*] Come, darling.
    [*Avril trips out, and Basil follows her in a way that he deems to be stately.*

Poges. I hope they'll do no damage, now.

Souhaun. Oh, never fear ; Basil sits the saddle like a centaur.
    [*The movement of horses' hooves is heard, then a trot, getting fainter till it dies away.*

Poges [*exasperated*]. God send he doesn't frighten the horse. More decent of him had he remained here to get this telephone going. They all seem to be determined here to keep us away from every semblance of civilisation ! [*To Souhaun — stormily*] Will you, for God's sake, try to get O'Killigain to do something to get this thing in order ? [*He goes over to where Souhaun is busy with the curtains and pulls the curtains out of her*

hands, then flings them on the floor.] D'ye hear, d'ye hear
what I'm saying to you, woman ?

Souhaun [*losing patience and seizing him, and shaking him
roughly*]. What d'ye think you're doing, you old dim-
eyed, old half-dead old fool ! I'll disconnect you as
well as the telephone if you don't learn to behave
yourself ! You settled on coming here, and you'll put
up with the annoyances !

Poges [*protestingly*]. Eh, eh, there ! It was you who persuaded me to come to this god-forsaken hole !

Souhaun [*shaking him more fiercely*]. You're a liar, I didn't !
It was you yourself who were always pining to see the
little squirrels jigging about on the trees, and see the
violets and primroses dreaming in the budding stir of
spring ! [*She pushes him violently from her.*] Another
snarly sound out of you, and I'm off to live alone.

Poges [*gloomily*]. You can well afford to be independent
now, since, like a fool, I settled five hundred a year on
you.
    [*During this contest Cloyne has appeared at the left
    entrance and now gives a judicious cough.*

Souhaun [*quickly — to cover dispute from Cloyne*]. We'll
decide on this stuff, then, for the curtains, Cyril, dear.

Poges. It'll look delightful, darling. [*Pretending to see
Cloyne for the first time.*] Oh, what do you want ?

Cloyne. Canon Creehewel's outside an' would like to have
a few words with you, if you're not too busy.

Poges [*showing irritation*]. Oh, these priests, these priests !
Thick as weeds in this poor country. Opposed to every
decent thought that happens not to have come from

them. Ever on guard to keep the people from growing out of infancy. No one should give them the slightest encouragement. Oh, if the misguided people would only go back to the veneration of the old Celtic gods, what a stir we'd have here! To the delightful, if legendary, loveliness of — er — er — er — what's his name, what's her name, what's their name? I have so often said it, so often in my mind, the chief, or one of the chief gods of the ancient Celts?

Souhaun. Was it Gog or Magog, dear?

Poges [*with fierce scorn*]. Oh, no, no, no; try to think a little, if you really want to assist me. Can't you remember that Gog and Magog were two Philistinian giants killed by David, or Jonathan, or Joshua, or Joab, or Samson, or someone? It's the old Celtic god I have in mind, the one — what was his name?

Souhaun. Gulliver?

Poges. Oh no; not Gulliver!

Souhaun. Well, I don't know the hell who it was.

Poges [*slapping his thigh exultantly*]. Brobdingnag! That was the fellow — the fellow that ate the nine nuts — or was it seven? — plucked from the tree hanging over the well near the world's end.

Cloyne. What am I to say to the Canon, sir?

Poges. What does he want; did you ask him what he wants?

Cloyne. He says he just wants to drop a word or two of thanks for the fifty pounds you sent him.
  [*A murmur of voices is heard outside. It comes nearer and the sound seems excited.*

Poges [*listening*]. What's that, now ?

1st Workman's Voice [*outside*]. Keep his head up.

3rd Workman's Voice [*outside*]. You're home, sir, you're home now.

> [*They come in supporting Basil by the arms, followed by the 2nd Workman, holding Basil's coat-tail. Basil is pale, and has a frightened look on his face. His lovely coat is spattered with mud and, in some places, torn. The 1st Workman is carrying the tall hat, now looking like a battered concertina.*]

Poges [*anxiously*]. What's this ; what's happened ?

1st Workman [*soothingly*]. He's all right, sir ; just a little shock. We seen him crawling towards the house an' went to his help. His horse flung him. [*Whispering to Poges*] He shouldn't be let on anything more mettlesome than a rocking-horse, sir.

Souhaun [*running to Basil*]. Are you much hurt, Basil, dear ?

Basil [*brokenly*]. Bruised, bruised from head to foot.

Poges [*with irritation*]. Well, why the hell didn't you stay here and help me to get the telephone fixed ?

Basil. Why didn't you hold me back by force ? Oh, why did you let me go !

Souhaun [*anxiously*]. Where's Avril ?

Basil [*ignoring her query*]. Oh, I should never have ventured upon an Irish horse ! Irresponsible, irresponsible, like the people. When he wouldn't go, I gave him just a little jab with the spur — [*moaningly*] — and the brute behaved like a wild animal, just like a wild animal !

1st Workman [*soothingly — to Souhaun*]. He's not hurt much, ma'am ; came down in th' grass on his poor bum.

Souhaun. But where's Avril ? [*Shaking Basil's shoulder*] Where's Avril ?

Basil. Gone !

Souhaun. Gone ?

Basil. Away with O'Killigain. He came bounding up to help Avril and abused me for falling off. Then they cantered away together. [*Loudly and a little shrilly*] Naked and unashamed, the vixen went away with O'Killigain !

　　[*Plaster falls and a hole appears in the ceiling, almost directly over the fireplace ; then a thin rope, with a bulb attached to its end, comes dangling down, followed by the face of a heavily Yellow-bearded Man, who thrusts his head as far as it can go through the hole.*

Yellow-bearded Man [*to those below*]. Hay, hay there ; is this where yous want the light to go ?

Poges [*with a vexatious yell when he sees where the rope hangs*]. No it isn't, no it isn't, you fool ! [*Indicating a place near the centre and towards the back*] There, there's where it's wanted ! Where my desk will be.! Oh, they're knocking down more than they're building up !

Yellow-bearded Man [*soothingly*]. Don't worry ; just a little mistake in measurement, sir. Never fear, we'll hit th' right spot one o' these days ! The one thing to do, sir, is to keep cool.

　　[*He takes his head out of the hole and disappears, leaving Poges furious.*

Poges [*shouting up at the hole*]. Who are you to order me to keep cool ? I won't keep cool. I refuse to keep cool !

Souhaun [*to Poges*]. Here, help me in with poor Basil till he drinks some brandy and lies down for a little.
  [*Poges takes one arm, Souhaun takes the other, and they lead Basil out of the room.*

Poges [*to Basil — helping him out*]. I hope you realise the sterling trouble you give people by your damned refusal to recognise your limitations !

Basil [*petulantly*]. Carry me out, man ; carry me out !

Cloyne [*as they pass*]. What am I to do with the Canon, sir ?

Poges [*ferociously*]. Tell him I'll give him another cheque if he gets the telephone fixed for me before the night is out !
  [*Basil, Souhaun, and Poges go out by the left entrance ; Cloyne by that on the right, leaving the men standing together in a corner of the room.*

2nd Workman [*pensively*]. Th' spirit of th' Grey o' Macha's in our Irish horses yet !

1st Workman [*excitedly*]. Did yous hear that, eh ? Did yous hear what he just let dhrop ? That the lassie o' th' house went off with O'Killigain riding naked through the locality !

2nd Workman. Stark naked she was, too. Didn't I know well be th' cut of her jib that she was a hop, step, an' lep of a lassie ! An' right well she looked too !

1st Workman. Th' sight near left me eyes when I seen her go prancin' out without as much as a garther on her to keep her modesty from catchin' cold.

3rd Workman. This'll denude the disthrict of all its self-denyin' decency.

1st Workman [*excitedly jumping upon a seat to get nearer to the hole in the ceiling*]. Cornelius, eh, there, Cornelius !
  [*The yellow-bearded head is thrust through the hole again.*

Yellow-bearded Man. What's up ?

1st Workman. Didja hear th' terrible thing that's afther happenin' ?

Yellow-bearded Man. No ; what terrible thing ?

1st Workman. The lassie o' th' house's gone careerin' all over th' counthry on horseback with only her skin as a coverin' !

Yellow-bearded Man [*horrified*]. G'way !

3rd Workman [*up to him*]. An' th' poor men workin' in th' fields had to flee to th' ditches to save th' sight of their eyes from th' shock o' seein' her !

Yellow-bearded Man [*with aggravated anguish in his voice*]. Oh, isn't it like me to be up here outa sight o' th' world, an' great things happenin' !

CURTAIN

ACT II

The same as in the preceding Act.

The two portraits, one of Stoke, the other of Poges, are now hanging on the wall at back, between the windows. Bright-green curtains, broadly striped with red, are on the windows. A Jacobean armchair has been added to the two stiff pew-like seats beside the fireplace. The table is to the left, so that two mattresses, one beside the other, can be seen, with their heads against the wall and their feet towards the front. On these, wrapped round with rugs and blankets, are Poges and Stoke. Some thick rolled-up floor rugs are lying against the wall. A bunch of pampas grass is in the earthenware jug standing on the table. The rejected crimson curtain stuff is lying over one of the pew-like seats. A walking-stick — Basil's — is leaning against the wall, near to where he is lying.

It is about half-past seven on a cold and misty morning. A few misty beams of sunlight are coming in through the windows, paling the light of a lighted lantern standing between the two beds.

The two men are twisting about uneasily on the mattresses; when Poges twists to the right, Basil twists to the left, and vice versa. Then Poges, wearing a blue beret with a black bow at the side, lifts his head a little and glances over at Basil. He is in that drowsy state felt by a man who has spent long hours of the night trying to get to sleep and failing to do so.

Before the scene is disclosed, the hooting of owls is heard first; then the faint lowing of cattle, grunting of swine, crowing of cocks, bleating of sheep; then, vigorously from various directions the whistling of the chorus of The Farmer's Boy.

Poges [after he has twisted about several times — half to himself, half to Basil]. Good God, isn't it cold ! [*Basil is silent.*] Eh, Basil, are you awake ? How d'ye feel now ?

Basil [*with a faint groan*]. Stiff as hell still ! It's a mercy I'm alive. And, on the top of it, Avril to make a laughing-stock of me by enjoying herself with O'Killigain.

Poges [*sympathetically*]. It was damned mean of her, Basil. She's inclined that way, I'm afraid. You'll have to keep a strong hand over her, my boy.

Basil [*with a deep groan*]. I can't — now.

Poges. Why can't you, man ?

Basil. A month before we came here I did a very foolish thing.

Poges. Oh ?

Basil [*mournfully*]. Settled five hundred a year on her for life.

Poges. Oh ! [*A fairly long pause.*] Basil, Basil, I did the same to Souhaun !

Basil. We're done for, Cyril.

Poges [*in a sprightly way*]. No, no ; a month in the country'll make us young again. We'll be as lively as goats in no time. Besides, we can always cautiously hint at an increase in the settlement.

Basil [*gloomily*]. With the workers always striking for higher wages, it'll have to remain a hint.

Poges [*as gloomily*]. It's damnable, Basil. If much more is given to them, how's a poor man to live ? [*He sinks back on the mattress and pulls the clothes over his head. Outside a cock crows loudly, followed by the call of a cuckoo. Clicking his tongue exasperatedly — from under the clothes.*] Dtch, dtch, dtch! Isn't it a good thing those birds aren't in the house! [*The cock crows again, much louder this time, and the cuckoo calls again. Popping his head from under the clothes.*] Damn that cock and cuckoo! Did you hear that cock crowing, Basil, and the cuckoo calling?

Basil. Deafening, aren't they! And the owls, too, all the night. Jungle noises!

Poges. The country's not going to be so quiet as I thought. Still, I'm glad we came.

Basil. So am I, really. These sounds are just part of the country's attractions — pleasant and homely.

Poges. And stimulating, Basil, stimulating. Look at the sunlight coming in through the windows — another dawn, Basil; another life. Every day in the country brings another chance of living a new life.

Basil [*enthusiastically*]. And we're going to live it, eh, what, Cyril?

Poges [*enthusiastically*]. Oh, boy, ay!
    [*Souhaun appears at the back entrance, left, and Avril at entrance to the right. Both are wearing fur coats over their night-dresses, and shiver a little.*

Souhaun [*plaintively*]. For goodness' sake, will you two men get up and do something. Cloyne's fallen down in a dark passage and hurt her wrist, and she can't do much.

Poges. Oh?

Avril. And something will have to be done to heat the rooms — we were almost frozen last night.

Poges. Ah ! Well, we weren't scorched with the heat either.

Souhaun. Well, stir yourselves, and you'll soon get warm. O'Killigain and his men are already at work, and will want to be coming in and out of here.

> [*The cock crows louder than ever, and is joined by many more, a few of them at a great distance, so that the sounds are heard but faintly ; these are mingled with the barking of dogs, the lowing of cattle, the bleating of sheep, the twittering of birds, the grunting of pigs, and the cackling of hens.*

Avril. There, you hear ; everything's alive but you two.

Poges. Well, we'll be in the midst of them all in a second.

> [*The two women withdraw. Basil and Poges, with the clothes wrapped round them, sit up, and dive down again. After a second or two they sit bolt-upright again, and again dive down.*

Poges [*shivering*]. Ooooh, Basil, cold !

Basil [*shivering*]. Bitter, bitter ! What would I not give now for a cosy flat ; a cosier bed ; and a blazing hot-water bottle ! [*They lie quiet for a short time.*

Poges. There's nothing for it but to plunge out of the summer into the black and bitter winter.

Basil. You say the word.

Poges. Ready ! Steady ! Go !

> [*They climb laboriously out of the beds. When they get out, it can be seen that they have been fully dressed, even*

to their heavy topcoats and scarves wound round their necks.

Poges [*blowing on to his hands and rubbing them*]. Ooooh, crisp, isn't it ? Healthy, though. Ooooh ! Where the hell's that Barney, that he hasn't a fire lighted for us ? Oooh ! One would want to be on his tail all day. [*Shouting*] Barney, Barney ! [*Barney comes in holding some logs in the crook of his right arm, and a lantern in his left hand. Cloyne follows, with some paper and a bellows. Her left wrist is bandaged. Barney is wearing a topcoat, and has a muffler round his neck. Cloyne, too, is wearing a heavy coat. They both go over to the fireplace. As they come in*] Ah, here we are. Bit nippy, Barney ; sharp, but beneficial. [*To Cloyne*] You'll have to be more careful with the steps and passages. Mind your feet coming in, mind your head going out. Oooooh ! [*To Basil*] You better slip off, and give the others any help you can. [*As Basil is going*] What about your walking-stick ?

Basil [*moving stiffly*]. I must try to do without it—about the house, anyway.

> [*He takes the lantern that is beside his bed, and goes out, limping a little.*

Poges [*to the other two*]. Well, what do the pair of you think of the country, eh ? And the house ? Better than any your old Kings of Tarara had, eh ?

Cloyne [*effusively*]. I'm sure it'll be lovely, sir, when we settle down.

> [*Poges has been jerking his arms about in an effort to drive the cold from his body. Cloyne begins to fold the clothes on the beds, and tidy them up.*

Poges. Of course it will. We'll enjoy it all ; we'll feel

younger ; we will *be* younger. The air, fresh air, pure air, exhilarating air, will be able to get at us. [*He sucks in his breath and blows it out again.*] Ooooh ! Soon we won't know ourselves. We'll eat better, sleep better ; flabby muscles will become firm, and we'll realise that we are alive, alive, alive-O. Think of the walks we'll have ; so much to see, so much to hear, so much to smell ; and then to come back, nicely tired, to such a lovely house. A life for the gods !

Cloyne. Wondherful, wondherful, sir.

Poges. Now I must be off to swallow down a cup of tea, for there's a lot to be done, a lot to be done yet.

                  [*He hurries off out of the room.*

Cloyne. The poor oul' codger !

Barney. Comin' down to this back o' God-speed place for rest an' quietness ! Afther all that science has thried to do for us, goin' back to lantherns an' candles. Th' only electric light he'll allow in a Tudor house is one over his own desk ! Runnin' in the face o' God Almighty's goodness — that's what it is.

Cloyne. They'll get tired of it before us.

Barney. I can tell you, I'm tired of it already. Looka the place we're livin' in : doors everywhere shaped like doors o' dungeons ; passages dark as hell when it was first formed ; crackin' your head when you're goin' in, and breakin' your toe when you're goin' out ; an' I'm tellin' you, it's only beginnin'.

Cloyne. It might be worse.

Barney [*striking a match to light the paper*]. We're goin' to be worse, I'm tellin' you.

Cloyne. We can't be worse than we are.

Barney [*as the flames of the paper die down*]. There's no chance o' kindlin' here. Why did you say, then, that we might be worse ?

Cloyne. Well, so, indeed, an' we might.

Barney. How can we be worse, woman, when we're as bad as we can be ?

Cloyne. Simply be bein' worse than we were.

Barney. How can we be worse than we were, when we're as bad as we can be, now.

Cloyne. You'll see we'll be worse before we're betther.

Barney. Damn these logs ! Isn't that what I'm sthrivin' to dhrive into your head ?

Cloyne. What are you sthrivin' to dhrive into me head ?

Barney. That we'll be worse than we were before we're as bad as we are now, an' in a week's time we'll be lookin' back with a sigh to a time, bad as it could be then, that was betther than the worst that was on top of us now.

[*Poges bustles in again. The heavy topcoat is gone and he is now dressed in bright-blue shorts, emerald-green jersey, brown shoes, and the scarf is still round his neck. He has a cup of tea in his hand, and he is sipping it as he comes into the room. He is miserably cold, but he puts on a brisk air, sorting it out in his mind that to be cold in the country is natural, to be ignored as far as possible, and to be countered by a smiling face, a brisk manner, and the wearing of brilliant clothes denoting freedom of movement and utter disregard of the common rules of convention. He is feeling far from comfortable, but*

    thinks this shouldn't be shown; for the colder you are,
    and the more uncomfortable you feel, the brisker you must
    be, and the hardier you'll get.

Poges. Here we are again! Ready for anything now.
[*Losing his gay attitude when he sees that the fire isn't lighted.*]
Isn't the fire lighted yet? What are you doing,
Barney? Being in the country's no reason why we
should be frozen to death.

Barney. I can't get a spark out of it, afther all me
sthrivin'.

Poges [*testily*]. You can't light logs with a bit of paper,
man. Oh, use your brains, Barney, use your brains.

Barney. An' what else have I got to light them with?

Poges. Small sticks, man; put some small sticks under
them.

Barney. An' will you tell me where I'm goin' to get the
small sticks? Isn't the nearest shop a dozen miles
away?

Poges. Well, if there's no sticks, sprinkle a little paraffin
on them.

Barney [*sarcastically*]. An' where am I goin' to get the
paraffin? There's no oil wells knockin' about here.

Poges [*severely*]. Don't be funny. You've got to remember
you're in the country now.

Barney. Isn't it meself that's gettin' to know it well!

Poges. We've got to do things for ourselves: there's no
chance of pushing a button to get things done here.

Barney. Sure, I'm beginnin' to think you're right.

Poges. Can't you see that those logs are too big?

Barney, I think I do, unless me sight's goin' curious.

Poges [*hotly*]. Well, then, why don't you do it!

Barney. Arra, do what?

Poges [*loudly*]. Make them smaller, man!

Barney [*calmly and sarcastically*]. An' how?

Poges. And how? Why, with an axe, of course.

Barney [*losing his temper — loudly*]. An' where's the axe, an' where's the axe?

Poges. There must be an axe knocking about somewhere.

Barney. There's nothin' knockin' about here but a bitther breeze whirlin' through the passages that ud make the very legs of a nun numb!

Cloyne [*trying to mollify things*]. Sure, the poor man's back-broken an' heart-broken thryin' to kindle it, sir.

Poges [*who has been waving his arms and stamping his feet while his teeth chatter — turning fiercely on Cloyne*]. You mind your own business, girl! [*Seeing her putting the mattresses by the wall.*] Have we got to sleep down here again tonight?

Cloyne. Ay, an' yous have. Th' other rooms are too damp still. Sure, Mr. O'Killigain says that it'll take a month of fierce fires to dhry them out.

Poges [*testily*]. Mr. O'Killigain says this, and Mr. O'Killigain says that! I'm getting tired of what Mr. O'Killigain says. If we have to sleep here, you or Barney'll have to stay up all night keeping the fire going, or we'll be frozen in our sleep. [*His eye catches sight of the telephone. He goes over to it and lifts the receiver.*] Not a sound ! No, oh no ; not a bit of a hurry. [*Angrily to Cloyne*] Go out, girl, and send in the boy who's working at this telephone. [*With a low moan*] Ireland !

> [*Cloyne goes out by the doorway on the right leading to the entrance hall. After a few seconds the loud lowing of a cow is heard, followed by a scream from Cloyne, who rushes frantically back into the room, pale and trembling.*

Cloyne [*breathlessly rushing back into the room, falling on the floor, and catching Poges wildly by the legs*]. Save me ! Stuck his head into me face, th' minute I opened the door. Mother o' God, I'll never see th' light of another day with th' fright I got !

Poges [*alarmed*]. What is it, what is it, woman ?

Cloyne [*almost incoherent*]. A bull, a wild bull, out in th' enthrance hall !

Barney [*frantically*]. A wild bull ! We're all desthroyed.

Poges [*trying to release himself from Cloyne's hold*]. Let me go, girl ! Let me go, or I can't defend myself. If he comes in here, the whole of us'll be horned !

Cloyne [*frantically*]. My legs have given undher me. Let me hold on to you, sir — it's me only hope !

Poges [*to Barney*]. Put the table to the doorway, man, and help to bar him out — quick, quick, man ! And a mattress. [*To Cloyne while Barney is pushing the table and a mattress to the door*] Why didn't you clap the door in his face, you fool ?

Cloyne. Wasn't he half into the hall before I'd the door

half open ! Oh, sir, what are we goin' to do ? Oh, please go, sir, an' thry an' shove him out !

[*The bellow of the animal is heard outside in the hall.*

Poges [*half dead with panic*]. My God, woman, you can't shove bullocks about ! [*Shouting*] Souhaun, there's a wild bull in the house ! Help, O'Killigain, help. [*To Barney*] Run, run, man, and get Mr. Stoke to bring down the gun. Oh, go quick, man ! An' keep well out of range. [*Barney runs off. Shouting*] O'Killigain, help ! Can't you let me go, girl ?

Cloyne [*still clinging to him*]. Carry me off, sir, please. Don't leave me here to die alone ! Maybe he won't be able to climb the stairs afther us. Oh, when I came to th' counthry, I never thought there'd be wild animals on th' door-step !

[*Basil appears at one of the entrances at the back ; he moves forward stealthily and extends a gun to Poges.*

Basil [*nervous*]. What is it, what is it ?

Poges. A bull, out in the hall.

Basil. Who let him in ? Damn it, such carelessness ! You must be on guard in the country, you know. Here, take the gun, man.

Poges [*angrily — to Basil*]. Come out, come out in the open, man, and be ready to use the gun if he comes into the room ! [*Shoving the gun from him.*] You use it, man ; weren't you an A.R.P. man ?

Basil [*indignantly*]. I never did anything more than clay-pigeon shooting ! Let whoever let the damned animal in, let the damned animal out ! [*He pokes Poges with the gun.*] Here, take this, and down him — you're nearer the bull than I am.

Poges [*angrily*]. I'm not a toreador, am I ? And don't
point, don't point the gun at me ! Lower the barrel,
man ; oh, lower the barrel ! D'ye want me to die two
deaths at once ? What's the advantage of your passing
through Oxford if you can't face a bull with a gun in
your hand ? Be a man, man, and not a mouse.

Basil [*keeping well in the passage, and only showing his nose*].
Telephone the police, the fire brigade, or something.

Poges [*violently*]. Don't you know the kind of a country
we're in ! There's no police, no fire brigade, no telephone ! Come here, if you won't use the gun, and
help me carry this girl away out of danger.
   [*The cow puts a stylised head, with long curving horns,
   over the barricade and lets out a loud bellow. Cloyne
   spasmodically tugs the legs of Poges, making him lose his
   balance so that he topples to the floor, after a frantic
   effort to save himself.*

Cloyne. Oooh, sir, save me !

Poges [*with a wild shout as he is falling*]. My God, he's on
top of us ! We're done for ! Help !
   [*Basil throws the gun into the room and runs for his life.*

Barney [*in the far distance*]. Sing out, sir, if you want any
assistance !
   [*Someone is heard stirring outside where the animal is ;
   this stir is followed by the voice of the 1st Workman
   shooing the cow out of the hall. After a few moments,
   Poges slowly sits up and listens.*

1st Workman [*shouting outside*]. Eh, oick, oick, eh, yeh gett ;
ay, ay, oick oick !
   [*Poges gets up on to his feet, shaking a little, and going over,
   picks up the gun and, steadying himself on it, stands over*

the prostrate Cloyne, who is almost in a faint, bundled up on the floor, with her face hidden in her hands. Shortly after, the 1st Workman appears at the entrance with a bucket of coal and some sticks. He looks over the table, astonished to see the prostrate Cloyne, and Poges standing near with a gun in his hand.

Poges [*stormily*]. Where the hell did that bull come from ? who owns her ? who let that bull come tearing into a private house ?

1st Workman. Bull, sir ?　Oh, that wasn't a bull, sir.　[*He pushes the table back to its place.*]　Jest a harmless innocent cow, sir.　Frightened the poor girl, now, did it ? [*Cunningly*] But I see it didn't frighten you, sir.

Poges [*flattered*]. No, no, not me.　[*To Cloyne*] Here, girl, get up on your feet.　[*Loudly*] It wasn't a bull ; I knew it couldn't be a bull !　and it's gone, so get up. [*Putting down the gun.*]　Get up !　[*With the help of the 1st Workman and Poges, Cloyne gets up on her feet.*]　There now, be off with you.　Get Miss Avril to give you a stiff glass of whiskey, and you'll be all right.　And take this gun back to Mr. Basil.

　　　[*He picks up the gun and hands it to the shaking Cloyne.*

Cloyne. Oh, sir, this place is worse than a jungle in th' desert !

Poges. Go on, go on !　I thought you Irish were a brave people.

　　　[*He is shaky himself, but he stiffens himself to conceal the tremors.*

Cloyne [*going out with the gun*]. For ages now, it's bulls I'll be dhreamin' of, an' there's ne-er a lock on me door either !

Poges. Fainting, shouting, screaming, and running about
for nothing ! No nerves, no nerves, no spirit ; no
coolness in a crisis.

1st Workman [*craftily*]. An' did they all think it was a
bull, sir ? An' you stood your ground. Looka that
now. Prepared for anything, sir.

Poges [*taking it all in*]. The other fellow, Mr. Basil, ran for
his life ; think of that — ran for his life !

1st Workman. Did he, now ?

Poges. British, too, think of that ; surprising and dis-
appointing, very. [*Briskly and a little anxiously*] Still,
I must acquaint the police. I can't have cows or bulls
wandering about the rooms of Ormond Manor.

1st Workman [*who has started to light the fire*]. One o' th' ladies
sent me in to light a fire for you. [*Placatingly*] Sure,
sir, she was only the cow me friend brought this
mornin' so that, when you had a minute, you could
run out an' look her over. A fine animal, sir. She got
loose an' wandhered in when she found th' door open.
She's betther than th' best that was in th' cattle raid
o' Cooley.
   [*Souhaun comes in by a back entrance followed by Avril.
   She is carrying a black vase, striped with blue, and has a
   jazzy overall on one of her arms. Avril carries a blue
   bowl, striped with black. They are carrying them very
   carefully, as if they were very precious indeed.*

Souhaun. What's all this commotion about a bull ? We
had to stop Basil from trying to throw himself out of a
window !

Avril. And Barney got out on top of the roof.

Poges. Oh, nothing, nothing at all ; a stray cow in the garden mooed, and Basil lost his head and Cloyne lost her feet.

Avril. But Barney, when he was rushing past, said that you were out here roaring for help !

1st Workman. Roarin' for help, is it ? Indeed an' he wasn't, for I can testify to that, but standin' here, cool as you like, he was, waitin' for the worst.

Souhaun. Well, if we're to stay in the country, we'll have to get used to all kinds of animals, big and small.

Poges [*shaking his head*]. I'm convinced now that poor Basil can't be wholly English. There's a weak joint somewhere.

Souhaun [*leaving the overall on a seat*]. There's your overall, dear, to wear when you're working, and we're taking your precious Annamese vase and Cambodian bowl to our room for safety, till everything's straight.

Poges. Oh, that's right, if anything happened to either of them, I'd pass out. Lift the vase up, dear, till I see it a second. [*She lifts it up.*] Oh, Lord, isn't it lovely ? [*To Avril*] The Cambodian bowl too. [*She lifts it over her head.*] A little too high, dear; just go down on one knee. [*She does so.*] Aaah ! Precious, precious ! The chaste form, the tender planes, the refined colouring ; the exquisite design, the *tout ensemble* — they go down into the undiscoverable deeps of the heart !

1st Workman. Arra, be God, indeed an' they do, sir.

Avril [*languishingly*]. A background of eau-de-nil would set them off to their full advantage.

Souhaun [*cocking her eye at them*]. Oh no, Avril ; Chinese white's the pure and proper background for them.

Avril. Eau-de-nil.

Souhaun. Chinese white, dear.

Poges. Neither. Chrome yellow's the tone. A warm and pure cloak, as it were, for the chaste bodies of the vase and the bowl. [*He goes over and touches them tenderly.*] My darling treasures ! Take them off, and lay them down with circumspection. Mind the step going out.
 [*Souhaun and Avril go slowly and stately out, carrying the vase and the bowl as if they were precious relics.*

1st Workman [*to Poges who has come over to the fireplace where a fine fire is blazing now*]. There y'are, sir ; a fire that'll warm y' up an' make your mind easy.

Poges [*stretching out his hands to the fire*]. Good, great, grand ! Are you the workman who knows all the stories and legends of Ireland since the world began ?

1st Workman. No, no, not me, sir ; it's Philib you mean — th' powerful man with th' powerful beard. [*Touching his forehead.*] Some say he isn't all there, but a wondherful man, ay, indeed, is Philib. Does a man good to talk to him.

Poges. I'll have a chat with him, the first chance I get.

1st Workman [*looking round the room with a ravishing air*]. This is a wondherful house, so it is. It's an honour to be workin' in it. Afther hundhreds o' years standin' in frost, rain, an' snow, frontin' th' winds o' the world, it's a marvel it isn't flat on its face, furnishin' only an odd shelther for a sthray fox ; but here it stands, an' we all waitin' for a windy winther ud stagger it an' send it tottherin' down.

Poges [*indignantly*]. Tottherin' down ! What d'ye mean, tottherin' down ? The place is as firm as a lighthouse. Tottherin' down, indeed !

1st Workman [*repelling the idea that he thought of such a thing*]. Tottherin' down, is it ? Now who, in th' name o' God, save a sure an' safe fool ud think it was tottherin' down ? Not me, now ; oh no, not me. Tottherin' down me neck ! Isn't the grand oul' house goin' to show, soon an' sudden, a sign of what a fine residence it was when the quality harnessed their horses for a hunt be the risin' rim o' th' dawn, or sat down in their silks an' satins to their evenin' meal in the shadowy shine o' th' golden candles !

Poges. Purple nights and golden days, my friend. [*He sighs.*] Aah !

1st Workman [*with a long, deep, imitative sigh*]. Aah ! We'll never set eyes on the like o' them again, sir ; th' sparklin' carriages comin' an' goin', th' steeds throttin' nicely an' neatly, or movin' at a gallop, always elegant, on a visit to me lord here, or me lady there, with th' sky above in a fair swoon o' pride for th' fine things movin' about below ; an' they full o' grace, an' decked out in the grandeur o' th' West Indies an' th' East Indies, sobered down a thrifle for use in a Christian counthry, the women's bosoms asway with jewels, like a tendher evenin' sky, alive with stars. An' th' gentlemen, just a dim step down, but elegant too, in finery fair, with ruffles an' lace, with cutaway coats an' vests embroidhered, each holdin' a cane to keep them steady, an' all halo'd with scents to ring them round from th' smell o' th' poor an' dingier world at work or play !

Poges [*enthusiastically*]. Those were handsome days. [*He fixes a plume of pampas grass in his beret.*] When shall we look upon their like again? [*He folds the crimson curtain stuff round him as if it were a cavalier's cloak.*] The lawns and ramparts still are here, and we shall be the men! [*He snatches up Basil's walking-stick.*] The plume in the hat, the velvet cloak over the shoulder, the tapering rapier in the hand! [*He makes a vicious lunge at the 1st Workman, who narrowly dodges the pass.*] Die, varlet!

1st Workman [*remonstratively*]. Eh, eh, there; careful, sir, be careful! Be careful how yeh prod!

Poges [*leaning on the stick as if it were a sword — sorrowfully*]. Where are the kings and queens and warriors now? Gone with all their glory! The present day and present men? Paltry, mean, tight, and tedious. [*Disgustedly*] Bah!

1st Workman. What are we now, what are we all, but a tired thribe thryin' to do nothin' in th' shortest possible time? Worn away we are, I'm sayin', to shreds and shaddas mouldin' machines to do everything for us. Tired, is it? Ay, tired an' thremblin' towards th' edge of th' end of a life hardly worth livin'!

Poges [*gloomily pacing up and down*]. Not worth living, not worth living.

1st Workman [*with greater energy*]. Time ago, an' we gave a ready ear to one speakin' his faith in God an' his neighbour; but now, there's so many gabbers goin' that there's hardly a listener left. Sure, that in itself is as sharp a punishment as a lease o' hell for a long vacation. It's meself is sayin' ourselves came late, but soon enough to see the finery fade to purple dust, an' the glow o' th' quality turn to murmurin' ashes.

Poges [*striking the attitude of a clumsy cavalier*]. We won't let them perish completely ! We'll keep the stern old walls standing. We'll walk where they walked, sit where they sat, and sleep where they slept !

1st Workman. An' talk as they talked too.

Poges [*wildly*]. Our pride shall be their pride, our elegance their elegance, and the banner of the Ormonds shall fly from the battlements again ! The King, the King, God bless him !

1st Workman [*warningly*]. I wouldn't say too much about the King, sir ; we're a little touchy about kings down here in Clune na Geera.

> [*From outside is heard a scream from Souhaun and a squeal from Avril ; then the sound of running feet, and the crash of breaking chinaware. After a moment or so, Souhaun pitches into the room from the left entrance at back, and Avril from the right one. Souhaun is holding the top rim of the vase in her hand, and Avril the butt of the bowl. When he sees the damage, the 1st Workman slinks off.*]

Poges [*furiously*]. What the hell's all this ?

Avril [*breathlessly*]. Rats !

Souhaun [*breathlessly*]. Gigantic creatures !

Avril. Here.

Souhaun. There.

Both [*together*]. Everywhere !

Poges [*in anguish*]. Oh, look at what's left of my Annamese vase and Cambodian bowl ! A hundred pounds of the best for each, and then only when I happened to catch

the cunning Keeper drunk in the Bazaar of Singapore.
What the hell were the pair of you thinking of ?

Souhaun. Rats.

Avril. Here, there, and everywhere.

Poges [*wildly*]. You evil-handed dolts to destroy my two
best treasures ! You'll pay for them, you'll pay for
them !

Avril [*scornfully*]. We'd look well thinking of them, and
we running for our lives.

Souhaun. You can imagine what it was when Basil is up
there now on guard with the gun.

Poges [*mockingly*]. Oh, he's the boy to shoot down wild
animals. [*Imploringly*] For God's sake go up and take
the gun off him or he'll send a bullet through the body
of some human being ! And for the future, you and
your friend keep your awkward hands off any treasures
I may have left.

Souhaun [*scornfully*]. Treasures ! Who told you that the
Annamese vase and your old Cambodian bowl were
treasures ?

Poges. Everyone who saw them, woman !

Souhaun. Ay, to humour you. Well, let me tell you they
weren't more valuable than a second-hand vase or
bowl bought at a Woolworth sale. That's the fact,
and it's best to know it.

Poges [*with quiet emphasis*]. And who gave you that in-
formation ?

Avril. Couldn't anyone, not a fool, see what they were
the minute they saw them ?

Souhaun. The minute Mr. O'Killigain set eyes on them, he said that they went from Derby in thousands to Singapore and Saigon for suckers to buy them !

Poges [*with furious scorn*]. Oh, indeed, did he ? Oh, an authority on what kind of art d'ye call it in Clune na Geera ? I'll test them. I'll send them to the Curator of the Wallace Collection. We'll see. Mr. O'Killi-gain — good God !

    [*He takes the pieces from Avril and Souhaun and puts them on the table. Cloyne appears at an entrance at back with a troubled look on her face.*

Cloyne. Here, they've gone and dumped the garden tools an' the roller right in front of the hall door ! And the roller's so close that when you want to go out or come in you have to climb over it.

Poges. Tell whoever brought them to bring them to the back and put them in the shed, fool !

Cloyne. How can I tell him when him an' the lorry's gone ?

Poges [*furiously*]. And why didn't you tell him before he went ?

Cloyne. An' didn't I now ? He just said that the back was threnched be the workmen an' he hadn't time to build pontoon bridges.

Poges. What a country ! What a people ! [*Viciously — to Souhaun*] And you encourage them, because you and your friend Avril are Irish too !

Souhaun. If you ask me, you're not such a shining paragon of goodness yourself.

Poges [*explosively*]. I believe in efficiency ! I demand efficiency from myself, from everyone. Do the thing thoroughly and do it well : that's English. The word given, and the word kept : that's English. [*Roaring*] And I'm an Englishman !

Souhaun. You are indeed, God help you !

Cloyne. An' what are we goin' to do about the garden tools an' th' roller ?

Souhaun [*in a bustling and dominant way, catching up the jazz-patterned overall and putting it on Poges*]. Here, if we waste any more time talking, the house will never be ready to live in. Put this on, and go and bring the roller from the front door through here, out of the way, to the back. When you've done that, bring the garden tools to the back too, and let us see your grand English efficiency at work while I and Avril do some of the hundred things remaining to be done.

[*She gives him a push from her, and she and Avril hurry away out by one of the back entrances.*

Cloyne [*warningly*]. It seems a heavy roller, sir, so mind you don't sthrain yourself when you're pullin' it.

Poges [*testily*]. Go away, go away, girl ; I'm not an invalid. [*Cloyne goes. Poges moves over to the blazing fire and stretches out his hands to the flame. The 2nd Workman comes in by left entrance at back wheeling a barrow filled with bricks. He is a powerful man of fifty, with gleaming eyes and wide and strong beard. As he comes nearer, Poges turns to give him greeting. Warmly*] Good day, good sir ; it's a cold day that's in it, surely.

2nd Workman [*eyeing Poges curiously*]. Ay is it, for them

who has to brave it, an' can't stand all day in front of
a sturdy fire like a kingly Pharaoh.

Poges [*a little nonplussed*]. Quite, yes, yes, quite. Everyone tells me the place round here is a rich storehouse
of history, legend, and myth ?

2nd Workman [*with a little scorn in his voice*]. It's a little
they know an' little they care about those things. But
the place has her share o' histhory an' her share o'
wondhers.

Poges [*flatteringly*]. And I'm told you have a rare stock of
them yourself.

2nd Workman. Ay, indeed, I have me share o' wondhers,
new an' old.

Poges [*trying to be Irish*]. Looka that, now. Arra, whisht,
an' amn't I told it's strange stories you do be tellin' of
the noble things done by your fathers in their days, and
in the old time before them.

2nd Workman [*sinking into a meditative mood*]. When less
than a score of the Fianna brought back the King of
England prisoner, invaded Hindostan, an' fixed as
subjects the men of all counthries between our Bay o'
Dublin and the holy river that gave to holy John the
holy wather to baptize our Lord.

Poges [*astonished*]. I never heard that one before.

2nd Workman [*with murmuring scorn*]. An' where would th'
like o' you hear it, man ? That was in the days o'
Finn Mac Coole, before his hair was scarred with a
hint o' grey ; the mighty Finn, I'm sayin', who stood
as still as a stone in th' heart of a hill to hear the cry of
a curlew over th' cliffs o' Erris, the song of the black-

bird, the cry o' the hounds hotfoot afther a boundin' deer, the steady wail o' the waves tumblin' in on a lonely shore ; the mighty Finn who'd surrendher an emperor's pomp for a place with the bards, and the gold o' the King o' Greece for a night asleep be the sthream of Assaroe !

Poges [*solemnly*]. A great man, a great man, surely ; a great man gone for ever.

2nd Workman [*sharply*]. He's here for ever ! His halloo can be heard on the hills outside ; his spear can be seen with its point in the stars ; but not with an eye that can see no further than the well-fashioned edge of a golden coin.

Poges [*moving back a step — a little awed*]. You see these things, do you ?

2nd Workman. I hear sthrange things be day, an' see sthrange things be night when I'm touched be the feel of the touch of the long-handed Lugh. When the Dagda makes a gong o' the moon, an' the' Sword o' Light shows the way to all who see it.

Poges. Aah !

2nd Workman. Then every rib o' grass grows into a burnished fighter that throws a spear, or waves a sword, an' flings a shield before him. Then Ireland crinkles into a camp, an' kings an' sages, queens an' heroes, saints an' harpers stare me in the face, an' bow, an' pass, an' cry out blessing an' vict'ry too, for Heber's children, with the branch of greatness waving in their hands !

Poges [*sadly*]. And there it ends !

2nd Workman [*giving Poges a drowsy glance*]. I'm thinkin' it might have been well for some if the end an' all was there ; but it sthretches out to the sight of a big dim ship with a followin' fleet in the great dim distance, with a stern-fac'd man in the blue-gold coat of the French Armee, standin' alone on th' bridge of the big dim ship, his eyes fixed fast on the shore that was fallin' undher the high-headed, rough-tumblin' waves o' the sea !

Poges [*awed into interest — murmuringly*]. A big dim ship and a following fleet, carrying a man in the blue-gold coat of the French Armee — who was he, and when was that, now ?

2nd Workman. Th' man was Wolfe Tone, and the time was yestherday.

Poges. Yesterday !

2nd Workman. The man was there, but the fleet was a golden dhream, always comin' in an' ever goin' out o' th' Bay o' Banthry !

　　[*O'Killigain has come in at the commencement of the 2nd Workman's musing, unnoticed by the dreaming worker, and barely noticed by the interested Poges, listening intently to what is being said, and a little awed by the influence of the 2nd Workman. O'Killigain comes softly over, and stands a little behind but close to the dreaming workman.*

Poges [*bending towards the 2nd Workman*]. And who was the man in the blue-gold coat of the French Armee ?

2nd Workman. He was a great Irish soldier and a great Irish friend to the people of no property in Ireland.

O'Killigain [*very softly*]. And there are others.

2nd Workman [*softly too, but not so softly*]. And there are others ; for through the roads of the four green fields goes Shane the Proud, with his fine head hidden, waving away his more venturesome friends from the horns of a bull, the hoofs of a horse, the snarl of a dog, an' th' smile of an Englishman.

Poges [*going back a step*]. The smile of an Englishman !

2nd Workman [*unheeding the interruption*]. An' in the midst of them all is Parnell standing still ; unheeding he stands with a hand on his breast, his white face fixed on the East, with his wine-coloured eyes flashin' hathred to England !

O'Killigain [*very softly*]. And there are others.

2nd Workman [*with a glance at O'Killigain*]. They came later, an' haven't wandhered fully back to where they cleared a way for a gropin' people, but they will come, an' stare us into the will to take our own again.

Poges [*detaching himself from the spell*]. And do none other of those you know, good man, see the things that you see ?

2nd Workman. Barrin' a few an' O'Killigain there, they see these things only as a little cloud o' purple dust blown before the wind.

Poges. That's very sad.

2nd Workman. Barrin' O'Killigain there an' a few, what is it all now but a bitther noise of cadgin' mercy from heaven, an' a sour handlin' o' life for a cushion'd seat in a corner ? There is no shout in it ; no sound of a slap of a spear in a body ; no song ; no sturdy winecup in a sturdy hand ; no liftin' of a mighty arm to push back the tumblin' waters from a ship just sthrikin' a storm. Them that fight now fight in a daze o' thradin' ; for buyin' an' sellin', for whores an' holiness, for th' image o' God on a golden coin ; while th' men o' peace are little men now, writin' dead words with their tiny pens, seekin' a tidy an' tendher way to the end. Respectable lodgers with life they are, behind solid doors with knockers on them, an' curtained glass to keep the stars from starin' !

[*The 2nd Workman stoops, lifts the shafts of the barrow, and is about to go out.*

Poges [*to 2nd Workman — placatingly*]. My own great-grandfather was Irish, I'm told, and my grandmother was a kind of a Scotswoman.

2nd Workman [*going out with the barrow slowly*]. That's not such a lot, an' you're not sure of any of it either.

Poges. What a strange, odd man ! I couldn't get half of what he was trying to say. Are there many like him ?

O'Killigain. Millions of them, though few of them have tongues so musical.

Poges. He rather took to me, I think, and looks upon me as a friend.

O'Killigain [*ironically*]. He looks upon you, and all Englishmen, as a rascal, a thief, and a big-pulsed hypocrite.

Poges [*indignantly*]. Good God, but that's pure ignorance. Where would the world be without us ?

O'Killigain. The giddy globe would wobble, slow down, stand still, and death would come quick to us all.

Poges [*a little puzzled by this remark*]. Eh ? Quite. Well, no, not so bad as that, you know, but near it, damned near it.

[*Souhaun runs in with a look of dark annoyance on her face.*

Souhaun. Oh, look at you standing here still, and so much to be done — [*her voice rises*] — so much to be done, so much to be done ! I asked you to get the roller away from the door an hour ago, and here's Barney after twisting his wrist trying to climb over it standing in the same old place ! [*She catches him by the overall.*] Come, for God's sake, and take the damn thing out of the way !

Poges [*pulling her hand away from the overall — angrily*]. Oh, have some decency, order, and dignity, woman ! Can't you see I'm having a serious discussion with O'Killigain ? [*He turns swiftly on O'Killigain.*] We, sir, are a liberty-loving people, and have always striven to preserve perfect — perfect, mind you — freedom of thought, not only in our own land, but throughout the whole world ; but that anyone should be permitted to hold opinions such as are held by that lunatic just gone out, and are apparently held by you, sir, too, is a perfect scandal and disgrace !

Souhaun. Oh, there's no use of you trying to ride your high horse here in Clune na Geera !

Poges [*stormily*]. I'm not trying to ride my high horse here in Clune na Geera ! What is said in Clune na Geera is a matter of very little importance indeed. But every right-minded man the world over knows, or ought to know, that wherever we have gone, progress, civilisation, truth, justice, honour, humanity, righteousness, and peace have followed at our heels. In the Press, in

the Parliament, in the pulpit, or on the battlefield, no
lie has ever been uttered by us, no false claim made,
no right of man infringed, no law of God ignored, no
human law, national or international, broken.

O'Killigain [*very quietly*]. Oh, for God's sake, man, don't
be pratin' like a pantaloon priest !

Souhaun [*trying to push Poges from the room — impatiently*].
Go out and get the garden roller !

Poges [*loudly*]. I say, sir, that Justice is England's old
nurse ; Righteousness and Peace sit together in her
common-room, and the porter at her gate is Truth !

O'Killigain [*quietly, but sarcastically*]. An' God Himself is
England's butler !

Poges [*roaring with rage*]. That's a vile slander, sir !

O'Killigain. Whether it is or no doesn't matter much,
for in a generation or so the English Empire will be
remembered only as a half-forgotten nursery rhyme !

Poges [*fiercely as Souhaun is pushing him out*]. An opinion
like that deserves the jail !

Souhaun [*giving him a last strong push out into one of the back
entrances*]. Oh, go on ! [*She goes over towards O'Killigain
and stands looking shyly and a little archly at him.*] What
a naughty man you are to provoke him into such a
tantrum ! [*After a slight pause.*] I hear terrible things
about you, Mr. O'Killigain.

O'Killigain. Oh ?

Souhaun. That you are a great man for the girls !

O'Killigain. A pretty girl shows me a sign that God is
smilin'.

Souhaun [*archly*]. It's well I need the gay an' youthful gloss of pretty Avril, or it's shelterless I'd be from all your stormy moods !

O'Killigain [*gallantly*]. When I look at you close I see you a week or two oldher than your younger friend, an' when you go as bright about the house, an' dhress as gay as she does, you look like an earlier summer kissin' a tardy spring goodbye.

Souhaun. More than twenty years younger than the old fool Poges I am of course. It's ridiculous for me to be with him. I have a nice little income of my own now, and it's like a young bird I feel that has just got command of its restless wings. [*She pauses for a moment.*] You really do believe that I am as pretty as Avril ? You're not just teasing me, are you ?

O'Killigain. Not I. You are one o' th' fine sights of this world. [*He lilts :*]

> There are many fair things in this world as it goes,
> The blue skies of summer, th' flushing red rose,
> But of all th' fair, blossoming things that men see,
> A comely-built lass is th' nearest to me,
> A comely-built lass is th' dearest to me !

And you are a comely-built lass.

Souhaun [*coming near to him and stroking his arm*]. Your poor arm, wounded for the sake of others. What's your name ?

O'Killigain. My name ? O'Killigain, of course.

Souhaun. No, no, your more familiar name ; the name your girl would call you by ?

O'Killigain. Jack.

Souhaun [*lingering over it*]. Jack.　What a dear name, Jack!
What a dear name — [*she suddenly stands on tiptoe and
kisses him*] — Jack!

> [*She is running out by the entrance on the right when she
> bumps into Poges laboriously pulling in a gigantic roller
> as high in diameter as he is tall.　The heavy iron side-
> discs are vividly painted in panels of red, white, blue,
> green, and yellow.　When the roller is pulled into the
> room, it can be seen that the 1st Workman is pushing it
> behind.*

Poges [*angrily, as Souhaun bumps into him*]. Eh, eh, there,
look where you are going, can't you?

Souhaun [*amazed at the size of the roller*]. God bless us,
Cyril, what on earth's that you're carting into the
house?

Poges [*petulantly*]. Can't you see what it is?　The roller
you told me to bring through here to the back.　The
roller, the roller I bought to roll the lawn.

Souhaun. But it's too big, man.

Poges. No, it isn't too big.　The man who sold it to me
said that the bigger it was, the more effective it would
be.

Souhaun. But you'll never be able to pull a mighty thing
like that.

Poges. And what's to prevent me from pulling it?
Amn't I pulling it now?　A child of ten could pull it,
the man said; well-balanced, you know, the man said.
Easy to pull, and easier to propel, the man said.

Souhaun. You've just been taken in, Cyril.　The thing's
altogether too big.　[*To the 1st Workman*] Isn't it?

1st Workman. It looks a size too large to me, ma'am.

Poges. The grass in this district needed a special big roller to level it, the man said, and this was the roller to level it.

1st Workman. Sure, that roller ud level a hill.

O'Killigain. The grass'll give way undher that, right enough.

Souhaun. The cheek of declaring that a child of ten could pull it like a toy.

1st Workman. G'way, ma'am, an' did he really say that now ?

Poges. One pull over the lawn with that roller would be enough for the season, the man said.

O'Killigain. An', faith, so it would, an' for every season afther too.

1st Workman. Sure, an' wouldn't a specially powerful horse himself wilt undher a thing like that ! Whoever gave you that, man, musta taken it off an oul' steam-roller.

[*The 3rd Workman appears at entrance to right and proceeds to take an enjoyable interest in what is happening.*

3rd Workman. Mother o' God, looka what he's after buyin' be th' name of a roller ! Isn't it a shame, now, to have imposed on a poor, simple, inoffensive man with a vehicle like that !

Poges [*defiantly*]. It's a bargain, I know it's a bargain ; the man said it's a bargain.

Souhaun [*mockingly*]. The man said, the man said — ay, and you swallowed everything the man said.

O'Killigain [*to 1st Workman*]. Give Mr. Poges a hand to take this machine out of the sight of mortal men.

Poges [*obstinately*]. I'll take it myself, thank you all. Once you got the knack of balancing it, the man said, you could turn it with your little finger, and I believe what the man said.

O'Killigain [*to 3rd Workman*]. Here, you go on back to your work ; go on, off you go !
[*He follows the 3rd Workman out of the room. Poges gives a mighty push to the roller, propelling it slowly to one of the entrances at the back. The 1st Workman goes over and helps him to push it.*

Poges [*fiercely — to 1st Workman*]. Let go, you ! I'll manœuvre it myself. Let go, I tell you !

1st Workman [*as fiercely — to Poges*]. Can't you see, man, the declivity runnin' down the passage that'll lead you, if the roller once gets outa hand, into God knows where ?

Poges [*with a roar into the face of the 1st Workman*]. Let go !
[*The 1st Workman, startled, suddenly lets go his hold on the roller and the roller shoots forward down the declivity, Poges going with it, like a flash of lightning. Heard as he is careering down the passage — with anguish in his voice*] Help !
[*There is a pause of a few moments, then a thud is heard, followed by a rumbling crash of falling bricks and mortar ; then silence again.*

Souhaun [*with vehement rage — running out*]. The blasted fool ! He has rocked the house and killed himself and hasn't made his will !

1st Workman [*staring down the passage*]. Right through the wall he's gone ! [*He runs to where the hole is in the ceiling,*

gets a seat and stands on it. Calling up to the hole] Eh,
Cornelius, eh, quick !
[*The face of the Yellow-bearded Man appears at the hole,
and he thrusts down his head as far as it will go.*

Yellow-bearded Man. Well, what's up now ?

1st Workman [*excitedly*]. The oul' man, the oul' fool, has
gone right through the wall with the roller, an' shook
the house — bang !

Yellow-bearded Man. Didn't I think it was an earthquake !
[*Testily*] An' don't be tellin' me these things while
I'm up here. Can't you wait till I'm down in th' world
o' men, and can enjoy these things happenin' !
[*He angrily takes his head out of the hole. The 1st Workman
gets down from the seat and runs out by entrance on right.*

1st Workman [*running out*]. Mr. O'Killigain, Jack, eh,
Jack !
[*Souhaun returns, followed by Cloyne and Barney leading in
the frightened Poges, powdered with the dust of the falling
mortar. Souhaun arranges a mattress for him on which
he squats, supported by pillows.*

Souhaun. You were warned, you were warned, and you
would have your own way. It's fortunate you are,
indeed, that none of your bones is broken.

Poges [*moaningly*]. Brandy, get me some brandy. [*Barney
goes out and comes back with a glass, brandy, and soda-water.
He fills out a glassful and gives it to Poges. After he has drunk
the brandy — to Cloyne and Barney*] Go way, you two, and
don't stand there gaping at me ! [*They go. Musingly*]
What a rascal that man must be who sold me the roller !
In this simple country, among a simple people, where

the very air is redolent with fairy lore, that such a dangerous and materialistic mind should be lurking!

Souhaun. For God's sake, man, talk sense.

Poges [*shaking his head sorrowfully*]. A gay and charming people, but irresponsible, utterly irresponsible.
[*O'Killigain appears at the right entrance with a cloudy look on his face.*

O'Killigain. Look here, that Basil of yours is goin' about the grounds carrying a fully-cocked gun at a dangerous angle. He'll do harm. Send someone to take it off him, or I'll twist it out of his hands myself! And you'll want to be more careful yourself, or you'll have th' oul' house down!

Poges [*indignantly*]. Oh, what a conceited fool that fellow is — going about to do dangerous damage for want of a little common sense and caution. I don't believe he ever fired a gun in his life. [*To Souhaun*] Go out, dear, and take it off him, before he shoots somebody — and go quick! [*Souhaun runs out by the entrance on the right, and O'Killigain is following her when Poges speaks to him, and halts him at the entrance.*] Oh yes, Mr. O'Killigain, a word please. [*He drinks some more brandy.*] Er, just a word. People are saying — there's a rumour going about that you and — and Miss Avril are — are, well, seen together at times.

O'Killigain. Well?

Poges. Well? Damn it, man, she's a lady, Mr. Stoke's a gentleman, and you're only a — a tradesman!

O'Killigain. Well?

Poges. Well? Oh, don't be welling me! The week she was away from here was bad enough, and very

suspicious.   She had the damned cheek to say she was
with you.

O'Killigain. So she was.

Poges. So she was, was she? Well, it's dishonourable,
and it will have to stop.

O'Killigain. And who'll stop it?

Poges [*firmly*]. I and Mr. Stoke will stop it.

O'Killigain [*quietly*]. You pair of miserable, old, hypo-
critical, wizened old getts, I'd like to see you trying!

Poges [*choking with rage*]. Get out of the house, and come
here no more! I'll write to your parish priest!
I'll—— [*A shot rings out in the grounds outside.*] Good
God, the fool has shot somebody!
  [*O'Killigain goes off in a hurry.   There is a pause.   Then
  the yellow-bearded face is thrust through the hole in the
  ceiling as far as it can go, and shouts down at Poges
  sitting like Buddha on the mattress:*

Yellow-bearded Man [*down to Poges*]. He's shot her, shot her
dead, the poor little innocent creature! Th' charmin'
little thing full o' gaiety an' go!

Poges [*very frightened, up to the Yellow-bearded Man*]. Shot
who, shot who, man? Is it the young lass?

Yellow-bearded Man. Without warnin' he done it, without
a flicker of an eyelid he sent her into the unknown!

Poges [*murmuring in agony*]. Avril! Oh, my God, little
Avril. The curse of the Irish thorn-tree is on us!
The little lass gone. [*Near swooning*] Cut down like a
coloured bubble! The fairies must be manœuvring,
and they'll get me next, maybe. Sweet little Avril the
first to go!

Yellow-bearded Man [*savagely*]. Twenty-five pounds, an' not
a penny less, he'll pay for it, or I'll have the heavy law
on him. I'd ha' let you have her at first for the twenty,
but in some compensation for th' agony of seein' the
poor thing sink down into death, I'll have to get the
other five, or I'll have the heavy law on him !

Poges [*sitting up suddenly*]. What are you talking about,
man ? What's shot, who's killed ?

Yellow-bearded Man. Be th' way, you don't know that that
lean, skulkin' friend o' yours has shot dead me poor
little innocent, poor little cow ! [*Sarcastically*] He
thought it was a bull !

Poges [*bewildered*]. Oh, what a terrible country to have
anything to do with ! My precious vase is gone, my
beautiful bowl is broken ; a wall's demolished, and an
innocent animal's shot dead : what an awful country
to be living in ! A no-man's land ; a waste land ; a
wilderness !

CURTAIN

ACT III

Before the room appears, the sounds of falling rain and swishing winds are heard; and these go on, at intervals, throughout the scene.

The same as in the preceding Act; but some more articles of furniture have been added to the room. Between the entrance to the right at the back, and the right wall, stands what is said to be a Jacobean china-cabinet, filled with old pieces of china. At each side of the larger entrance on the right stands an armoured figure, comical-looking things, with long sharp points protruding where the man's nose (if a man were inside the suit) would certainly be; each figure, standing stiff, holds a long halberd well out from his body. Over these are, crossed, pennons, green and blue, fixed on the wall.

A blazing fire is in the fireplace. No one is in the room. After a moment Poges, dressed in his jazz-patterned overall, with a paper in his hand, runs in and rushes over to the telephone.

Poges [*into the mouthpiece — hurriedly*]. Get me — Oh, good evening, good evening. This is Mr. Poges, Ormond Manor. Get me St. Paul, London : 123. The house is getting on all right, thank you. Be quick, please. [*Warmly*] There's no — seems — in it; I am in a hurry. Oh, the ladies are quite well, sir. No, no, no; I don't want to go to an all-night dance to hear Irish songs sung! I want St. Paul! Eh? No, St. Peter won't do; please don't try to be funny; I am on very serious business. Get me the number I want at once! [*He takes the mouthpiece from his mouth and gives vent to a roaring growl of anger.*] Whether it won't matter a hundred years from now isn't the point, sir. [*Shouting*] Damn it, get me St. Paul! [*Bursting with rage*] No

579

wonder I use bad language. Is this the way business
is done here? No wonder this country's as it is.
What's wrong with it? [*Roaring*] Everything's wrong
with it! You what? You hope my stay here will
help to civilise me a little! [*He looks stupefied; then he slams
the receiver on the hook. Almost instantly the 'phone rings.
He whips off the receiver again and puts it to his ear.*] What
the hell does this — Eh? Who are you? St. Paul?
Good God! This is Poges, Bradford. Oh, it's an
awful place. People helpless, superstitious, and
ignorant. I want you to get me five hundred shares
in the Welldonian Cement Co.; shares are bound to
jump, the minute the bombing starts seriously. They
have jumped? Ah. What, a fiver a share, now?
Well, get me two fifty. What? Not one to be had?
[*Clicking his tongue*] Dtch, dtch. Run on them, eh?
One wouldn't imagine there'd be so many trying to
cash in on splintered bodies. The world, the world,
Bradford! Yes, yes, of course; if there's any going,
snap them up. Righto. Goodbye.

> [*He hangs up the receiver. Barney appears at the entrance
> on the right.*

Barney. Canon Creehewel would like to speak to you, sir.

Poges. Right; send the Canon in to me.

> [*Barney goes; and, in a second or so, the Canon comes in.
> He is inclined to be portly, has rather a hard face, head
> bald at the front, with bushy greying hair at the back of
> his head and over his ears. He is wearing a soft hat,
> sodden with rain, which he puts on the end of the table
> when he comes in; and a long dark cloak, glistening with
> rain too. He comes over eager — to Poges, with a smile
> on his face, and outstretched hand.*

Canon. Ah, my dear friend, I'm so glad to have a chance

of a word with you. How are you liking Clune na
Geera ?

Poges. Splendid, though the weather has been cold and
very wet. Take your cloak off.

Canon [*taking off his cloak. When his cloak is off, it can be
seen that his clothes fit nicely*]. Isn't it a nuisance ; and
we're in for more of it, by all accounts. If it goes on
much more, the district will be a dismal swamp.

Poges [*indicating a seat*]. Sit down, Canon, sit down.
Glass of sherry ?
          [*The Canon sits, and Poges sits too, opposite the Canon.*

Canon. No, thanks. I drink rarely. [*Apologetically*] Good
example, you know. Well, welcome, my dear sir, to
our district. You have a very beautiful house here.
An old house, but a fine one. It is almost a sacred
thing to keep an old thing from dying, sir ; for whatsoever things are just, whatsoever things are honest,
whatsoever things are pure, whatsoever things are
lovely and of good report, are invariably found close to,
and, sometimes, intimately enclosed in the life and
being of ages that have passed, and in the life of men ·
and women who have gone away before us.

Poges [*gratified*]. I wholeheartedly agree with you, reverend
sir. I feel it, I know it.

Canon. With all its frills, its frivolities, its studied
ceremonial, however gaily-coloured its leisure may
have been, the past had in it the core of virtue ; while
the present swirl of young life, I'm saying, with its
feverish sthrut of pretended bravery, its tawdry carelessness about the relation and rule of religion to man,

with all its frantic sthretching of pleasure into every second of life, contains within it a tawny core of fear that is turning darker with every chime of the passing hours !   [*The rain and wind are plainly heard.*

Poges [*leaning towards the Canon — eagerly*]. We must lengthen our arm back to the past and pluck back some of the good things that haven't gone away as far from us as the dead who knew them.

Canon. A worthy enterprise, dear sir, and I hope you and your good people will be a help to us here to bring some of the slow movement of the past into the reckless and Godless speed of the present. [*He leans over towards Poges till their heads nearly touch.*] You and yours can do much to assist the clergy to keep a sensible check on the lower inclinations of the people, a work which should be near the heart of every sensible and responsible man with a stake in the country.

Poges. I'll do all I can. [*Leans back with an air of business importance.*] From the practical point of view, how am I to help ?

. *Canon* [*dropping a little into the idiom of the district*]. Help us to curtail th' damned activity of the devilish dance halls ! Open a dance hall, and in a month or less the innocent disthrict becomes worse than your Leicester Square in London when the night has fallen. If the dance halls are allowed to go ahead without the conthrol of the clergy an' responsible people, God will go from Clune na Geera !

Poges [*shocked*]. Good God ! Such a condition of things among a simple, charming, and pastoral people amazes me.

Canon [*warming to it*]. Arra, wouldn't it sicken you, when the hot days come, to see fools of oul' men an' fools of oul' women too, settin' a bad example, goin' about nearly naked, in their coloured shorts, an' brazen-fac'd lasses mixed among them in low-cut bodices, defiant short skirts, or shorter trousers, murdherin' modesty with a restless an' a reckless hand !

Poges. A lamentable state of affairs entirely, sir.

Canon [*rising and going over close to Poges — intensely*]. An' like Eden, sir, we've a snake in our garden too !

Poges. Oh !

Canon. O'Killigain !

Poges. Ah !   [*The wind and the rain are plainly heard.*

Canon. Guard your womenfolk from him, for no woman is safe with that man. He publicly defends the wearing of low-necked blouses by brazen hussies ; he stands be the practice of courting couples walking the highways and byways be night. Why, one moonlight night, meetin' my curate dhrivin' home a lasciviously-minded girl, O'Killgain tore the stick from the curate's hand an' smashed it into pieces ! A dangerous man, my dear sir, a most dangerous man.

Poges [*a little nervously*]. I'm what you'd call a foreigner down here, and so couldn't interfere with O'Killigain personally ; but what I can do to help you, I certainly will, in any other way.

Canon. Thank you — I guessed you would. Your fifty pounds have helped a lot already. And now I've taken up a lot of your time and must go. [*He takes up his hat.*] By the way, how's the workman I sent you getting along ?

Poges. Which one ?

Canon. The one doing your electric light — a yellow-bearded fellow.

Poges [*emphatically*]. Oh, he's getting along splendidly !

Canon. I'm glad to hear it. A good fellow — a Knight of St. Columbus.

Poges. Well, now, I never knew Columbus was a saint.

Canon [*smiling indulgently*]. Oh yes indeed ; a great Irish saint.

Poges. I always thought he was an American.

Canon. An American ; who ?

Poges. Christopher Columbus.

Canon [*smiling*]. Oh, there were two Columbuses, one Irish and the other — er — American.

    [*As the Canon is about to move away, Avril, followed by Souhaun, dances into the room from an entrance at the back. She is dressed in a low-cut blouse, short tailor-made skirt, and soft leather high boots moulded to her calves and reaching to just below her knees ; and looks, indeed, a very tempting and desirable young hussy. She has a mackintosh over her arm. Souhaun, too, is dressed in very short shorts of a vivid crimson and a black V-necked jersey, looking as enticing, in a more mature way, as young Avril herself. Poges is a little embarrassed, but the good Canon does not flicker an eyelid. Souhaun whips off Poges' overall and shows him in a green jersey and brown shorts.*

Souhaun. You mustn't receive the Canon, dear, in an overall !

Avril. I say, Cyril, old boy, when are we going to get that damned bathroom ? It's a bit thick trying to have a bath in a basin.

> [*She sees the Canon and stops to gaze at him.*

Poges [*introducing her*]. Mr. Stoke's — er — wife — Miss Avril, Canon. [*Introducing Souhaun*] My — er — wife, Miss Souhaun.

Canon [*bowing graciously — to Avril*]. My dear young lady. [*To Souhaun*] Madam, I'm very pleased to know you.

Avril [*nodding to Canon — to Poges*]. Well, when are we going to have a decent bathroom, old cock o' th' walk ?

Poges [*deprecatingly*]. The Canon's here, Avril.

Canon [*jovially*]. Youthful spirits, sir, youthful spirits.

Poges. We'll have a bathroom if we can fit one in without injuring the harmony of the old house. The Tudor period never saw a bathroom. This generation's getting soft, Canon ; we want hardening.

Avril. Bunkum !

Poges [*indignantly*]. It's anything but bunkum ! Shakespeare had to do without one.

Souhaun. But surely, dear, you must know that the Tudor people knew nothing about the use of steam ?

> [*Basil now appears at an entrance at the back, and when he sees the company, he stays there and listens. He is dressed in a yellow jersey and black shorts. No one notices him.*

Poges [*petulantly*]. Steam ! We stand here, in the centre, not of a house, but of a great civilisation, and you mention steam !

Souhaun. In the centre of a hot bath, dear, I can remain in the centre of your civilisation.

Basil [*joining in — looking like a statue in the doorway*]. Not precisely, Souhaun, for it would require, or at least postulate, a full and concentrated retirement through the avenues of thought back to the time of which the visible surroundings are vividly, but quiescently reminiscent. The conception of the conscious thoughts, interrelating with the — with the outward and inward action and reaction of all — or most of the bodily senses, incorporating the outward vision of sight with the inward vision of the inward conception of the — of the fragmentary stumuli — er — stimuli, into a perfect and harmonious whole ; a thing, if I may be allowed to say so, if not impossible, is at least improbable, sitting down, or indeed even standing up, in the middle of a hot bath.

Avril [*with mock enthusiasm*]. Hooray !

Poges [*to the Canon*]. Mr. Stoke, Canon ; cousin to the uncle of a K.G., and passed through Oxford.

Canon. Really ? Well, well, remarkable connections. [*In the far distance a faint clap of thunder is heard ; the Canon cocks his ear to listen.*] I must be off. Bad sign. The soft rain that's falling may change to a downpour, and I've a long way to go.
  [*Canon puts on his cloak. Barney and Cloyne come in carrying a heavy Jacobean chair between them.*

Souhaun. Ah, the Jacobin chair. [*Indicating the way*] Out in the entrance hall, Barney.

Poges. Let's look at it a second. [*Barney and Cloyne pause.*]
Ah, Canon, old things take a lot of beating.

Canon. They do, they do, sir.   Well, I must go now.

Poges [*halting him*]. One second, sir. [*He goes to the table,
writes a cheque, and hands it to the Canon.*] Another little
trifle to keep things going, Canon.

Canon. Twenty-five pounds ! Oh, thank you, and God
bless you, my very dear sir.

Souhaun. You must come to dinner some night.

Canon. I will, I will, with pleasure ; goodbye all.
          [*Midst a murmur of goodbyes the Canon goes out.*

Poges [*indignantly*]. Never showed the slightest interest
in the Jacobin chair. Ignorance ; Irish ignorance !
[*Angrily — to Cloyne and Barney, who are holding the chair
like a salesman displaying a piece of silk*] Bring the damned
thing into the entrance hall, will you, and don't stand
there like fools !
   [*Cloyne, in her hurry, jerks the chair from Barney's hold and
   it bumps to the floor.*

Poges. Oh, butter-fingers, d'ye want to destroy it ?
That's a Jacobin chair, man, a Jacobin chair !

Barney [*with a yell as he carries out the chair with Cloyne*].
Well, if I let a damned chair fall, I didn't knock a
wall down !

Poges. Impudent rascal. The more you do for them the
less they think of you ! [*He bustles into his overall
again.*] Now to business. What'll we do first ? The
rugs ?

Souhaun. There's no use of trying the rugs till you get

your quattrocento bureau in position. Then we'll be able to see if the colour of the rugs suits the bureau.

[*Avril has put on her mackintosh and sidled over to the entrance on right, leading to the hall, and is about to slip out when Basil darts to her side and catches her arm.*

Basil. Where are you slipping off to?

Avril. I'm going for a brisk walk along the bank of the brimming river. I'm fed-up carrying things about to get this foolish old house in order.

Poges. In this weather? Nonsense!

Basil. A good idea; I'll go with you, darling.

Avril [*with a malevolent look at him*]. Wouldn't you like to, eh? Take my advice and don't! [*To Poges*] Ay, in this weather.

[*She goes quickly, leaving Basil, undecided, looking after her.*

Basil [*bitterly*]. She's going to go with O'Killigain!

Souhaun. Nonsense. She can't be out of your sight for a minute but you imagine the girl's with O'Killigain. The rain'll soon send her back. [*To Poges*] You see about locking the bureau, while I get the men to carry it in for you.

[*Poges goes by one of the entrances at the back.*

Basil [*going towards entrance at back*]. I tell you the jade's gone after O'Killigain.

Souhaun [*warningly*]. If I were you, Basil, I shouldn't press hard after little Avril; you are a little too consequential to please her always.

Basil [*maliciously — as he goes out*]. And you, me lady, are a lot too old to please O'Killigain at any time!

[*Souhaun stands stiff for a few moments; then she goes
quickly to the entrance to the hall and is seen beckoning for
one of the workmen.*]

Souhaun [*calling*]. One of you, come here, please.
   [*The 2nd Workman comes into the room and stands near the
   entrance, looking quietly at Souhaun.*]

Souhaun. Send Mr. O'Killigain in to me, please.

2nd Workman. He's gone to the station to see afther a
wagon-load o' bricks.

Souhaun [*slowly, after a pause*]. By himself?

2nd Workman [*after a pause*]. With th' handsome young
woman. [*A pause.*] You're a handsome woman yourself; you're Irish too; an' y'ought to be sensible.

Souhaun [*slowly — a little surprised*]. Am I not sensible,
good man?

2nd Workman [*earnestly*]. Your shinin' eyes can always say
you are; an' soon you'll tire o' nestin' in a dusty nook
with the hills outside an' th' roads for walkin'.

Souhaun. I will, will I?

2nd Workman [*with his eyes looking steadily in hers*]. Ay will
you, an' dance away from a smoky bragger who thinks
th' world spins round on th' rim of a coin; you'll
hurry away from him, I'm sayin', an' it's a glad heart'll
lighten th' journey to a one'll find a place for your little
hand in th' white clouds, an' a place for your saucy
head in th' blue o' th' sky.

Souhaun [*with a touch of mockery*]. Yourself, for instance?

2nd Workman. It's waitin' warm, he'll be, to please you,
highly, an' show you wondhers of a manly manner.

Souhaun [*laughing, with a little catch in the laugh*]. A daughter of the Ormond with a workman !

2nd Workman [*raising his head proudly and looking steadily at her*]. An oldher name is an O'Dempsey, an' an oldher glory's in the name than the honour thrown to th' Earl o' Ormond when he crouched for favour at the English feet !

> [*The 2nd Workman looks at Souhaun and Souhaun looks at the 2nd Workman for a moment, then she turns and goes slowly out by right entrance at back.*

3rd Workman [*appearing at the back left entrance*]. Here, Philib, what'r you doin' ? You're to give us a hand to get in the oul' codger's bureau.

> [*The two of them go out by the entrance to the left at back. After a second or two, the sound of scuffling and of voices are heard just outside the narrow entrance through which the two men have gone out, then Poges comes in with an anxious look on his face, turns and concentrates his gaze on the entrance. Presently the end of a big gilded desk-bureau comes in sight round the corner, with the three workmen puffing, pulling, pushing, and scuffling it along, each giving orders to the other two, to the concern of poor old Poges. When the bureau comes to the entrance, it can be seen to be a very tight fit.*

1st Workman. A little to the ayste, there, a little more to the ayste, can't yous !

2nd Workman. No, west, west ; can't yous see it'll jam if yous cant it to the ayste ? To th' west, I'm tellin' yous !

Poges [*anxiously*]. Easy, boys, easy, now ; take care, take great care ; that's a thing you won't meet every day, you know. I had an anxious time while it was coming over.

3rd Workman [*taking no notice of Poges*]. Where th' hell are yous shovin'? Are yous blind, or wha'? No squirming'll get it in that way. [*Recklessly*] Here, throw th' thing up on its hind legs an' let her go!

Poges [*loudly and anxiously*]. Eh, there, eh; steady, steady. Careful how you handle that. It's not a thing to throw up on its hind legs. I can't have a precious thing like that scratched and mangled. That's a quattrocento piece of furniture, and there isn't another piece like it in the world.

1st Workman [*to the others*]. Hear what the gentleman's sayin' to yous! Amn't I tired tellin' yous yous ud look long before yous ud find such a piece o' furniture in th' whole o' Clune na Geera? Yous can't fling a thing like this about the way you'd fling about an oul' kitchen chair. [*To Poges*] Amn't I right, sir?

Poges. Yes, yes; quite right, my man. Thousands of people would give a fortune to possess a thing like that bureau. So gently, boys, gently. The slightest scratch will do irreparable damage.

1st Workman. See, boys, it's a quattrocento lump o' furniture, an' so needs gentle handlin'. [*To 2nd Workman*] You, Philib, there, give it a sudden swing to the ayste, an' while she's swingin' we'll shoot her ahead.

2nd Workman [*angrily*]. How am I goin' to give her a sudden swing to the ayste when there's no purchase to get a grip of her? Squattrocento or nottrocento, I'm not goin' to let it whip a slice outa my hand!

3rd Workman [*thoughtfully*]. Th' only way to get it in proper is to get a sledge-hammer an' knock down some o' th' archway.

Poges [*indignantly*]. Knock down some of the archway !
You'll do no such thing ! You'll be suggesting that
the house should be knocked down next. There's no
sledge-hammer to be brought within sight of this
precious bureau. [*Leaning over towards the men*] Listen :
this is a piece of quattrocento — understand that, the
whole of you, please !

1st Workman [*to the others*]. There, now, what did I tell
yous ? Yous hear what the gentleman says.

Poges. It ought to go in easily, if you knew your job.
The driver of the furniture van looked at this entrance
and told me not to worry, that the bureau would slide
in without the slightest trouble.

1st Workman [*scornfully*]. Is it Larry Lunigan said that,
now, did he ? Don't mind anything Larry Lunigan
says, sir. If your head was split he'd say it was only a
scratch, to keep your heart up.

3rd Workman. Even if you were dead he'd tell your wife
to wait, an' say you never could be sure of anything.
An' we're not furniture shifters, sir.

Poges. Well, I'm sure of one thing : that bureau is
coming into this room, and coming in without a
scratch.

3rd Workman. 'Course it is.

1st Workman. Time an' patience'll do it.

Poges [*looking closely at the bureau — in anguish*]. Oh, my
God, there's the stone wall eating into its edge ! Get
it away, pull it out, shove it in, you fools ! [*As they
shove*] Wait, wait !

1st Workman [*soothingly*]. I shouldn't worry, sir; a shavin' or two off is th' worst that can happen to it.

Poges. Wait, wait a second. I'll go and get some cushions and pillows to guard the sides from the wall.
[*He runs out by the adjoining entrance for the cushions.*

1st Workman. J'ever see such an oul' fustherer in your life? You'd think the thing was on its way to the kingdom of heaven th' way he's cryin' over it.

3rd Workman. With a look on his ugly oul' gob like the tune th' oul' cow died of.

1st Workman. A quattrocento, mind you, says he.

3rd Workman. Seven hundred years an' more old, says he. Well, it's near time it met its death anyhow.

1st Workman. Here, let's get it in before he comes back billowin' with cushions. It's well able to take a knock or two.

2nd Workman. Here's th' crowbar he wouldn't let us use. [*He lifts up a big crowbar.*] We'll inch it in be main strength. Now, boys, get your shoulders to the quattrocento while I heave with th' bar! [*To the 1st Workman*] Start a shanty, Bill, to give us encouragement.

1st Workman [*chanting quickly, while they all brace themselves*]:
What shall we do with th' dhrunken sailor,
What shall we do with th' dhrunken sailor,
What shall we do with th' dhrunken sailor,
Early in th' mornin'?

All [*together — shoving and tugging vehemently*]:
Pull away, an' up she rises,
Pull away, an' up she rises,

Pull away, an' up she rises,
Early in th' mornin' !

[*Poges rushes in with some cushions in his arms. He is
frantic when he sees what the men are doing.   As he rushes
in he is accompanied by a peal of thunder, louder than the
last, but still fairly faint.   As he comes to a halt near the
bureau the peal ends.*]

Poges [*enraged*]. What, in the devil's name, are you trying
to do ? Do you want to burst it to bits ? Oh, why
did I ever bring my poor quattrocento to a country like
this ! Shove it from the wall, shove it from the wall
till I put a cushion in !

1st Workman. Sure, it won't go far enough away from
the wall to fit a cushion, man.

Poges [*frantically*]. Do what you're told, do what you're
told. [*He drops the cushions, seizes the edge of the bureau and
tries to pull it from the wall.*] Here, somebody, help
me !

[*Before he is aware of it, the 1st Workman leaps on to the
top of the bureau to cross over to him, his heavy hobnailed
boots scraping the top of it.*]

Poges [*shouting at him*]. Get down, get down, man !

1st Workman [*astonished*]. Amn't I only comin' across to
help you.

Poges [*yelling at him*]. That's a quattrocento, that's a
quattrocento, man !

1st Workman. Sure, I know it is.

Poges. Then get off it, get off it — sticking your hobnailed boots through and through it !

1st Workman [*lifting up a foot so that the sole of the boot can be seen*]. Is it that, sir ? Sure, th' nails are worn so soft an' smooth they wouldn't mark th' wing of a butther-fly.

Poges [*roaring*]. Get down, get down at once !
[*The 1st Workman jumps off the bureau back among his mates.*

2nd Workman [*muttering loudly*]. It ud be a godsend to some I know if they opened their eyes to th' signs an' wondhers showin'.

Poges. Now, no talk ; and don't do anything till I give the order.

Men. All right, sir ; go ahead ; we're waitin'.

Poges. When I say go, you swing it to the right, while I swing it to the left.   Are you all ready ?

1st Workman. Ready an' waitin' an' willin'.

Poges. Go !
[*They all swing to the left, and Poges's foot is caught between the bureau and the archway.   He lets a squeal out of him.*

Poges [*in anguish*]. Release my foot, my foot's caught ! Why did you all swing left ? Don't you know right from left ?

3rd Workman. You should have said ayste, sir.

Poges. Shove it off, shove it from my foot !

1st Workman [*placing the crowbar between archway, against the column, and the bureau*]. Now, boys, all together — heave yo-ho ! [*There is a mighty heave from them, one with*

*the bar, the others with their shoulders. The bureau moves
slowly; a crack is heard; the column snaps with the push of
the bar against it and falls over the bureau, which suddenly
shoots forward right into the middle of the room, the men
stumbling after it. The men look triumphantly at the bureau,
the 1st Workman leaning on the crowbar like a warrior leaning
on his spear. Poges rubs his foot and contemplates the damage
to the bureau and the entrance.]* There she is for you now,
sir; right where you want her to be.

3rd Workman. I knew well patience ud do it in the end.

Poges. Oh, look at the bureau and look at the entrance !

1st Workman [*confidently*]. Oh, a spot o' cement an' a lick
o' white paint'll make th' entrance look as young as
ever again.
　　*[Souhaun comes in, followed by Cloyne and Barney, who
　　are carrying a rug between them. They leave it on the
　　floor. Basil is wearing very wide plus-fours.*

Souhaun. We're getting the house into some kind of
order at last. [*She sees the damage.*] Oh, who's caused
all the wreckage ?

Poges [*sarcastically*]. Your very clever countrymen, dear.

Basil [*mockingly*]. And the high opinion they have of
themselves.

2nd Workman. There is sweet music in the land, but not
for th' deaf ; there is wisdom too, but it is not in a
desk it is, but out in th' hills, an' in the life of all
things rovin' round, undher th' blue sky.

Poges [*angrily and despairingly*]. Take this broken column away and be off to your work again. Leave us, leave us, before the house falls !

[*The workmen take away the column and go out by entrance leading to the hall.*

Souhaun. Let us try the rugs, for God's sake ! I can't go out o' th' room but there's damage done. [*Cloyne and Barney spread on the floor a rug scattered over with brightly-coloured geometrical patterns. Cloyne and Barney then go out; the rest stare at the rug.*] Rather gay-looking for the floor of a Tudor house, dear.

Basil [*decidedly*]. Too bright and too modern.

Poges. Where ? how ? why ?

Basil. The Tudors, my dear sir, were a sensible and sober people, and wouldn't tolerate anything that was vulgar or, shall I say, conspicuous.

Souhaun [*with some mockery*]. You see, darling, it was taste, and not steam, that was everything in those days.

Basil. Quite, Souhaun ; taste was the Tudor — er — er — *monumentum aere perennius.*

Poges. I don't know everything, my dear sir ; but I do know something about the period that this house — er — exemplifies ; in fact, the period was so riotous in colour that the men's breeches had one leg blue, the other leg red, or vice versa.

Basil [*with a patronising laugh*]. Ah, old boy, that wasn't the Tudor period.

Poges. What period was it, then ?

Souhaun. The Hiawatha period.

Poges [*indignantly — to Souhaun*]. This is no joke, please. [*To Basil*] What period was it, then ?

Basil [*airily*]. Not the Tudor period, certainly ; no, certainly not, old boy.

Poges [*contemptuously*]. Pshaw ! You don't know it your-self.

> [*From the entrance at back the 2nd Workman appears wheeling a barrow filled with bricks. Passing by the disputants, on his way to the hall entrance, he wheels the barrow over a rug.*

Poges [*shouting at him*]. Where the hell are you going with your dirty barrow ?

2nd Workman [*dropping the shafts of the barrow and turning to answer Poges*]. I'm bringin' a barrow o' bricks to O'Killigain, sir.

Basil. Oh, he's back, is he ?

Poges. What the hell do you think you're doing, man ?

2nd Workman. Amn't I after tellin' you, I'm bringin' a barrow o' bricks to O'Killigain ?

Poges. What d'ye mean, trundling your dirty barrow over a handsome rug laid out for inspection ?

2nd Workman. What d'ye want me to do ? Take th' barrow o' bricks up in me arms an' fly over it ?

Basil [*with great dignity*]. Take it away at once, sir, and don't show impertinence to your betters.

2nd Workman [*eyeing Basil with scorn*]. Jasus, looka what calls itself a betther man than me !

> [*O'Killigain appears at the entrance leading to the hall.*

Poges [*earnestly* — *to the 2nd Workman*]. My man, you're cheeking a cousin of a K.G. whose family goes back to — to — [*turning to Basil*] — William the Conqueror, isn't it ?

Basil [*stiffening* — *with proud complacency*]. Further back, old boy — Alfred ; the last man of the last family fell at the battle of Hastings.

Poges [*impressively*]. There, you see.

Souhaun [*with a sign of mockery in her voice*]. And the ancient gentleman passed through Oxford, too.

O'Killigain [*from the archway*]. The city of dissolute might !

2nd Workman [*with mock deference*]. D'ye tell me that, now ? Why didn't you make me aware of all that glory before I began to speak ? Isn't it an alarmin' thing to hear of the ancientology of a being that I took to be an ordinary man ! An' what might be the ancient gentleman's ancient name ?

Poges. Basil Horatio Nelson Kaiser Stoke.

2nd Workman. A right worthy name. It mayn't have a musical sound, but it has a steady one. There's no flightiness in that name. An' now, would you like to know mine ?

Poges [*amusedly*]. Here, be off with you to your work ; as if your name mattered much.

2nd Workman. Me name's O'Dempsey, of the clan that were lords of Offaly ere his ancient highness here was a thousand years from bein' born ; a clan that sthretches back as far as the time before an Englishman thought of buildin' a weedy shelther ; an' further

back to a day or two afther th' one when the sun herself was called upon to shine.

[*He takes hold of the shafts of the barrow preparatory to
starting off.*

Poges [*contemptuously*]. You don't look it, my poor man !

2nd Workman [*as he wheels the barrow out*]. I feel it ; an' th'
river's risin'.

Poges [*severely — to O'Killigain*]. You really oughtn't to
allow, much more encourage, this silly, ignorant, and
superstitious conceit among your men ; it is something
close to scandalous !

O'Killigain [*quoting*]. They go their own gait : looking
carelessly in the faces of presidents and governors, as
to say, *Who are you?*

Poges [*imperatively*]. Well, it's not going to be heard in
this house ! The bobtag and ragtail must be made to
keep their free-and-easy manners at a distance. Dignity
reigns here.

[*A louder peal of thunder is heard in the distance, and the
room darkens a little.*

O'Killigain. It's raining.

Poges. Eh ?

O'Killigan. It's raining hard.

Souhaun [*shivering*]. And growing cold.

O'Killigain. And old things are perishing.

2nd Workman [*appearing at entrance*]. We're knocking off,
O'Killigain, for the rain is heavier an' the winds are
keen.

O'Killigain. You do well to knock off, for it is waste of time to try to butthress up a tumbling house.

Souhaun [*over to the 2nd Workman*]. The house'll be lone-some without you.

2nd Workman. Come, then, an' abide with the men o' th' wide wathers, who can go off in a tiny curragh o' thought to the New Island with th' outgoin' tide, an' come back be th' same tide sweepin' in again !

Poges [*mockingly — to Souhaun, clapping her on the back*]. There's a high and hearty invitation to you, me lady !
                                        [*Avril comes in and dances over to Basil.*

Souhaun [*gleefully poking Poges in the ribs — to 2nd Workman*]. A long sail on the widening waters, no less ; what gift is offered when the tide returns, good man ?

2nd Workman. With firm-fed men an' comely, cordial women there'll be laughter round a red fire when the mists are risin', when th' roads an' fields are frosty, an' when th' nights is still.

Souhaun [*in a mocking voice — to Poges*]. There now, dear, is there anything more in the world than these that you can give ?

Poges [*with pretended dismay*]. He has me beaten ; what am I going to do at all, at all ?

2nd Workman. A portion, too, with them who, ruddy-faced, were first in battle, with crimson cloak, white coat, an' silver belt studded with splendour by a cunning hand ; a portion, too, with them of paler faces an' dhressed in dimmer clothes, who, fearless, stepped a straight way to th' gallows, silent an' darin' in th' midst of a yelled-out Sassenach song !

Souhaun [*trying to speak mockingly, but developing a slight catch in her voice; for she has been moved by the 2nd Workman's words*]. Where is the lady who would be slow to give a man with such a coaxing way an invitation to her pillow ?

Avril [*who sees her friend is affected. She comes closer to her, and touches her on the arm*]. Souhaun, Souhaun, come an' show me your newest dhresses, an' don't stay listenin' to his thrancin' talk. Don't leave me alone with them.

Souhaun [*shaking off Avril's hand. Falling into the Irish idiom*]. Let me be, girl, for it's right an' lovely listenin' to a voice that's makin' gold embroidery out o' dancin' words.

Poges [*angry and a little nervous*]. It's time to put an end to all this nonsense !

O'Killigain [*ignoring Poges's angry exclamation — to Avril*]. An' you, young girl, sweet bud of an out-spreading three, graft yourself on to the living, and don't stay hidden any longer here. Come where the rain is heavy ,where the frost frets, and where the sun is warm. Avril, pulse of me heart, listen to me, an' let longin' flood into your heart for the call of life. The young thorn-three withered away now, can awaken again, an' spread its fragrance around us. Spit out what's here, an' come where love is fierce an' fond an' fruitful. Come, lass, where there's things to say an' things to do an' love at the endings !

2nd Workman. Jack has spoken fair, an' there's no handsome hindrance near to stop yous. What's here but a creakin' grandeur an' poor witherin' talk ; salt food without a dhrink to go with it ; an' a purple dhryness turnin' timidly to dust !

O'Killigain [*coming close to Avril*]. Aren't my words a star in your ear, lass? Haven't you heard them? They've hit your young breast, lass. Come with me, I say; come away from where rich ignorance is a blessing, an' foolishness a gift from God! Come to th' house on th' hill: the door is open, the fire's alight on the hearth, and the table's laid with a clean white cloth.

Avril. Let another go in by the door; let another eat at the table; let another sit by the fire. Why didn't you come for me, O'Killigain, before the young thorn-tree had shed its blossom, and before the stems began to die?

O'Killigain. I'd other things to do. While you were livin' your lesser life, an' singin' your dowdy songs, I was fightin' in Spain that you might go on singin' in safety an' peace. [*He grips her arm*] I've come for you, now, me love.

Avril [*emotionally and anxious*]. I cannot go where things are said and things are done, for love has had no voice in the beginning of them! [*She tries to free her arm*] Oh, Jack, let me go — you're hurting me!

O'Killigain. It's O'Killigain gives the pressure of comfort and of care. D'ye mind th' hurt when th' hurt's th' hurt of love?

Avril [*passionately*]. Yes, I do! Oh, no, no; I don't, O'Killigain! I don't, I don't! Your pressure on my arm presses on my heart, too. Oh, go away an' leave me lonely!

[*She breaks away and runs to Souhaun, who puts an arm around her.*

O'Killigain. Avril, come out of th' guttherin' candlelight

here to where th' wind puts a flush on the face, ruffles
th' hair, and brings a catch to the breath ; come to th'
one you want ; come to th' man who needs you !

2nd Workman [*to Souhaun*]. An' you, Souhaun, sturdy lily
o' Clune na Geera, come into the love that can fix or
flutther th' stars o' th' sky an' change th' shinin' moon
into a lamp for two. Come to th' one you need ;
come to th' man who wants you !

Souhaun [*half joking, all in earnest*]. If you only had a horse
handy, I'd ride away with you !

2nd Workman [*quietly*]. He's outside waitin'. A loan
from Mr. O'Killigain. An animal can gallop glorious
the livelong day undher th' sound of a steady voice an'
th' touch of a steady hand.

Souhaun [*greatly moved*]. N-no !

2nd Workman [*firmly*]. Yes.

Basil [*rising out of astonishment — to Poges, angrily*]. How
long are you ready to stick this, man ? Send these
impudent fellows away !

Poges [*as if awaking from a stupor — furiously to the two
men*]. Get out, the two of you ! We haven't lived
long enough here to be touched with your insanity !
Get out !

Souhaun [*to 2nd Workman — gently*]. I'll see ; I'll do
whatever Avril advises. [*To Avril*] Come, dear, till we
think out a wonderful answer.

O'Killigain [*to Avril as she is going out*]. Be ready : I'll call,
and come to take you when the river rises !
[*He goes out.*

2nd Workman [*to Souhaun as she is going out after Avril*]. I'll wait outside be th' good gallopin' horse till th' snowy-breasted pearl comes to shimmer on me shouldher.

[*He goes out after O'Killigain.*

Poges [*furious and mocking*]. When the river rises ! Come with me and be my love ! Come into the garden, Maud. Were ever fools so foolish !

Basil [*in angry glee*]. And the fellow with the galloping horse outside ! Boot, saddle, and away ! I never expected to see and hear the like, even in this odd country. [*Slapping Poges on the back — jokingly*] You'd better watch out for the sound of the galloping horse !

Poges [*slapping Basil on the back*]. And you keep an ear open for O'Killigain's call when the river rises !

Basil [*in a mock tragical voice*]. Beware the sound of a galloping horse !

Poges [*in the same manner*]. Beware of O'Killigain's call !
[*Poges goes over to the bureau, opens a drawer, takes some papers out of it, and looks at them ; then he sits down at the bureau, and arranges things in order to write a letter.*

Basil. And, for God's sake, did you hear that vulgar fellow chatting about making the moon do something or other ?

Poges [*arranging things on the bureau*]. Poor crazy fool. They're all a bit demented. Must be the climate. Most amusing.

Basil [*gloomily*]. Yes, amusing up to a point, but hardly reassuring ; no. [*He comes nearer to Poges.*] I don't like it, Poges.

Poges [*a little startled*]. Eh ?

Basil. Well, it isn't exactly comfortable to be living in a community of crazy people, is it ? It may even become dangerous.

Poges [*sitting up straight*]. That's a serious thought, Stoke. Now that you mention it, I do feel the insidious influence of the place. We might become demented too.

Basil. If they allowed us to live long enough.

Poges. Good God, what a thought ! I must have a talk with you about this when I finish this letter.

Basil. You saw for yourself how this influence is even affecting the girls.

Poges [*emphatically*]. The girls ? There you are wrong, Stoke. No, no, not the girls, man. They were just humbugging the poor fools. Nonsense ; not the girls.

Basil [*about to go out*]. You watch. Come up to our room when you've finished the letter, will you ?

Poges. At once. [*Basil goes out. Poges takes some paper, and writes the date on the top right corner. Then he pauses, and evidently begins to think of what has happened. Shaking his head slowly from side to side — musingly*]. Erin, the tear and the smile in thine eye.

    [*He clears his throat with a cough, and settles down to write. The room becomes darker. He has hardly been writing a minute when a curious face appears round the corner of the entrance leading to the hall. It is the stout little face of a little man dressed in neat black clothes covered with a saturated fawn-coloured mackintosh. Big spectacles cover his eyes. A huge fiery-red beard spreads over his chest like a breastplate, reaching to his belly, and*

extending out from his body like a fan turned downwards.
He wears a black jerry hat. When he speaks he is found
to have a little voice. He carries a blackthorn stick in his
hand. As he peeps round he sees Poges at the bureau, and
pulls in his head again. He thrusts it forward again,
steps out, and comes into full view. He pulls his coat
straight with a jerk and smoothes his trousers, and then
comes with a trot into the room, right over to Poges, bends
over towards him, and greets him in a hearty manner. He
is the Postmaster of the village.

Postmaster. An honour it is, sir, to meet the owner of such
a fine house. A house with a histhory. A house
where the genthry joined themselves to merriment and
danced th' stars to sleep ! [*He dances clumsily round the*
room, singing] See me dance the polka, see me dance the
polka, see me dance the polka, as I have done before.
[*He suddenly stops and comes close to Poges.*] I hope I see
you well, sir ? I bear a message from the Postmaster.

Poges [*amazed*]. I am well, thank you ; and what is your
message from the Postmaster ?

Postmaster. When I was outside, an' heard you coughin',
it's well I knew be th' sound of th' cough that the
cough was th' cough of a gentleman.

Poges [*impatiently*]. Yes, yes ; but what is your message ?

Postmaster. Well, as genuine gentleman, you'll be th'
first to agree that a Postmaster with a small wife an'
a large family, an' hardly any salary — I near forgot to
mention that — hardly any salary at all, if the thruth
was told, as a thrue gentleman, you'll agree that a man
like that is handicapped, an' has a claim on a gentleman's sympathy.

Poges. But I can't make his wife bigger or his family smaller, can I?

Postmaster. Sure, I know you can't, an' that's not what the Postmaster's complainin' about. [*He leans over Poges.*] But th' poor man needs sleep, he needs his share o' sleep.

Poges [*humouring him — thinking his visitor is out of his mind*]. Yes, yes; of course, the poor man needs sleep. We all need sleep. That's a fine stick you have in your hand, sir; can I see it?

Postmaster [*holding up the stick and stretching it away from Poges*]. Ay, ay, a fine blackthorn. There y'are; look at it as long as you like — [*warningly*] — but don't lay a finger on it. There's a stick could give a man a crack a man ud remember!

Poges [*nervous*]. Oh? I can't see it well from here; let me take it in my hand for a moment.

Postmaster. Sorra a second you're goin' to have it in your hand. That stick has never been outa me father's hand an' it has never been outa mine. D'ye know why?

Poges. No, friend, I don't.

Postmaster. Guess, now, guess.

Poges [*smiling sweetly*]. I haven't the slightest idea, friend; I couldn't guess.

Postmaster. This's th' very stick that me oul' fellow made a swipe at Parnell with — th' scandaliser of Ireland's holy name, a swipe that, had it got home, ud a laid Parnell up for a month o' Sundays! Now, as a thrue gentleman, wouldn't you say I was right?

Poges. Yes, yes ; quite right.

Postmaster. Well, havin' settled that, let's settle th' other : amn't I right in sayin' that every man should have his share o' sleep ?

Poges. Yes, yes ; of course.

Postmaster. Well, then, amn't I right in sayin' that th' poor Postmaster should have his share o' sleep too ?

Poges. To be sure. [*Rising from his seat*] Now, I must be going. [*A fairly loud clap of thunder is heard, followed by the sound, first of a trotting horse, then of one going off at a gallop. They listen till the sounds die in the distance.*] A horse going off at a gallop. [*He makes a move away*] I must go to see what's wrong.

Postmaster [*waving him back with the stick*]. Wait a minute — I'm not done yet. You've just said the poor Postmaster should have his share o' sleep — didn't you ?

Poges [*impatiently*]. Yes, yes, friend.

Postmaster. I knew you'd say that. [*He stretches out his hand to Poges.*] Lave it there. [*He shakes hands with Poges.*] Now I won't have to be keepin' one eye open an' me ear glued to the bell, for fear of a toll call or a thrunk call, afther ten o'clock at night, an' I settlin' down for a cosy sleep.

Poges [*the truth dawning on him*]. Oh, so you're the Postmaster, are you ? So it was you who delayed me when I wanted St. Paul ?

Postmaster. Didn't you know that ?

Poges. The telephonic system here is an all-night one, isn't it ?

Postmaster. 'Course it is, but that says nothin'.

Poges [*decidedly*]. Look here, my man ; I'm a business man, and have to make calls at all hours of the night ; I can't be thinking of every man having an honest night's sleep.

Postmaster. 'Course you can't ; it's only the poor Postmaster that you've got to keep in mind.

Poges [*severely*]. Look here, my man, as long as I pay for the service, the service will have to be supplied. Good day.

Postmaster. There isn't a gentleman in th' whole disthrict ud think, except in th' case o' sudden death or disasther, of givin' a tinkle afther th' hand o' th' clock had passed the figure of half-past nine o' night.

Poges. Take yourself and your stick away out of the house, man !

Postmaster [*mimicking him*]. Take yourself and your stick away outa the house, man. Is it comin' down here to teach us good manners an' feelin' y'are, an' you puttin' a surly gob on you when you're asked to fall in with the sensible an' thried institutions of the neighbourhood ?

> [*While they have been talking together, the room has darkened still more, and Poges sharply tugs the string that puts on the light; the wind has risen and can be heard occasionally blowing through the trees outside, and even shaking the old house.*

Poges [*in a rage*]. Go on, get out !

> [*As he says this, a long, loud peal of thunder is heard.*

Postmaster. D'ye hear that ? There won't be many thrunk

calls goin' for a while, an' th' poor Postmaster'll have a sweeter night's sleep than some I know. [*He bends towards Poges.*] When — the river — rises !

[*The room has darkened; the wind rises; the one light in the room flickers. The Postmaster and Poges watch it. Then the Postmaster turns to go, but halts when a Figure of a man is seen standing at the entrance leading to the hall. He is dressed from head to foot in gleaming black oilskins, hooded over his head, just giving a glimpse of a blue mask, all illumined by the rays of flickering lightning, so that The Figure seems to look like the spirit of the turbulent waters of the rising river. The Postmaster goes back, startled, till he is beside Poges, and the two men stand and stare at the ominous Figure. Basil, Barney; and Cloyne appear at the entrances at back, each holding a lighted lantern in his and her hand. They are very frightened. They too hold up their lanterns and stare at The Figure.*]

Basil. The river is rising !

Barney. Risin' high !

Cloyne. An' will overwhelm us all !

The Figure [*in a deep voice*]. The river has broken her banks and is rising high ; high enough to come tumbling in on top of you. Cattle, sheep, and swine are moaning in the whirling flood. Trees of an ancient heritage, that looked down on all below them, are torn from the power of the place they were born in, and are tossing about in the foaming energy of the waters. Those who have lifted their eyes unto the hills are firm of foot, for in the hills is safety ; but a trembling perch in the highest place on the highest house shall be the portion of those who dwell in the valleys below !

[*The lightning ceases for a moment; the entrance becomes dark, and The Figure disappears.*

Poges [*frantic*]. What shall we do? what must we do? what can we do?

Basil [*in anguish*]. We're lost!

Cloyne [*sinking down on her knees*]. King o' th' Angels, save us!

Barney [*clasping his hands*]. Amen! A nice pass we've come to when we have to call for help in a Tudor house! [*To Basil and Poges*] It's the evil livin' of you two buckos that has brought this disaster upon us!

Poges [*bawling*]. Souhaun, Souhaun! O'Killigain, help!

Basil [*roaring at Poges*]. You made us come down here!

Poges [*roaring at Basil*]. You're a liar, it was you!

Postmaster [*bringing down the blackthorn stick with a bang on the quattrocento bureau*]. Eh, order, order, law an' order there; steady! Measures o' safety to be taken. [*Thrusting his stick towards Poges — sharply*] Has the highest room in the house a way to the roof — quick!

Poges [*answering at once*]. Yes.

Cloyne [*in anguish*]. Th' roof — oh, my God!

Postmaster [*rapidly*]. Up with us all with bread and wine, with firewood and coal, and an axe. Up!

Poges. An axe?

Postmaster. To hack whatever suitable furniture we can get into a raft if we're swirled off th' roof. [*Driving Cloyne and Barney before him*] Up!

Poges [*loudly*]. Souhaun, Souhaun, where's Souhaun?

Basil [*impatiently*]. Come on, and come up.
  [*Avril comes in from one of the back entrances. She is covered with a green mackintosh, and a coloured scarf, peasant-wise, is over her head. She carries a small case. She passes between the two men without a word, and stands still near the entrance leading to the hall, looking out before her.*

Poges [*staring at her*]. What are you doing here? What are you watching? [*Avril stands still and silent.*] Where's Souhaun, where's Souhaun?

Avril [*quietly — without looking round*]. She's gone.

Poges. Gone? How? Where?

Avril [*quietly — still not moving*]. Gone with the wind; gone with the waters; gone with the one man who alone saw something in her!

Poges [*raging*]. What, with that loud-mouthed, ignorant, superstitious, low-born, half-mad Irishman! Oh, she's nicely rooked me! She was with him on the galloping horse that galloped away, was she? Oh, she's nicely rooked a simple, honest, loving-hearted, foolish man! She's gone, is she?

Avril. An' well it would be if I was with her.

Poges. You damned slut, are you in your mind as bad as she is?

Avril [*indicating Basil*]. The mind that went with him is as bad as the mind that went with you.

Basil [*sneeringly*]. You lost the chance you had to get away from it.

Avril. He said he'd come when the river rises.

O'Killigain [*outside — loudly*]. Avril !

Avril [*with a start of joy*]. O'Killigain ! O'Killigain !
[*O'Killigain appears, his trench coat drenched and his hair
soaking, at the entrance.*

O'Killigain. My barque is waiting, love ; come !
[*Avril picks up the case and runs to O'Killigain.*

Basil. Honest, decent woman, she carries the booty of
her friends in her pack !

Avril [*quietly*]. I gave more than I got, you gilded monkey.
It's winnowed of every touch of life I'd be if I stayed
with th' waste of your mind much longer. [*She taps
the case.*] Th' thrinkets I wormed out of you are all
here, an' here they stay, for th' wages were low for
what was done for you.

Poges [*sneering*]. And gentleman O'Killigain will happier
be with a harlot's fortune !

O'Killigain [*good-humouredly*]. Of course he will. Th'
good things of this life are good for all, an' a pretty girl
looks handsomer in arms that are fit and fond to hold
her. You have had your day, like every dog. Your
Tudors have had their day, and they are gone ; and th'
little heap o' purple dust they left behind them will
vanish away in th' flow of the river. [*To Avril*] Come,
love, to my little house up on th' hill.
[*He goes out with Avril. After a moment the sound of oars
are heard splashing the waters, and O'Killigain is heard
singing.*

O'Killigain [*singing : other voices, outside, join in the chorus*] :

Come from the dyin' an' fly from th' dead,
Far away O !
An' now, with th' quick, make your home an' your bed,
With a will an' a way, away O !

Then away, love, away,
Far away O !
To live any life that is looming ahead,
With a will an' a way, away O !

Away from all mouldherin' ashes we row,
Far away O !
Takin' th' splendour of livin' in tow,
With a will an' a way, away O !

Then away, love, away,
Far away O !
Where th' lightning of life flashes vivid we go,
With a will an' a way, away O !

    [*Poges stands still, listening till the song fades away in the
       distance. Suddenly Basil clutches his arm.*

Basil [*frantically*]. Look, the waters are tumbling towards
   us ! Run, man !
    [*He tears up the passage while Poges follows more slowly.*

Poges [*going out*]. My poor little quattrocento, the waters
   are about to cover thee ! My comfort's gone, and my
   house of pride is straining towards a fall. Would to
   God I were in England, now that winter's here !
    [*He disappears down the passage as the green waters tumble
    into the room through the entrance from the hall.*

CURTAIN

COME FROM THE DYIN'

Come from the dy-in' an' fly from the dead

Far___ a-way O!___ An' now, with the quick, make your

home an' your bed, With a will and a way a-way

O! Then a-way, love__, a-way,

Far___ a-way O!___ To live an-y life that is

looming a-head, With a will an' a way a-way O!

THE MAID OF BUNCLODY

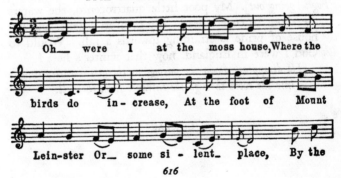

Oh___ were I at the moss house, Where the

birds do in-crease, At the foot of Mount

Lein-ster Or___ some si-lent___ place, By the

streams of Bun - clo - dy Where all

plea - sures do__ meet, And__ all I would

ask is One kiss from you, sweet.

O'KILLIGAIN'S LILT

They may rail at this life, from the hour I be-gan it, I

found it a life full of kind-ness and bliss; And un-

-til they can show me some hap - pi - er pla - net, More

so - cial and bright, I'll con - tent me with this.

THERE ARE MANY FAIR THINGS IN
THIS WORLD

There are ma-ny fair things in this world as it goes, The

blue skies of__ sum-mer, the flush-ing red rose, But of

all the fair blossom-ing things that men see, A -

come‑ly‑built lass is the near‑est to me, A
come‑ly‑built lass is the dear‑est to me.

HEY, HEY, THE COUNTRY'S HERE

Ru‑ral scenes are now our joy, Farm‑er's boy,
Milk‑maid coy, Each like a new‑ly paint‑ed toy
CHORUS
In the bosk‑y coun‑try. Hey, hey, the country's here, The
country's there, It's ev‑'ry where, We'll have it, now, last
thing at night, And the ve‑ry first thing in the morn‑ing!

THERE'S LIFE WITH TH' LASSES

Come in or go out or just stay at the door, With a
girl on each arm an' one stand‑ing be‑fore, Sure, the
more that I have, the more I a‑dore, For there's
much slower
life with the lass‑es, says Ro‑ry O' More!

618

Red Roses for Me

To Dr. J. D. Cummins
in memory of the grand chats
around his surgery fire

My thanks to Bridgid Edwards
for setting down the airs to the songs

CHARACTERS IN THE PLAY

MRS. BREYDON

AYAMONN BREYDON, *her son*

EEADA
DYMPNA } *Mrs. Breydon's neighbours in the house*
FINNOOLA

SHEILA MOORNEEN, *Ayamonn's sweetheart*

BRENNAN O' THE MOOR, *owner of a few oul' houses*

A SINGER, *a young man with a good voice*

ROORY O'BALACAUN, *a zealous Irish Irelander*

MULLCANNY, *a mocker of sacred things*

REV. E. CLINTON, *Rector of St. Burnupus*

SAMUEL, *verger to the church*

INSPECTOR FINGLAS, *of the Mounted Police, and the Rector's churchwarden*

1ST MAN
2ND MAN } *neighbours in the next house to Breydons'*
3RD MAN

DOWZARD } *members of St. Burnupus' Select Vestry*
FOSTER

A LAMPLIGHTER

1ST RAILWAYMAN

2ND RAILWAYMAN

SCENES

ACT I.—Two-roomed home of the Breydons.

ACT II.—The same.

ACT III.—A Dublin street, beside a bridge over the river Liffey.

ACT IV.—Part of the grounds round the Protestant Church of St. Burnupus. In this Act the curtain is lowered for a few minutes to denote the passing of a few hours.

TIME.—A little while ago.

Act I

The front one of two rather dilapidated rooms in a poor working-class locality. The walls, whitewashed, are dwindling into a rusty yellowish tinge. The main door, leading to the hall, is at the back, a little towards the right. The fireplace is in the right-hand wall, and a brilliant fire is burning in the large, old-fashioned grate. In the centre of the room is an old ebony-hued table on which stands a one-wick oil-lamp, its chimney a little smoky from the bad oil in the reservoir. Some books lie on the table, some paper, coloured chalks, a pen, and a small bottle of ink. In the left wall, up towards the back, is the door leading to the second room. Below this door is a horsehair sofa showing signs of old age. On it, to the head, is a neatly folded bundle of sheets and blankets, showing that it is used as a bed during the night. To the left of the main door at back is a large basket used by actors when on tour. On the other side of this door is an ordinary kitchen dresser on which some of the crockery is on the ledge, for the upper shelf is filled with a row of books, by the look of them second-hand. Over the basket, on the wall, is tacked a childlike brightly-coloured pastel of what is meant to be a copy of one of Fra Angelico's angels blowing a curved and golden trumpet ; and beside it is a small coloured reproduction of Constable's " Cornfield ". In the same wall, towards the back, is a large, tall window, nearly reaching the ceiling, and, when one is in front of it, the top of a railway signal, with transverse arms, showing green and red lights, can be seen. Under this window, on a roughly made bench, stand three biscuit tins. In the first grows a geranium, in the second, musk, and in the third, a fuchsia. The disks of the geranium are extremely large and glowing ; the tubular blooms of the golden musk, broad, gay, and rich ; and

*the purple bells of the fuchsia, surrounded by their long white
waxy sepals, seem to be as big as arum lilies. These crimson,
gold, and purple flowers give a regal tint to the poor room.
Occasionally in the distance can be heard the whistle of an engine,
followed by its strenuous puffing as it pulls at a heavy rake of
goods wagons. A chair or two stand about the room.*

*It is towards the evening of a mid-spring day, and the hour
would make it dusk, but it is darker than that, for the sky is
cloudy and rain is falling heavily over the city.*

*Ayamonn and his mother are in the room when the scene
shows itself. He is tall, well built, twenty-two or so, with
deep brown eyes, fair hair, rather bushy, but tidily kept, and
his face would remind an interested observer of a rather handsome, firm-minded, thoughtful, and good-humoured bulldog. His
mother is coming up to fifty, her face brownish, dark eyes with a
fine glint in them, and she bears on her cheeks and brow the
marks of struggle and hard work. She is dressed in a black
jacket, fitting close, marred by several patches, done very neatly,
dark-blue skirt, a little faded, and rather heavily-soled boots. At
the moment this is all covered with a rich blue velvet cloak,
broidered with silver lace, and she is sitting on a kitchen chair
covered with a dark-red, rather ragged cloth.*

*Ayamonn wears a bright-green silk doublet over which is a
crimson velvet armless cloak bordered with white fur. The back
part of the cloak is padded so as to form a big hump between his
shoulders. Across his chest is a dark-green baldric from which
hangs a scabbard. A cross-hilted sword is in his hand. On his
head he has a black felt hat with narrow turned-up rims. A
black band goes round the hat, and a crimson feather sticks up
from it. His legs are in heavy, black, working corduroy
trousers, and he wears heavy hobnailed boots. She and he are in
an intensely listening attitude.*

Mrs. Breydon [*whispering over to Ayamonn*]. She's gone ;

wanted to borra something else, I suppose. They're feverish with borrowing in this blessed house !

Ayamonn. Damn her for a troublesome fool ! Where's this I was when the knock came ?

Mrs. Breydon. I was just goin' to say
     Ay, an' for much more slaughter after this,
     O God ! forgive my sins, and pardon thee !

Ayamonn [*looking at the floor*]. Oh yes ! [*He recites*] —
     What, will th' aspiring blood of Lancaster
     Sink to the ground ? I thought it would have
         mounted. [*He holds the sword aloft, and stares at it*]
     See how my sword weeps for the poor king's
         death !
     O, may such purple tears be always shed
     For those that wish the downfall of our house !
     If any spark of life be yet remaining,
     [*He stabs at the floor*] Down, down to hell ; and say
         I sent thee hither !

     [*A knuckle-knock is heard at the door. Ayamonn and Mrs. Breydon stiffen into a silent listening attitude. A fine baritone voice, husky with age, is heard speaking outside.*

Voice. Is anyone in or out or what ? [*Louder raps are given as Ayamonn steals over, and places his back to the door.*] Eh, in there — is there anyone movin', or is the oul' shack empty ?

Mrs. Breydon [*in a whisper*]. Oul' Brennan on the Moor. He was here before, today. He's got his rent for his oul' houses, an' he wants to be told again that the Bank of Ireland's a safe place to put it.

Ayamonn [*warningly*]. Ssshush !

Voice. No answer, eh? An' me afther seein' a light in
th' window. Maybe they are out. For their own
sakes, I hope they are; for it's hardly an honourable
thing to gainsay a neighbour's knock.

[*The sound of feet shuffling away is heard outside, and then
there is silence for a few moments.*

Mrs. Breydon. He's gone. He's always a bit lively the
day he gets his rents. How a man, with his money,
can go on livin' in two rooms in a house an' sthreet
only a narrow way betther than this, I don't know.
What was he but an oul' painter an' paperhanger,
starvin' to save, an' usin' his cunnin' to buy up a few
oul' houses, give them a lick o' paint, and charge the
highest rent for th' inconvenience of livin' in them!

Ayamonn. I wish he'd keep himself and his throubles far
away from me now. I've higher things to think of
and greater things to do than to be attached to the
agony of an old fool for ever afraid a fistful of money'll
be snatched away from him. Still, he isn't a miser,
for he gives kids toys at Christmas, and never puts less
than half a crown on the plate in church on Sundays.

Mrs. Breydon. So well he may!

Ayamonn. What was he sayin' when he was here before?

Mrs. Breydon. Oh, th' usual question of askin' me what I
thought about the Bank of Ireland; mutterin' about
somebody not payin' the rent; and that his birthday's
due tomorrow.

Ayamonn [*looking at the chair*]. I'll have to get a loan of a
chair with arms on, and someway make them golden to
do the thing proper in the Temperance Hall; and
I'll paint for the back of it, on thin cardboard, a

cunning design of the House of Lancaster, the red rose, so that it'll look like a kingly seat.

Mrs. Breydon. Th' killin' o' th' king be th' Duke o' Gloster should go down well, an' th' whole thing should look sumptuous.

Ayamonn. So it will. It's only that they're afraid of Shakespeare out of all that's been said of him. They think he's beyond them, while all the time he's part of the kingdom of heaven in the nature of everyman. Before I'm done, I'll have him drinking in th' pubs with them !

Mrs. Breydon. I don't know that he'll go well with a Minstrel Show.

Ayamonn. He'll have to go well. If only King Henry doesn't rant too much, saw the air with his hands, and tear his passion to tatthers. The old fool saw someone do it that way, and thinks it must be right. [*With a sigh.*] I daren't attempt to recite my part now, for Oul' Brennan on the Moor's waitin' and listenin' somewhere down below ; so I'll just get it off by heart. How old does he say he'll be tomorrow ?

Mrs. Breydon. Only seventy-six, he says, an' feelin' as if he was lookin' forward to his twenty-first birthday.

Ayamonn. Well, he won't have long to wait.

Mrs. Breydon [*slyly*]. He was muttherin', too, about some air or other on the oul' piano he has at home.

Ayamonn [*springing up from where he has been sitting*]. It's one o' mine he's put an air to ! [*He rushes from the room and returns in a few moments.*] He's not there ; gone home, I suppose. [*Irritably*] I wish you'd told me that at first.

Mrs. Breydon. I'd thry to rest a little, Ayamonn, before you go to work. You're overdoing it. Less than two hours' sleep today, and a long night's work before you. Sketchin', readin', makin' songs, an' learnin' Shakespeare : if you had a piano, you'd be thryin' to learn music. Why don't you stick at one thing, an' leave the others alone ?

Ayamonn. They are all lovely, and my life needs them all.

Mrs. Breydon. I managed to get on well enough without them. [*A pause. She goes over to the window and tenderly touches the fuchsia.*] There's this sorryful sthrike, too, about to come down on top of us.

Ayamonn [*sitting in the red-covered chair and reading Shakespeare — quietly and confidently*]. There'll be no strike. The bosses won't fight. They'll grant the extra shilling a week demanded.

Mrs. Breydon [*now fingering the musk*]. I thought this Minstrel Show was being run to gather funds together ?

Ayamonn [*impatiently*]. So it is, so it is ; but only in case the strike may have to take place. I haven't much to do with it, anyway. I'm with the men, spoke at a meeting in favour of the demand, and that's all.

Mrs. Breydon. You'll undhermine your health with all you're doin', tearin' away what's left of your time be runnin' afther—— [*She checks herself, and becomes silent.*

Ayamonn [*lowering his book to his lap — angrily*]. Go on — finish what you started to say : runnin' afther who ?

Mrs. Breydon. Nobody, nobody.

Ayamonn. Runnin' afther Sheila Moorneen — that's what was in your mind to say, wasn't it ?

Mrs. Breydon. If it was aself; is there a new law out that a body's not to think of her own thoughts.

Ayamonn [*sharply*]. What have you got against the girl?

Mrs. Breydon. Nothing. As a girl, I'd say she's a fine coloured silken shawl among a crowd of cotton ones. A girl I'd say could step away from the shadowy hedges where others slink along, tiltin' her head as she takes the centre of the road for the entherprisin' light o' day to show her off to everyone. Still——

[*She stops speaking again.*

Ayamonn. Ay, but still what? You've a maddenin' way of never finishing some of your sentences.

Mrs. Breydon [*braving it out*]. She's a Roman Catholic; steeped in it, too, the way she'd never forgive a one for venturin' to test the Pope's pronouncement.

Ayamonn. And who wants to test the Pope's pronouncement? Life and all her vital changes'll go on testing everything, even to the Pope's pronouncement. D'ye think I've laboured as I have, and am labourin' now, to furnish myself with some of the greatness of the mighty minds of the past, just to sink down into passive acceptance of the Pope's pronouncement? Let the girl believe what she may, reverence what she can : it's her own use of her own mind. That she is fair to look upon, charming to talk with, and a dear companion, is well and away enough for me, were she even a believer in Mumbo Jumbo, and had a totem pole in her front garden.

Mrs. Breydon. There's worse still than that in it.

Ayamonn. Worse, is there? An' what may that be?

Mrs. Breydon. She's th' child of a sergeant in the Royal Irish Constabulary, isn't she?

Ayamonn. Well, she can't help it, can she?

Mrs. Breydon. I know that; but many have murmured again' a son of mine goin' with the child of a man crouchin' close to their enemy.

Ayamonn. Everything, it seems, is against her, save herself. I like herself, and not her faith; I want herself, and not her father.

Mrs. Breydon. The bigger half of Ireland would say that a man's way with a maid must be regulated by his faith an' hers, an' the other half by the way her father makes his livin'.

Ayamonn. And let the whole world join them! Fair she is, and her little ear's open to hear all that I thry to say, so, were she the child of darkness aself, I'd catch her hand and lead her out and show her off to all men.

Mrs. Breydon. She wouldn't be a lot to look at afther she'd wended her way through poverty with you for a year an' a day.

Ayamonn. She gives no honour to gold; neither does her warm heart pine for silks and satins from China and Japan, or the spicy isles of Eastern Asia. A sober black shawl on her shoulders, a simple petticoat, and naked feet would fail to find her craving finer things that envious women love.

Mrs. Breydon. Ah, go on with you, Ayamonn, for a kingly fool. I'm tellin' you th' hearts of all proper girls glow with the dhream of fine things; an' I'm tellin' you, too, that the sword jinglin' on th' hip of Inspector Finglas, the red plume hangin' from his menacin' helmet, an' th' frosty silver sparklin' on his uniform, are a dazzle o' light between her tantalised eyes an' whatever she may happen to see in you.

Ayamonn. Tell me something else to add to my hope.

Mrs. Breydon. Go on readin', an' don't bother to listen to your mother.

Ayamonn [*going over and gently putting his hands on her shoulders*]. I do listen, but I am drifting away from you, Mother, a dim shape now, in a gold canoe, dipping over a far horizon.

Mrs. Breydon [*with a catch in her voice*]. I did an' dared a lot for you, Ayamonn, my son, in my time, when jeerin' death hurried your father off to Heaven.

Ayamonn. It's I who know that well : when it was dark, you always carried the sun in your hand for me ; when you suffered me to starve rather than thrive towards death in an Institution, you gave me life to play with as a richer child is given a coloured ball. [*He gently lifts up her face by putting a hand under her chin.*] The face, the dear face that once was smooth is wrinkled now ; the eyes, brown still, that once were bright, have now been dimmed by a sthrained stare into the future ; the sturdy back that stood so straight, is bending. A well-tried leaf, bronzed with beauty, waiting for a far-off winter wind to shake it from the tree.

Mrs. Breydon [*gently removing his hand from her chin*]. I have a tight hold still. My back can still bear many a heavy burden; and my eyes, dimmer now than once they were, can still see far enough. Well, I betther take this fancy robe from off me, lest it give me gorgeous notions.

[*She takes off her robe, and leaves it carefully folded on the basket, then goes over and arranges the fire. Ayamonn looks thoughtfully out of the window, then takes off cloak, sword, and hat, leaving them carefully on the basket.*

Ayamonn [*musingly*]. He'll hardly come tonight in this

rain. If he does, I'll get him to read the King's part, and do mine over again.

Mrs. Breydon. Who's to come tonight?

Ayamonn. Mullcanny : he's searching Dublin for a book he wants to give me ; and, if he got it, he was to bring it tonight — *The Riddle of the Universe.*

Mrs. Breydon. That's another one I wouldn't see too much of, for he has the whole neighbourhood up in arms against his reckless disregard of God, an' his mockery of everything solemn, set down as sacred.

Ayamonn. Oh, Tim is all right. The people are sensible enough to take all he says in good part ; and a black flame stands out in a brightly-coloured world.

Mrs. Breydon. You don't know them, if you say that ; he'll meet with a mishap, some day, if he doesn't keep his mouth shut.

Ayamonn. Nonsense.

[*She has quietly slipped a shawl around her, and is moving to the door so silently as to seem to want to prevent Ayamonn from noticing her movements, when the door opens and Eeada, Dympna, Finnoola, and several men, appear there. The three women come a little way into the room; the men stay around the door. All their faces are stiff and mask-like, holding tight an expression of dumb resignation; and are traversed with seams of poverty and a hard life. The face of Eeada is that of an old woman; that of Dympna, one coming up to middle age ; and that of Finnoola, one of a young girl. Each shows the difference of age by more or less furrows, but each has the same expressionless stare out on life.*

[*Dympna is carrying a statue of the Blessed Virgin, more than two feet high, in her arms. The figure was once a*

*glory of purest white, sparkling blue, and luscious gilding;
but the colours have faded, the gilt is gone, save for a spot
or two of dull gold still lingering on the crown. She is
wearing a crown that, instead of being domed, is castellated
like a city's tower, resembling those of Dublin ; and the
pale face of the Virgin is sadly soiled by the grime of the
house. The men are dressed in drab brown, the women in
a chill grey, each suit or dress having a patch of faded
blue, red, green, or purple somewhere about them.*

Eeada [*to Mrs. Breydon*]. Could you spare a pinch or two of
your Hudson's soap, Mrs. Breydon, dear, to give the
Blessed Virgin a bit of a wash? [*To all in general*]
Though I've often said it's th' washin' that's done
away with the bonnie blue of th' robe an' th' braver
gold of its bordhers an' th' most o' th' royalty outa th'
crown. Little Ursula below's savin' up her odd
pennies to bring Her where She'll find a new blue
robe, an' where they'll make the royalty of th' gilt
glow again ; though whenever she's a shillin' up, it's
needed for food an' firin' ; but we never yet found
Our Lady of Eblana averse to sellin' Her crown an'
Her blue robe to provide for Her people's need. [*Mrs.
Breydon gives half a packet of soap powder. Gratefully*]
Thank you, ma'am, an' though y'are of a different
persuasion, Our Blessed Lady of Eblana's poor'll bless
you an' your fine son for this little tribute to Her
honour and circumspect appearance before the world.

The Rest [*murmuring*]. Ay will She, an' that's a sure thing.
[*They open a way for Eeada to pass out, with Dympna
carrying the statue, following in a kind of simple procession. Mrs. Breydon is moving slowly after them.*

Ayamonn [*who has noticed her under his eyes*]. You're not
going out again, surely — on a night like this, too ?

Mrs. Breydon. Not really ; only down the road to Mrs. Cashmore's. She's not too well ; I promised I'd dhrop in, and see to a hot dhrink or something for her before she wandhered off to sleep.

Ayamonn [*irritably*]. You think more of other homes than you do of your own ! Every night for the past week you've been going out on one silly mission or another like an imitation sisther of charity.

Mrs. Breydon. I couldn't sit quiet knowin' the poor woman needed me. I'd hear her voice all through the night complainin' I never came to give her a hot dhrink, settle her bed soft, an' make her safe for th' lonely hours of th' slow-movin' night.

Ayamonn. A lot they'd do for you if you happened to need help from them.

Mrs. Breydon. Ah, we don't know. A body shouldn't think of that, for such a belief would dismay an' dismantle everything done outside of our own advantage. No harm to use an idle hour to help another in need.

Ayamonn. An' wear yourself out in the process ?

Mrs. Breydon [*with a sigh*]. I'll wear out, anyway, sometime, an' a tired ould body can, at least, go to its long rest without any excuse.

> [*As she opens the door to go out, Sheila appears on the threshold. She is a girl of about twenty-three, fairly tall, a fine figure, carrying herself with a sturdiness never ceasing to be graceful. She has large, sympathetic brown eyes that dim, now and again, with a cloud of timidity. Her mouth is rather large but sweetly made ; her hair is brown and long, though now it is gathered up into a*

thick coil that rests on the nape of her neck. She is dressed in a tailor-made suit of rich brown tweed, golden-brown blouse, and a bright-blue hat. These are now covered with a fawn-coloured mackintosh, darkened with heavy rain, and a hastily folded umbrella is dripping on to the floor. She comes in shyly, evidently conscious of Mrs. Breydon's presence; but fighting her timidity with a breezy and jovial demeanour. Mrs. Breydon tries, but can't keep a little stiffness out of her greeting.

Sheila. Oh! good evening, Mrs. Breydon. What a night! I'm nearly blown to bits; and the rain — oh, the wind and the weather!

Mrs. Breydon. You must be perished. Take off your mac, and come over to the fire. Get Ayamonn to make you a cup o' tea, and bring you back to life again.

Sheila. No, really; I'm burning — the battle with the wind and the rain has made me warm and lively.

Ayamonn. Hey ho, the wind and the rain, for the rain it raineth every day. Sit down and take the weight off your legs.

Sheila. Not worth while, for I can't stop long. [*To Mrs. Breydon*] Going out on a night like this, Mrs. Breydon?

Ayamonn [*hastily*]. She has to go: got an urgent call from a poor sick neighbour.

Sheila [*hesitatingly*]. What is it? Could . . . could I do it for you?

Ayamonn [*decidedly*]. No, no, you couldn't. The woman knows my mother. It's only to see her safe and warm in bed for the night; Mother won't be long.

Mrs. Breydon. Good night, Miss Sheila ; perhaps you'll be here when I come back.

Sheila. I don't think so. I must go almost at once.

Mrs. Breydon. Well, good night, then.

> [*She goes out, and Ayamonn goes over to Sheila, kisses her, and helps her off with the mac.*

Sheila. You shouldn't let your mother go out on a night like this — she's no longer a young woman.

Ayamonn. I don't like to interfere with her need to give help to a neighbour. She likes it, and it does her good.

Sheila. But the rain's coming down in sheets, and she's got but a thin shawl round her shoulders.

Ayamonn [*impatiently*]. Oh, she hasn't very far to go. Let's think of greater things than the pouring rain and an old woman on her way to smooth pillows on a sick bed. Look ! — [*he feels her skirt*] — the hem's wringing. Better dry it at the fire. Turn round and I'll unfasten it for you.

Sheila [*forcing his hand away*]. It's nothing — you are thinking now of your own pleasure. You weren't so eager to see me when I was knocking at the door a while ago.

Ayamonn. You ! But it was Old Brennan o' the Moor that was there.

Sheila. Before him, I was there. He hammered at the door too.

Ayamonn [*angry with himself*]. And I thinking the rapping was that of a pestering neighbour ! I might have guessed it wasn't, it was so gentle.

Sheila. After trying to slip in unnoticed, there I was left with the whole house knowing I was at the door, and when I ran down, I heard them yelling that the stylish-dressed pusher was trying to get into Breydon's again! A nice time I'll have with my people when they hear it.

Ayamonn. I was doing my Shakespeare part, and didn't want disturbance, so there I was, standing stiff and breathless like a heron in a pond, keeping my dear one away from me! [*Going over and taking her in his arms*] Well, it's all over now, and here you are in my arms, safe and sure and lovely.

Sheila [*struggling away from him*]. No, it's not all over; and don't press me so hard; don't ruffle me tonight, for I feel a little tired.

Ayamonn [*peevishly*]. Tired again? Well, so am I, more than a little tired; but never too tired to put a sparkle into a welcome for a loved one.

Sheila. Oh, Ayamonn, I do want you to be serious for one night.

Ayamonn. Very well, very well, Sheila. [*He moves away from her, and stands at the other side of the fire.*] Let us plan, then, of how we can spin joy into every moment of tomorrow's day.

Sheila. That's why I hurried here to see you — I can't be with you tomorrow.   [*There is a long pause.*

Ayamonn. Why can't you be with me tomorrow?

Sheila. The Daughters of St. Frigid begin a retreat tomorrow, to give the Saint a warm devotion, and Mother insists I go.

Ayamonn. And I insist that you go with me. Is the Saint Frigid more to you than the sinner Ayamonn? Would you rather go to the meeting than come to see me? [*A pause.*] Would you, would you, Sheila?

Sheila [*in a hesitant whisper*]. God forgive me, I'd rather còme to see you.

Ayamonn. Come then; God will be sure to forgive you.

Sheila. I daren't. My mother would be at me for ever if I failed to go. I've told you how she hates me to be near you. She chatters red-lined warnings and black-bordered appeals into my ears night and day, and when they dwindle for lack of breath, my father shakes them out of their drowsiness and sends them dancing round more lively still, dressed richly up in deadly black and gleaming scarlet.

Ayamonn. Sheila, Sheila, on the one day of the month when I'm free, you must be with me. I wouldn't go to a workers' meeting so that I might be with you.

Sheila. There's another thing, Ayamonn — the threatened strike. Oh, why do you meddle with those sort of things!

Ayamonn. Oh, never mind that, now. Don't be like a timid little girl ensconced in a clear space in a thicket of thorns — safe from a scratch if she doesn't stir, but unable to get to the green grass or the open road unless she risks the tears the thorns can give.

Sheila. Oh, Ayamonn, for my sake, if you love me, do try to be serious.

Ayamonn [*a little wildly*]. Oh, Sheila, our time is not yet come to be serious in the way of our elders. Soon

enough to browse with wisdom when Time's grey
finger puts a warning speck on the crimson rose of
youth. Let no damned frosty prayer chill the sunny
sighs that dread the joy of love.

Sheila [*wildly*]. I won't listen, Ayamonn, I won't listen !
We must look well ahead on the road to the future.
You lead your life through too many paths instead of
treading the one way of making it possible for us to
live together.

Ayamonn. We live together now ; live in the light of the
burning bush. I tell you life is not one thing, but
many things, a wide branching flame, grand and good
to see and feel, dazzling to the eye of no-one loving it.
I am not one to carry fear about with me as a priest
carries the Host. Let the timid tiptoe through the
way where the paler blossoms grow ; my feet shall be
where the redder roses grow, though they bear long
thorns, sharp and piercing, thick among them !

Sheila [*rising from the chair — vehemently*]. I'll listen no
more ; I'll go. You want to make me a spark in a
mere illusion. I'll go !

Ayamonn. Rather a spark from the althar of God, me
girl ; a spark that flames on a new path for a bubbling
moment of life, or burns a song into the heart of a poet.

Sheila. I came here as a last chance to talk things quiet
with you, but you won't let me ; so I'll go. [*As he
seizes her in his arms*] Let me go ! [*Pleadingly*] Please,
Ayamonn, let me go !

Ayamonn. I tell you it is a gay sight for God to see joy
shine for a moment on the faces of His much-troubled
children.

Sheila [*fearfully*]. Oh, don't bring God's name into this, for it will mean trouble to the pair of us. And your love for me lasts only while I'm here. When I'm gone, you think more of your poor painting, your poor oul' Ireland, your songs, and your workers' union than you think of Sheila.

Ayamonn. You're part of them all, in them all, and through them all ; joyous, graceful, and a dearer vision ; a bonnie rose, delectable and red. [*He draws her to him, presses her hard, lifts her on to his lap, and kisses her.*] Sheila, darling, you couldn't set aside the joy that makes the moon a golden berry in a hidden tree. You cannot close your ear to the sweet sound of the silver bell that strikes but once and never strikes again !
[*The door opens, and the head of Brennan o' the Moor looks into the room. It is a bald one, the dome highly polished ; the face is wrinkled a lot, but the eyes are bright and peering. A long white beard gives him a far-away like-ness to St. Jerome. He is dressed in a shabby-genteel way, and wears a long rain-soaked mackintosh. A faded bowler hat is on his head.*

Brennan. Oh, dear, dear, dear me !
[*He comes into the room showing that his back is well bent, though he still has a sturdy look about him. A strap around his body holds a melodeon on his back. Sheila and Ayamonn separate ; he rises to meet the old man, while she stares, embarrassed, into the fire.*

Ayamonn. Now what th' hell do you want ?

Brennan [*taking no notice of Ayamonn's remark — taking off his hat in a sweeping bow*]. Ah, me two sweet, snowy-breasted Dublin doves ! Me woe it is to come ramblin' in through marjoram moments scentin' the serious hilarity of a genuine courtin' couple. I'm askin' now what's the dear one's name, if that isn't thresspassin' on others who are in a firmer condition of friendship? Though, be rights, it's a fair an' showy nosegay I should be throwin' through a shyly opened window into the adorable lady's lap.

Sheila [*shyly*]. Me name is Sheila.

Brennan. Sheila is it? Ay, an' a Sheila are you. Ay, an' a suitable one too, for there's a gentle nature in the two soft sounds, an' a silver note in the echo, describin' grandly the pretty slendher lass me two ould eyes are now beholdin'.

Ayamonn [*going over and catching him by an arm to guide him out*]. I can't see you now, old friend, for the pair of us are heavily harnessed to a question that must be answered before either of us is a day older.

Brennan. Sure I know. An' isn't it only natural, too, that young people should have questions to ask and answers to give to the dewy problems that get in th' way of their dancin' feet?

Ayamonn [*impatiently*]. Come again, old friend, when time has halted us for an hour of rest.

Brennan. It isn't me, I'm sayin', that would be dense enough to circumvent your longin' to be deep down in the silent consequence of regardin' each other without let or hindrance. [*He goes towards Sheila, eagerly, pulling Ayamonn after him.*] It's easy seen, sweet lady, that you're well within the compass of your young man's knowledge, an' unaware of nothin', so I may speak as man to lady, so with cunnin' confidence, tell me what you think of the Bank of Ireland?

Ayamonn. Oh, for goodness' sake, old man. Sheila's no intherest in the Bank of Ireland. She cares nothing for money, or for anything money can buy.

Brennan [*staring at Ayamonn for a moment as if he had received a shock*]. Eh ? Arra, don't be talkin' nonsense, man ! Who is it daren't think of what money can buy ? [*He crosses to the door in a trot on his toes, opens it, looks out, and closes it softly again. Then he tiptoes back to Sheila, bends down towards her, hands on knees, and whispers hoarsely*] I've just a little consideration of stocks and bonds nestin' in the Bank of Ireland, at four per cent — just enough to guard a poor man from ill, eh ? Safe an' sound there, isn't it, eh ? [*To Ayamonn*] Now, let the fair one speak out on her own. [*Twisting his head back to Sheila.*] Safe there as if St. Pether himself had the key of where the bonds are stationed, eh ?

Sheila. I'm sure they must be, sir.

Brennan [*with chuckling emphasis*]. Yehess ! Aren't you the sensible young lady ; sure I knew you'd say that, without fear or favour. [*Turning towards Ayamonn.*] What do you say ? You're a man, now, of tellin' judgement.

Ayamonn. Oh, the State would have to totther before you'd lose a coin.

Brennan [*gleefully*]. Go bang, absolutely bang ! Eh ?

Ayamonn. Go bang !

Brennan. Bang ! [*To Sheila*] Hear that, now, from a man climbin' up to scholarship ? Yehess ! Stony walls, steely doors, locks an' keys, bolts an' bars, an' all th' bonds warm an' dhry, an' shinin' safe behind them.

Sheila. Safe behind them.

Brennan [*gleefully*]. Ay, so. An' none of it sthrollin' into Peter's Pence. [*Chuckling.*] Wouldn't the Pope be mad if he knew what he was missin' ! Safe an' sound. [*To Ayamonn*] You think so, too, eh ?

Ayamonn. Yes, yes.

Brennan [*soberly*]. Ay, of course you do. [*To Sheila — indicating Ayamonn*] A good breed, me sweet an' fair one, brought up proper to see things in their right light.

Ayamonn [*catching him impatiently by the arm*]. And now, old friend, we have to get you to go.

Brennan. Eh ?

Ayamonn. To go ; Sheila and I have things to talk about.

Brennan [*suddenly*]. An' what about the song, then ?

Ayamonn. Song ?

Brennan. Th' one for the Show. Isn't that what brought me up ? At long last, afther hard sthrainin', me an' Sammy have got the tune down in tested clefs, crotchets, an' quavers, fair set down to be sung be anyone in thrue time. An' Sammy's below, in his gay suit for the Show, waitin' to be called up to let yous hear th' song sung as only Sammy can sing it.

Ayamonn. Bring him up, bring him up — why in hell didn't you tell me all this before ?

Brennan [*stormily*]. Wasn't I thryin' all the time an' you wouldn't let a man get a word in edgeways. [*Gesturing towards Sheila.*] He'll jib at singin' in front of her. [*He whispers hoarsely towards Sheila.*] He's as shy as a kid in his first pair o' pants, dear lady.

Ayamonn [*impatiently pushing him out of the room*]. Oh, go on, go on, man, and bring him up.   [*Brennan goes out.*

Sheila [*earnestly*]. Wait till I'm gone, Ayamonn; I can't stop long, and I want to talk to you so much.

Ayamonn [*a little excited*]. Oh, you must hear the song, Sheila; they've been working to get the air down for a week, and it won't take a minute.

Sheila [*angrily*]. I've waited too long already! Aren't you more interested in what I want to say than to be listening to some vain fool singing a song?

Ayamonn [*a little taken aback*]. Oh, Sheila, what's wrong with you tonight? The young carpenter who'll sing it, so far from being vain, is as shy as a field-mouse, and you'll see, when he starts to sing, he'll edge his face away from us. You do want to hear it, Sheila, don't you?

Sheila [*appealingly*]. Let it wait over, Ayamonn; I can come to hear it some other time. I do want to say something, very serious, to you about our future meetings.

Ayamonn [*hastily*]. All right then; I'll hurry them off the minute the song's sung. Here they are, so sit down, do, just for one minute more.

[*But she goes towards the door, and reaches it just as Old Brennan returns shoving in before him a young man of twenty-three, shy, and loth to come in. He is tall, but his face is pale and mask-like in its expression of resignation to the world and all around him. Even when he shows he's shy, the mask-like features do not alter. He is dressed in a white cut-away coat, shaped like a tailed evening dress, black waistcoat over a rather soiled shirt-*

front, frilled, and green trousers. He carries a sheet of manuscript music in his hand. Brennan unslings his melodeon from his back, fusses the young Singer forward; bumping against Sheila, who has moved towards the door, he pushes her back with a shove of his backside; and puts Ayamonn to the other end of the room with a push on the shoulder.

Brennan [*as he pushes Sheila*]. Outa th' way, there! Stem your eagerness for a second, will yous? All in good time. Give the man a chance to get himself easy. [*As he pushes Ayamonn*] Farther back, there, farther back! Give the performer a chance to dispose himself. Isn't he a swell, wha'? The centre group's to be dhressed the same way, while th' corner men'll be in reverse colours — green coats, black trousers, an' white vest, see? Th' whole assembly'll look famous. Benjamin's lendin' all the set o' twelve suits for five bob,'cause o' th' reason we're runnin' th' Show for. [*To Sheila — in a hoarse whisper*] You stare at the fire as if he wasn't here. He's extravagant in shyness, an' sinks away into confusion at the stare of an eye — understand?

[*She slowly, and a little sullenly, sits down to stare into the fire. The door is opened, and in comes Roory O'Balacaun with a small roll of Irish magazines under an arm. He is a stout middle-aged man, dressed in rough homespun coat, cap, and knee-breeches, wearing over all a trench coat.*

Roory. Here y'are, Ayamonn, me son, avic's th' Irish magazines I got me friend to pinch for you. [*He looks at the Singer.*] Hello, what kind of a circus is it's goin' on here?

Ayamonn. Mr. Brennan Moore here's organising the singers for the Minsthrel Show to help get funds in case we have to go on sthrike, Roory.

Roory. I'm one o' th' men meself, but I don't stand for a foreign Minsthrel Show bein' held, an' the Sword of Light gettin' lifted up in th' land. We want no coon or Kaffir industry in our country.

Brennan [*indignantly*]. Doesn't matter what you stand for before you came here, you'll sit down now. Thry to regard yourself as a civilised member of the community, man, an' hold your peace for th' present. [*To the Singer*] Now, Sam, me son o' gold, excavate the shyness out of your system an' sing as if you were performin' before a Royal Command !

Roory [*with a growl*]. There's no royal commands wanted here.

Brennan [*with a gesture of disgusted annoyance*]. Will you for goodness' sake not be puttin' th' singer out ? I used the term only as an allegory, man.

Roory. Allegory man, or allegory woman, there's goin' to be no royal inthrusions where the Sword o' Light is shinin'.

Ayamonn. Aw, for Christ's sake, Roory, let's hear the song !

Brennan [*to the Singer, who has been coughing shyly and turning sideways from his audience*]. Now, Sam, remember you're not in your working clothes, an' are a different man, entirely. Chin up and chest out. [*He gives a note or two on the melodeon.*] Now !

Singer [*singing*] :
 A sober black shawl hides her body entirely,
 Touch'd by th' sun and th' salt spray of the sea ;
 But down in th' darkness a slim hand, so lovely,
 Carries a rich bunch of red roses for me.

[*He turns away a little more from his audience, and coughs shyly.*

Brennan [*enthusiastically*]. Sam, you're excellin' yourself! On again, me oul' son!

Singer [*singing*] :
Her petticoat's simple, her feet are but bare,
An' all that she has is but neat an' scantie;
But stars in th' deeps of her eyes are exclaiming
I carry a rich bunch of red roses for thee!

Brennan [*after giving a few curling notes on the melodeon*]. A second Count McCormack in th' makin'! An' whenever he sung *Mother Mo Chree*, wasn't there a fewroory in Heaven with the rush that was made to lean over an hear him singin' it!
[*While Brennan has been speaking, the door has opened, and Mullcanny now stands there gaping into the room. He is young, lusty, and restless. He is wearing fine tweeds that don't fit too well; and his tweed cap is set rakishly on his head. He, too, wears a mackintosh.*

Mullcanny. Is this a home-sweet-away-from-home hippo-dhrome, or what?

Brennan [*clicking his tongue in annoyance*]. Dtchdtchdtch!

Mullcanny. An' did I hear someone pratin' about Heaven, an' I coming in? [*To Brennan — tapping him on the shoulder*] Haven't you heard, old man, that God is dead?

Brennan. Well, keep your grand discovery to yourself for a minute or two more, please. [*To the Singer*] Now, Sam, apologisin' for th' other's rudeness, the last verse, please.

Singer [*singing*] :
> No arrogant gem sits enthron'd on her forehead,
> Or swings from a white ear for all men to see ;
> But jewel'd desire in a bosom, most pearly,
> Carries a rich bunch of red roses for me !

Brennan [*after another curl of notes on the melodeon*]. Well, fair damsel and gentlemen all, what do you think of the song and the singer ?

Ayamonn. The song was good, and the singer was splendid.

Mullcanny. What I heard of it wasn't bad.

Singer [*shyly*]. I'm glad I pleased yous all.

Roory [*dubiously*]. D'ye not think th' song is a trifle indecent ?

Mullcanny [*mockingly*]. Indecent ! And what may your eminence's specification of indecency be ? [*Angrily*] Are you catalogued, too, with the Catholic Young Men going about with noses long as a snipe's bill, sthripping the gayest rose of its petals in search of a beetle, and sniffing a taint in the freshest breeze blowing in from the sea ?

Brennan [*warningly*]. Lady present, lady present, boys !

Roory. It ill becomes a thrue Gael to stand unruffled when either song or story thries to introduce colour to the sabler nature of yearnin's in untuthored minds.

Brennan [*more loudly*]. Lady present, boys !

Sheila [*rising out of the chair and going towards the door*]. The lady's going now, thank you all for the entertainment.

[*To Ayamonn*] I won't stay any longer to disturb the important dispute of your friends.

Ayamonn [*going over to her*]. Don't be foolish, Sheila, dear ; but if you must go, you must. We'll see each other again tomorrow evening.

Sheila [*firmly*]. No, not tomorrow, nor the next night either.

Ayamonn [*while Brennan plays softly on the melodeon to hide embarrassment*]. When then ?

Sheila. I can't tell. I'll write. Never maybe. [*Bitterly*] I warned you this night might be the last chance of a talk for some time, and you didn't try to make use of it !

Ayamonn [*catching her arm*]. I made as much use of it as you'd let me. Tomorrow night, in the old place, near the bridge, the bridge of vision where we first saw Aengus and his coloured birds of passion passing.

Sheila [*wildly*]. I can't ; I won't, so there—oh, let me go !
    [*She breaks away from him, runs out, and a silence falls on the room for a few moments.*

Roory [*breaking the silence*]. Women is strange things ! Elegant animals, not knowin' their own minds a minute.

Brennan [*consolingly*]. She'll come back, she'll come back.

Ayamonn [*trying to appear unconcerned*]. Aw, to hell with her !

Singer [*faintly*]. Can I go now ?

Brennan. Wait, an' I'll be with you in a second.

Mullcanny [*to Ayamonn*]. I just dropped in to say, Ayamonn, that I'll be getting Haeckel's *Riddle of the Universe* to-morrow, afther long searching, and I'll let you have it the minute it comes into my hand.

[*The door is suddenly flung open, and Eeada, followed by Dympna and Finnoola, with others, mingled with men behind them, rushes into the room in a very excited state. She comes forward, with her two companions a little behind, while the rest group themselves by the door.*

Eeada [*distractedly*]. It's gone She is, an' left us lonesome; vanished She is like a fairy mist of an early summer mornin'; stolen She is be some pagan Protestan' hand, envious of the love we had for our sweet Lady of Eblana's poor!

Chorus. Our Lady of Eblana's gone!

Ayamonn. Nonsense; no Protestant hand touched Her. Where was She?

Dympna. Safe in Her niche in th' hall She was, afther Her washin', lookin' down on the comin's an' goin's of Her strugglin' children: an' then we missed Her, an' th' niche was empty!

Chorus. Our Lady of Eblana's gone!

Single Voice. An' dear knows what woe'll fall on our poor house now.

Brennan. An' a good job, too. [*Passionately*] Inflamin' yourselves with idols that have eyes an' see not; ears, an' hear not; an' have hands that handle not; like th' chosen people settin' moon-images an' sun-images, cuttin' away the thrue and homely connection between the Christian an' his God! Here, let me and me singer out of this unholy place!

[*He pushes his way through the people, followed by the Singer, and goes out.*

Eeada [*nodding her head, to Ayamonn*]. All bark, but no bite ! We know him of old : a decent oul' blatherer. Sure, doesn't he often buy violets and snowdhrops, even, for little Ursula, below, tellin' her she mustn't put them before a graven image, knowin' full well that that was th' first thing she'd hurry home to do. An' she's breakin' her young heart below, now, because her dear Lady has left her. [*Suspiciously*] If oul' Brennan had a hand in Her removal, woe betide him.

Mullcanny [*mocking*]. Couldn't you all do betther than wasting your time making gods afther your own ignorant images ?

Ayamonn [*silencing him with a gesture*]. That's enough, Paudhrig. [*To Eeada*] Tell little Ursula not to worry. Her Lady'll come back. If your Lady of Eblana hasn't returned by tonight, I'll surrender my sleep afther my night's work to search for Her, and bring Her back safe to Her niche in the hall. No one in this house touched Her.

Eeada. An' you'll see She'll pay you back for your kindness, Ayamonn — [*looking at Mullcanny*] — though it's little surprised I'd be if, of Her own accord, She came down indignant, an' slipped off from us, hearin' the horrid talk that's allowed to float around this house lately.

Mullcanny [*mocking*]. Afraid of me, She was. Well, Ayamonn, I've some lessons to get ready, so I'll be off. I'll bring you the book tomorrow. [*To the crowd — mocking*] I hope the poor Lady of Eblana's poor'll find Her way home again.

[*He goes out through a surly-faced crowd.*

Ayamonn [*to Eeada*]. Don't mind Mullcanny. Good

night, now ; and don't worry about your dear statue. If She doesn't come back, we'll find another as bright and good to take Her place.

Eeada [*growling*]. The fella that's gone'll have a rough end, jeerin' things sacred to our feelin'.

[*They all go out, and Ayamonn is left alone with Roory. Ayamonn takes off his doublet, folds it up, and puts it back in the basket. He goes into the other room and comes back with oilskin coat and thigh-high leggings. He puts the leggings on over his trousers.*

Ayamonn [*putting on the leggings*]. Th' shunting-yard'll be a nice place to be tonight. D'ye hear it ?

[*He listens to the falling rain, now heavier than ever.*

Roory. Fallin' fast. That Mullcanny'll get into throuble yet.

Ayamonn. Not he. He's really a good fellow. Gave up his job rather than his beliefs — more'n many would do.

Roory. An' how does he manage now ?

Ayamonn. Hammering knowledge into deluded minds wishing to be civil servants, bank clerks, an' constables who hope to take the last sacraments as sergeants in the Royal Irish Constabulary or the Metropolitan Police.

Roory. By God, he's his work cut out for him with the last lot !

[*The door is again opened and Eeada sticks her head into the room.*

Eeada. Your mother's just sent word that the woman she's mindin's bad, an' she'll have to stay th' night. I'm just runnin' round meself to make your mother a cup o' tea.

Ayamonn [*irritably*]. Dtch dtch — she'll knock herself up
before she's done ! When I lock up, I'll leave the
key with you for her, Eeada.
          [*He lights a shunter's lantern and puts out the lamp.*

Eeada. Right y'are.   [*She goes.*

Roory. What kid was it sketched th' angel on th' wall ?

Ayamonn. Oh, I did that. I'd give anything to be a
painter.

Roory. What, like Oul' Brennan o' th' Moor ?

Ayamonn. No, no ; like Angelico or Constable.

Roory [*indifferently*]. Never heard of them.

Ayamonn [*musingly*]. To throw a whole world in colour on
a canvas though it be but a man's fine face, a woman's
shape asthride of a cushioned couch, or a three-
bordered house on a hill, done with a glory ; even
delaying God, busy forgin' a new world, to stay awhile
an' look upon their loveliness.

Roory. Aw, Ayamonn, Ayamonn, man, put out your
hand an' see if you're awake ! [*He fiddles with the books
on the table.*] What oul' book are you readin' now ?

Ayamonn [*dressed now in oilskin leggings and coat, with an
oilskin sou'wester on his head, comes over to look at the book in
Roory's hand, and shines the lantern on it*]. Oh, that's
Ruskin's *Crown of Wild Olive* — a grand book — I'll
lend it to you.

Roory. What for ? What would I be doin' with it ?
I've no time to waste on books. Ruskin. Curious
name ; not Irish, is it ?

Ayamonn. No, a Scotsman who wrote splendidly about a

lot of things. Listen to this, spoken before a gathering of business men about to build an Exchange in their town.

Roory. Aw, Ayamonn — an Exchange ! What have we got to do with an Exchange ?

Ayamonn [*impatiently*]. Listen a second, man ! Ruskin, speakin' to the business men, says : " Your ideal of life is a pleasant and undulating world, with iron and coal everywhere beneath it. On each pleasant bank of this world is to be a beautiful mansion ; stables, and coach-houses ; a park and hot-houses ; carriage-drives and shrubberies ; and here are to live the votaries of the Goddess of Getting-on — the English gentle-man——"

Roory [*interrupting*]. There you are, you see, Ayamonn — th' *English* gentleman !

Ayamonn. Wait a second — Irish or English — a gentle-man's th' same.

Roory. 'Tisn't. I'm tellin' you it's different. What's in this Ruskin of yours but another oul' cod with a gift of the gab ? Right enough for th' English, pinin' afther little things, ever rakin' cindhers for th' glint of gold. We're different — we have th' light.

Ayamonn. You mean th' Catholic Faith ?

Roory [*impatiently*]. No, no ; that's there, too ; I mean th' light of freedom ; th' tall white candle tipped with its golden spear of flame. The light we thought we'd lost ; but it burns again, sthrengthenin' into a sword of light. Like in th' song we sung together th' other night. [*He sings softly :*]

Our courage so many have thought to be agein',
Now flames like a brilliant new star in th' sky;
And Danger is proud to be call'd a good brother,
For Freedom has buckled her sword on her thigh.

Ayamonn [*joining in*] :
Then out to th' place where th' battle is bravest,
Where th' noblest an' meanest fight fierce in th' fray,
Republican banners shall mock at th' foemen,
An' Fenians shall turn a dark night into day!
[*A pause as the two of them stand silent, each clasping the
other's hand.   Ayamonn opens the door to pass out.*

Roory [*in a tense whisper*]. Th' Fenians are in force again,
Ayamonn; th' Sword o' Light is shinin'!
[*They go out, and Ayamonn closes the door as the Curtain
falls.*

ACT II

The same as in Act I.

It is about ten o'clock at night. The rain has stopped, and there is a fine moon sailing through the sky. Some of its rays come in through the window at the side.

Ayamonn, in his shirt-sleeves, is sitting at the table. He has an ordinary tin money-box in his hand, and a small pile of coppers, mixed with a few sixpences, are on the table beside him. He is just taking the last coin from the slit in the box with the aid of a knife-blade. His mother is by the dresser piling up the few pieces of crockery used for a recent meal. The old one-wick lamp is alight, and stands on the table near to Ayamonn. Several books lie open there, too.

Ayamonn. There's th' last one out, now. It's quite a job getting them out with a knife.

Mrs. Breydon. Why don't you put them in a box with a simple lid on?

Ayamonn. The harder it is to get at, the less chance of me spending it on something more necessary than what I seek. [*He counts the money on the table.*] One bob — two — three — an' sixpence — an' nine — three an' nine-pence ; one an' threepence to get yet — a long way to go.

Mrs. Breydon. Maybe, now, th' bookseller would give you it for what you have till you can give him th' rest.

Ayamonn [*in agony*]. Aw, woman, if you can't say sense, say nothing ! Constable's reproductions are five shillings second-hand, an' he that's selling is the bastard that nearly got me jailed for running off with his Shakespeare. It's touch an' go if he'll let me have it for the five bob.

Mrs. Breydon [*philosophically*]. Well, seein' you done without it so long, you can go without it longer.

Ayamonn [*with firm conviction*]. I'll have it the first week we get the extra shilling the men are demandin'.

Mrs. Breydon. I shouldn't count your chickens before they're hatched.

Ayamonn [*joking a little bitterly*]. Perhaps our blessed Lady of Eblana's poor will work a miracle for me.

Mrs. Breydon [*a little anxiously*]. Hush, don't say that! Jokin' or serious, Ayamonn, I wouldn't say that. We don't believe in any of their Blessed Ladies, but as it's somethin' sacred, it's best not mentioned. [*She shuffles into her shawl.*] Though it's a queer thing, Her goin' off out of Her niche without a one in th' house knowin' why. They're all out huntin' for Her still.

[*The door opens, and Brennan comes in slowly, with a cute grin on his face. He has a large package, covered with paper, under his arm.*

Brennan. Out huntin' still for Her they are, are they? Well, let them hunt; She's here! A prisoner under me arm!

Mrs. Breydon [*indignantly*]. Well, Mr. Brennan Moore, it's ashamed of yourself you should be yokin' th' poor people to throubled anxiety over their treasure; and little Ursula breakin' her heart into th' bargain.

Ayamonn. It's god-damned mean of you, Brennan! What good d'ye think you'll do by this rowdy love of your

own opinions — forcing tumult into the minds of
ignorant, anxious people ?

Brennan [*calmly*]. Wait till yous see, wait till yous see,
before yous are sorry for sayin' more. [*He removes the
paper and shows the lost image transfigured into a figure looking
as if it had come straight from the shop : the white dress is
spotless, the blue robe radiant, and the gold along its border
and on the crown is gleaming. He holds it up for admiration.
Triumphantly*] There, what d'ye think of Her now ?
Fair as th' first grand tinge of th' dawn, She is, an'
bright as th' star of the evenin'.

Mrs. Breydon. Glory be to God, isn't She lovely ! But
hurry Her off, Brennan, for She's not a thing for
Protestant eyes to favour.

Ayamonn [*a little testily*]. Put it back, Brennan, put it back,
and don't touch it again.

Brennan. Isn't that what I'm going to do ? Oh, boy
alive, won't they get th' shock o' their lives when they
see Her shinin' in th' oul' spot. [*He becomes serious.*]
Though, mind you, me thrue mind misgives me for
decoratin' what's a charm to the people of Judah in th'
worship of idols ; but th' two of you is witness I did it
for the sake of the little one, and not in any tilt towards
honour to a graven image.

Mrs. Breydon [*resignedly*]. It's done now, God forgive us
both, an' me for sayin' She's lovely. Touchin' a thing
forbidden with a startled stir of praise !

Ayamonn. Put it back, put it back, man, and leave it
quiet where you got it first.
  [*Brennan goes out, looking intently out, and listening,
  before he does so.*

Mrs. Breydon. He meant well, poor man, but he's done a
dangerous thing. I'll be back before you start for
work. [*With a heavy sigh.*] It won't take us long to
tend her for the last time. The white sheets have
come, th' tall candles wait to be lit, an' th' coffin's
ordhered, an' th' room'll look sacred with the bunch of
violets near her head. [*She goes out slowly — as she goes*]
Dear knows what'll happen to th' three children.

    [*Ayamonn sits silent for a few moments, reading a book, his
    elbows resting on the table.*]

Ayamonn [*with a deep sigh — murmuringly*]. Sheila, Sheila,
my heart cries out for you ! [*After a moment's pause, he
reads :*]

    But I am pigeon-livered, an' lack gall
    To make oppression bitther ; or, ere this,
    I should have fatted all th' region kites
    With this slave's offal : Bloody, bawdy villain !

Oh, Will, you were a boyo ; a brave boyo, though, and
a beautiful one !

    [*The door opens and Old Brennan comes in, showing by his
    half-suppressed chuckles that he is enjoying himself. He
    wanders over the room to stand by the fire.*]

Brennan [*chuckling*]. In Her old place she is, now, in Her
new coronation robe ; and funny it is to think it's the
last place they'll look for Her.

Ayamonn. I'm busy, now.

Brennan [*sitting down by the fire*]. Ay, so you are ; so I see ;
busy readin'. Read away, for I won't disturb you ;
only have a few quiet puffs at th' oul' pipe. [*A pause.*]
Ah, then, don't I wish I was young enough to bury
meself in th' joy of readin' all th' great books of th'

world. Ah ! but when I was young, I had to work hard.

Ayamonn. I work hard, too.

Brennan. 'Course you do ! Isn't that what I'm sayin' ? An' all th' more credit, too, though it must be thryin' to have thoughtless people comin' in an' intherferin' with the golden movements of your thoughts.

Ayamonn. It's often a damned nuisance !

Brennan. 'Course it is. Isn't that what I'm sayin' ? [*As the door opens*] An' here's another o' th' boobies entherin' now. [*Roory comes in, and shuts the door rather noisily.*] Eh, go easy, there — can't you see Ayamonn's busy studyin' ?

Roory [*coming and bending over Ayamonn*]. Are you still lettin' oul' Ruskin tease you ?

Ayamonn [*angrily*]. No, no ; Shakespeare, Shakespeare, this time ! [*Springing from his chair*] Damn it, can't you let a man alone a minute ? What th' hell d'ye want now ?

Brennan [*warningly*]. I told you he was busy.

Roory [*apologetically*]. Aw, I only came with the tickets you asked me to bring you for the comin' National Anniversary of Terence Bellew MacManus.

Ayamonn. All right, all right ; let's have them.

Roory. How many d'ye want ? How many can you sell ?

Ayamonn. Give me twelve sixpennies ; if the sthrike doesn't come off I'll easily sell that number.

Roory [*counting out the tickets which Ayamonn gathers up and puts into his pocket*]. I met that Mullcanny on the way with a book for you ; but he stopped to tell a couple of railwaymen that the Story of Adam an' Eve was all a cod.

Brennan [*indignantly*]. He has a lot o' the people here in a state o' steamin' anger, goin' about with his bitther belief that the patthern of a man's hand is nearly at one with a monkey's paw, a horse's foot, th' flipper of a seal, or th' wing of a bat !

Ayamonn. Well, each of them is as wonderful as the hand of a man.

Roory. No, Ayamonn, not from the Christian point of view. D'ye know what they're callin' him round here ? Th' New Broom, because he's always sayin' he'll sweep th' idea of God clean outa th' mind o' man.

Brennan [*excited*]. There'll be dire damage done to him yet ! He was goin' to be flattened out be a docker th' other day for tellin' him that a man first formin' showed an undoubted sign of a tail.

Ayamonn. Ay, and when he's fully formed, if he doesn't show the tail, he shows most signs of all that goes along with it.

Roory. But isn't that a nice dignity to put on th' sacredness of a man's conception !

Brennan [*whisperingly*]. An' a lot o' them are sayin', Ayamonn, that your encouragement of him should come to an end.

Ayamonn. Indeed ? Well, let them. I'll stand by any honest man seekin' th' truth, though his way isn't my way. [*To Brennan*] You, yourself, go about deriding many things beloved by your Catholic neighbours.

Brennan. I contest only dangerous deceits specified be the Council o' Thrent, that are nowhere scheduled in th' pages of the Holy Scriptures.

Roory. Yes, Ayamonn, it's altogether different; he just goes about blatherin' in his ignorant Protestant way.

Brennan [*highly indignant*]. Ignorant, am I? An' where would a body find an ignorance lustier than your own, eh? If your Council o' Thrent's ordher for prayers for the dead who are past help, your dismal veneration of Saints an' Angels, your images of wood an' stone, carved an' coloured, have given you the image an' superscription of a tail, th' pure milk of the gospel has made a man of me, God-fearin', but stately, with a mind garlanded to th' steady an' eternal thruth!

    [*While they have been arguing, Mullcanny has peeped round the door, and now comes into the room, eyeing the two disputants with a lot of amusement and a little scorn. They take no notice of him.*

Roory. Sure, man, you have the neighbourhood hectored with your animosity against Catholic custom an' Catholic thought, never hesitatin' to give th' Pope even a deleterious name.

Brennan [*lapsing, in his excitement, into a semi-Ulster dialect*]. We dud ut tae yeh in Durry, on' sent your bravest floatin' down dud in th' wathers of th' Boyne, like th' hosts of Pharaoh tumblin' in the rush of th' Rud Sea! Thut was a slup in th' puss tae your Pope!

Mullcanny. You pair of damned fools, don't you know that the Pope wanted King Billy to win, and that the Vatican was ablaze with lights of joy afther King James's defeat over the wathers of the Boyne?

Roory. You're a liar, he didn't !

Brennan. You're a liar, it wasn't !
  [*They turn from Mullcanny to continue the row with themselves.*

Brennan. Looksee, if I believed in the ministhration of Saints on' Angels, I'd say thut th' good Protestant St. Puthrick was at the hud of what fell out at Durry, Aughrim, on' th' Boyne.

Roory [*stunned with the thought of St. Patrick as a Protestant*]. Protestant St. Pathrick ? Is me hearin' sound, or what ? What name did you mention ?

Brennan. I said St. Puthrick — th' evangelical founder of our thrue Church.

Roory. Is it dhreamin' I am ? Is somethin' happenin' to me, or is it happenin' to you ? Oh, man, it's mixin' mirth with madness you are at thinkin' St. Pathrick ever looped his neck in an orange sash, or tapped out a tune on a Protestant dhrum !

Brennan [*contemptuously*]. I refuse to argue with a one who's no' a broad-minded mon. Abuse is no equivalent for lugic — so I say God save th' King, an' tae hull with th' Pope !

Roory [*indignantly*]. You damned bigot — to hell with th' King, an' God save th' Pope !

Mullcanny [*to Ayamonn*]. You see how they live in bittherness, the one with the other. Envy, strife, and malice crawl from the coloured slime of the fairy-tales that go to make what is called religion. [*Taking a book from his pocket*] Here's something can bear a thousand tests, showing neatly how the world and all it bears upon it came into slow existence over millions of years, doing away for ever with the funny wonders of the seven days' creation set out in the fairy book of the Bible.

Ayamonn [*taking the book from Mullcanny*]. Thanks, Pether, oul' son ; I'm bound to have a good time reading it.

Mullcanny. It'll give you the true and scientific history of man as he was before Adam.

Brennan [*in a woeful voice*]. It's a darkened mind that thries tae lower us to what we were before th' great an' good God fashioned us. What does ony sensible person want to know what we were like before the creation of th' first man ?

Ayamonn [*murmuringly*]. To know the truth, to seek the truth, is good, though it lead to th' danger of eternal death.

Roory [*horror-stricken — crossing himself*]. Th' Lord between us an' all harm !

Brennan [*whispering prayerfully*]. Lord, I believe, help Thou mine unbelief.

Mullcanny [*pointing out a picture in the book*]. See ? The human form unborn. The tail — look ; the os coccyx sticking a mile out ; there's no getting away from it !

Brennan [*shaking his head woefully*]. An' this is holy Ireland !

Roory [*lifting his eyes to the ceiling — woefully*]. Poor St. Pathrick !

Mullcanny [*mockingly*]. He's going to be a lonely man soon, eh ? [*To Ayamonn*] Keep it safe for me, Ayamonn. When you've read it, you'll be a different man. [*He*

goes to the door] Well, health with the whole o' you,
and goodbye for the present.   [*He goes out.*

Roory. Have nothin' to do with that book, Ayamonn,
for that fellow gone out would rip up the floor of
Heaven to see what was beneath it. It's clapped in
jail he ought to be !

Brennan. An' th' book banned !

Ayamonn. Roory, Roory, is that th' sort o' freedom you'd
bring to Ireland with a crowd of green branches an' th'
joy of shouting ? If we give no room to men of our
time to question many things, all things, ay, life itself,
then freedom's but a paper flower, a star of tinsel, a
dead lass with gay ribbons at her breast an' a gold comb
in her hair. Let us bring freedom here, not with
sounding brass an' tinkling cymbal, but with silver
trumpets blowing, with a song all men can sing, with
a palm branch in our hand, rather than with a whip
at our belt, and a headsman's axe on our shoulders.

[*There is a gentle knock at the door, and the voice of Sheila
is heard speaking.*

Sheila [*outside*]. Ayamonn, are you there ? Are you in ?

Brennan [*whispering*]. The little lass ; I knew she'd come
back.

Ayamonn. I don't want her to see you here. Go into the
other room — quick. [*He pushes them towards it.*] An'
keep still.

Roory [*to Brennan*]. An' don't you go mockin' our Pope,
see ?

Brennan [*to Roory*]. Nor you go singlin' out King Billy
for a jeer.

Ayamonn. In with yous, quick !

Brennan. I prophesied she'd come back, didn't I, Ayamonn ? that she'd come back, didn't I ?

Ayamonn. Yes, yes ; in you go.

> [*He puts them in the other room and shuts the door. Then
> he crosses the room and opens the door to admit Sheila.
> She comes in, and he and Sheila stand silently for some
> moments, she trying to look at him, and finding it hard.*

Sheila [*at last*]. Well, haven't you anything to say to me ?

Ayamonn [*slowly and coldly*]. I waited for you at the bridge
today ; but you didn't come.

Sheila. I couldn't come ; I told you why.

Ayamonn. I was very lonely.

Sheila [*softly*]. So was I, Ayamonn, lonely even in front
of God's holy face.

Ayamonn. Sheila, we've gone a long way in a gold canoe
over many waters, bright and surly, sometimes sending bitter spray asplash on our faces. But you were
ever listening for the beat from the wings of the angel
of fear. So you got out to walk safe on a crowded
road.

Sheila. This is a cold and cheerless welcome, Ayamonn.

Ayamonn. Change, if you want to, the burning kiss falling
on the upturned, begging mouth for the chill caress of
a bony, bearded Saint. [*Loudly*] Go with th' yelling
crowd, and keep them brave, and yell along with them !

Sheila. Won't you listen, then, to the few words I have
to say ?

Ayamonn [*sitting down near the fire, and looking into it, though he leaves her standing*]. Go ahead ; I won't fail to hear you.

Sheila. God knows I don't mean to hurt you, but you must know that we couldn't begin to live on what you're earning now — could we ? [*He keeps silent.*] Oh, Ayamonn, why do you waste your time on doing foolish things ?

Ayamonn. What foolish things ?
    [*A hubbub is heard in the street outside ; voices saying loudly " Give him one in the bake " or " Down him with a one in th' belly "; then the sound of running foot-steps, and silence.*

Sheila [*when she hears the voices — nervously*]. What's that ?

Ayamonn [*without taking his gaze from the fire*]. Some drunken row or other.   [*They listen silently for a few moments.*

Ayamonn. Well, what foolish things ?

Sheila [*timid and hesitating*]. You know yourself, Ayamonn : trying to paint, going mad about Shakespeare, and con-sorting with a kind of people that can only do you harm.

Ayamonn [*mockingly prayerful — raising his eyes to the ceiling*]. O Lord, let me forsake the foolish, and live; and go in the way of Sheila's understanding !

Sheila [*going over nearer to him*]. Listen, Ayamonn, my love ; you know what I say is only for our own good, that we may come together all the sooner. [*Trying to speak jokingly*] Now, really, isn't it comical I'd look if I were to go about in a scanty petticoat, covered in a sober black shawl, and my poor feet bare ! [*Mocking*] Wouldn't I look well that way !

Ayamonn [*quietly*]. With red roses in your hand, you'd look beautiful.

Sheila [*desperately*]. Oh, for goodness' sake, Ayamonn, be sensible ! I'm getting a little tired of all this. I can't bear the strain the way we're going on much longer. [*A short pause.*] You will either have to make good, or——   [*She pauses.*

Ayamonn [*quietly*]. Or what ?

Sheila [*with a little catch in her voice*]. Or lose me ; and you wouldn't like that to happen.

Ayamonn. I shouldn't like that to happen ; but I could bear the sthrain.

Sheila. I risked a big row tonight to come to tell you good news : I've been told that the strike is bound to take place ; there is bound to be trouble ; and, if you divide yourself from the foolish men, and stick to your job, you'll soon be a foreman of some kind or other.

Ayamonn [*rising from his seat and facing her for the first time*]. Who told you all this ? The Inspector ?

Sheila. Never mind who ; if he did, wasn't it decent of him ?

Ayamonn. D'ye know what you're asking me to do, woman ? To be a blackleg ; to blast with th' black frost of desertion the gay hopes of my comrades. Whatever you may think them to be, they are my comrades. Whatever they may say or do, they remain my brothers and sisters. Go to hell, girl, I have a soul to save as well as you. [*With a catch in his voice*] Oh, Sheila, you shouldn't have asked me to do this thing !

Sheila [*trying to come close, but he pushes her back*]. Oh, Ayamonn, it is a chance ; take it, do, for my sake !

    [*Rapid footsteps are heard outside. The door flies open and Mullcanny comes in, pale, frightened, his clothes dishevelled, and a slight smear of blood on his forehead. His bowler hat is crushed down on his head, his coat is torn, and his waistcoat unbuttoned, showing his tie pulled out of its place. He sinks into a chair.*

Ayamonn. What's happened ? Who did that to you ?

Mullcanny. Give's a drink, someone, will you ?

    [*Ayamonn gets him a drink from a jug on the dresser.*

Mullcanny. A gang of bowseys made for me, and I talking to a man. Barely escaped with my life. Only for some brave oul' one, they'd have laid me out completely. She saved me from worse.

Ayamonn. How th' hell did you bring all that on you ?

Mullcanny [*plaintively*]. Just trying to show a fellow the foolishness of faith in a hereafter, when something struck me on the head, and I was surrounded by feet making kicks at me !

    [*A crash of breaking glass is heard from the other room, and Brennan and Roory come running out of it.*

Roory. A stone has done for th' window ! [*He sees Mullcanny.*] Oh, that's how th' land lies, is it ? Haven't I often said that if you go round leerin' at God an' His holy assistants, one day He's bound to have a rap at you !

Brennan. Keep away from that window, there, in case another one comes sailin' in.

    [*Immediately he has spoken, a stone smashes in through the window. Brennan lies down flat on the floor ; Mull-*

*canny slides from the chair and crouches on the ground;
Roory gets down on his hands and knees, keeping his head
as low as possible, so that he resembles a Mohammedan
at his devotions; Sheila stands stiff in a corner, near the
door; and Ayamonn, seizing up a hurley lying against
the dresser, makes for the door to go out.*

Brennan. I guessed this was comin'.

Ayamonn [*angrily*]. I'll show them !

Sheila [*to Ayamonn*]. Stop where you are, you fool !
    [*But Ayamonn pays no attention to the advice and hurries out
    of the door.*

Roory [*plaintively and with dignity — to Mullcanny*]. This
    is what you bring down on innocent people with your
    obstinate association of man with th' lower animals.

Mullcanny [*truculently*]. Only created impudence it is that
    strives to set yourselves above the ape's formation,
    genetically present in every person's body.

Brennan [*indignantly*]. String out life to where it started,
    an' you'll find no sign, let alone a proof, of the dignity,
    wisdom, an' civility of man ever having been associated
    with th' manners of a monkey.

Mullcanny. And why do children like to climb trees, eh ?
    Answer me that ?

Roory [*fiercely*]. They love it more where you come from
    than they do here.

Sheila [*from her corner*]. It's surely to be pitied you are,
    young man, lettin' yourself be bullied by ignorant
    books into believing that things are naught but what
    poor men are inclined to call them, blind to the glorious
    and eternal facts that shine behind them.

Mullcanny [*pityingly*]. Bullied be books — eternal facts — aw ! Yous are all scared stiff at the manifestation of a truth or two. D'ye know that the contraction of catharrah, apoplexy, consumption, and cataract of the eye is common to the monkeys ? Knowledge you have now that you hadn't before ; and a lot of them even like beer.

Roory. Well, that's something sensible, at last.

Brennan [*fiercely*]. Did they get their likin' for beer from us, or did we get our likin' of beer from them ? Answer me that, you, now ; answer me that !

Roory. Answer him that. We're not Terra Del Fooay-geeans, but sensible, sane, an' civilised souls.

Mullcanny [*gleefully*]. Time's promoted reptiles — that's all ; yous can't do away with the os coccyges !

Brennan. Ladies present, ladies present.

Roory [*creeping over rapidly till his face is close to that of Mullcanny's — fiercely*]. We stand on the earth, firm, upright, heads cocked, lookin' all men in th' face, afraid o' nothin' ; men o' goodwill we are, abloom with th' blessin' o' charity, showin' in th' dust we're made of, th' diamond-core of an everlastin' divinity !

Sheila [*excitedly*]. Hung as high as Gilderoy he ought to be, an' he deep in the evil of his rich illusions, spouting insults at war with th' mysteries an' facts of our holy faith !

Brennan [*to Sheila*]. Hush, pretty lady, hush. [*To the others*] Boys, boys, take example from a poor oul' Protestant here, never lettin' himself be offended be a quiver of anger in any peaceable or terrified discussion.

Now, let that last word finish it ; finis — the end, see ?

Roory [*angrily — to Brennan*]. Finis youssell, you blurry-eyed, wither-skinned oul' greybeard, singin' songs in th' public streets for odd coppers, with all th' boys in th' Bank of Ireland workin' overtime countin' all you've got in their front room !   Finis you !

Brennan [*indignantly*]. An office-boy, in a hurry, wouldn't stop to pick up from th' path before him the few coins I have.   An' as for being withered, soople as you I am, hands that can tinkle a thremblin' tune out of an oul' melodeon, legs that can carry me ten miles an' more, an' eyes that can still see without hardship a red berry shinin' from a distant bush !

[*The door opens and Ayamonn and his mother come in. She runs over to the blossoms at the window, tenderly examining the plants growing there — the musk, the geranium, and the fuchsia.*

Mrs. Breydon [*joyfully*]. Unharmed, th' whole of them. Th' stone passed them by, touchin' none o' them — thank God for that mercy !

Ayamonn. What th' hell are you doin' on your knees ? Get up, get up. [*They rise from the floor shamefacedly.*] Th' rioters all dispersed. [*To Mullcanny*] Mother was th' oul' one who saved you from a sudden an' unprovided death.   An' th' Blessed Image has come back again, all aglow in garments new.   Listen !

[*A murmur of song has been heard while Ayamonn was speaking, and now Eeada, Dympna, Finnoola, and the Men appear at the door — now wide open — half backing into the room singing part of a hymn softly, their pale faces still wearing the frozen look of resignation; staring at the Image shining bright and gorgeous as Brennan has*

*made it for them, standing in a niche in the wall,
directly opposite the door. Eeada, Dympna, Finnoola,
and the Men singing softly —*

> Oh ! Queen of Eblana's poor children,
> Bear swiftly our woe away;
> An' give us a chance to live lightly
> An hour of our life's dark day !
> Lift up th' poor heads ever bending,
> An' light a lone star in th' sky,
> To show thro' th' darkness, descending,
> A cheerier way to die.

Eeada [*coming forward a little*]. She came back to Her poor
again, in raiment rich. She came back ; of Her own
accord. She came to abide with Her people.

Dympna. From her window, little Ursula looked, and
saw Her come in ; in th' moonlight, along the street
She came, stately. Blinded be the coloured light that
shone around about Her, the child fell back, in a
swoon she fell full on the floor beneath her.

1st Man. My eyes caught a glimpse of Her too, glidin'
back to where She came from. Regal an' proud She
was, an' wondrous, so that me eyes failed ; me knees
thrembled an' bent low, an' me heart whispered a
silent prayer to itself as th' vision passed me by, an' I
fancied I saw a smile on Her holy face.

Eeada. Many have lived to see a strange thing this
favoured night, an' blessin' will flow from it to all
tempered into a lively belief ; and maybe, too, to
some who happen to be out of step with the many
marchin' in the mode o' thruth. [*She comes a little
closer to Mrs. Breydon. The others, backs turned towards the
room, stand, most of them outside the door, a few just across*

the threshold, in a semicircle, heads bent as if praying, facing towards the Image.] Th' hand of a black stranger it was who sent the stones flyin' through your windows ; but ere tomorrow's sun is seen, they will be back again as shelther from th' elements. A blessin' generous on yous all — [*pause*] — except th' evil thing that stands, all stiff-necked, underneath th' roof !

Mullcanny [*mockingly*]. Me !

Sheila [*fiercely*]. Ay, you, that shouldn't find a smile or an unclenched hand in a decent man's house !

Mullcanny. I'll go ; there's too many here to deal with — I'll leave you with your miracle.

Ayamonn. You can stay if you wish, for whatever surety of shelther's here, it's open to th' spirit seeking to add another colour to whatever thruth we know already. Thought that has run from a blow will find a roof under its courage here, an' a fire to sit by, as long as I live an' th' oul' rooms last !

Sheila [*with quiet bitterness*]. Well, shelter him, then, that by right should be lost in the night, a black night, an' bitterly lonely, without a dim ray from a half-hidden star to give him a far-away companionship ; ay, an' a desolate rest under a thorny and dripping thicket of lean and twisted whins, too tired to thry to live longer against th' hate of the black wind and th' grey rain. Let him lie there, let him live there, forsaken, forgotten by all who live under a kindly roof and close to a cosy fire !

Mullcanny [*with pretended alarm*]. Good God, I'm done, now ! I'm off before worse befall me. Good night, Ayamonn.

Ayamonn. Good night, my friend.   [*Mullcanny goes out.*

Brennan. We're keepin' decent people out of their beds —
so long, all.

Roory. I'll be with you some o' th' way, an' we can finish
that argument we had.   Good night all.
     [*He and Brennan go out together, closing the door after them.
     Sheila stands where she was, sullen and silent.*

Mrs. Breydon. Shame on you, Sheila, for such a smoky
flame to come from such a golden lamp !   [*Sheila stays
silent.*]   Tired out I am, an' frightened be th' scene o'
death I saw today.   Dodge about how we may, we come
to th' same end.

Ayamonn [*gently leading her towards the other room*]. Go an'
lie down, lady ; you're worn out.   Time's a perjured
jade, an' ever he moans a man must die.   Who
through every inch of life weaves a patthern of vigour
an' elation can never taste death, but goes to sleep
among th' stars, his withered arms outstretched to
greet th' echo of his own shout.   It will be for them
left behind to sigh for an hour, an' then to sing their
own odd songs, an' do their own odd dances, to give a
lonely God a little company, till they, too, pass by on
their bare way out.   When a true man dies, he is buried
in th' birth of a thousand worlds.
     [*Mrs. Breydon goes into the other room, and Ayamonn closes
     the door softly behind her.   He comes back and stands
     pensive near the fire.*

Ayamonn [*after a pause*]. Don't you think you should go
too ?

Sheila [*a little brokenly*]. Let me have a few more words
with you, Ayamonn, before we hurry to our separation.

Ayamonn [*quietly*]. There is nothing more to be said.

Sheila. There's a lot to be said, but hasty time won't stretch an hour a little out to let the words be spoken. Goodbye.

Ayamonn [*without turning his head*]. Goodbye.

[*Sheila is going slowly to the door when it partly opens, and half the head of Eeada peeps around it, amid an indistinct murmur as of praying outside.*

Eeada [*in half a whisper*]. Th' Protestan' Rector to see Mr. Breydon. [*The half of her head disappears, but her voice is heard saying a little more loudly*] This way, sir; shure you know th' way well, anyhow.

[*The door opening a little more, the Rector comes in. He is a handsome man of forty. His rather pale face wears a grave scholarly look, but there is kindness in his grey eyes, and humorous lines round his mouth, though these are almost hidden by a short, brown, pointed beard, here and there about to turn grey. His black clothes are covered by a warm black topcoat, the blackness brightened a little by a vivid green scarf he is wearing round his neck, the fringed ends falling over his shoulders. He carries a black, broad-brimmed, soft clerical hat and a walking-stick in his left hand. He hastens towards Ayamonn, smiling genially, hand outstretched in greeting.*

Rector. My dear Ayamonn. [*They shake hands.*

Ayamonn [*indicating Sheila*]. A friend of mine, sir — Sheila Moorneen. [*Moving a chair.*] Sit down, sir.

[*The Rector bows to Sheila; she returns it quietly, and the Rector sits down.*

Rector. I've hurried from home in a cab, Ayamonn, to see you before the night was spent. [*His face forming grave lines*] I've a message for you — and a warning.

[*The door again is partly opened, and again the half head of Eeada appears, mid the murmurs outside, unheard the moment the door closes.*

Eeada. Two railwaymen to see you, Ayamonn ; full house tonight you're havin', eh ?

[*The half head goes, the door opens wider, and the two railwaymen come into the room. They are dressed drably as the other men are, but their peaked railway uniform caps (which they keep on their heads) have vivid scarlet bands around them. Their faces, too, are like the others, and stonily stare in front of them. They stand stock still when they see the Rector.*

1st Railwayman [*after a pause*]. 'Scuse us. Didn' know th' Protestan' Minister was here. We'll wait outside till he goes, Ayamonn.

Ayamonn. Th' Rector's a dear friend of mine, Bill ; say what you want, without fear — he's a friend.

1st Railwayman [*a little dubiously*]. Glad to hear it. You know th' sthrike starts tomorrow ?

Ayamonn. I know it now.

2nd Railwayman. Wouldn' give's th' extra shillin'. Offered us thruppence instead — th' lowsers ! [*Hastily — to Rector*] 'Scuse me, sir.

1st Railwayman [*taking a document from his breast pocket*]. An' th' meetin's proclaimed.

Rector [*to Ayamonn*]. That's part of what I came to tell you.

1st Railwayman [*handing document to Ayamonn*]. They handed that to our Committee this evening, a warrant of warning.

Rector [*earnestly — to Ayamonn*]. I was advised to warn you, Ayamonn, that the Authorities are prepared to use all the force they have to prevent the meeting.

Ayamonn. Who advised you, sir — th' Inspector ?

Rector. My churchwarden, Ayamonn. Come, even he has good in him.

Ayamonn. I daresay he has, sir ; I've no grudge against him.

Rector [*convinced*]. I know that, Ayamonn.

Ayamonn [*indicating document — to 1st Railwayman*]. What are th' Committee going to do with this ?

1st Railwayman. What would you do with it, Ayamonn ?

Ayamonn [*setting it alight at the fire and waiting till it falls to ashes*]. That !

2nd Railwayman [*gleefully*]. Exactly what we said you'd do !

Sheila [*haughtily*]. It's not what any sensible body would think he'd do.

1st Railwayman [*ignoring her*]. Further still, Ayamonn, me son, we want you to be one of the speakers on the platform at the meeting.

Sheila [*bursting forward and confronting the railwaymen*]. He'll do nothing of the kind — hear me ? Nothing of the kind. Cinder-tongued moaners, who's to make any bones about what you suffer, or how you die ? Ayamonn's his reading and his painting to do, and his mother to mind, more than lipping your complaints in front of gun muzzles, ready to sing a short and sudden death-song !

1st Railwayman [*a little awed*]. To see Ayamonn we came, an' not you, Miss.

2nd Railwayman [*roughly*]. Let th' man speak for himself.

Ayamonn [*catching Sheila's arm and drawing her back*]. It's my answer they're seeking. [*To railwaymen*] Tell the Committee, Bill, I'll be there ; and that they honour me when they set me in front of my brothers. The Minstrel Show must be forgotten.

Sheila [*vehemently — to the Rector*]. You talk to him ; you're his friend. You can influence him. Get him to stay away, man !

Rector. It's right for me to warn you, Ayamonn, and you, men, that the Authorities are determined to prevent the meeting ; and that you run a grave risk in defying them.

2nd Railwayman [*growling*]. We'll chance it. We've barked long enough, sir ; it's time to bite a bit now.

Sheila [*to Rector*]. Warning's no good ; that's not enough — forbid him to go. Show him God's against it !

Rector [*standing up*]. Who am I to say that God's against it ? You are too young by a thousand years to know the mind of God. If they be his brothers, he does well among them.

Sheila [*wildly*]. I'll get his mother to bar his way. She'll do more than murmur grand excuses.

[*She runs to the door of the other room, opens it, and goes in. After a few moments, she comes out slowly, goes to the chair left idle by the Rector, sits down on it, leans her arms on the table, and lets her head rest on them.*

Ayamonn. Well?

Sheila [*brokenly*]. She's stretched out, worn and wan, fast asleep, and I hadn't the heart to awaken her.

Rector [*holding out a hand to Ayamonn*]. Come to see me before you go, Ayamonn. Be sure, wherever you may be, whatever you may do, a blessing deep from my breast is all around you. Goodbye. [*To the railwaymen*] Goodbye, my friends.

Railwaymen. Goodbye, sir.

 [*The Rector glances at Sheila, decides to say nothing, and goes towards the door; Ayamonn opens it for him, and he goes out through the semicircle of men and women, still softly singing before the Statue of the Queen of Eblana's poor. Sheila's quiet crying heard as a minor note through the singing.*

   Oh, Queen of Eblana's poor children,
   Bear swiftly our woe away,
   An' give us a chance to live lightly
   An hour of our life's dark day!

CURTAIN

ACT III

A part of Dublin City flowering into a street and a bridge across the river Liffey. The parapets are seen to the right and left so that the bridge fills most of the scene before the onlooker. The distant end of the bridge leads to a street flowing on to a point in the far distance; and to the right and left of this street are tall gaunt houses, mottled with dubious activities, with crowds of all sorts of men and women burrowing in them in a pathetic search for a home. These houses stand along another street running parallel with the river. In the distance, where the street, leading from the bridge, ends in a point of space, to the right, soars the tapering silver spire of a church; and to the left, Nelson's Pillar, a deep red, pierces the sky, with Nelson, a deep black, on its top, looking over everything that goes on around him. A gloomy grey sky is over all, so that the colours of the scene are made up of the dark houses, the brown parapets of the bridge, the grey sky, the silver spire, the red pillar, and Nelson's black figure.

On one of the bridge parapets a number of the men seen in the previous scenes are gathered together, their expressionless faces hidden by being bent down towards their breasts. Some sit on the parapets, some lounge against the gaunt houses at the corner of the street leading from the bridge, and, in one corner, a man stands wearily against the parapet, head bent, an unlit pipe dropping from his mouth, apparently forgotten. The sun shines on pillar and church spire, but there is no sign of sun where these people are.

On the pavement, opposite to where the men sit, nearer to this end of the bridge, sit Eeada, Dympna, and Finnoola, dressed so in black that they appear to be enveloped in the blackness of a dark night. In front of Eeada is a drab-coloured basket in which cakes and apples are spending an idle and uneasy time. Dympna has a shallower basket holding decadent blossoms, and a drooping bunch of violets hangs from a listless hand.

Eeada [*drowsily*]. This spongy leaden sky's Dublin ; those tomby houses is Dublin too — Dublin's scurvy body ; an' we're Dublin's silver soul. [*She spits vigorously into the street.*] An' that's what Eeada thinks of th' city's soul an' body !

Dympna. You're more than right, Eeada, but I wouldn't be too harsh. [*Calling out in a sing-song way*] Violets, here, on'y tuppence a bunch ; tuppence a bunch, th' fresh violets !

Eeada [*calling out in a sing-song voice*]. Apples an' cakes, on'y tuppence a head here for th' cakes ; ripe apples a penny apiece !

Dympna. Th' sun is always at a distance, an' th' chill grey is always here.

Finnoola. Half-mournin' skies for ever over us, frownin' out any chance of merriment that came staggerin' to us for a little support.

Eeada. That's Dublin, Finnoola, an' th' sky over it. Sorrow's a slush under our feet, up to our ankles, an' th' deep drip of it constant overhead.

Dympna. A graveyard where th' dead are all above th' ground.

Eeada. Without a blessed blink of rest to give them hope. An' she cockin' herself up that she stands among other cities as a queen o' counsel, laden with

knowledge, afire with th' song of great men, enough
to overawe all livin' beyond th' salty sea, undher
another sun be day, an' undher a different moon be
night.   [*They drowse, with heads bent lower.*

1st Man [*leaning wearily against the parapet*]. Golden
Gander'll do it, if I'm e'er a thrue prophet. [*Raising
his voice a little*] He'll flash past th' winnin' post like an
arra from th' bow, in the five hundhred guinea West's
Awake Steeplechase Championship.

2nd Man [*drowsily contradicting*]. In me neck he will!
He'd have a chance if it was a ramble. Copper
Goose'll leave him standin', if I'm e'er a thrue prophet.

Eeada [*waking up slightly*]. Prophets? Do me ears deceive
me, or am I afther hearin' somebody say prophets?

Dympna. You heard a murmur of it, Eeada, an' it's a bad
word to hear, remindin' us of our low estate at th'
present juncture. Th' prophets we once had are well
hidden behind God be now, an' no wondher, for we
put small pass on them, an' God in His generous
anger's showin' us what it is to be saddled with
Johnnies-come-marchin'-home, all song an' shirt an'
no surety.

Finnoola [*shaking her head sadly*]. A gold-speckled candle,
white as snow, was Dublin once; yellowish now,
leanin' sideways, an' guttherin' down to a last shaky
glimmer in th' wind o' life.

Eeada. Well, we've got Guinness's Brewery still, givin'
us a needy glimpse of a betther life an hour or so on a
Saturday night, though I hold me hand at praisin' th'
puttin' of Brian Boru's golden harp on every black
porther bottle, destined to give outsiders a false im-

pression of our pride in th' tendher an' dauntless
memories of th' past.

[*The Rector and the Inspector appear at the farther end of the
bridge, and come over it towards where the men and
women are. The Rector is dressed in immaculate black,
wears a glossy tall hat, and carries a walking-stick. He
has shed his topcoat, but wears his green scarf round his
neck. The Inspector is clad in a blue uniform, slashed
with silver epaulettes on the shoulders, and silver braid
on collar and cuffs. He wears a big blue helmet, back
and front peaks silver-bordered, and from a long silver
spike on the top flows a graceful plume of crimson hair.
On the front is a great silver crown throned on a circle of
red velvet. A sword, in a silver scabbard, hangs by his
side. He is wearing highly-polished top-boots. They
both pause on the bridge, the Rector looking pensively down
over the parapet at the flowing river.*]

Inspector. It was a great wedding, sir. A beautiful bride
and an elegant bridegroom ; a distinguished congregation, and the Primate in his fine sermon did justice to
the grand occasion, sir. Fittingly ended, too, by the
organ with *The Voice that Breathed o'er Eden.*

Rector [*apparently not very interested*]. Oh yes, yes ; quite.

Inspector. Historic disthrict, this, round here : head-
quarters of a Volunteer Corp in Grattan's time — not,
of course, that I agree with Grattan. A great-great-
grandfather of mine was one of the officers.

Rector. Oh yes ; was he ?

Inspector. Yes. Strange uniform he wore : richly black,
with sky-blue facings, a yellow breast-piece, ribbed with
red braid, and, capping all, a huge silver helmet having
a yellow plume soaring over it from the right-hand side.

Rector [*smiling*]. Your own's not too bad, Mr. Church-warden.

Inspector. Smart ; but a bit too sombre, I think, sir.

Eeada [*whining towards them*]. On'y a penny each, th' rosy apples, lovely for th' chiselurs — Jasus ! what am I sayin' ? Lovely for th' little masters an' little misthresses, stately, in their chandeliered an' carpeted dwellin'-houses ; or a cake — on'y tuppence a piece — daintily spiced, an' tastin' splendid.

Dympna [*whining towards them*]. Tuppence, here, th' bunch o' violets, fit for to go with th' white an' spotless cashmere gown of our radiant Lady o' Fair Dealin'.

Eeada [*deprecatingly*]. What are you sayin', woman ? That's a Protestan' ministher, indeed, gentleman, Dympna !

Dympna. Me mind slipped for a poor minute ; but it's pity he'll have on us, an' regulate our lives with what'll bring a sudden cup o' tea within fair reach of our hands.

Eeada. Apples, here, penny each, rosy apples, picked hardly an hour ago from a laden three ; cakes tuppence on'y, baked over scented turf as th' dawn stepped over th' blue-gowned backs o' th' Dublin Mountains.

Dympna. Tuppence a bunch, th' violets, shy an' dhrunk with th' dew o' th' mornin' ; fain to lie in the white bosom of a high-born lady, or fit into th' lapel of a genuine gentleman's Sunday courtin' coat.

[*The Rector takes a few coins from his pocket and throws them to the women, who pick them up and sink into silence again.*

Inspector. Swift, too, must have walked about here with the thorny crown of madness pressing ever deeper into his brain.

Rector [*indicating the men and women*]. Who are these ?

Inspector [*indifferent*]. Those ? Oh, flotsam and jetsam. A few of them dangerous at night, maybe ; but harmless during the day.

Rector. I've read that tens of thousands of such as those followed Swift to the grave.

Inspector. Indeed, sir ? A queer man, the poor demented Dean ; a right queer man.
[*A sleepy lounger suddenly gives a cough, gives his throat a hawk, and sends a big spit on to one of the Inspector's polished boots, then sinks back into sleep again.*

Inspector [*springing back with an angry exclamation*]. What th' hell are you after doing, you rotten lizard ! Looka what you've done, you mangy rat !
[*He takes hold of the lounger and shakes him sharply.*

2nd Man [*sleepily resentful*]. Eh, there ! Wha' th' hell ?

Inspector [*furiously*]. You spat on my boots, you tousled toad — my boots, boots, boots !

2nd Man [*frightened and bewildered*]. Boots, sir ? Is it me, sir ? Not me, sir. Musta been someone else, sir.

Inspector [*shaking him furiously*]. You, you, you !

2nd Man. Me, sir ? Never spit in public in me life, sir. Makin' a mistake, sir. Musta been someone else.

Rector. Inspector Finglas ! Remember you wear the King's uniform ! Quiet, quiet, man !

Inspector [*subsiding*]. Pardon me. I lost my temper. I'm more used to a blow from a stone than a dirty spit on my boot.

Rector [*shuddering a little*]. Let us go from here. Things here frighten me, for they seem to look with wonder on our ease and comfort.

Inspector. Frighten you ? Nonsense — and with me !

Rector. Things here are of a substance I dare not think about, much less see and handle. Here, I can hardly bear to look upon the same thing twice.

Inspector. There you are, and as I've said so often, Breydon's but a neat slab of a similar slime.

Rector. You wrong yourself to say so : Ayamonn Breydon has within him the Kingdom of Heaven. [*He pauses.*] And so, indeed, may these sad things we turn away from.   [*They pass out.*

Eeada [*thinking of the coins given*]. Two tiny sixpences — fourpence a head. Oh, well, beggars can't be choosers. But isn't it a hard life to be grindin' our poor bums to powder, for ever squattin' on the heartless pavements of th' Dublin streets !

Dympna. Ah, what is it all to us but a deep-written testament o' gloom : grey sky over our heads, brown an' dusty streets undher our feet, with th' black an' bitther Liffey flowin' through it all.

Eeada [*mournfully*]. We've dhrifted down to where there's nothin'. Younger I was when every quiet-clad evenin' carried a jaunty jewel in her bosom. Tormented with joy I was then as to whether I'd parade th' thronged sthreets on th' arm of a 16th Lancer, his black-breasted crimson coat a sight to see, an' a black plume droopin' from his haughty helmet ; or lay claim to a red-breasted Prince o' Wales's Own, th' red plume in his hat a flame over his head.

Dympna. It was a 15th King's Own Hussar for me, Eeada, with his rich blue coat an' its fairyland o' yellow braid, two yellow sthripes down his trousers, an' a red bag an' plume dancin' on his busby.

Eeada. Lancers for me, Dympna.

Dympna. Hussars for me, Eeada.

Eeada. An' what for you, Finnoola?

Finnoola. What would a girl, born in a wild Cork valley, among the mountains, brought up to sing the songs of her fathers, what would she choose but the patched coat, shaky shoes, an' white hungry face of th' Irish rebel? But their shabbiness was threaded with th' colours from the garments of Finn Mac Cool of th' golden hair, Goll Mac Morna of th' big blows, Caoilte of th' flyin' feet, an' Oscar of th' invincible spear.

Eeada [*nudging Dympna*]. That was some time ago, if y'ask me.
   [*Brennan comes slowly over the bridge from the far side. His melodeon is hanging on his back. He looks around for a likely place to play. He leans against a parapet, some distance off, and unslings his melodeon from his back.*

Eeada. Here's that oul' miser creepin' after coppers, an' some bank bulgin' with what he has in it already.

2nd Man [*waking suddenly, spitting out vigorously, and speaking venomously*]. Rowlin' in th' coin o' th' realm—bastard!
   [*He sinks into a coma again.*

Brennan [*giving himself confidence*]. Evenin', ladies an' gentlemen. Good thing to be alive when th' sun's kind. [*They take no heed of what he says. Brennan sighs; then plays a few preliminary notes on the melodeon to make sure it is in tune.   He begins to sing in a voice that was once a mellow baritone, but now is a little husky with age, now and again quavering a little on the higher notes in the song. Singing :*]

I stroll'd with a fine maid far out in th' counthry,
Th' blossoms around us all cryin' for dew ;
On a violet-clad bench, sure, I sat down beside her,
An' tuck'd up my sleeves for to tie up her shoe.
An' what's that to anyone whether or no
If I came to th' fore when she gave me th' cue ?
She clos'd her eyes tight as she murmur'd full low,
Be good enough, dear, for to tie up my shoe.

Eeada [*with muttered indignation*]. Isn't that outrageous, now ; on a day like this, too, an' in a sober mood !

Dympna. In front o' decent women as well !

1st Man [*waking up suddenly*]. Disturbin' me dhreams of Golden Gandher gallopin' home to win in a canther !

Brennan [*singing*] :
Th' hawthorn shook all her perfume upon us,
Red poppies saluted, wherever they grew,
Th' joyous exertion that flaunted before me,
When I tuck'd up my sleeves for to fasten her shoe.
An' what's it to anyone, whether or no
I learn'd in that moment far more than I knew,
As she lifted her petticoat, shyly an' slow,
An' I tuck'd up my sleeves for to fasten her shoe ?

The heathery hills were all dancin' around us,
False things in th' world turn'd out to be thrue,
When she put her arms round me, an' kiss'd me an'
    murmur'd,
You've neatly an' tenderly tied up my shoe.

An' what's that to anyone whether or no,
I ventur'd quite gamely to see th' thing through,
When she lifted her petticoat, silent an' slow,
An' I tuck'd up my sleeves for to tie up her shoe?

[*Some pennies have been thrown from the windows of the houses. Brennan picks them up, and taking off a shabby, wide-brimmed hat, bestows a sweeping bow on the houses. During the singing of the last verse of the song, Ayamonn and Roory have strolled in, and have listened to the old man singing while they leant against the balustrade of the bridge. The scene has grown darker as the old man is singing his song, for the sun is setting.*

2nd Man [*waking up suddenly*]. Off with you, old man, thinkin' to turn our thoughts aside from th' way we are, an' th' worn-out hope in front of us.

1st Man [*waking up — wrathfully*]. Get to hell outa that, with your sootherin' songs o' gaudy idleness!

Eeada. Makin' his soul, at his age, he ought to be, instead o' chantin' ditties th' way you'd fear what would come upon you in th' darkness o' th' night, an' ne'er a sword be your side either.

3rd Man. Away with you an' your heathen songs to parts renowned for ignorance an' shame!

Finnoola. Away to where light women are plenty, an' free to open purple purses to throw you glitterin' coins!

[*Brennan slings his melodeon on to his back, puts his hat back on his head, and wends his way across the bridge.*

Roory [*as he passes*]. Isn't it a wondher, now, you wouldn't sing an Irish song, free o' blemish, instead o' one thickly speckled with th' lure of foreign enthertainment?

[*Brennan heeds him not, but crosses the bridge and goes out.
The men and women begin to sink into drowsiness again.*

Ayamonn. Let him be, man ; he sang a merry song well, and should have got a fairer greeting.

Roory [*taking no notice of Ayamonn's remark — to the men and women*]. Why didn't yous stop him before he began ? *Pearl of th' White Breasts,* now, or *Battle Song o' Munster* that would pour into yous Conn's battle-fire of th' hundhred fights. Watchman o' Tara he was, his arm reachin' over deep rivers an' high hills, to dhrag out a host o' sthrong enemies shiverin' in shelthers. Leadher of Magh Femon's Host he was, Guardian of Moinmoy, an' Vetheran of our river Liffey, flowin' through a city whose dhrinkin' goblets once were made of gold, ere wise men carried it with frankincense an' myrrh to star-lit Bethlehem.

Eeada [*full of sleep — murmuring low*]. Away you, too, with your spangled memories of battle-mad warriors buried too deep for words to find them. Penny, here, each, th' ripe apples.

Dympna [*sleepily — in a low murmur*]. Away, an' leave us to saunter in sleep, an' crave out a crust in the grey kingdom of quietness. Tuppence a bunch the fresh violets.

Finnoola [*sleepily*]. Run away, son, to where bright eyes can see no fear, an' white hands, idle, are willin' to buckle a sword on a young man's thigh.

1st Man [*with a sleepy growl*]. Get to hell where gay life has room to move, an' hours to waste, an' white praise is sung to coloured shadows. Time is precious here.

2nd and 3rd Men [*together—murmuringly*]. Time is precious here.

Ayamonn. Rouse yourselves ; we hold a city in our hands !

Eeada [*in a very low, but bitter voice*]. It's a bitther city.

Dympna [*murmuring the same way*]. It's a black an' bitther city.

Finnoola [*speaking the same way*]. It's a bleak, black, an' bitther city.

1st Man. Like a batthered, tatthered whore, bullied by too long a life.

2nd Man. An' her three gates are castles of poverty, penance, an' pain.

Ayamonn. She's what our hands have made her. We pray too much and work too little. Meanness, spite, and common pattherns are woven thick through all her glory ; but her glory's there for open eyes to see.

Eeada [*bitterly — in a low voice*]. Take your fill of her glory, then ; for it won't last long with your headin' against them who hold the kingdom an' who wield th' power.

Dympna [*reprovingly*]. He means well, Eeada, an' he knows things hid from us ; an' we know his poor oul' mother's poor feet has worn out a pathway to most of our tumbling doorways, seekin' out ways o' comfort for us she sadly needs herself.

Eeada [*in a slightly livelier manner*]. Don't I know that well ! A shabby sisther of ceaseless help she is, blind to herself for seein' so far into th' needs of others. May th' Lord be restless when He loses sight of her !

Finnoola. For all her tired look an' wrinkled face, a pure white candle she is, blessed this minute by St. Colm-kille of th' gentle manner, or be Aidan, steeped in th' lore o' Heaven, or be Lausereena of th' silver voice an' snowy vestments — th' blue cloak o' Brigid be a banner over her head for ever !

The Other Two Women [*together*]. Amen.

Roory [*impatiently*]. We waste our time here — come on !

Ayamonn. Be still, man ; it was dark when th' spirit of God first moved on th' face of th' waters.

Roory. There's nothin' movin' here but misery. Gun peal an' slogan cry are th' only things to startle them. We're useless here. I'm off, if you're not.

Ayamonn. Wait a moment, Roory. No-one knows what a word may bring forth. Th' leaves an' blossoms have fallen, but th' three isn't dead.

Roory [*hotly*]. An' d'ye think talkin' to these tatthered second-hand ghosts'll bring back Heaven's grace an' Heaven's beauty to Kaithleen ni Houlihan ?

Ayamonn. Roory, Roory, your Kaithleen ni Houlihan has th' bent back of an oul' woman as well as th' walk of a queen. We love th' ideal Kaithleen ni Houlihan, not because she is false, but because she is beautiful ; we hate th' real Kaithleen ni Houlihan, not because she is true, but because she is ugly.

Roory [*disgusted*]. Aw, for God's sake, man !

[*He hurries off angrily.*

Eeada [*calling scornfully after him*]. God speed you, scut !

Ayamonn [*placing a hand softly on Eeada's head*]. Forget him, an' remember ourselves, and think of what we can do to pull down th' banner from dusty bygones, an' fix it up in th' needs an' desires of today.

[*The scene has now become so dark that things are but dimly seen, save the silver spire and the crimson pillar in the distance; and Ayamonn's head set in a streak of sunlight, looking like the severed head of Dunn-Bo speaking out of the darkness.*]

Finnoola. Songs of Osheen and Sword of Oscar could do nothing to tire this city of its shame.

Ayamonn. Friend, we would that you should live a greater life ; we will that all of us shall live a greater life. Our sthrike is yours. A step ahead for us today ; another one for you tomorrow. We who have known, and know, the emptiness of life shall know its fullness. All men and women quick with life are fain to venture forward. [*To Eeada*] The apple grows for you to eat. [*To Dympna*] The violet grows for you to wear. [*To Finnoola*] Young maiden, another world is in your womb.

Eeada [*still a little gloomily*]. Th' soldiers will be chasin' us with gunfire ; th' polis hoppin' batons off our heads ; our sons an' husbands hurried off to prison, to sigh away th' time in gloomier places than those they live in now.

Ayamonn. Don't flinch in th' first flare of a fight. [*He looks away from them and gazes meditatively down the river.*] Take heart of grace from your city's hidden splendour. [*He points with an outstretched hand.*] Oh, look ! Look there ! Th' sky has thrown a gleaming green mantle over her bare shoulders, bordhered with crimson, an' with a hood of gentle magenta over her handsome head — look !

[*The scene has brightened, and bright and lovely colours
are being brought to them by the caress of the setting sun.
The houses on the far side of the river now bow to the
visible world, decked in mauve and burnished bronze; and
the men that have been lounging against them now stand
stalwart, looking like fine bronze statues, slashed with
scarlet.*

Ayamonn. Look! Th' vans an' lorries rattling down th'
quays, turned to bronze an' purple by th' sun, look like
chariots forging forward to th' battle-front.

[*Eeada, rising into the light, now shows a fresh and virile
face, and she is garbed in a dark-green robe, with a
silvery mantle over her shoulders.*

Eeada [*gazing intently before her*]. Shy an' lovely, as well as
battle-minded!

[*Dympna rises now to look where Ayamonn is pointing. She
is dressed like Eeada, and her face is aglow. The men
have slid from the parapets of the bridge, turning, too, to
look where Ayamonn is pointing. Their faces are aglow,
like the women's, and they look like bronze statues,
slashed with a vivid green. Finnoola rises, last, and
stands a little behind the others, to look at the city
showing her melody of colours. Finnoola is dressed in a
skirt of a brighter green than the other two women, a
white bodice slashed with black, and a flowing silvery
scarf is round her waist.*

Finnoola. She's glowin' like a song sung be Osheen himself, with th' golden melody of his own harp helpin'!

1st Man [*puzzled*]. Something funny musta happened,
for, 'clare to God, I never noticed her shinin' that way
before.

2nd Man. Looka the loungers opposite have changed to

sturdy men of bronze, and th' houses themselves are gay in purple an' silver !

3rd Man. Our tired heads have always haunted far too low a level.

Ayamonn. There's th' great dome o' th' Four Courts lookin' like a golden rose in a great bronze bowl ! An' th' river flowin' below it, a purple flood, marbled with ripples o' scarlet ; watch th' seagulls glidin' over it — like restless white pearls astir on a royal breast. Our city's in th' grip o' God !

1st Man [*emotionally*]. Oh, hell, it's grand !

Eeada. Blessed be our city for ever an' ever.

Ayamonn [*lifting his right hand high*]. Home of th' Ostmen, of th' Norman, an' th' Gael, we greet you ! Greet you as you catch a passing hour of loveliness, an' hold it tightly to your panting breast ! [*He sings :*]
Fair city, I tell thee our souls shall not slumber
Within th' warm beds of ambition or gain ;
Our hands shall stretch out to th' fullness of labour,
Till wondher an' beauty within thee shall reign.

The Rest [*singing together*] :
We vow to release thee from anger an' envy,
To dhrive th' fierce wolf an' sly fox from thy gate,
Till wise men an' matrons an' virgins shall murmur
O city of splendour, right fair is thy fate !

Ayamonn [*singing*] :
Fair city, I tell thee that children's white laughter,
An' all th' red joy of grave youth goin' gay,
Shall make of thy streets a wild harp ever sounding,
Touch'd by th' swift fingers of young ones at play !

The Rest [*singing*] :
We swear to release thee from hunger an' hardship,
From things that are ugly an' common an' mean ;
Thy people together shall build a brave city,
Th' fairest an' finest that ever was seen !

> [*Finnoola has been swaying her body to the rhythm of the song, and now, just as the last part is ending, she swings out on to the centre of the bridge in a dance. The tune, played on a flute by someone, somewhere, is that of a Gavotte, or an air of some dignified and joyous dance, and, for a while, it is played in fairly slow time. After some time it gets quicker, and Ayamonn dances out to meet her. They dance opposite each other, the people around clapping their hands to the tap of the dancers' feet. The two move around in this spontaneous dance, she in a golden pool of light, he in a violet-coloured shadow, now and again changing their movements so that she is in the violet-coloured shadow, and he in the golden pool.*

Eeada [*loudly*]. The finest colours God has to give are all around us now.

Finnoola [*as she dances*]. The Sword of Light is shining !

1st Man [*exultantly*]. Sons an' daughters of princes are we all, an' one with th' race of Milesius !
> [*The dance comes to an end with Ayamonn and Finnoola having their arms round each other.*

Eeada. Praise God for th' urge of jubilation in th' heart of th' young.

1st Man. An' for th' swiftness of leg an' foot in th' heart of a dance.

2nd Man. An' for th' dhream that God's right hand still holds all things firmly.

[*The scene darkens slightly. Ayamonn loosens his hold on Finnoola and raises his head to listen to something. In the distance can be heard the sound of many feet marching in unison.*

Finnoola [*a little anxiously*]. What is it you're listenin' to ?

Ayamonn. I must go ; goodbye, fair maid, goodbye.

Finnoola. Is it goin' to go you are, away from the fine things shinin' around us ? Amn't I good enough for you ?

Ayamonn [*earnestly*]. You're lovely stayin' still, an' brimmin' over with a wilder beauty when you're dancin' ; but I must go. May you marry well, an' rear up children fair as Emer was, an' fine as Oscar's son ; an' may they be young when Spanish ale foams high on every hand, an' wine from th' royal Pope's a common dhrink ! Goodbye.

[*He kisses her, and goes across the bridge, passing out of sight on the farther bank of the river. The figures left behind have shrunk a little ; the colours have faded a good deal, and all look a little puzzled and bewildered. The loungers have fallen back to the walls of the houses, and, though they do not lie against them, they stand close to them, as if seeking their shelter. There is a fairly long pause before anyone speaks. They stand apart, as if shy of each other's company.*

Eeada [*murmuringly*]. Penny each, th' ripe apples. Who was it that spoke that time ? Jasus ! I musta been dhreamin'.

Dympna [*in a bewildered voice*]. So must I, th' way I thought I was lost in a storm of joy, an' many colours, with gay clothes adornin' me.

Finnoola [*puzzled and dreamy*]. Dhreamin' I musta been when I heard strange words in a city nearly smothered be stars, with God guidin' us along th' banks of a purple river, all of us clad in fresh garments, fit to make Osheen mad to sing a song of the revelry dancin' in an' out of God's own vision.

Eeada [*murmuringly, but a little peevishly*]. For God's sake give over dwellin' on oul' songs sung by Osheen, th' way you'd be kindlin' a fire o' glory round some poor bog-warbler chantin' hoarse ditties in a sheltered corner of a windy street. [*Very sleepily*] Th' dewy violets, here, on'y tuppence a bunch — Jasus, apples I mean !
   [*Now the tramp-tramp of marching men is heard more plainly.*

Dympna [*a little more awake*]. Tuppence each, the bunch of vio—— What can that be, now ?

1st Man [*gloomily, but with a note of defiance in his voice*]. Th' thramp of marchin' soldiers out to prevent our meetin' an' to stop our sthrike.

2nd Man [*in a burst of resolution*]. We'll have both, in spite of them !
   [*The scene darkens deeply now. In the pause following the 2nd Man's remark, nothing is heard but the sound of the tramping feet ; then through this threatening sound comes the sound of voices singing quietly, voices that may be of those on and around the bridge, or of those singing some little distance away.*

Voices [singing quietly] :
  We swear to release thee from hunger and hardship,
  From things that are ugly and common and mean ;
  Thy people together shall build a great city,
  The finest and fairest that ever was seen.

CURTAIN

ACT IV

Part of the grounds surrounding the Protestant church of St. Burnupus. The grounds aren't very beautiful, for they are in the midst of a poor and smoky district; but they are trim, and, considering the surroundings, they make a fair show. An iron railing running along the back is almost hidden by a green and golden hedge, except where, towards the centre, a fairly wide wooden gate gives admittance to the grounds. Beyond this gateway, on the pathway outside, is a street lamp. Shrubs grow here and there, and in the left corner, close to the hedge, are lilac and laburnum trees in bloom. To the right is the porch of the church, and part of the south wall, holding a long, rather narrow window, showing, in coloured glass, the figures of SS. Peter and Paul. Some distance away from the porch is a rowan tree, also in blossom, its white flowers contrasting richly with the gay yellow of the laburnum and the royal purple of the lilac. The rest of the grounds are laid out in grass, except for the path leading from the gateway to the entrance of the church. It is a warm, sunny evening, the Vigil of Easter, and the Rector is sitting on a deck-chair, before a table, on which are some books and papers. He is evidently considering the services that are to be held in the church on the following day.

The Rector is wearing a thick black cassock lined with red cloth, and at the moment is humming a verse of a hymn softly to himself, as he marks down notes on a slip of paper before him. A square black skull-cap covers his head.

Rector [*singing to himself, softly*] :
    As Thou didst rise from Thy grim grave,
    So may we rise and stand to brave

Th' power bestow'd on fool or knave ;
We beseech Thee !

[*The verger comes out from the porch and walks towards the Rector. He is bald as an egg, and his yellowish face is parched and woebegone-looking. He is a man of sixty, and shows it. His ordinary clothes are covered with a long black mantle of thin stuff, with a small cape-like addition or insertion of crimson velvet on the shoulders.*]

Rector [*noticing the verger beside him*]. Hymn 625 : we must have that as our opening hymn, Samuel.

Samuel. It's got to go in, sir.

Rector. As you say — it's got to go in. Did you want to speak to me, Samuel ?

Samuel. Excuse me, sir, for what I'm agoin' to say.

Rector [*encouragingly*]. Yes, yes, Samuel, go on.

Samuel [*mysteriously*]. Somethin's afther happenin', sir, that I don't like.

Rector [*turning a little in his chair.*]. Oh ! What's that, Sam ?

Samuel. Mr. Fosther was here this mornin' runnin' a hand through th' daffodils sent for Easther, an' found somethin' he didn't like.

Rector. Yes ?

Samuel. It's not for me to remark on anything that manœuvres out in front o' me, or to slip in a sly word on things done, said, or thought on, be th' pastors, masthers, or higher individuals of th' congregation ; but, sometimes, sir, there comes a time when a true man should, must speak out.

Rector [*with a sigh*]. And the time has come to say something now — what is it, Sam ?

Samuel [*in a part whisper*]. This mornin', sir, and th' dear spring sun shinin' through th' yellow robes of Pether an' th' purple robes o' Paul, an' me arrangin' th' books in th' pews, who comes stealin' in, but lo and behold you, Fosther an' Dowzard to have a squint round. Seein' they're Select Vesthrymen, I couldn't ask them why they were nosin' about in th' silence of th' church on an ordinary week-day mornin'.

Rector [*patiently*]. Yes ; but a long time ago, you said something about daffodils.

Samuel. I'm comin' at a gallop to them, sir.

Rector. Good ; well, let's hear about the daffodils.

Samuel. Aha, says I, when I seen th' two prowlers with their heads close together, whisperin', aha, says I, there's somethin' on th' carpet.

Rector. Is what you have to tell me something to do with Dowzard and Foster, or the daffodils ?

Samuel. Wait till you hear ; sometimes Fosther an' Dowzard'll be to th' fore, an' sometimes th' daffodils. What can these two oul' codgers be up to? says I, sidlin' up to where they were, hummin' a hymn.

Rector. Humming a hymn ? I'm glad to hear it ; for I'd be surprised to hear either of them humming a hymn.

Samuel. Me it was, sir, who was hummin' th' hymn ; for in a church, I like me thoughts to go with th' work I'm doin', if you know what I mean.

Rector [*impatiently*]. It'll be nightfall before you get to the daffodils, man.

Samuel. Wait till you hear, sir. There I was gettin' close to them be degrees, when, all of a sudden, didn't Fosther turn on me, shoutin' "Are you goin' to be a party to th' plastherin' of Popish emblems over a Protestan' church?"

Rector. Popish emblems?

Samuel. Th' daffodils, sir.

Rector. The daffodils? But they simply signify the new life that Spring gives; and we connect them in a symbolic way, quite innocently, with our Blessed Lord's Rising. And a beautiful symbol they are: daffodils that come before the swallow dares, and take the winds of March with beauty. Shakespeare, Sam.

Samuel [*lifting his eyes skywards and pointing upwards*]. Altogether too high up for poor me, sir. [*He bends down close to the Rector's ear.*] When he seen the cross o' daffodils made be Breydon, he near went daft. [*A pause, as if Samuel expected the Rector to speak, but he stays silent.*] God knows what'll be th' upshot if it's fixed to the Communion Table, sir. [*Another slight pause.*] Is it really to go there, sir? Wouldn't it look a little more innocent on th' pulpit, sir?

Rector [*in a final voice*]. I will place it myself in front of the Communion Table, and, if Mr. Foster or Mr. Dowzard ask anything more about it, say that it has been placed there by me. And, remember, when you say Mr. Foster and Mr. Dowzard, it's to be Mr. Breydon too. [*He hands some leaflets to Samuel.*] Distribute these

through the pews, Sam, please. The arranging of the
flowers is finished, is it ?

Samuel. Yessir ; all but the cross.

Rector. I will see to that myself. Thanks, Sam.
    [*Samuel goes off into the church, and the Rector, leaning
    back in his chair with a book in his hand, chants softly.*

Rector [*chanting*] :
        May wonders cease when we grow tame,
        Or worship greatness in a name ;
        May love for man be all our fame,
        We beseech Thee !
    [*As he pauses to meditate for a moment, Mrs. Breydon is seen
    coming along, outside the hedge. She enters by the gate,
    and comes over to the Rector. Sheila has come with her,
    but lags a little behind when they enter the grounds. The
    Rector rises quickly from his chair to greet Mrs. Breydon.*

Rector [*warmly*]. My dear Mrs. Breydon ! Hasn't it been
a lovely day ? The weather promises well for Easter.

Mrs. Breydon. It would be good if other things promised
as well as the weather, sir.

Rector. We must be patient, and more hopeful, my friend.
From the clash of life new life is born.

Mrs. Breydon. An' often new life dies in th' clash too.
Ah, when he comes, sir, speak th' word that will keep
my boy safe at home, or here.

Rector [*laying a gentle hand on her arm*]. I wish I could, dear
friend ; I wish I could.

Mrs. Breydon. His mind, like his poor father's, hates what
he sees as a sham ; an' shams are powerful things,

mustherin' at their broad backs guns that shoot, big
jails that hide their foes, and high gallows to choke th'
young cryin' out against them when th' stones are
silent.

Rector. Let those safely sheltered under the lawn of the
bishop, the miniver of the noble, the scarlet and
ermine of the judge, say unto him, this thing you
must not do ; I won't, for sometimes out of the
mouths of even babes and sucklings cometh wisdom.

Sheila. If what's against him be so powerful, he is helpless ; so let this power go on its way of darkened
grandeur, and let Ayamonn sit safe by his own fireside.

> [*To the left, on the path outside the hedge, the Inspector, in
> full uniform, appears, evidently coming to see the Rector;
> on the right, followed by the men and women of the
> previous scenes, appears Ayamonn. He and the Inspector
> meet at the gate. The Inspector and he halt. The
> Inspector indicates he will wait for Ayamonn to pass, and
> Ayamonn comes into the grounds towards the Rector.
> The Inspector follows, but, in the grounds, stands a
> little apart, nearer the hedge. The men and women
> spread along the path outside, and stay still watching
> those in the grounds from over the hedge. They hold
> themselves erect, now; their faces are still pale, but are
> set with seams of resolution. Each is wearing in the
> bosom a golden-rayed sun. Brennan comes in and, crossing
> the grass, sidles over to sit down on the step of the porch.*

Rector [*shaking Ayamonn's hand*]. Ah, I'm so glad you've
come ; I hope you'll stay.

Ayamonn [*hastily.*] I come but to go. You got the cross of
daffodils ?

Rector. Your mother brought it to us ; it will hang in

front of our church's greatest promise. Come and
place it there with your own loyal hands, Ayamonn.

Inspector. Loyal hands engaged in rough rending of the
law and the rumpling-up of decency and order ; and
all for what ? For what would but buy blacking for
a pair of boots, or a sheet of glass to mend a broken
window !

Brennan [*from his seat on the porch's step*]. He's right, Ayamonn, me son, he's right : money's the root of all evil.

Ayamonn [*to the Inspector*]. A shilling's little to you, and
less to many ; to us it is our Shechinah, showing us
God's light is near ; showing us the way in which our
feet must go ; a sun-ray on our face ; the first step
taken in the march of a thousand miles.

Inspector [*threateningly*]. I register a lonely warning here
that the people of power today will teach a lesson many
will remember for ever ; though some fools may not
live long enough to learn it.

Mrs. Breydon. Stay here, my son, where safety is a green
tree with a kindly growth.

Men and Women [*in chorus — above*]. He comes with us !

Sheila. Stay here where time goes by in sandals soft,
where days fall gently as petals from a flower, where
dark hair, growing grey, is never noticed.

Men and Women [*above*]. He comes with us !

Ayamonn [*turning towards them*]. I go with you !

Inspector [*vehemently*]. Before you go to carry out all your
heated mind is set to do, I warn you for the last time
that today swift horses will be galloping, and swords
will be out of their scabbards !

Rector [*reprovingly — to Inspector*]. I hope you, at least, will find no reason to set your horses moving.

Inspector [*stiffly*]. I'll do my duty, sir ; and it would be a good thing if someone we all know did his in that state of life unto which it has pleased God to call him.

Rector [*losing his temper*]. Oh, damn it, man, when you repeat the Church's counsel, repeat it right ! Not *unto which it has pleased God to call him*, but *unto which it shall please God to call him*.

Inspector [*losing his temper too*]. Damn it, man, do you believe that what the fellow's doing now is the state of life unto which it has pleased God to call him ?

Rector [*hotly*]. I have neither the authority nor the knowledge to deny it, though I have more of both than you, sir !

[*The Inspector is about to answer angrily, but Sheila catches his arm.*

Sheila. Oh, cancel from your mind the harder things you want to say, an' do your best to save us from another sorrow !

Inspector [*shaking off Sheila's hand roughly, and going to the gateway, where he turns to speak again*]. Remember, all ! When swords are drawn and horses charge, the kindly Law, so fat with hesitation, swoons away, and sees not, hears not, cares not what may happen.

Mrs. Breydon [*angrily — up to the Inspector*]. Look at th' round world, man, an' all its wondhers, God made, flaming in it, an' what are you among them, standing here, or on a charging horse, but just a braided an' a tasselled dot !

[*The Inspector hurries off, to pause, and stands outside the hedge, to the right, the men and women shrinking back a little in awe to give him a passage.*

Mrs. Breydon [*to Ayamonn*]. Go on your way, my son, an' win. We'll welcome another inch of the world's welfare.

Rector [*shaking his hand*]. Go, and may the Lord direct you ! [*He smiles.*] The Inspector's bark is louder than his bite is deep.

Ayamonn. For the present — goodbye !
[*Ayamonn hurries away through the gate, pausing, outside the hedge to the left, turning to give a last look at the Inspector.*

Inspector. Bear back, my boy, when you see the horsemen charging !
[*He goes out by the right, and Ayamonn goes out left, followed by the men and the women. There is a slight pause.*

Rector [*briskly — to banish a gloomy feeling*]. Now, Mrs. Breydon, you run along to the vestry, and make us a good cup of tea — I'm dying for one. [*To Sheila*] You'll join us, Miss Moorneen, won't you ?

Sheila [*immediately anxious*]. Oh no, thanks. I . . . I shouldn't even be here. I'm a Catholic, you know.

Rector. I know, and I'd be the last to ask you do anything you shouldn't ; but rest assured there's no canonical law against taking tea made by a Protestant. Off you go, and help Mrs. Breydon. I'll join you in a moment.
[*Sheila and Mrs. Breydon go off by the south wall of the church.*

Brennan [*as the Rector is gathering his books and papers from the table*]. Hey, sir ; hey there, sir ! It won't shatther th' community at large this disturbance, will it, eh ?

Rector. I hope not.

Brennan [*with a forced laugh*]. No, no, of course not. Bank of Ireland'll still stand, eh ? Ay. Ravenous to break in, some of them are, eh ? Ay, ay. Iron doors, iron doors are hard to open, eh ?

Rector [*going off to get his tea*]. I suppose so.

Brennan. Ay, are they. He supposes so ; only supposes — there's a responsible man for you !
    [*The verger comes into the porch and bends over Brennan.*

Samuel [*in a hoarse whisper*]. Come in an' have a decko at our grand cross.

Brennan. Cross ? What cross ?

Samuel. One o' daffodils for Easther, to be put in front of th' Communion Table.

Brennan. Popery, be God !
    [*Booing is heard a little distance away, followed by the rattling fall of a shower of stones.*

Brennan. What's that ; what's happenin' ?

Samuel [*going to back, and looking down the street*]. A crowd flingin' stones ; flingin' them at two men runnin' for their life.

Brennan [*nervously*]. Let's get into the church, quick. Throuble's beginnin' already.
    [*They both go into the church, and Samuel closes the door. A crowd can be heard booing. Men and women, among them Eeada, Finnoola, Dympna, the Railwaymen, and the*

> *Lurchers who were on the bridge, pass across outside the
> hedge. The Leader carries a red flag, and all march with
> determination. They are all singing the following song:*

Leaders [*singing*] :
   If we can't fire a gun, we can fire a hard stone,
   Till th' life of a scab shrivels into a moan ;

Crowd [*chorusing*] :
   Let it sink in what I say,
   Let me say it again —
   Though the Lord made an odd scab, sure, He also
   made men !

Leaders [*singing*]:
   Th' one honour he'll get is a dusty black plume,
   On th' head of th' nag taking him to the tomb ;

Crowd [*chorusing*] :
   Let it sink in what I say,
   Let me say it again :
   Th' scab's curs'd be th' workers, book, candle an'
   bell !

> [*They cross over and disappear. After a pause, Dowzard
> and Foster come running in ; they hurry through the
> gateway, and dash over to the church's porch.*
> [*Dowzard is a big, beefy, red-faced man, rolls of flesh pouring
> out over the collar of his coat. His head is massive and
> bald, with jet-black tufts behind his ear, and a tiny fringe
> of it combed across high over his forehead. Foster is small
> and scraggy, with aggression for ever lurking in his cranky
> face, ready to leap into full view at the slightest oppor-
> tunity. His cheeks and lips are shaven, but spikes of
> yellowish whiskers point defiantly out from under his chin.
> His voice is squeaky and, when it is strengthened in*

anger, it rises into a thin piping scream. Both are
dressed in the uniforms of railway foremen, blue cloth,
with silver buttons, and silver braid on Dowzard's
peaked hat and coat-sleeves, and gold braid on those of
Foster. Both have their coats tightly buttoned up on
them. They take off their peaked caps and wipe sweat
from their foreheads. Dowzard pushes the door.

Dowzard. We're safe here in th' grounds ; Church
grounds sacred. Unguarded, verminous villains —
Papists, th' lot o' them !

Foster [*venomously*]. On' one o' their leaders a Select
Vestryman. On' thot domned Rector stondin' by
him. Steeped in Popery : sign o' th' cross ; turnin'
eastward sayin' th' Creed ; sung Communion — be
Gud, it's a public scondal !

Dowzard. Some o' them stones scorched me ear passin'
by. We shouldn't have worn our uniforms. Gave us
away. I knew we were in for it when they called us
scabs.

Foster. Scobs themselves ! Smoky, vonomous bastards !
I tull you I'd wear me uniform in th' Vutican. [*He*
unbuttons his coat and shows that he is wearing a vivid orange
sash, bordered with blue.] Thor's me sash for all tae see.
You should ha' stud with me, mon ; stud like th'
heroes o' Dully's Brae !

Dowzard [*shouting and knocking at door*]. Ey, there, in there,
come out, open th' blasted door an' help a half-dead
man !
 [*The church door is opened, and the Rector, followed by the*
 verger and Brennan, comes out into the grounds.

Rector. What's wrong ; what has happened ?

Dowzard. Th' Pope's bullies with hard stones have smitten us sore. Honest men, virtuous an' upright, loyal to th' law an' constitution, have this day been smitten sore with Popish stones — oh, me poor head !

Foster. St. Bartholomew's Day's dawnin' again, I'm tullin' yous, an' dismumbered Protestants'll lie on all th' sthreets !

Rector. You can't be badly hurt when you complain so grandly.

Foster. Stand up for th' ruffians be makin' luttle of our hurts, so do, ay, do. [*Noticing Brennan who has edged towards the gate and is about to go away.*] Eh, you, aren't you goin' to stay an' put tustimony to the fullness o' th' Protestan' feth ?

Brennan [*with slight mockery*]. Ay, I would, an' welcome, if I hodn't to go, forbye, at this hour of on uvery day, I mak' ut a rule tae be sturdy in th' readin' of a chapther o' God's word so's I won't hold on tae wordly things too strongly.   [*He goes out.*

Foster [*fiercely*]. A jully-fush Protestant ! [*To the Rector*] Look see, I tull you th' fires o' Smithfield 'ull be blazin' round Protestant bodies again, an' coloured lights 'ull be shown in th' Vatican windows soon !

Dowzard. An' we'll be th' first to go up in th' flames.

Rector [*laughing contemptuously*]. Nonsense, oh, nonsense.

Foster [*almost screaming*]. It's not nonsense, mon ! Every sable-robed Jesuit's goin' about chucklin', his honds twitchin' to pounce out on men like me here, an' Eddie Dowzard there, tae manacle us, head, hond, and fut, for th' wheel, th' thumbscrew, an' th' rack, an'

then finish us up at th' stake in a hoppy Romish auto-
dey-fey ! The Loyola boyos are out to fight another
buttle with th' men o' King Bully !

Rector [*amused*]. Well, let the Loyola boyos and King
Bully fight it out between them. I'm too busy to join
either side. Goodbye.

Foster [*catching his arm as he is going — viciously*]. You're
no' goin' tae be lut slide off like thot, now, with your
guilty conscience, mon. There's things to be done,
and things tae be ondone in yon church, there ; ay, ay.

Rector [*quietly*]. Indeed ?

Foster [*angrily — to Dowzard*]. Uh, speak, speak a word,
mon, on' don't leave ut all tae me.

Dowzard. First, sir, we want you to get rid o' Breydon
from the Vesthry an' from th' church.

Rector. Oh, indeed ?

Foster [*almost screaming*]. It's no' oh, indeed ; answer th'
question — plain yes or no !

Rector [*coldly*]. Gentlemen, Mr. Breydon stays in the
Vestry till the parishioners elect someone else ; as for
the church, God has seen fit to make him a member of
Christ, and it is not for me, or even for you, gentlemen,
to say that God did wrong.

Dowzard [*sneeringly*]. An' when did that wondherful thing
hoppen ?

Rector. At his baptism, as you yourself should know.

Foster [*with an agonised squeal*]. Popery, Popery, nothin' but
Popery ! Th' whole place's infusted with it !

[*The verger appears at the porch door with the cross of daffodils in his hand. It has a Keltic shape, the shafts made of the flowers, and the circle of vivid green moss. The verger shows it to Dowzard, behind the Rector's back, and Dowzard sidling over, takes it from him, the verger returning into the church again.*

Rector. And now be good enough, Mr. Foster, to let my arm go.

[*In the distance, a bugle-call sounding the charge is heard. Foster lets go of the Rector's arm ; and they all listen.*

Foster [*gleefully*]. Aha, there's the bugle soundin' th' charge, an' soon the King's horses an' th' King's men'll be poundin' th' riothers undher their feet ! Law an ordher in th' State an' law an' ordher in th' Church we must have. An' we're fightin' here as they're fightin' there — for th' Crown an' ceevil an' releegious liberty !

[*The sound of galloping horses is heard, followed by several volleys of rifle-fire. They all listen intently for a few moments.*

Foster [*gleefully*]. Hear that now ? Your Breydon fullow'll soon be doshin' in here for th' church to hide him.

Rector. The cross of Christ be between him and all harm !

Dowzard [*dancing out in front of the Rector, holding out the cross — with exultant glee*]. The cross — a Popish symbol ! There y'urre, see ? A Popish symbol flourished in th' faces o' Protestant people ! [*With a yell*] Ichabod !

Foster [*venomously*]. I'll no' stick it, no ; I'll no' stick it. Look-see, th' rage kindlin' godly Luther is kindlin' me ! Here, go, gimme a holt of thot. [*He snatches the cross of flowers from Dowzard, flings it on the ground, and dances on it.*] Th' bible on' th' crown ! The twa on' a half, th' orange on' blue ; on' th' Dagon of Popery undher our Protestant feet !

Dowzard [*wildly*]. Th' dhrum, th' dhrum, th' Protestant dhrum !

    [*While Foster and Dowzard have been dancing about and shouting their last few words, the men and women have run frightened along the path, behind the hedge. Those running from the right, turn, and run back to the left ; those running from the left, turn, and run back to the left again, passing each other as they run. They suddenly see the men and women running about behind the hedge, and at once plunge into the porch, almost knocking the Rector down.*

Foster [*as they fly — to the Rector*]. Out uh th' way, mon, out uh th' way !

    [*After a pause Eeada comes running through the gate, into the garden, over to the Rector.*

Eeada [*beseechingly*]. Oh, sir, please let me into the church, till all th' sthrife is over — no place's safe with the soldiers firin' an' th' police runnin' mad in a flourish o' batons !

Rector [*reassuringly*]. Be calm, be quiet, they won't touch a woman. They remain men, however furious they may be for the moment.

Eeada. Arra, God help your innocence ! You should ha' seen them sthrikin' at men, women, an' childher. An' me own friend, Dympna, in hospital gettin' her face laced with stitches, th' way you'd lace a shoe ! An' all along of followin' that mad fool, Breydon !

Rector. Go in, then. [*To the verger, who has come to the entrance*] See her safe.

    [*Eeada and the verger go into the church. Finnoola comes*

slowly along the path outside the hedge, holding on to the railings as she moves, step by step. When she comes to the gateway, she sinks down to the ground and turns a white and distorted face towards those in the grounds.

Finnoola [*painfully*]. For th' love o' God, one of you tell me if th' Reverend something Clinton's here, or have I to crawl a long way further?

Rector [*hurrying over to her*]. He's here; I'm he, my good woman. What is it you want of me?

Finnoola. I've a message for you from Ayamonn Breydon.

Rector [*eagerly*]. Yes, yes; where is he?

Finnoola. He's gone.

Rector. Gone? Gone where?

Finnoola. Gone to God, I hope.   [*A rather long pause.*

Rector [*in a low voice*]. May he rest in peace! And the message?

Finnoola. Yes. He whispered it in me ear as his life fled through a bullet-hole in his chest — th' soldiers, th' soldiers. He said this day's but a day's work done, an' it'll be begun again tomorrow. You're to keep an eye on th' oul' woman. He wants to lie in th' church tonight, sir. Me hip's hurt; th' fut of a plungin' horse caught me, an' I flat on th' ground. He sent a quick an' a long farewell to you. Oh, for Christ's sake get's a dhrink o' wather! [*The verger runs for a drink.*] We stood our groun' well, though. [*The verger comes back with the water, and she drinks.*] Now I can have a thrickle of rest at last.

          [*She stretches herself out on the ground.*

Rector. Where did you leave him? Where is he lying

now ? [*She lies there, and makes no answer. He picks up the broken cross of flowers and is silent for a few moments. With head bent low—sorrowfully*] Oh, Ayamonn, Ayamonn, my dear, dear friend. Oh Lord, open Thou mine eyes that I may see Thee, even as in a glass, darkly, in all this mischief and all this woe !

[*The curtain comes down to indicate the passing of some hours. When it rises again, it is evening. The lamp over the porch door is lighted, and so is the church, the light shining through the yellow robe of St. Peter and the purple robe of St. Paul from the window in the church's wall. The church organ is playing, very softly, a dead march. The lamp on the path, outside the hedge, isn't yet lighted. The dark figures of men and women can be faintly seen lining themselves along the hedge. Mrs. Breydon is standing in the grounds, near to the gateway. Foster and Dowzard stand on the steps of the porch. A little in front, with his back turned towards them, stands the Rector, now with white surplice over his cassock, his stole around his neck, and the crimson-lined hood of a Doctor of Divinity on his shoulders. Sheila, holding a bunch of crimson roses in her hand, stands under the rowan tree. Partly behind the tree, the Inspector is standing alone. A lamplighter comes along the path, carrying his pole with the little flower of light in the brass top. He lights the lamp on the path, then comes over to peer across the hedge.*]

Lamplighter. What's up ? What's on ? What's happenin' here ? What's they all doin' now ?

1st Man. Bringin' th' body o' Breydon to th' church.

Lamplighter. Aw, is that it ? Guessed somethin' was goin' on.

1st Man. He died for us.

Lamplighter. Looka that, now! An' they're all ac-couthered in their best to welcome him home, wha'? Aw, well, th' world's got to keep movin', so I must be off; so long!   [*He goes.*

Dowzard [*speaking to the Rector's back*]. For th' last time, sir, I tell you half of the Vestry's against him comin' here; they don't want our church mixed up with this venomous disturbance.

Rector [*without moving, and keeping his eyes looking towards the gateway*]. All things in life, the evil and the good, the orderly and disorderly, are mixed with the life of the Church Militant here on earth. We honour our brother, not for what may have been an error in him, but for the truth for ever before his face. We dare not grudge him God's forgiveness and rest eternal because he held no banner above a man-made custom.

Foster [*savagely*]. Aw, looksee, I'm no' a mon to sut down on' listen to a tumblin' blether o' words — wull ye, or wull ye not, give intil us?
     [*In the distance a bagpipe is heard playing* Flowers of the Forest. *Mrs. Breydon's body stiffens, and Sheila's head bends lower on her breast.*

Rector. It is a small thing that you weary me, but you weary my God also. Stand aside, and go your way of smoky ignorance, leaving me to welcome him whose turbulence has sunken into a deep sleep, and who cometh now as the waters of Shiloah that go softly, and sing sadly of peace.
     [*As he is speaking, the lament ceases, and a moment after, a stretcher bier, bearing the covered-up body of Ayamonn,*

*appears at the gateway. It is carried down towards the
church, and the Rector goes to meet it.*

Rector [*intoning*]. Lord, Thou hast been our refuge from
one generation to another. For a thousand years in
Thy sight are but as yesterday. [*He chants :*]
 All our brother's mordant strife
 Fought for more abundant life ;
 For this, and more — oh, hold him dear.
 Jesu, Son of Mary, hear !

 Gather to Thy loving breast
 Ev'ry laughing thoughtful jest,
 Gemm'd with many a thoughtful tear.
 Jesu, Son of Mary, hear !

 When Charon rows him nigh to shore,
 To see a land ne'er seen before,
 Him to rest eternal steer.
 Jesu, Son of Mary, hear !

 [*The bier is carried into the church, and, as it passes, Sheila
 lays the bunch of crimson roses on the body's breast.*

Sheila. Ayamonn, Ayamonn, my own poor Ayamonn !
 [*The Rector precedes the bier, and Mrs. Breydon walks beside
 it, into the church, the rest staying where they are.
 There is a slight pause.*

Dowzard. We'd betther be goin'. Th' man's a malignant
Romaniser. Keep your eye on th' rabble goin' out.

Foster [*contemptuously*]. There's little fight left in thom,
th' now. I'll no' forgive thot Inspector fur refusin' to
back our demond.
 [*They swagger out through the gateway and disappear along
 the path outside the hedge, as those who carried the bier
 come out of the church.*

2nd Man. That's the last, th' very last of him — a core o' darkness stretched out in a dim church.

3rd Man. It was a noble an' a mighty death.

Inspector [*from where he is near the tree*]. It wasn't a very noble thing to die for a single shilling.

Sheila. Maybe he saw the shilling in th' shape of a new world.
> [*The 2nd and 3rd Men go out by the gateway and mingle with the rest gathered there. The Inspector comes closer to Sheila.*

Inspector. Oughtn't you to go from this gloom, Sheila ? Believe me, I did my best. I thought the charge would send them flying, but they wouldn't budge ; wouldn't budge, till the soldiers fired, and he was hit. Believe me, I did my best. I tried to force my horse between them and him.

Sheila [*calmly*]. I believe you, Inspector Finglas.

Inspector [*gently catching her by the arm*]. Tom to you, dear. Come, Sheila, come, and let us put these things away from us as we saunter slowly home.

Sheila [*with a quiver in her voice*]. Oh, not now ; oh, not tonight ! Go your own way, and let me go mine, alone tonight.

Inspector [*taking her hand in his*]. Sheila, Sheila, be sparing in your thought for death, and let life smile before you. Be sparing in thought of death on one who spent his life too rashly and lost it all too soon. Ill-gotten wealth of life, ill-gone for ever !

Sheila [*withdrawing her hand from his gently*]. Oh, Tom, I hope you're right ; you are right, you must be right.

[*They have walked to the gateway, and now stand there together, the men and women along the hedge eyeing them, though pretending to take no notice.*

Inspector. You'll see it clearer, dear, when busy Time in space has set another scene of summer's glory, and new-born spring's loud voice of hope hushes to silence th' intolerant dead.

Sheila [*musingly*]. He said that roses red were never meant for me ; before I left him last, that's what he said. Dear loneliness tonight must help me think it out, for that's just what he said. [*Suddenly — with violence*] Oh, you dusky-minded killer of more worthy men !

[*She runs violently away from him, and goes out, leaving him with the men and women, who stand idly by as if noticing nothing.*

Inspector [*after a pause*]. What are ye doing here ? Get home ! Home with you, you lean rats, to your holes and haunts ! D'ye think th' like o' you alone are decked with th' dark honour of trouble ? [*Men and women scatter, slowly and sullenly, till only Brennan, with his melodeon on his back, is left, leaning by the gate. To Brennan*] Heard what I said ? Are you deaf, or what ?

Brennan [*calmly*]. I'm a Protestant, an' a worshipper in this church.

Inspector. One of the elect ! So was Breydon. Well, keep clear of unruly crowds — my men don't wait to ask the way you worship when they raise their arms to strike.

[*He goes slowly away down the path. A few moments pass, then the Rector and Mrs. Breydon come out of the church. He arranges a shawl round her shoulders.*

Rector. There ; that's better ! My wife insists you stay the night with us, so there's no getting out of it.

Mrs. Breydon. She's kind. [*She pauses to look at the rowan tree.*] There's th' three he loved, bare, or dhrenched with blossom. Like himself, for fine things grew thick in his nature : an' lather come the berries, th' red berries, like the blood that flowed today out of his white body. [*Suddenly — turning to face the church.*] Is it puttin' out th' lights he is ?

Rector. Yes, before he goes home for the night.

Mrs. Breydon. Isn't it a sad thing for him to be lyin' lonesome in th' cheerless darkness of th' livelong night !

Rector [*going to the porch and calling out*]. Sam, leave the lights on tonight.
                    [*The church, which had dimmed, lights up again.*

Rector. He's not so lonesome as you think, dear friend, but alive and laughing in the midst of God's gay welcome. Come.
    [*They slowly go through the gate and pass out. The verger comes from the church and swings the outer door to, to lock up for the night. Brennan comes down into the grounds.*

Samuel [*grumbling*]. Light on all night — more of his Romanisin' manœuvres.

Brennan. Eh, eh, there ; houl' on a second !

Samuel. What th' hell do you want ?

Brennan. Just to sing a little song he liked as a sign of respect an' affection ; an' as a finisher-off to a last farewell.

Samuel [*locking the door*]. An what d'ye take me for ? You an' your song an' your last farewell !

Brennan [*giving him a coin*]. For a bare few minutes, an'
leave th' door open so's th' sound'll have a fair chance
to go in to him. [*The verger opens the door.*] That's it.
You're a kind man, really. [*Brennan stands facing into
the porch, the verger leaning against the side of it. Brennan
unslings his melodeon, plays a few preliminary notes on it, and
then sings softly :*]

A sober black shawl hides her body entirely,
Touch'd be th' sun an' th' salt spray of th' sea ;
But down in th' darkness a slim hand, so lovely,
Carries a rich bunch of red roses for me !

[*The rest of the song is cut off by the ending of the play.*

CURTAIN

RED ROSES FOR ME

A so-ber black shawl hides her bod-y en-ti-re-ly, Touch'd by th' sun and th' salt spray of th' sea; But down in th' dark-ness a slim hand, so love-ly, Car-ries a rich bunch of red ro-ses for me.—

TH' BOULD FENIAN MEN

Our cour-age so ma-ny have thought to be age-in', Now flames like a bril-liant new star in th' sky; An' Dan-ger is proud to be call'd a new bro-ther, Since Freedom has buckled her sword on her thigh. Then out to th' place where th' bat-tle is brav-est, Where th' noblest an' meanest fight fierce in th' fray, Re-pub-lic-an ban-ners shall mock at th' foe-men, An' Fen-ians shall turn a dark night in-to day!

OH, QUEEN OF EBLANA'S POOR CHILDREN

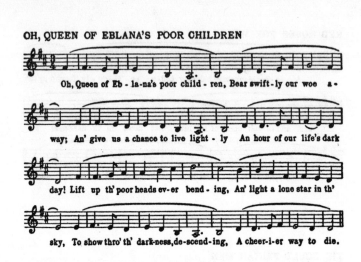

Oh, Queen of Eb - la-na's poor child - ren, Bear swift-ly our woe a-

way; An' give us a chance to live light - ly An hour of our life's dark

day! Lift up th' poor heads ev-er bend - ing, An' light a lone star in th'

sky, To show thro' th' dark-ness, de-scend-ing, A cheer-i-er way to die.

I TUCK'D UP MY SLEEVES

I stroll'd with a fine maid far out in th' coun-try, Th'

blos-soms a-round us all cry-in' for dew;— On a

dai-sy deckt bench, sure, I sat down be-side her, An' tuck'd up my sleeves for to

tie up her shoe. An' what's that to a-ny one wheth-er or no, If I

came to th' fore when she gave me th' cue? She clos'd her eyes tight as she

mur-mured full low, Be good e-nough, dear, for to tie up my shoe.

FAIR CITY

Fair ci-ty; I tell thee our souls shall not slum-ber With-in th' warm beds of am-bi-tion or gain; Our hands shall stretch out to th' full-ness of la-bour, Till won-dher an' beau-ty with-in thee shall reign!

WE BESEECH THEE

As Thou didst rise from Thy_ grim grave, So may we rise to stand and brave Th' pow'r be-stow'd on fool_ or knave._ We be-seech Thee!

THE SCAB

If we can't fire a gun, we can fire a hard stone, Till th' life of th' scab shriv-els in-to a moan. Let it sink in what I say, Let me say it a-gain— Tho' th' Lord God made an odd scab He al-so made men!

725

BROTHERS

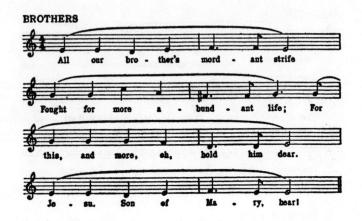

All our bro - ther's mord - ant strife

Fought for more a - bund - ant life; For

this, and more, eh, hold him dear.

Je - su, Son of Ma - ry, hear!

Bedtime Story

CHARACTERS IN THE PLAY

the good guy JOHN JO MULLIGAN, *a clerk*
angelic, sweet ANGELA NIGHTINGALE, *a gay lass*
fishy DANIEL HALIBUT, *a clerk — friend to Mulligan*
MISS MOSSIE, *a very respectable lodging-house keeper*
A POLICEMAN
A DOCTOR
A NURSE

Names ironic

SCENE

A bachelor-flat in Dublin.

TIME.—The present.

The sitting-room of the bachelor-flat rented by John Jo Mulligan from Miss Mossie, owner of one of the old houses of Dublin, decayed a little, but still sternly respectable, and kept presentable by her rigid attention to it. She has divided it into lodgings for respectable young gentlemen. A rather dull though lofty room. To the right is an ordinary gas fire ; over it a mantelpiece on which is a clock, flanked on either side by a coloured vase ; over these, on the wall, a square, gilt-framed mirror. Further up, towards back, is a door leading to Mulligan's bedroom. By the back wall, near this door, is a small bookcase with a few books sprawled out on its shelves ; and on top is a pale-green vase holding a bunch of white pampas grass. To the left of this is a window, now heavily curtained with dull, brown hangings. In the window's centre is a stand holding a coloured flower-pot containing some kind of a palm plant. Further on is a picture of a whitewashed cottage, well thatched with straw, a brown pathway before the door, with purple heather growing in tufts on its edges, and, in the distance, the dark-blue peaks of hills, all surmounted by a bright blue sky. In the side wall on the left is the door leading to the rest of the house. On this door several overcoats are hanging. To the left of it is an umbrella-stand in which are a walking-stick and two umbrellas, one newer than the other. Close to the fireplace is an armchair clad in dark-green leather, and further away, at an angle, is a settee to hold two, clad in the same colour. In the room's centre is a round table covered with a red table-cloth. On the table are a photograph or two, a vase of chrysanthemums, and a book, open, with its face turned down, so that the place might not be lost when the reader left it aside. The room is lighted from a bulb hanging from the centre of the ceiling ; the light is softened by being covered with a yellow parchment shade. A standard lamp

stands on the floor a little way from the sitting-room door,
towards the window, its light mollified by a deeply-fringed red
silk shade.   A key is sticking in the keyhole of the sitting-room
door.   A pair of Mulligan's tan shoes are beside the fireplace.
It is three or four of a cold, sleety January morning.

The fire is unlit, the room in darkness, when, presently, the
bedroom door opens, and Mulligan comes into the sitting-room,
showing the way to himself by the light of an electric torch.   He
is but half dressed, in blue shirt, bright-checked, baggy plus-fours,
and coloured-top stockings.   He is a young man of twenty-four
or -five ; tall, but not thin.   His hair is almost blond, and he
wears it brushed back from his forehead, which is too high for the
rather stolid face, giving him, at times, the look of a clown
having a holiday.   His upper lip has a close-cropped moustache.
He is a constitutionally frightened chap, never able to take the
gayer needs of life in his stride — though he would be glad to
do it, if he could ; but he can never become convalescent from a
futile sense of sin.   His clean-shaven face shows a very worried
look.   He comes into the room cautiously, waving the light over
the floor, the table, the chairs, as if looking for something — as
a matter of fact, he is ; then returns to the door to peep into the
bedroom.

Mulligan [*sticking his head into the room — in a cautious*
    whisper]. I can't see the thing anywhere.   Sure you
    left it out here ?   [*There is no reply to the question.*]   I
    say I can't find it anywhere out here.   [*There is no reply.*
    He mutters to himself as if half in prayer] I shouldn't have
    done it ; I shouldn't have done it !   I musta been
    mad.   Oh, forgive me !   [*He clicks his tongue, and peeps*
    into the room again.]   Dtch dtch !   Gone asleep again !
    [*Whispering*] Angela !   Angela !   [*In a louder whisper*]
    Are you awake ?   Eh, Angela ?

Angela [*within the room — sleepily*].   Wha' ?

Mulligan [*echoing her*]. Wha', wha'! [*To himself*] Oh, it was a mad thing to do. Miserere mei. [*Speaking into room with irritation*] Have you forgotten what you sent me out to get? [*Appealingly*] Please try to arouse yourself, Angela!

Angela [*within*]. Wha'?
　　[*Silence again for a few moments while Mulligan flashes the light on to the clock.*]

Mulligan. It's going to four o'clock in the morning, Angela.

Angela [*within*]. Didja get the lipstick?

Mulligan [*testily*]. I've told you I can't see it anywhere.

Angela [*sleepily*]. Have another look — there's a dear. I know I left it out there somewhere.

Mulligan [*shivering a little*]. It's nothing like a tropical climate out here, you know.

Angela [*sleepily*]. It's easy to li' the fire, isn't it?
　　[*Mulligan crosses to the fireplace, turns the gas tap, and sees that the meter wants another shilling. He irritatedly turns the tap off, and, crossing quickly back to the bedroom, knocks over the vase of flowers on the table, sending the water spilling over the table and on to the floor.*]

Mulligan [*half to himself and half to Angela — with annoyance*]. There's the vase down! Wather into me shoes and all over the floor! [*Putting his head into the bedroom again*] I've knocked the vase down now! The place is flooded! And I can't light the fire — the meter needs another shilling.

Angela [*sleepily*]. Look in me han'bag, somewhere about. Maybe there's a bob in it.

[*In desperation, Mulligan goes to the cupboard, opens it, takes out a wallet from which he takes a shilling, goes back to fireplace, puts it in the slot, and lights the fire. Then he returns to the bedroom door.*

Mulligan [*putting his head into the bedroom again*]. Angela, are you up yet? The whole place is flooded. [*He gets no answer.*] You're not going asleep again, are you? Angela!

Angela [*within — sleepily*]. What time is it?

Mulligan [*in a loud and impatient whisper*]. I told you long ago. It's going to four o'clock in the morning. That friend of mine I told you of, will be back any minute from his all-night dance, before you slip away, if you don't hurry.

Angela [*from within*]. And what if he is? If he knew what had been going on in here, he'd be sorry he ever went to the dance.

Mulligan. Looka, Angela, I don't feel a bit funny about it. We should never have done it. Please get up, and face the situation. Remember your solemn promise to slip off when things were still.

[*Angela appears at the door. She is a girl of twenty-five to twenty-seven, tall, trimly-formed, and not without dignity. Her hair is auburn, inclining towards redness. She is something of a pagan.*

[*At present, she is dressed in her cami-knickers, covered by Mulligan's brown dressing-gown, and her bare feet are thrust into Mulligan's slippers. Far and away too good a companion of an hour, a year, or a life, for a fellow like Mulligan.*

Angela [*from the doorway*]. D'ye like the dark because your
deeds are evil, or what? ~~Switch on the light~~ for God's
sake, man, and let's have a look at each other before
you banish your poor Eve from her Mulligan paradise.

Mulligan [*as he switches on the light*]. I was afraid someone
outside might see it, stay to look, might hear our
voices, and wonder.

Angela. Wonder at what?

Mulligan. At hearing a girl's voice in my room at this
time of night or morning.

Angela [*mockingly*]. And isn't it a sweet thing for a girl's
voice to be heard in a man's room at this time o' the
night or morning?

Mulligan [*almost tearfully*]. You know it's not; not as
we're situated. You know you did wrong to practise
on a body who didn't know enough. Situated as we
are, without divine warrant, it's not proper. We're
in the midst of a violent sin, and you should be
ashamed and sorry, instead of feeling sinfully gay about
it. It's necessary to feel sorry for a sin of this kind.

Angela. You were quite gay when we were coming in,
boy, weren't you? You've had your few bright
moments, and you've given a sparkle to your life, so
don't spoil it all. It may well be more serious for me
than it is for you. [*She shivers.*] Burrr! It's cold
here! I'll come back when the room's warmer, and
make myself ready to meet the respectable world.
  [*She goes back into the bedroom, while he stands at the
    bedroom door for a few moments, not knowing what to do.*

Mulligan [*eyes raised appealing to the ceiling*]. Oh, that one'll

be well punished for her gaiety and carelessness in sin !
Oh, when will I forget this night's doings ?   Shattering
fall !   The very next day after me Novena too !   [*He
peeps into the bedroom.*]   Don't get too cosy there, or you
won't want to move.   Move we must, and soon.   [*He
goes to the cupboard, relocks it, and puts the key in his pocket ;
then he goes to the armchair, sits down in it, and starts to
put on his shoes.   Putting on a shoe — in a half-prayer*]
Sweet Saint Panteemalaria, get me outa this without
exposure.   [*He clicks his tongue*]   Dtch dtch !   Soaking
wet !   and I'll be a cautious goer from this out — I
promise.   [*He goes over to bedroom door again with but one
shoe on, and peeps in.*]   Angela, room's warm now ;
quite warm.   The time's flying, mind you.   [*There is
no reply.*]   Aw, God, have you gone to sleep again !
Please, Miss Nightingale, please have some regard for
others !

Angela [*from within — sleepily*].   Did you find it ?

Mulligan.   Find what, find what ?

Angela.   Me lipstick you were looking for ?

Mulligan.   No, no, I didn't ;   must be in there somewhere.

Angela.   I remember I had it when you had me perched
on your lap.   Remember ?

Mulligan [*as if to someone in sitting-room*].   Oh, don't be
reminding me of things !   [*Into the bedroom*]   No, I
don't remember.   Oh, for goodness' sake, get up !

Angela.   All right, all right.   Put out a glass of wine, and
I'll be out in a minute.

   [*Mulligan goes to the cupboard, unlocks it, and takes out a
   bottle of wine and a glass.   He locks the cupboard again,
   leaving the key in the keyhole.   He goes to the table, fills*

*out a glass of wine, and leaves it, with the bottle, on the
table, in readiness for Angela.*

[*He sits down in the armchair, puts on the other shoe, then
winds a woollen muffler round his neck, puts on a
pullover and coat that have been hanging over the back
of a chair, and finally places a trilby hat on his head.
As he does these things, he occasionally mutters to himself.*

Mulligan [*busy with the wine for Angela*]. Not a single
thought has she for what might happen to me if
discovery came. Utterly abandoned to her own
intherests. [*As he sits in chair putting on the second shoe —
in a full-blown prayer*] Oh, gentle Saint Camisolinus,
guardianess of all good young people, get between me
and this petticoated demonsthrator of sinful delusion,
and I'll be O.K. for evermore. I will, I promise !

[*Angela comes into the room at last, and makes quick for
the fire. She has put on her stockings — silk ones — and
skirt, a short, well-tailored one of darkish green, with
broad belt of dark red and black buckle. She carries a
brown jersey over her arm, and her shoes in her hand.*

Angela [*throwing her shoes on to the armchair, and stretching
her hands to the fire*]. Burrr ! It's cold out here still !
I thought you said the room was warm ? [*She notices
how he's dressed.*] All ready for the journey, eh ? Soon
we'll be skiing down the stairs, wha' ? Praying to all
the saints you know to see me out, eh ?

[*She puts the jersey on over her head before the mirror over
the fireplace, and pats it down smoothly over her breast
and shoulders.*

Angela. We have to face the hard, cold facts now, haven't
we, dear ?

Mulligan. We've got to think now of what would become
of me if you were discovered here.

Angela [*mockingly*]. Really? Of course, when one thinks of it, that becomes the one important problem.

Mulligan [*not noticing the mockery*]. It is, actually. You see, Angela, the head of my department's a grand Knight of Columbanus, an uncompromising Catholic, strict in his thought of life, and if he heard of anything like this, I'd — I'd be out in the bleaker air, quick; the little gilt I have on life would be gone; I'd run to ruin! God help me!

Angela [*prompting him*]. And then there's Father Demsey?

Mulligan. Then there's Father Demsey whose right-hand man I am in the Confraternity and at all Saint Vincent de Paul meetings, with his " We can safely leave that matter with Mr. Mulligan ", or " John Jo will do this for us ". You see, it's a matter of importance to more than me. So, come on — we betther get off at once.

Angela [*rising from the chair, and drinking the glass of wine*]. Angela's bright eyes, her scarlet lip, fine foot, straight leg, and quivering thigh have lost their charm for Mr. Mulligan. He's all for go-ahead godliness now! [*She pours out another glass of wine and drinks it.*] And what is to become of me? You don't care, and I don't care either.

> [*She moves about the room in a slow, semi-reckless rhythm as she lilts — Mulligan following her trying to get her quiet again.*

Angela [*lilting and moving about*] :
>> I don't care what becomes of me,
>> I don't care what becomes of me.

Mulligan [*shuffling after her as she moves as well as he can — in a low, anguished voice*]. Angela, please! Sit down, do!

Angela [*lilting*] :
> I don't care if I'm out till two,
> I don't care for the man in blue.

Mulligan [*following her*]. Please, Miss Nightingale, be serious ! The landlady'll hear you, and then we'll be done !

Angela [*lilting*] :
> I don't care what the people say,
> Here, there, and everywhere ;

Mulligan [*appealing to the ceiling*]. Saint Curberisco, help me !

Angela [*in a final burst*] :
> For I'm going to be married in the morning,
> So tonight, boys, I don't care !

[*Facing towards Mulligan.*] Sometime or other, we have to face out of all we get into : face out of getting into bed with a woman no less than face out into silence from the glamour of prayer ; face out of summer into winter ; face out of life into death !

Mulligan [*crossing himself*]. Your talk's near blasphemy, Angela ! Now you're going where you shouldn't venture. You'll bring a curse down on me, if you're not careful ! Please be more discreet.

Angela. They're facts.

Mulligan. We're not fit for facts now.

Angela [*facing him fiercely*]. You stand there mustering up moans for yourself, and never once realise that you've ruined me ! Yes, ruined me !

Mulligan [*startled*]. Oh, God, d'ye hear her ! Ruined you ? Oh, come, now, don't thry to act the innocent.

Angela. It's you who's acting the innocent, but it won't work. I was only an innocent kid till I met you. You led me on and destroyed all confidence in the goodness of me own nature! You never, never ceased from persuasion till you got me here. I wasn't even to take off my hat, if I was the least bit suspicious. We were just to sit quiet discussing Yeats's poems. You were to sit ice-bound in your chair.

Mulligan [*indignantly*]. I led you on! Angela Nightingale, you're inventing things. It was you insisted on coming, because you didn't like restaurants. A sorry thing for me I ever listened to you!

Angela [*ignoring his remarks*]. It's me's the sorry soul for listening to you. You promised a quiet hour of poetry, but we were hardly here when you began to move. Yeats's poems soon flew out of your head and hand. You got as far as "I will arise and go now, and go to Innisfree"; then before the echo of the line was hushed, you had me clapped down on your knee. [*She becomes tearful.*] That was the start of my undoing. What am I going to do!

Mulligan [*lifting his eyes to the ceiling*]. There's lies! [*Facing her*] Astounded I was, when without a word of warning, I found you fitting into me lap! [*Coming closer to her — fervently*] The thruth is, if you want to know, that all the way to here, I was silently praying to a bevy of saints that you'd stay torpid in any and every emergency of look or motion!

Angela. You took care to leave your saints out on the doorstep; ay, and shut the door in their faces, too. You gave your solemn word, before I'd take one step to this place, that you'd be as harmless as an image in a looking-glass. I trusted you. I had heard you were a good boy. I thought you were a gentleman.

Mulligan. What about your uplifting can-can round the table while I was reading Yeats's poem ?

Angela [going her own way]. You made me believe you'd keep the width of a world between us while we were together, so's to avoid accidents. You said anyone who knew you would tell me you had a profound respect for girls ; that you were slow in love-making.

Mulligan [with insistence]. The can-can ; what about the can-can around the table ?

Angela [with a great wail in her voice]. And then you stunned me with your speed !

Mulligan [with greater insistence]. I'm asking you what about the can-can you danced around the table while I was thrying to read " I will arise and go now, and go to Innisfree " ?

Angela [acting the innocent]. What can-can ? What are you talking about ? I don't know what you mean by can-can.

Mulligan. I mean the dance that uplifted your skirt out of the way of your movements and juggled a vision of spiritual desolation into a mirage of palpitating enjoyments.

Angela [appealing to the world at large]. Oh, d'ye hear the like o' that ! Meanness is most of you to try to put the cloak of your own dark way round my poor shoulders ! The dance I did could be done by an innocent figure in a nursery rhyme. You were bent on this awful mischief from the first. I sensed it when I walked with you — something evil hovering near. Oh, why didn't I follow me intuition ! [*She begins to be hysterical.*] And I thought you such a nice man ; and now, after fencing me in with shame, you're making out I gave you the stuff to make the fence around me. Oh, the infamy of it ! [*She moves rapidly up and down the room, clasping and unclasping her hands.*] Oh, what shall I do, where shall I go, what shall I say !

Mulligan [*getting very frightened*]. Angela, calm yourself. Speak lower, or you'll wake Miss Mossie, and we'll be ruined. Sit down ; do, please !

Angela [*fluttering about and staggering a little*]. I'm undone, undone completely. I won't be able to look any honest woman in the face ; I won't be able to shake the hand of any honest man I meet ; my future's devastated ! [*She presses a hand to her heart.*] I'm not feeling well ; not at all well ; you'd better get Miss Mossie.

Mulligan [*horrified and very agitated*]. Angela !

Angela [*staggering towards the chair*]. Not well at all. I feel I'm going to faint ! No, no ; yes, yes — I am going to faint !

   [*She sinks down on the chair, stretches out, and closes her eyes.*

Mulligan [*falling on a knee before her — well frightened now*]. Angela, don't ! Angela, dear, wake up ! [*Lifting his eyes to the ceiling.*] Saint Correlliolanus, come on, and deliver us from utther desthruction !

Angela [*plaintively and faintly*]. Wather !

Mulligan [*panic-stricken*]. No, wine ! [*He rises from his knee, pours out a glass of wine, and brings it to her.*] Oh,

Angela, why did you let yourself get into such a state ? Here, take it quietly in sips. [*As she drinks it*] Sip, sip, sip. That should do you good. Hope no one heard you. Miss Mossie sleeps with one ear cocked. [*He strokes her hand.*] You'll soon be all right, and able to slip away in a few minutes.

Angela [*noticing the ring on the hand stroking hers*]. Pretty ring ; garnet set in gold ; precious garnet didn't you say ?

Mulligan [*none too sure of what he should say*]. Yep. Not much value though.

Angela. Why's it on the little finger ?

Mulligan. Knuckle's too big on the right one ; won't go over it.

Angela [*fingering it*]. Let me see it in me hand. [*He hesitates, then takes it off, and gives it to her with reluctance. Putting it on the engagement finger*] Fits me to a nicety. How did you come by it ?

Mulligan. An uncle left it in my care when he went on a job to Hong Kong. He never came back, and as no one asked about it, I made it my own.

Angela. Oh ? Lucky one. [*She looks up into his face, smiling archly, displaying the finger with the ring on it*] Looks like we were an engaged couple, John Jo, dear, wha' ?

Mulligan. An engaged couple ? [*With an uneasy and constrained laugh*] Yis ! Funny thought, that ; quite. Feeling bether ?

Angela. Seem to ; hope it won't come over me again.

Mulligan [*fervently*]. God forbid ! What about taking off our shoes, and making a start ? [*He takes off his.*

Angela [*taking off her shoes*]. I suppose we must go some-time.

Mulligan [*trying to speak carelessly*]. Let's have the ring back, dear.

Angela [*as if she'd forgotten it*]. The ring? Oh, yes; I near forgot. [*She fiddles with it; then suddenly straightens herself to listen.*] Is that the sound of someone at the door below?

Mulligan [*agitated again*]. Oh God, if it's Halibut home from the dance we'll have to wait till he settles down! I wish you'd gone when the going was good!

Angela [*who has taken off her shoes — rising from the chair*]. Come on, we'll chance it!

Mulligan [*pushing her back*]. Chance it! We can't afford to chance it. [*Going over to the door leading to rest of the house*] I'll reconnoitre down, and make sure the way's clear, before we chance it.

> [*He goes out of the room, is absent for a few moments, while Angela swallows another glass of wine; then he returns hastily, a hand held up warningly for silence.*

Mulligan [*in a frightened whisper*]. Near ran into him on the stairs. Thank God it was so dark. Just had time to turn back. We'll have to wait now till he settles in. [*He listens at the door, shuts it suddenly, and glides over to Angela.*] Quick! He's gone by his own place, and is coming up here! [*He catches her by the arm, hurries her across the room, and shoves her into the bedroom.*] Get in, and keep silent for God's sake!

> [*As he shoves her in, a knock is heard at the sitting-room door. Mulligan shuts the bedroom door, slides over to the chair, sits down, takes the book from the table, and pretends to be reading.*

[*Another knock is heard at the door, then it opens, and Mr.
Daniel Halibut is seen standing there. He is a man of
twenty-five, a little below medium height, inclining to
be plump. His hair is reddish, and a thick moustache
flowing from his upper lip hides his mouth. Sometimes
his hand tries to brush it aside, but the moment the hand
is removed, it falls back into its old place at once. A
fawn-coloured overcoat covers an informal evening-suit —
dinner-jacket and black tie. A black homburg hat is on
his head. He comes in as one who is full of himself as
if he had done himself well at the dance, and as one who
feels himself a man of the world above the cautious and
timorous Mulligan. His hat and coat are damp.*]

*But, is
not !*

Halibut [*coming into the room*]. Ha, there you are, me son,
rotten night out ; sleet. Coming up, I could have
sworn I seen you coming down the stairs.

Mulligan [*in pretended surprise*]. Me coming down the
stairs ? At this time of the morning ? What would I
be doing on the stairs at this hour ?

Halibut. Well, what are you doing up at this time of
the morning ?

Mulligan. I found it impossible to sleep, so got up to see
if a bit of Yeats's poetry would make me drowsy.

Halibut. Is it Yeats, is it ? God, man, he wouldn't let
you sleep ; drive you nuts ! All people liking Yeats
are all queer. He's all questions. What am I ? Why
am I ? What is it ? How did it come ? Where will
it go ? All bubbles. Stuck up in the top of his ould
tower, he sent the bubbles sailing out through a little
loophole to attract the world outside. And all the
little writers copied them, and blew bubbles of their
own, till you could see them glistening among the

things of the althar, or shining in the hair of the girl you were courting.

Mulligan [*with an obvious yawn*]. Well, Yeats has made me sleepy, anyway. [*He flings the book on the table, and goes to get out of the chair.*] I'll be off to bed again.

Halibut [*shoving him back into the chair*]. Wait till I tell you. You should ha' been at the dance. There never was a grander occasion; divel a grander ever! The place was fair gushing with girls. And only a few who'd make you shut your eyes if they were sitting on your knee. A hilariously hopeful whirlwind of skirt and petticoat, John Jo, when a waltz was on!

Mulligan [*getting up and edging Halibut towards the sitting-room door*]. Go to bed, now, like a good fellow. I'm tired. We'll talk about it tomorrow. Goodnight.

Halibut [*edging Mulligan back towards the fireplace*]. Wait till I tell you. You are a boyo. You'd never guess who was there? Your old flame of a week — Jessie! She told me things! When will you wake up? When he asked me out for the first time, says she, I expected a hilarious night at a dance or a music-hall, says she; I near fainted, says she, when, instead, he asked me to go with him to Benediction! Mulligan's management of maidens! Oh, John Jo, when will you wake up?

Mulligan [*annoyed, pushing Halibut towards the door*]. If I elect to keep from danger, that's my affair. Looka, Dan, I've got to get up early to go to Mass on my way to the office, so be a good fellow, and go. I'm not concerned with girls.

Halibut. Betther if you were. [*He pushes Mulligan back*

toward the fireplace again.] You'd sleep betther at night for one thing. [*He puts an arm around Mulligan, and forces him into being a partner.*] Roamin' in th' gloamin', eh? Oh, boy! [*Lilting*] With a lassie by yeer side. Oh, it's lovely to go roamin' in th' gloamin'!

Mulligan [*angrily — struggling from Halibut's hold, and rather roughly forcing him to the door*]. Aw, lay off it, damn it, Dan! I'm in no mood for a Highland fling! Please go to your own room, and leave me in peace — I'm done in! [*He shoves him out and closes the sitting-room door.*

Halibut [*as he's being shoved out*]. All right, if that's the way you feel. It'd be a good thing to put your hand on a girl's knee, and chance it.
[*Mulligan listens at the door for a few moments. Then he gets down on his knees, and puts an ear to the floor. He rises, goes to the bedroom door, opens it, and calls Angela out.*

Mulligan. Now, Angela; now's our time. No delay, please.

Angela [*going behind the curtains on the windows*]. What kind of a night or morning is it? [*From behind the curtains*] Christ! It's snowing or something! [*She comes from behind them, goes to the door, and takes one of Mulligan's coats hanging there.*] I must have a coat.
[*Angela puts the coat on.*

Mulligan [*in a faint protest*]. Eh, Angela, that's me best one.

Angela [*taking an umbrella from the stand*]. And an umbrella, too.

Mulligan. That's me best umbrella.

Angela. Never mind, dear. I'll let you have it back when you hand me into the taxi on the all-night rank. Let's hurry now, boy. [*Mulligan opens the door cautiously, listens a moment ; takes a torch from a pocket, and shines it forth, then leads the way from the room, shutting the door gently behind him. Both of them are in their stockinged feet. After a few moments have passed, the door suddenly flies open, and Angela hurries in, followed by Mulligan wearing a look of agony on his face. They carry their shoes under their arms. As she comes in*] You louser, you'd have let me go off without it ! Didn't care a damn once you were rid of me. And all I have for another fortnight is in that handbag !

Mulligan [*appealingly*]. Speak lower, Angela, or you'll have the Mossie one down on top of us ! I just can't remember you having a handbag when you first came in.

Angela [*angrily*]. You can't remember ! Well, I had one, and a good one, too, and I've got to get it — see ! D'ye mean to hint I'm making it up ?

Mulligan [*in agony*]. No, no ; but for God's sake, speak easy ; please, Angela !

Angela [*leaving her shoes down, and pulling the cushions off the settee and throwing them on the floor*]. Well, then, find it for me. Mind you, had I been down the street when I missed it, I'd have banged the door down to get in to get it !

Mulligan [*leaving his shoes down, and pulling the table about, pulling the chairs from the wall, and pulling the umbrella-stand away, to look behind them*]. This is terrible ! I'll be ruined if I'm discovered. What colour was it ?

Where had you it last ?   Where d'ye think you could have put it ?

Angela. I don't know, fool.   It was a dark-green one I bought last week, and gave five pounds for.   I got confused and forgot about everything when you started to pull me on to your knee.

Mulligan. But we can't stay to look for it.   Miss Mossie'll soon be going about with her candle in her hand.

Angela. I'm not going without it !   I think I remember you snatching it outa me hand when you started to pull me on to your lap.

Mulligan. Oh, give over about me pulling you on to me lap, and give us a hand to look for it !   [*He runs into the bedroom, and starts to search there, flinging the bedclothes about.   In bedroom*] I can't see it anywhere here, so I can't.

Angela [*tearfully*]. And I was to come here only for a quiet glass of wine and a biscuit.   That's what you said, and kept repeating ; and I believed you, oh, I believed you !

Mulligan [*coming out of bedroom*]. No sign of it there.

Angela [*marching up and down the room, clasping and unclasping her hands*]. Oh, isn't this a nice end to a quiet glass of wine and a biscuit !

Mulligan. Get a hold of yourself.   What sort was it ?

Angela. A pure morocco leather one, dark green, with initials on it filigreed in mother o' pearl.

Mulligan [*impatiently*]. Yis, yis ; [*anxiously*] but how much was in it altogether ?

Angela. Fifteen pounds odd.

Mulligan [*aghast*]. Good Lord !

Angela. And the lipstick you couldn't find musta been in it too ; silver-cased and all ; and a lovely bracelet watch waiting to be mended. Oh, what will I do ! Oh, yes, and a silver brooch I wanted to get a pin for. What will I do, what will I do ?

Mulligan. You slip off, and when I come back, I'll search high and low for it.

Angela [*with rising nervous tension*]. And how am I to fare till you find it ? You wouldn't turn a hair if I was willing to go in my shift ! John Jo Mulligan, you're a dasthard ! It would be the price of you to let Miss Mossie and the whole house know the sort you are !

Mulligan. For God's sake, Angela ! What d'ye want me to do ; only tell me what you want me to do ?

Angela [*moving about distracted*]. And to think I thought I was safe with you ! [*Her glance falls on the cupboard, and she makes a bee-line for it.*] Could it have got in here ?

Mulligan [*hastily*]. No, no ; it couldn't have got in there.

Angela [*drawing out a leather wallet*]. What's this ?

Mulligan [*going over to take wallet from her*]. Nothing there but a few private letters, and a lot of bills.
   [*But before he can reach her to get it away, she has whisked a bundle of notes from it.*]

Angela [*giggling — a little hysterical*]. John Jo's hidden treasure. [*She counts them rapidly.*] Eighteen pounds ten. All fresh ones too. Nice to handle.

Mulligan. They're not mine. I'm minding them for a friend. You can put them back.

Angela [*mockingly*]. At once, dear. I'll mind them for you, dear. [*She takes a cheque-book out of the wallet.*] A cheque-book, too. [*As he comes closer*] Keep your distance, keep your distance, or I'll claw the gob off you !

Mulligan. I was only going to give you a few of them to tide you over, dear.

Angela [*fiercely*]. You were? How sweet of you ! I'll have them all, you primly-born yahoo. And more. [*She raises her voice*] And more !

Mulligan [*whisperingly*]. All right, all right, only keep calm ; keep quiet.

Angela [*indicating the cheque-book*]. Make me out a cheque for five pounds like a decent, honest man.

Mulligan [*taking a fountain pen from his pocket, and settling down to write*]. All right ; anything to pacify you.

Angela [*patronisingly patting his head*]. You're not the worst, John Jo. You're really a pleasant chap when you get going. Make a cheque out for ten, darling, to compensate for the goods in the handbag. Ten, dear ; that's all now. Well, we've had a right good time together. Pity I can't stay longer. See you again soon, when you're feeling frisky, eh ? Naughty boy ! [*She has taken the cheque from the dazed Mulligan, put it in his wallet, and now straightens herself to go, taking her shoes off the floor, and putting them under an arm. At the door*] I know my way down, so don't you stir. I'll steal away like a maid of Araby. I'll be seeing you. Be good.

  [*Dazed and stunned, Mulligan sits still for a few seconds ; then he gets up from the chair to look around him.*

Mulligan [*rising from the chair*]. Fully-fledged for hell, that one, and you never noticed it ! Oh, John Jo, John Jo !

[*He suddenly stiffens.*]　She had no handbag !　She never
had a handbag !　Oh, Christ, she's codded me !　[*He
looks in the cupboard, then looks over the table.*]　She's taken
away me wallet, too !　Me umbrella !

[*He runs out of the room to follow her, so agitated that he
leaves door wide open behind him.　There are a few
moments of silence ; then Miss Mossie appears at the
open door with a lighted candle in a candlestick in her
hand.　She is a short, stout woman of thirty-five or so.
She is dressed in a brown skirt reaching to her ankles,
and we get a glimpse of black stockings sinking into a
pair of stout black shoes.　Her dark hair is gathered
into a knob, and made to lie quiet on the nape of her
neck.　She wears a yellow jumper, and a brown Jaeger
topcoat is flung over her shoulders.　She wears spectacles.
She looks into the room for a moment, a look of perplexed
anxiety on her face, then turns aside to call to Halibut.*]

Miss Mossie.　Mr. Halibut, Mr. Halibut, come up, come
up quick !　[*Halibut appears at the door.　He is now
wearing a pair of blue pyjamas, covered by a dressing-gown
of dark red, and his bare feet are slippered.*]　Oh, Mr.
Halibut, what can the matter be ?　Oh, dear, what can
the matter be ?

Halibut [*agog with excitement*].　What's up, Miss Mossie ?

Miss Mossie [*coming into the sitting-room, followed by Halibut*].
Looka the state of the room ;　and Mr. Mulligan's just
run out into the street in his stockinged feet !

Halibut [*astonished*].　No ?　How d'ye know he went out
into the street ?

Miss Mossie.　I seen him go.　I heard something stirring
when I was putting on me jumper, so I looked out,

and there was Mr. Mulligan scuttling down the stairs. Walking in his sleep, he musta been. He had an air on him as if he was enraptured within himself; a look as if he was measuring life and death together to see which was tallest.

Halibut. Is that right? Coming back from the dance, I thought I saw him on the stairs, too, but when I came up, he was sitting reading Yeats's poems. Said he couldn't sleep. I warned him against the poems.

Miss Mossie [*coming over to the bedroom door, and opening it*]. Oh, looka the state of this room, too! Everything flung about.

Halibut [*awed*]. Looks like he had a wild fit, or something!

Miss Mossie. Something terrific! This isn't just disarray, Mr. Halibut — it's an upheaval! You don't think it could be that something suddenly went wrong in him?

Halibut [*startled by a thought*]. Wrong in him, Miss Mossie? What could go wrong in him?

Miss Mossie. A quietly-disposed man like Mr. Mulligan doesn't do this [*indicating disorder of rooms*] without something whizzing within him.

Halibut [*frightened*]. You mean in his mind?

Miss Mossie [*firmly*]. We must act. We can't let him roam the streets or do any harm here. I'll phone the police and a doctor, and I'll slip out for the constable that usually stands at the street corner. [*They move to the sitting-room door.*] I'll go now. You stay on the lobby here in the dark, and watch over him if he comes back.

Halibut [*dubiously*]. I'm not a strong man, Miss Mossie.

Miss Mossie. After all, Mr. Halibut, we don't want to be murdhered in our beds.

Halibut [*crossing himself*]. God forbid, Miss Mossie !

Miss Mossie. And the odd thing is, he'd be doing it with the best intentions. If he comes back, he may still be asleep, so don't shout at him and wake him too suddenly. Just humour him, unless he gets violent.

Halibut [*picturing in his mind all that might happen*]. Ay, violent — that's the danger !

Miss Mossie. Then you'll just have to close with him, and hold him till the constable comes.

Halibut [*panic-stricken*]. Close with him ? Hold him till the constable comes ? But, woman alive, I'm not gifted that way !

Miss Mossie. You'll do your best, I know ; if he overcomes you, it won't be your fault.

Halibut. Don't you think it would be only prudent to have a poker handy ?

Miss Mossie. Too violent-looking. [*Indicating a corner of the lobby*] There's the bit of curtain-pole I use to push the window up — you can keep that handy ; but don't let him guess why you have it. [*She takes the key from the inside and puts it in the keyhole on the outside of the door.*] There now, if the worst comes, you can fly out and lock him safely within the room.

Halibut. It sounds easy, but it's really a desperate situation.

Miss Mossie. Don't let him see you're frightened. Keep him under command. That's what me sisther did with me when I used to walk in my sleep a few years ago.

Halibut [*stricken with confused anxiety*]. What, you used to sleep-walk, too?

Miss Mossie. That's why I dhread the habit coming back to me, for then you never know whether you're always asleep and never awake, or always awake and never asleep. I'll be off now. You'll be quite safe if you only keep your wits about you.

> [*She goes off with her candle, leaving a world of darkness to poor Halibut. There is a silence for a few moments, then the watcher in the darkness, and any who are listening, hear a patter of feet on stairs outside, and the voice of Mulligan calling out loudly the name of Miss Mossie several times. Then a great bang of a closing door; dead silence for a moment, till Mulligan is heard calling again.*

Mulligan [*outside*]. Dan, Dan, are you awake? Dan Halibut, are you awake, man? [*Mulligan appears on the lobby just outside the sitting-room door. He is talking to himself, a haggard, lost, and anxious look on his face, and he is a little out of breath. His coat and hat are damped by the falling sleet outside; his feet wet. He pauses on the lobby, and waves his electric torch about till its beam falls on the silent and semi-crouching Halibut.*] Oh, it's here you are? Thought you were in bed fast asleep. Called you, but got no answer. What a night! Twenty-eight pounds ten gone with the wind! [*He lifts a cushion from the floor to look under it.*] It's not there! [*He flings it viciously away. To Halibut*] What has you here in the dark and the cold?

Halibut. Just shutting the window to keep it from rattling.

Mulligan [*going into the sitting-room*]. We must do something. Miss Mossie's gone rushing hatless out into the
darkness and the sleet. Hatless, mind you ! Looked
as if she was sleep-walking again. A one-time habit
of hers, did you know ? You'll have to go after her.

Halibut [*coming a little way into the room, but staying close
to the door, holding the sprig of curtain-pole behind his back*].
I know, I know ; but what were you doing out in the
sleet and the darkness *yourself*? And in your stockinged
feet, too, look at them !

Mulligan. Me ? Couldn't sleep ; felt stifled ; went out
for some fresh air. Didn't think of shoes. Something
whizzing in me mind. [*A little impatiently*] But you
dress and go after Mossie. See what's wrong with her.
Several times, before you came, she came into my
room, fast asleep, at dead of the night, with a loving
look on her face. We can't afford to let ourselves be
murdhered in our sleep, Dan. [*He flops into chair.*]
Saint Fairdooshius, succour me this night.

Halibut [*bewildered with anxiety, eyes lifted to ceiling in a
low appeal*]. Oh, sweet Saint Slumbersnorius, come to
me help now ! [*To Mulligan*] All right ; yes. I'll
settle you in first. You go to bed, John Jo, quiet. Go
to bed, go to bed, and go asleep, and go asleep !

Mulligan [*looking at Halibut curiously — a little impatiently*].
I've told you I can't sleep. Twenty-eight pounds ten,
and my fine leather wallet gone forever !

Halibut [*in a commandingly sing-song way*]. Never mind.
Put them out of your thoughts, and go to bed, go to
bed, and go to sleep, and go to sleep — I command !

Mulligan [*half rising from his chair so that Halibut backs*

towards the door — staring at Halibut in wonderment].
What's wrong with you, Halibut ? [*He sinks back into
the chair again, and Halibut returns into the room.*]   Me
best coat and best umbrella, too !   Gone.

[*His glance happens to fall on his hand, and he springs out
of the chair with a jump, sending Halibut backing swiftly
from the room again.*

Mulligan.   Me ring !   I never got it back !

Halibut [*straying cautiously back into the room again*].   Money,
best coat, best umbrella, wallet, and ring !   When did
you lose all these things, man ?

Mulligan.   A minute or so ago ;   no, no, an hour ago ;   two
hours ago ;   more.   [*He leans his arms dejectedly on the
table, and buries his head on them.*]   I di'n't lost them, Dan ;
I gave them away, flung them all away !

Halibut.   In an excess of charity of having too many
possessions, or what ?   You know, I've warned you,
John Jo ;   often warned you.

Mulligan [*raising his head from his arms — resentfully and
suspiciously*].   Warned me ?   How warned me ?

Halibut.   I warned you that running out to devotions
morning and night, and too much valuable time spent
on your knees, would upset you one day or another.
And, now, you'll have to admit that these things
couldn't have happened to you if you had had a girl
with you tonight.

Mulligan [*with a wail of resentment*].   Oooh !   Don't be a
blasted fool !   [*He notices that Halibut has something behind
his back.*]   What's that you have behind you ?

Halibut [*trying to be carelessly funny*].   Me tail.   Didn't you know ? I'm a wild animal. [*He wags the piece of curtain-pole.*] Now, the wild animal says you're to go to bed, go to bed, and go to sleep, and go to sleep. Obey the wild animal at once !

Mulligan [*slowly rising from the chair, staring anxiously and suspiciously at Halibut*]. What's amiss with you, Halibut ? Are you sleep-walking, too ? Leave down that curtain-pole. Don't be acting the goat, man. [*Coaxingly — as Halibut brings the piece of curtain-pole to his front*] Go on, Dan, oul' son, leave the thing down !

Halibut. As soon as you're safely settled in bed, John Jo. Then I'll pop out after Mossie. To bed ; to bed ; and go to sleep, go to sleep — I command !

Mulligan [*fear having come on him — suddenly seizes the wine-bottle by the neck, and holds it as a club, running to window, swinging back the curtains, and trying to open it*]. God Almighty, I'm alone with a lunatic ! [*Shouting — as he tries to open the window*] Help !

Halibut. I'll not let you destroy yourself — come away from that window, or I'll flatten you !

Mulligan [*wheeling round, still holding bottle by the neck to use it as a club, and facing towards Halibut*]. Looka, Halibut, leave that club down. [*Coaxingly*] Now, be sensible, Dan, like a good chap, and drop that club.

Halibut. Drop that bottle first, I say ; drop that bottle first !

Mulligan. Drop that club, I tell you. [*Fiercely*] Drop that club !

Halibut [*dancing up and down — panic-stricken*]. Put that bottle down ! Put it down, and go to bed, I tell you !

Mulligan [*dodging about*]. Drop that club at once, Halibut !

Halibut. Put that bottle down immediately !

Mulligan. I command you !

Halibut. I command you !
[*They have been dodging about without coming near to each other ; Halibut swinging the piece of curtain-pole to and fro in front of him for protection. In one of the blind swings, the pole slips from his hand, and sails out through the window, causing a great sound of falling glass. They both stare at the window — dumbfounded for a few moments.*

Mulligan [*exultingly*]. Aha, I've got you now !
[*But Halibut has fled from the room, banged the door after him, and locked it from the outside. Mulligan hurries to the door and presses his back to it. Then Miss Mossie's voice is heard outside.*

Miss Mossie [*outside*]. Oh, what's happened ? I feared it would end in violence ! Mr. Halibut, Mr. Halibut, are you much hurted ?

Mulligan [*shouting through the door to Miss Mossie*]. Miss Mossie ; here, Miss Mossie !

Miss Mossie [*from outside*]. Oh, Mr. Mulligan, what have you done to poor, innocent Mr. Halibut ? We've found him lying in a dead faint out here on the lobby.

Mulligan [*indignantly — shouting outwards*]. Poor, innocent Mr. Halibut ! What has he not tried to do to me !

He rushed in here, lunacy looking out of his eyes, and tried to shatther me with a club, with a club ; tried to murdher me ! Now he's locked me in.

Miss Mossie [*soothingly*]. Now isn't that a shame ! What a naughty man he is ! Never mind now. You go to your chair and sit down by the fire, and I'll get the key to open your door. Everything will be all right, Mr. Mulligan.

Mulligan [*indignantly*]. Everything isn't all right now ! I'll live no longer in the same house with Halibut !

Miss Mossie [*coaxingly*]. Do go and sit down by the fire, Mr. Mulligan, there's a dear. I'll bring you a hot drink, and we'll talk about things ; do, now, like a good man. [*Mulligan goes to the fireplace, and sits down in the armchair. He lights a cigarette and puffs it indignantly. After a few moments, the door opens, and Miss Mossie lets into the room a big, topcoated and helmeted policeman, the doctor with his case, wearing an anxious look on his face, and a nurse, enveloped with a dark-blue cloak on the left side of which is a white circle surrounding a large red cross. She carries the usual nursing-suitcase in her hand. Miss Mossie is in the midst of them, and Halibut, in the rear, with a ghastly pale face, rises on his tiptoes to gaze over their shoulders. All but Halibut form a semicircle round Mulligan's back, who puffs away, unconscious of the entrance of the crowd. Bending sidewise from behind the policeman to speak to the sitting Mulligan*] Now, Mr. Mulligan, we'll see what all this little disturbance was about, and what was the cause of it, and then we'll be all — er — O.K., eh ? And I've brought in a few kind friends to help me.

Mulligan [*rising from his chair in blank surprise, and almost echoing Miss Mossie*]. A few friends to help you ? [*He turns around to face Miss Mossie, but is confronted by the big, helmeted policeman, the doctor, and the nurse. He slides back into the chair almost in a dead faint. Falling back into the chair*] Good God !

CURTAIN

I DON'T CARE WHAT BECOMES OF ME

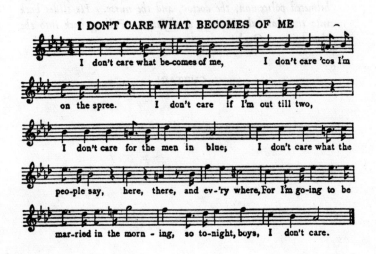

I don't care what be-comes of me, I don't care 'cos I'm
on the spree. I don't care if I'm out till two,
I don't care for the men in blue; I don't care what the
peo-ple say, here, there, and ev-'ry where, For I'm go-ing to be
mar-ried in the morn - ing, so to-night, boys, I don't care.

ROAMIN' IN THE GLOAMIN'

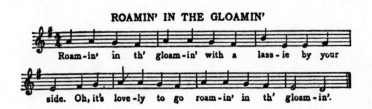

Roam-in' in th' gloam-in' with a lass-ie by your
side. Oh, it's love-ly to go roam-in' in th' gloam-in'.

A MORALITY COMEDY IN ONE ACT

Time to Go

CHARACTERS IN THE PLAY

MICHAEL FLAGONSON, *proprietor of a tavern*

BULL FARRELL, *proprietor of a general stores*

MRS. FLAGONSON, *Flagonson's wife*

BARNEY O'HAY, *farmer owner of five acres*

COUSINS, *farmer owner of twenty acres*

CONROY, *farmer owner of a hundred and fifty acres*

SERGEANT KILLDOOEY, *of the Civic Guards*

1ST CIVIC GUARD

2ND CIVIC GUARD

WIDDA MACHREE, *who has asked too much for a cow*

KELLY FROM THE ISLE OF MANANAUN, *who has given too little for it*

A YOUNG MAN

A YOUNG WOMAN

———

SCENE

Outside of Flagonson's Tavern and Bull Farrell's General Stores on the edge of an Irish country town, a day or so after a fair.

TIME.—The present.

The scene is the butt-end of an Irish town, small and untidy. To the left, part of Flagonson's Tavern façade can be seen. There are the door and a window to the right of it ; the roof is of slate, and a smoke-grimed chimney is sending out a little trickle of smoke. Over the doorway is a notice declaring that BEER AND SPIRITS FOR ALL can be had there ; between the window and the door is a larger notice holding the printed announcement on it of LUNCHES, DINNERS, AND TEAS — AD LIB ; the Latin phrase done out in larger letters. The front wall is brickwork half-way up, the rest is covered with a patchy rough-cast. A little way from the door are a rough wooden bench and a few kitchen chairs ; and a few tankards stand on the table.

Opposite to the Tavern stands the General Stores of Mr. Bull Farrell, jutting out far enough to show the wide doorway, a window, and part of the front wall. Along the wall is a board having on it the words BULL FARRELL. GENERAL STORES. FROM A NEEDLE TO AN ANCHOR. Arranged along the wall, leaning against it, are a new hoe, a dung-fork, a spade ; in front of them a new wheelbarrow, a dust-bin, a large box, and an eight-stone sack of phosphate. On the slated roof is a smoke-begrimed chimney from which ascends a little trickle of smoke.

Beyond these two establishments is a road going across, and smaller ways lead past in front of the Tavern and the General Stores. In the background is a scrubby field with a vista of a few cottages, thatched, in the distance. On the edge of the field, close to the edge of the road, are the remains of two trees, one near the Tavern and the other near the General Stores. Their branches are withered, and they look as if they had been blasted by lightning. A string of various-coloured bunting, triangular *in shape, connects Tavern and Stores, and a tiny string of the same bunting hangs over the Tavern door and over the door of the General Stores. Each has a small Papal flag, perpendicular stripes of white and yellow, stuck out from the upper part of the windows.*

Over all is a lovely magenta-coloured sky, fleeced here and there by clouds, rosily-silver wherever the sun touches them.

Flagonson is standing by the edge of the table, his arse leaning against it. He is a man of fifty-five, big-headed, and strongly built. His hair, once a brilliant red, is now badly chaffed with grey. Although his belly is beginning to advance too far into the world, he is a well-formed, upstanding man. He is mechanically wiping a tankard with a cloth.

Bull Farrell, owner of the General Stores, is very different from Michael Flagonson. He is a wisp of a man, looking as if a shove would send him with speed flying out of the world. Although but forty years of age, he is quite bald, but his upper lip clings on to a thick, dark, truculent moustache. He is dressed in tweeds, and has a high, stiff, white collar round his neck, encircled with a black tie. A dark-blue apron protects his trousers from dust damage. Flagonson too wears a collar, not quite so high as that worn by Farrell; a low-necked dark waistcoat, with white front, and a black bow nestling under the stuck-out wings of the collar. His apron is a white one. Bull Farrell is standing in his doorway looking towards Flagonson.

Flagonson [*with a glance at the decorations*]. How lonesome an' woebegone the decorations look now the crowd's gone.

Bull [*glancing at them, too*]. Ay, with the coloured booths, the shoutin' of buyin' and sellin', the swearin' an' fightin' gone with th' crowd too, it's a bit lonely like. [*He glances at the decorations again.*] I dunno why you put them up. Waste of time; waste of money.

Flagonson [*indicating those over Bull's door*]. You've a token hangin' there yourself.

Bull. Me great-grandfather bought them for some meetin' in honour of Dan O'Connell. They cost me nothin'.

Flagonson. An' what about the Papal flag?

Bull [*gloatingly*]. I nailed that off a kid bangin' the window with it to th' point of breakin'; and when I threatened the police on him, he was damned glad to get away without it.

Flagonson. The polis is the only ones to put th' fear o' God in them.

Bull. Only for them, they wouldn't leave a thing standin' in th' town. Durin' th' Fair, they had me plagued. I daren't ha' left a thing standin' outside, or it would have been gone while I was winkin'.

Flagonson. Well, it's all cold an' calm now, anyhow. Nothin' left of all the burly business but big farmer Conroy an' little farmer Cousins still arguin'. Cousins wants to sell an' Conroy says he wants to buy, though, afther twelve hours of talkin', they're no nearer to an agreement yet.

Bull [*coming from the door, and leaning towards Flagonson — confidentially*]. Conroy sees somethin' in them cattle, though no-one else can. Conroy's a cute one. He says he wants only to do a good turn to poor Cousins. [*He throws back his head, and gives a loud guffaw.*] Conroy doin' a good turn! He's takin' a helluva time to do it. Slow, but sure!

Flagonson. I dunno. Maybe he has a soft spot in him somewhere.

Bull [*with surprised indignation*]. Soft spot ? Why, man alive, Conroy ud take the gold from a holy saint's halo an' shove it in th' bank !

Flagonson [*after a pause*]. I wondher what happened to that fine-lookin' woman in th' black dhress and the bright blue cloak thryin' to sell her cow to th' upstandin' chap in the saffron kilt an' th' gay, green shawl ?

Bull. She sold it all right to him, Barney O'Hay was tellin' me ; an' then she went east an' he went west, leadin' th' cow home.

Flagonson. It wasn't what you'd call a bulky Fair. I've seen betther, an' I've seen worse.

Bull. So've I ; but you musta made a bundle, seein' the house was packed all th' day an' half-way into th' night.

Flagonson [*a little sharply, touched with envy*]. An' isn't the sufferin' road out there worn away with the constant caravan of donkey-cars, pony-cars, an' motor-cars, loaded to th' brims, carryin' off stuff from your stores, so that you musta been ladlin' money into your positive possessions !

Bull [*placatingly*]. Don't grudge me mine, Mick, an' I won't grudge you yours.

Flagonson [*cheerily*]. God forbid I did, Bull, for it wouldn't be a Christian thing to do. Though me own takin's timidly topped last year's, I'd say I never seen a quieter Fair : all noise, a noise of bargainin', with a little laughter an' gaiety lost in th' commotion.

Bull. An' why was that ? Because the young are goin' who aren't already gone. Because there's ne'er a one, lad or lass, in th' disthrict between seventeen an' thirty. An' why are they gone?

Flagonson. To betther themselves, God help them! Even me own Judy an' Jack, up in Dublin, want me to settle them in London, where there's a betther openin', they say, God help them. Ay, an openin' into th' world that shuts them out from God!

Bull [*contemptuously*]. Ay, so our clergy say. [*He throws back his head, and laughs contemptuously.*] Th' clergy! Ireland's a bird sanctuary for them. Priest-puffin island!

Flagonson [*with some remonstrance in his voice*]. Now, Bull, now, Bull, dhraw it mild about th' clergy; not but I'd agree that it's hard to have an aysey mind with th' clergy pullin' out of us from all quarthers.

Bull. An' why th' hell haven't you got the spunk to fight some of their pirate pinchin'? What with their blue sisthers of th' poor, the white nuns of th' needy, th' brown sisthers of our crippled companions, we're rooked in th' mornin's, an' rooked at night, if our doors aren't bolted!

Flagonson [*loosing his thoughts*]. With church collectors runnin' along every road an' passable path, an' hoppin' over every stile, pattherin' at your doors like hailstones in a storm! With their "Th' collector from Bona Mors, Mr. Farrell"; "th' collector, Mr. Farrell, for th' new presbytery be the new church"; "Mr. Farrell, th' collector for the Foreign Missions"; till a body's lightened of a lot he had to put away for a rainy day!

Bull [*remonstratively indignant*]. Then why don't you fight it, man? [*He goes forward, and assumes a semi-fighting pose.*] Why don't you sthruggle against it, man? What ails you that you won't stand firm?

Flagonson [*half hesitatingly*]. I will, I will, Bull; you'll see.

Bull [*scornfully*]. You will, you will; I'll see, I'll see! When will I see? You've been sayin' that for years! Abnegate, I say, then, if you're a man, man.

Flagonson [*trying to be positive*]. I will; I must. This pinchin' be th' priests of th' little we have is gettin' unconthrollable!

Bull. Isn't that what I'm afther tellin' you! Priest-puffin island. An' it's not a shillin' they want, or even half-a-crown; oh, no; th' mineemus now asked from a poor thrader is a pound, if you please. And if a pound's given, they'll say with a blisterin' glance, " If you're only givin' a pound, Mr. Farrell, you might as well make it one pound one ". Am I to be the one lone figure left standin', like a pillar without any support, to fight against this convulsion of givin' against our will? Is there ne'er a man but meself left in th' land? Are we to become only a scared an' scatthered crowd? Are you goin' to do anything, or are you not?

Flagonson [*with heated resolution*]. I am! [*He bangs a tankard on the table.*] I will, I will; I must!

Bull [*with scornful impatience*]. You must, you will! There's no surety in your tankard-dhrummin'. [*Savagely*] But will you, man; will you, will you?

[*Two cyclists, a Young Man and a Young Woman, have come in from around the Tavern, pushing their bicycles along the road. He is simply dressed in tweeds and wears a tweed cap; his trouser-ends are thrust into his socks.*

She wears a dark jersey and green slacks. When they speak, they do so quickly, as if in a somewhat excited hurry. To Bull:

Young Man [*in quick excitement*]. How far from here, sir, is the remains of the Abbey of Ballyrellig?

Bull. Th' oul' graveyard with th' ruins in it is it you mean?

Young Man. It must be: th' one with the chapel of Saint Kurrakawn in it.

Young Woman [*rapidly*]. A lovely crypt with groined arches, supported by lovely semi-columns, decorated with lovely foliage an' faces.

Bull. D'ye tell me that, now? Well, if what it is is what yous want, it's more'n fifteen miles farther on. But th' whole thing's lost, man, in thickets, brambles, an' briars.

Young Man [*still speaking quickly*]. There's still a pathway to it, I'm told.

Bull. D'ye tell me that, now?

Young Woman. We simply must see it before we go away. It's just a dhream!

Bull. D'ye tell me that, now?

Young Man [*to Young Woman*]. We'll want a meal first, dear. [*To Flagonson*] Can we have a fairly substantial one, sir?

Flagonson [*with quiet assurance*]. Indeed, yous can; anything in reason; we're here to enthertain.

[*He indicates the notice on the wall.*

[*The Young Man and Young Woman wheel their bicycles towards the General Stores, and leave them leaning against the back wall.*

Young Man [*glancing inquiringly at the Young Woman*]. A nice chop would make a good start?

Flagonson. A right royal start, if the chops were to be had, sir.

Young Woman [*after a pause — to the Young Man*]. A few nice, lean rashers, Ned, would do just as well.

Flagonson. Ay, miss, an' fat ones, either, if there was any to be had. You don't expect us to kill a pig to provide yous with rashers, do yous?

Young Man [*annoyed and disappointed*]. Well, what have you, then?

Flagonson. What about a boiled egg, a powerful cup o' tay, an' as much bread as you like to get down yous?

Young Woman [*with a glance at the Young Man*]. That'll have to do, Ned.

Flagonson [*indicating the Tavern door*]. In with yous, then, an' th' lady inside'll give yous all yous can conveniently want. [*The Young Man and Young Woman go rather slowly into the Tavern. To Bull*] Shockin' th' way the young demand things nowadays!

Bull. Their effervesacatin' spirits nowadays is incontrollable!

[*Widda Machree appears around the back of the General Stores, walking along the road. She is a young woman of thirty. Her face is pale, well chiselled, and pure-looking. She wears a coloured scarf over her head, peasant-wise, so that the round of her face only is seen. A bright blue cloak draped from her shoulders half covers a black skirt and blouse. She wears black stockings and shoes. She is straightly built and slim, and has a semi-plaintive air, though this is occasionally changed into a humorous, half-cynical manner. She looks about her for a moment, and then speaks to the two men.*

Widda Machree [*plaintively*]. I'm Widda Machree : me sweetheart died the day we were to wed, an' neighbours gave me the name I go by now. I'm in great throuble, gentlemen. I can't stay aysey by the big turf fire an' th' hearth swept clean. I have to thravel now along th' big bog road, because of a sin, gentlemen ; an ugly, mortal sin, an' a mean one, too. Ochone, oh, ochone !

Flagonson. A bad burden to have on a conscience, ma'am.

Widda Machree. Ay ; I'm but a wandherin' cloud o' conscience. There's ne'er a green glen left in Erin for me now. Never on Lady Day agin will I wear me dhress of speckled velvet, or sew the silver buckles on me shining shoon. O ochone, ochone !

Bull. No good'll come be dwellin' on it, ma'am.

Flagonson. You're th' lady was bargainin' with th' kilted gentleman over th' sale of your cow, aren't you ?

Widda Machree. That thransaction was me undoin', gentlemen. I thought I could rise above th' temptation, but I sank below it. I'll sit down a second. [*She sits down on the bench.*] I'm tired searchin' for th' kilted gentleman. If he happens to pass by here, hold him till I call again. Kelly's th' name. [*She gets up and swings round on her toes in a kind of dance, chanting :*]

> Has anybody here seen Kelly?
> K ee double ell y ;
> Has anybody here seen Kelly,
> Kelly from the Isle of Man-an-aun!

I must settle accounts with him. Oh, ochone, I did a mean sin as well as a mortal one.

Bull. You looked sensible enough when I seen you bargainin' away with th' kilted man, opposite Trinity Church.

Widda Machree. At Trinity Church I met me doom, gentlemen. Givin' so much of me peace of mind to gain so little. Oh, miserere mei! I'll never go near th' church again till th' wrong's righted an' me soul feels free. But who am I tellin'? Sure you two musta often felt th' same way yourselves, for yous musta shot a gay lot o' rogueries into th' world in your time.
> [*The quiet, matter-of-fact way that the last remark is made seems to stun the two men for a few moments, and they stand, silent, staring at her.*

Bull [*after a rather long pause*]. I can tell you, ma'am, that the last remark you made is an entirely disilushunnary designation! There's ne'er a wisp of dishonesty to be found in either of our two firms!

Widda Machree. Don't crown your rogueries with a lie on top of them, good man. Didn't every soul I met comin' along here tell me yous were th' two most meritorious rogues in th' disthrict, an' that Canon Bullero commends all yous do because of the whack he gets out of it?

Flagonson [*indignantly*]. Looka here, ma'am, I'm not anxious to have mortal sins any way adjacent to me respectable house ; an' th' bench you're occupyin' is meant for customers only.

Widda Machree. Your hint is tellin' me it's time to go, sir.

Bull [*coming nearer, and bending towards her till his face is close to hers — fiercely*]. An' with me fond farewell, let you tell all you meet that Bull Farrell hides no roguery undher the registered comfort of any priest's connivance, havin' refused to sanction th' givin' of ad libeetitum donations for th' period of sinny quaw non !
    [*Widda Machree rises from her seat, bows to the two men, and walks with slow dignity to the road.   As she reaches it, the Young Man and the Young Woman come hurrying from the Tavern, both, evidently, in a deep state of indignation.   They make for where their bicycles are. Mrs. Flagonson comes to the door to watch their departure. She is thirty-five, and not at all bad-looking.   She is dressed neatly in a brown skirt and black bodice.   A coloured cotton apron protects the skirt and the breast of the bodice.*

Young Man [*holding his bicycle ready to go — angrily*]. A nest of daylight robbers !   Five shillin's each for a crumb of bread, a cup of tea, and an egg wouldn't sit tight in a thimble !   Daylight robbery !

Mrs. Flagonson [*going over to Flagonson, and prodding him in the back with her forefinger*]. Not a word, mind you, Michael.
        [*She returns to the Tavern, and disappears within it.*

Young Man [*sadly*]. Times have changed !   When Brian Boru reigned, jewels an' costly garments could be left on the hedges without a soul thinkin' of touchin' them. But now !

Young Woman. I wondher what would Brian Boru think of it if he was alive today !

Young Man [*passionately*]. Or the Fenians before him, who set honour an' thruth before comfort or safety. High hangin' to ye on a windy night, yeh bunch of incandescent thieves !

> [*The Young Man and his companion go out indignantly, neither of the two men responding in any way. Widda Machree gazes fixedly at the two men for some moments during a short silence following the departure of the two young people. During the silence, the sound of coins jingling together is heard coming from Tavern and General Stores.*

Widda Machree [*thoughtfully*]. A dangerous sound ; a sound not to be mingled with the gentle jingle of the Mass bell. Take warnin' from me, gentlemen, who lost her virtue for a few lousy coins. Yous may go smilin' through th' world, gentlemen, but yous won't go smilin' through heaven. Let yous put more value into what yous give an' less into what yous get, before it's too late.

Bull [*determinedly*]. Looka, you ; go where you're goin' with less blather. We're not in th' same category, ma'am.

Widda Machree [*after a slight pause*]. Looka, you ; if sins were written on people's foreheads, th' two of yous would pull your caps well down over your eyes !

Flagonson. Please go, ma'am ; we're reticent people, an' not interested in th' bouncing uttherance of things meant for the veiled ear of a priest.

Widda Machree. I'm goin', me lad. [*She starts on her way.*]

I've warned yous. [*The sound of clinking coins, coming from the General Stores and the Tavern, which had faded, becomes clear again.*] Aha, there's th' dangerous sound again, boys !

> [*She begins to sing, and again weaves herself into a dancing movement, wheeling round on her feet, and ending the chant just as she disappears around the Tavern.*

Widda Machree [*singing*] :
Jingle coins, jingle coins, jingle all the day.
Count them all an' wrap them up an' tuck them safe away.
Jingle coins, jingle on till life has pass'd away,
Then change to foolish cries of woe upon th' judgement day !

Flagonson. Sounds a bit suspicious to me, Bull.

Bull. Suspicious ? Didn't she tell her own story herself ? A brazen bitch, Mick, an' a desiduous one, too !

Flagonson. Committin' mortal sin, mind you, with a go-boy in a sumptuous saffron kilt an' a gay green shawl.

Bull [*solemnly*]. I always had me doubts about them laddos goin' about in kilts, Mick. On occasions of this kind, a kilt's an unpredictable garment for any man to be wearin'. [*He comes closer.*] She'll excite th' neighbours against us if she's not conthrolled. I shouldn't wondher if she was a Red !

Flagonson [*shocked*]. No, no, God forbid ! We must let the clergy know at once !

Bull [*throwing back his head for a guffaw*]. Th' clergy ! Priest-puffin island again. Not th' clergy, man, but th' polis !

[*Barney O'Hay appears round the gable-end of the General Stores, and comes down from the road to Bull. He is a man of forty-five, thin and stringy. The evidence of continual toil and ever-present anxiety shows in the lines of his face which is seamed like a man of seventy. He is dressed in an old pair of khaki trousers, a shabby tweed coat, a little too short for him, and a well-worn waistcoat. A faded bowler hat covers his head, and his boots are patched. The one bright thing about him is a white, tall collar and brown tie which are symbols connecting him with the better-off farmers. He carries a blackthorn stick. He tries to walk briskly, but his steps are stiff; and his effort to smile cheerily but fills his face with a deeper gloom.*

Barney [*as he comes in*]. God save th' two men!

Flagonson
Bull } [*together — very coldly*]. You, too, O'Hay.

Barney [*coming down to Bull as briskly as he can*]. Morra, Mr. Farrell — I've great news for you, so I have.

Bull [*doubtfully*]. Huh, have you?

Barney [*breezily*]. Ay have I; news'll cock y'up with pride an' pleasure.
  [*Flagonson has cocked his ears, though pretending to be indifferent.*

Bull [*irritably*]. Well, out with it, if it's good news.

Barney [*almost smacking his lips because of having something to say sure to please Farrell*]. Canon Whizzer's spreadin' it all over th' disthrict about you givin' him twenty pound this mornin'. Outa modesty, says he, Misther Farrell asked me to keep it secret; but, says he, such devotion is a thing to be told as an example to others. [*There is a dead silence. Seeing Bull glaring at him angrily, Barney looks at Flagonson, only to see him glaring angrily at Farrell. Haltingly*] I hope there's nothin' wrong.

Flagonson [*to the world in general*]. God Almighty, a man never knows what he's shakin' hands with nowadays ! What a quare sthress I'd have been in had I gone all out to provoke th' clergy ! You'd think deception would have lessened its dimensions in this year of our anno domino !
    [*Mrs. Flagonson comes from the Tavern and goes over to Flagonson.*

Mrs. Flagonson [*prodding Flagonson with her forefinger in the back*]. Come, Michael, help feed th' chickens.
    [*She returns to the Tavern, and Flagonson follows her meekly.*

Flagonson [*half to himself and half to the world — as he goes into the Tavern*]. An' he only afther condemnin' a poor, decent woman for simply makin' a mistake ! [*He throws his head backwards, and gives a loud, mocking guffaw.*] Priest-puffin island ! D'ye get me, Mr. Bull Farrell !

Bull [*roughly and loudly to Barney*]. Well, what d'ye want, blatherer ?

Barney [*frightened*]. I just came to get th' bag o' phosphates from you.

Bull. When you plank down a tenner of what you owe, you'll get it.

Barney [*half wailing*]. I couldn't, I couldn't, Misther Farrell.

Bull. You couldn't, you couldn't ! You sold your pigs, didn't you ?

Barney [*plaintively*]. Ah, sir, for next to nothin'. Th' kitchen leavin's I collected didn't make them prime. Th' slovenly bitches round here put tea-leaves, cabbage stalks, an' orange peel into it. How could any animal fatten itself on that stuff ?

Bull. Gimme th' ten pounds you got for them, an' I'll let you have th' phosphate.

Barney. It was th' same with me acre o' hay — th' drouth banished all th' good out of it ; an' th' acre o' spuds was mostly smalleens. I can't give th' tenner at once, sir.

Bull [*almost shouting*]. Then get to hell outa here, then, if you can't !
>   [*He turns away, goes into Stores, comes back to the door, where he stands, sourly smoking his pipe.*
>   [*Barney goes back, abashed, to lean against the wall of the Stores, disconsolate.*
>   [*Conroy and Cousins come in from the Tavern end ; Conroy briskly, Cousins more slowly, a harassed look on his face. Conroy is middle-aged, Cousins about thirty years old. Conroy a man of a hundred and fifty acres, Cousins a man of twenty acres. Conroy wears cord breeches, Cousins corduroy ones ; Conroy brown leggings, Cousins black ones, soiled with cow-dung ; Conroy wears a sparkling bowler hat, Cousins a rumpled tweed hat. Both wear coats of dark-coloured cloth, and both carry sticks : Conroy's a fine, thick malacca cane, Cousins' a blackthorn. They come to the table.*

Cousins [*following Conroy in*]. I just couldn't, Misther Conroy ; I've taken fifteen pounds off already.

They're fine beasts either for milkin' or beef; all-round animals, an' worth every penny of me first askin'.

Conroy [*turning to look at Cousins pitifully*]. None o' them would win a fourth prize at a thin-stock show, man. I know a beast when I see one. It'll take an age of feedin' before them beasts is the kinda cattle you're dhreamin' they are.
> [*Bull, becoming interested in the bargaining, comes out from the door, and listens intently. Barney O'Hay gradually straightens up from the wall, and becomes interested too.*

Cousins. You prodded them with your stick till your arm ached, an' couldn't make a dint. A healthy herd they come from. There's growin' goodness in them beasts, I'm tellin' you.

Conroy [*laying a caressing hand on Cousins' arm*]. Looka here, Cousins, I'm only thryin' to do a neighbour a good turn. I really don't want your beasts; they'll only be in th' way. Don't be too graspin', man! Here, take off another five pounds, an' I'll allow them to be mine.

Cousins [*shaking off Conroy's arm — indignantly*]. Five pounds, is it? I'll dhrive them home first! [*He makes to go off, and reaches the road, where he pauses.*] Is that your final offer, Misther Conroy?

Conroy [*up to him*]. Here, then — four pounds off: that, or nothin'!

Cousins [*coming back again*]. Here, I'll split that as a favour — two off, an' that's me final word.

Conroy. Three, then. Is it a bargain? If not, I'm done. [*He holds a hand out to Cousins.*] Come on, man; put your hand there!

Cousins. Two ten, or nothin'. Here, two fifteen, then. Nothin' fairer. [*He holds a hand out.*] Before I go !

Conroy [*bringing his hand down on Cousins' with a loud smack*]. Done ! A dhrink for th' two of us. [*He raps on the table with his stick.*] Flagonson ! Two whiskies !
    [*Flagonson brings out the drinks and leaves them on the table. Conroy and Cousins take them up to drink when Kelly from the Isle of Mananaun comes round by way of the Tavern. He is tall and straight. He wears a saffron kilt and a green shawl is draped from a shoulder. A black balmoral hat, with a green feather sticking up from it, covers his head. A silver pin-brooch shines in his shawl. His face is pale and grave-looking, though occasionally showing a satirical line in it. He halts on the road, and looks towards the men.*

Kelly [*down to the men*]. Did any of yous, by any chance, see a fine lady pass by ? A lady with a fair face, gathered in a little with grief, but with ne'er a hint o' guile in it ?

Flagonson [*with a wave of the hand — to Kelly*]. Go away, go away, we're busy people here.

Kelly [*musingly, as if to himself*]. A mortal sin torments my coming in and my going out ; a mortal sin and a mean one. [*To the men*] Gentlemen, I must find the lady, and get back my good name.

Flagonson [*impatiently — with an angrier wave of his hand*]. Go away, man ; we're busy people here, I'm tellin' you !

Kelly. So I see ; all bent down over the thought of gain. [*A pause.*] Yous are all very close to hell now, gentlemen. Take warnin' be me who gave too little for what I got.

Cousins [*quickly*]. You bet th' poor lady's price down too low?

Kelly. No, no; I gave her what she asked, but she asked too little for what she gave.

Cousins [*excited*]. Didja hear that, Misther Conroy? He didn't give th' lady a fair price. A mortal sin — there's sense in that, now.

Conroy [*fiercely — to Cousins*]. Sense in it, you fool, because it suits yourself.

Cousins. Th' gentleman's right — I didn't get half o' what I gave was worth.

Kelly. It's a curse on us all, brother: givin' too little for what we get.

Conroy [*angrily — to Kelly*]. You must be th' boyo who th' Sergeant told me was spreadin' ideas about incitin' to discontentation everywhere. I can tell you, th' polis'll soon be on your tail!

Flagonson [*to Kelly*]. Who are you, anyway? No-one even knows your name.

Kelly [*doing the dance the Widda did, but turning round the reverse way — lilting*] :

> Th' name I'm called is Kelly,
> K ee double ell y ;
> Th' name I'm called is Kelly,
> Kelly from the Isle of Mananaun !

Go on, gentlemen, with your gettin' of gain while the great big world keeps turnin'.

Conroy [*jeeringly*]. G'wan, you, an' find your lady, an' cuddle her into agreein' with your curious theologicality.

Bull [*maliciously*]. Lady is it ? Seems like she's a one would settle down in a ditch with a donor.

Kelly [*calmly*]. Aha, so you've bad minds along with th' love of gain. You thry to pin on others th' dirty decorations that may be hangin' on your own coats. [*He points, one after the other at Conroy, Bull, and Flagonson. Lilting :*]
Who were you with last night ?
Who were you with last night ?
Will you tell your missus when you go home
Who you were with last night ?

Flagonson [*in anguished indignation*]. This is more than a hurt to us : this hits at the decency of the whole nation !

Kelly [*pointing his forefinger straight at Conroy*]. Do you go to Mass ?

Conroy [*spluttering*]. Do I go to Mass ? Of course I go to Mass, sir !

Kelly. An' don't you feel odd an' outa place there, thinking of gains in the week gone, and th' gains of th' week to come ?

Conroy. Me outa place there ! What th' hell d'ye mean, man ?

Barney [*bursting out from his somewhat obscure corner, and standing forth to confront Kelly*]. I'll not stand here to hear Misther Conroy insulted ! I'll have you know Misther Conroy's chairman of the Catholic Young Men's Society ; that Misther Conroy's name's down for th' medal of St. Silvesther ; that Misther Conroy's a Grand Knight of St. Columbanus ; an' that Misther

Conroy's a particular friend of Monsignor Moymelligan's !

Kelly. Aha, but is Misther Conroy a particular friend of th' saints ?

Conroy [*furiously*]. I'm not goin' to stand here an' see th' saints insulted ; an' I'll not stand here, either, to listen to your unannounceable mysteries that would shear all companionable manners from our business consortations !

Cousins [*soothingly*]. Aysey, Misther Conroy ; aysey !

Conroy [*raging*]. Good God, what are we payin' the Civic Guards for ! Where are th' loafers hidin' ? Is a man like me to be hunted into an indetermination rage by th' unsponsored, piseudo religiosity of a kilted bum ! I'll soon put th' law on his heels ! [*He rushes on to the road past Kelly, then turns to face him.*] You musta come from some quare place, I'm thinkin', to be makin' a mock of all the things we hold so sacred. I'll settle you !

[*He makes to rush off behind the Tavern. Kelly points a forefinger towards his back, and emits a sharp, short whistle, and Conroy suddenly stops dead in his rush, and stands stiff, one leg stretched out before the other, having stopped in the act of finishing a step forward. The others look on with amazement and some alarm.*

Kelly [*down to the surprised men — somewhat humorously*]. See ? A pointing finger can stop him in his stride. As long as it points, he stays put. But a stretched arm would soon grow tired, so I'll send him off on his errand of mercy.

[*He again emits a short, sharp whistle, lowers his arm, and Conroy resumes his rush, apparently unaware of what*

has happened. The others, a little frightened, draw
gradually away from Kelly, towards the protection of the
houses — Flagonson and Cousins to the Tavern, and
Bull and Barney towards the General Stores, till they
are half hidden standing in the entrance to each.

Kelly. Don't be slinkin' off like as if yous had murdhered
Nellie O'Flaherty's beautiful dhrake. [*The clink of*
coins is heard again in Tavern and Stores.] Aha, that's
how th' harp o' Tara sounds today! What's it
playin'? [*The tune of "Jingle Bells" is softly heard.*]
I am in my sleep, an' don't waken me. A signature
song! [*Going slowly away behind the General Stores,*
lilting as he crosses :]
Jingle coins, jingle coins, jingle all th' day,
Jingle them at night again, for coins have come to stay.
Jingle coins till silent Death comes in his frozen sleigh
To gather yous an' all your coins, an' jingle yous away!
   [*He disappears around the back of the General Stores. The*
      rest, by this time, are hidden within Tavern and Stores,
      their heads only peeping out around the jambs of the
      doorways.

Flagonson [*peeping out from behind the door*]. Is he gone?

Cousins [*coming out a little way from the Tavern door*]. Yis.
No sign of him now.

Bull [*coming out of the Stores*]. We should have faced him
out; should've stood up to him; defied him. We're
not worums!

Flagonson [*decisively*]. No, Bull, no. There was magic in
that figure, man. When he pointed at me and asked
me who I was with last night, I felt it slippin' up an'
down me spine.

TIME TO GO 785

Cousins [*timidly*]. All th' same, he said one thing worth thinkin' of when he told us it was a mortal sin to give too little for a thing you're buyin'.

Barney [*assertively*]. Misther Conroy was right ; he musta come from some quare place, for to bring in th' topic of religion outa hours shows a quare mind. [*He suddenly listens.*] I hear a step. Someone's comin' again.

> [*They all make for Tavern and Stores, and try to peep round the doorways towards the road. The Sergeant comes stealthily in along the road, looking fearfully to right and left. He comes down till he is close to the Tavern.*

Sergeant [*in towards the Tavern — in a loud whisper*]. Misther Farrell, are yous there ? [*He hurries across to the Stores, and whispers towards the door.*] Misther Flagonson, are yous there ?

> [*The four men, affected by the stealthiness of the Sergeant, become stealthy too. They come out of Tavern and Stores to gather round him, heads bent inwards towards each other, and shoulders crouched low.*

Flagonson. What is it, Sergeant ? What has you goin' about gathered up like a cod in a pot ?

Sergeant [*warningly*]. Hush ! Thry to feel unconscious of all wrong-doin'. Thry to look, not like the gaums yous are, but like innocent ones.

Bull [*impatiently*]. What sorta talk's this, Sergeant ?

Sergeant. Hush, I'm sayin'. Not so loud. Th' west's asleep. Th' Inspector says to me, Killdooey, he says, find out th' antecedents of th' person.

Flagonson. Ah, the antecedents.

Sergeant. An' no names mentioned, Sergeant, says he, for identification might prove dangerous. [*He suddenly looks down at each arm.*] Now which is me right arm an' which is me left one ?

Bull [*indicating it*]. That's your right one. Godamit, man, don't you know one arm from t'other yet ?

Sergeant [*not noticing Bull's remark*]. Folly it up to Carlow, he says.

Barney. Folly what up to Carlow, man ?

Sergeant [*whispering low*]. Th' person, sir. Folly th' person, says th' Inspector, even if th' person goes up to Carlow.

Cousins. We don't get th' dhrift of what you're dhrivin' at, Sergeant.

Sergeant [*seizing Flagonson by the arm*]. Looka, Bull Farrell, I love a lassie. D'ye know ?

Flagonson [*bewildered*]. Yis, yis, I know.

Sergeant [*lilting*] :
     A bonnie Hielan' lassie :
[*In a loud and positive burst of song :*]
     She's as pure as th' lily in th' dell !

Flagonson. Yis, yis, you can tell us about that again. What's throublin' us is what's throublin' you ?

Sergeant [*dreamily*]. Ay, ay ; it's th' person who's goin' about dividin' th' people into fightin' over what th' person says.

Cousins [*impatiently*]. An' what, in God's name, is th' person actually sayin', Sergeant ?

Sergeant [*dreamily*]. Th' person's in th' throes of a mortal sin for sellin' a cow to someone, an' askin' too much for it, so th' person's sayin' ask less than you'd like to get for a thing you're sellin'.

Cousins [*indignantly*]. No, no ; that's against all law an' livability !   Where's th' freedom our poor boys died to get, if a body daren't ask for what he wants for a thing he's sellin' ?   You're mixin' things up, Sergeant ; th' kilted person passin' here said th' very opposite !

Sergeant. Th' skirted person, you mean ?

Cousins. Th' kilted person, I'm sayin'.

Flagonson [*excitedly*]. We forgot th' first one !

Sergeant. Which first one, what first one ?

Flagonson. A person opposin' in appearance th' person we have in mind now.

Sergeant [*putting a hand to his brow to help in very deep thought*]. Then th' person has two presenceses.   [*He pauses, then stretches out his right arm in front of him.*] We'll get to th' bottom of it, sure's this is me left arm !

Barney [*in a whisper — to Bull*]. Is he dhrunk or what ?
   [*Barney has been watching the Sergeant for some time with intensity, and now moves very gradually away from the group, keeping still a watch on the Sergeant.*

Sergeant [*dreamily*]. Comin' through th' rye to here, I felt shaky.   I thried to whistle, but no sound came to me assistance.   I sucked in an' I blew out, but ne'er a single sound came to me assistance.   [*He puts his face close to Bull's, and whispers*] Looka, Inspector, I feel like — what do I feel like ?   I feel like th' man who sthruck O'Hara ! [*He takes his face away from Bull's, and begins to sing, accompanying, at first, with so sudden a sway that the others (except Barney) catch hold of him and are forced to join in the movement. The Sergeant goes on accompanying the words with the movements which the words seem to suggest (at times, somewhat violent), and those clinging to him are forced to move with him. Singing and carrying on mime movements :*]

> First we mopp'd th' floor with him,
> Dragg'd him up an' down th' stairs ;
>
> Then we had another go, undher tables, over chairs.
> Such a sight you never saw —
> Before he'd time to say his prayers,
>
> Rags an' bones were all we left
> Of th' man who sthruck O'Hara !

Barney [*shrinking back towards the Stores*]. God Almighty, th' fella's touched !

Flagonson [*agonised*]. Aw, pull yourself together, Sergeant !
[*The Sergeant, with an effort, straightens himself as if for parade. Outside, the voice of Widda Machree is heard lilting quietly the chorus of " I Know Where I'm Goin' ".*]

Widda Machree [*lilting, outside*] :
> I know where I'm goin',
> And I know who's goin' with me ;
> I know who I love,
> But th' dear knows who I'll marry !

[*Widda Machree comes in from the back of the General Stores. The men sense her presence, and stand tense in a semicircle together, their backs to the road along which the Widda is walking. She looks down towards them.*

Just as she comes in, the Sergeant wilts away again, crouching and tense as the rest are.

Bull [*in a whisper — to the Sergeant*]. Now or never, Sergeant, thry to pull yourself together !

Widda Machree. God save yous all. I feel me journey's endin'. [*She lilts and wheels around in a kind of dance :*]
        Has anybody here seen Kelly ?
        Kay ee double ell y ;
        Has anybody here seen Kelly ?
        Kelly from th' Isle of Mananaun !
[*Down to the men*] Have yous seen a spirit, or what, yous are so silent ? Have yous no music in yous save the din of the market-place ?

Bull [*whispering passionately to the Sergeant*]. Now, Sergeant, up, an' answer her !

Widda Machree. No picture in your minds but a warrant for an arrest, or a bill demandin' pay for goods delivered ?

Sergeant [*in a whisper to Bull*]. I have to wait for reinforcements !

Widda Machree. You is neither fit for heaven nor to take th' floor at Phil the Fluther's Ball ! [*From around the back of the Stores, opposite to where the Widda Machree stands, Kelly comes. He halts when he sees her, and both gaze silently at each other for some moments. Then each holds out arms to the other as they come close.*] My brother !

Kelly. My sisther ! [*Offering her a purse*] Take all I kept from you ; and take th' cow back, too, for I gave less than I should when I was buying.

Widda Machree [*offering him a purse*]. Take back all you

gave, an' keep th' cow, for I asked more than I should when I was sellin'.

Kelly
Widda Machree} [*together*]. Forgive !

> [*They enter into each other's arms.*

Kelly. More than sisther !

Widda Machree. More than brother !

> [*A blast from a police whistle is heard ; the Sergeant leaps to life, and Conroy, followed by two Civic Guards, rushes in, the 1st Civic Guard still blowing his whistle. They halt for a second when they see the two embracing, and look on for a second.*

Conroy [*excitedly*]. There they are — the ruffians ! Surround them ; hold them tight !

1st C. Guard [*waving papers in the air*]. We've got th' warrants indictin' them for breaches of th' peace.

2nd C. Guard [*waving papers in the air*]. An' a full-blown certificate from Doctor Simples showin' neither of them non compos mentis.

Flagonson ⎫　　Handcuff them !
Bull　　　⎬ [*in unison*]. Put them behind bars at once.
Barney　 ⎪　　Solitary confinement for th' pair o' them.
Cousins　⎭　　Yis, yis ; th' sight of them unsettles us.

> [*Widda Machree and Kelly are handcuffed, the Sergeant and the 1st Civic Guard placing themselves beside Kelly, while the 2nd Civic Guard takes charge of Widda Machree.*

Conroy. Go on, Sergeant, dhrag them off before we hear

more of their lies, one sayin' " Give more when you're buyin' ' ", an' th' other sayin' " Ask less when you're sellin' ' ".

Kelly [*to Conroy*]. Th' sayin's, sir, are but two sides of the same thruth.

Conroy [*angrily*]. Will you take away th' deludherin' louser, Sergeant, an' not be lettin' him go on talkin' !

Kelly [*pointing to the blasted trees*]. Soon yous'll all be no more than are these two barren, deadened trees. Then when yous are silent stiffs, others will count your coins.

Sergeant [*laying a hand on Kelly's shoulder*]. Come on, me man, to where you'll be cured into seein' things as we all see them.

2nd C. Guard [*laying a hand on Widda Machree's shoulder*]. An' you, me woman, come along to where your poor mind'll be mended.

Kelly [*to Widda Machree*]. It is time to go, sisther.

Widda Machree [*to Kelly*]. It is time to go, brother.

Kelly [*embracing and kissing her*]. Goodbye, fair sweetheart.

Widda Machree [*kissing him*]. Goodbye, my love.
  [*The Sergeant, followed by the 1st Civic Guard, leads out Kelly by way of the Stores ; the 2nd Civic Guard leads out Widda Machree by way of the Tavern. As they go, Kelly and the Widda Machree perform their wheeling dance they did before, while Kelly says his last farewell, and Widda Machree says hers.*

Kelly [*wheeling quietly in his semi-dance, as he goes out*] :
        Goodbye to holy souls left here,
        Goodbye to man an' fairy ;

Widda Machree [*wheeling quietly in her semi-dance as she goes out*] :

> Goodbye to all of Leicester Square,
> An' th' long way to Tipperary.

Conroy [*taking off his hat and mopping his head with a big handkerchief*]. What a dispicable pair ! Thank th' holy saints that that danger's past. [*To Cousins*] Now let us settle up in peace.

> [*He takes a wallet from his pocket, is about to open it, when he cocks an ear to listen.*
> [*The tune of " Jingle Coins ", accompanied by voices singing the words, is heard, sung and played softly, as if coming from a great distance.*

Voices [*with accompaniment*] :

> Jingle coins, jingle coins, jingle all the day,
> Jingle them at night again, for coins have come to stay.
> Jingle them till silent Death comes in his frozen sleigh
> To gather you and all your coins, and jingle yous away !

Conroy. Is that th' sound of singin' somewhere I hear ?

Cousins. Yis ; seems to be something familiar.

Bull. The Civic Guards cod-actin' in th' barracks down th' road.

> [*Conroy opens his wallet as he stands by the table, and is about to count out notes, when the Sergeant and 1st Civic Guard rush in from behind the Stores. They are in a great state of excitement.*

Sergeant [*to the others — breathless*]. Did he go this way ? We seen him flash by here. Are yous dumb ? Answer !

Conroy. Who, who, man ?

Sergeant. Kelly from th' Isle of Mananaun. Just slid out
o' th' handcuffs, out of our hold, an' was gone !
  [*The 2nd Civic Guard rushes in, panic-stricken, from
  around the Tavern.*

2nd C. Guard [*hysterically*]. Did she go this way ? I seen
her flashin' by. Goddamnit, answer !

Conroy. Who, who, man ?

2nd C. Guard. Th' lady, th' hussy. Just slid outa me
grip, an' was gone !

Conroy [*with a furious shout*]. Then go afther them an' get
them, you blasted fools !
  [*The Sergeant and the 1st Civic Guard rush out in one
  direction, the 2nd Civic Guard in the other.*
  [*The tune of " Jingle Coins " played on trumpet and drum
  becomes loud and clear now, and all stand tensely to
  listen. The two barren trees in the background suddenly
  flush with blossom, foliage, and illuminated fruit.*

Bull [*listening*]. They're mockin' us in some place or
another ; in some place unknown.

Cousins [*excitedly pointing to the trees*]. Look, looka th'
threes !

Barney [*falling on his knees*]. Jayayus, a miracle !

Cousins [*falling on his knees*]. They musta been saints !
  [*Bull and Flagonson now fall on their knees, too, and all
  face towards the glowing trees.*
  [*After a few moments, Mrs. Flagonson appears at the
  Tavern door, goes over to Flagonson, taking no notice of
  what has happened, and prods her husband in the back
  with her forefinger.*
  [*The glowing trees begin to fade as soon as Mrs. Flagonson
  prods her husband in the back.*

Mrs. Flagonson [*prodding her husband*]. Come in, Michael, an' help me tot up th' takin's.

[*Without a word, Flagonson gets up and follows his wife into the Tavern, and the glowing trees fade away utterly, becoming dead and barren again. The others rise a few moments afterwards, stand still for a second or so, then look sheepishly at each other.*

Conroy [*roughly to Cousins*]. Come on in, an' let's settle up in quietness for th' scrawls o' cattle I was a fool to buy.   [*He goes into the Tavern.*

Bull [*to Barney*]. No use o' you stayin' here. Bring me th' tenner, or you'll get no phosphate from me.

[*He goes into the Stores.*

[*Barney turns slowly away and makes for the road to go home, and on the way out Cousins stops him with a question.*

Cousins [*to the dejected Barney*]. Didja see anything, Mr. O'Hay? I wondher what was it I seen?

Barney. If I seen anything, an' if you seen anything, what was seen was only an halleelucination!

[*He goes dejectedly on his way, and Cousins goes slowly into the Tavern.*

END OF THE PLAY

HAS ANYBODY HERE SEEN KELLY?

Has an-y-bo-dy here seen Kel-ly?

Kay ee dou-ble ell y; has an-y-bo-dy here seen

Kel-ly? Kel-ly from the Isle of Man-an-aun.

JINGLE COINS, JINGLE COINS

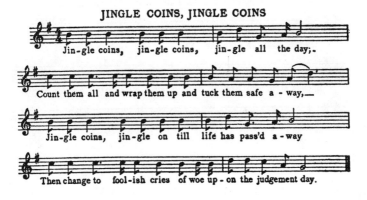

Jin-gle coins, jin-gle coins, jin-gle all the day;.

Count them all and wrap them up and tuck them safe a-way,—

Jin-gle coins, jin-gle on till life has pass'd a-way

Then change to fool-ish cries of woe up-on the judgement day.

WHO WERE YOU WITH LAST NIGHT

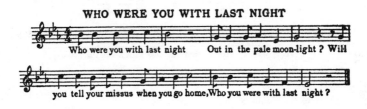

Who were you with last night Out in the pale moon-light? Will

you tell your missus when you go home, Who you were with last night?

I LOVE A LASSIE

I love a lass-ie, a bon-nie Hie-lan' las-sie, she's as
pure as the li - ly in the dell.

THE MAN WHO STRUCK O' HARA

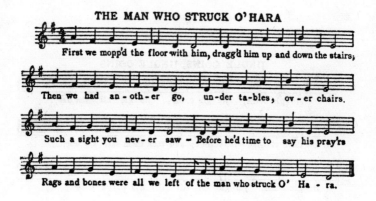

First we mopp'd the floor with him, dragg'd him up and down the stairs;
Then we had an-oth-er go, un-der ta-bles, ov-er chairs.
Such a sight you nev-er saw – Before he'd time to say his pray'rs
Rags and bones were all we left of the man who struck O' Ha - ra.

I KNOW WHERE I'M GOING

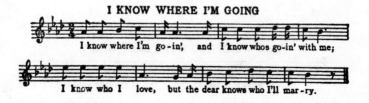

I know where I'm go-in', and I know whos go-in' with me;
I know who I love, but the dear knows who I'll mar-ry.

UNDER EACH PLAY is listed first, the theatre and date of the original production; second, the date of publication. The listing is in order of production, except for unproduced plays, which are listed in order of writing. This chronology was prepared by Randolph Goodman, Brooklyn College.

The Robe of Rosheen (one act)
    Written c. 1918
    Unproduced
    The Plain People, Republican periodical, Dublin, c. 1918
The Frost in the Flower (one act)
    Written 1919
    Unproduced
    Unpublished
The Harvest Festival (one act)
    Written c. 1920
    Unproduced
    Unpublished

The Crimson in the Tri-Color (one act)
    Written c. 1921
    Unproduced
    Unpublished
The Shadow of a Gunman
    Abbey Theatre, Dublin, April 9, 1923
    In *Two Plays*, 1925
Cathleen Listens In (one act)
    Abbey Theatre, Dublin, October 1, 1923
    Unpublished
The Cooing of the Doves (one act)
    Written 1923
    Unproduced, later revised and used as Act II
      of *The Plough and the Stars*
    Unpublished
Juno and the Paycock
    Abbey Theatre, Dublin, March 3, 1924
    In *Two Plays*, 1925
Nannie's Night Out (one act)
    Abbey Theatre, Dublin, September 29, 1924
    Unpublished
The Plough and the Stars
    Abbey Theatre, Dublin, February 8, 1926
    Published 1926
The Silver Tassie
    Apollo Theatre, London, October 11, 1929
    Published 1928
Within the Gates
    Royalty Theatre, London, February 7, 1934
    Published 1933

The End of the Beginning (one act)
Abbey Theatre, Dublin, February 8, 1937
In *Modern Short Plays,* Guy Boas, editor,
1935
The Star Turns Red
Unity Theatre, London, March 20, 1940
Published 1940
Red Roses for Me
Olympia Theatre, Dublin, April, 1943
Published 1942
Purple Dust
Boston Tributary Theatre, Boston, Mass.,
December 6, 1944
Published 1940
Pound on Demand (one act)
American Repertory Theatre, New York,
January, 1947
In *Collected Plays,* 1951
Oak Leaves and Lavender
Lyric Theatre, Hammersmith, London, May,
1947
Published 1946
Cock-a-Doodle-Dandy
The People's Theatre, Newcastle-on-Tyne,
December, 1949
Published 1949
Hall of Healing (one act)
Yugoslav-American Hall, New York, May 7,
1952
In *Collected Plays,* 1951

Bedtime Story (one act)
>Yugoslav-American Hall, New York, May 7,
>>1952
>In *Collected Plays*, 1951

Time to Go (one act)
>Yugoslav-American Hall, New York, May 7,
>>1952
>In *Collected Plays*, 1951

The Bishop's Bonfire
>Manuscript completed 1954
>Unproduced
>Unpublished